Modernizing the U.S. Census

Barry Edmonston and Charles Schultze, Editors

Panel on Census Requirements in the Year 2000 and Beyond

Committee on National Statistics

Commission on Behavioral and Social Sciences and Education

National Research Council

NATIONAL ACADEMY PRESS

Washington, D.C. 1995

This project is supported by funds provided by the Bureau of the Census, U.S. Department of Commerce, under contract number 50-YABC-2-66008.

Library of Congress Catalog Card No. 94-69488

International Standard Book Number 0-309-05182-7

Additional copies of this report are available from: National Academy Press, 2101 Constitution Avenue, N.W., Box 285, Washington, D.C. 20418

Call 800-624-6242 or 202-334-3313 (in the Washington Metropolitan Area)

B493

PANEL ON CENSUS REQUIREMENTS IN THE
YEAR 2000 AND BEYOND

CHARLES L. SCHULTZE (*Chair*), The Brookings Institution, Washington, D.C.

MARGO ANDERSON, Department of History, University of Wisconsin, Milwaukee

DOUGLAS M. DUNN, Consumer Services, AT&T, Basking Ridge, New Jersey

IVAN P. FELLEGI, Statistics Canada, Ottawa, Ontario, Canada

STEPHEN·E. FIENBERG, Department of Statistics, Carnegie Mellon University

CHARLES P. KINDLEBERGER, St. Louis Community Development Agency, St. Louis, Missouri

MICHEL A. LETTRE, Maryland Office of Planning, Baltimore, Maryland

JAMES N. MORGAN, Institute for Social Research, University of Michigan

WILLIAM A. MORRILL, Mathtech, Inc., Princeton, New Jersey

RICHARD F. MUTH, Department of Economics, Emory University

JANET L. NORWOOD, The Urban Institute, Washington, D.C.

EROL R. RICKETTS, Center for Social Research, City University of New York*

TERESA A. SULLIVAN, Department of Sociology, University of Texas, Austin

KARL TAEUBER, Department of Sociology, University of Wisconsin, Madison

JAMES TRUSSELL, Office of Population Research, Princeton University

BARRY EDMONSTON, *Study Director*
CONSTANCE F. CITRO, *Senior Staff Officer*
JUANITA TAMAYO LOTT, *Research Associate*
MICHELE L. CONRAD, *Senior Project Assistant*
MEYER ZITTER, *Consultant*

---

*Served until August 12, 1994.

Acknowledgments

The panel's report is the result of the efforts of many people. The panel was established under the auspices of the Committee on National Statistics. Miron Straf, director of the committee, was instrumental in developing the study and provided guidance and support to the panel and staff. The committee, with Burton Singer and, later, Norman Bradburn, as chairs, had responsibility for the establishment of the panel and for review of the final report. Three committee members devoted thoughtful hours to reading and commenting on the final report: John Geweke, Noreen Goldman, and Dorothy Rice. We also appreciate comments on the final report that we received from Tom Jabine and Bruce Petrie, members of the Panel to Evaluate Alternative Census Methods; Duane Steffey, study director of that panel; and six anonymous reviewers selected by the report review committee of the National Academy of Sciences. The panel would like to acknowledge the contributions of Porter Coggeshall, Robert Hauser, and Henry Riecken, who supervised the National Research Council review of our report.

At the beginning of its activities, the panel was pleased to be briefed by U.S. Representatives Harold Rogers and Thomas C. Sawyer on their views of the decennial census and their thoughts on criteria for future censuses. We also thank Barbara Bryant, who was director of the Bureau of the Census during the initial phases of the panel's work, and Harry Scarr, who was acting director for the latter period of our work, for their presentations to the panel and their helpful assistance to our requests for information.

We received continuing cooperation and assistance from the staff and management of the Bureau of the Census, including in particular Charles Alexander, Art Cresce, Greg Diffendal, Jim Dinwiddie, Jerry Gates, Jay Keller, Joe Knott,

John Long, Robert Marx, Lawrence McGinn, Nampeo McKenney, Susan Miskura, Mary Mulry, Lorraine Neece, Janice Pentercs, Gregg Robinson, John Thompson, Robert Tortora, and Signe Wetrogan.

We acknowledge with gratitude the assistance we received from the many individuals, in addition to those from the Bureau of the Census, who met regularly with the panel: Katherine Wallman and Maria Gonzalez, Office of Management and Budget; TerriAnn Lowenthal, Shelly Wilkie Martinez, and George Omas, House Subcommittee on Census, Statistics, and Postal Personnel; David McMillen, Senate Subcommittee on Government Information and Regulation; and Bruce Johnson, Jack Kaufman, and Chris Mihm, General Accounting Office.

Special thanks are due to the large number of individuals and organizations who consulted with the panel about their requirements for census data, their perception of content needs, and their appraisal of alternative methods for collecting census data. We owe a considerable debt of thanks to these people, who are listed in Appendix N.

We also thank the consultants to the panel—Larry Barnett, Jonathan Entin, Ed Goldfield, Samuel Issacharoff, Daniel Levine, Evelyn Mann, Mary Nenno, and George Wickstrom—who provided drafts of background papers. We appreciate the assistance of Margaret Mikyung Lee, who prepared a Congressional Research Service report on legal issues concerning the census and discussed legal issues with the panel on several occasions. Philip Fulton of the Bureau of Transportation Statistics provided the panel with expertise on transportation data and assisted greatly with the preparation of Appendix G. Juanita Tamayo Lott coordinated the activities of the panel's working group on race and ethnicity data; she directed the preparation of Chapter 7 and Appendix K. Meyer Zitter was responsible for coordinating the panel's work on the needs for small-area data and the usefulness of administrative records for the census and for intercensal estimates. He helped to prepare background papers and supporting tables for Chapter 8 and Appendices A, B, I, J, K, and L.

Eugenia Grohman, associate director for reports in the Commission on Behavioral and Social Sciences and Education, was responsible for editing the report and made valuable suggestions about its structure. We acknowledge the contribution of her superb editing skills in the preparation of this report. Our report also benefited from a final editing by Christine McShane and Elaine McGarraugh, also of the commission staff.

No panel with a task as complex and as difficult to focus as ours could perform its duties without an excellent, well-managed staff. In particular, the overall report would not have been possible without the dedicated efforts of three staff members. We are enormously indebted to Michele Conrad, senior project assistant, who cheerfully undertook any task requested by panel members. She was responsible for the panel's survey of state data centers. She prepared background papers on business as well as state and local needs for census data, presented in the report as Appendices E and F. She also edited the materials that have become Appendix H. Constance Citro, senior staff officer, made major contributions to the panel's work. She coordinated two of the panel's working groups, one on census data requirements for reapportionment and redistricting and the other on the special requirements for census long-form information. She directed the preparation of Chapters 1 and 6 and Appendices A and C. More than this, she worked with the study director from beginning to end in reviewing and revising drafts of the report, offering intelligent and constructive advice on the panel's work, and helping on all the tasks needed to bring the report to publication. Finally, we are uniquely indebted to study director, Barry Edmonston, who managed the overall strategy for the panel's work, organized and managed a complex set of activities, and nudged us on to meet our deadlines. His intellectual contributions are embedded throughout our work.

I wish to close by expressing my profound appreciation to fellow panel members for their willingness to devote long hours and their special knowledge to the development and writing of the report. They have worked together well and patiently, a critical element in such a comprehensive review of the needs for the census. A number of panel members prepared background papers for our discussions. Some of their contributions appear in the appendices; others have been incorporated into the text.

Charles L. Schultze, *Chair*
Panel on Census Requirements
in the Year 2000 and Beyond

Contents

Preface

In 1992 the Congress mandated that a study of the fundamental require-ments for the nation's decennial census be undertaken by the National Academy of Sciences-National Research Council. The mandate was in part in response to the costs and large relative undercount of minority groups in the 1990 census: there were higher per unit costs than previous censuses and higher rates of cover-age error (net undercount of the population) than in the 1980 census.

As specified by the legislation, the Panel on Census Requirements in the Year 2000 and Beyond, under the Committee on National Statistics, was estab-lished (Decennial Census Improvement Act of 1991, Public Law 102-125) to study:

(1) means by which the Government could achieve the most accurate popu-lation count possible; and

(2) consistent with the goal under paragraph (1), ways for the Government to collect other demographic and housing data.

In the words of the legislation, the panel was directed to consider such matters as:

• ways to improve the Government's enumeration methods, especially with regard to those involving the direct collection of data from respondents;

• alternative methods for collecting the data needed for a basic population count, such as any involving administrative records, information from subnational or other surveys, and cumulative or rolling data-collection techniques;

• the appropriateness of using sampling methods, in combination with basic data-collection techniques or otherwise, in the acquisition or refinement of population data, including a review of the accuracy of the data for different levels of geography (such as States, places, census tracts and census blocks);

• the degree to which a continuing need is anticipated with respect to the types of data (besides data relating to the basic population count) which were collected through the last decennial census; and

• with respect to data for which such a need is anticipated whether there are more effective ways to collect information using traditional methods and whether alternative sources or methodologies exist or could be implemented for obtaining reliable information in a timely manner.

With respect to each alternative proposed, the panel was directed to include:

• an evaluation of such alternative's relative advantages and disadvantages, as well as an analysis of its cost effectiveness; and

• for any alternative that does not involve the direct collection of data from individuals (about themselves or members of their household), an analysis of such alternative's potential effects on (i) privacy; (ii) public confidence in the census; and (iii) the integrity of the census.

Our mission was to respond to Congress's interest in rethinking the census, both the requirements for the data currently collected in the census and methods of conducting the census at less cost and with improved coverage.

Our panel approached its task in several ways. We worked closely with Census Bureau staff to understand the cost structure of the census and the reasons for cost escalations since 1970. We also worked with Census Bureau staff to model the likely cost implications of various changes to census methodology. We reviewed the available literature and consulted with others in the field on the pros and cons of different ways of conducting the census, including radical changes, such as conducting a sample census or basing the census entirely on administrative records; fundamental reforms of current census methodology, such as the use of sampling to follow up nonresponding households; and numerous changes in census procedures.

We also met with a wide range of user groups to understand their requirements and uses for census data and the likely consequences of no longer collecting the items they now use or of collecting those items by some other means. We conducted two in-depth case studies of census data use, one for transportation research and planning and the other for housing research and planning. We did not, however, review the content of the census questionnaire on an item-by-item basis. No outside panel can substitute for the process by which data users, most importantly, federal government agencies, debate the relative merits of including in the census an item on, say, commuting, versus an item on, say, disability or national origin. We did review the evidence on whether the content of recent censuses, taken as a whole, has contributed to such problems as rising costs and coverage errors and whether there is a case on these grounds for reducing the number of items.

As part of its response to the congressional mandate and at the specific request of the Department of Commerce and the Bureau of the Census, the Committee on National Statistics convened a separate Panel to Evaluate Alternative Census Methods to conduct a complementary study. In addition to these two panels, the Department of Commerce established an extensive advisory structure for the census, consisting of a policy committee of federal agency officials with needs for census data, a technical committee of knowledgeable staff, and an advisory committee with members from outside organizations with a stake in the census.

Our review of possible census methodologies overlaps in some respects the work of the Panel to Evaluate Alternative Census Methods. That panel's report and this one cover some of the same ground, but from differing perspectives. The Panel to Evaluate Alternative Census Methods focused primarily on technical issues of implementation and evaluation of promising methodologies. Our panel focused on issues of the cost structure for the census, ways to achieve the most accurate population count, and requirements for census content. Both emphases are important, and we note that on major issues of needed methodological improvements the two panels reached very similar conclusions. (The final report of the Panel to Evaluate Alternative Census Methods, *Counting People in the Information Age*, was published in 1994.)

Our panel (in contrast to the Panel to Evaluate Alternative Census Methods) devoted considerable attention to questions of census data use, including the rationale for users' needs for census information and whether those needs could be satisfied by some means other than the census itself. Early in our deliberations, we investigated the legal requirements for census data to support reapportionment and redistricting at the federal, state, and local levels of government and whether those requirements ruled out any of the changes in census methodology that have been proposed. We also reviewed the legal requirements for census data to support other program and policy needs of federal agencies. Some of our early findings were presented in an interim report in May 1993 and a letter report in November 1993; these are integrated in this report.

We urge prompt consideration of our findings and recommendations by Congress and the Census Bureau so that the needed changes in the census process can be made in time to realize their full benefits for the 2000 census.

Charles L. Schultze, *Chair*
Panel on Census Requirements
in the Year 2000 and Beyond

Modernizing the U.S. Census

Summary

The obligation for the federal government to conduct a census or decennial enumeration of the population for the purpose of apportioning the Congress is part of the Constitution. But the census provides the nation with essential data that go well beyond a simple population count. The information available from the census is widely used by governments at all levels for planning and administrative purposes, by business firms, by academic researchers, journalists, educators, writers, and community and nonprofit organizations. Although much valuable information about the U.S. population—race, income, employment, housing conditions, and other social and economic data—is collected by periodic surveys and from analysis of administrative records, only the census provides data covering a wide range of population characteristics for small geographic areas and small population groups. Census information is needed by the federal government for reapportionment of seats in the Congress, and by states for drawing congressional districts that meet the requirements of the Voting Rights Act. At the federal level, Congress has enacted laws requiring the use of census data to apportion federal funds to states, cities, school districts, and other governmental units under a wide variety of statutes, and they are used by many federal agencies to design, administer, and evaluate their programs.

The decennial censuses are planned and conducted with a high degree of professional competence. Nevertheless, some important problems have emerged over the past several decades. First, after decreasing from 1940 to 1980, the overall net undercount of the population increased in 1990 (to 1.8 percent, up from 1.2 percent in 1980). Moreover, in 1990, the difference in the net undercount between the black and nonblack populations rose to 4.4 percentage points,

1

the highest level since 1940 (the earliest census for which estimates of this type are available). Differential undercounts for blacks, Hispanics, and others cause concern because of their implications for such important uses of census information as legislative redistricting and fund allocation. Second, the existence of an initial census count and a subsequent and separate estimate from a postcensal evaluation survey for 1990 gave rise to divisive political arguments and legal suits over which set of numbers would be the official ones to be used for these important purposes.

Third, the costs of taking the census have escalated sharply, even after allowing for inflation and population growth. One of the reasons for that cost escalation, disturbing in its own right, has been a drop in the percentage of households who cooperate by filling out and returning the mail questionnaire. The 1970 decennial census cost $231 million. If adjustments are made to reflect the rise in prices and wages and the growth in the number of households between 1970 and 1990, with a further adjustment to take account of the increased costs associated with the decline in the mail response rate, the cost of conducting a 1970-type census in 1990 would have been about $1.3 billion. The actual cost of the 1990 census was $2.6 billion, twice as much. Although it has been argued that a major cause of the cost increase was due to costs associated with the long form (the longer questionnaire sent to 1 in 6 housing units in 1990), the panel's analysis of the relationship of content and cost led us to conclude that the content of the census did not produce the added costs. More generally, the panel has found that moderate changes in content do not have a significant effect on census costs.

In spite of considerable effort, the panel was unable to pin down, item by item, the causes of the cost increases. The panel believes, however, that a major part of the cost increase was driven by the response of the Census Bureau to several outside pressures. Most important, there was an increased and politically powerful demand for accurate population counts for very detailed geographical subdivisions and in hard-to-enumerate areas. Simultaneously, public cooperation with the census process, as measured by mail response rates, declined and was lowest in precisely those areas for which the pressures for an accurate count were greatest. The Census Bureau responded by pouring on resources in highly labor-intensive efforts to attempt to count every last person.

OVERALL CONCLUSIONS AND RECOMMENDATION

The panel's first task was to investigate whether and to what extent various types of essential data can best be collected by the decennial census or by other means. Our second task was to consider and recommend the most cost-effective methods of conducting the census and otherwise collecting census-type data. We evaluated a wide range of methods for meeting the requirements of the decennial census, including radical proposals that would sharply alter the way the data are collected, substantial changes in the context of the traditional census, and incremental changes in the census.

The basic recommendation of this report follows from four central conclusions:

1. It is fruitless to continue trying to count every last person with traditional census methods of physical enumeration. Simply providing additional funds to enable the Census Bureau to carry out the 2000 census using traditional methods, as it has in previous censuses, will not lead to improved coverage or data quality.

2. It is possible to improve the accuracy of the census count with respect to its most important attributes by supplementing a reduced intensity of traditional enumeration with statistical estimates of the number and characteristics of those not directly enumerated.

3. Once a decision is made to use statistical estimation for completing the count, a thorough review and reengineering of census procedures and operations could achieve substantial cost savings in the next census, even as accuracy is being improved.

4. With regard to proposals to drop the long form in the next decennial census and substitute a continuous monthly survey to obtain relevant data, substantial further research and preparatory work are required to thoroughly evaluate the likely effect and costs of these proposals. Continuous measurement deserves serious consideration as a means of providing more frequent small-area data; however, the necessary research and evaluation cannot be completed in time for the 2000 census. Therefore, the 2000 census should include the long form.

Our analysis leads to one overarching recommendation for a substantially redesigned census in order to contain costs, reduce error in the population count, and improve data quality. We believe that significant changes in the census, which the Census Bureau in large part is planning to test, can achieve significant improvements in the data and at the same time make it possible to realize significant reductions in costs.

A REDESIGNED CENSUS

Statistical Estimation

The panel concludes that physical enumeration or pure "counting" has been pushed well beyond the point at which it adds to the overall accuracy of the census. Moreover, such traditional census methods still result in a substantial undercount of minority populations. Techniques of statistical estimation can be used, in combination with the mail questionnaire and a reduced scale of follow-up of nonrespondents, to produce a better census at reduced costs.

Efforts to follow up individually those who fail to return the mail questionnaire should be simplified and truncated after a reasonable effort based on several criteria (see Chapter 5), and statistical sampling should be used to estimate the number and characteristics of the nonrespondent households that remain. In addition, evaluation surveys should be undertaken to improve the overall count and reduce the differential undercount.

Statistical estimation techniques have long been used in the census for a number of purposes, including close-out procedures, determining vacant units, and imputation of missing census responses. The use of statistical methods for sampling nonrespondents and surveys to complete the count is formal recognition that modern statistical procedures can improve the process, reduce costs, and produce better data for the country as a whole and for large areas and population groups by reducing the differential undercount. (It is also true, however, that the use of statistical techniques would increase the variability for small areas somewhat.) In our judgment, so long as a good-faith effort at physical enumeration is made, completing the estimates by statistical techniques would meet constitutional requirements.

The Census Bureau is planning large-scale tests in 1995 to help design the appropriate combination of enumeration and statistical estimation. The 2000 census should integrate enumeration and estimation to produce the best single estimate of the population and of the characteristics of the population, rather than two separate estimates—an initial count and a subsequent adjustment.

> **Recommendation 5.1 The panel recommends that the Census Bureau make a good-faith effort to count everyone, but then truncate physical enumeration after a reasonable effort to reach nonrespondents. The number and characteristics of the remaining nonrespondents should be estimated through sampling.**

> **Recommendation 5.2 To improve the census results, and especially to reduce the differential undercount, the panel recommends that the estimates achieved through physical enumeration and sampling for nonresponse be further improved and completed through survey techniques. The census should be designed as an integrated whole, to produce the best single-number count for the resources available. The Census Bureau should publish the procedures used to produce its final counts, as well as an assessment of their accuracy.**

Improving Response

Essential to the success of a redesigned census are efforts to improve the response to the mail questionnaire and also the completeness of the address list to which the questionnaires are sent. The Census Bureau should continue to stress the mandatory nature of the census. An expectation that the census is not mandatory would affect adversely efforts to increase the mail response rate and would undercut the improvements otherwise obtainable through a redesigned census. The Census Bureau has already conducted a number of field tests of improved procedures, such as the use of respondent-friendly census forms, designed to improve mail response rate, lower costs, and raise accuracy; the results to date have been promising.

Recommendation 5.3 The panel recommends that the Census Bureau incorporate successfully tested procedures to increase the initial response rate in the 2000 census, including the use of respondent-friendly questionnaires and expanded efforts to publicize the mandatory nature of the census.

To improve the master address file and other components of census operations, the Census Bureau should develop partnerships with state and local governments and the U.S. Postal Service.

Recommendation 5.4 The panel recommends that the Census Bureau develop cooperative arrangements with states and local governments to develop an improved master address file and that Congress amend Title 13 of the U.S. Code to permit sharing of this file for statistical purposes with state and local governments and the federal statistical system.

Recommendation 5.5 The panel recommends that the U.S. Postal Service and the Census Bureau continue to work together to improve the decennial census. We endorse an expanded role for the U.S. Postal Service in the 2000 census in several areas: (a) development, maintenance, and improvement of an accurate address file for the nation's residential housing units, (b) checking the address list prior to the census to improve accuracy, (c) delivery of the mailed forms, and (d) ascertainment of the vacancy status of housing units during the census.

Reducing Costs

On the basis of preliminary estimates provided by the Census Bureau and our own analysis, we judge that the use of the specific cost-savings techniques that we recommend—principally, truncation and sampling for nonresponse follow-up—would have reduced the costs of the 1990 census by $300 to $400 million. But, as noted earlier, $1.3 billion of the cost increase in the census between 1970 and 1990 is not explained by rising prices, increased numbers of households to be counted, and the effects of the decline in the mail response rate. We believe that these cost increases stemmed principally from efforts to meet strong pressures for highly accurate counts of detailed area and population group by means of highly intensive operations seeking to make a physical count of every last person. This view leads us to believe it is possible to achieve additional cost savings—beyond the $300 to $400 million—by means of a thorough-going "reengineering" of the entire census process in the context of the new census design in which statistical estimation is integrated with direct enumeration into a single-number census.

If censuses in 2000 and beyond rely on statistical methods to improve population coverage, then *all* procedures for enumerating the population need to be reconsidered in this new context. Such a fundamental rethinking of the census has the greatest potential for cost reductions. A thorough reexamination should consider issues of data collection, data processing, and data dissemination, such as: How many district offices are needed? How long do they need to be open? What staffing and supervisory personnel are needed? Has automation improved the census process commensurate with cost increases? How much of the product line can shift from print to electronic media? Given the use of statistical estimation to complete the count, which coverage improvement operations can be scaled back or eliminated?

As one means of undertaking a serious and successful reengineering effort, we recommend that the Census Bureau develop a plan for conducting the new "integrated single-number" census in 2000 that would eliminate a substantial fraction of the $1.3 billion increased costs between 1970 and 1990, with a target for cost savings much larger than the $300 to $400 million already identified. The Census Bureau should identify what would have to be done to meet a target for substantial cost savings and spell out the consequences both for its operations and for the quality of the resulting census.

Since we have not been able to pinpoint the specific components of operations and procedures that led to the cost increase from 1970 to 1990, we cannot predict the full magnitude of the cost reduction that would be feasible while still producing a high-quality census. But we are convinced that a good-faith effort to develop such a plan would identify important cost savings that could be made without a significant sacrifice of quality. These savings could result from reengineering all census operations in the context of a single-number census in which enumeration and statistical estimation are fully integrated.

Recommendation 5.6 We recommend that the Census Bureau undertake a thorough reexamination of the basic structure, organization, and processes by which the decennial census is conducted to

obtain the full cost-saving potential of the proposed redesigned census. As one part of its reexamination, the Census Bureau should develop a plan for the 2000 census that eliminates a substantial fraction of the $1.3 billion cost increase (in 1990 dollars) from 1970 to 1990 that is not accounted for by the growth in housing units and the decline in the mail response rate. The target for this plan should be much more than the $300 to $400 million we have already identified.

Support for the New Design

The Census Bureau should settle expeditiously on a new census design that contains a reasonable rate of direct enumeration combined with greater reliance on statistical estimation. Such a design can produce not only lower costs, but also improved accuracy for the single most important variable: the count of population, particularly by race and ethnicity. Because people not familiar with statistical sampling and survey techniques may be alarmed by some of the characteristics of a census that relies more heavily on sampling and statistical estimation, the Census Bureau should undertake a sustained program of public education about this plan well in advance of the 2000 census.

Recommendation 5.7 The panel recommends that the Census Bureau publicize, as soon as possible, its plan for implementing a redesigned census. It should then move to obtain early commitment for the new plan from both Congress and data users.

CENSUS CONTENT AND THE LONG FORM

Historically, the census has collected additional content beyond the minimum set of items needed from all households for the constitutional purposes of reapportionment and redistricting. Since 1960, most of the additional data have been collected on a separate long form sent to a fraction of households (most households have received a short form). These additional data are widely used and serve many important public purposes. The nation needs the breadth of information for small areas and small population groups that these census data now provide.

Conclusion 6.1 The panel concludes that, in addition to data to satisfy constitutional requirements, there are essential public needs for small-area data and data on small population groups of the type and breadth now collected in the decennial census.

The process for determining the content of the census (both the short and the long forms) has involved bringing together federal agencies and balancing their data needs against considerations of questionnaire length and feasibility. Views of other data users have also been sought. This process has worked well and should be maintained and strengthened.

Conclusion 6.2 The panel concludes that the process of determining the census content by involving federal agencies and eliciting the views of other users has worked well in the past and should be continued. In our judgment, the process would be strengthened by increasing the oversight and coordination role of the chief statistician in the Office of Management and Budget.

In 1990, the long form—sent to approximately 1 in 6 households, or about 15 million of the nation's 92 million households—had 58 items in addition to the 13 on the short form. Its length and complexity have led to some suggestions that dropping the long form would significantly improve the census mail response rate and substantially lower costs. It has been variously suggested that much of the lost data could be replaced by the use of administrative records or by a large-scale and continuing sample survey of households.

Our work does not support these suggestions. In our judgment:

• The long form has not been responsible for the decline in response rates or the increase in costs in the last several censuses: the number of questions has been roughly the same for a number of decades, and the sampling rate has declined as a percentage of households.

• Available evidence indicates that the overall effect on response rates of dropping the long form would not be large (about a 1 percentage point increase) and, in any event, would apply only to the 1 in 6 households that currently receive the long form. The evidence also suggests that the long form does not increase the undercount or adversely affect the differential undercount by race to any significant extent.

• Given the necessity of conducting a decennial census, the inclusion of a long form questionnaire for a large sample of households is a cost-effective way of obtaining highly valuable information.

Conclusion 6.3 The panel concludes that the marginal cost of incremental data on the decennial census is low. In particular, we conclude that the extra cost of the census long form, once the census has been designed to collect limited data for every resident, is relatively low.

One proposal to reduce the burden of the census long form on each household that receives it is to spread out the long-form content over several, somewhat shorter forms, in an approach called matrix sampling.

Recommendation 6.1 The panel recommends that the Census Bureau evaluate the merits of a matrix sampling approach that uses several intermediate forms in place of a single long form to reduce respondent burden. The Census Bureau should examine the effects on:

- **satisfying data users' needs;**
- **mail return rates;**
- **sampling and nonsampling errors (including item nonresponse rates);**
- **operational problems; and**
- **data processing and estimation problems that could affect the usefulness of the information, particularly for multivariate analysis.**

Another approach to reducing respondent burden, which the Census Bureau has recently been investigating, is to drop the long form from the census and substitute a continuous measurement survey—that is, a large monthly survey of perhaps 200,000 to 500,000 households. By averaging the results of the monthly surveys over a period of 3 to 5 years, more timely long-form-type data, accurate enough for use in relatively small geographic areas, could be produced. At the state level and for large metropolitan areas, estimates could be made by averaging over much shorter periods. In its preliminary work, the Census Bureau has speculated that the costs of the new continuous measurement survey over a decade could be roughly offset by the cost savings from dropping the long form from the census and by other cost reductions that might be achieved in intercensal operations.

The panel has followed the ongoing plans of the Census Bureau with great care and interest. Although we believe that the proposed continuous measurement system deserves serious evaluation, we conclude that much work remains to develop credible estimates of its net costs and to answer many other fundamental questions about data quality, the use of small-area estimates based on cumulated data, how continuous measurement could be integrated with existing household surveys, and its advantages compared with other means of providing more frequent small-area estimates. In our judgment, it will not be possible to complete this work in time to consider the use of continuous measurement in place of the long form for the 2000 census.

**Conclusion 6.4 The panel concludes that the work to date on con-
tinuous measurement has overestimated the savings from dropping
the long form, understated the cost of a continuous measurement
system, and not sufficiently examined feasible alternatives for meeting the nation's needs for more timely long-form-type data at reasonable overall cost. We conclude that it will not be possible to
complete the needed research in time to make the critical decisions
regarding the format of the 2000 census. We therefore do not recommend substituting continuous measurement for the long form in
the 2000 census.**

For the longer term, the Census Bureau's program of research on continuous
measurement should be expanded and redirected in a framework that considers
alternative cost-effective ways to meet the needs of data users for intercensal
estimates and how efforts to that end can be integrated with the overall federal
statistical system.

**Recommendation 6.2 The panel recommends that the Census Bu-
reau broaden its research on alternatives for more frequent small-
area data to encompass a wider range than continuous measurement, as currently envisaged. In that context, the Census Bureau
should examine the cost-effectiveness of alternatives, the ways in
which they meet user needs, and the manner in which continuous
measurement or other alternatives could be integrated into the
nation's system of household surveys. The research program should
be carried out in cooperation with the federal statistical agencies
that sponsor household surveys and should include evaluation of
the quality of important data elements, the frequency and modes of
data collection, and the manner in which results would be presented,
as well as methods for introducing change over time.**

Summarizing our conclusions about the content of the 2000 census, we see
the long form as a cost-effective means of collecting needed data, and we conclude that there is no feasible alternative to the long form for 2000.

**Recommendation 6.3 The panel recommends that the 2000 census
include a large sample survey that obtains the data historically gathered through a long form.**

DATA ON RACE AND ETHNICITY

Historically, the decennial census has included questions on race and
ethnicity and provided classifications for respondents to check. The number and

character of the classifications have changed over time as social attitudes have changed, as changes have occurred in the racial and ethnic makeup of the population, and as the needs for race and ethnicity data by governments and society have evolved. The short-form questions on race and ethnicity in the 1990 census included 15 categories or subcategories listed in the question on race and 4 categories in the question about Spanish/Hispanic origin.

In recent decades these data have become particularly significant. The growing public concern about problems related to racial and ethnic discrimination has emphasized the need for accurate demographic data on race and ethnicity. The Voting Rights Act of 1965 (as amended), together with court interpretations, has substantially expanded the need for race and ethnicity data at the small-area level for congressional redistricting and other purposes. At the same time, the disturbing growth in the differential undercount in the 1990 census for ethnic and racial minorities has called attention to problems with the demographic data on race and ethnicity collected by the census.

At present, there are growing but conflicting public pressures for enlarging and changing the race and ethnicity classifications used in the census. The census form provides for self-identification of race and ethnicity by respondents. But the presumption that only one classification per respondent is appropriate is being challenged by the growing heterogeneity of American households as a result of rising immigration, increased interracial and interethnic marriages, greater numbers of people with multiple racial identities, and expanded recognition in recent decades of the fluidity of race and ethnicity classifications. The design of future censuses must take these changes into account.

Conclusion 7.1 The panel concludes that there are inherent ambiguities to racial and ethnic status. We recognize that reporting of this status in the census has multiple meanings for respondents and that the context of reporting affects how people self-identify.

Conclusion 7.2 The panel concludes that the census questionnaire must be developed as a well-tested means for obtaining nationally useful data on race and ethnicity to meet constitutional and legally mandated federal requirements and for other legislative and program needs and informational purposes.

Recommendation 7.1 The panel recommends that the Census Bureau expand its examination and testing of race and ethnicity questions to provide comprehensive information on: (1) public understanding of the concepts and acceptability of questions, (2) compatibility among the several census items and the utility of crosstabulations, (3) the comparability of census data to race and ethnicity data collected in other federal surveys or obtained from

administrative records, and (4) the quality of data for small areas and specific groups. This research needs to be given a high priority so that the results may be incorporated into the review of Statistical Directive 15 currently being conducted by the Office of Management and Budget.

Recommendation 7.2   The panel recommends that the Office of Management and Budget issue a revision of Statistical Directive 15 sufficiently early to provide adequate time for planning and testing for the 2000 census and coordinated implementation of changes by all affected agencies.

SOME RADICAL ALTERNATIVES TO THE CENSUS

The panel evaluated a number of proposals for radically different ways of collecting the data now provided in the decennial census before deciding to recommend a redesigned census combining traditional enumeration with greater use of statistical estimation. (These alternatives are discussed in Chapter 4 of the report, prior to the discussion of the redesigned census in Chapter 5 and census content issues in Chapters 6 and 7. This Summary reverses the order of the discussion.)

There are three critical requirements for census data to which the panel attached great weight in assessing alternative data collection methods. First, for constitutional, legislative, and many other legitimate reasons, households, people, and their characteristics must be associated with specific geographic locations— with residential addresses. Second, and of particular importance since the enactment of the Voting Rights Act, data are required on the racial and ethnic identification of people, again associated with residential addresses. Third, there is a range of critical needs for small-area data that include information on a wide variety of population characteristics.

A National Register

A population register is a special type of administrative record, a system maintained by the mandatory continuous registration of all residents. If each individual is issued an identification number (like a Social Security number), a register can be cross-referenced to administrative records to provide a wide variety of data linked to addresses. To be useful for census-type data, people would be legally required to update their addresses at periodic intervals with the governmental unit that keeps the register.

A national register has the advantage of timely data availability (more frequently than once every 10 years). If the cost of operating a population register is absorbed by other administrative uses, then the additional cost of using the data for statistical purposes may be relatively low; however, the United States has no such system in place. Moreover, proposals to create a register would raise privacy and civil rights concerns almost surely sufficient to make it unacceptable in the American culture, and, without a high degree of public cooperation, a national register would produce low-quality data.

Conclusion 4.1 The panel concludes that a national register for the United States is not a feasible replacement for the decennial census.

An Administrative Records Census

There are three potential ways in which administrative records—such as records of the Social Security Administration, the Internal Revenue Service, and the vital statistics systems of state and local governments—can be used to supplant or supplement the decennial census: (1) administrative records could substitute for the entire census; (2) a very simple census could be taken with only a few basic questions and other necessary census-type information obtained from administrative records; and (3) administrative records could be used in the taking of the regular census—for example, by helping to find hard-to-reach population groups—and to improve the quality of intercensal data. Only the first two options represent radical alternatives to the conventional census because administrative records are already used to assist in the census.

The possible use of administrative records to take the place of all or a major part of the census is hampered by several factors. No single set of administrative records is complete enough for the data needed, so that large-scale linkage of records from different systems would be likely to be required, leading to increased costs and privacy problems. Many sets of records (e.g., the bulk of Social Security files) lack up-to-date addresses. There would be political, social, and statistical reliability problems inherent in requiring that ethnicity and race data be supplied as part of administrative records. It would be very difficult to "unduplicate" administrative records when data from several different record systems are combined without the availability of a comprehensive and uniform personal identification number. Nevertheless, the use of administrative records in the census can be expanded, and we suggest ways in which this can be done.

Conclusion 4.2 The panel concludes that an administrative records census is not a feasible option for 2000.

A Census Conducted by the U.S. Postal Service

Since the U.S. Postal Service regularly visits the vast majority of residences in this country, some have suggested that it be given the task of collecting decennial census data by delivering a questionnaire to every residence and conducting the basic census enumeration, with the Census Bureau responsible for designing the questionnaire and tabulating the results. This suggestion does not deal with the fact that the most difficult and costly task of the census is collecting information from those who have failed to return the mail questionnaire, either through direct follow-up visits or by survey techniques. For neither of these tasks is the Postal Service a suitable or cost-effective vehicle. The hourly costs of letter carriers are more than three times the hourly costs of census enumerators in the 1990 census. A joint study by the Census Bureau and the U.S. Postal Service concluded, for a variety of reasons, that it would not be practical for letter carriers to replace census enumerators.

Conclusion 4.3 The panel concludes that the decennial census cannot be conducted by the U.S. Postal Service in any way that would be cost-effective or an improvement over the conventional census.

The U.S. Postal Service and the Census Bureau can greatly assist each other in census-related activities, and we make specific recommendations to foster that cooperation.

A Sample or Rolling Census

Two sample survey approaches are possible for completely replacing the conventional census. One is the use of a large sample survey to produce an estimate of the total U.S. population and its characteristics at a single point in time. Some have referred to such a large survey for estimating the population as a *sample census*. The other approach is a rolling census, which entails the complete enumeration of the population in such a manner that the sample enumerated at any given time is a random sample of the whole population. One option for a rolling census is an annual 1-in-10 sample survey designed to enumerate the entire population over a 10-year period.

The key challenge to a sample census is that the Constitution calls for a complete count of the population at one point in time. Also, by all the available evidence, household surveys experience higher net undercoverage rates and more severe differential undercoverage than does the complete-count census. Furthermore, a sample census would require the development of an accurate sampling frame (e.g., a complete list of all dwellings in the United States) from which to draw the sample. For a rolling census, the cost is likely to exceed the cost of a conventional census. Finally, public acceptability of either a sample census or a rolling census is likely to be low because both lack the high-profile, attendant publicity, and historic image of the decennial census.

Conclusion 4.4 The panel concludes that a rolling or sample census is not an acceptable replacement for the 2000 decennial census.

INTERCENSAL SMALL-AREA DATA

The availability of accurate demographic and related data for small areas—cities, counties, school districts, neighborhoods, and other small geographic areas—is most important for the efficient planning and operation of many federal, state, and local government activities, for large numbers of business firms, and for research in many areas. A wide variety of government agencies has come to place great reliance on small-area data, and the decennial census is a key source for such information. Not only is it used directly, but it can also be combined with more current data from other sources to produce additional information. The census data themselves, however, suffer from the disadvantage of progressive obsolescence as people move and economic conditions change over the 10 years between censuses. In a mobile population such as that of the United States, this obsolescence is particularly rapid.

Although the enhancement of current annual surveys might, at some additional cost, provide more timely estimates for larger geographic areas (states, metropolitan areas, and populous counties and cities), the cost of surveys large enough to supply annual data for small areas would be prohibitive. We commented above on the proposal to substitute a continuous measurement survey for the decennial long form that would produce a 3- or 5-year moving average of small-area data. So far there has been little support from small-area data users for such a move. Still, the Census Bureau, in the redirected research program that we recommend, should carefully explore the response of users to the proposal.

The most cost-effective way of improving the availability of intercensal small-area data is likely to be the expanded use of federal, state, and local administrative records to supplement decennial census data. By conducting experiments with the use of administrative records, the Census Bureau could gradually build a reservoir of knowledge about the potentials and the limitations of such records and the modifications in records that would be needed to make them useful for statistical purposes. Efforts along this line would strongly benefit from the expansion of mutually cooperative arrangements among the Census Bureau, federal agencies, and state and local governments.

Recommendation 8.1 The panel recommends that the Census Bureau work to improve the amount, quantity, and frequency of small-area intercensal data:

• The Census Bureau should conduct experiments with federal administrative records for deriving more frequent small-area intercensal data estimates. At a minimum, the panel recommends that the Census Bureau geocode several large federal administrative record systems and use them to produce small-area estimates.

• **The Census Bureau should work with state and local governments to enhance the quantity and frequency of small-area data.**

Recommendation 8.2 The panel recommends that the Census Bureau give a single unit sole responsibility to exploit administrative records and produce small-area intercensal estimates on a frequent basis. Its work on administrative records should examine geographic consistency and quality. The unit should develop methods for increasing geographic content; establishing consistency of federal, state, and local administrative data; augmenting content on national records; augmenting usefulness of the resulting information through modeling; and computerizing approaches to database management to facilitate the use of administrative data in a census. If the content of administrative records can be improved for use in preparing small-area estimates, that is desirable, but the major purpose of the unit would be to produce small-area intercensal estimates.

In support of each recent census, the Census Bureau created a master file of residential addresses and, in 1990, linked that file to a geographic reference system (called TIGER), which provides map locations for physical features including roads, streets, and address ranges. The panel has been informed that the Census Bureau and the U.S. Postal Service are well along in the development of a cooperative arrangement under which the vast bulk of the master address file for the census and the associated TIGER system would be kept continuously updated. On the basis of preliminary estimates provided by the Census Bureau, the 10-year cost of keeping these files updated is, to a first approximation, no higher than the cost incurred each decade to build them from scratch.

The updated address files would be a major tool that state and local governments could use, in combination with decennial census data and currently available information from administrative records and other sources, to improve small-area data during intercensal periods. At the same time, such local uses of the address file would greatly contribute to its completeness. An address file that is complete and accurate and geographically referenced to small areas will also support the redesigned census, with its increased reliance on sampling and statistical estimation to determine the number and characteristics of nonrespondents. To make possible an accessible continuously updated national address file, politically acceptable changes in the laws and regulations governing census information would need to be worked out in order to make the address file (without information about residents) available to cooperating state and local governments for statistical purposes only.

The Census Bureau should examine the cost and coverage of a continuously updated national address file and geographically referenced database. The examination should evaluate its use as a sampling frame for large federal household surveys, its use for geographically referencing administrative records for small-area intercensal estimates, and possible savings that would offset its costs.

Recommendation 8.3 **If the cost estimates for continually updating the master address file and associated geographic-referencing database (including costs by the Census Bureau and others) are comparable to the cost of one-time updating just prior to the census, the panel recommends that development proceed. If the cost estimates are higher, then the clear advantages of the continuously updated address system should be weighed against the additional costs. If a decision is then made to continue, the Census Bureau should proceed with the necessary steps, including the necessary accompanying safeguards, to make the master address file available for statistical purposes to the federal statistical system and to cooperating state and local governments.**

1

The Role of the Census

The United States will conduct its next population census in 2000—the twenty-second such census since the nation was founded. The Constitution of the United States, article I, section 2, specifically requires a decennial census to provide information for reapportionment of seats in the U.S. House of Representatives, which, by extension, also means providing information to redraw congressional district boundaries:

> Representatives . . . shall be apportioned among the several States which may be included within this Union, according to their respective numbers. . . . The actual Enumeration shall be made within three Years after the first Meeting of the Congress of the United States, and within every subsequent Term of ten Years, in such Manner as they shall by Law direct.

Censuses in the nineteenth century were ad hoc operations, carried out initially by U.S. marshals and then by temporarily employed enumerators under the supervision of a census office that was set up anew and disbanded each decade. In 1902 an act of Congress established a permanent Bureau of the Census, now lodged within the Department of Commerce, that assumed responsibility for planning and supervising the census on a professional basis (see Anderson, 1988).

The modern census in the United States is a complex series of operations, involving a long lead time for planning and a multitude of steps in execution. The basic methodology for recent censuses includes the following steps (variations in the process occur in some instances: for example, census enumerators deliver unaddressed questionnaires to rural households—see Appendix B):

19

- the advance preparation of a master list of addresses;
- the mailout of questionnaires to all addresses on the list with the request that each household complete the questionnaire and return it by mail;
- the follow-up by enumerators for questionnaires that are not returned and to obtain answers to missing items (some of this follow-up is done by telephone);
- a series of checks to strive for more complete coverage of the population;
- computerized processing of the questionnaires and tabulation of the results; and
- a program to evaluate the quality of the enumeration.

With regard to content, the U.S. census has almost from the very beginning obtained added information about the population beyond the absolute minimum required for reapportionment and redistricting. Since 1940, the census has also obtained information on the nation's housing stock. In the most recent census in 1990, about 104 million questionnaires were mailed out (or delivered by census enumerators).[1] Five of every six of those questionnaires ("short forms") asked households to respond to 6 questions for each person in the household and 7 questions on the housing unit. The remaining one-sixth of the questionnaires ("long forms") asked households to respond to an additional 35 questions on the household members and 23 questions on the housing unit (see Appendix A).

In other words, the 1990 census, like every census since 1940, included a sample survey as part of the complete enumeration. The 1940 census was the first to have enumerators ask questions of a sample of the population; the 1960 census was the first to have the Postal Service deliver (unaddressed) questionnaires and initiated the use of separate, printed short and long forms (the latter containing additional items asked of a sample of households).

In many respects, the 1990 census was a very successful operation, particularly considering the difficulties inherent in attempting to enumerate a large and diverse population. It was, however, expensive—in both total dollars ($2.6 billion) and costs per housing unit ($25). Moreover, these costs exceeded the costs of previous censuses, even allowing for inflation, decline in mail response rates, and growth in the number of households. Like previous censuses, the 1990 census also had errors. Most prominent and politically sensitive—because of the implications for the distribution of legislative seats and funding for government programs—were differential coverage errors, in which some population groups and geographic areas were counted less thoroughly than others. Despite the increased amount of money spent on the 1990 census, there was a somewhat higher net undercount of the total population than in 1980, as measured by the technique of demographic analysis (1.8 percent compared with 1.2 percent), and a somewhat larger difference between the net undercount rates for minorities and whites.

Following the 1990 census there was growing concern that census costs might continue to climb with no likelihood of gains in the completeness of coverage. Fueling this concern was the evidence of declining public cooperation with the census—in 1990, only 74 percent of households mailed back their questionnaire compared with a return rate of 81 percent in 1980, thereby adding costs to send out enumerators to follow up the nonresponding households. (The mail return rates cited refer to the percent of *occupied* households that sent back a questionnaire; the mailback rates for all housing units, including occupied and vacant, were lower.) To obtain an independent assessment of how best to address these concerns, Congress asked the Committee on National Statistics to establish the Panel on Census Requirements in the Year 2000 and Beyond. Our panel was asked to evaluate the need for the data in the census, to consider whether needed data are better collected in the census itself or by some other data collection system, and, in general, to identify changes to the census that could ameliorate the twin problems of coverage errors and high costs.

OVERVIEW OF THE REPORT

In the remainder of this introductory chapter, we summarize our findings and conclusions about users' requirements for census data and the extent to which these data serve important public policy purposes (appendices provide detailed reviews of various types of census data uses). We also outline the criteria—including implications for content, cost, quality of information, feasibility, timeliness, and public acceptability—that we used to evaluate proposed changes in census methods, including alternatives to the census itself for collecting needed content. Chapter 2 briefly reviews the history of coverage problems in the census, and Chapter 3 reviews in detail the cost structure of the 1990 census and the patterns and reasons for the marked escalation in census costs over the past few decades.

The next four chapters address issues of method and content for the 2000 census, with reference to our evaluation criteria. Chapter 4 considers the merits of radical alternatives that have been proposed to replace current census methodology (e.g., establishing a national population register). Chapter 5 considers fundamental reforms to the current census process, such as the use of sampling in nonresponse follow-up. Chapter 6 discusses issues related to the overall census content, including whether the long form, which goes to a sample of households, adversely affects the costs and coverage of the basic census and whether a system of continuing household mail surveys could replace the long form. Chapter 7 considers the needs for census data on the important content items of race and ethnicity and the problems associated with obtaining such data.

Finally, Chapter 8 discusses issues and possible approaches for obtaining more frequent small-area estimates between censuses. Appendices provide additional information on specific topics.

THE NEED FOR CENSUS DATA

Before we consider how best to conduct the census, or whether and how to replace the traditional census process in whole or in part with some other data collection system, we should be clear about the data requirements that a census (or a comparable alternative) must satisfy. We review below data needs for reapportionment and redistricting, which are constitutionally mandated, and other data needs, for which a rationale must be established.

Data Needs for Reapportionment and Redistricting

The bedrock purpose of the census is to provide data for legislative reapportionment and redistricting. Over the last few decades, legislation and court rulings have extended this basic constitutional mandate for the census. Court decisions implementing the "one-person, one-vote" principle have required the census to produce data that will support legislative reapportionment and redistricting for all levels of government with a very high degree of accuracy. The census, therefore, cannot merely count the population, but must determine precisely where people live. Also, the Voting Rights Act, as originally enacted in 1965 and continued and amended several times since, has required the census to produce not only population counts by age but also data on race and ethnic origin at a very fine geographic level of detail. Although the Voting Rights Act and court decisions do not specify the census as the source of such data, the census (or a comparable replacement for it) is the only practical source (see Appendix C).

The legal requirements for census data for purposes of legislative reapportionment and redistricting determine several key features that a census must have. First, the census must include an attempt at a complete enumeration of the entire country at one point in time. Second, the census must provide basic data (e.g., age and race) at the smallest possible geographic level, namely, the census block. Data at the block level are needed not so much for themselves as to permit legislative districts to be drawn by combining blocks to meet court-mandated criteria for equal populations across districts and appropriate representation of minority groups under the Voting Rights Act.

Other Data Needs

Given the constitutionally grounded requirement for a census with such basic information as age, race, and sex (these items are necessary as well to ensure that people are counted once and only once), what additional content is needed? The census is unique among the statistical activities of the federal government in that it provides data on a range of topics that are reasonably accurate for small geographic areas and also small subgroups of the population (e.g., small ethnic and occupational groups). The federal government sponsors many surveys that provide more in-depth information on a particular subject (e.g., income, transportation, housing, educational attainment), but such surveys provide estimates only for relatively large geographic areas (e.g., regions, states, and metropolitan areas). Administrative records systems also provide useful information, but they typically pertain to a particular population group (e.g,. recipients of social security and public assistance benefits) and have limited content. The census alone provides a broad range of information that can be cross-tabulated for small geographic areas (and small subgroups).

One question is whether all this information is serving important purposes. Another question is whether collecting all this information materially impairs the accuracy and increases the costs of obtaining the minimal set of items that is needed for the census's primary purpose. A third question is whether some other data collection system could better serve to obtain needed content or whether the census itself remains a cost-effective vehicle for this purpose. We address the latter two questions in Chapter 6. Here we consider the value of the additional content that is currently collected in the census.

Federal Agency Needs for Census Data

We begin by looking at the legal requirements for census content in federal statutes and agency regulations. It is dangerous to push too hard for a requirement that each and every item on the census must be legally mandated. Some items lacking legal mandates may be needed for such important purposes as improving census coverage. Also, the determination of the length and content of the census questionnaire is not well served by requiring agencies to seek statutory approval for each item. Such a process could result in an *increase* in census content and, in any event, should not substitute for a decision process that makes deliberate trade-offs among agency needs, considered all together, and that takes into account the changing needs for data to inform current and emerging policy concerns as well as those from the past.

Nonetheless, it is important to determine whether the census content is required to serve important federal policy and program purposes. We reviewed materials compiled by the Census Bureau and the Office of Management and Budget on the federal mandates for items in the 1990 census (see Appendix M). The results are quite clear: almost all census items are required by federal government agencies to meet specific mandates. For some items, legislation requires the item and specifies that it be obtained from the census. For other items, the legislation requiring the item does not specify the census as the source, although the census (or a comparable replacement for it) is the only practical source. For a few items, there is no legislation but a requirement generated by agency program operations.

Listed below are just a few of the many examples of legislatively mandated items (see Appendix M for others):

• The Elementary and Secondary Education Act requires data on the poverty status of school-age children by school district to allocate federal compensatory education funds. School districts vary in size from entire cities or counties to small towns or even smaller districts. At the present time, only the census long-form sample provides the necessary small-area data on income for determining the proportion of poor school-age children in each district.

• The 1975 and later amendments to the Voting Rights Act require the director of the Census Bureau to determine political jurisdictions (counties, municipalities, and townships) that must implement procedures for bilingual voting to protect the rights of language minorities. These determinations are currently made from long-form census data on mother tongue, citizenship, educational attainment, and English-language ability, together with information on age, race, and ethnicity.

• Title 42, Section 1786, of the U.S. Code requires the Department of Agriculture Food and Nutrition Service to obtain census data by state and county to determine the number of women, infants, and children whose families have incomes below the maximum income limit for the Special Supplemental Nutrition Program for Women, Infants, and Children (WIC).

• Various sections of the U.S. Code require the Department of Agriculture Rural Development Administration to use census data on income for tracts and counties to allocate grant funds and determine loan interest rates for several assistance programs (e.g., the Emergency Community Water Assistance Program and the Water and Waste Disposal Loan and Grant Program).

Just a few of the other applications of census data by federal agencies that are based on authorizing legislation include:

• The Immigration and Naturalization Service uses census data for governmental units on place of birth, citizenship, year of entry, and other characteristics to prepare congressionally required reports and for program planning and evaluation purposes.

• The Equal Employment Opportunity Commission uses census labor force data by zip code to analyze statistical evidence in class action charges of employment discrimination.

• The Department of Transportation uses census data on disability for traffic analysis zones to monitor compliance with the Federal Transit Act and the Americans with Disabilities Act.

In addition, the census serves important functions in the federal statistical system. Some of these functions, such as providing denominators for vital rates (e.g., birth and death rates) and reweighting household sample surveys to more accurately reflect the distribution of the population (such surveys invariably have higher coverage errors than the census itself), involve the basic census content on age, race, and sex. Other uses of census data by federal statistical agencies involve additional content items, for example:

- The census address list serves as the sampling frame for many federal surveys, saving agencies the expense of developing such a frame (with the exception of areas of new construction). Often, such census content items as income and occupation are used to make the survey sample design more cost-effective.
- Census data on income and other characteristics are used by the Bureau of Economic Analysis in developing regional, state, and local-area personal income estimates. In turn, these estimates are used by federal agencies in formulas that allocate federal funds for such programs as Medicaid and Aid to Families with Dependent Children.
- Census data on place of work and other characteristics are used by the Office of Management and Budget to define metropolitan statistical areas, which in turn have many applications in federal programs.

Needs of Other Data Users

Reviewing federal agency uses of census data made it clear to us that the items in the 1990 census were there to serve important federal agency purposes. No item was included because it served exclusively the interest of some other community (e.g., business, academia).[2] Of course, many other organizations and individuals in addition to federal agencies—state and local governments, business organizations, universities and other research institutions, nonprofit organizations, the media, students, and individual citizens—make use of census data, often in conjunction with data of their own. Indeed, since the availability of computer-readable data files beginning with the 1970 census, there has been an explosion in the use of census data by all kinds of users for all kinds of purposes (see Appendices C-H).

In some cases, these uses are a direct consequence of federal mandates—for example, states and local governments need certain items to obtain federal aid and to satisfy the requirements of the Voting Rights Act. In other instances, there is no direct link to a federal requirement, but the uses nonetheless serve federal purposes in a broad sense.

Thus, local governments make extensive use of small-area census data to identify target populations for services and to allocate facilities and resources to serve target populations most effectively. For example, they may use census tract or block group data on a variety of characteristics to locate health clinics or to determine the need for establishing programs to serve groups of new immigrants. Such analyses, properly carried out, help make best use of scarce local tax dollars—and of state and federal tax dollars that go to localities to support programs and services.

Often such analyses use data from other sources—for example, local governments frequently map local administrative data (e.g., on hospital admissions, clinic visits, school enrollment) to the same geographic areas for which they obtain census data, in order to determine rates of service use, indicators of unmet need, and the like. For these kinds of uses, the administrative data add an important element, but the array of census data is the linchpin that makes the analysis possible.

Businesses also make extensive use of census data. Some business uses—for example, to evaluate progress in hiring disadvantaged groups by analyzing occupation and demographic characteristics of local labor markets—directly serve public purposes established in federal legislation and court actions. Other business uses—for example, to help determine the best site for a plant or retail outlet by analyzing socioeconomic and demographic characteristics in different locations—serve public purposes indirectly by helping to make the best use of scarce investment dollars for expansion and redirection of business operations.

Research uses of census data serve a public purpose by advancing knowledge that in turn often has policy implications. For example, analysis of census data on patterns of internal migration contributes to understanding of the factors that influence regional growth and decline. Also, analysis of census data on the numbers, characteristics, and destinations of groups of new immigrants is directly relevant to current highly visible policy issues surrounding the benefits and burdens of immigration to the United States.

Finally, census data serve the important purpose of informing the public—through the media and other dissemination channels (e.g., libraries). Citizens benefit from information on the characteristics of their locality or their population group—individually and in comparison with other localities or groups—in performing many civic functions, such as voting, organizing to support legislation, and otherwise participating fully in a democratic society.

Proposals are sometimes made that data users should pay for collecting needed census information. These proposals miss the mark in several respects. First, from our review, there are no items included in the census solely to serve other users and not also to meet a federal agency requirement; hence, there are no items that could be charged off to private organizations or other nonfederal users. To the contrary, their uses of census information represent an added return on the federal investment in census data collection and one that is very cost-effective: once the data have been collected and tabulated for federal purposes, the cost of providing them to others is normally quite small.[3] Moreover, having census data available to all and not just to those who pay is an important factor in maximizing the added returns from census data use (e.g., small businesses or poor localities are not disadvantaged in this regard).

Second, although federal agencies could be asked to pay for "their" items, there are problems with such an approach. Many items, such as income and education, are needed as analytical variables by almost all agencies. Also, such a financing system would complicate planning for the census, in that the scope of the questionnaire could be uncertain until very late in the decade. Finally, given the need for agencies to have their items included in the census in order to carry out their mandates, it is unlikely that agencies would opt out of the census. Hence, to have agencies pay for items would at best amount to a rearrangement of federal budget dollars with little or no impact on overall census costs and, more likely, would add to costs given the need for added coordination.

Conclusion About Data Needs

We believe that the need for census content (beyond the minimum set of items) is clear. By this statement, we do not mean to endorse each and every item nor to suggest that the overall content could not be reduced somewhat. But we do mean to endorse the necessity and usefulness of data on a range of topics that can be cross-tabulated for small areas and small groups.

Hence, the issue, in our minds, comes down to whether there is some other mechanism that can obtain equivalent data, either at lower cost then adding content to the basic census or at about the same cost but with other benefits (e.g., greater frequency of data). We address this issue in Chapter 6 in our discussion of the cost and coverage effects of the long form and possible alternatives to it. In Chapter 8, we discuss more generally alternatives for obtaining more frequent small-area data between censuses.

CRITERIA FOR EVALUATING APPROACHES TO THE CENSUS

There are some major national policy choices involved in considering requirements and techniques for the decennial census. The panel sees its role as one of identifying those choices and providing analysis to make informed decisions possible. Some major options for conducting future censuses illustrate the dilemma in thinking about what a future census should look like. First, should the census be a highly intensive physical enumeration with a complete physical follow-up of all nonresponses, or should physical enumeration efforts be reduced through the use of sample-based follow-up? Should the census include an intensive effort to physically count every person, or should it rely on various statistical techniques for adjustment? The trade-offs, in this case, involve costs, accuracy, and the acceptability of statistical adjustment. A second choice involves how to implement the basic requirements of court decisions mandating equality in population size of voting districts. Both the court decisions and the Voting Rights Act—grounded firmly in the Constitution, including the Fourteenth and Fifteenth amendments—mandate census data requirements. Third, what level of information beyond basic demographic detail must be provided every 10 years for small areas or small population groups? A large number of programs and funding allocation are based on decennial census data. Data from surveys or administrative records could be used to provide more timely estimates, albeit with less geographic detail than the census. Administrative records can provide estimates for small areas with selected content that is designed and reported for administrative purposes. To what extent can alternative sources meet reasonable needs, and at what cost?

Our conclusions on the merits of proposed changes in the census, including radical alternatives, fundamental reforms, and minor alterations, are based on several criteria. Most important among them are the following:

- *Information content and statistical quality.* Under this rubric, we asked such questions as: Does the proposed alternative provide a range of information for small geographic areas and population groups? Specifically, does it provide data needed for constitutional purposes and for other required uses by federal government agencies? Does the alternative reduce or increase errors in the data, such as coverage errors, sampling errors, and other biases?
- *Operational feasibility and costs.* Under this heading, we asked: What are the costs of the alternative, including developmental costs and likely steady-state operating costs? What are the implications for work flow and organization of the census process? Would legislation be required to implement the alternative?
- *Dissemination.* Can the alternative provide data more frequently than every 10 years? How rapidly after data collection can output be provided? Can output be provided for locally defined and changing geographic areas? In addition, we asked whether various aspects of the census data collection process could be used, perhaps in combination with other sources, to provide better intercensal information.
- *Public acceptability.* Will the alternative be acceptable to the public, or will it suffer by comparison to the high profile and historic image of the traditional census? Will a reasonably large proportion of households respond with accurate information? Will the data produced be politically acceptable for constitutional and legislative purposes?

Using these criteria, we considered ways for the U.S. census in 2000 to provide a rich array of needed data for small areas and small population groups at reduced costs and with acceptable quality. Most of the focus of this report is on planning for the 2000 census. It may not be possible, however, to fully implement all of the reforms advocated in this report in 2000, and thus the 2000 census may be a transition to a fully redesigned census in 2010 and beyond. We therefore have considered ways to improve estimates throughout the decade following 2000 and to achieve possibly even greater reform of the methodology for censuses in the year 2010 and beyond.

NOTES

[1] As it turned out, about 92 million questionnaires went to occupied households, and the remainder were sent to units that were determined to be vacant or no longer residential.

[2] The items on appliances that were included in the 1960 and 1970 censuses (e.g., whether the household had a washing machine or dryer—see Appendix A) are often cited as examples of content provided to serve exclusively business marketing interests. However, these items were asked primarily because they represented important indicators for federal agencies of standard-of-living differences across the country; their use by the private sector was secondary. They may have been retained on the questionnaire for one too many censuses, but they were requested and justified by federal agencies.

[3] People do pay some minimal amount for census data at present. The sale of census data normally includes the reproduction and publication costs.

2

Population Coverage and Its Implications

Although the census count of the U.S. population has never been complete, public concerns about the incompleteness have increased in recent decades. The census is the sole basis for apportionment of congressional seats and is relied on heavily for the distribution of federal funds. Improved statistical and demographic techniques permit the Census Bureau to estimate the incompleteness of the census with greater accuracy than in the past. Thus, concern about census incompleteness springs, ironically, from the improved professional work of Census Bureau staff and from extraordinary expectations for a "complete" census count.

Some undercount of the population occurs in all censuses. This chapter reviews what is known about census coverage for recent U.S. censuses. The chapter also discusses two major implications of census incompleteness: political representation at the congressional level and the distribution of federal funds that are allocated on the basis of population.

COVERAGE ESTIMATES

Coverage estimates, which measure the extent to which the census counts all the people, are made by two methods. One method is to conduct a large sample survey in conjunction with the decennial census (called the Post-Enumeration Survey, PES, in 1990), match all individuals in the survey to those reported in the census, and then estimate the number of unenumerated people in the census by age, sex, and race. The second method, demographic analysis, is to develop an estimate of the population independent of the census, using birth and death records for previous years, immigration and emigration data, and previous censuses.

Demographic estimates are the primary means for comparing coverage for censuses over time for the nation as a whole. Demographic analysis has two main methodological weaknesses. One is deficiencies in the data—particularly the immigration and emigration data. The magnitude of illegal alien flows into and out of the United States in recent decades is unknown, as is the magnitude of emigration of citizens and legal resident aliens. The second shortcoming is that demographic analysis cannot provide estimates by states or other subnational areas. Demographic estimates of coverage (see Table 2.1) show that the net national undercount (the number of people omitted minus the number overcounted) was estimated at 7.0 million in 1940, 6.3 million in 1950, 5.6 million in 1960, 5.5 million in 1970, 2.8 million in 1980, and 4.7 million in 1990. The undercount rate dropped from 5.4 percent in 1940, to 4.1 percent in 1950, 3.1 percent in 1960, 2.7 percent in 1970, and 1.2 percent in 1980, then rose to 1.8 percent in 1990 (Robinson et al., 1993:13).

Coverage Errors

Based on the criterion of net undercount, the 1990 census was somewhat worse than the 1980 census. Comparisons of net undercount, however, fail to reveal some other kinds of deficiencies in census counting. Net undercount figures reflect three elements:

(a) People who were not counted in the census or who were omitted from the census in their proper place or residence. These people are called *omissions*.

(b) People who were enumerated more than once, were ineligible to be counted in the census (e.g., babies born after Census Day), or were counted at their incorrect place of residence. These people are called *erroneous enumerations*.

(c) People whose existence was ascertained (by the judgment of the enumerator or other evidence) but whose characteristics were missing and so had to be "borrowed" from another enumerated person. These people are called *substitutions*.

The combination of erroneous enumerations and substitutions (b and c) can be added together to produce the total number of *counting errors*, which in 1990 were estimated to include 16 million people. A substantial proportion of counting errors are people who were incorrectly placed in the wrong geographic areas, resulting in an omission in the correct location and an erroneous enumeration in the incorrect location. From the national perspective, people assigned to an incorrect location were counted in the population (and thus not part of the na-

TABLE 2.1 Net Population Undercount in the Census by Demographic Analysis, 1940-1990

Undercount Rates and Numbers	1940	1950	1960	1970	1980	1990
Total						
Population (millions)	131.7	150.7	179.3	203.3	226.6	248.7
Undercount rate (%)	5.4	4.1	3.1	2.7	1.2	1.8
Number undercounted (millions)	7.0	6.3	5.6	5.5	2.8	4.7
Nonblacks						
Population	118.8	135.7	160.5	180.7	199.9	218.2
Undercount rate	5.0	3.8	2.7	2.2	0.8	1.3
Number undercounted	5.9	5.2	4.3	4.0	1.6	2.9
Blacks						
Population	12.9	15.0	18.9	22.6	26.7	30.5
Undercount rate	8.4	7.5	6.6	6.5	4.5	5.7
Number undercounted	1.1	1.1	1.3	1.5	1.2	1.8
Difference: black-nonblack net undercount rate	3.4	3.6	3.9	4.3	3.7	4.4

Note: Alaska and Hawaii became states in 1959. For 1950 and earlier, the population data and undercount estimates are for the 48 coterminous states. For 1960 and after, the data include Alaska and Hawaii.

Source: Population data: Bureau of the Census (1993b, Table 1). Undercount rates: Robinson et al. (1993).

tional undercount), but they do produce counting errors in the census for subnational geographic areas.[1]

For people missed from the census or counted at the wrong location (called omissions), Ericksen and DeFonso (1993) estimated the number in 1990 at 20 million people; they estimate net undercount of about 4 million, which is quite close to the estimate of 4.7 million, cited earlier, on the basis of demographic analysis. Both omissions and counting errors were higher in 1990 than in 1980; *omissions increased proportionately more than counting errors*, so the result was a larger net undercount. The sum of both types of census error, omissions and counting errors, is called the *gross coverage error*. The gross coverage error was 23-25 million people for the 1980 census and 36 million for the 1990 census. There was a substantial increase in the gross coverage error between the 1980 and 1990 censuses.

A point to bear in mind when evaluating estimates of omissions and counting errors (and hence the level of gross coverage error) is that, for the nation as a whole and for large geographic areas, many of these errors cancel out. Thus, a significant number of people who are included in the number of omissions because they were missed at the correct location are also included in the number of counting errors because they were counted but at the wrong location. Perhaps 40-50 percent of counting errors represent people who were also counted as omissions, for which the two classifications balance out (see Hogan, 1993:Table 7). However, for small areas, these kinds of geographic location errors may make a difference.

Undercount by Subgroups

According to the 1990 estimates by demographic analysis, almost three-fourths of the net national undercount were nonblacks (primarily whites). The rate of undercount, however, was over four times higher for blacks than for nonblacks, 5.7 and 1.3 percent, respectively (Robinson et al., 1993:13).[2] Figure 2.1 presents undercount rates for blacks and nonblacks from 1940 to 1990, as well as the difference between the nonblack and black rates. In the 1990 census, the undercount rate for both men and women was also about 4 to 5 times higher for blacks than for nonblacks; it varied from 8.5 percent for black men to 0.6 percent for white women.

Demographic analysis of the difference between black and nonblack net undercount rates shows modest changes from 1970 to 1990. In 1940, the black net undercount rate was 3.4 percentage points higher than the nonblack rate. By 1970, the difference had increased to 4.3 percentage points. The differential undercount by race was reduced somewhat in the 1980 census, to 3.7 percentage points. By 1990, even with continuing efforts to reduce the differential undercount, the difference had increased to 4.4 percentage points, slightly higher than at the beginning of the massive effort in 1970.

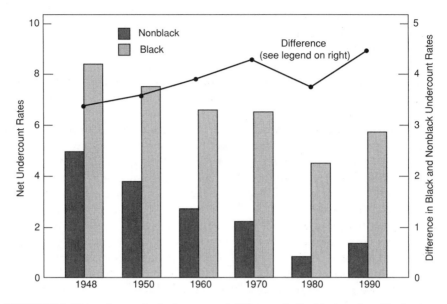

FIGURE 2.1 Net undercount rates by race and difference in the black and nonblack rates, 1940-1990.

Net undercount rates estimated from the PES were also higher for Asian and Pacific Islanders, Hispanics, and American Indians and Alaskan Natives in the 1990 census. The undercount of the Asian and Hispanic groups is likely to have been influenced by the relatively large numbers who are foreign-born, people who may not have understood census questionnaires and procedures.

By age, undercount numbers and rates from demographic analysis varied widely, from a negative undercount rate (indicating census overcount) for white women ages 15 to 24, to a positive undercount of 14 percent for black men ages 30 to 34. Black girls and boys under age 5 were missed at an 8.6 and 8.2 percent rate, respectively; black girls and boys ages 5 to 9 were missed at a 7.5 percent and 7.7 percent rate, respectively. The undercount rate peaked for all men at ages 25 to 29, but at about 4.5 percent for nonblack men and 12.7 percent for black men. For black women, the undercount rate ranged from minus 7.7 (indicating census overcount) to 4.9 percent for each age group above age 20.

The estimates of net undercount from demographic analysis differ in reliability because of differences in the basic data used to prepare them. The result is that estimates of census error are more reliable for whites than for blacks and other race and ethnic groups. Estimates of the omitted population are selective by race, sex, and age. Men and women ages 25 to 60, together with children under age 10, made up more than 90 percent of those not counted. Even more narrowly, almost two-thirds of the estimated omitted population consists of two groups: children under age 10 and men ages 25 to 39. These findings, along with evidence of higher underenumeration rates for minority groups, are useful for assessing the effect of using statistical methods to improve the enumerated count.

Some information is known about the geographic distribution of the net undercount from the 1990 PES. Figure 2.2 displays estimates of the net undercount rates for the 1990 census by state. States are classified into five categories: very low and low net undercount, average undercount, and high and very high net undercount. States with a population of the most undercounted groups tended to have higher net undercount rates. States in the South and Southwest had net undercount rates higher than the national average. States in New England and the Midwest tended to have lower than average net undercount rates. New York, Maryland, and the District of Columbia are distinctive with higher net undercount rates than their neighboring states.

The undercount is higher in cities than in other areas, and the people missed in the census are disproportionately concentrated in larger cities. The most serious problems of conducting the census seem to occur in inner cities, despite intensive efforts to count the population in those areas.

There are several implications of undercount for minority groups. In political representation and funding based on population, undercounted groups get less credit for their population than they are due. Political districts drawn relative to population are "overpopulated" for undercounted areas (i.e., overpopulated means a larger actual population, including people who were unenumerated, than counted in the census). Overpopulated districts result in underrepresentation of minority areas (i.e., fewer districts) at all levels of government—federal, state, and local—that base political representation on population size.

Errors in Small-Area Data

The accuracy of the census population counts can have different meanings in different contexts. For example, for a government program with cutoff points for state funding, the degree of inaccuracy is critical only when a state population is close to the point at which funding decisions would be affected. For congressional redistricting or for local-area decisions that involve relatively small areas, the relative accuracy of the population count for blocks and aggregations of blocks is important. In response to the panel's request for information about the accuracy of small-area data in the 1990 census, the Census Bureau provided special analysis of census blocks from the PES. That block-level analysis revealed several types of errors in data from a stratified sample of 5,290 PES clusters in the 1990 census (Diffendal, 1994).[3]

More than 25 percent of the clusters had no erroneous inclusions—housing units assigned to the sampled cluster that are actually outside the search area. In the census, for clusters with erroneous enumeration, duplication occurs fairly often (in about 25 percent of the total clusters).

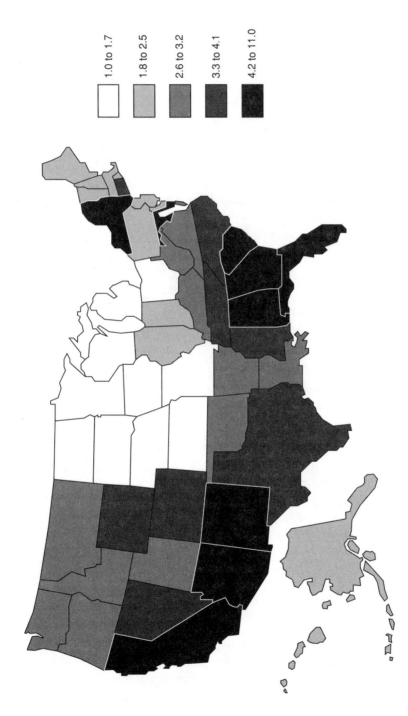

1.0 to 1.7
1.8 to 2.5
2.6 to 3.2
3.3 to 4.1
4.2 to 11.0

FIGURE 2.2 Net undercount rates for states, 1990.

The distribution of erroneous inclusions is skewed; most of them occur in a small proportion of clusters. About 1 percent of the clusters (about 50 out of 5,290 clusters) in the 1990 census account for more than one-third of erroneous inclusions. This means that relatively few areas contribute a substantial proportion of erroneous inclusion errors to the census.

The most common types of census nonmatches—the situtation in which the PES results are not matched to census results—are: (1) nonmatch with other persons in the household matched (occurs in more than one-half of clusters), (2) nonmatch with the entire household missed for a matched address (occurs in more than one-third of clusters), and (3) nonmatch with the entire household missed for a missed housing unit (occurs in about one-fifth of clusters). Typically, for the three common types of nonmatches, there are only 3 to 6 cases per cluster, of about 30 housing units per cluster. Census nonmatches are also concentrated in a relatively few number of clusters. The initial analysis by Diffendal does not reveal if clusters with a high proportion of erroneous enumerations are in vacation areas, wealthy suburbs, or other areas where the overcount may be biased in favor of the more mobile segment of the population and among those who have more than one residence.

The analysis presented in Diffendal (1994) is a good beginning to understanding the quality of small-area census data. It would be useful to see further research on the overlap of erroneous enumerations and census nonmatches (showing possible joint occurrence in the same clusters) and on the sum of erroneous enumerations, census nonmatches, and substitutions (i.e., the level of gross error).

In addition to the errors in small-area data discussed above, there are other sources of error, including the errors in the information provided by respondents and in data processing. Regarding nonsampling erros, Appendix L provides information from the 1990 census on errors stemming from nonresponse to items in the census questionnaire.

IMPLICATIONS OF UNDERENUMERATION

Underenumeration in the census has serious political, economic, and social implications. The decennial population count, reported in the census, affects the state apportionment of seats in the U.S. House of Representatives and the geographic boundaries for congressional districts, state legislative districts, and city council districts. Under the "equal proportions" methods for federal apportionment, a shift of relatively few people could result in the change of a state's representation.

For all state and local districts, the possibility that undercoverage will have an effect on a district's boundaries depends on the size of the district; the coverage rates by age, sex, and race; the distribution of the population by age, sex, and race; and the undercoverage rates of contiguous districts.

Effects on Congressional Apportionment

If undercoverage were eliminated, population would increase in areas with a large number of such high-undercount groups as minorities and inner-city residents. An estimate of what the 1990 census results would have been, if surveys were used to complete the count, can be obtained by using PES information to make a correction for each state's population. If used in 1990, a correction, using a set of adjustment factors taking age, sex, race, region, and urban-rural characteristics into account, would have been made for each of 7 million census blocks in the nation.

The number of congressional seats is fixed at 435: an addition of a congressional seat for one state means that another state loses a seat. Congressional apportionment of seats in the House of Representatives is based on the method of equal proportions. In this method, each of the 50 states receives one congressional seat, no matter what its population. Next, a priority value is calculated for the nth seat for each state (for example, n equals 2 for a state's second seat after it has received the first seat), using the state's apportionment population multiplied by the factor:

$$\frac{1}{\sqrt{n(n-1)}}.$$

The factor decreases as the number of seats increases: the factor equals 0.71 for the second seat and 0.41 for the third seat. The state with the largest priority value receives the next congressional seat. When each state has exactly one congressional seat, the state with the largest population receives the 51st seat. But, after it does, the population apportionment factor is recalculated and compared with the priority value for all other states to decide which state receives the 52nd seat. The repeated calculation of priority values and assignment of congressional seats continue until all 435 seats are distributed. One state will receive the 435th congressional seat, and the state with the highest priority value for the 436th seat will not receive one.

Adding population to a state will increase the priority values for the state, but it will not necessarily increase the likelihood of gaining an additional seat. The critical question for a state is whether a change in its priority value affects the assignment of the last several congressional seats. Corrections to the census population count would typically change the congressional delegations for those few states with priority values close to the 435th cutoff.

As illustrated in Table 2.2, Washington received the 435th seat in the reapportionment based on the 1990 census. If Washington's population had been 10,200 persons fewer, or 0.21 percent of the state's total, it would not have qualified for the 435th seat. At the same time, Massachusetts failed to qualify to gain another seat by a population of 12,607, or 0.21 percent of its total population.

TABLE 2.2 Apportionment Population for States, 1990

House Seat	State	Number of Seats in House Delegation	Apportionment Population	Population Change Required Amount	Percent
		Possible Losers			
428	California	52	29,839,250	−236,002	−0.79
429	Texas	30	17,059,805	−104,241	−0.61
430	Mississippi	5	2,586,443	−15,648	−0.61
431	Wisconsin	9	4,906,745	−29,004	−0.59
432	Florida	23	13,003,362	−72,490	−0.56
433	Tennessee	9	4,896,641	−18,900	−0.39
434	Oklahoma	6	3,157,604	−9,036	−0.29
435	Washington	9	4,887,941	−10,200	−0.21
		Possible Winners			
436	Massachusetts	11	6,029,051	+12,607	+0.21
437	New Jersey	14	7,748,634	+22,698	+0.29
438	New York	32	18,044,505	+98,765	+0.55
439	Kentucky	7	3,698,969	+34,258	+0.93
440	California	53	29,839,250	+401,972	+1.35
441	Montana	2	803,655	+11,002	+1.37
442	Arizona	7	3,677,985	+55,242	+1.50
443	Georgia	12	6,508,419	+109,885	+1.69

Source: Passel (1991).

What would have happened to the reapportionment process if the state populations had been corrected using the PES, as was debated in 1990? It is difficult to determine exactly how the application of the PES results to the 1990 census would have affected actual congressional reapportionment, because the adjustment would have been done for small geographic areas; the calculation here uses average PES values to estimate the state's population data (Passel, 1991, presents the calculation cited here). Applying the average PES values to the 1990 state population counts, three states would have gained a congressional seat: Georgia (a 12th seat), Montana (a 2nd seat), and California (a 53rd seat). The losing states would have been Oklahoma, Pennsylvania, and Wisconsin. It should be noted that very small population differences affect the assignment of congressional seats close to the cutoff—regardless of whether the decisions are based on population figures including or excluding corrections for undercoverage. Because of California's large population size, relatively small percentage changes in its population could add or subtract a congressional seat; California shows up as both a possible winner and possible loser in Table 2.2. In this instance, the correction would have resulted in a distribution of congressional seats that is not substantially different from the allocation of seats based on the uncorrected counts.

Congressional redistricting would be affected to a greater extent than apportionment because virtually all congressional districts, except for those in single-state districts, would have their boundaries changed by adjusted census block data. Moreover, a census that is corrected for undercoverage in the physical enumeration would affect the redistricting for state legislatures and city councils, which rely on decennial census data.

Effects on Distribution of Federal Funds

The undercount also affects the distribution of federal and state funds, which are allocated on the basis of population. Funds for education, health, transportation, housing, community services, and job training are all allocated to geographic areas on the basis of population size and social and economic factors. In 1990 the federal government disbursed about $125 billion to state and local governments, and nearly half of this amount was distributed using formulas involving census population data. Several studies have examined the effect of adjusting for census undercount on the distribution of funds to state and local governments. All studies of the 1970 and 1980 censuses concluded that the impact of census population adjustment on grant allocations would be small.[4]

More recently, Murray (1992) has reported results for the 1990 census. The total federal allocation for grants involving census population counts was $58.7 billion in 1989, or about $236 per capita for eligible population jurisdictions. However, adjusting the allocation for the undercount would not simply result in an additional $236 per unit of net undercount for several reasons. First, population is only one of several factors in many federal formula grant allocations; in such programs, an increase of population results in only a partial increase in funding. Second, although many grant allocations increase with population gains, there are some programs (such as the Community Development Block Grant Program in the Department of Housing and Urban Development) in which funding is reduced with population growth. Finally, and most important, federal grant formulas are largely fixed in their total amount. In reality, as the total U.S. population is increased by correcting for the undercount, smaller amounts of funds per capita would be available for allocation. If, for example, a fixed sum was apportioned among geographic areas on the basis of population size alone and the population of every geographic area doubled, there would be no change in funds allocated to any area.

Table 2.3 shows the effects of correcting for the census undercount on 108 federal programs that are affected by population counts. Overall, the 108 programs had obligations of $58.7 billion in 1989, with five major programs accounting for $51.8 billion of the total. Of the major programs, Medicaid is the largest, and the Highway Planning and Construction Program is the second largest. As shown in the third column of Table 2.3, the overall obligation per capita for all federal programs was $236 in 1989. When each state and relevant local jurisdiction is adjusted for undercount, some states and local areas lose and some gain.[5] The overall amount per net undercounted person among gaining areas is about $56, considerably less than the average per capita obligation. Only 34 to 42 percent of areas would gain because of using corrected population counts. Many governments with only modest population undercounts would not, in fact, actually gain additional federal grant monies. The effect on redistribution of federal funds would be modest: only 0.32 percent, or about $190 million, of the total federal obligations would be altered by correcting the population count.

By definition, the distribution of money under these programs would change if there were a *differential* change in the population count. The effect of the undercount on each state's share of a fixed total of funds distribution depends on state characteristics. Moreover, the amount of money gained and lost is obviously related not only to the estimated undercount rate, but also to population size.

In federal funding allocation programs, social and economic factors as well as population counts are used. The use of these other factors points to the importance of enumeration and accurate data concerning the people counted for optimal program planning and equitable distribution of funds. The reduction of population undercount and the improvement of accuracy of collected data are both important for the Census Bureau, which needs to provide accurate data to ensure the fair funding of federal programs.

Because in the 1990 census blacks and other minority groups had a larger undercount than whites—as in prior censuses—minorities and the communities in which they live have been disadvantaged in federal and other programs in

TABLE 2.3 Effects of One Method of Adjustment for Net National Undercount on Annual Federal Obligations to State and Local Governments, 1989 Obligations with 1990 Population Census Data

Program	Obligation Level[a] (billions)	Obligation Per Capita in Eligible Population	Per Capita Amount Per Miscount Among Gainers	Percentage of Funds Redistributed	Percentage of Jurisdictions Gaining
Social Service Block Grants	$2.7	$10.79	$3.78	0.53	42
Highway Planning and Construction	13.4	45.58	13.17	0.42	42
Rehabilitation Services	1.4	5.78	5.15	1.35	42
Medicaid	34.0	136.75	38.67	0.55	34
Community Development Block Grants	2.2	15.13	13.47	0.97	39
103 Other Programs	6.9	26.67	8.50	0.46	42
Total—108 Programs	$58.7	$236.00	$56.00	0.32	34-42

[a]The obligation levels for the first five programs include total assignments of the program, totaling $53.7 billion. The actual amount distributed to the 50 states and the District of Columbia was $51.8 billion.

Source: Murray (1992).

which population is an important factor for fund allocation. Representatives of the black, Asian and Pacific Islander, Hispanic, and American Indian and Alaskan Native populations have stressed their concerns about improvements in population coverage for their groups.

The analysis in this chapter reports reapportionment rates and funding allocation levels for state and local governments. However, much of the effect of population coverage is at the substate level, although there are few data to document those effects. Of those variables currently measured, population coverage varies primarily by housing characteristics (tenure and types), race, sex, and age. The possible shifts in legislative representation and possible shifts in state and local monies would be greater at substate levels than demonstrated above for federal reapportionment and funding allocation, because of the greater heterogeneity in population characteristics across small areas than across larger areas.

NOTES

[1]The reasons why people who were counted at the wrong location are both an omission and an erroneous enumeration and why substitutions are treated as coverage errors has to do with the way in which coverage and the net undercount are estimated by a postenumeration survey (see Chapter 5). Because the postenumeration survey, by design, selects people in a sample of areas, it detects errors in geographic residence as well as omissions and erroneous enumerations at the national level.

[2]Alternate estimates for the undercount from the PES showed rates that were more than 6 times higher for blacks than for whites, 4.6 and 0.7 percent, respectively (Hogan and Robinson, 1993:18). Undercount rates were 3 time higher for Asians, 7 times higher for Hispanics, and 17 times higher for American Indians than for whites.

[3]PES clusters are small areas of the country that are sampled for the survey, prior to the selection of individual housing units. PES clusters were either a census block or collection of blocks in 1990, chosen as the primary sampling unit for the survey. The purpose of selecting clusters is to get the most reliable results per unit of costs.

[4]Because formula grant allocations depend on factors other than population, the disbursements can be affected by errors in other data. Siegel (1975) argued that the underreporting of income in the 1970 census affects grant allocations more than population undercoverage.

[5]Not all local jurisdictions are eligible for all federal allocation formula grants. The Community Development Block Grant program, for example, is restricted to cities and towns with 50,000 or more population and to urban counties.

3

Census Cost Increases and Their Causes

The cost of census activities has increased sharply since 1960. In 1990 dollars, the 1960 census cost about $520 million. The 1990 census cost $2.6 billion, an increase of 400 percent after adjusting for inflation (U.S. General Accounting Office, 1992). Population and, more important, the number of housing units have increased over this period but, even after making allowances for these factors, cost escalation has been severe.

The average cost of the census was less than $10 dollars per housing unit in 1960 (in 1990 constant dollars) and was still only $11 per housing unit for the 1970 census. It escalated to $20 per housing unit in 1980 and $25 in 1990, an increase of 150 percent in real terms over 30 years.

GENERAL FACTORS

A substantial decline in the population's response rate to the mailed census questionnaire, from 78 percent in 1970 to 65 percent in 1990, has been an important cause of the cost escalation, although far from the only one (U.S. General Accounting Office, 1992:36).[1] In 1990, households that did not mail back their questionnaires were personally visited, as many as six times, in an attempt to collect census information. If mail response rates continue to decline, as they have done for the past several censuses, the national mail response rate may be less than 60 percent in 2000.[2] The U.S. General Accounting Office (1992:41) estimates that the 2000 census would cost $4.8 billion, in 1992 dollars, if the 2000 census is conducted using the same methods as the 1990 census.[3]

If increased census costs had resulted in census improvements, particularly

44

in better coverage and a decreased differential undercount of minorities, it would be possible to argue the merits of costs versus coverage. However, as demonstrated in Chapter 2, both the overall percentage undercount and the differential undercount (the difference of the undercount between the black and nonblack populations) apparently worsened in the 1990 census (Robinson et al., 1993). It is of course possible that the net undercount and differential undercount might have been even worse in 1990 if less had been spent on the census. Some may claim that even greater funding was needed in 1990 to decrease the undercount. However, we cannot assess these hypothetical claims in the absence of evidence. The observable evidence is that substantially more was spent on the 1990 census, and the undercount did not improve. The fact that spending more money did not produce a more accurate census was, in large part, at the center of the criticisms levied at the 1990 decennial census.[4]

Costs have been affected by increased legal demands for accurate small-area data (see Appendix C for extended discussion of legal requirements for census data). The "one-person, one-vote" rulings of the Supreme Court in the 1960s and the Voting Rights Act of 1965 as extended and amended in the past 30 years have substantially expanded the requirement for accurate population data, cross-classified by age and ethnicity at the small-area level, for legislative redistricting and related purposes. And although the statutes do not specify the geographic level of detail that is required, the census now provides it at the level of individual census blocks in order to provide flexible building blocks for subsequent reaggregation by census data users. Also, over the past three decades, the number of congressional statutes calling for the use of demographic and related data to apportion federal funds among states and localities has mushroomed. Although the statutes often do not specify the use of data based on the decennial census, in practice the use of census data for these purposes is ubiquitous in the absence of alternative sources.

During this 30-year period there has also been a virtual explosion among state and local governments and private business firms in the development of computer data banks and computer models based on the use of census data at the block level for purposes of planning and operations. This has generated another set of demands for accurate small-area data. It has also raised important questions about relationships among federal, state, and local governments and private business firms with respect to the appropriate development and use of large-scale geocoding and geographic data systems (discussed in Chapter 8).

These developments, the ways that the Census Bureau has responded to them, and the ways in which they are perceived by the public have interacted with each other both to raise the costs of taking the census and to generate increased perceptions of inequity in the resultant census statistics. Thus, for example, the depressed response rate is typically lowest precisely in areas with high concentrations of minority groups, leading to substantially increased costs in an effort to minimize differential undercount and produce accurate data. Despite these efforts, the results still fall short of meeting heightened public demands for fairness and evenhandedness in redistricting legislatures and apportioning public monies. In turn, the Census Bureau over recent decades has sought to deal with the combined pressures of falling response rates and increased demands for detailed, geographically fine-grained and accurate data principally through the use of highly labor-intensive enumerative techniques for follow-up and coverage improvement.

SPECIFIC FACTORS AND MARGINAL COSTS

The increase in census costs in recent decades has been dramatic. Expressed in dollars of 1990 purchasing power, the full cycle costs of the decennial census rose from a little over $520 million in 1960 to $2,600 million for the 1990 census. The fourfold increase in costs over a 30-year period arises from several factors, including factors not directly attributable to census operations themselves. Three key factors need to be considered, looking at costs in constant dollars: census content, the growth of population and housing units, and declines in mail response rates.

Census Content

Congressional concern with census cost escalation has led to a search for remedies for the 2000 census. One suggestion has been to reduce census content, perhaps by eliminating the long-form census questionnaire. Every person in the United States was asked during the 1990 census for some basic demographic information (including race, age, relationship to household head, and sex) on a short-form questionnaire. In addition, a 1-in-6 sample of people was given a more detailed long-form questionnaire with questions about income, schooling, occupation, and related social and economic items. Residents in smaller governmental areas, with populations of about 2,500 or less, were sampled at a rate of 1 in 2 in order to obtain sufficient responses for accurate estimates of smaller areas. People in areas with about 2,000 or more housing units were sampled at a 1-in-8 rate. Special rules were made for people in group quarters and those residing in areas in which special enumeration was required. Overall, the sample design for the long form produced a sample of 1 in every 6 households in the nation. But, with one caveat, we do not believe that the content of the census is driving cost increases and coverage problems (see Chapter 6 on the special issue of the cost of the long form).

Some items on the long-form census questionnaire, such as those pertaining to income, may be subject to greater than average response error and require more follow-up verification. But the long-form questionnaire has remained at relatively constant length for the past four censuses, whereas costs have increased dramatically. Furthermore, the sampling rate for the long-form questionnaire has declined, a change that should have yielded lower overall costs.[5] The panel acknowledges the congressional concern about substantial cost escalations in the census; however, we do not find evidence that census content is a primary factor producing the cost increases.

Although we believe it most unlikely that the addition or subtraction of a limited number of questions would significantly affect overall census costs, it is certainly possible that very large differences in the complexity and length of the census questionnaire might affect public willingness to cooperate, reduce the response rate, and through that route affect costs—although, even then, such cost increases can affect only some 17 percent of households, since all other households are already receiving only the short form. There is some evidence on this point from recent Census Bureau experiments with a very truncated form. We note the historical evidence that strongly suggests that matters of content have not been a major driving force behind the recent and threatened rise in census costs.

The length of the census questionnaire has not changed appreciably during the 1960 to 1990 period. The sample of households receiving the sample long-form questionnaire has decreased slightly during the period. The sampling fraction has decreased from 1 in 4 in 1960 to 1 in 6 in 1990. During this period of four censuses, the questionnaire delivered to U.S. households included a short form with 17 questions in 1960, 18 in 1970, 15 in 1980, and 13 in 1990. The questionnaire length of the long form was 49 questions in 1960, 38 or 52 questions in 1970,[6] 65 questions in 1980, and 58 questions in 1990. Overall, the length of the long form has remained relatively constant, while the sampling fraction has declined. Hence, we cannot attribute any increased census costs to the content of the census.

Changes in Population and Housing

Some of the census cost increases can be attributed to growth in the population and the number of housing units to be counted. In Table 3.1, the first part summarizes some of the basic data relevant to analyzing costs for the four censuses beginning in 1960. The second part converts the nominal costs to dollars of constant 1990 purchasing power and shows them on a per housing unit basis. Since census costs depend primarily on the expense of delivering a mail questionnaire to a household or having an enumerator visit a housing unit, it is more realistic to relate cost growth to the rise in the number of housing units rather than to population growth. Even when housing units are vacant and contain no household, there is a cost to ascertaining that fact, so that the number of housing units rather than the number of households is the relevant unit to consider for cost analysis. Between 1960 and 1970 census costs, when adjusted for the growth in inflation and in the number of housing units, increased only modestly (see the last line in Table 3.1); thereafter costs grew rapidly. Overall, the growth

TABLE 3.1 Factors Associated with Increases in Census Costs, 1960-1990

	Decennial Census Cycle			
	1960	1970	1980	1990
Basic Data				
Full-cycle census costs[a]	$120	$231	$1,136	$2,600
(in millions, nominal dollars)				
Population (in millions)	179.3	203.3	226.5	248.7
Housing units (in millions)	58.9	70.7	90.1	104.0
Mail response rates (in percent)	—[b]	78	75	65
Derived Data				
Census costs in 1990 dollars				
(in millions)[c]	$523	$744	$1,795	$2,600
Cost per housing unit (in 1990 dollars)	$9	$11	$20	$25

[a]Total census costs are shown in Figure 2.6 of a report from the U.S. General Accounting Office (1992) and in original source documents from the Census Bureau. We should note, however, that Figure 2.6 of the General Accounting Office report is mislabeled as showing costs in constant 1990 dollars. The graph shows costs in current dollars. Total expenditures for the 1970 census, for instance, were $231 million, which are shown in that amount in the General Accounting Office graph.

[b]The 1960 census was not conducted using primarily mailout/mailback questionnaires.

[c]Using GDP implicit price deflator to adjust to 1990 dollars.

of housing units accounts for about $350 million of the cost increases from 1970 to 1990.[7]

Mail Response Rates

Some of the cost growth per housing unit can be attributed to the fall-off in mail response rates.[8] If a mail questionnaire was not returned to the census office, a field worker visited the address in an attempt to count the household. Under the 1990 census procedures, as many as six visits could have been made. Census Bureau staff have provided estimates that under 1990 census procedures a decline of 1 percentage point in the mail response rate would increase costs by 0.67 percent.[9] Between 1970 and 1990 the mail response rate fell 13 percentage points, a decline that translates into a $225 million cost increase.[10] However, this estimate assumes the existence of the highly labor-intensive cost structure of 1990. If, instead, the same adjustment percentage for the decline in the response rate is applied to the lower cost base of 1970, the resulting cost increase would have been only about $95 million.[11] The change in response rates has been qualitative as well as quantitative. Not only has the number of nonrespondents increased, but they are also increasingly difficult to locate and enumerate. The cost impact based only on the decline of mail response rates probably underestimates the impact using the 1970 cost base. Thus, we estimate that somewhere between $95 and $225 million of cost increases between 1970 and 1990 can be attributed to the fall in the response rate. And the higher number is valid only if one accepts as "necessary" all of the other cost increases between 1970 and 1990.

Table 3.2 summarizes the cost analysis to this point. Of the roughly $1.9 billion inflation-adjusted cost increase between 1970 and 1990, only $445 to $575 million can be explained by growth in the number of housing units and the decline in the mail response rate. Cost increases not explainable by these factors amounted, at the lower end of the range, to some $1.3 billion, a rise of 100 percent relative to the 1970 base, after adjustment for changes in housing units and response rates.[12]

Other Factors

Having taken into account housing unit growth, mail response rate declines, and inflationary changes, we must conclude that other factors account for the

TABLE 3.2 Increases in Census Costs, 1970 to 1990 (in 1990 dollars, in millions)

Census Costs	1970	1990
Nominal census costs (in millions)	$231	$2,600
Census costs in 1990 dollars (in millions)	$744	$2,600
Housing units (in millions)	70.7	104.0
Cost per housing unit, in 1990 dollars	$11	$25

Factors Behind Cost Increases	1970-1990
Total census cost increase, in 1990 dollars (in millions)	$1,856
Less increase due to:	
• Growth in housing units, in 1990 dollars (in millions)	$350
• Decline in mail response rates, in 1990 dollars (in millions)	$95-225
Equals unexplained increase, in 1990 dollars (in millions)	$1,281-1,411

remaining cost increases. These other factors account for a sizable proportion of overall census cost increases. We are unable to account for $1.3 billion, or almost three-fourths of the total 1970 to 1990 cost increases. This unexplained portion of census cost increases is not contributed by inflation, by population or housing growth, or by declines in the mail response rates. What other factors account for the increases?

The persistent disparity in the undercount of different population groups, with undercount rates greater for minorities than for others, coupled with the consequences of greater demands for accurate small-area data, has generated pressures on the Census Bureau to expand substantially its efforts to decrease the differential undercount and to produce more detailed accurate data. The results, which still did not satisfy public demands in the 1990 census, have led to a highly labor-intensive and expensive effort to enumerate the U.S. population.

Many questions have been raised about the educational qualifications of census enumerators. It seems likely that there have been declines in their education levels and job skills. For earlier censuses, a more abundant supply of part-time, motivated, better-educated housewives formed a large portion of the temporary census staff. With declines in married-couple households and increases in the proportion of women working full time, there are relatively fewer women with these qualifications available for part-time census employment. The panel attempted to examine this issue but has not been able to acquire data on either the educational qualifications for the temporary census labor force or the relationship between educational qualifications and productivity. It is therefore difficult to assess the impact of this factor on census staff productivity and on overall census costs.

Census Cost Changes

The panel reviewed some of the specific procedures that have been associated with cost changes in the 1980 and 1990 censuses. Our review raised questions about the justification for these cost increases. All costs for the following five areas are in 1993 dollars. The cost estimates and census cost headings are taken from Neece and Pentercs (1994).

(1) Census Planning Activities. The cost of planning direction and review increased from about $30 million for the 1970 census to $105 million for the 1990 census. Most of this threefold increase seems to be associated with headquarters management, since it explicitly does not include geography, address list development, content planning, or statistical research and evaluation. What is not known adequately is what has been bought for the extra expense and was it worth the price.

(2) Data Collection. The biggest single increase reported in Census Bureau cost figures is related to what is called data collection: from $378 million in

1970 to $1.4 million in 1990. The unit cost of data collection (per housing unit) was $5.51 in 1970 and $13.86 in 1990. More district offices were created and kept open longer, the supervisory ratios were reduced considerably, the method of payment was changed from piece rate (with exceptions for specially difficult areas and for the final cleanup work) to hourly rates. Paying hourly rates seems to be particularly open to abuse by very short-term employees working in an almost entirely decentralized (and necessarily only loosely supervised) mode. What is more striking about these cost increases is that they occurred despite heavy investments in automation. This whole activity, more than any other, needs a fresh examination in the new environment for taking future censuses.

(3) Data Processing. The two census data processing components, data processing and data processing systems, had combined costs that increased from $122 million in 1970 to $433 million in 1990. Given the fact that computer power per unit of expenditure increased at an exponential rate during the past 20 years, this is one area where the panel would have anticipated at most a modest level of growth in overall expenditures, particularly since there appear to be no offsetting savings elsewhere in the census system. The explanations by the Census Bureau staff concern an increase in automation, not whether this improved the process or its results by a factor commensurate with the observed cost increases.

(4) Data Dissemination. The costs of data tabulation and publication increased fivefold: from $22 million in 1970 to $114 million in 1990. This increase, too, seems to raise questions about whether improvements were commensurate with cost increases. How much detail should be pretabulated and how much produced on demand? How should the product line change from print to electronic media? Are the quite modest gains in timeliness worth the substantial cost increases?

(5) Census Testing. The costs for test censuses and dress rehearsals increased from $10 million in 1970 to $78 million in 1990. Yet the shift in methodology from the 1960 to 1970 census (to a mailout/mailback census for most of the country) was arguably more fundamental than methodological changes implemented since. Also, very few changes were made in terms of content, and these tended to be deletions. The panel supports research and testing for new methods and new content, but with an emphasis on a critical and strategic approach to testing: the Census Bureau should concentrate on testing a selected few high-priority items for inclusion in the next census.

Census Staff Productivity

The panel studied changes in labor productivity by examining the number of housing units and the total population enumerated by census staff in the 1960, 1970, 1980, and 1990 censuses. Based on census data assembled by Beresford

TABLE 3.3 Comparison of Population Enumerated in the Census and Number of Census Bureau Personnel Taking the Census, 1960 to 1990

Panel A	1960	1970	1980	1990
Total Population (millions)	179.3	203.3	226.5	248.7
Total Housing Units (millions)	58.9	70.7	90.1	104.0
Undercount Rate (%)				
Total	3.1%	2.7%	1.2%	1.8%
Blacks	6.6%	6.5%	4.5%	5.7%
Nonblacks	2.7%	2.2%	0.8%	1.3%
Difference in black and nonblack rates	3.9%	4.3%	3.7%	4.4%
Number of District Offices	399	393	412	449
Time Period Open (months)	3-6	4-6	6-9	9-12
Staff				
Headquarters	1,846	2,186	4,081	6,763
Field	187,500	223,038	458,523	510,000[a]
Processing	2,000	2,600	5,400	11,000
Total	191,346	227,824	468,004	527,763
Average Hourly Pay				
Manager	$3.35	$5.88	$9.41	$15.25
Field supervisor	2.75	4.68	7.37	12.00
Crew leader	1.95	2.96	4.66	8.50
Enumerators	1.60	2.56	4.03	7.50
Clerks	1.70	2.32	3.66	5.75

Panel B: Productivity ratio = housing units/number of staff	1960	1970	1980	1990
Headquarters	31,907	32,342	22,078	15,378
Field	314	317	197	204
Processing	29,450	27,192	16,685	9,455

Panel C: Percent change in productivity ratio by decade	1960-1970	1970-1980	1980-1990
Headquarters	+1.4%	−31.7%	−30.3%
Field	+1.0%	−37.8%	+ 3.6%
Processing	−7.7%	−38.6%	−43.3%

TABLE 3.3 Continued

Panel D: Percent change in productivity ratio since 1960	1970	1980	1990
Headquarters	+1.4%	−30.8%	−51.8%
Field	+1.0%	−37.3%	−35.0%
Processing	−7.7%	−43.3%	−67.9%

*a*The 1990 census staff number has been adjusted to make it comparable with earlier censuses. The Census Bureau reports that there were 650,000 field staff in 1990 (Beresford, 1993). This number includes an unknown number of persons who took training, received training pay, and then voluntarily quit. Beresford (1994) provides preliminary estimates that the average field staff worked 22 days, with 2 days for training. If there were 150,000 quitters, the field staff estimate would be: 650,000 − 150,000 + (2/22 × 150,000) = 513,635, which we round to 510,000.

Note: Beresford relies on Census Bureau estimates for the staff numbers in Panel A. The Census Bureau provides different sources of information for each census, but there are no comparable records for prior censuses.

Source: Beresford, 1993, 1994.

(1993), Table 3.3 summarizes trends in staff productivity. During the 1960 to 1990 period, as the Census Bureau increased efforts to reduce the undercount, the number of enumerated households (or persons) per census employee decreased. The organization of census staff changed over the period. The number of district offices increased, from 399 in 1960 to 449 (plus 9 in Puerto Rico) in 1990. Also, the organization of district offices evolved during this period, with the addition of 13 regional offices in 1990 that provided oversight to the data collection efforts of district offices. District offices also stayed open longer, increasing their operational period from 3 to 6 months in 1960 to 9 to 12 months in 1990.[13] The length of operation for local census offices is comparatively long for the U.S. census, compared with the national censuses of other countries.

The numbers shown in the table have limitations. A major limitation to the staff figures, which are from the Census Bureau, is that no full-time-equivalent data are available for the field staff. Full-time-equivalent numbers for field staff were developed as a necessary part of the 1990 census administrative budget process; however, no figures are available for actual employees. Data for headquarters and processing are for full-time staff, but (as discussed below) it is not known how long the temporary field staff worked on the census. It is thought by census staff that a substantial proportion of the field staff worked for only a short period in 1990. Also, we do not have data on the actual hours worked. Lack of hourly information is a problem particularly for interpreting trends in productivity of temporary staff because they generally work for a limited period of time, ranging from a few days to several months. If, as appears to be the case for 1990, turnover in the temporary staff is particularly high, then the observed staff numbers are higher than the unknown full-time-equivalent figures. Such higher temporary staff numbers, with turnover, will also evidence lower productivity.

Panel A of the table shows that there was a substantial increase in staff for headquarters, field operations, and data processing. Compared with 1960, the 1990 census staff was almost 3 times larger to count 1.4 times more people and 1.8 times more households. The 1990 census employed many people as census enumerators who received training but did not actually carry out census work. The panel has no estimates from the Census Bureau of the numbers of enumerators who were trained and did not work, although Table 3.3 includes assumptions that there was a substantial proportion of the total number of enumerators—150,000 of the 650,000 hired enumerators—who received training and voluntarily departed without actually working on the census.

Panel B reports the basic productivity ratio by dividing the number of housing units by the number of staff. We assume that the major cost of the census is related to the number of housing units because census questionnaires must be prepared, delivered, and processed for each housing unit.[14] But the number of housing units increased more rapidly than the population, increasing the number of units requiring census questionnaires and follow-up for nonresponse. Overall census costs are affected more by the number of housing units than by population numbers. In 1960, about 31,907 housing units were processed by each headquarters staff person. This productivity ratio increased slightly, by 1.4 percent (see Panel C), between 1960 and 1970; decreased substantially, by 31.7 percent, between 1970 and 1980; and declined a further 30.3 percent between 1980 and 1990. Overall (see Panel D), productivity for headquarters staff dropped 52 percent over the four censuses from 1960 to 1990.

The field staff includes the bulk of employees working on the decennial census. Most of the field staff are temporary workers and receive salaries considerably lower than those of the permanent staff in headquarters or those handling the processing of the census. For this examination, numbers of full-time-equivalent employees are preferable, but such numbers were not reported for the 1990 census. The numbers recorded for the census field staff include all employees who worked on the census, including some persons who worked only a few days. Our understanding is that turnover in temporary field staff was higher in the 1990 census than in prior censuses. The best estimate from those familiar with the 1990 census is that about 150,000 of the 650,000 field staff quit after receiving two days of training. Adjusting for the quitters, we estimate an equivalent of about 510,000 for the number of field staff who worked throughout the enumeration period on the census.[15]

From 1960 to 1990, there was a decrease in the number of housing units per temporary field staff, from about 314 in 1960 to 204 in 1990, a decrease of about 35 percent over the period. A factor in the decrease of the total number of housing units per field staff in 1990 is that mail response rate was lower than

1980, increasing the proportion of housing units requiring personal follow-up.[16] The major declines in field staff productivity occurred between 1970 and 1980.

Finally, the processing staff increased from about 2,000 in 1960 to 11,000 in 1990, a 4.5-fold increase. (Processing staff receive average salaries that are lower than headquarters employees.) There were sharp decreases in productivity ratios during the period, from 29,000 housing units enumerated per processing staff in 1960 to 27,000 in 1970, a 7.7 percent decline, followed by a 39 percent decline in 1980 and a further 43 percent decline in 1990—a cumulative decrease of 68 percent over the four censuses.

SUMMARY

The costs of taking the census have escalated sharply, especially since 1970. Even after adjusting 1970 wages and prices to 1990 levels and allowing for the growth of the number of housing units and the decline of the mail response rates, an unexplained increase in census costs of approximately $1.3 billion between 1970 and 1990 remains.

There are important caveats to cost analysis of the census over the past 20 years. The work done by census staff (both field and headquarters staff) changed drastically during the 20-year period as the Census Bureau tried increasingly complex and labor-intensive approaches. Although the figures in this chapter emphasize productivity data, we note that the cost increases are primarily associated with issues of census design and not management.

The rise in costs did not produce a "better" census, at least as measured by the accuracy with which the total population or its major components were counted. We believe that a large part of the cost increase was driven by the way in which the Census Bureau responded to several important outside pressures: there was an increased demand for accurate population counts at very detailed geographic subdivisions and in hard-to-enumerate areas for purposes of congressional and legislative redistricting and otherwise carrying out the Voting Rights Act and its amendments. At the same time, public cooperation with the census process, as measured by the mail response rate, declined and was lowest precisely in the areas in which the pressures for an accurate count were greatest. The Census Bureau responded by pouring on resources in highly labor-intensive enumeration efforts to count every last person. For example, census district offices remained open for longer durations and the supervisory ratios increased during the period.

It is widely believed among those associated with the census process over the last several decades that the quality of the temporary personnel employed during the decennial census deteriorated over the period, as evidenced by higher turnover and lower productivity. Although we have not been able to assess the quantitative importance of this phenomenon, the view is so widespread as to lend it some credence.

Our deliberations have led us to two general observations about the problems and issues outlined above. First, there are no conceivable changes in the collection of census data that will simultaneously meet all of the following objectives: (1) continue a highly intensive census effort, relying principally on physical enumeration and labor-intensive follow-up techniques, to overcome the consequences of a declining mail response rate; (2) provide detailed and reliable block-level data for redistricting and the Voting Rights Act; (3) provide the other housing and demographic data widely demanded for cross-tabulation at the level of small geographic areas; (4) reduce the differential undercount; and (5) keep costs from growing rapidly. There is, in short, no magic bullet.

Second, from an inspection of recent trends in census costs, the panel concludes that efforts to increase differential coverage, especially through highly labor-intensive enumeration techniques, are a key factor driving up costs. Moreover, efforts to improve differential coverage (i.e., the percentage difference of population counted for whites and minorities) have had increasingly diminishing returns (coverage was better in 1980 than 1970, but there were no such gains in 1990). Differential coverage improvement efforts have been carried to the point at which additional effort and expense may yield little or no improvement in coverage or in decreasing subgroup differences in net undercount. Expensive efforts to improve census coverage are understandable given such forces as the impetus of the Voting Rights Act to provide detailed data on race and ethnicity at the block level. Nonetheless, it is appropriate to ask if this continued effort to improve differential coverage, which has been so far unsuccessful and has increased census costs, is necessary for future censuses.

NOTES

[1]The denominator for census mail response rates includes both unoccupied and occupied housing units.

[2]Overall mail response rates were 78 percent in 1970, 75 percent in 1980, and 65 percent in 1990 (U.S. General Accounting Office, 1992). If mail response rates dropped at the rate of change of 1970 to 1990, then the projected response rate in 2000 would be 55 percent.

[3]The GAO calculation assumes continued population and household growth during the decade and a decrease in the mail response rate from 65 to a range of 55 to 59 percent, involving about 50 million nonrespondent households.

[4]Examining census costs and the national net undercount rate over the 1960 to 1990 period, the general trend has been moderate improvements in overall coverage accompanied by substantial cost increases. The 1980 census seems atypical in the overall trend, achieving a much lower overall net undercount rate but doubling real costs per household. After the achievements of the 1980 census, the 1990 census was not able to continue the general trend of coverage improvements.

[5]Costs associated with attempts to improve coverage are related, to a great extent, to missing households. The problem for much of the undercoverage is not that households were delivered a questionnaire and did not respond, but that households were not located and sent a questionnaire in the first place. There are two different kinds of coverage costs associated with the long form: (1) the extra costs of getting a long-form questionnaire delivered to each sample housing unit and (2) the additional cost of getting information from mail nonrespondents.

[6]The 1970 census long form used a matrix sampling approach with separate samples of 5 percent and 15 percent of households selected. The 5 percent sample had a long form with 52 questions, and the 15 percent sample had 38 questions.

[7]This assumes that census costs rise in proportion to housing. Actually, costs probably rise a little less than proportionately. If so, the unexplainable part of the cost increase is a little larger.

[8]We refer to both mail response and mail return rates in this report. Mail return rates are the proportion of forms mailed back by occupied housing units. Mail response rates are calculated on the basis of all housing units, including vacant units. Because about 10 percent of housing units are vacant, mail response rates tend to be slightly lower than mail return rates.

[9]The actual census cost changes associated with the mail response rate show a complicated picture. Initial declines in response rates produce increases of about $14 to $15 million for each percentage point change. For greater magnitudes of declines in the mail response rate, decreases in 4 or more percentage points, there is an increased cost of about $17 to $18 million for each percent point change. For each percentage point increase in mail response rates, there is a decline of about $16 million in total census costs.

[10]Although mail response rates declined for the census from 1970 to 1990, especially in the 1980 to 1990 period, similar declines did not occur in major federal household surveys. Federal surveys, however, are typically face-to-face or a combination of mail with telephone or interviewer follow-up. The census is primarily a mail questionnaire, with personal visits for nonresponse follow-up. A recent review of nonresponse in 47 major federal demographic and establishment surveys revealed that there was little evidence of declining response rates during the 1982 to 1991 period (Gonzalez et al., 1994). There were some increases, however, in refusal rates in demographic surveys. It is unclear why the census mail response rate declined substantially more than the secular trend for major surveys, unless there were improvements made in household surveys that were not duplicated in the census.

[11]We derive the cost estimate using the 1970 census cost base by multiplying 13 percentage points (the 1970 to 1990 mail response decline) times the .0067 (the assumed census costs per mail response point decrease) times the estimated census costs. The estimated census costs, in constant dollars, would be

the cost per household of the 1970 census ($10.52 in 1990 constant dollars) times the number of households in 1990 (104 million), or $1.09 billion.

[12]We have used the change in the gross domestic product (GDP) deflator as the measure of inflation, which rose 222 percent from 1970 to 1990. But the central conclusions of this section are unchanged if other general measures of inflation are substituted. The chain weight GDP price index rose by 207 percent. We also attempted to construct a special weighted index reflecting the increase in the wages, fringes, and costs of goods and services purchased for the census. The full set of data was not available to construct such an index, but we estimate that it might show an increase in the range of 237 to 245 percent. Even with the upper end of this range as a measure of inflation, "unexplained" cost increases over the 1970 to 1990 period would still amount to over $1.2 billion (compared with the $1.3 billion cited in the text).

[13]About 110 district offices, called master district offices, were open as long as 18 to 20 months during the 1989 and 1990 fiscal years. Master district offices managed address list development activities in the year prior to the 1990 census.

[14]During the period from 1960 to 1990, the number of persons per housing unit decreased. Such a decrease would reduce the length of the personal interview for nonresponse follow-up, but the impact on enumerator productivity and census costs would probably be slight. The relationship between censuses and household size is also affected by other factors. First, there is generally a positive relationship between household size and census mail response rates. Smaller households typically have lower mail response rates, which contribute to increased costs. Second, declines in household size have been associated with increases in nontraditional households (households different from married couples with or without children present). Nontraditional households, for various reasons, increase the difficulty and cost of census enumeration. Finally, households with fewer people increase the difficulty of making personal contact during nonresponse follow-up, the most expensive phase of census operations.

[15]The Census Bureau intentionally "overtrained" the number of enumerators because past experience showed that many enumerators resign before census operations end. The goal was to have a sufficient number of people trained so that there would be enough workers available during the daily peak activity.

[16]Census Bureau analysis (Keller, 1994) suggests that actual production rates during the nonresponse follow-up operation in the 1990 census (interviews completed by enumerators per hour) increased from 1980 to 1990. Census staff believe that these production gains can be attributed to improved training, better management reports, and incentive payments.

4

Radical Alternatives

There are several ways in which a population can be counted. A conventional modern population census attempts to provide a count of all the people within a territory at a specified time. A census normally involves eight elements: (1) a definition of the population to be considered as part of the census; (2) determination of the content to be included on the census questionnaire, usually based on an extensive examination of users' needs; (3) careful testing of alternative questionnaire wordings and formats; (4) systematic preparation of lists of dwellings in which the population lives; (5) the hiring and training of enumerators; (6) the distribution of questionnaires and use of enumerators to question either the whole population or only those people who did not satisfactorily complete their questionnaires; (7) the processing and analysis of the census questionnaires; and (8) dissemination of statistical summaries using a variety of media. Within the general description, there are many variants of the specific procedures.

Several radical alternatives to a conventional census have been proposed for the United States. This chapter discusses four of them: a national register for the basic census, an administrative records census, a census conducted by the U.S. Postal Service, and a rolling or sample census. This chapter examines the characteristics of each of these alternatives and presents the panel's conclusions about their feasibility for the needs now met by the decennial census.

In a conventional modern census, most countries depend on either enumerators to visit the household or staff to compile results from mail questionnaires. Some countries, such as Canada, have enumerators deliver questionnaires directly to each household. The U.S. census relies primarily on a mailing address for every dwelling unit and then uses the U.S. Postal Service for delivery of a mail questionnaire. If questionnaires are not returned, the census office then directly contacts the households that have not responded.

As noted above, there are many different specific procedures and widely different levels of intensity for achieving coverage. Some countries distribute their census questionnaires, do a "reasonable" follow-up, and accept some net undercount. In contrast, the U.S. census operation is a very intensive attempt to contact every housing unit and obtain demographic information for every person in the household. As part of its activities, the U.S. census operation involves an intensive effort to prepare an accurate address list, has enumerators active in the field for a longer time than other census operations, and makes as many as six attempts to follow up all nonrespondents. This intensive U.S. census is now very expensive. One major census design alternative, therefore, is for a less intensive, cheaper census.

A NATIONAL REGISTER FOR THE BASIC CENSUS

A national population register could replace the conventional census with the continuous recording of individual data, possibly linked to other records, for every resident of the United States. In order to provide data required for apportionment and redistricting (and for other purposes) the register would need to report the precise geographic location of everyone, that is, his or her residential address.

In spite of the challenges of such a system, population registers have been successfully developed in several nations, including Belgium, the Netherlands, Switzerland, and the Scandinavian countries. The Swedish system has its roots in the seventeenth century, and the Dutch register has been operating for more than a century. A similar system was instituted in the United Kingdom during World War II but was discontinued.[1]

A population register must be continuously updated to retain its usefulness. Also, a register needs to be linked to other records as people move, change their marital status, change jobs (and incomes), increase their formal education, have children, and die. Such a register can be maintained continuously only if there is a legal requirement for individuals to report all changes of addresses and certain other changes in status. Furthermore, massive record linkage (in order to obtain required information from other administrative record systems) is generally possible at reasonable cost only if all individuals are issued unique identifiers and if these identifiers are recorded on the main administrative system.

A register-based system, by itself, can supply basic demographic information about the population. Basic demographic data could include a person's birth date and birthplace, sex, and race or ethnicity (if requested by some form and if identity is assumed to be fixed). Through record linkage (or mandatory reporting to the register), information can also be obtained on marital status, children, and family and household structure. Further linkage to tax records can provide income information.

A register system for the United States would have to be designed to meet user requirements for census information content and statistical quality. The first critical requirement would be to provide data required for legislative needs (especially to fulfill the requirements of the Voting Rights Act): individual data by age and race and ethnicity for small geographic areas. Such data would require that all persons be identified by race and ethnicity, a severe challenge for current birth records, which record the race and ethnicity of parents but not of newborns, and immigration records, which do not collect data on the race or ethnicity of immigrants. An additional problem would exist for illegal aliens, for whom there is no likelihood of successful registration.

There are a number of options for a basic register that could be used in the United States. One option is a multipurpose register based on population and housing data. Basic register data could include administrative records as well as statistical data. A prerequisite for such a system in the United States would be required registration of all international and internal migrants.[2] Even if such registration were publicly acceptable, it would be difficult to maintain a register of international migrants in the face of a net gain of about 200,000 to 300,000 new illegal aliens annually. (The net figure hides gross illegal flows that are probably 5 to 10 times larger than the net flows). Also, the United States maintains no emigration records at all for the some 200,000 or so residents (native-born or foreign-born with U.S. citizenship) who depart each year and settle permanently in another country.

Data from a population register could be more timely than those from a conventional census. Annual estimates for small areas could be provided and updated as changes occur in geographic boundaries. Time-series comparisons would be improved with more frequent estimates for population data. A national population register with basic demographic data would also provide a powerful sampling frame for surveys for more general use. Having continuously updated demographic data, with an associated national address list, would make it possible to develop more effective sampling schemes with less expensive data collection.

A register-based census has a technical limitation in that the range of topics and their definitions are limited. Some census topics are not covered by current administrative records that might be linked with a register, and it may not be reasonable to add questions to administrative forms solely because data are needed for statistical purposes. Such data would therefore have to be collected in other ways—e.g., data on labor force status. For topics not covered by administrative records, a population register, even after linkage with other administrative records, would provide no estimates. Supplementary data could be collected by sample surveys, but to provide census-type detail on occupation, education, travel to work patterns, and other social and economic variables would require samples comparable to that of the current census long form at least once every 10 years. The need for surveys would offset some of the savings that a register operation might provide compared with the census.

Sweden offers an example of how a country with an administrative register deals with topic limitations in the register. Unlike Denmark, which has relied wholly on its register-based census since 1981, Sweden has retained a census questionnaire since 1970, but it asks only for information that is not in the administrative records. The 1990 Swedish census questionnaire asked about economic activity, housing, household composition, and education; the data are then linked to the central population register to provide the full array of needed information.

On balance, the experience of countries operating register-based systems is that the ongoing costs are cheaper than those of a conventional census (Redfern, 1989). The peaking of resources is reduced, and large-scale field operations for data collection are not required. However, cost savings are achieved only if the information content of the register, supplemented through record linkage, is adequate.

Data from a population register can be produced more quickly and more frequently than data from a conventional census. The experience of countries operating population registers seems to be that the ongoing operation of the system lends itself to the prompt preparation of summary reports and aggregate data reports. Moreover, detailed information can be produced from the system as required on the usually limited variables that are recorded on it. Still, the system is sensitive to technical problems, particularly since the administrative files for the system with which it needs to be linked periodically are not centrally controlled. Linking administrative records would be a challenge for the United States in several regards: there are many administrative files that are controlled by state and local governments, and it would be a problem if the files changed without proper attention to the impact on the population register.

Strong political and cultural opposition is likely to the introduction of a unique individual numbering and compulsory registration system in the United States. The prospect of ongoing linkage of federal, state, and local government data would be opposed by many people. The requirement for notification of changes of address would also be felt to be onerous by many residents. Advocates concerned about privacy issues have already raised questions about adequate protection for federal administrative databases. Such advocates would be naturally concerned about the creation of a national database, on every U.S. resident, that would be continuously updated with changes in individual characteristics, including current residence. Access to state and local databases, especially for a centrally controlled population register, is also problematic. To be maintained continuously, there would need to be ways for individuals to update easily and regularly changes in their social and economic characteristics and their current residence. A population register would require universal compliance in registration from U.S. citizens and resident aliens. If the population register were not universally accepted, its use in lieu of census data would lead to serious quality, cost, and public acceptability problems.

There are numerous advantages, for operational and financial reasons, for some countries to use national registers. But, for the foreseeable future, there would be major disadvantages for the United States, including a possible lack of public cooperation stemming from privacy issues about the required data matching and record linkage, which in addition to being concerns for their own sake, could lead to poor-quality data and lack of population coverage.

Conclusion 4.1 The panel concludes that a national register for the United States is not a feasible replacement for the decennial census.

Although a national register is not a feasible alternative for the 2000 census, the long-run possibilities may be more positive. Demands for universal health care with "portable" individual policies may produce a basic register of the population with such limited content as age, sex, marital status, and current address. The pendulum of public perception may shift toward the use of administrative records for labor certification, under the pressure to deal with illegal immigration, for example. If there were a relatively complete listing of the population, maintained up to date for routine administrative purposes, it might become attractive to consider the feasibility of a national register to replace the traditional census. A national register, as implemented already in several countries, offers frequent data at reasonable cost.

AN ADMINISTRATIVE RECORDS CENSUS

Another radical alternative to a conventional census involves the use of administrative records. During the past decade, some European countries (mostly in Scandinavia) have linked additional administrative records to their central population register and have discontinued direct-inquiry censuses. Denmark, Finland, and the Netherlands now rely on population counts and essential characteristics from their central records, although they supplement their national data with sample surveys. Other countries, such as Sweden, now canvass the population with a short-form census and use administrative records to provide information that, in turn, does not need to be asked in the census. A critical question is whether it is desirable for the United States to consider developing methods for a population census using administrative records *without* the support of a continuous population register—something that has not been attempted in any country yet.

Assessing this broad option in brief terms, the panel concludes that administrative records cannot be adapted in the near future (by 2000) to meet even relaxed demands for detailed demographic information for small geographic areas. It would be extremely difficult to redesign current administrative data as a substitute for census data to meet the Voting Rights Act requirements for data on race and ethnicity for small geographic areas. No federal or state administrative system now possesses race and ethnicity data for the U.S. population, combined with coverage of all households and accurate information on current address.

Other limitations of existing administrative records include the accuracy of address information and the paucity of demographic and socioeconomic variables that are included (see Appendix J for details). The panel agrees with a letter report from the Panel to Evaluate Alternative Census Methods to the director of the Census Bureau (Bradburn, 1992), which finds that it is not feasible to consider the use of a census based on administrative records for 2000.

It is important to look beyond the 2000 census for an evaluation of a possibly more effective use of administrative records. Recent research suggests that a high proportion of the U.S. population is included in one or more existing administrative records (Sailer et al., 1993). The coverage of administrative records may well expand in the future. Moreover, if it becomes important to use records for census purposes, efforts could be made to expand the content and improve the quality of the records over the next two decades. An administrative records census may be a real alternative in 2020, but not if work does not begin soon in order to accumulate experience in working with the records. The potential population coverage of administrative records is an important area for further consideration, and more research is needed.

Consideration of the use of administrative records as a complement or substitute for the current census must address several issues. Whereas it is true that the coverage of some administrative record systems is high and expanding, no single record system covers the entire population. Two examples provide an illustration. The Internal Revenue Service (IRS) collects information from its annual tax returns and related information documents; however, it is a challenge to produce estimates of nonfilers who do not show up in their administrative records. As another example, the Social Security Administration (SSA) maintains a register of Social Security accounts. Increasingly, infants are registered with the SSA at birth and, because immigrants need to obtain a Social Security account, the country is moving toward a universal registration system. Emigrants, however, are not recorded in any administrative system.[3] There also persist significant flows of illegal aliens into the United States, with a net gain of perhaps 200,000 or more illegal entrants annually and approximately 2 million illegal residents currently (Bean, Edmonston, and Passel, 1990). Illegal aliens often use fraudulent Social Security documents or other people's account numbers. There is therefore a need to assess differential coverage for administrative records systems and to examine whether a procedure could be developed to use administrative records for a census count.

Information on racial and ethnic identification must be provided by the census. There are no race and ethnicity data in IRS records, and Social Security records do not contain such information for everyone. Birth registration certificates now include the race and Hispanic status of the mother (and sometimes of the father, with all states participating by 1994), but the information on race is kept confidential by the state vital registration system.[4] Moreover, there are questions about the racial and ethnic identity of the many children who are born to parents of different racial origin or ethnicity. Can we presume the racial or ethnic identity of an adult on the basis of information from a birth certificate? Our nation has continually changed its sense of race and ethnicity classification over time. Even if a record system included race and ethnicity information for the entire population, the categories may change (as was done during recent censuses when a category for Asian and Pacific Islander was added), and the entire population would need to be resurveyed. Finally, there are concerns about the differences in the reporting of race and ethnicity in a nonthreatening census context and in administrative records.

Current administrative records are particularly problematic on race and ethnicity data. Little is known about the coverage of various minority groups in administrative record databases. Some databases do not include information on race. Nor is information on coverage by race available from those with data on race. Data on small population groups, such as American Indians, are likely to be a special problem because geographic coding is difficult in isolated rural areas and coverage is unknown.

Race data in SSA files (the Summary Earnings Record file in particular), the major federal database with demographic information for the U.S. population, have been declining in quality (Irwin, 1984:4-1 to 4-3). The race question for a Social Security applicant used the categories of *white*, *black*, and *other* until 1980. In 1980, the race/ethnicity question was altered and the listed categories were *white*, *black*, *American Indian*, *Asian and Pacific Islander*, and *Spanish*. The race/ethnicity question was voluntary, however, and a substantial proportion of applicants, especially in some large metropolitan areas, has not provided their race/ethnicity self-identity on forms since 1980.

Because no national files other than those of the SSA contain specific race/ethnicity information, it is important to note three limitations of these files. First, for individuals registering before 1980 and reporting "other" for their race, the specific racial/ethnic identification is not known. Second, a significant proportion of persons who applied for a Social Security number during the past 14 years did not provide a racial/ethnic identification. Third, many Social Security numbers are currently issued to infants, whose parents apply for a Social Security number for the newborn at the time of birth. The race of a newborn is uncertain, because not all children necessarily have parents of the same race or ethnicity, nor will the race of a newborn necessarily be the same race or ethnicity reported by the person when an adult. Regardless of the racial or ethnic uncertainty of the newborn, no information on the race or ethnicity of a child is transferred to SSA files because there is no record on the birth certificate of the race or ethnicity of the child. Birth certificates indicate only the race and ethnicity of the mother, and the information is not forwarded to the SSA. As a combination of the above limitations, current files are substantially incomplete or inadequate for race/ethnicity information for an administrative records census.

Besides the challenge of obtaining essential race and ethnicity information from administrative records, there are serious doubts that current records (from either the federal, state, or local governments) could provide most of the information currently collected in the long-form census questionnaire. Could records be redesigned to collect this information? Would large surveys be used in conjunction with a census based on administrative records?

The coverage of various major administrative records databases varies greatly. The IRS files have relatively high coverage of the population, especially if efforts are made to take into account miscellaneous tax records and people who may not file tax returns every year (Sailer et al., 1993). Additional people might be added to tax files from other databases, including elderly persons from the Medicare files and other groups of people from state and local files for welfare, Medicaid, and Food Stamps. At this moment, the coverage of an administrative records census cannot be precisely estimated because of extensive and unknown overlap between files, and because estimates of duplicates in specific files vary greatly. Finally, it is also clear that an administrative records census would need to depend on supplementary administrative records data on people in group quarters (prisons, jails, hospitals for the mentally ill, and other places for long-term residence in a group setting).

A reference date for an administrative records census requires careful study because various administrative records databases are updated at different times for different reasons and would have varying degrees of completeness if used for a specific census date. For example, deaths are not necessarily noted in a timely fashion in administrative records.

A basic census requires the correct geographic location for each respondent. Because the mailing address is not always the same as the residential address, an administrative records census would require a current residence for every person. One possibility would be to require an added question on residential address for the annual tax return, which would still not provide actual residential location for a substantial proportion of the population.

Administrative records do not provide family relationships for households. Neither IRS nor other administrative records identify the relationships among persons at an address that would permit the determination of families. Yet family-based statistics are critical outputs from the census. This is a serious problem because family-based statistics are among the most important data produced by the census.

A final issue for examination is the accuracy of the address for individuals in administrative records. The census needs to allocate individuals to small areas. This can be done if individuals can be assigned to a specific dwelling unit, then placed within census blocks. However, this requires that administrative records be current and have an accurate street address. In some cases administrative records lacking up-to-date, accurate addresses could be linked to another record system that provides such addresses. In this case, the challenge is to link several individual records at the household level. Finally, and most important, is the issue that IRS data (and other records) often use business address or a tax accountant's address for tax information. These are issues for future research to examine.

The costs of data collection for an administrative records census would be spread among many federal, state, and local agencies. An administrative records census would require that the Census Bureau have access to a large number of individual files for matching and linking. It might be necessary to enact legislation to permit access to needed administrative records databases for matching and linkage. The pulling together of administrative records would be a complex, demanding task, though not a task beyond the capabilities of current information processing technology. The total cost of an administrative records census is uncertain. Countries with a uniform identification system and a long tradition of accepting registration have relatively low costs associated with their population registers. The experience of other countries provides little applicable information for the potential costs in the United States, a country with no existing system and no uniform identification system across major records systems.

Output from an administrative records census could be produced in a timely fashion and in a manner similar to that from a conventional census. Detailed information could be produced for geographic areas, including small geographic areas with geographically referenced data. Census output from an administrative records census may be limited in a number of important ways, however. First, coverage is likely to be lower than in the conventional census because currently undercounted groups are not necessarily included in administrative records. Illegal aliens in the United States are particularly unlikely to be included in an administrative records census. Second, small-area information could be subject to significant errors if the accuracy of address information is weak or if the issue of residential versus filing address is not remedied. Third, content would be limited to that of administrative records, even if current records were redesigned to include some additional data items. Moreover, administrative record systems are vulnerable to technical problems and changes, particularly if contributed files are not centrally controlled by the Census Bureau.

An administrative records census would require the creation of a central data bank of virtually all people in the country, with linked information from files currently stored completely separately. The accurate linkage of different databases would be best accomplished with a unique individual identifier, such as a Social Security number. How would the public react to the creation of a data bank? What would be the public's willingness to provide Social Security numbers for major records, realizing that the purpose was to link various individual records for statistical information only? The issue of privacy and confidentiality of administrative records requires considerable investigation before one could consider the replacement of the conventional census with an administrative records census. The panel does not make a judgment about what the public acceptability would be for an administrative records census. We do note, however, that there would be strong political pressures against an administrative records census.

Although administrative records have been used to support census-taking for several years, the use of administrative records to take a full census is unlikely in the near future. The unique quality of self-reported race and ethnicity data, collected every 10 years by the census in an evolving format, cannot be duplicated by current administrative records.

Furthermore, an administrative records census faces a critical technical problem: the requirement to be able to unduplicate records. If there is reliance on several systems of administrative records, then the records must be unduplicated in order to prevent an overcounting of the population. More research and testing is needed on technical issues, including undercoverage, reporting errors, race and ethnicity data, and unduplication.

The Census Bureau has used administrative records to support census activities in the past. We endorse the use of administrative records to improve census coverage. The Census Bureau should intensify its efforts to use administrative records, recognizing that expanded use of administrative records must be an evolutionary process. In particular, we recommend (see Chapter 8) more intensive work with administrative records for preparing intercensal estimates.[5] As experience is gained with records, we support experimentation to ensure their potential use for supplementing and complementing decennial census content.

Conclusion 4.2 The panel concludes that an administrative records census is not a feasible option for 2000.

A CENSUS CONDUCTED BY THE U.S. POSTAL SERVICE

The U.S. Postal Service and its letter carriers have played an important role in prior censuses. Chapter 5 reviews the role played by the Postal Service in recent censuses.

One radical alternative for a future census would be to have the entire field operation of the census conducted by the U.S. Postal Service. The U.S. Postal Service would deliver and collect census questionnaires using its own staff. Letter carriers would then collect information from all households that did not respond to the mail questionnaire. The role of the U.S. Postal Service would be limited to the actual field operation—all data would be transmitted to the Census Bureau.

The letter carriers might collect information directly from household members, and they might know enough about the household to provide substitute information. Major savings on the cost of nonresponse follow-up could be made if letter carriers could provide a limited amount of basic information on nonrespondents, without having to contact the household. Even if letter carriers knew this minimal information for some households on their mail delivery route, however, it is unlikely that they would be highly accurate (on age, for example) or that they would know such information for all households. And having postal employees classify household members by race and ethnicity might be objectionable to many people. Moreover, streamlining of mail delivery operations in recent years has reduced the contact that letter carriers have with many of their residential customers.

This radical alternative has been examined by a joint group from the U.S. Postal Service and the Census Bureau (Green and Scarr, 1993). Their examination of this alternative reveals:

• It would not be cost-effective for either the U.S. Postal Service or the Census Bureau for the U.S. Postal Service to administer directly the census field operations. In conducting the 1990 census, it took about 36 million staff hours to contact nonrespondents. If this amount of work were handled by the U.S. Postal Service, it would have taken about 20 hours of overtime per week for about 5 weeks for *every* letter carrier. This assumes that every letter carrier would cooperate and would be willing (under current union rules) to work this amount of overtime.

• The average U.S. Postal Service letter carrier costs about $23.50 per hour in total costs for regular time worked. This can be contrasted with the average hourly pay of about $7.50 (including benefits) that was paid to the average census enumerator in 1990. The rate for overtime census interviewing by letter carriers would be even higher, four times the rate for a census enumerator. Obviously, there is no benefit to the U.S. Postal Service, or to postal customers who pay the costs, for letter carriers to contribute their time without reimbursement. Overall, the cost of letter carriers is much higher than census enumerators, on an average hourly basis, and would significantly increase census costs.

• The U.S. Postal Service and its letter carriers are not well acquainted with the occupants of residential addresses. Many letter carriers do not actually go door-to-door. Many households receive their mail at central boxes in apartment buildings or in new suburban areas. Many other people use postal mailboxes.

For over 25 years, almost all new mail delivery points in residential areas have been served through cluster boxes, making it unnecessary for the letter carrier to go door-to-door. A letter carrier serving newer residential areas rarely sees customers and often does not even see the residential housing units. Most rural letter carriers do not go to the customers' doors, but deliver to mailboxes along roads that are often some distance from the customers' houses. In addition, all mail delivery is done during business hours when most people are not at home.

• Rural areas would present special problems for the delivery of census questionnaires by the U.S. Postal Service. Special procedures would need to be developed because rural letter carriers do not go to the actual rural house. In some parts of the country, the U.S. Postal Service delivers mail at central postal offices through individual mail boxes. The actual physical location of the mail recipient is not known. Nor is it known whether more than one family or household member may share a mailbox. In other areas, rural route boxes are located at major intersections or on roadways. Again, the physical location of the residence is not known.

• There would be legal concerns about U.S. Postal Service administration of the field operations of the census. Privacy issues might affect what letter carriers can do in obtaining information from nonrespondents. The public perception of the U.S. Postal Service might be adversely affected: How would the public view the U.S. Postal Service if it were involved in collecting and reporting personal information to others? People may have serious concerns about reporting information to letter carriers who deliver their mail every day. Finally, its possible legal responsibilities for the quality of the data and legal repercussions would be a concern for the U.S. Postal Service.

The Census Bureau and the U.S. Postal Service concluded that there are many ways in which cooperation on the census and other activities has been mutually beneficial. They also agreed that there are important new ways for an enhanced role for the U.S. Postal Service in future censuses. But they concluded that the "best way to use the expertise of the U.S. Postal Service letter carriers is not through the collection of actual census data" (Green and Scarr, 1993:8). The U.S. Postal Service gains no real advantage in taking on the responsibilities for census field operations. The primary objective of the U.S. Postal Service is to collect and deliver mail. Taking on census field operations would mean that the organization would divert attention from other tasks without gaining any important return. Overall, the U.S. Postal Service believed that the use of letter carriers to conduct census interviews "would have a negative impact on the ability of the Postal Service to deliver the mail" (Green and Scarr, 1993:6). We concur with the conclusions of this joint group.

Conclusion 4.3 The panel concludes that the decennial census cannot be conducted by the U.S. Postal Service in any way that would be cost-effective or an improvement over the conventional census.

It should be noted that the panel believes that there is an expanded role for the Postal Service in census operations in future censuses (Chapter 5 describes the expanded role) and for improving the Census Bureau's intercensal national address list (Chapter 8 outlines this activity).

A ROLLING OR SAMPLE CENSUS

With regard to the constitutional requirements for the census, it is clear that a basic enumeration is required to meet constitutional requirements for reapportionment. Such an effort, in effect, is required also because of the need for small-area data for redistricting—including one-person, one-vote needs and Voting Rights Act requirements (see Appendix C for a legal and political history). For these reasons, census designs that do not include a complete enumeration of the population once a decade are not reasonable options on legal and practical grounds. We also have considered these designs from a practical perspective in the discussion below.

In a sample census, only some of the population would be counted. In a rolling census design, different parts of the population would be surveyed every year. Several variants of a rolling census design have been proposed. One design proposes a full census (including short-form and long-form content) of one-tenth of the nation's counties to be conducted every year (Horvitz, 1986). A different sample of counties would be covered every year of the decade. Horvitz submits that accurate data on internal migration could be developed from each year's one-tenth census to use in developing population estimates for the counties not covered that year. However, as the design does not provide for even a minimal census of the entire country at a single point in time, it would fail to meet the constitutional requirement that reapportionment counts be based on an attempt at a complete enumeration of the entire population.

Another design variant proposes to survey a less clustered sample of one-tenth of the population each year, cumulating the estimates over 1, 2, or more years to increase their reliability for small geographic areas (Kish, 1981, 1990). The proposed one-tenth sample would provide state estimates of reasonable reliability; however, use of these estimates would encounter the constitutional barrier to a sample census. Averaging the estimates from each year's sample over a 10-year period reduces their sampling error, but these estimates would not pertain to a year chosen for reapportionment but rather to the average experience of states and other areas over the prior 10 years. Not being based on an attempt at complete enumeration at a given time, they would, at a minimum, raise the question of whether they meet the constitutional requirement. Moreover, the cumulated estimates would be far more out of date with regard to the distribution of the population than would be estimates from the current census.[6]

Designs that attempt to spread over the decade the collection of some of the information that is now obtained in the census merit evaluation as to their benefits and costs. It is worth considering if such a design would provide more timely data and higher coverage and whether, even if these were to occur, they would offset higher costs. There appears to be a legal consensus, however, that such designs must include a minimal complete census every tenth year to satisfy the constitutional requirement for reapportionment.[7]

From the methodological perspective, it is not even clear how one would go about conducting a sample census. Obtaining a sufficient degree of accuracy for reapportionment (and other purposes) would require the development of a frame from which to draw the sample. In the census, the frame would be the list of addresses that is used to mail out census questionnaires.[8] In addition to developing the address list, it would be necessary to carry out activities to determine the list's accuracy for purposes of obtaining a proper random sample of *people*, as the list would likely include nonresidential addresses (e.g., businesses) as well as exclude some residences. One such evaluation activity might be to conduct a second independent survey either before or after the sample census itself, which, at a minimum, would have to ascertain the number, age, and sex of respondents. As a result of all these activities, for all intents and purposes, the Census Bureau would quickly wind up conducting virtually a complete census.

A sample census, assuming that it could be effected, would face other problems. An important difficulty is that, by all the available evidence, household surveys experience higher net undercoverage rates and more severe differential undercoverage than does the complete-count census.[9] Errors of undercoverage and differential undercoverage that arise from the use of sampling can be adjusted by evaluation surveys. But the extent of such adjustment would be very large in a census that relied completely on sampling. Another problem that could contribute to coverage errors is the likely difficulty of publicizing a sample census in which there is no intent to try to contact everyone. Finally, there would appear to be some questions regarding the likelihood of achieving significant cost savings over a complete census.[10]

A rolling census would provide more regular information and, on average during the decade, would be more current at the time of use. Annual or regular output could be provided for small geographic areas and for small population groups, but the availability and detail of output would depend on sample sizes. Estimates for the nation and for subnational areas and groups would be affected by adjustment from sampling, coverage, and enumeration errors. Information for small areas, such as city blocks used for purposes of redistricting, would have to be based on data averaged over several years—raising both legal issues and problems of interpretation (e.g., regarding the meaning of such data as a moving average of income from a rolling census).

The cost of a rolling census would be more stable and less peaked than a conventional census. Expertise could be developed, and training would be more cost-effective. The work flow for the Census Bureau would be less disruptive. Regular contacts with the surveyed population would offer chances for improvement of procedures. Regular surveys would offer the opportunity to implement a transition to new census questions, while maintaining a time trend for older questions. The high-risk nature of a one-time conventional census would be reduced. But the cost of carrying out a rolling census, with sample data collected to replace the conventional long form, backed by the need to collect decennial data with benchmark information, would almost certainly exceed the cost of a conventional census.

Output would be more frequent and could be produced more quickly. Because of the rolling nature of the sample, special procedures would need to be developed for aggregating data of sufficient sample size for small-area estimates. There would be pressure to produce results quickly and delays would be less acceptable than for the conventional census. For a large rolling census, there would be increasing pressures to maintain the data online, with periodic inclusion of the latest sample survey data.

There is no reason to anticipate that public acceptability would decline for a rolling census. However, the survey nature of the data collection would lack the high profile and historic image of the conventional census (see Chapter 6 for a discussion of data collection through a continuous measurement survey). Noncompliance would increase for a rolling census, compared with a similar decennial census, because of the survey nature of the operation. All factors being equal, the response rates and coverage would be poorer for a rolling census. There is also a special problem to note: the rolling census would be capable of providing current data on many topics that are the subject of regular sample surveys—e.g., employment, unemployment, income, and education. Given the high-quality measurements achieved for these variables by ongoing surveys, the rolling census is most unlikely to replicate their results. Having competing estimates of, say, average family income or unemployment rates may undermine confidence in the rolling census and ultimately in the nation's statistical system. Also, having two sets of estimates may lead to question about duplication and suggestions for dropping at least one of the surveys. Sponsoring agencies would understandably favor continuation of their high-quality survey and would therefore not be supporters, in this circumstance, of a rolling census.

The panel does not recommend a rolling or sample census on substantive grounds. A sample census would face serious problems in coverage (a greater proportion of the population would be included in the final count through sampling and statistical estimation), would not provide substantial cost savings, and could not be publicized as a complete count of the population. Moreover, there are some types of data (i.e., transportation information) that appear to be best collected at one point in time. A rolling census provides little advantage for overall census data and is likely to cost much more than the conventional census.

Conclusion 4.4 The panel concludes that a rolling or sample census is not an acceptable replacement for the 2000 decennial census.

NOTES

[1]See Redfern (1987) for a review of the use of population registers, in association with administrative records, for censuses.

[2]International migration also affects the conventional census, which counts all residents of the United States at the time of the census, including illegal immigrants. Undercount estimates and procedures to correct the physical enumeration would also include undocumented aliens in the country.

[3]It is true that permanent emigrants do not pay taxes and would cease to appear actively in some administrative records. It would still be difficult to determine emigrant status solely on evidence that someone no longer files tax forms.

[4]The SSA is looking at ways to resume the collection of race and ethnicity information from birth certificates. But in 1994 these data are not reported to the SSA from birth certificates.

[5]Technically, this is a difference between postcensal (estimates after a census) and intercensal (estimates made between two existing census) procedures. We refer generally to estimates in the period between censuses as intercensal, ignoring the complexity of different demographic procedures.

[6]For reapportionment and redistricting in 2001, 2011, and so on, conventional census data would be about 1 year old, whereas the cumulated estimates would be centered mid-decade, making them 6 years old. See Fellegi (1981) for a detailed critique of the Kish proposal, including conceptual and operational aspects.

[7]The Census Bureau is currently evaluating continuous measurement designs that include a year-zero census together with rolling surveys throughout the decade to obtain long-form items and update short-form items (see Alexander, 1993). See the discussion in Chapter 6 for additional material on continuous measurement designs.

[8]This line of argument does not necessarily apply to all sample surveys, many of which can make use of area frames.

[9]For example, in March 1986, the Survey of Income and Program Participation and the March Current Population Survey covered only 80-82 percent of black men ages 16 and older and 93 percent of nonblack men ages 16 and older. Coverage ratios were somewhat higher for women. (Coverage ratios compare the estimates from a survey, using the initial survey weights that take into account the sample fraction and household nonresponse, with the corresponding census-based population figures not adjusted for undercount. See Citro and Kalton, 1993:Table 3-12; see also Shapiro and Kostanich, 1988.)

[10]The full cost of creating the address list would be incurred; moreover, the need for reliable small-area estimates would preclude the clustering of field operations, as is typically done in smaller household surveys.

5

A Redesigned Census

Chapters 2 and 3 identify two central problems with the current approach to taking the decennial census: costs have escalated rapidly while accuracy, as measured by both the overall and the differential undercount, has decreased. In this chapter, the panel identifies and makes recommendations for reducing the cost and improving the accuracy of the census.

Our overarching recommendation for a substantially redesigned census follows from three central conclusions:

1. The massive employment of enumerators, in an attempt to count every last household that fails to return a census mail questionnaire, cannot produce an accurate and cost-effective census. Long before that objective could be achieved, diminishing returns set in, so that only small gains are achieved at great budgetary cost.

2. After a reasonable and cost-effective effort to make a physical count of the population, the use of sample surveys and statistical estimation techniques to complete the count can produce greater accuracy than the traditional approach— especially with respect to the critical problem of differential undercount. We consider the use of statistical estimation to supplement the physical count to be the best possible realization of the actual enumeration required by the Constitution.

3. Once it is accepted that statistical estimation can be used with accuracy to complete the counting process, substantial cost savings can be achieved by redesigning the census process from the ground up to take advantage of this change.

As background to our detailed recommendations, this chapter first outlines two approaches to taking the decennial census: the traditional census and a redesigned census. The chapter then discusses the major components of the second approach, identifies the critical choices that will have to be made in designing such an approach, and makes specific recommendations for the basic strategy that should be used. The chapter then considers and recommends a number of additional measures that could improve the accuracy and lower the costs of the next census. Finally, it proposes a fundamental review and reengineering of all census procedures to take advantage of the full cost-reducing potential of the new approach.

TWO APPROACHES TO COUNTING THE POPULATION

The traditional approach, used in the 1990 census, relies completely on intensive efforts to achieve a direct count (physical enumeration) of the entire population. The alternative approach, an integrated combination of enumeration and estimation, also starts with physical enumeration, but completes the count with statistical sampling and survey techniques. Figure 5.1 is a schematic presentation of the two approaches.

The enumerative approach, labeled the traditional census on the left-hand side of the figure, begins with the construction of an address register, including elaborate procedures to improve its comprehensiveness.[1] Census forms are then mailed to a comprehensive list of residential addresses, with instructions to mail back the completed questionnaire. Not all households return their completed mail questionnaire within a reasonable period of time. For households that do not respond to the mail questionnaire (35 percent of all housing units and 26 percent of all occupied housing units in 1990), census enumerators undertake an intensive follow-up effort to determine whether the unit is occupied and, if so, to contact the household and elicit responses. Repeat visits are made, administrative records are sometimes examined, and special programs to contact particular groups (e.g., homeless people) are carried out. This process is continued for an extended period of time to enumerate physically every household and all the people in every household.

Extensive special programs have been directed toward coverage improvement in recent censuses. These programs are expensive, both in absolute terms and often in terms of the cost per person or housing unit. Special coverage improvement programs have included:

- movers check—a follow-up of people reporting a change of address to the U.S. Postal Service during the census enumeration period;
- prelist recanvass—in prelist areas, a recheck of the address list during the second stage of follow-up;
- vacant/delete check—a recheck in the field of housing units originally

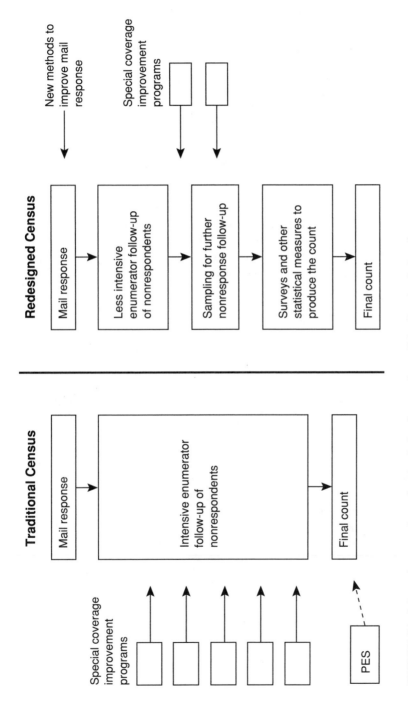

FIGURE 5.1 Schematic comparison of major design features for traditional and redesigned census.

classified as vacant or as "delete" because they were not residential—this was done on a sample basis in 1970 and for all units in 1980 and 1990;

 • causal count—a campaign to find persons missed from the census by contacting community organizations or visiting places frequented by transients; and

 • nonhousehold sources program—matching administrative records to census lists for selected areas.

Citro and Cohen (1985:Tables 5.2 and 5.3) present cost and effectiveness data on these programs for the 1970 and 1980 censuses.

The results from the mail response, enumerator follow-up, and intensive special coverage improvement efforts are combined to produce the actual enumeration of the U.S. population—both as a whole and for subdivisions down to the block level.

Even though a highly labor-intensive effort is undertaken to obtain a completed questionnaire for every household, the resulting estimates contain errors. As we noted in Chapter 2, the 1990 census produced a net undercount of 1.8 percent for the nation as a whole. This net undercount included overcounting in some areas and among some groups, which was more than offset by undercounting among other areas and groups. Blacks and Hispanics, Asian and Pacific Islanders, American Indians and Native Alaskans, renters, and residents of poor inner-city areas were undercounted by larger percentages than the nation as a whole. To detect these errors, a highly intensive survey of a representative sample of areas throughout the country was conducted after the physical enumeration efforts ceased.

In 1990, on the basis of a sample of areas, the difference between the census count and the count produced by the Post-Enumeration Survey (PES) was used to calculate statistical estimates—by area, racial group, and other relevant demographic characteristics—of the net undercount or overcount contained in the census data. After a series of legal battles, it was decided _not_ to use the results of the PES to correct the initial 1990 census count, either nationally or in smaller areas. The enumerative count remained the official 1990 census estimate, used to make reapportionment and redistricting decisions and for other purposes.

This enumerative approach has been subject to the two basic failings discussed in Chapters 2 and 3: high and rapidly rising costs and high differential undercount. We therefore propose for the redesigned census the approach of statistical estimation to correct the enumerative count, not as a simple add-on to the traditional census but as a completely new point of departure. By so doing we address not only the issue of differential undercount (which could have been done in 1990), but also the issue of high costs. Statistical estimation, regarded not as an add-on as was done in 1990 but as an integrated aspect of census taking, allows a fundamental reengineering of the entire census design.

The alternative approach, labeled the redesigned census on the right-hand side of Figure 5.1, combines an initial stage of direct counting (physical enumeration) with various statistical estimation techniques. Correctly designed, this approach involves more than a simple layering of a postenumeration survey on top of a traditional labor-intensive physical enumerative design. Rather, every stage of the census, including the initial stage of physical enumeration, is designed with the awareness that statistical sampling and estimation are available to remedy deficiencies and improve coverage. This approach permits the elimination of all operations that add relatively little to accuracy but have high unit costs. Indeed, it permits the reengineering of the entire traditional phase of the census with this guiding principle. Moreover, this approach produces an integrated single-number census, rather than the confusing and politically divisive result of the 1990 process, in which the enumeration produced an official census count, but the PES produced another set of numbers.

The redesigned census starts, just as in the first approach, with the mailing of census forms to an address list. The redesigned census includes new methods to improve the mail response. The new methods—including respondent-friendly questionnaires, Spanish-language questionnaires for Hispanic areas, use of reminder postcards, and motivational messages to increase mail return—will decrease costs by reducing the need for personal nonresponse follow-up. A substantial program to track down those who do not respond by the designated date is carried out using census enumerators, but with significantly less intensity and of shorter duration than in the first approach. The follow-up includes a judicious combination of a second mailing to nonrespondents, follow-up by telephone, and personal visit. The follow-up, area by area, is designed with four guiding principles: (1) a reasonable attempt should be made to follow up all nonresponding households; (2) all areas should have as an objective a reasonably high response rate; (3) follow-up should be terminated after a reasonable attempt (e.g., several calls to the same household rather than as many as six calls, as was done in the 1990 census); and (4) the entire duration of field operations should be limited (e.g., 4-5 months rather than 9 to 12 months, as was done in the 1990 census). The use of these physical enumerative techniques is *truncated* after a reasonable effort has been made (see below for a discussion of the criteria for when to truncate).

Once the follow-up is truncated, intensive surveys are taken of some sample fraction (e.g., one in four, or some fraction) of nonrespondents to get the full range of census information from the nonrespondents in those areas. On the basis of these results, statistical techniques are used to estimate, for all nonrespondents, what has to be added to the mail responses and the truncated follow-up to arrive at what the traditional census count would have been had the follow-up effort expended on the sample been implemented for all nonresponding households. The use of sampling techniques to follow up nonrespondents is called sampling for nonresponse follow-up.

The less intensive the 100 percent follow-up and the smaller the sampling fraction, the larger the cost saving but the greater the probability of errors in the count for small geographical areas. A highly accurate count for the nation as a whole could be achieved with a modest degree of physical enumeration of households and a relatively small sampling fraction. But the possibilities of substantial sampling error in any given small area, which would result in either an overestimate or underestimate of the count for that area, would be high. More intensive 100 percent follow-up and higher sampling fractions would raise costs but reduce the spread of errors in small areas. It should be noted, however, that in the traditional approach, with its effort at full physical enumeration, the range of errors in the count for small areas is still substantial.

Independent of sampling for nonresponse, a further survey is taken of all households in a sample of areas to complete the census process by providing estimates of those people who were missed by previous operations. (These two important roles for the use of sampling are explained further in the box on page 81, which is based on Steffey and Bradburn, 1994.) Unlike the traditional census, in which a PES survey is taken to evaluate the final count, the redesigned census would have an integrated coverage measurement survey for the purpose of estimating the number and characteristics of those missed by the prior stages of the census.[2] These are the people missed by all traditional census approaches (see Chapter 2). Overcounting, which is also detected by the PES, could also be taken into account by a coverage measurement survey. In addition, information on birth, death, and immigration might be used to check or supplement the surveys. It is this final count that is published as the official population count of the United States, for the nation, for all geographic areas, and for all the various demographic characteristics of the population.

There are various schemes for exactly how these various elements should be combined and what emphasis should be placed on each. But they would all substitute some degree of statistical estimation for the expensive 1990 effort to try to count by physically enumerating—with incomplete success—every last person. In spite of several decades of attempts to improve population coverage through direct enumeration, inequities continue to exist in the census undercount by race and for geographic areas. Statistical methods to detect these inequities now exist that are feasible for use in the 2000 census.

We endorse the goal of producing the best population census by counting, assignment (allocating households and persons based on good evidence—see below), and statistical estimation. In a new census environment whose last steps involve statistical estimation, the initial phases of the census would be constructed in such a way that every person would have an opportunity to be physically counted, and the Census Bureau would make a good-faith effort to count physically every person through the construction of an accurate and complete mailing list, the use of mail questionnaires, and reasonable efforts to follow-up all nonrespondent households. Following attempts to physically enumerate nonrespondents to the mail questionnaire, first through 100 percent follow-up and

The Roles of Sampling in the Census Bureau's One-Number Census

In 1990, the official census figures were based on a census process that consisted of three basic steps: (1) constructing a list of addresses, (2) obtaining responses that could be linked to the address list, and (3) following up to obtain responses from those initially missed. In addition, a coverage measurement process was designed to estimate the size of the population that was missed in previous steps of the census process. Two sets of population totals were produced, with and without corrections based on coverage measurement, and an ex post facto decision was made about whether to accept the corrected totals. This "adjustment" decision proved to be controversial because it occurred in a highly politicized environment in which interested parties perceived themselves as winners or losers, depending on which set of numbers was chosen.

For the 2000 census, the Census Bureau has proposed the concept of a "one-number census," one that will provide "the best possible single set of results by legal deadlines, . . . based on an appropriate combination of counting, assignment, and statistical techniques" (Miskura, 1993). In the Census Bureau's definition, counting refers to all methods for direct contact with respondents, including mail questionnaires, personal visits, and telephone calls. Assignment refers to the use of information from administrative records to add people to the count for a specific geographic location without field verification. Statistical techniques for estimation include imputation procedures, sampling during follow-up of nonrespondents, and methods for measuring census coverage. These three components of a one-number census are designed to complement one another. In particular, the results from coverage measurement will be fully integrated into the official census estimates (Miskura, 1993).

Sampling will be used in the new census process in two distinct ways. The first is in *nonresponse follow-up.* After initial contact and follow-up activities, a sample of households or blocks containing households that did not respond are selected for further follow-up. Estimates, based on the sample, are made of the numbers and characteristics of those who would have responded to the follow-up had it been conducted on the entire population. This use of sampling is proposed primarily to reduce costs by reducing the use of expensive follow-up procedures. It has other advantages too: it can reduce the time needed for the follow-up process, thereby allowing more time for coverage measurement. And, although it contributes to variability through sampling error, it can reduce other kinds of errors.

The second way in which sampling will be used in the one-number census is in *coverage measurement.* A sample survey is conducted from which estimates are made of the numbers and characteristics of those not counted in previous steps of the census process, including those who are not accounted for in the nonresponse follow-up step. This use of sampling is designed to improve the accuracy of the census.

In 1990, sampling was used in a coverage measurement process (See Figure 5.3) for evaluation purposes and for possible use as a basis for official population estimates, with a decision on the latter deferred until after the results of the sample were examined. The previous steps of the census process were designed to be used as the basis for reported census figures independently of the coverage

continued on next page

measurement process. In the proposed one-number census, coverage measurement is conceived as an essential part of census-taking and not just as an evaluation of other census operations. In particular, it is not regarded as a method of producing a second set of population estimates that competes with the population estimates obtained without its use. Coverage measurement, which includes sampling, statistical estimation based on the sampling, and statistical modeling, will be integrated with the other census-taking operations. Hence, this phase of census-taking is called *integrated coverage measurement.*

The fundamental innovation of a one-number census is that an appropriate methodology for integrated coverage measurement is established before the census is carried out, with the recognition that results at previous steps cannot be regarded on scientific grounds as viable alternatives to the final, best set of official population estimates. It also allows for more optimal design of other census operations.

Source: Adapted from Steffey and Bradburn (1994).

then through sampling, the census would use survey-based statistical estimation to complete the final official population count.

As mentioned earlier, there are several additional specific ways to achieve cost savings in the future integrated single-number census, including: respondent-friendly questionnaires and other improved procedures for increasing mail response rates, truncating census operations earlier to minimize the lengthy work period for district offices and census field staff, and increased use of U.S. Postal Service employees for such operations as vacancy checks of housing units. But, most important, statistical estimation at the final stage of census operations and abandonment of the target of physically counting everyone permit a complete reengineering of the basic census operation in light of the new census context. Thus, numerous expensive coverage improvement operations used in the 1990 census can be reviewed with an eye to elimination as unnecessary (compare the left and right sides of Figure 5.1).

As a guide to the exposition below, we note that there are four key stages in the redesigned census (see the right-hand side of Figure 5.1) leading to the final official population count: mail response, enumerator follow-up, sampling for further nonresponse follow-up, and a survey together with other statistical estimation techniques to complete the count. Ways to improve the mail response are described later in a section entitled "Improve Response Rates." Issues relating to enumerator follow-up are covered in several sections of the next major section, in which we discuss decreasing the intensity of nonresponse follow-up and truncation of enumeration after a reasonable effort. After describing a reasonable effort at enumerator follow-up, we discuss the role for "Sampling for Nonresponse Follow-Up" in a separate section. We describe the role of an integrated coverage survey in a later section entitled "Survey-Based Methods to

Complete the Count." With the use of statistical estimation (the integrated coverage measurement survey) built into the redesigned census, the entire process of census enumeration needs to be reengineered. Under the new procedures of a redesigned census, there would be a reduction of special coverage programs that are no longer cost-effective. The reengineered census, along with a review of some specific census operations, is presented below in a major section entitled "A Reengineered Census."

Census Bureau Plans

The panel would like to recognize that the Census Bureau is actively working on plans and conducting research on much of what is described in this chapter. Much of the material reported here is based on ongoing census research. The Census Bureau, however, has not yet prepared a specific proposal for the 2000 census design. Census Bureau plans for the 2000 census will be informed by results of census tests in 1995.

The Census Bureau will carry out a major test of census design options at four sites in 1995. The test will examine the following methods:

1.   Sampling for the follow-up of nonrespondents to the mail questionnaire.

2.   Statistical methods to estimate separately the number and characteristics of people missed because their housing unit was missed, people missed within enumerated housing units, and people who were erroneously enumerated.

3.   Coverage questions for a complete listing of household members.

4.   Mailout of Spanish-language questionnaires.

5.   Target methods to count historically undercounted populations.

6.   Counting persons with no usual residence.

7.   Making census questionnaires more widely available by placing unaddressed questionnaires in accessible locations (e.g., stores and post offices).

8.   Respondent-friendly questionnaire design and a full mail strategy for improved mail response.

9.   Telephone response as a follow-up option.

10.   Real-time automated matching for record linkage.

11.   Using the U.S. Postal Service to identify vacant and nonexistent housing units.

12.   Electronic imaging to scan respondent-friendly census forms and to capture data.

13.   Cooperating with the U.S. Postal Service for the continuous updating of a national housing address file.

14.   Collecting long form-type data using matrix sample forms (two or more sample forms with only a subset of the questions).

Results from the 1995 census tests, and continued tests from 1996 to 1998, will be important for operational plans for the 2000 census. At the moment, the Bureau of the Census (1993a) proposes to conduct a "one-number census" that will use statistical methods integrated into the census process. Except for a one-number census, the Census Bureau has not made a formal commitment to the specific recommendations that the panel makes in this chapter for a redesigned census. Moreover, we propose a much more extensive redesign of the 2000 census.

In recent congressional testimony, Harry Scarr, the acting director of the Bureau of the Census, stated that the 1995 census tests would provide important results for planning the 2000 census, including: (1) detailed evaluations of sampling for nonresponse follow-up and sampling as part of statistical estimation for census coverage, (2) operational and cost information for new sampling and estimation methods, and (3) evaluation of the effect of new methods on errors in census data (Scarr, 1994). The 1995 census test will also examine the quality of the census address lists, in a cooperative venture in which U.S. Postal Service delivery addresses are used

Legal Issues of Statistical Estimation

As part of its examination of alternative methods for counting the population, the panel examined the legal issues for the greater use of statistical estimation. The requirement for effort at complete enumeration does not necessarily rule out the increased use of sampling as part of the census. Sampling has several potential uses that are worth inspection for increased use in future censuses.

It is important to distinguish among three potential uses of sampling in the census. The first is to estimate the number and characteristics of people who were not found even after attempts at nonresponse follow-up and people who were counted more than once or should not have been counted. This use of sampling to complete the count is referred to as an integrated coverage measurement survey in Figure 5.1. The second broad use of sampling in a census is sampling within the actual process of physical enumeration. The number of nonresponding households is known, so the purpose of sampling the nonrespondents is to estimate their characteristics. The third broad use of sampling is to take a sample of the population at the beginning of the census. In such a "sample" census, no attempt would be made to enumerate every person. The panel discusses this option in Chapter 4.

In the panel's judgment, the spirit of the constitutional, legislative, and judicial history regarding enumeration is compatible with the use of sampling as part of the census process, so long as that process includes a reasonable effort to reach all inhabitants. Specifically, we believe that census designs that use sampling for the follow-up stage of census operations (after an initial reasonable attempt has been made to collect a census questionnaire from everyone) and for the final stage of census operations for an estimate of the population not counted by physical enumeration (using an integrated coverage measurement survey for statistical estimation to complete the count) would meet both substantive and legislative requirements for reapportionment. Such designs also have the potential to increase census accuracy and reduce census costs (see Appendix C for a discussion of the legislative requirements for the census).

Precedents from previous censuses exist for the use of sampling. Several court cases have explicitly upheld the constitutionality of an adjustment based on a survey (such as the PES in the 1990 census), citing the importance of having data as accurate as possible for reapportionment and redistricting.[3] The question of the legality of sampling for follow-up for nonresponse has never been explicitly raised in the courts; however, language used in the relevant court cases would clearly seem to be consistent with its use.

Court decisions on census issues have deferred to the Census Bureau on technical issues. The panel's review of legal issues in Appendix C does not provide grounds for concern that courts will question the expanded use of sampling in the census (i.e., sampling for nonresponse follow-up or a sample survey to estimate the number and characteristics of people missed in the physical enumeration). Courts have accepted the use of sampling in prior censuses, and we propose a more extensive use of sampling in the 2000 census. After a review of past court decisions, the panel expects that the courts will continue to accept the technical decisions made by Census Bureau staff, including the use of sampling in a good-faith effort to count the population, in a redesigned census.

BASIC ELEMENTS OF A NEW CENSUS DESIGN

The conventional mailout/mailback census operation that the Census Bureau has conducted for the 1970, 1980, and 1990 census can schematically be thought of as involving five stages: (1) the development and checking of a master address list prior to the census, (2) the physical enumeration of the population through the mailing of the census questionnaires several days before April 1 (Census Day) and the collection of the returned questionnaires, (3) the follow-up of those housing units that do not return the census questionnaire, (4) a variety of coverage improvement activities, and (5) checks on the census coverage. One critical area that would be affected by our proposal is point (3).

Decreasing the Intensity of Nonresponse Follow-Up

In practice, the follow-up of *all* nonrespondents is a costly procedure—the precise magnitude of the cost depends on the intensity of the effort. Follow-up of nonrespondents was directed by each of the 449 district offices in the 1990 census. Follow-up began about three weeks after Census Day, with enumerators directed to contact households who had not yet returned their questionnaires. At the end, as a last resort, enumerators were directed to ask neighbors, landlords, or others who might be familiar with the household occupants to provide basic demographic and housing information.

Somewhat different procedures were followed in a small number of areas either in which mail addresses did not exist or in which it would not have been feasible to rely on mail questionnaires for the census. For areas lacking mail addresses—primarily rural areas with central postal mailboxes—census staff used a "list-enumerate" procedure. This procedure involved census staff's identifying each of the housing units in a geographic area, listing the units with an identifiable location (e.g., the three-story house on the northwest corner of the intersection of Belnap Road and County Road Five), and then directly enumerating the occupants. The list-enumerate procedure was also used in some inner-city areas for which the mail return rates had been very low and for which the population coverage had been poor under the traditional mailout/mailback approach.

Not only is there a direct expense to follow up each nonresponding household with the intensity employed in the 1990 census, but there are also substantial additional infrastructure costs when the duration of follow-up is prolonged.[4] There has been a gradual increase in the length of time that census district offices remain open during the census, which increases costs for rental of the physical space and equipment and boosts the personnel costs for all district office employees. For the 1960 census, district offices were open for 3 to 6 months; for the 1970 census, offices were open for 4 to 6 months; for the 1980 census— coinciding with the large unit cost increases (discussed in Chapter 3)—offices were open for 6 to 9 months; finally, for the 1990 census, as a result of earlier opening to improve the address listing and lengthened follow-up of nonrespondent households, district offices were open for 9 to 12 months.

Sampling for Nonresponse Follow-Up

Reducing the intensity of the 100 percent follow-up of nonrespondents and a subsequent sample-based follow-up of the remaining nonrespondents can maintain an acceptable level of data quality while yielding major cost savings. A reduced effort on highly labor-intensive nonresponse follow-up, using less expensive telephone follow-up and having many fewer personal visits, would result in substantial cost savings.

After a reasonable effort at 100 percent follow-up, a sample of the remaining nonrespondents would be followed up intensively, perhaps with attempts to contact one of every three or four nonrespondents.[5] The nonresponse follow-up would use the same census enumerators who worked on the initial census follow-up, although fewer enumerators would be needed for follow-up on a sample basis. This sample would be used to estimate the fraction of units vacant and the characteristics of all remaining nonrespondents. The sample might be based on areas or on households: one of four census blocks in selected small areas or one of every four households might be selected. More intensive effort could be directed to obtaining information from these sampled nonrespondents, while still reducing aggregate follow-up costs. The sampled nonrespondents would be used to provide estimates for the other nonrespondents, assuming, as in other survey research, that they are a reasonable sample of all nonrespondents.

Truncation of Enumeration After a Reasonable Effort

Reduced intensity of physical enumeration, which we label truncation, when combined with statistical estimation techniques to complete the count, far from degrading the overall quality of the census, will improve the accuracy of the final count of the nation as a whole, for large demographic groups, and for populous areas. But in choosing the extent and the specific pattern by which the intensity of physical enumeration is reduced, two issues have to be considered. *First*, greater reliance on statistical estimation will increase the variability of the count in small areas. *Second*, excessively early truncation of physical enumeration would mean that only a modest fraction of the population would be directly counted in some hard-to-enumerate areas, and such truncation could lead both to unfavorable public reactions and to an erosion of the compliance with the mandatory nature of the census. It is important, therefore, to design a set of criteria for choosing the degree and methods of truncation that would minimize these problems, while still achieving significant cost-saving and improving the quality of the overall census results.

If the census data collection period is shortened or truncated, significant savings would result from the early curtailment of field operations. A truncated census would involve the closing of hundreds of district offices, with savings in staff and overhead expenses associated with the prolonged continuation of data collection.

It should be noted that consideration of a truncated census assumes some use of statistical estimation in order to produce the final census count. It makes no sense to curtail census operations when the counting of the population is not complete unless there are plans to conduct statistical surveys for completing the count as well as estimating the characteristics of nonrespondents.

A truncated census design should be considered in terms of two factors, completion rates (the percentage of households counted before 100 percent follow-up ceases and sampling begins) and public perceptions of the attempt to count everyone: the sooner that sampling for nonresponse follow-up begins, the greater the cost savings but the greater the risk of public perception that "not everyone was counted." As noted above, the panel's concern with a reasonable period of enumerator-intensive follow-up before moving to sampling for follow-up is not a worry about the quality of population coverage. Rather, the panel is concerned that an excessively early truncation of census follow-up activities may be perceived by the public as not trying to count the entire population. This, in turn, could lower mail response rates, raise costs, and lower the quality of the census for small areas. The panel believes that it is important to maintain both the actuality and the public perception that the census is mandatory and that the census makes the attempt to count every person. We comment on this issue at the end of this chapter.

Alternative Techniques of Truncation

There are three possible ways to truncate full-scale direct enumeration after a reasonable effort: (1) after a given date, (2) after a given fraction of the population has been counted in an area, and (3) after a given amount of resources for enumeration has been used in each area. In practice, the most cost-efficient and politically feasible technique for truncation would be some combination of these or similar criteria.

In an approach using truncation after a given date, labor-intensive follow-up would be undertaken for a specified period of time, which would be the same for all areas of the country. Various dates for truncating census operations are possible. The problem, of course, is that with reasonable truncation dates, there would be wide variations in completion rates across geographic areas. Three possible dates—April 21, June 2, and June 30—are useful for illustration because in 1990 about two-thirds of census questionnaires were completed by April 21, about 90 percent by June 2, and almost all by June 30.

An alternative technique for truncation is to cease 100 percent follow-up operations in an area after a given fraction of the population has been counted. For example, if a goal of 90 percent enumeration is set as a goal for every area, then some areas with very high rates of return for the mail questionnaire might have personal visits for nonresponse follow-up only on a sample basis. Areas with low mail return rates would have 100 percent nonresponse follow-up until the 90 percent coverage goal is achieved. Attempting to achieve a minimum count implies a longer period of physical enumeration in low-response areas. Yet, even after prolonged attempts to count 90 percent of the housing units in an area, there may be some low-response areas that do not reach the goal. In those cases, it might be wise to consider the use of a given date for truncation.

Another technique for truncation would be to spend a set amount of resources for each estimated nonrespondent, by areas. Census staff would estimate prior to the census the probable size of the nonrespondent population, using results from the 1995 and other census tests, and allocate funds by areas, with roughly the same amount of money per nonrespondent. Areas with high mail return rates (and a lower number of nonrespondents) would receive fewer funds than areas with low mail return rates.

The optimal strategy is likely to involve a combination of all three techniques. Experience with the 1995 census tests and more detailed planning by census staff will be needed to arrive at a combined strategy that is cost-efficient. A politically feasible strategy would also need to take into account the fact that some nonresponse follow-up would be desirable for all areas, regardless of how successful the response to the mail questionnaire, and that low-response areas should see a reasonable intensity of nonresponse follow-up rather than see physical enumeration terminate at a set date.

What Determines a Reasonable Effort

A critical issue for truncation of intensive 100 percent nonresponse follow-up is the determination of what constitutes a reasonable effort. The discussion above concluded that a redesigned census should involve a combination of truncation after a given date, after a given fraction of the population has been counted, and after a given amount of resources has been used. The objectives of the 100 percent follow-up should be: to achieve a minimum response rate, to terminate follow-up after reasonable attempts to contact nonrespondents, and to limit the duration of follow-up activity.

The optimal combination of procedures for an actual census requires information on each of the truncation approaches, separately and in combination. The panel has considered all various alternative strategies, but statistical information available to the panel has been limited to truncation by date. The panel searched for information to document other ways to truncate 100 percent follow-up but learned that data from the 1990 census provide only selected information. Analysis of data from the 1995 census tests and perhaps further testing are required to provide sufficient information for a final strategy.

The panel can illustrate the effects of truncation for the one approach for which data are available: truncation by date. Very early truncation would produce the most savings, but in many hard-to-enumerate areas early truncation would leave a large percentage of the estimated population uncounted. A large percentage of uncounted people has two serious effects. One effect is on statistical estimation: the use of survey-based methods to complete the census count is more accurate when a relatively high percentage of the population is counted through direct enumeration. A redesigned census should therefore aim to count a reasonably high proportion of the population through the mail questionnaire and nonrespondent follow-up.

The second serious effect of very early truncation is the problem of perception and misunderstanding, noted above. Early truncation in hard-to-enumerate areas may be seen as a lack of interest in achieving an accurate count in these areas, even though survey methods would be used to produce the final census count. Some residents of hard-to-enumerate areas may believe that the census is not mandatory, thereby further complicating efforts to achieve an accurate count.

Completion Rates. Considerable variation would exist for the completion rates for a truncated census (before a sample of nonrespondents is taken) for geographic areas and for major racial groups. Table 5.1 presents coverage estimates in the 1990 census for various demographic groups. This table shows the percentage of population counted, for three dates and a nontruncated census, relative to the final PES population estimate. On April 21, three weeks after Census Day, most of the mail questionnaires were returned but little nonresponse follow-up occurred. Over two-thirds of the national population was counted by April 21, although there were substantial variations among major race and Hispanic groups: only one-half of the American Indians were counted but over 70 percent of the nonblack (primarily white) population was counted. On June 2, after about six weeks of 100 percent nonresponse follow-up, the national population was 89 percent counted. A gap in coverage rates persisted, however, with an 11 percentage point difference between blacks (79 percent coverage) and nonblacks (90 percent coverage). By June 30, as the census enumeration drew to a close, the national count was relatively complete (relative to the final PES estimate) and the race and Hispanic differences in coverage rates narrowed. In summary, if truncation were applied consistently by date across the nation, there would be substantial differences in coverage rates between race and Hispanic groups.

We can illustrate further what is known from the 1990 census about completion rates that would have occurred if the 1990 census had been truncated at various dates (see Table 5.2). The results are classified by some major census characteristics: list/enumerate areas, urban/rural, and census divisions. This table is based on tabulations from the PES clusters for the 1990 census. Each column shows the proportion of PES clusters with less than 50 percent of the final responses complete. As of April 21, three weeks after Census Day—when there would have been negligible follow-up of nonresponses to the mail questionnaire—16 percent of the PES clusters in the nation still had less than 50 percent of the final responses complete. By June 2, with about 6 weeks of nonresponse follow-up, only 3 percent of the nation's PES clusters still had less than 50 percent of the final responses complete.

There is considerable variation in completion rates by characteristics of PES clusters. The collection of household responses is much slower in clusters with list/enumerate procedures (list/enumerate procedures refer to census operations in which the enumerator personally lists housing units in an area, then distributes census questionnaires to each unit). List/enumerate operations are required in a few areas in which no adequate mailing list can be prepared prior to the census. Most list/enumerate areas are rural areas without individual mailboxes for each housing unit or American Indian lands with scattered housing units. In both rural areas and American Indian lands, census enumerators travel the area to list each housing unit and then enumerate it personally. As shown in the second row of Table 5.2, there was a higher proportion of list/enumerate clusters with less than 50 percent responses complete for the first several weeks of nonresponse

TABLE 5.1 Final PES Estimates and Population Coverage for Truncated Census Counts by PES Coverage Measurement for Major Race and Ethnic Groups, 1990 Census

Demographic Group	April 21 Coverage (Percent)	June 2 Coverage (Percent)	June 30 Coverage (Percent)	Nontruncated Census Coverage (Percent)	Final PES Estimates (thousands)[a]
Total	68.7	88.5	96.3	98.4	252,713
American Indian	50.2	82.0	93.2	95.5	2,052
Asian and Pacific Islander	62.7	84.0	95.1	97.7	7,447
Black	53.6	78.6	92.6	95.6	31,377
Hispanic	57.3	80.5	92.1	95.0	23,521
Nonblack	70.8	90.0	96.8	98.8	221,336

[a]The total number of people in each group is based on the final PES estimate.

follow-up. After about 6 weeks of nonresponse follow-up, however, the completion rates for low-response clusters were similar for list/enumerate areas and other areas.

There were few substantial differences in the completion rates by date for larger and smaller urban areas and rural areas. Rural areas were affected by a higher proportion of areas requiring list/enumerate procedures. After several weeks of nonresponse follow-up, there were similar levels of clusters with less than 50 percent of final response complete for urban and rural areas.

Regional levels of clusters with less than 50 percent of final responses complete were affected by the requirements for list/enumerate procedures (which affects the New England area, for example) and regional patterns in the tardiness of nonresponse follow-up. There were particularly lengthy follow-up periods on American Indian lands before the response rates were adequate: even after 6 weeks of nonresponse follow-up, 21 percent of the PES clusters still had less than 50 percent of the final responses complete. Several regions—Northeast, Middle Atlantic, South Atlantic, East South Central, and Pacific—also required longer duration of follow-up, compared with the remaining regions, before the proportion of clusters with less than 50 percent of final response complete falls to relative low levels.

TABLE 5.2 Proportion of PES Clusters With Less Than 50 Percent of Final Responses Complete, by Date of Census Operations, 1990 Census

Type of PES Cluster	Sample Size	April 21	May 5	May 19	June 2	June 30
Total	4,949	.16	.11	.07	.03	.00
List/Enumerate						
Yes	359	.52	.21	.06	.04	.00
No	4,590	.13	.11	.07	.03	.00
Urban/Rural						
Urban, 250,000+	2,153	.15	.12	.08	.03	.00
Urban,< 250,000	1,730	.13	.10	.06	.02	.00
Rural	1,066	.23	.12	.06	.03	.00
Census Divisions						
American Indian	39	.54	.41	.31	.21	.00
Northeast	297	.25	.15	.07	.03	.00
Middle Atlantic	709	.20	.15	.10	.05	.00
South Atlantic	652	.17	.14	.09	.04	.00
East South Central	514	.13	.11	.08	.03	.00
West South Central	674	.11	.09	.05	.01	.00
East North Central	646	.12	.08	.04	.01	.00
West North Central	420	.09	.04	.02	.01	.00
Mountain	422	.19	.10	.04	.02	.00
Pacific	576	.20	.14	.07	.03	.00

These illustrative results demonstrate the perceptual problems of attempting to use an automatic cutoff date for follow-up census operations. If all non-response follow-up were curtailed on May 19, after 4 weeks of follow-up operations, the final responses would be far from complete in a substantial proportion of small areas. This line of reasoning would therefore suggest that truncating census follow-up should, for reasons of cost-efficiency and political feasibility, be determined by a combination of date, percentage complete, and resources expended. We believe that a mixture of criteria for truncation would give a better combination of cost savings and coverage improvement.

We note that a purely truncated census does not seem feasible to the panel. A truncated census, in a pure form, would cease census physical enumeration before everyone had been physically enumerated and eliminate any sampling for follow-up, relying only on a postenumeration survey to estimate the uncounted population. We conclude that such a census would not, by design, represent a good-faith effort to count every resident and so would not meet the minimum legal requirements of a census of the U.S. population. But we conclude that decreasing the intensity of follow-up, in the context of attempting to contact every person, and using sampling to follow up the most difficult-to-locate non-respondents, does represent a good-faith effort, and it would reduce costs.

Cost Savings. Cost estimates for a redesigned census under various truncation assumptions are available from the Census Bureau only for truncation by date. Further work is needed by census staff to develop the mix of physical enumeration, sample follow-up, and statistical estimation that would represent the best trade-off between the partly competing objectives of maintaining low sampling errors for small-area estimates and reducing census costs. However, the panel did work with Census Bureau staff, using the Bureau's census cost model, to develop a set of illustrative estimates of cost savings that could have been achieved in 1990 through a particularly simple combination of truncation and sampling for nonresponse follow-up. We selected four illustrative dates for truncation and applied them across the country: April 21, May 18, June 2, and June 30. We consider two alternative levels of sampling for nonresponse follow-up for illustration: 50 percent and 25 percent.

We examine illustrative cost savings assuming two levels of mail response rates. One level is the actual mail response rate experienced in the 1990 census (65 percent). The second level is an improved mail response rate that might be experienced in the 2000 census (71 percent). Of course, it is impossible to forecast the mail response rate for the 2000 census, partly because public cooperation with the census has been declining over time and may level off or worsen in the future, but also because the 2000 census should include a number of improvements that would increase mail response rates over what might have been expected if 1990 methods were used.

For these cost estimates, we assume a mail response rate for census questionnaires that is higher than that experienced for the 1990 census. Based on the Simplified Questionnaire Test (SQT) and the Appeals and Long-Form Experiment (ALFE) (these recent tests are discussed in a later section), it is clear that mail response rates of census questionnaires can be increased with respondent-friendly questionnaires and the treatment of a prenotice letter, reminder postcard, and replacement questionnaire, either separately or in combination. We assume that a short form would have a mail return rate of 77 percent, the observed completion rate for a respondent-friendly short form with the appeal "Your response is required by law" and a standard confidentiality emphasis (Tortora, 1993). The respondent-friendly long form was not tested with a variety of appeals in the ALFE study. A respondent-friendly long form had an observed completion rate of 56 percent, with no appeal (Tortora, 1993). We assume that the appeal had the same impact on long-form mail response rates as on the tested short-form rates. Because there was a 29 percent decline in the proportion of nonrespondents for the short form with appeal, we make a similar assumption for the long form: we assume that a respondent-friendly long form with an appeal "Your response is required by law" and a standard confidentiality emphasis would have a completion rate of 69 percent. The respondent-friendly forms and the use of an appeal have not been implemented in an actual census environment, in which the mail response rates are likely to be higher. We assume for cost estimates that there is a 5 percent higher overall response rate than in the test results. Combining the assumed mail return rates for the short and long forms, adjusting for vacant housing units, and assuming a higher response in a census environment, we assume an overall mail response rate of 71 percent as an estimate for the 2000 census.

The cost estimates also include the cost of a census evaluation survey, assuming that the cost is similar to the 1990 PES. We assume, therefore, that a truncated census with sampling for nonresponse follow-up would include the costs for a survey to complete the count.

Table 5.3 presents the estimated cost savings for the combination of truncation and sampling for nonresponse follow-up. The top panel shows the savings assuming the 1990 mail response rates; the lower panel shows the savings assuming a higher mail response rate, in the context of what might be expected for a redesigned 2000 census. For a census in which full-scale follow-up activities are terminated at a reasonably early date—around May 18, for example—significant cost savings can be expected—as well as high sampling errors in those areas in which the final count has to be based on sample follow-up to a significant extent. With the 1990 census response rates and 25 percent sampling for nonresponse follow-up, there would be a cost saving of $468 million. With extra efforts for improving the mail response rates (which cost more money), there would be an expected higher mail response rate (see lower panel of the table) and fewer nonrespondents for sampling. The cost saving in this situation, for a

TABLE 5.3 Cost Savings for the Census Long and Short Forms for Combinations of Truncation and Sampling for Nonresponse Follow-Up (in millions of 1990 dollars)

Truncation Date	50 Percent Sampling for Nonresponse Follow-Up	25 Percent Sampling for Nonresponse Follow-up
Cost Savings With 1990 Census Mail Response Rate of 65 Percent		
June 30	$ 62	$ 64
June 2	$ 168	$ 224
May 18	$ 324	$ 468
April 21	$ 391	$ 557
Cost Savings Assuming Final Mail Response Rate of 71 Percent		
June 30	$ 89	$ 92
June 2	$ 183	$ 226
May 18	$ 303	$ 413
April 21	$ 351	$ 482

Source: Keller (1993a and 1993b); Neece (1993); Pentercs (1993a and 1993b); and Tortora (1993).

census truncated on May 18 and with 25 percent of nonrespondents sampled for follow-up, would be $413 million.

The cost savings above for a census truncated by date and with 25 percent sampling for nonresponse range from $413 to $468 million, depending on assumptions about the census mail response rate. The panel believes that a redesigned census would best be conducted using a combination of criteria for truncating the 100 percent follow-up of nonrespondents. Using a combination of criteria might result in a longer period of 100 percent follow-up in hard-to-enumerate areas, which would decrease the projected cost savings. The panel's judgment is that cost savings of $300 to $400 million, in 1990 dollars, is a reasonable figure to use for contemplating the effect of truncation with sampling for nonresponse follow-up.

Higher response rates not only reduce the costs of nonresponse follow-up, but also reduce the number of questionnaires that would need to be sampled for follow-up or estimated from a survey to complete the count. However, the use of sampling for follow-up would introduce additional variation in sampling errors among different groups and areas. In assessing the importance of sampling errors, it is important to understand two points: (1) under present techniques, there are significant nonsampling errors for small areas (Appendix L presents information on imputation for missing responses—one type of nonsampling error) and (2) the new census design that the panel recommends will provide more accurate measures of the population count for the total and for various groups for the nation as a whole and for larger geographic areas.

We have considered a variety of cost estimates, for different times of truncation, different rates of sampling for nonresponse follow-up, and different levels of mail response rates. The panel does not recommend any particular date for truncation, and indeed does not recommend a uniform national truncation date. Nevertheless, based on simulations that could be carried out using 1990 data, it is our belief that cost savings (in 1990 dollars) approaching $300 to $400 million might be achieved in the 2000 census through the use of a shorter period of full-scale follow-up and sampling for nonresponse follow-up.

Recommendation 5.1 The panel recommends that the Census Bureau make a good-faith effort to count everyone, but then truncate physical enumeration after a reasonable effort to reach nonrespondents. The number and characteristics of the remaining nonrespondents should be estimated through sampling.

Survey-Based Methods to Complete the Count

After the return of the mail questionnaire, a reasonable but truncated enumerator follow-up, and the use of sampling for further follow-up, surveys would be used to improve and complete the count. There are various design possibilities for the use of such surveys to estimate census undercoverage used to complete the count. One approach involves a postenumeration survey in which a sample of areas is revisited by specially trained enumerators who try to do a complete census count. This approach is "do it again, but better." A second approach involves an independent survey that is matched to the census to provide net coverage estimates. This survey approach is "do it again, independently."

The 1990 Post-Enumeration Survey followed the second approach of conducting a concurrent independent survey. We present, first, a simple overview of how the PES works to correct for coverage problems in the physical enumeration of the population. In 1990, the PES sample was a resurvey of the population (actually, people living in a sample of areas, in the 1990 design), independent of the census. The results of the PES were matched against census records, providing an estimate of the numbers erroneously included in the census (gross overcount) and a basis for estimating numbers missed from the census (gross undercount).[6] For the undercount estimates, let N_c be the number of persons counted in the census, let N_p be the number of persons counted in the PES, and let N_{cp} be the number of persons counted in both. Then, if being counted in the census is independent of being counted in the PES, the probability of being counted in both is the product of the probabilities of being counted in the census and in the PES: $N_{cp}/N = (N_c/N)(N_p/N)$, so that $N = N_c N_p/N_{cp}$, where N is the true population.

The actual conduct of the PES in the 1990 census was somewhat more complicated than just described. The postenumeration survey operation involves finding people who were omitted from the census and deleting people who were included in the census but found to be erroneously enumerated. The postenumeration survey-census match for people, as indicated above, is done for a variety of demographic groups and by selected types of residence. The postenumeration survey counts for a given group (e.g., black women ages 30-44 in urban areas of the Midwest who own their own homes) in the sample areas are compared with the estimated number of similar people obtained in the census. The comparison is used to estimate the net undercount for such people, producing a coverage measurement factor that can be used to correct estimates from other similar areas. The box on page 98 presents more detailed description of the steps that were taken in the PES and the preparation of adjustment factors for dealing with the census undercount. Hogan (1993) discusses the specific operations, methods, and results for the 1990 PES.

There are several important assumptions for the postenumeration survey-type adjustment of the physical enumeration of the census. The first assumption is that the probability of being recorded in the census is the same for each person in the population, and likewise the probability of being recorded in the postenumeration survey is the same for each person in the population. The second assumption is that the probability of a person's being recorded in the postenumeration survey is independent of whether he or she was recorded in the census. The notion of independence in sampling is a statistical one: independence means that the two events (census enumeration and postenumeration survey counting for the sample population) occur without relation to, and with no influence on, the occurrence of the other one. In practice, it means that the postenumeration survey needs to be operationally independent of census operations; it needs to develop its own address lists, to use enumerators who did not canvass the area for the census, and to arrive at its own count of the sample population. The third key assumption for the postenumeration survey is homogeneity (i.e., that each member of the population has an equal chance of being captured in the census enumeration or in the survey). Unfortunately, heterogeneity, or the lack of an equal chance of being in the census or survey, has the same effect as lack of independence, so that the effect of heterogeneity cannot be distinguished from lack of independence.

The 1990 PES calculations were, in practice, carried out for a strata of persons (defined by geographic location, sex, age, ethnicity, place size, and owner/renter status) within which the three key assumptions above are tenable. The 1990 design used 1,392 strata for the coverage estimates. Nonetheless, the existence of a group of people who, because of their residential situation or desire to evade authorities, have zero probability of being counted in the census or the postenumeration survey undermines the assumption of homogeneity and

The 1990 Census Correction Process

Step 1. An area probability sample of about 5,000 blocks was selected. The "block" was essentially a city block in urban and suburban areas and a well-defined geography in rural areas.

Step 2. The 5,000 sample blocks generated two probability samples of people. The "E" or enumeration sample consisted of all persons in the 1990 physical enumeration in those blocks. The "P" or population sample consisted of all persons counted in an independent enumeration of blocks conducted some time following the physical enumeration. Together, the two samples comprised the Post-Enumeration Survey (PES).

Step 3. The P sample persons were matched to lists of persons counted in the physical enumeration. The objective was to determine which sample persons were counted in the physical enumeration and which were not.

Step 4. Each E sample enumeration was either matched or not matched to a P sample enumeration. E sample enumerations were ultimately designated as correct or erroneous.

Step 5. The data were screened for incomplete, missing, or faulty items. All missing data were completed by statistical imputation techniques.

Step 6. Estimates of the total population were calculated within each of 1,392 poststrata based, in part, on the characteristics of the PES sample. The poststrata were mutually exclusive and spanned the entire U.S. population.

Step 7. The 1,392 ratios, called raw "adjustment factors," were "smoothed" to reduce sampling variability. (Smoothed adjustment factors were obtained by shrinking the raw adjustment factors toward a predicted value from a multiple regression model, with the degree of shrinkage determined by the quality of the predictor and the inherent sampling variability in the raw factor.)

Step 8. The smoothed adjustment factors were applied to the physical enumeration, block by block, for each of the 7 million blocks in the nation.

Source: Fienberg (1992—adapted from Wolter, 1991).

leads to a downward bias in the postenumeration survey estimate of the undercount.

The 1990 PES was used to produce ratio estimates from the sample of blocks (5,290 block clusters) to the rest of the population. But there were special problems with the 1990 evaluation survey because the sample was too small for use in preparing small-area adjustments and sampling variability led to elaborate forms of statistical smoothing. If plans for a one-number census in 2000 proceed, an adequate sample can be designed that will overcome the special statistical problems of the 1990 survey. As the Census Bureau moves to implement a census that relies on survey methods to complete the count, it becomes even more important to have a method for coverage adjustment than it was in 1990. A redesigned one-number census will rely on the quality of its evaluation survey.

Alternatives to the postenumeration survey, such as CensusPlus (described below), also take the form of a ratio estimate from a sample of blocks to the nation. The nature of work in those blocks and the statistical estimation within them may be quite different from previous work with the 1990 PES. Alternative methods have different assumptions, and one aspect of the 1995 census test will be to make a comparison between a postenumeration survey estimate and CensusPlus. At the moment, the postenumeration survey has become the standard for census adjustment. The Census Bureau will need to acquire evidence that CensusPlus or some alternative is going to be superior.

Results from the postenumeration survey-type estimation would be used to produce estimates for small areas, down to the level of the individual census blocks, for all population groups throughout the country. The report of the Panel to Evaluate Alternative Census Methods (Steffey and Bradburn, 1994) contains a discussion of the methods that will be required for incorporating people and households into the individual blocks, including the creating of units in such a way that total number of counts for smaller areas equals the counts for larger areas comprising the collection of smaller areas.

The 1990 PES involved 165,000 housing units and identified a net undercount of 1.6 percent and substantial differential undercount related to age, sex, and racial groups and by geographic area. For the 1995 census tests, the Census Bureau currently proposes to use a survey-based method to complete the count, called CensusPlus, that is designed to run concurrently with the main census operations. The CensusPlus method would involve operating a survey behind the regular census operations in the same blocks. CensusPlus would carry out an intensive enumeration in a sample of blocks with the objective of obtaining a complete enumeration of the population. The assumption of complete coverage for CensusPlus would then be used for comparisons with the census enumeration to derive correction factors. But no final decision has been made about the survey method that would be used to complete the census count in the 2000 census. The PES was used in 1990 and much is known about its operational feasibility and costs; tests with CensusPlus in 1995 will provide comparable information about this alternative.

Whether a postenumeration survey, CensusPlus, or some combination of the two survey designs is used in the 2000 census, it is important to emphasize that its principal use is to complete the census—i.e., that the survey is not designed to evaluate the census but is an integral part of the census. This is a fundamental departure—it is the only feasible approach largely to eliminate the differential undercounts historically observed in U.S. censuses. Furthermore, the approach can serve as a springboard for a complete reengineering of the enumeration-based part of the census. Indeed, traditionally the enumeration had to carry the full burden of producing a complete census. Using only physical enumeration resulted in a variety of extremely intensive and costly approaches, particularly when used in combination. Knowing that the count resulting from physical enumeration (with sample follow-up of nonrespondents) will be completed by a final survey should permit the Census Bureau to redesign all preceding operations with a view to reducing reliance on the less cost-effective approaches to enumeration. Indeed, as we've said, we are advocating a complete reengineering. We shall return to this point in the last two sections of this chapter.

A survey-based method to complete the count has several benefits for the redesigned census. A major one is reduced costs. The traditional census has, in recent decades, increased the use of intensive enumeration efforts in a futile attempt to physically count every person. This effort has produced diminishing returns. Trying to directly enumerate everyone in a large and diverse population has become prohibitively expensive, yet it is unlikely that spending more money will reduce net overall or differential undercoverage. A less expensive approach is to realize that modern statistical methods can assist in improving the census count and to rely on those methods for future U.S. censuses, thereby reducing the intensive follow-up effort that was used in the previous two censuses.

The second benefit of integrated statistical estimation is improved accuracy with respect to the count and differential undercount for the nation as a whole as well as large areas and groups. Using high-quality special surveys to complete the count will enable the Census Bureau to use data-quality enhancements (e.g., intensive efforts to find hard-to-enumerate persons) that would be too expensive to use for the entire population. Such a high-quality survey can then be used to estimate the number and characteristics of the people missed by the census and take them into account in completing the official count.

Although the use of statistical methods to complete the census count will increase variability for very small areas, there will be benefits from cost savings and improved overall coverage. Whatever the adjustment factors used in an integrated coverage measurement system, the adjustments will become much coarser as geographic detail becomes smaller. There is fervent debate among demographers and statisticians about the best methods to be used for completing the census count for small geographic areas. We note that the conventional 1990 census approach also produces large variability for small-area estimates (as described earlier). The panel believes that further work on the census methods to be used for producing small-area estimates is needed before a decision should be made.

The Census Bureau has published, for each modern census in the past 50 years, a comprehensive description of the procedures followed in enumerating the population, together with an assessment of the quality of the data. Separate census publications routinely note nonresponse rates and information on allocation rules and rates (Appendix L provides an example of allocation information

from the 1990 census, cited in this report for our panel's examination of the
quality of data on race and ethnicity). The panel urges the Census Bureau to
continue this tradition of conscientious documentation of census procedures and
to provide for the redesigned 2000 census the materials needed for proper use of
census data and for independent scrutiny of the accuracy of census data.

> **Recommendation 5.2 To improve the census results, and especially
> to reduce the differential undercount, the panel recommends that
> the estimates achieved through physical enumeration and sampling
> for nonresponse be further improved and completed through sur-
> vey techniques. The census should be designed as an integrated
> whole, to produce the best single-number count for the resources
> available. The Census Bureau should publish the procedures used to
> produce its final counts, as well as an assessment of their accuracy.**

ADDITIONAL MEASURES TO IMPROVE ACCURACY
AND REDUCE COSTS

Improve Response Rates

Research by the Census Bureau in recent years provides evidence that the
mail response rates to the census questionnaire can be improved, compared with
the 1990 experience. Work with the Simplified Questionnaire Test and the
Appeals and Long-Form Experiment suggest several improvements: respondent-friendly questionnaires, pre- and post-mailout reminders, use of replacement questionnaires, use of appeals to the mandatory nature of the census, and
telephone reminders. Taken together, these changes could significantly improve
the mail response rates for the 2000 census. Although the panel is not able to
provide a specific estimate of the mail response rate for the 2000 census (none of
these improvements has yet been used in a census environment), we believe that
these improvements would at least halt the decline in census mail response rates
in recent censuses.

A Simplified Questionnaire Design

Work on the SQT conducted by the Census Bureau in early 1992 was designed to address issues in relation to response rates for the short form. Chapter
6 discusses the results of the SQT tests.

Results from the SQT confirm that changes in the short-form content, design, and collection procedures can improve census response rates. Higher response rates reduce the need for follow-up interviews, including the time for
follow-up interviewing and the training time for more interviewers. However,
the use of replacement questionnaires—and other measures to improve response

rates—incur additional costs that need to be considered when weighing the benefits from higher response rates. Additional costs involve the mailing and printing costs of a reminder postcard or a replacement questionnaire, the possibly higher costs of printing and processing a respondent-friendly census questionnaire, and the use of telephone calls to urge nonrespondents to mail in their questionnaires. There may be additional costs to respondent-friendly forms that may increase machine costs for processing and tabulation. Optimizing for respondent ease may increase response rates, but it may also increase machine costs. All extra costs must be weighed against the cost savings from increased mail response rates. Some methods to increase mail response rates may not, after careful study, yield an overall net cost savings.

Respondent-Friendly Long Forms and the Use of Appeals

The Census Bureau conducted the Appeals and Long-Form Experiment in 1993 with two objectives: to determine the influence of two types of respondent-friendly construction on response rates for the census long form and to determine the influence of three types of appeals on response rates to the census short form. The ALFE work involved the use of methods to improve mail response rates that had been learned from the SQT. Results from the ALFE test are described in greater detail in Chapter 6.

The ALFE research leads to two conclusions for taking the census. First, it is possible to improve the census long form by designing it as a more respondent-friendly questionnaire. Second, stressing the mandatory nature of the census ("Your response is required by law") substantially improves the mail completion rates. Although the ALFE study did not test directly the use of a mandatory appeal with the long form, the results suggest that it may be possible to increase the long-form mail completion rates by as much as 15 percentage points by using a respondent-friendly questionnaire and stressing the mandatory and confidential nature of the census.

> **Recommendation 5.3 The panel recommends that the Census Bureau incorporate successfully tested procedures to increase the initial response rate in the 2000 census, including respondent-friendly questionnaires and expanded efforts to publicize the mandatory nature of the census.**

Partnerships with State and Local Governments

In rethinking census operations for the future, the Census Bureau needs to develop new partnerships. One of the two most important partnerships needed is with state and local governments. The other is with the U.S. Postal Service, discussed in the next section.

The Census Bureau needs to work with state and local governments to improve understanding of the new methods for the 2000 census, changes in census enumeration operations, and the use of integrated coverage measurement. The 2000 census will have different methods for coverage improvement, with a decreased reliance on intensive and expensive direct enumeration. Local and state governments need to be informed about these new approaches and to understand how they will affect census operations in their areas. Congress should evaluate the Census Bureau for its success in establishing cooperative state and local programs.

A special goal for improved cooperation between the Census Bureau and local governments is to reach agreement on the housing address list for the decennial census. Approximately one-half of census undercount is attributable to missed housing units. Local governments have often criticized past censuses because they believe that housing units exist that were not counted by the census. However, the census address list has been deemed confidential by the Census Bureau so that local governments have not been able to make direct comparisons between their address list and the list used for the census. It would be valuable to have a new partnership in which local governments and the Census Bureau work together to construct the best possible address list for the census. Such a partnership would also reduce a major source of disagreement about the accuracy of the population count reported in the census.

The panel discusses the sharing of the Census Bureau's address list in two places in this report: in this chapter and in Chapter 8, where we discuss a continuously updated address file. In both instances, an important aspect of the sharing of census address lists is the confidentiality restriction on the Census Bureau contained in Title 13, the federal legislation governing the Census Bureau's activities. The current interpretation of Title 13 by the Census Bureau is that it does not permit the agency to allow others to examine the list of individual addresses that it assembles for the decennial census. We discuss these issues more fully in Chapter 8, in a section entitled "Title 13 Concerns."

Recommendation 5.4 The panel recommends that the Census Bureau develop cooperative arrangements with states and local governments to develop an improved master address file and that Congress amend Title 13 of the U.S. Code to permit sharing of this file for statistical purposes with state and local governments and the federal statistical system.

Partnership with the U.S. Postal Service

The second major partnership needed is between the Census Bureau and the U.S. Postal Service. Historically the U.S. Postal Service has had an important role in the decennial census, delivering and returning the bulk of the census questionnaires by mail. In 1990, the letter carriers delivered about 90 million census questionnaires to individual households. Whereas such work may be considered part of the normal duties of the U.S. Postal Service, it is critical that the questionnaire be delivered correctly and on time. This section reviews the current role of the U.S. Postal Service and the panel's suggestions for an expanded role in future census activities.

Current Role

The U.S. Postal Service has played key roles in several steps in recent censuses. First is development and improvement of the census address list. Beginning about 2 years prior to the 1990 census, the U.S. Postal Service provided assistance in several phases of advance census address checking. Using either commercial mailing lists or census enumerators, the Census Bureau prepared preliminary address lists for rural areas, small and medium towns, and major urban centers. U.S. Postal Service letter carriers checked each address on their mail routes, made corrections, identified duplicates and undeliverable addresses, and added missing addresses. About 75 million addresses were checked in this work. These verifications and corrections were completed by the U.S. Postal Service by April 1989. The letter carriers then completed a final review of the mail addresses in February and March 1990, immediately before the mailing of census questionnaires. For this operation, address lists were checked again to identify missing, duplicate, and undeliverable addresses.

The second step is providing the prompt and accurate delivery of census questionnaires. U.S. Postal Service letter carriers delivered all census questionnaires to housing units in the short period before Census Day (April 1, 1990). This was a massive, coordinated delivery operation, with more than 90 million questionnaires, which had to ensure that every household received the proper questionnaire at the proper time. The important role of the letter carriers in accurate and timely delivery of questionnaires cannot be overstated.

The third step is automated sorting of mail returns. About 66 million completed mail questionnaires were returned to either 1 of the 346 district offices or 1 of 7 special processing offices.[7] The U.S. Postal Service designated a special zip+4 postal code for each census office to ensure the timely and efficient return of questionnaires. The Census Bureau printed these zip+4 postal codes on the return envelope, and postal facilities sorted the returns with their automated equipment. These arrangements helped to improve the speed of and logistics for the delivery of the completed questionnaires at the processing centers.

The fourth step involved checks for correct address for matched questionnaires. Several 1990 census programs encouraged people to complete a questionnaire if they thought that they had not been enumerated. About 3 million questionnaires were received through this program. The Census Bureau was required to match the address of the questionnaires with the census address list to ensure the correct enumeration of persons at their usual residence. If the address on the questionnaire could not be matched, the address was sent to the U.S. Postal Service for verification. Addresses classified as deliverable addresses by the U.S. Postal Service and the people corresponding to these addresses were then added to the census.

Finally, the U.S. Postal Service was involved in the census closeout address check. During the final period of the nonresponse follow-up operation, some district offices used the U.S. Postal Service to obtain information about unenumerated addresses. These district offices provided an address card for each unenumerated address to the U.S. Postal Service and asked for a limited amount of information about the address (type of structure, occupancy status on Census Day, and the number of occupants on Census Day). The results of this limited operation in 1990 were that 142,000 address cards were sent to the U.S. Postal Service and 35,000 were returned. Only 17 percent of the returned cards provided the number of Census Day occupants. The Census Bureau concluded that more controlled research was needed to determine the usefulness of this limited information from letter carriers in the final stages of follow-up of non-respondents.

Expanded Role

In the panel's judgment, the U.S. Postal Service should continue to play a strong role in the decennial census. In addition to the tasks noted above, there are several other ways in which the U.S. Postal Service might support the conduct of the census. Some new ways are outlined in a letter of agreement from the U.S. Postal Service and the Census Bureau (Green and Scarr, 1993), which we summarize here.

Maintenance of a continuously updated residential address list. Census-taking relies heavily on an accurate and complete address list. The Census Bureau and the U.S. Postal Service are working on an arrangement to share address information. Such an arrangement would start with the 1990 census address list as a base and then develop a permanent and continuously maintained list of addresses. The updating would rely on the firsthand knowledge of letter carriers—who gain through their daily work information about the inventory and location of housing unit addresses. During the course of their normal duties, letter carriers would record the existence of each unit to which mail is delivered on their routes. These records would be collected by the U.S. Postal Service into a single national file of address information.

The proposed methodology is to periodically link the continuously updated U.S. Postal Service address information with Census Bureau address files. Such a linkage would reveal addresses missing from the census list. A contribution of the Census Bureau to the joint work would be linkage to its geographic files and maps. With updating of new addresses, the linkage would also reveal new streets. Following the identification of missing streets, the Census Bureau would provide maps with information of interest to the U.S. Postal Service for its route and mail delivery planning. Such collaborative work may require legislative changes for the sharing of address information. We address cost issues and the desirability for an ongoing national address file in more detail in Chapter 8.

Identification of vacant housing units. Because the misclassification of occupied housing units can cause coverage errors in the census, in the 1990 census at least two enumerator visits were made to each potentially vacant address. Census costs could be reduced if one or more of these enumerator visits were eliminated by relying on the local letter carrier to ascertain the vacancy status of the housing unit. The letter carrier may also be able to complete the work more quickly because he or she visits each address almost every day. Ascertaining the vacancy status more promptly, closer to Census Day, would improve the data quality of the census.

Encouragement of local efforts to convert rural addresses to addresses with house numbers and street names. Unlike city addresses, rural addresses do not provide both a mailing address and a unique physical location for the housing unit. Many rural addresses use a rural route and box number, a post office box, or general delivery. Such rural addresses are a problem for both the U.S. Postal Service (because they present difficulties for automated sorting of addresses for more efficient mail delivery) and the Census Bureau (because they are difficult to handle in automated matching for assignment of geographic codes). The decennial census needs to assign every individual to a specific small area of geography in order to fulfill the data requirements for legislative redistricting. The census could not, for example, simply record thousands of people residing at the specific location of a central post office. Therefore, regardless of the location and nature of the mailing address, the census must be able to associate a specific physical location for the residence of each family and individual recorded in the census. Because city-style addresses allow more efficient routing of emergency services (fire, policy, and ambulance), many rural areas of the nation are converting to city-style addresses. Both the U.S. Postal Service and the Census Bureau will benefit from these conversions.

> **Recommendation 5.5 The panel recommends that the U.S. Postal Service and the Census Bureau continue to work together to improve the decennial census. We endorse an expanded role for the U.S. Postal Service in the 2000 census in several areas: (a) development, maintenance, and improvement of an accurate address file**

for the nation's residential housing units, (b) checking the address list prior to the census to improve accuracy, (c) delivery of the mailed forms, and (d) ascertainment of the vacancy status of housing units during the census.

A REENGINEERED CENSUS

The panel is extremely concerned about the costs and the accuracy of future censuses. The previous sections have detailed ways in which net census costs could be reduced by $300 to $400 million, principally by truncating the follow-up stage of census operations after a reasonable effort and by relying on sampling for nonresponse follow-up. We have also reviewed ways to improve the completeness of the census count for the total population and for subgroups through the use of integrated coverage measurement as the last stage in arriving at the final population count (the "actual enumeration" called for in the Constitution). We emphasize that the use of integrated coverage measurement affords the opportunity to realize yet additional cost savings in the census by means of a thoroughgoing "reengineering" of the entire census process.

Basing the census on the use of statistical estimation to compensate for the unavoidable undercoverage that occurs in traditional census enumeration means that the entire procedure of census enumeration and processing operations can and should be rethought. In the past, the direct enumeration operations have sought, at great expense, to count every person. If a person was not counted, he or she was omitted from the final census count except as imputed in census allocation procedures. Under the redesigned census we propose for future censuses, the uncounted population will be estimated by relatively inexpensive survey-based statistical techniques, and the final count will include both the estimated as well as the directly counted population. It should be possible, therefore, to greatly reduce the costly intensive effort to count every person directly. Since such a reduction would eliminate those operations having the least relative cost-effectiveness, there is the potential to realize substantial savings.

The "unexplained" increases in census costs that occurred over the period 1970 to 1990 amounted to $1.3 billion. (By unexplained increases, we mean the cost increases that are not explained by wage and price increases, the growth in the number of housing units, and the decline in the mail response rate.) We were not able to decompose analytically the causes of these increases, in terms of specific operational and managerial decisions. However, we strongly believe the cost increases stemmed heavily from efforts, during a period of declining public cooperation with the decennial census, to meet strong political pressures for accurate counts by area and population group through the application of highly expensive and labor-intensive efforts to make a physical count of every person. As just one example, field offices stayed open for 9 months in 1990, compared with 6 months in 1980, and 3 to 4 months in 1970.

Not only were there cost increases as the result of new programs intended specifically to improve coverage (e.g., rechecking every housing unit originally determined to be vacant), but also substantial cost increases occurred in major components of the census (Chapter 3 includes a more detailed description of the cost components). Thus, in five key categories, in 1990 dollars, costs increased from 1970 to 1990: by $75 million for census planning activities, $1,022 million for data collection, $311 million for data processing, $92 million for data dissemination, and $68 million for census testing (but note that these increases have not been adjusted for the growth in the number of households or the decline in the mail response rate). The total of unexplained cost increases, as we noted earlier, amounts to $1.3 billion in constant 1990 dollars. Given these large increases from 1970 to 1990, we are convinced that abandonment of the goal of physically counting every person and completely rethinking all of the census operations in the context of the new design would make possible substantial additional savings—for example, through reducing some expensive coverage improvement programs that would no longer be needed if statistical measures were used to complete the count.

With the adoption of a new census design that includes integrated coverage measurement to complete the count, there is an opportunity and a need for knowledgeable census staff to review every aspect of census operations to identify procedures that are no longer necessary or that can be redesigned to be more cost-effective. This review of costs would be similar to the kinds of reengineering that corporations (and agencies of government) have undertaken in recent years to rethink and streamline their production processes.

A reengineering effort would probably begin with a more detailed examination of previous census operations, which might determine that particular expenditures (and expenditure increases) were well justified in light of the overall design for past censuses. However, we propose a new census design; hence, the question is not whether a particular operation was justified in the past but whether it is needed in the future and, if so, whether it can be streamlined in some manner, combined with other operations, or otherwise made more cost-effective. Thus, the review must go beyond a line-by-line audit to consider each operation in the context of the overall approach that is proposed for the 2000 census, namely, one in which statistical estimation plays an important role along with direct enumeration.

To put it another way, it is critical to challenge the attitude that the census needs to be improved without regard to costs and cost-effectiveness. Given the legal challenges to the Census Bureau in recent decades, one can understand such an attitude. But the panel believes that a more productive approach would be to reengineer census operations for greater cost-effectiveness in the context of the proposed census redesign. At this writing, we are unaware of any activities by the Census Bureau to carry out the extensive census reengineering that we propose. We urge the Census Bureau to commit to and carry out as soon as possible such a reengineering effort, in which the basic structure and organization as well as all operations and managerial techniques of the census are reviewed with the goal of reducing costs while maintaining the essential quality of the results.

We have identified $300 to $400 million in net savings that could be achieved by specific innovations—principally, the use of truncation and sampling for nonresponse follow-up. But for a reengineering effort to be successful, we believe it essential to present census planners with a target for cost savings that presents a genuine challenge to encourage new thinking. As one managerial technique to help identify cost savings, we propose that the Census Bureau flesh out the best possible plan to produce a new census for 2000 at a total cost (adjusted for increases in housing units and prices since 1990) that would eliminate a substantial fraction of the $1.3 billion "unexplained" increase in costs between 1970 and 1990, with a target for cost savings much larger than the $300 to $400 million we have already identified. The Census Bureau should then evaluate this plan in terms of its effects on the quality of resulting data products.

We argue that substantial cost savings are reasonable for the purpose of this planning exercise; that is, a target for planning a reengineered integrated single-number census in 2000 that would cost substantially less than the 1990 census (after allowing for changes in prices and household numbers). Our rationale for such a goal follows. The 1990 census cost $1.86 billion more (in constant dollars) than the 1970 census. Of this total, about $450 to $580 million is explained by the increase in housing units and the decline in the census mail response rate, leaving remaining cost increases of $1.3 billion (see Table 3.2). We have estimated potential net savings from truncating 100 percent follow-up after a reasonable effort and relying on sampling to complete the non-response follow-up operation of $300 to $400 million. Even more important, the new census design would use statistical estimation to complete the count. As a consequence, operations and procedures need no longer be designed to try to count every last person, an effort to which we have assigned major responsibility for the $1.3 billion cost increase from 1970 to 1990.

The questions that should be examined in this planning exercise include: How many district offices are needed for the census? How long do they need to be open? How many enumerators are required for a less intensive physical enumeration? What is the most cost-effective method of payment for enumerators? What levels of staffing and supervisory personnel are needed? Given the use of statistical estimation to complete the count, which coverage improvement operations can be scaled back or eliminated? How can automation be integrated into census field activities so as to reduce the combined costs of people and systems? How can data processing be made more efficient? How much of the product line can shift from print to electronic media?

Since we have not been able to identify the specific elements of the 1970 to 1990 cost increase, we cannot predict the full magnitude of the savings that would be feasible while still producing a high-quality census. But we are convinced that a good-faith effort to develop such a plan would identify important cost savings that could be made without a significant sacrifice of quality.

We emphasize that a planning target—eliminating a substantial fraction of the 1970 to 1990 "unexplained" cost increases is just that—a planning target. In its review, the Census Bureau should identify what would have to be done to meet a target and spell out the consequences both for its operations and for the quality of the resulting census. Even if it is ultimately deemed infeasible to achieve the full magnitude of the savings set as a target for the exercise while still maintaining the quality of the census, a good-faith effort could still identify substantial cost savings, as all census operations are reengineered for a single-number census in which physical enumeration and statistical estimation are fully integrated.

> **Recommendation 5.6 We recommend that the Census Bureau undertake a thorough reexamination of the basic structure, organization, and processes by which the decennial census is conducted to obtain the full cost-saving potential of the proposed redesigned census. As one part of its reexamination, the Census Bureau should develop a plan for the 2000 census that eliminates a substantial fraction of the $1.3 billion cost increase (in 1990 dollars) from 1970 to 1990 that is not accounted for by the growth in housing units and the decline in the mail response rate. The target for this plan should be much more than the $300 to $400 million we have already identified.**

BUILDING PUBLIC SUPPORT

The census involves a joint commitment of the government and the American people. The government—involving federal, state, and local agencies—attempts to communicate with the people in a detailed and specific way by sending out census questionnaires and receiving replies. The American people expect a fairly apportioned Congress, equitable distribution of monies from government programs, and accurate and useful data on themselves. From this perspective, a census with incomplete or poor-quality data may be considered to be a failure of the mutual commitment of the government and the people about the census. The failure may come about from a failure by the government to provide an appropriate set of questions or methods for collecting information about those questions, a failure to indicate to the American people that it is important to respond to the census questionnaire, a failure to send out a questionnaire that is properly perceived and understood (a questionnaire that is hard to understand or is not in the language of the respondent), or a failure to send out a questionnaire or provide a way of responding that can be acted on in the social setting in which the respondent resides.

The census process may also break down from adverse publicity or the widespread reluctance of the American people to participate in the census, or a combination of both. Unfavorable or sensational news that ridicules the census or its questions or highlights charges of discrimination adversely affects the mail return rates and increases the cost of data collection for nonrespondents. Thus, the process of the census program involves not only the attempt to publicize the census favorably in the mass media, but also sending messages to the public about all aspects of the census process that can be received, understood, accepted, and acted on.

The actual counting of the population in the census depends on explaining census operations to the people and on building a mutual agreement for the undertaking. The challenge for the 2000 census will be to conduct a public education campaign early enough to allow scrutiny of all the new features of a census that is fundamentally changed.

We believe that the next U.S. census should be fundamentally redesigned to provide greater accuracy at lower cost. If a redesigned census is decided on, the methods should be determined by the Census Bureau, with technical advice from appropriate sources.

The Census Bureau will need to state publicly the methods it proposes to follow in the census. If the 2000 census is redesigned, it is critical to state those methods as soon as possible in order to obtain comments from government agencies at the federal, state, and local levels, from census data users, and from the public. The procedures finally decided on will need to be announced well in advance of Census Day, 2000. Allowing a reasonable period for public comments suggests that the redesigned census, in its broad features, needs to be presented publicly within the next year or so.

Recommendation 5.7   The panel recommends that the Census Bureau publicize, as soon as possible, its plan for implementing a redesigned census. It should then move to obtain early commitment for the new plan from both Congress and data users.

NOTES

[1]Appendix B outlines the key steps in the traditional census process, describing by year the activities undertaken in the 1990 census.

[2]A survey does not necessarily have to come after the sampling for nonrespondents in some designs proposed for statistical estimation of undercoverage for the 2000 census. This independent survey for coverage estimation could occur during the census.

[3]The recent case of *City of New York* v. *U.S. Department of Commerce* (1993, Eastern District, New York) is the latest court decision that discusses, in part, the statistical methods that might be used for the conduct of the census; Appendix C presents a fuller discussion of legal issues.

[4]Available evidence from the 1980 census indicates that the costs per follow-up interview increase with the more calls that are attempted for nonresponding households. Citro and Cohen (1985: Appendix 6.2) discuss information on follow-up procedures in the 1980 census and illustrate the costs for a census that uses reduced follow-up callbacks or sampling in the nonresponse follow-up.

[5]See the report of the Panel to Evaluate Alternative Census Methods (Steffey and Bradburn, 1994:97-105) for a more detailed discussion about the possible operations for nonresponse follow-up.

[6] The joint use of the PES and census to estimate the "true" population size is a type of dual-system estimation. Dual-system estimation is generally used in many ways to estimate human and animal populations. For biological research, animals are caught in a survey and then matched against the number caught at later times or who are spotted in a count of an area. Biologists refer to these estimates as capture-recapture estimates. For demographic research, the dual-system estimation is used to provide an estimate of coverage for the census.

[7]The 1990 census operated 449 district offices, plus 9 in Puerto Rico. Only 346 offices processed completed mail questionnaires.

6

Census Content

An important part of the panel's charge was to consider the needs for census data and whether those needs are better met by the census itself or by some other data collection system. In responding to this part of our charge, we did not attempt to determine the merits of each and every item in the census. We believe it would be inappropriate for us to substitute our judgment on specific items for that of federal government agencies and others who use the data. Rather, we sought to determine in broad terms whether the kinds of data now collected in the census, beyond those items required for the constitutionally mandated purposes of reapportionment and redistricting, serve important public purposes.

In our review (see Chapter 1 and Appendices D-H and M), we determined that federal agencies require census-type data on small areas and small population groups for legally mandated purposes (e.g., for allocation of funds and enforcement of antidiscrimination laws) and, more broadly, to implement and evaluate government programs and policies. We also determined that other data users—such as state and local governments, researchers, and business organizations—require census-type data for purposes that directly or indirectly serve the public interest. Our conclusion, therefore, is one of unequivocal support for the importance of census-type information: the nation needs to have the breadth of data for small areas and small population groups that the census now provides.

Conclusion 6.1 The panel concludes that, in addition to data to satisfy constitutional requirements, there are essential public needs for small-area data and data on small population groups of the type and breadth now collected in the decennial census.

On the basis of this conclusion, we undertook the following tasks:

- to review in broad terms the process by which the census content is decided;
- to assess whether the content beyond that required for constitutionally mandated purposes of reapportionment and redistricting—largely the information now collected from the census long form—adversely affects census costs and coverage; and
- to evaluate the merits of a continuous measurement data collection system (i.e., a large, continuing monthly mail household survey) as a possible replacement for the census long form.

In considering census content, we also reviewed the difficult issues posed by the collection of data on race and ethnicity. These data are vitally needed not only for redistricting under the Voting Rights Act and court decisions, but also for many other program, policy, planning, and research purposes. The results of this analysis are in Chapter 7.

THE PROCESS FOR DETERMINING CENSUS CONTENT

In recent decades, the process of determining the questions to include in the census has involved a council or committee of federal agency representatives, coordinated by the Statistical Policy Office of the Office of Management and Budget (OMB). The Census Bureau has generally determined the dimensions of the "envelope," that is, the overall length of the short and long form, and has weighed in on the desirability of including questions for such purposes as coverage improvement and historical continuity. It has also evaluated questions in terms of their fitness and feasibility in a census context (thus, some questions, such as religion, are considered inappropriate for the census, and others are determined to be too complex or too subject to misinterpretation to provide reliable responses from a mail questionnaire). Within this framework, federal agencies have argued for items to serve their program and policy needs and have made trade-offs as needed. In recent censuses the Census Bureau has also sought input from states and cities and the public, through such mechanisms as public meetings. These meetings have generated a long list of potential new items to include in the census. Ultimately, however, federal agency data needs take precedence, and not even all of the agencies' proposed items can be accommodated because of the limits set by the Census Bureau on feasibility and questionnaire length.

OMB has a formal role in approving the questionnaire under the terms of the Paperwork Reduction Act. Indeed, in 1988, OMB disapproved the questionnaire for the census dress rehearsal and, by extension, for the 1990 census. OMB requested that seven housing items be moved from the short to the long form, that three housing questions on the long form be deleted entirely, and that the size of the long-form sample be reduced from about 16 million households (about 1 in 6) to 10 million households, with possible use of a variable-rate sampling plan. After appeals and analysis by data users and statistical work by the Census Bureau and others on the sample size, OMB rescinded most of the changes it had requested. A few housing items were moved from the short to the long form, and a variable-rate sampling plan was adopted (see Choldin, 1994).

Congress also plays a role because the secretary of commerce is required to provide to Congress the list of topics proposed for inclusion in the census no later than 3 years before Census Day and to provide the proposed list of specific items no later than 2 years before Census Day. For the 1990 census, Congress altered the question on race from the format originally proposed by the Census Bureau.

Congress has already been involved in the questionnaire for the 2000 census. Some members have argued that the questionnaire should be limited to basic items that are needed for key federal purposes. In response, the Census Bureau proposed to include in the 1995 census test only those items that are required by law to be collected in the census. From a review of legislation and agency documents, the Census Bureau classified items into three categories: (1) items mandated by law to come from the census; (2) items required by law although not necessarily from the census, but for which there is no reasonable alternative source; and (3) items not mandated but needed for agency program purposes. Restricting the questionnaire to the items in the first two categories would have little effect on the content of either the long form or the short form compared with 1990—most items are required by law. Restricting the questionnaire to the items in the first category, however, would considerably shorten both the long and short forms because many laws do not specifically name the census as the data source (see Bureau of the Census, 1993a, and Appendix M). The prospect that the test census content in 1995 (and, consequently, the 2000 census) might be restricted to items mandated in a strict sense led several agencies (notably, the Department of Transportation) to explore obtaining legal mandates for needed items they believed could be obtained in a cost-effective manner only from the census.

Subsequently, the Census Bureau proposed to include virtually all of the 1990 content in the 1995 test, and agencies have put in abeyance, at least for the time being, efforts to mandate specific items. We support the Census Bureau's decision for the test: information is needed on the mail return rates and costs of the long form in the context of the important changes in census methodology that will be tested in 1995 (see the panel's letter report: Schultze, 1993). That information is needed whether or not the 2000 long form is ultimately reduced in length or replaced by another data collection method, such as the continuous measurement system currently under consideration at the Census Bureau (see below).

In the process of determining the census content, there is a need to balance many factors, including program and policy data requirements, limitations on questionnaire space, and feasibility considerations and costs, as well as a need to make some provision for historical continuity. Inevitably, trade-offs must be made. That such trade-offs result from a full consideration of the range of agency needs and other relevant factors in a broad context is a positive benefit of the process as it has operated to date. The process would be likely to be impaired if a decision were made that all items must have explicit legislative mandates to be included in the census. Such a requirement could lead to individual initiatives by agencies and congressional committees to mandate items that could make it harder to control the size of the questionnaire or balance data needs across agencies.

We support the continuation of a process for determining census content that involves the relevant federal agencies and data users. However, we believe that the integrity of the process would be enhanced by strengthening the oversight role of the chief statistician in OMB. For example, the Office of the Chief Statistician could take a lead in organizing agency meetings to consider such issues as the trade-offs between collecting data in the census itself or in other ways. That office brings a useful breadth of perspective, which encompasses the needs of program agencies for census data as well as of other users, including statistical agencies. That office also brings a concern for such issues as the feasibility of asking questions in a census context.

Conclusion 6.2 The panel concludes that the process of determining the census content by involving federal agencies and eliciting the views of other users has worked well in the past and should be continued. In our judgment, the process would be strengthened by increasing the oversight and coordination role of the chief statistician in the Office of Management and Budget.

THE LONG FORM

Given the importance of the broad range of data for small areas and small population groups that the census currently collects, the main question is whether those data should be collected as part of the census or by some other means. Is the census the right vehicle to collect additional questions beyond the minimum required for reapportionment and redistricting? Do the added questions—principally those on the census long form, which is sent to a sample of households—increase the costs of the census and impair the quality of the data?

The argument for the view that the long form is a problem for the census can be formulated as follows: respondents find the long form unduly burdensome because of its length and complexity; this burden lowers the overall mail return rate and also lowers item response rates for people who do send back a form;

both of these effects, particularly the former, increase census costs; and the lower mail return rate may also contribute to population undercoverage.

Questions about the long form are of intense interest to almost every user of census data and elicit strong opinions on all sides. Many data users are impassioned in their defense of the long form, implicitly rejecting the idea that it hurts the basic census enumeration and arguing for the need for the rich multivariate data that it provides for small areas and small population groups. Others see the long form as a threat to the cost and quality of the census data that are needed to serve the basic constitutional purposes. In light of this controversy, in this section we review the evidence about the effects of the long form on census costs, mail return rates, and coverage.

Costs

The long form adds costs to the census in a number of ways, including: extra printing costs, extra postage, additional follow-up for every percentage point that the mail return rate for the long form is less than that for the short form, additional editing and follow-up for item nonresponse, coding of such items as industry and occupation, and additional data processing and publication costs. However, the long form, which is essentially a large sample survey on top of the massive effort undertaken for the complete (short-form) census, represents a marginal addition to total census costs. Moreover, the costs associated with the long form do not explain the escalation in census costs that has occurred.

Over the period from 1960 to 1990, the long form became *less* rather than more of a burden on the population and a smaller component of the census. The sample size of the long form was reduced from 25 percent of the households in the 1960 census to about 17 percent of the households in the 1990 census, i.e., 1 in 6. (In the variable-sampling rate design used, in small places the sample size was 1 in 2 of households, and in large census tracts the sample size was 1 in 8 of households.) Over this period, the number of questions remained about the same (the number increased somewhat from 1960 to 1980 but declined from 1980 to 1990—see Appendix A).

According to Miskura (1992), the total costs of the long form, including follow-up and all other costs, may have contributed 9 to 10 percent ($230 to $250 million) to the $2.6 billion costs of the census in 1990. More recent estimates that were provided to the panel from the Census Bureau's cost model suggest that the marginal cost of the long form in the context of the 1990 census methodology may range from $300 to $500 million, or 11 to 19 percent of total 1990 census costs. The added cost due to the somewhat lower mail return rate for long forms compared with short forms in 1990 (see below) is a relatively minor component of the total. Because relatively few households were sent the long form, the lower long-form mail return rate reduced the combined short- and long-form mail return rate (based on occupied housing units) by less than 1 percentage point: 74.1 percent for short and long forms combined and 74.9 percent for the short form alone. Using the Census Bureau's estimate that each percentage point drop in the mail return rate contributed 0.6 percent to total costs, this percentage point difference increased census costs by about $16 million.

The changes that are contemplated for the redesigned 2000 census, such as truncation and sampling for nonresponse follow-up, would reduce the cost of the long form. (We discuss in greater detail the likely costs of the long form in the context of a new census design in the section below on continuous measurement.) Also, just as the long form itself represents a marginal addition to census costs, so, too, marginal reductions in the content of the long form would likely have very limited effects on census costs. It is certainly important to scrutinize all proposed content items to determine their usefulness and appropriateness for inclusion in the census, but eliminating a few items will not produce much cost saving.

Conclusion 6.3   The panel concludes that the marginal cost of incremental data on the decennial census is low. In particular, we conclude that the extra cost of the census long form, once the census has been designed to collect limited data for every resident, is relatively low.

Mail Return Rates

The long form increases the burden of the census on the population, which may in turn reduce response rates relative to the short form. We noted above that the burden in terms of the proportion of households receiving the long form has declined progressively from 1960 to 1990; also, the number of questions has changed relatively little over the period. In this section, we review the evidence on mail return rates in the 1980 and 1990 censuses and the results of experiments to improve response.[1]

Effects in 1980 and 1990

The effect of the long form on mail return rates in 1980 was minimal (see Bureau of the Census, 1986): the mail return rate (which covers occupied housing units) was 81.6 percent for the short form and 80.1 percent for the long form, a difference of 1.5 percentage points.[2] Return rates were considerably higher in decentralized, easy-to-enumerate suburban district offices than in centralized, hard-to-enumerate urban offices, but the disparity in return rates differed little by type of form. Return rates varied by census regional office—from 77 percent overall in the Dallas and New York City regional offices to 85 percent in Detroit and Chicago, but the largest difference in return rates between short and long forms was 3.5 to 3.6 percentage points (in Dallas and Los Angeles).

The long form had a somewhat greater effect on mail return rates in 1990 than it had in 1980. The long-form mail return rate was 4.5 percentage points below the short-form mail return rate (70.4 percent versus 74.9 percent), compared with the difference of 1.5 percentage points in 1980. There is some evidence that the long-form/short-form differential in return rates was greater in hard-to-enumerate areas: district offices in central cities had the largest short-form/long-form difference—6.9 percentage points—compared with the national average of 4.5 (see Thompson, 1992). Since only one-sixth of all households received the long form, however, the difference in return rates reduced the overall mail return rate by less than 1 percentage point.

Indeed, what stands out about mail return rates in the 1990 census is not the relatively minor difference between the short-form and long-form rates, but the overall decline in the mail return rate. A 1990 survey to find out why people did not send back their questionnaires showed that most of the reasons cited apply to either form (Kulka et al., 1991): three-fourths of nonrespondents said they never received a form, or never opened it, or filled it out but never mailed it back; the remainder said they opened the form but did not start to fill it out or did not complete filling it out.

Experiments to Improve Response

Because declines in the mail return rate affect census costs, the Census Bureau moved quickly after the 1990 census to conduct experiments with both the short and the long forms to determine ways to increase response. In 1992 the Census Bureau conducted the Simplified Questionnaire Test (SQT) to assess the impact on mail return rates of reducing the number of questions on the short form and of making the form more user-friendly (see Dillman et al., 1993). The SQT tested five different short forms: the form used in 1990 (with wording updated to 1992) as a control; the "booklet" form, which contained all of the 1990 content but in a user-friendly format; the "micro" form, which contained no housing items and asked only for name, age, sex, race, and ethnicity; the micro form with a request for Social Security number added; and the "roster" form, which asked only for name and age (birth date). Every form except the control was in a user-friendly format.

The appropriate comparison for evaluating the effect of questionnaire length on response to the SQT is to look at the booklet, micro, and roster forms. There was virtually no difference in response between the micro and the roster forms. Both the micro and the roster forms achieved higher return rates overall—by 4.1 to 4.6 percentage points—than the booklet form.[3] However, these improvements were largely in areas that were relatively easy to enumerate in 1990; the improvements in hard-to-enumerate areas were much less impressive: 1.9 to 2.4

percentage points compared with 4.4 to 4.8 percentage points in the easy-to-enumerate areas. The effects of a user-friendly format were just the opposite: overall, the user-friendly booklet form achieved a higher return rate than the control form by 3.4 percentage points. The effect was most pronounced in hard-to-enumerate areas: the difference was 7.6 percentage points in these areas, compared with 2.9 percentage points in easy-to-enumerate areas.

The SQT and a subsequent experiment, the Implementation Test (IT), also provided evidence on the effects of such strategies to improve response as the use of a prenotice letter, a reminder postcard, a stamped return envelope, and a replacement questionnaire (see Census Data Quality Branch, no date). The IT, which used the micro short form for all treatments, found that the use of a prenotice letter increased response rates by 6 percentage points, and the use of a reminder card increased response rates by 8 percentage points (the effects were larger in areas that were relatively easier to enumerate in 1990). There were no significant effects from the use of a stamped return envelope. From comparing the IT treatment that combined the use of a prenotice letter and reminder card with the results of the SQT for the micro form (the SQT used a prenotice letter, a reminder card, and a replacement questionnaire for all treatments), the Census Bureau estimated that the use of a second or replacement questionnaire increased response rates by 10 to 11 percentage points.

The Census Bureau conducted a third experiment in 1993 with user-friendly long forms and appeals to increase response—the Appeals and Long-Form Experiment (ALFE) (see Treat, 1993). For the long-form component, ALFE tested four different forms: the same 20-page long form used in 1990 (with wording updated to 1993) as a control; a 28-page user-friendly long form in a booklet format (with all of the questions for each household member preceding the questions for the next member); a 20-page user-friendly row-and-column long form; and the same 8-page booklet short form used in the SQT. The format of the booklet long form was expected to be more conducive to response than the format of the row-and-column long form, but the increased page length of the booklet long form was expected to be an impediment to response. None of the forms included any type of motivational appeal.

Overall, the booklet long form increased return rates by 4.1 percentage points compared with the 1990 long form. In contrast, there were no statistically significant effects of the user-friendly row-and-column format. Whether the booklet long form might have increased return rates by an even higher percentage if its page length had been the same as the 1990 long form cannot be determined from the experiment. By type of response area, the booklet long form increased the return rate in areas that were easy to enumerate in 1990 but had no effect in hard-to-enumerate areas.

All of the ALFE long forms achieved substantially higher return rates than the 1990-type long form that was used in the 1986 National Content Test (NCT): the difference in return rates between the ALFE and the NCT 1990-type long forms was 10.3 percentage points.   Based on evidence from experiments with mailing strategies to increase response, Treat (1993) surmises that the difference in return rates was due to the use of a prenotice letter and a reminder postcard in the ALFE, which were not used in the NCT.

The ALFE booklet short form achieved substantially higher return rates than did the booklet long form: the difference was 11.3 percentage points overall, 10.8 percentage points in easy-to-enumerate areas, and 15.3 percentage points in hard-to-enumerate areas. However, one cannot conclude that such a wide differential would occur under census conditions of extensive publicity and outreach.

As a separate part of the ALFE, the use of three different types of motivational appeals was tested, emphasizing, respectively, the benefits of the census, the confidentiality of the data, and the mandatory nature of responding. The first two types of appeals had very little effect; however, a strong emphasis on the mandatory aspect increased the return rate by 10 to 11 percentage points. Unfortunately, the appeals portion of the experiment was conducted only with the short form, so that no information is available about possible effects on response to the long form. In general, the ALFE leaves many questions unanswered about the long form, such as the effects on return rates of different page lengths or the difference between short- and long-form return rates with a mandatory appeal, particularly when carried out in the context of a national census (with its attendant publicity and legitimacy).

Conclusions

Overall, the evidence is clear that the problems with mail return rates experienced in the 1990 census characterized the short form almost to the same degree as the long form. The Census Bureau's experiments with different form types and lengths and with other aspects of the mailout process (the use of a prenotice letter, a reminder postcard, a replacement questionnaire, motivational appeal, etc.) have identified some promising ways to increase mail returns by households for both the short and long forms.

Features of the mailout not related to the forms as such (e.g., motivational appeal, use of replacement questionnaire) seem to be particularly effective in increasing mail return rates. With regard to the forms themselves, there is evidence that making both the short form and the long form more user-friendly improves response somewhat, particularly (in the case of the short form) in hard-to-enumerate areas. There is also evidence that reducing the length of the short form—the form that most households receive—helps response to a limited extent.

It may be that implementing the various improvements to the mailout process, including making the short form shorter and more user-friendly, will widen the differential between the short-form and long-form mail return rates. One must assess the evidence cautiously, however, because none of the tests of improvements to the short and long forms and the comparative effects on mail return rates has yet been conducted in anything approaching a census environment. (The decision to include the long form in the 1995 census test is critically important in this regard.) Also, a wider differential in the context of a considerably higher overall mail return rate has very different implications from a wider differential at the level of the rate in 1990. Finally, it is important to remember that the long form, however it is designed, goes to relatively few households.

Coverage

Coverage errors in the 1990 census, specifically people missed within households, were higher for forms obtained by enumerators compared with forms that households filled out and mailed back themselves. The reason, presumably, is not because the enumerators did a poor job, but because people who do not mail back their questionnaires also do not respond well to follow-up. Thus, the percentage of people in the 1990 Post-Enumeration Survey (PES) who were not matched to the census although their housing unit was matched (within-household misses) was 11.6 percent for enumerator-filled returns compared with 1.8 percent for mail returns (Siegel, 1993; see also Keeley, 1993).[4]

This difference means that the somewhat lower mail return rates for long forms in 1990 could have had the effect of increasing coverage errors. Overall, however, the effect of the long form on within-household misses of people in 1990 was trivial (Siegel, 1993) because most people (5 out of 6) did not receive the long form; the difference between short-form and long-form mail return rates was not large (4.5 percentage points); and rates of within-household misses were virtually the same for short and long forms within type of return—1.9 and 1.8 percent for short-form and long-form mail returns and 11.7 and 11.3 percent for short-form and long-form enumerator-filled returns. Thus, the nonmatch rate for people in enumerated households, combining mail and enumerator-filled forms, was 4.2 percent for short forms and 4.4 percent for long forms, not a statistically significant difference.[5]

The contemplated change in methodology for the 2000 census to take account of coverage errors and complete the count by means of statistical estimation essentially renders the effect of the long form on coverage moot. To the extent that there is an effect, it will be taken care of in the estimation process (see Chapter 5). Other changes, such as the use of sampling for nonresponse follow-up, would also minimize the effects of lower long-form mail return rates on coverage.

Matrix Sampling

Although the long form had relatively little effect on mail return rates and almost no effect on coverage in 1990, it does represent a burden on households in the census sample. One proposal to reduce the burden on these households—and, thereby, perhaps improve response—is to employ matrix sampling. This approach divides the long-form sample into subgroups, each of which receives a different, shorter version of the long-form questionnaire with a subset of the content. Matrix sampling was used in the 1970 census, which had two intermediate-length forms that included some questions in common. It was also used to a lesser extent in the 1960 census for the housing items (see Appendix A).

We understand that the Census Bureau currently plans to include a full long form and an intermediate-length form in the 1995 test, which should provide valuable information about optimal form length in the context of a user-friendly design and other improvements to census methodology.[6] We support this decision, which recognizes the need to test content in the context of design, rather than trying to separate the two.

There are many issues about matrix sampling that need to be addressed before making a decision about its use in the 2000 census. All other things being equal, data users are most likely to prefer a single long form for the reason that every variable can be cross-tabulated with every other variable. Also, a single long form provides the maximum sample size (for a given overall sampling rate) and facilitates data analysis. In addition, a single long form is likely to be easier to control in the field. However, because each version of the long form in a matrix sampling scheme is reduced in length, there may be a positive effect on mail return rates and item nonresponse rates, which may in turn reduce the costs associated with follow-up. Also, there may be ways to minimize operational and data processing and analysis problems associated with matrix sampling. Information is needed on the balance of the positive and negative implications of this approach for reducing respondent burden.

We encourage the Census Bureau to conduct a comprehensive analysis, with the results from the 1995 test and other information, of the cost-effectiveness of matrix sampling in comparison with a single long-form design.

Recommendation 6.1 The panel recommends that the Census Bureau evaluate the merits of a matrix sampling approach that uses several intermediate forms in place of a single long form to reduce respondent burden. The Census Bureau should examine the effects on:

- **satisfying data users' needs;**
- **mail return rates;**
- **sampling and nonsampling errors (including item nonresponse rates);**
- **operational problems; and**
- **data processing and estimation problems that could affect the usefulness of the information, particularly for multivariate analysis.**

CONTINUOUS MEASUREMENT

The Census Bureau has recently devoted considerable energy to investigating a continuous measurement system as a possible alternative to the long form. In such a system, the long-form content would be ascertained through an ongoing monthly mail survey of a large sample of households, and the census itself would be limited to a short form.[7] Two concerns have driven the interest in such a system. The first—which we believe is misplaced—is that the long form adversely affects the coverage of the census itself and substantially increases costs. The second, quite legitimate concern is that census information, whether from the short or the long form, quickly becomes out of date. For example, information on poverty rates for school-age children at the school district level, which is used to allocate federal compensatory education funds, is available only once a decade.[8]

These concerns have led the Census Bureau to develop a proposal for a continuous measurement system to replace the census long form (see, e.g., Alexander, 1993, 1994a, 1994b). The system would involve a mailout/mailback survey conducted each month of a large sample of households, with telephone and personal follow-up for nonresponse. The system would provide reliable estimates on an annual (or more frequent basis) for such large geographic areas as states and large metropolitan statistical areas. By cumulating data for several years, the system would provide reliable estimates for small geographic areas. For the smallest areas for which the long form currently provides data (census tracts and block groups) it would be necessary to cumulate data over a 5-year period to obtain reliable estimates. Once the system is in full operation, small-area estimates could be provided each year on the basis of 5-year cumulated moving averages.

In addition to more frequent data for both small and large geographic areas, the hope is that a continuous measurement system would improve data quality because it would be possible to use a trained, permanent staff for data collection, rather than temporary staff hired for the census once a decade. Continuous measurement could have other benefits. For example, a regularly updated master address file would be required for continuous measurement, and such a file could also have uses for other data collection and analysis efforts. Costs for continuous measurement data collection would be spread out over the decade rather than cycling between a trough and a peak as happens now, which could facilitate efficient management of the operation. However, the success of the system, particularly the provision of small-area estimates from cumulated data, would depend on consistent annual appropriations at the level needed.

We support the further investigation of continuous measurement and of other alternatives for providing more frequent small-area estimates between censuses (see Chapter 8). We are concerned, however, that the current program of research and development for continuous measurement is moving much too quickly into an operational phase when key issues about the concept remain to be addressed. One important issue obviously concerns costs, in comparison with both the long form and other alternatives for providing more frequent data. Also, fundamental questions about data quality, about user needs (particularly how to interpret and work with cumulated, moving-average estimates), and about the very important relationship of the continuous measurement system to ongoing household surveys have not been but must be carefully considered.[9]

Limited operational tests, such as the Census Bureau proposes to conduct in 1995 (see Alexander, 1994b), can provide useful information with which to evaluate some aspects of costs and data quality for a continuous measurement system. Even more useful and, indeed, critical, in our view, are extensive consultations with data users and other federal statistical agencies, along with low-cost research activities that can address user needs and concerns. The Census Bureau's current plans include such activities (e.g., simulating the behavior of cumulated moving-average statistics with existing data). But the emphasis of current studies is on a series of operational tests that rapidly increase in scope and cost, leading up to a final decision at the end of 1997 on whether to drop the census long form from the 2000 census and replace it with continuous measurement. This schedule is much too ambitious in our view, given all of the questions that need to be answered about continuous measurement, as well as alternatives to it, before a decision of such importance can be made.

In sum, the panel supports a careful examination of continuous measurement along with other alternatives, as a possible way to improve the timeliness of small-area data. But we do not believe that the Bureau of the Census can have sufficient information in time in order to make a decision to drop the long form from the 2000 census.

Costs

Much of the discussion to date about replacing the long form with continuous measurement has assumed that the decision would be cost neutral. The assumption, in public presentations, has been that sufficient savings could be made by a combination of dropping the census long form and achieving efficiencies from integrating various operations of continuous measurement with other components of the federal statistical system to fund a full 10-year cycle of continuous measurement. However, this assumption is very much open to question.

A strong case can be made that a continuous measurement system that provides small-area estimates from cumulated 5-year data with the same reliability as those obtained from the long form once every 10 years would have a full-cycle cost 1.5 to 3 times greater than that of the long form itself. The reasons for the likely cost disadvantage of continuous measurement are as follows. For continuous measurement to yield small-area estimates based on cumulating data over 5 years, the sample size over 10 years must be of the same order as *twice* the long-form sample size. Furthermore, because the long form is an add-on to the basic census, it has intrinsic cost advantages over a continuing survey:

• The long-form survey is carried out with the immense publicity of the decennial census, which should yield higher response rates than a comparably executed survey.

• An entire field organization—field representatives, supervisors, physical space, manuals, and other field staff and materials—is available for the short form; only marginal additional costs are attributable to the long form.

• The address register is prepared for the short form; no extra cost from this source is involved in having a long-form survey as part of the census. By contrast, significant costs are likely to be involved to maintain the master address file for every single block in the country on a regular basis over a 10-year period, even if some of these costs will result in lower address register costs for the census itself.

• Mailing unit costs (mailout, mailback, check-in against the address register) are much cheaper for the long form than for continuous measurement because every housing unit in the census mailout/mailback areas receives a form, and only the marginal extra cost of mailing a heavier questionnaire is attributable to the long form.

There may be some cost disadvantages of the long form compared with continuous measurement. Because the census requires that a high volume of work be completed within a short time, there is little opportunity to achieve efficiencies from the application of continuous process improvement techniques. For the same reason, the long form may incur higher costs on a per unit basis for such elements as data processing equipment (because more equipment must be available to process a given number of cases within the short time available). However, on balance, we believe it likely that the cost advantages of the long form compared with continuous measurement substantially outweigh the disadvantages. Hence, we believe that a continuous measurement program would likely cost substantially more than the long form for the same level of sampling accuracy. In order to show the comparison, we first consider the cost savings of dropping the long form.

Cost Savings from Dropping the Long Form

In comparing the long form with continuous measurement, the first requirement is a realistic estimate of the savings from dropping the long form from the census. Materials supplied by Jay Keller and his Census Bureau colleagues suggest that the marginal costs of the long form—in the context of the census as it was conducted in 1990—are $300 to 500 million (in 1990 dollars). For an appropriate comparison with the proposed continuous measurement system, these estimates need to be modified to reflect a design that ends up with an 18 percent nonresponse, of which only one-third of the nonresponding households are followed up, to correspond to the proposed continuous measurement system, which will follow up only about one-third of an estimated 18 percent of nonrespondent households that remain after mailback and an initial telephone follow-up (see below).

Such a design would correspond roughly with a plan in which 100 percent census follow-up operations are truncated about May 18, and then one-third of the remaining nonrespondents are followed up. By May 18, the census would have followed up all nonrespondents to the mailout for 4 weeks, completing census questionnaires for more than 80 percent of households—similar to the level reached by continuous measurement through mail response and telephone follow-up. We have estimates from the Census Bureau that the combined savings on such a census operation (for the short and long forms) would be about $470 million (using numbers interpolated from Edmonston, 1994). Assuming that follow-up costs on the long form are a disproportionate share of the total, an expected saving on the long-form operation alone of about $100 million seems reasonable.

Hence, the comparable cost of the long form survey is about $200 to $400 million. Even the high end of this range significantly alters the cost comparisons between the long form and a full cycle of continuous measurement.

Continuous Measurement Cost Estimates

The Census Bureau originally proposed a sample size for continuous measurement of 500,000 housing units per month, which would provide small-area estimates of comparable reliability with the 1990 long form (see Alexander, 1993). The full-cycle (10-year) costs of this proposal were estimated at about $1 billion, or 2 to 3 times the estimated marginal cost of the long form ($300 to 500 million) in the context of the 1990 census methodology. Moreover, we believe that these costs are likely to be underestimated (see below).

The Census Bureau's current proposal is for a continuous measurement survey with a monthly sample size of 250,000 housing units (see Alexander, 1994a, 1994b). This sample size would provide small-area estimates with about 25 percent higher sampling errors than estimates from the 1990 long form. The full-cycle (10-year) costs for a continuous measurement survey of 250,000 housing units per month have been estimated at about $615 million.[10] This amount is 1.5 to 3 times the estimated marginal cost of the long form in the context of a redesigned census that uses sampling for nonresponse follow-up ($200 to $400 million). (Sampling for nonresponse follow-up in the census would also increase the sampling errors of small-area estimates, although it is not clear by how much.)

The $615 million estimate relies on a large number of assumptions—some rather severe. To reproduce the estimate, we use the following cost factors derived from Alexander (1994a) (see below for details):

Cost Factor	Monthly Cost (millions)
Mailout of questionnaires	$1.48
Telephone follow-up	0.96
Personal follow-up, "regular" areas	1.19
Personal follow-up, very rural areas	0.68
Fixed costs	0.83
Total costs per month	5.14
Total costs per decade	$616.80 (rounded to $615)

This estimate assumes a total of 250,000 questionnaires are mailed out each month and 135,000 are returned, at a cost per response of $11, for a total cost of $1.48 million per month. (The estimated number of mailed back questionnaires represents a mail return rate of 60 percent of occupied housing units, assuming that 10 percent of addresses to which questionnaires are sent, or 25,000 units, turn out to be vacant.)

The estimate further assumes there are 115,000 attempted telephone follow-ups (250,000 housing units minus 135,000 mail returns), of which 50,400 respond, at $19 per response, for a total cost of $0.96 million per month. (The estimated telephone response rate is based on several assumptions: 25,000 of the 115,000 addresses are vacant units with no telephone; of the remaining 90,000 occupied units, telephone numbers are located for about 65 percent, and, of these, about 85 percent respond.)

After mail return and telephone follow-up, 39,600 households remain. Personal follow-up for these households is conducted on a sample basis: in 85 percent of areas ("regular" areas), the sampling rate is 1 in 3; in the remaining very rural areas, the sampling rate is 1 in 5 (for an overall sampling rate of about 31 percent). The estimated 25,000 vacant units are followed up in the same way. The cost to attempt a personal interview in regular areas is $65, and the cost to attempt a personal interview in very rural areas is $350 (because of higher travel costs).[11] In total, personal follow-up is attempted in one-third of the cases in regular areas (11,200 households plus 7,100 vacant units) at a unit cost of $65, or $1.19 million per month. In very rural areas, personal follow-up is attempted in one-fifth of the cases (1,200 households plus 750 vacant units) at a unit cost of $350, or $0.68 million per month.

Finally, the estimate includes $0.83 million per month of (unspecified) fixed costs. This estimate amounts to 16 percent of total monthly costs.

In summary, the survey design for continuous measurement assumes the following approximate distribution for the original 225,000 households (leaving aside the 25,000 vacant units): 60 percent respond to the mail survey, 22 percent respond to the telephone follow-up, 6 percent are contacted by personal visit, and the remaining 12 percent are not contacted. After all of the follow-up is carried out as specified, there are still some 27,200 households of the 225,000 selected (or 12 percent) that are left as nonrespondents by survey design (i.e., of the 39,600 households that are nonrespondents after the telephone follow-up, only 12,400 are sent for personal interview follow-up).

The total monthly cost for continuous measurement, under the scenario just outlined, is $5.14 million. Over 10 years, the continuous measurement operation would cost about $615 million (rounding to the estimate provided by Alexander to the panel). The intensity of operations under this proposal corresponds to one of the contemplated truncated census designs with sampling for nonresponse follow-up for which the marginal cost of the long form is estimated at $200 to $400 million. Hence, the estimated costs for continuous measurement are 1.5 to 3 times the estimated marginal cost of the long form under a similar design. Furthermore, as noted above and discussed below, we believe there are missing elements for which cost information is needed. Overall, we believe that a realistic estimate of the costs of the continuous measurement is likely to be higher than the estimates developed to date.

Missing Cost Data

To prepare a more complete estimate of the costs of continuous measurement would require more careful consideration of several questions and issues:

• What cost components does the assumed cost of $11 per completed mail interview include? This estimate, which seems unrealistically low, must cover paper costs, printing the questionnaires, printing envelopes, logistics (getting the questionnaires to the right places both on their way out and on their way back), postal costs for mailout and mailback, checking in the questionnaires, training staff to edit the questionnaires, data entry, computer editing, and handling of edit rejects.

• What is the cost to maintain the master address file, block by block, for every quarter for a 10-year period at a level of coverage completeness commensurate with that achieved by the long form embedded in the census? Also, what is the cost to deal with rural addresses that are not yet in city-style format?

• What is the net cost increase required to maintain a continuously updated geographic referencing system, linked to the master address file, for a 10-year period compared to the one-time updating work involved in the census?

• What cost components are included in the estimate of fixed costs, which amount to 16 percent of total costs? Specifically, what is the cost in maintaining a headquarters staff for continuous measurement over a 10-year period? Other than headquarters staff, what are the other fixed costs for continuous measurement for a 10-year period?

•   What is the cost if initial mail response rates are different than those projected? The Census Bureau estimates assume a 60 percent mail return rate from occupied housing units, which compares with a 70 percent mail return rate for the census long form. The latter rate was achieved with all the intense publicity and sense of legitimacy that can only derive from a national census. What is the evidence that a continuing survey would achieve a response as high as 60 percent? (In this regard, it would be useful to compare the response rates with other mail surveys conducted by the Census Bureau.)

According to Alexander (1994b), the assumed 60 percent mail return rate is based in part on results from the ALFE experiment, which suggest that such a rate could be obtained by improving the questionnaire package and the mailing process (e.g., having a prenotice letter, a reminder card, and a user-friendly questionnaire). Such improvements, however, would apply to the long form as well as to a continuing survey. In other words, an appropriate cost comparison must build in realistic assumptions about the response to a continuing survey that is not conducted under census conditions vis-à-vis the response that is obtained from a comparably designed long form as part of the census.

•   What is the cost associated with the operation of finding telephone numbers for 115,000 households each month for a 10-year period in order to contact households that did not return their questionnaire? Telephone numbers are also needed for households that mailed back but did not fully fill out their questionnaire; presumably, the questionnaire will ask for a telephone number for follow-up purposes. If the costs to locate telephone numbers are built into the unit cost of completed telephone interviews, what are those built-in costs?

•   What is the cost associated with attempted telephone calls that result in a telephone nonresponse? In the Census Bureau's calculations, telephone costs are computed as a unit telephone interview cost multiplied by the number of completed telephone interviews.

•   What is the cost of extra calls or other costs incurred due to edit failures (missing or inconsistent responses to questionnaire items), other than those built into the unit costs per completed mail return, telephone, or personal interview?

•   Finally, what are the costs associated with data processing and dissemination?

Other Cost Savings

Taking the Census Bureau cost estimates at face value, the costs of a continuous measurement system with a sample size of 250,000 housing units per month, when compared with the marginal cost of the long form executed with the use of truncation and sampling for nonresponse follow-up, leave a difference of $215 to $415 million to be made up through other savings. (This range is $615 million for the full-cycle costs of continuous measurement minus the estimated marginal cost of $200 to $400 million for the long form under a comparable design.)

One suggestion (see Alexander, 1994b) is that continuous measurement would reduce the costs of compiling the master address file for the census. The marginal costs to the continuous measurement scheme for updating the master address file throughout the decade are unknown. It is the panel's understanding that these costs are not currently included in the continuous measurement proposal. Moreover, little is known about the improved quality of the master address file that would be gained by using continuous measurement interviewing staff to check and update local-area address lists. Estimates of cost savings from the continuous updating of the master address file are speculative at this moment.

The data obtained by continuous measurement could also prove useful for existing surveys and estimates programs in a number of ways that cut costs. For example, continuous measurement data could provide a more efficient means of designing surveys of rare populations, by reducing the need for expensive screening surveys to identify eligible respondents.

All of these potential benefits of continuous measurement for the statistical system should be investigated carefully. However, at this stage, estimates of savings are highly speculative, and the likelihood that such savings could make up all or a significant fraction of the difference between the full-cycle costs of continuous measurement and the savings from dropping the long form must be viewed with skepticism.

Data Quality

Another important aspect of evaluating a continuous measurement system in comparison to the long form concerns data quality. In terms of sampling errors, the plan for continuous measurement that we have just reviewed will produce estimates for small geographic areas (when data are cumulated) that have sampling errors about 25 percent higher than the long form in the context of the 1990 census methodology. The sampling errors may be about the same as the long form in a redesigned census that uses truncation and sampling for nonresponse follow-up.

Some analysts anticipate that data quality in terms of nonsampling error (e.g., item nonresponse, reporting errors of various kinds) would be improved in a continuous measurement system over the long form and hence that the mean squared error (combining sampling and nonsampling error) would be no worse or even better. The assumption is that a continuous measurement system would achieve quality improvements because of the use of experienced interviewers and supervisors and generally the ability to monitor data collection in a more effective manner than can be achieved in the compressed and hectic schedule of the census.

It may well be that more experienced interviewers will improve the quality of the data obtained by telephone and personal follow-up. Such improvements could be important in light of evidence about data-quality problems with long forms (and short forms) that are obtained by census enumerators (see Appendix L).

On one important dimension of quality, however, completeness of within-household coverage, continuous measurement is likely to perform worse than the census long form. It is well known that household surveys rarely cover the population as well as the decennial census (see, e.g., Shapiro and Kostanich, 1988). For example, even after adjustment for nonresponse, the March Current Population Survey and the Survey of Income and Program Participation typically cover only 80 to 85 percent of black men and 90 to 95 percent of other people when compared with unadjusted census-based population estimates (i.e., estimates that have not been adjusted for the undercount in the census itself; see Citro and Kalton, 1993:Table 3-12).[12] Alexander (1993, 1994b) indicates that continuous measurement might do better than the Current Population Survey because it will include some features of the census, such as questions designed to improve within-household coverage. However, we believe that a major reason for improved coverage in the census relative to household surveys is the widespread and intense publicity and sense of legitimacy associated with the census, which cannot be replicated for continuous measurement (or other) surveys.[13] Because of the much lower intensity of planned follow-up of continuous measurement, its much larger scale of operation, and its incomparably lower expected unit costs compared with other household surveys, we see no reason to expect that continuous measurement would have improved coverage. Moreover, a lower intensity of follow-up would disproportionately affect those with traditionally high coverage errors: minorities, poor people, and mobile and transient populations. These are groups for which census long-form data are heavily used.[14]

Conceptual Issues with Cumulated Data

If a continuous measurement system is adequately funded throughout the decade, it promises users the benefits of more frequent estimates for both small and large geographic areas than are available from the census long form. At the same time, the use of cumulated data, collected on a continuing basis, to produce small-area estimates poses a number of analytical problems that must be addressed and resolved.

• *Reference Periods and Recall.* One issue with continuous measurement is the reference period that is used for each month's survey. For annual income, for example, one could ask respondents each month to report their income for the preceding 12 months or to report their income for the previous calendar year.

The former option reduces the length of recall but specifies a reporting period (the preceding 12 months) that is not natural for respondents (except for interviews that fall in January of each year). In addition, the data would need to be adjusted in various ways to produce calendar-year estimates. The latter option lengthens the recall for most respondents considerably: people will be asked as late as December about their income in the preceding calendar year. Yet it is well known that it is best to ask about income fairly soon after the end of the year when people are preparing to file their income tax returns. This is what happens in the current census, in which questionnaires are mailed out in late March. Similar problems of reference period and recall can apply to employment status, occupation, and industry, and other important variables on the long form.

• *Analysis Problems.* Data that refer to 5-year annual averages have different analytic issues than those for a single year. How does one compare the 5-year average of two municipalities, one of which was growing strongly, the other declining strongly, during the period? What is the meaning of median income when some of the income data refer to the beginning and some to the end of the 5-year averaging period?

• *Residence Rules.* Given the mobility of the U.S. population, there is a problem of how one assigns population consistently to different areas in different months and years.

• *Changes in Content or Design.* Surveys (and censuses) need to be modified from time to time, with regard to question wording and aspects of their design. Such changes always pose a problem for continuity of time series. In the case of continuous measurement, the problem is more acute because the key estimates for small areas require cumulated data and hence depend on stability in all aspects of the design, questionnaire, and operation of the survey.

Relation to Other Household Surveys

Much of the nation's most important social and economic information is collected in household surveys conducted by the Census Bureau for other agencies in the federal statistical system. The sponsoring agencies and the Census Bureau have for years conducted extensive research to improve the quality of such surveys as the Current Population Survey, the Health Interview Survey, and the National Crime Survey, as well as the Survey of Income and Program Participation, which is sponsored by the Census Bureau itself. Substantial sums are spent on these surveys to obtain detailed high-quality information on such topics as employment and unemployment, income, and health conditions. The system of continuous measurement currently planned by the Census Bureau will overlap in content with many of those surveys.

A continuous measurement survey would not provide the same refined measures or the detailed subject content of these other surveys, but it would provide the small-area detail that they do not. For key summary indicators, such as the unemployment rate or the poverty rate, less refined estimates would also be available from continuous measurement for larger geographic areas—the nation, regions, states, and larger metropolitan areas. These estimates would inevitably be compared with estimates from the other major federal household surveys. The very large sample size for continuous measurement and the fact that estimates for large areas could be provided on an annual or even more frequent basis would, at first glance, make continuous measurement an attractive source for key estimates.[15] The much lower unit costs of continuous measurement compared with existing surveys could lead to pressures to cut back the scope of existing surveys in order to reduce the overall costs of the federal statistical system.

But there are a number of reasons to continue to require information from current surveys. First, estimates from continuous measurement are likely to have much larger nonsampling errors than are estimates from the other surveys, given the crudeness of the mail questionnaire that must be used for continuous measurement. Moreover, some surveys like the Current Population Survey, which provide data widely used in macroeconomic analysis, are specifically designed to capture month-to-month fluctuations, a characteristic that would not be possessed by the continuous measurement survey. Finally, little is known about the quality of the data to be collected through continuous measurement and the manner in which those data compare to estimates from the existing household surveys. The collection procedures for continuous measurement, based on a mail survey with telephone and some personal interview follow-up for nonresponse, differ markedly from the personal interview and telephone collection with structured questionnaires used in the existing household surveys. Past research suggests that the nonsampling errors associated with self-enumeration in mail surveys are likely to be much larger than those in surveys conducted by personal visit or telephone.

We believe that the Census Bureau should develop methods for evaluating the quality of continuous measurement data compared with the other household surveys and for integrating estimates from continuous measurement with the other surveys before making any decision to proceed with implementation of a continuous measurement system. Otherwise, there is the prospect of competing estimates for key statistics without knowledge of how to interpret or reconcile them. The work that is needed on methods of integrating continuous measurement with other surveys in effect involves a complete redesign of the nation's household survey system; this work will take time.

Alternative Ways to Provide Small-Area Data

In conducting research on the costs and benefits of continuous measurement, it is important to broaden that research to examine the feasibility and cost-effectiveness of other means of obtaining more frequent small-area estimates.

Possible alternatives include expanding existing surveys, conducting a mid-decade census or large-scale survey, exploiting data from administrative records, or some combination of these approaches (see Chapter 8).

More broadly, it is important to consider competing uses within the federal statistical system for the additional funding that would otherwise be allotted to continuous measurement. In other words, if more complete estimates indicate, as it seems to us, that continuous measurement is likely to cost more than the savings from dropping the long form and other savings from integration with existing household surveys, then careful consideration should be given to alternative uses of that extra funding. The cost and benefits of a wider range of investments in the federal statistical system—whether to obtain more frequent small-area estimates by continuous measurement or by some other means or to meet other kinds of data needs—should be considered before deciding that continuous measurement is preferred.

Conclusions

For the short term, we conclude that it is not feasible for a continuous measurement system to replace the census as a means of collecting long-form type data. There are too many unanswered questions for which research is needed. Thus, credible estimates must be developed of the savings from dropping the long form (which we believe have been overestimated) and the costs of continuous measurement (which we believe have been underestimated). Also, many other issues remain to be addressed, such as data quality, conceptual issues of using cumulated data, the relationship of continuous measurement to existing household surveys, and the costs and benefits of continuous measurement compared with other methods for obtaining more frequent small-area data.

We do not believe that the needed research can be completed in time when decisions must be made about the content of the 2000 census. The Census Bureau has proposed a schedule for the development of continuous measurement that would lead to a dress rehearsal in 1997, with a decision at the end of that year on whether to drop the long form and proceed to implement continuous measurement beginning in 1998. Given all of the unresolved issues, we believe that this schedule is wholly unrealistic and that continuous measurement should therefore be ruled out as a replacement for the long form in 2000.

Conclusion 6.4 The panel concludes that the work to date on continuous measurement has overestimated the savings from dropping the long form, understated the cost of a continuous measurement system, and not sufficiently examined feasible alternatives for meeting the nation's needs for more timely long-form-type data at reasonable overall cost. We conclude that it will not be possible to complete the needed research in time to make the critical decisions

regarding the format of the 2000 census. We therefore do not recommend substituting continuous measurement for the long form in the 2000 census.

For the longer term, we support research on continuous measurement in the context of a broader program to evaluate alternatives for more frequent small-area data and how these alternatives could be integrated with existing household surveys. We encourage the Census Bureau, in cooperation with the other agencies of the federal statistical system, to undertake a comprehensive research program to evaluate the quality of the data that would be collected in continuous measurement; to design a new, modern, integrated system of household surveys; and to consider other sources of small-area estimates. This research, which has hardly begun, must be carried out before it is possible to effectively evaluate plans for a continuous measurement system.

Recommendation 6.2 The panel recommends that the Census Bureau broaden its research on alternatives for more frequent small-area data to encompass a wider range than continuous measurement, as currently envisaged. In that context, the Census Bureau should examine the cost-effectiveness of alternatives, the ways in which they meet user needs, and the manner in which continuous measurement or other alternatives could be integrated into the nation's system of household surveys. The research program should be carried out in cooperation with the federal statistical agencies that sponsor household surveys and should include evaluation of the quality of important data elements, the frequency and modes of data collection, and the manner in which results would be presented, as well as methods for introducing change over time.

CONCLUSIONS: CONTENT IN THE 2000 CENSUS

We have concluded that the long form is a cost-effective means to collect needed data for small areas and small population groups. The long form provides valuable information at reasonable marginal costs—which are likely to decrease with the redesign of the census process—and with little adverse effect on completeness of census coverage.

We have also concluded that there is no feasible alternative to including the long form in the 2000 census. This conclusion does not mean that there needs to be a long form as it existed in 1990: it may be possible, for example, to use matrix sampling to reduce the length of the form that is sent to any single household.

We see no prospect that a continuous measurement system can reasonably substitute for the long form in 2000. Such a system may ultimately prove advantageous, particularly for improving the frequency with which long-form content is obtained. But considerable added research and development must be undertaken before its use to replace the long form can be seriously considered. There is no likelihood in our view that the necessary research can be completed in time to make decisions about the 2000 census. Another possible alternative to the long form, administrative records, is not satisfactory at this time because no single record system (or feasible combination of systems) contains the needed information.

Hence, we recommend that the 2000 census include a sample survey that obtains the content associated with the census long form. The data can be obtained without jeopardizing the basic census operation and are vitally needed for important public policy purposes.

Recommendation 6.3 The panel recommends that the 2000 census include a large sample survey that obtains the data historically gathered through a long form.

NOTES

[1]The reason to use mail return rates (the proportion of forms mailed back from occupied housing units) rather than mail response rates (the proportion of forms mailed back from all housing units, including vacant units) is that the focus is on the effects of the long form on household behavior. Including vacant units in the denominator would overstate the extent to which the perceived burden of the long form induces households not to mail back their questionnaire. In contrast, the discussion of overall census costs and design in Chapter 5 used mail response rates because all units that need to be followed up, whether they turn out to be vacant or not, add costs.

[2]In the 1970 census the mail return rate was 87.8 percent for the short form and 85.5 percent for the long form, a difference of 2.3 percentage points. However, 1970 mail return rates are not strictly comparable with 1980 and 1990 rates because the 1970 mailout/mailback areas covered only 60 percent of the population compared with over 90 percent in 1980 and 1990 (see Appendix A).

[3]The micro form with a request for Social Security number had lower response rates than the micro form without this request, especially in areas that had low response rates in the 1990 census.

[4]The within-household nonmatch rates cited in the text are not the same as the within-household net undercount (because the nonmatch rates do not account for erroneous within-household enumerations, such as duplications).

[5]Also, coverage errors in the census that involve missing whole households or structures because they are not in the address list cannot be attributed to the type of form.

[6]The proposal is to test "nested" rather than matrix sampling as such; that is, the test will include a short form, an intermediate-length form with additional items, and a long form with all of the items on the intermediate-length form and some added items. However, it should be possible to use the results to simulate a matrix design that has two (or more) intermediate-length forms, each with some unique items as well as some items in common.

[7]Such a design is distinct from a rolling census, which would collect both short-form and long-form information over the course of the decade and not include a contemporaneous once-a-decade enumeration of the entire population; see Chapter 4.

[8]The Census Bureau is currently undertaking a program, at the request of Congress, to develop small-area intercensal poverty estimates; see Chapter 8.

[9]Many of these issues are raised in Alexander's papers (1993, 1994b), and a number of important issues are reviewed in documents prepared by the Bureau of the Census (1988a, 1988b) that evaluate two somewhat different versions of a proposed integrated system of area statistics that share some features with the proposed continuous measurement system.

[10]Alexander provided this estimate in communication with the panel. We were able to closely reproduce the estimate for the current proposed sample size of 250,000 housing units per month (see text) by using cost factors from Alexander (1994a:Attachment B), which provides detailed estimates for a continuous measurement survey with a somewhat smaller sample size of 233,000 housing units per month.

[11]The cost calculation shifts from completed interviews (in the case of mail and telephone responses) to attempted interviews in the case of personal visits. The assumption is that attempted but unsuccessful personal interviews do not save money since most of the cost is associated with making contact.

[12]Recent work by Shapiro et al. (1993) suggests that the difference between survey and census coverage is somewhat less pronounced when census over-counts are excluded from the comparison. Nonetheless, undercoverage in household surveys is significantly worse than in the census.

[13]One interesting question in this regard is whether response to the continuous measurement survey could be made mandatory like the census. Such a requirement could improve coverage, although it would represent a departure from current practice, in which household surveys are voluntary.

[14]Alexander (1994b:7) suggests that continuous measurement could make it possible to introduce corrective actions for such problems as poorer response in some areas (e.g., by assigning more effective interviewers or increasing the sampling rates in those areas).

[15]Some existing surveys (e.g., the Current Population Survey) publish monthly estimates; others publish quarterly or annual estimates. Current estimates from major federal household surveys are limited, however, to states and major metropolitan areas. The Census Bureau's plans for the continuous mea-

surement system call for quarterly processing of the data with estimates released 6 months after the end of a quarter. In addition, the Census Bureau plans to release annual data for all urban areas with 250,000 or greater population. However, user interest could lead to pressures to increase the frequency and timeliness of publication.

7

Data on Race and Ethnicity

Historically, the decennial census has included questions on race and ethnicity, although the specific questions asked and the categories for tabulating the answers have changed every 10 years. These changes have occurred because of shifts in the racial and ethnic makeup of the population, changes in social attitudes and political concerns, and the evolving needs of the federal government for data. The growing racial and ethnic diversity of the American population, changing attitudes about race and ethnicity, and the increasing use of census data have converged to make census questions on race and ethnicity the focus of attention and controversy. Those questions now play a special role in debates over census content, census methods, and public cooperation.

The Civil Rights Act of 1964 and the Voting Rights Act of 1965, with extensions, amendments, and court interpretations, have expanded the need for race and ethnicity data for all levels of geography, including individual blocks. These data are required for congressional and state election redistricting, for enforcement of federal, state, and local civil rights statutes, for allocation of funds and administration of programs at every level of government, and for many related purposes (see Appendix C). The decennial census is currently the primary source of race and ethnicity data to fulfill these many legal requirements. Without a change in the legal framework, the required race and ethnicity data need to be collected in the census. Coupled with survey information and data from administrative records, census data also satisfy other legislative and programmatic requirements for data on race and ethnicity.

Improvements in the measurement of errors in census data have fostered awareness in recent decades of the differential net undercounting of racial and ethnic minorities. Since the mid-1960s, this increased knowledge about the nation's policies and programs and their importance in these undercounts have contributed to increasing efforts and spending to improve the census. Data on race and ethnicity are involved, directly and indirectly, in most of the concern and contention about costs and quality of the 2000 census.

Two difficult issues have arisen with respect to the need for data on race and ethnicity in the census (see Statistics Canada and the Bureau of the Census, 1993, for an international review of census data on ethnicity).[1] One is the growing public pressure for revising and expanding race and ethnicity classifications in the census as the nation becomes more diverse. The other is increasing recognition of the fluidity and accompanying ambiguity of racial and ethnic identities for many people. These issues have been brought to the fore with the reliance of the census on self-identification of race and ethnicity, which began in the 1970 census. Self-identification has been viewed as an improvement over the historically discriminatory methods of designation, such as blood quantum and observer identification. These older methods carried the presumptions that a certain amount of ancestry determined a person's racial or ethnic identity, that an observer could identify a persons's race and ethnicity, that only one identification per respondent is appropriate, and that a person has the same identity in all situations in his or her lifetime. These presumptions are increasingly problematic with self-identification, especially at a time of growing heterogeneity of the American population, due not only to more diverse immigration but also to increased interracial and interethnic marriages. Moreover, self-identification in the census is not the same as in other surveys or on various types of forms. In the census, it is typically one member of the household who identifies his or her own race and the race of all other members of the household. The design of future censuses must take account of these issues.

The panel believes that underlying these important issues is a much more basic concern regarding the role of race and ethnicity data. In particular, there are inconsistencies between race and ethnicity categories required for legislative and administrative purposes and the census categories of race and ethnicity, which were designed for statistical purposes. Courts have already begun to litigate the classifications because of the discrepancy between the different conceptual approaches of the law and statistics. The legal approach views individuals as potential members of protected classes, as defined by statutes and judicial decisions. The statistical approach reflects an effort to provide a comprehensive demographic profile with data that may extend beyond legal considerations. The two approaches must be reconciled before the technical questions of questionnaire design, question placement (short or long form), and labeling of groups can be solved.

HISTORICAL CONTEXT

For over 200 years there have been both change and continuity in race and ethnicity data in the United States. The number of items related to race and ethnicity has increased and contracted over time as new populations have entered the United States or as selected populations have become important for policy purposes, such as a change in civil status. Table 7.1 displays the number and types of categories used in the race item of the census from 1850 to 1990. (For a discussion of the categories, see Mann, 1994.) An item on race has been included in every census since 1790, when the population was distinguished for apportionment purposes as the sum of free persons, Indians not taxed, and three-fifths of other persons. Article 1, Section 2, of the Constitution mandated the three-way race classification: within the context of race, free persons were understood to be whites; the persons counted as three-fifths were slaves and synonymous with blacks. This use of race data continued in censuses through the Civil War. The practice of the "one-drop rule"—which defined a person as black who had even one black ancestor—served to reinforce the identity of a person with any nonwhite ancestry as nonwhite.

The entry of new populations has motivated items related to ethnicity and national origin, which have been included in each census since 1850.[2] The questions first pertained to immigrants of European origins who were distinguished from the native-born white population. They were identified by several items related to nativity, parental birthplace, immigration, citizenship status, language status, and time of arrival in the United States. In contrast, immigrants of Asian origins were categorized as "aliens ineligible for citizenship," and they were counted in the race item as Chinese (beginning in 1870) and Japanese (beginning in 1890). By the 1890 census, the race item had expanded to eight categories: white, black, mulatto, quadroon, octoroon, Chinese, Japanese, and (American) Indian. The categories were a combination of color, tribal status, and Asian national origin. There was no single ethnicity item: in addition to previously asked items on birthplace, parents' birthplace, and citizenship status, the 1890 census included two language items: ability to speak English and mother tongue. It also included an item on number of years in the United States.

Classification by race and ethnicity became more complex in the twentieth century as more items were used to identify residents who enjoyed fewer rights than the native-born white citizenry. The race question continued to be characterized by both changing and continuing categories of color, tribal status, and Asian origins. Additional Asian categories were included to record the increased immigration from Asian countries that resulted from implementation of the 1965 Immigration and Nationality Act (which abolished the national origins system of the National Origins Act of 1924, as well as the Asiatic barred zone of the Immigration Act of 1917). Also during the twentieth century, several categories have been eliminated. For example, the Mexican category was used only once, in the race item of 1930, although it has resurfaced in the Hispanic origin item since 1970. Mixed-race categories, such as mulatto and part Hawaiian, were used for only brief periods, and none is presently used in the census.

Items related to ethnicity have also increased and decreased over time, and the exact wording of items has varied. Items have continued to revolve primarily around immigration, nativity, and origins. The 1920 census (which preceded the National Origins Act of 1924, which effectively restricted immigration from Europe) included 10 items related to ethnicity. In the post-1965 period, an important change in ethnic classification was the use of self-identification items to obtain data on ethnicity. This began with the 1970 census, when the Hispanic origin item was introduced. In the 1980 census, an open-ended ancestry item for all groups was included in the long form (McKenney and Cresce, 1993).

The race, Hispanic origin, and related ethnicity items on the census since 1970 are shown in Table 7.2 for the short form and Table 7.3 for the long form. These items are the result of changing policy and programmatic needs for race and ethnicity data and special research programs of the Census Bureau to test and improve the enumeration of racial minorities and persons of Hispanic origin in a mail-based census. The Spanish/Hispanic-origin item was first included in the 1970 census, and it was tested and refined in subsequent censuses (see Table 7.3). As the tables show, since 1970, there has been a proliferation of categories or subcategories to the question on race.

The write-in items in the 1990 census elicited more than 300 race responses, approximately 600 American Indian tribes, 70 different Hispanic-origin groups, and more than 600 ancestry groups. In addition to reporting identification with a specific racial group, respondents could indicate an "other" race identification in two ways: (1) by checking a circle on the questionnaire to indicate an "other" race, or (2) by writing a race in a box for "other races." Written "other race" responses numbered more than 9.8 million in 1990, including respondents who marked only the "other race" circle without specifying a race; of these, over 97 percent also indicated Hispanic origin. There were approximately 2.5 million write-ins to the "other race" category identified during the early automated coding and editing of the race item. In all, 41 percent were reclassified to one of the major race categories (white, black, American Indian/Alaskan Native, or Asian/Pacific Islander) during this automated process and thus were not included in the final counts for "other race."

CURRENT REQUIREMENTS

Foremost among the legal requirements for race and ethnicity data is the Voting Rights Act of 1965. As initially passed and subsequently amended (in 1970, 1975, 1982 and 1992), the Voting Rights Act prohibits states and political

TABLE 7.1 Census Race Categories, 1850-1990

Year	White	Black/Negro	Native Peoples	Chinese	Japanese	Other Asian or Pacific Islander	Other
1850[a]		Black, mulatto					
1860[a]		Black, mulatto	Indian[b]				
1870	White	Black, mulatto	Indian	Chinese			
1880	White	Black, mulatto	Indian	Chinese			
1890	White	Black, mulatto, quadroon, octoroon	Indian	Chinese	Japanese		
1900	White	Black	Indian	Chinese	Japanese		
1910	White	Black, mulatto	Indian	Chinese	Japanese		Other (+ write in)
1920	White	Black, mulatto	Indian	Chinese	Japanese	Filipino, Hindu, Korean	Other (+ write in)
1930[c]	White	Negro	Indian	Chinese	Japanese	Filipino, Hindu, Korean	Other races, spell out in full
1940	White	Negro	Indian	Chinese	Japanese	Filipino, Hindu, Korean	(Other races, spell out in full)
1950	White	Negro	American Indian	Chinese	Japanese	Filipino	(Other race-spell out)
1960	White	Negro	American Indian	Chinese	Japanese	Filipino, Hawaiian, part Hawaiian, etc.	
1970[d]	White	Negro or black	Indian (American)	Chinese	Japanese	Filipino, Hawaiian, Korean	Other (print race)
1980	White	Black or Negro	Indian (American), Eskimo, Aleut	Chinese	Japanese	Filipino, Korean, Vietnamese, Asian Indian, Hawaiian, Guamanian, Samoan	Other (specify)
1990	White	Black or Negro	Indian (American), Eskimo, Aleut	Chinese	Japanese	Filipino, Hawaiian, Korean, Vietnamese, Asian Indian, Samoan, Guamanian, other Asian or Pacific Islander	Other race

*a*In 1850 and 1860, free persons were enumerated on the form for "free inhabitants"; slaves were enumerated on the form designated for "slave inhabitants." For the free schedule, the instructions told the enumerators: "In all cases where the person is white leave the space blank in the column marked 'Color.'" For the slave schedule, the listed categories were black (B) or mulatto (M).

*b*Although this category was not listed on the census form, the instructions read:

5. Indians.—Indians not taxed are not to be enumerated. The families of Indians who have renounced tribal rule, and who under State or Territorial laws exercise the rights of citizens, are to be enumerated. In all such cases write "Ind." opposite their names, in column 6, under heading "Color."

9. Color.— Under heading 6, entitled "Color," in all cases where the person is white leave the space blank; in all cases where the person is black without admixture insert the letter "B;" if a mulatto, or of mixed blood, write "M;" if an Indian, write "Ind." It is very desirable to have these directions carefully observed.

*c*In 1930, the census questionnaires included "Mexican" as a race category.

*d*In 1970, on questionnaires used in Alaska, the categories "Aleut" and "Eskimo" were substituted for "Hawaiian" and "Korean."

TABLE 7.2 Race and Ethnicity Questions on the Short-Form Census Questionnaire, 1970, 1980, and 1990

1970 COLOR OR RACE	1980 IS THIS PERSON	1990 RACE
White	White	White
Negro or Black	Black or Negro	Black or Negro
Indian (Amer): print tribe	Japanese	Indian (Amer): print tribe
Japanese	Chinese	Eskimo
Chinese	Filipino	Aleut
Filipino	Korean	Asian or Pacific Islander:
Hawaiian	Vietnamese	Chinese
Korean	Indian (Amer): print tribe	Filipino
Other: print race	Asian Indian	Hawaiian
	Hawaiian	Korean
	Guamanian	Vietnamese
	Samoan	Japanese
	Eskimo	Asian Indian
	Aleut	Samoan
	Other: specify	Guamanian
		Other Asian or Pacific Islander: print race
		Other race: print race
	IS THIS PERSON OF SPANISH/ HISPANIC ORIGIN OR DESCENT?	IS THIS PERSON OF SPANISH/ HISPANIC ORIGIN OR DESCENT?
	No (not Spanish/Hispanic)	No (not Spanish/Hispanic)
	Yes, Mexican, Mexican-Amer., Chicano	Yes, Mexican, Mexican-Am., Chicano
	Yes, Puerto Rican	Yes, Puerto Rican
	Yes, Cuban	Yes, Cuban
	Yes, Other Spanish/Hispanic	Yes, Other Spanish/Hispanic print one group

NOTE: There were no Spanish/Hispanic-origin questions on the 1970 short form.

TABLE 7.3 Ethnicity and Related Questions on the Long-Form Census Questionnaire, 1970, 1980, and 1990

1970	1980	1990
15 percent sample Where was this person born? What country was his father born in? What country was his mother born in? What language, other than English, was spoken in this person's home when he was a child? **5 percent sample** Where was this person born? Is this person's origin or descent Mexican; Puerto Rican; Cuban; Central or South American, Other Spanish; No, none of these Is this person naturalized? When did he come to the United States to stay?	In what state or foreign country was this person born? Is this person a naturalized citizen of the United States? When did this person come to the United States to stay? Does this person speak a language other than English at home? What is this language? How well does this person speak English? What is this person's ancestry?	In what U.S. state or foreign country was this person born? Is this person a citizen of the United States? When did this person come to the United States to stay? Does this person speak a language other than English at home? What is this language? How well does this person speak English? What is this person's ancestry or ethnic origin?

subdivisions from imposing or applying any "standard, practice or procedure" for voting that will result in the abridgment of the right to vote "on account of race or color" or because a citizen "is a member of a language minority." Congress passed the legislation in 1965 to implement the guarantees of rights—particularly voting rights—in the Fourteenth and Fifteenth amendments to the Constitution. The definition of "race or color" was left implicit in the law; in practice, it meant "black" and "white" or "white" and "nonwhite." Congress added the coverage of "language minorities" in 1975 and specifically defined them as "persons who are American Indian, Asian American, Alaskan Native, or of Spanish heritage." Redistricting plans that "dilute" the votes of the "members of the protected class" come under the scrutiny of the law. In 1980 and 1990, therefore, state legislatures prepared redistricting plans that would not "dilute" the votes of minorities. There has been extensive litigation on these issues.

The Census Bureau has provided the population tabulations at the block level for the redistricting plans and their challengers. However, the Census Bureau collects these data under the authority of P.L. 94-171 (passed in December 1975), which does not specifically mention race and ethnicity tabulations; it was designed to provide timely total population counts for small areas to states and localities for redistricting purposes. The addition of the race and Hispanic-origin tabulations from the short form in 1980 was an administrative decision, in response to requests by the Department of Justice and state and local governments. The categories reported are those promulgated in the federal standard for race and ethnicity data, OMB Statistical Directive 15 (1977), which included four race groups: black, white, American Indian or Alaskan Native, and Asian or Pacific Islander; and one ethnic group, Hispanic origin. In 1990, race and Hispanic-origin data were cross-tabulated in the P.L. 94-171 file, and voting-age data were also reported.

Barring changes to the Voting Rights Act, the 2000 census will be required to provide race and ethnicity data for small geographic areas for the redistricting process. There are two challenges facing the Census Bureau in providing such data. The first is guaranteeing accurate and precise coverage of the minority and majority populations. Since the differential undercount of racial minorities is well known, the census without correction is itself a flawed standard and cannot provide accurate small-area data. The differential undercount has been the basis of lawsuits against the Census Bureau since 1970. The Department of Commerce has defended the Census Bureau against such lawsuits by noting that before 1990 there was no acceptable or tested method of distributing the known national undercount to small areas. Even in 1990, when an extensive evaluation was conducted to be able to adjust for the differential undercount, the accuracy of the adjustments for small areas was questioned.

In planning for the 2000 census, one of the major goals of the Census Bureau is to reduce the differential undercount. The Census Bureau plans to accomplish this through a series of fundamental changes in the way the census is conducted. One of these changes is to target potentially hard-to-count areas in advance so that special enumeration procedures will be used for the census there. Another change is the concept of an integrated one-number census, in which statistical estimation for missed persons will be directly incorporated in the census counts that are officially released. With such changes, it may be possible for Census Bureau to make inroads in correcting for the known differential undercount in the P.L. 94-171 redistricting file.

The second challenge the Census Bureau faces in providing race and ethnicity data for small geographic areas is the classification of various groups, which is currently mandated by OMB Directive 15, "Race and Ethnic Standards for Federal Statistics and Administrative Reporting," issued in 1977. Prior to that directive, federal agencies used their own categorization policies, leading to a recognition by several agencies of the need for a uniform set of race and ethnicity categories.

The OMB directive requires that race and ethnicity data, for both statistical and administrative purposes, be collected for a minimum set of categories: American Indian or Alaskan Native, Asian or Pacific Islander, black, Hispanic, and white. The directive explicitly allows the collection of additional detailed race and ethnicity categories, so long as they can be aggregated into the basic categories. Agencies should not, however, combine data from one major category with data from any of the other major categories. Individuals are not permitted multiple responses; however, a special exemption is made for the census to collect an "other" response.

Directive 15 has remained unchanged since it took effect in 1977. In 1993, the House Subcommittee on Census, Statistics, and Postal Personnel, chaired by Congressman Thomas C. Sawyer, held four informational hearings on Directive 15. At the July 1993 hearing, the Office of Management and Budget testified that the current administration planned to reconsider revision of the directive.

Directive 15 sets the framework for race and ethnicity data collected in the census, although the census has collected more detailed categories in the 1980 and 1990 censuses than required. Revisions to Directive 15 in the next few years would affect the 2000 census, possibly requiring additional major race and ethnicity categories, changing the specific groups within the major categories, and requiring the use of multiple responses.

In recent years, social scientists, some advocacy groups, and other data users have questioned the conceptual foundations behind the basic categories reported in OMB Statistical Directive 15 and hence the P.L. 94-171 tabulation. Advocacy groups have raised questions about including separate or new classifications for persons of multiracial parentage, for Native Americans, and for ethnic groups such as Arabs and people from the Middle East. The Census Bureau has also been asked by data users and service providers to furnish more data on smaller racial and ethnic groups for small geographical areas for program planning and evaluation, health studies, and fund allocation. To date, few if any challenges have questioned the use of the Statistical Directive 15 categories for the P.L. 94-171 files, although this might be a future implication of the issues raised about the directive. Thus far, the Census Bureau response has been to list subdivisions of the Statistical Directive 15 major categories or to accommodate other groups in three "other" write-in categories in the census: other race, other Asian and Pacific Islander, and other Spanish/Hispanic. In response, OMB has undertaken a major reconsideration of Directive 15 in consultation with a wide range of federal and nonfederal data users.

Census Bureau evaluation of the quality of race and ethnicity data suggests continuing classification problems (see Appendix K; McKenney et al., 1993; Cresce et al., 1992). For example, the Hispanic-origin item continues to have the highest allocation rate among short-form items. About 40 percent of Hispanics identified themselves as "other race" in the 1990 census question on race, which suggests that many respondents perceive "Hispanic" as a race rather than an ethnicity category. Moreover, as the Hispanic population has grown and as Hispanics increasingly identify themselves as "other race," this category has become larger than some "other race" categories.

Self-identification for race, Hispanic origin, and ancestry questions means that responses are based on self-perception and therefore are subjective, but at the same time, by definition, whatever response is recorded is an accurate response. Yet self-identification for many people is based on context; people have multiple identities that may differ by context. The political context for the current census categories—whether there are positive, neutral, or negative effects to identifying with a certain group—is only one context for identification. Race is a more salient concept for historically disadvantaged groups, particularly descendants of African American slaves. First-generation immigrants have tended to identify with their country of origin, though their children, in the second generation, have more complex patterns of identity. Even among whites, flux in identification is noted by inconsistency in reporting ancestry at different points in time. Waters (1990) suggests that many people have a range of choices and options in how they choose to identify. The increased number of people identified as American Indian and their high intermarriage rates, as well as the substantial intermarriage rates for several Asian and Pacific Islander and Hispanic populations, suggest that racial and ethnic identity is becoming more complex and may shift for a person over time as well as in social context. Racial and ethnic identity is likely to grow more complex as the pool of people with identity options increases. The high reporting of "European" as a first ancestry by American Indians and several Asian and Pacific Islanders groups may already reflect attempts to report on multiracial and multiethnic identities.

The purposes of collecting race and ethnicity data provide another context for self-identification. A person may respond differently to the same wording of questions, for example, when asked in the census and when asked in a job application form. Ivan Fellegi of Statistics Canada (private communication) provides an example of this sensitivity to racial self-identification. Self-reports of race were obtained from the Canadian Public Service Commission, the federal government's central personnel management agency, and compared with reports to the 1991 Census of Canada and to an employee survey. With results directly compared, individuals appear to make rather different reports of their racial status in the nonthreatening, anonymous context of the census: in the Canadian data, individuals were more likely to report minority racial status in the census than in the other two information systems.

Questionnaire design also can provide the opportunity for variations of self-reporting. It is clear that the actual wording of race and ethnicity questions can affect responses. For example, having an explicit box to check for Mexican origin self-identification results in more persons who classify themselves as Mexican than does an open-ended question to which persons can write in the classification "Mexican."[3] In the census, the race, Hispanic origin, and ancestry items may be viewed as variations of the same or similar concept, the overlap of concepts, or as different but related concepts depending on sequence, wording, and instructions. People who view them as the same or similar concepts provide consistent answers (or respond to one item and omit the others as redundant). In contrast, people who view the items as different may provide multiple responses.

On the basis of 1980 and 1990 census data, researchers have found that combinations of the race, Hispanic origin, and ancestry items yield different results in a person's self-identity, including: (1) people with the same racial and ancestry identity (e.g., white, German), (2) people with a race different from ancestry (e.g., African American, Irish), (3) people with one race and multiple ancestries (e.g., white, English, Russian), and (4) people with multiple racial identities (e.g., white, Vietnamese). As we noted above, the expansion of categories and of different combinations by which people self-identify is a response to immigration and interracial and interethnic unions, as well as changes in social attitudes, political pressures, and the evolving needs of the federal government for race and ethnicity data. This proliferation increases the possibility of fluidity and inconsistency of race and ethnicity reporting over time, as people may identify differently at different times or for different purposes.

FUTURE REQUIREMENTS

The problems of classification are likely to get much more complex as the ethnic and racial character of the American people changes. First, the official categories are themselves a product of the legislative debates of the 1970s, before the waves of immigration of recent years and the emergence of significant interracial marriage patterns and the resulting new generation of children with identities in two or more groups. Current public debate, as manifested in congressional and OMB hearings on Statistical Directive 15, has focused on the proliferation of new and finer classifications. There are, however, statistical and operational concerns that caution against large expansion of the number of categories. For new classifications, the completeness of coverage and accuracy of the national counts will be unknown, making it difficult to develop measures of undercount. The reliability of these counts from finer classification, especially for small geographical areas, will be questionable. Furthermore, small groups are not usually evenly distributed geographically but are quite concentrated, raising questions not just of reliability but of confidentiality and privacy (i.e., Census Bureau tabulation guidelines require that there is a minimum number of people in tabulated cells to protect the confidentiality of respondents). Operationally, the costs and burdens of collection, processing, and presentation of data about many ethnic and racial groups are significant. Although the expansion of race and ethnicity classifications is a recognition of the complexity of the racial and ethnic composition of the American population, the proliferation of categories may not be a practical solution.

More broadly, a close reading of the language of the Voting Rights Act and OMB Statistical Directive 15 reveals a conceptual confusion in categorization. The 1975 amendment to the Voting Rights Act defines "persons who are American Indian, Asian American, Alaskan Native or of Spanish heritage" as "language minorities." Directive 15 defines American Indians and Asian and Pacific Islanders as "racial" groups, regardless of language facility in English. The census questionnaire is in accord with Directive 15 and considers American Indians and Asian and Pacific Islanders, along with blacks and whites, as racial groups; it further includes tribal and subgroup delineations of these smaller populations. Similarly, the question on Spanish or Hispanic origin defines an "ethnic" identity. It does not measure language ability. Federal courts have begun to consider these issues in voting rights cases. In *Garza v. Los Angeles County Board of Supervisors*, expert witnesses testified that not all those who identified themselves as of Spanish origin in the 1990 census should be regarded as falling under the covered rubric of "persons of Spanish heritage," that is, a language minority (Grofman, 1992:218). Thus far, the courts have decided that self-identification places one in the group, so that "a response of Spanish origin on the census questionnaire" serves as the "defining characteristic of the covered population" (Grofman, 1992:218). The test of inclusion as a race or ethnicity classification would be an actual finding of a pattern of discrimination against a member of a protected class. However, since the current census question on race is not a question on language minority, but rather on racial or ethnic self-identity, future court challenges seem likely. Whatever the conceptual foundations should be, the census supports self-identification, implying that the census question must appear to be sensible and self-explanatory for respondents in terms of their own situation. For many Americans, multiple categories are a reality, irrespective of possible conceptual or legislative advantages for a univariate classification. It is probable that challenges to the current federal standards on race and ethnicity classification will become more serious in years to come and that the courts will challenge the Census Bureau to validate the conceptual foundations of race and ethnicity classifications.

CONCLUSIONS AND RECOMMENDATIONS

Because OMB Statistical Directive 15 is currently being reviewed, it seems prudent to continue research efforts to clarify the conceptual foundation of the classifications and to alert Congress to the conceptual confusion embedded in existing law and administrative procedures. As federal agencies and other data users have documented, the programmatic and policy considerations of the existing categories are important. What is problematic is being tied to these categories rigidly, especially as they may not fit current and future populations.

Conclusion 7.1 The panel concludes that there are inherent ambiguities to racial and ethnic status. We recognize that reporting of this status in the census has multiple meanings for respondents and that the context of reporting affects how people self-identify.

Conclusion 7.2 The panel concludes that the census questionnaire must be developed as a well-tested means for obtaining nationally useful data on race and ethnicity to meet constitutional and legally mandated federal requirements and for other legislative and program needs and informational purposes.

The growing diversity of the U.S. population, changes in the way people identify themselves, and variations in definitions of members of protected classes raise the fundamental question of whether current classifications are appropriate for the country's changing society and future legislative and other policy requirements. A research program on race and ethnicity for the 2000 census, which would now be starting very late in the planning cycle, can only begin to address some of these issues. A more extensive program of research on how persons identify themselves in terms of race and ethnicity is needed to promote meaningful classifications in a changing society. Such a program would include the extension of current, but limited, Census Bureau initiatives on cognitive research; testing of various combinations of the race, Hispanic-origin, and ancestry items; and testing for open-ended and multiple identifications. Allowing respondents to identify with more than one racial group, to report as multiracial, and to treat Hispanic origin as equivalent to a racial group may be more consistent with some respondents' self-perceptions, although it may be less consistent with other respondents' self-perceptions. Only systematic research can develop useful information on such issues.

Recommendation 7.1 The panel recommends that the Census Bu-

reau expand its examination and testing of race and ethnicity questions to provide comprehensive information on: (1) public understanding of the concepts and acceptability of questions, (2) compatibility among the several census items and the utility of
cross-tabulations, (3) the comparability of census data to race and
ethnicity data collected in other federal surveys or obtained from
administrative records, and (4) the quality of data for small areas
and specific groups. This research needs to be given a high priority
so that the results may be incorporated into the review of Statistical
Directive 15 currently being conducted by the Office of Management and Budget.

**Recommendation 7.2   The panel recommends that the Office of
Management and Budget issue a revision of Statistical Directive 15
sufficiently early to provide adequate time for planning and testing
for the 2000 census and coordinated implementation of changes by
all affected agencies.**

Needed planning activities include the review and redesign of respondent-
friendly forms, with special attention to the items on race and ethnicity. In
addition, because of the complexities involved, any proposed changes to these
items require consultation with affected groups and data users. Such consultation must occur prior to extensive tests as part of the planning cycle. Development of promotion and outreach programs for field tests also needs to be carried
out at this time, along with appropriate congressional review.

Any proposed changes of race and ethnicity items will have implications for
race and ethnicity data needed for statutory, legislative, and programmatic purposes that should be taken into consideration. These include drawing political
boundaries, funding allocations for various geographical levels, as well as the
quality of the data for small geographical areas and for such relatively small
racial and ethnic groups as American Indians.

NOTES

[1]Both Canada and the United States collect race and ethnicity data in their
censuses. About half of the countries of the world collect such data in their
censuses.

[2]Although the 1820 census contained a checkoff box or line pertaining to
foreign nationals, the use of that information is not clear; 1850 is the census date
usually cited by both historians and social scientists for the beginning of ethnic
items in the census.

[3]In 1990, the check-box resulted in more people responding to the Spanish/
Hispanic item and was significant for the Mexican-origin category only. This

relationship between check-box and write-ins did not hold for the write-ins to the Asian and Pacific Islander category in the race item: pre-1990 testing showed that more people provided Asian and Pacific Islander write-ins than reported in the check-boxes for the Asian and Pacific Islander groups.

8

Intercensal Small-Area Data

Small-area data are used for a variety of purposes, including the allocation of federal and state funds, public and private planning, determining the eligibility of a locality for funding or government programs, and scholarly research. The demand for accurate, timely, and consistent data for such areas—from counties to neighborhoods—has steadily increased as both public and private agencies have expanded and refined their uses of the data. State and local agencies use small-area data to monitor social conditions, such as unemployment, and to administer public services, such as selecting the locations of schools and public housing. The military use the data for recruitment purposes. Businesses use small-area data to formulate marketing strategies and to locate plants and stores.

The decennial census is currently the richest source of small-area data, but it provides this detail only once each decade, and it does not cover all topics and population subgroups with the accuracy and detail that data users would like. In addition, there are some kinds of data that are not collected efficiently in the census: data that require highly trained interviewers, long or complicated questionnaires, or from hard-to-identify populations. For example, data on homeless people or migratory and seasonal farmworkers are better collected through special surveys. Some major national surveys may provide accurate and timely information for the nation, but they usually provide detail for only a few large geographic areas. Consequently, users' needs for small-area information are met by the application of various estimation methods to census and survey data, but many of them use simplistic assumptions and out-of-date data sets.

The panel estimates, for example, that in fiscal 1989 $59 billion was distributed on the basis of 1980 census population data (see also Citro and Cohen,

1985). Poverty status in particular, especially among young children, is a major factor in the allocation of federal funds to states, counties, school districts, and other levels of local government. According to a recent report from the U.S. General Accounting Office (1990), 12 programs allocated more than $7.6 billion in fiscal 1989 on the basis of poverty data collected in the 1980 census. Of this total, education accounted for the largest share: some $4 billion was allocated in federal education funds through the use of census counts of school-age children in poverty.

Given the aging of census-based data over a decade and the possibility of substantial changes in both the specific characteristic under study and the relative standings of counties, cities, and other geographic entities, questions have been raised as to the effectiveness and equity of targeting funding allocations over time on the basis of the decennial census. The lack of up-to-date data with which to gauge changes in the size, composition, and distribution of the needy population between census years often complicates the efforts of program planners and administrators who are charged with carrying out programs to assist those most in need.

This chapter presents, first, a discussion of the needs for more frequent small-area data and past attempts to produce intercensal small-area data. The chapter then reviews current methods for producing small-area data, including an assessment of the major alternative methods. (For a discussion of the idea of a rolling census, see Chapter 4; for a discussion of continuous measurement, see Chapter 6). The third section examines in more detail one major source of information for producing small-area data, the use of administrative records. The final section discusses the use of a geographic reference system and address list for intercensal estimates.[1]

NEEDS FOR SMALL-AREA DATA

The problem of providing current estimates for small areas is not new. In 1972, for example, the enactment of revenue-sharing legislation called for the distribution of some $6 billion annually to states and local governments, under a formula that required current estimates of population and per capita income, as well as revenue tax effort, for each governmental unit eligible for revenue sharing allocations. Congress has enacted a variety of programs that allocate funds to local jurisdictions on the basis of current population estimates, including countercyclical revenue sharing, Aid to Families with Dependent Children, block grants for housing and related assistance, criminal justice equipment and programs, and employment and training assistance.

In some instances, the data requirements of the legislation were determined without clear understanding of the required data elements, the quality and timeliness of the existing data, or the feasibility of meeting the data requirements. In a very few instances, the data needs could be met fully by existing data; in most situations, however, the available data lacked either the precision or the timeliness that were called for or both, and new data collection efforts were begun. For example, the Current Population Survey (CPS) was expanded to provide annual average unemployment rates at the state level. Other legislation resulted in needs for new data—with all the attendant problems of funding, staffing, development, and time delays—such as the development of the National Crime Victimization Surveys. Finally, some legislative mandates could be met only through the implementation of new methodology; meeting the needs for data for general revenue sharing fell into this category. In too many instances, however, the methodologies were simply lacking or wholly inadequate to meet the needs. Whenever possible, of course, the most recent available data were used.

Timeliness

The specific challenge in preparing estimates for small geographic areas is that such areas can experience rapid population and economic changes. The smaller the geographic area, the greater the influence of migration and the possibility of rapid shifts in the local population or economic base. For example, a new suburban development or the migration of a group of immigrants to a city neighborhood can occur in just a few years. In such a case, decennial census information for a small area may no longer provide accurate information about the people, their education, income, and other characteristics. During periods of heavy and shifting immigration, such as has occurred in the United States during the past 20 years, census information presents an inadequate picture of the number and socioeconomic adjustment of small ethnic groups within 4 to 5 years after its collection. Small population groups are often affected more by these demographic changes and hence necessitate more frequent estimates.

Some data users, such as private for-profit companies, have increasingly developed alternative sources of information for making decisions about small areas. For decisions about site selection, advertising and promotional campaigns, and market research, they have increasingly acquired and generated transactional databases. Transactional database includes grocery store purchases, checking account monthly balances, and any event that is routinely recorded by businesses and can be linked to an individual or household. Some transactional data are now generated from cash registers and inventory controls for real-time estimates of change. Transactional data provide frequent small-area estimates for many businesses. Although the panel has not examined studies on the quality and usefulness of these data for federal and state government uses, they are probably of limited use for many important intercensal small-area estimates of persons, families, and households by social and economic characteristics, and they lack such important individual characteristics as race and ethnicity.

No matter how accurate small-area census data are at the time of collection, they lose currency as time passess. For areas undergoing rapid change, data that may have been relatively accurate at the time of collection may have become relatively inaccurate measures of the local area within several years. A full account of "errors" in the use of census data for small-area estimates involves two components. One stems from errors in the underlying census data. Data collected in the census, especially at the block level, have nonsampling errors and limitations, such as geocoding errors, response errors, and allocation for item nonresponse or imputed personal data. Census data also contain geocoding errors and response errors (e.g., someone gives too high or low an income figure). Users of small-area data, the panel believes, are often not well informed about the errors in census data. The other component derives from population shifts during intercensal years. It is the second source of change that produces, over the duration of a decade, the major cause of discrepancy between the original census information and the phenomenon that it is supposed to represent. With heavy immigration and substantial migration, population shifts dwarf any discrepancies that existed in the original census information.

From the perspective of the intercensal uses of census data, too much attention has been given to consideration of errors in the count and content, and too little attention has been given to errors of interpretation from changes over time. The panel believes that much of the error of interpretation derives from changes over time and not errors in the count or content. Broader recognition that errors in interpretation derive from changes over time would result in a healthy decrease in the false sense of accuracy of many census data.[2]

More timely information for certain small-area census items would offer substantial benefits for federal agencies, state and local governments, and other users of census data:

• Allocation of funds would be more accurately targeted with up-to-date small-area estimates.
• Municipalities, school districts, and other government agencies and business firms working with small-area data would be able to improve the decision-making process if more current data were available for their areas of management.
• Learning to work with administrative records (to provide more frequent data) would improve knowledge about the quality, limitations, and required improvements for these data.

Past Attempts to Produce Intercensal Small-Area Data

Most past attempts to produce small-area data have followed one of two very different approaches, survey-based data or model-based estimates. Survey-based estimates are derived directly through the collection of data: they usually require significant resources, both in dollar terms and in staff time, and specific measures of the reliability of the results are usually provided. Model-based estimates, in contrast, generally rely on the manipulation of existing data: they are far less costly and require far less staff, but their reliability cannot be directly measured and they are much more difficult to validate.

The survey-based approach is illustrated by the use of the Current Population Survey to produce state unemployment estimates to meet the needs of the Comprehensive Employment and Training Act of 1973 and the conduct of the Survey of Income and Education (SIE), which used a combination of a CPS sample and a specially designed sample to produce state-level estimates of poverty among children ages 5 to 17. The SIE, conducted in 1976, also was used to satisfy congressional mandates regarding the number of children and other people requiring bilingual education and guidance and counseling at the state level and to gather information for a number of other federal programs. The model-based approach was used at the federal level, in the preparation of population and per capita income estimates for revenue sharing, a program initiated in 1972 to distribute funds annually to more than 39,000 local governmental entities. It was also used by the New York State Department of Health (1988:1), which noted that "county-level poverty estimates for intercensal years have been perhaps the most needed, unavailable piece of data for program planning and monitoring in the health and human services fields."

Over the past two decades, the Census Bureau has had a program of producing intercensal estimates of the total national population, by selected characteristics such as age, sex, and race, that uses both survey-based and model-based approaches. The Census Bureau's program includes estimates for states, counties, and large metropolitan areas, and it is now experimenting with providing details on characteristics through the use of Internal Revenue Service (IRS) files. This resource was an essential element in the production of estimates of population and per capita income for use in meeting the requirements of the revenue sharing legislation in 1972, and it is continuing to play an important role in the Census Bureau's plans to develop systems to produce intercensal income distributions and measures of poverty for families and households at selected subnational levels. In spite of its 20-year duration, however, this program is in its earliest stages and its long-term success in providing needed intercensal small-area data is far from certain.

Without undertaking major new surveys, there is one survey-based and one model-based approach to improving intercensal estimates for small areas. One way is to use existing secondary sources by making modest enhancements, such as increasing the size or scope of existing national surveys. The scope for supplementary census information from national surveys is limited because of the relatively small size of the samples for small geographic areas; reliable information is therefore limited to areas with relatively large populations. A second way is to use administrative records that have national coverage. Administrative records include school information on age distribution and family relationship, Social

Security data with such details as disability records and pension status, and university and college graduation records with information about higher education.

Appendix I describes how these approaches have been used to produce intercensal small-area estimates, with four case studies on improving the frequency of the estimates. One study describes how the Department of Defense uses census data, administrative records, and large surveys to estimate the number of qualified military personnel in small areas. The second case study reports on the preparation of monthly employment and unemployment estimates by the Bureau of Labor Statistics (BLS), using sample survey data, administrative records, and statistical modeling to prepare monthly estimates for the 50 states, the District of Columbia, and 2,600 local areas. The monthly employment and unemployment estimates are used for planning and fund allocation for such federal programs as the Job Training and Partnership Act, the Economic Dislocation and Worker Adjustment Assistance Act, and the Urban Development Action Grant program. The third case study describes how the Census Bureau prepares annual estimates of income and poverty. The fourth case study discusses possible improvement of small-area intercensal estimates on seasonal and migrant farmworkers. Although a number of federal programs deals with farmworkers and the government spends over $500 million annually on those programs, there are few reliable data on a number of characteristics of farmworkers, which are needed for program planning and for purposes of allocating resources to state and local jurisdictions. The case study outlines how sample surveys, administrative records, and statistical methods could be used to provide annual estimates of farmworkers and their characteristics at the state level and annual estimates of the number of farmworkers in local areas.

The trade-offs between having more timely data for larger geographic areas and having more geographically precise data once every 10 years have been difficult for the panel to specify. On one hand, enlarging the sample size of the nation's large household surveys might provide quarterly or annual estimates for states and larger metropolitan areas, but the cost of providing annual estimates (not multiyear cumulative estimates from surveys) for small geographic areas would be prohibitive: it would require the equivalent of a census long form to be collected each year. On the other hand, the accuracy of small-area data collected once every 10 years declines significantly throughout the decade and so is inadequate for policy and program planning.

The panel believes that improvements in small-area estimates for the nation are needed. There are several different ways to improve the current amount and quantity of intercensal small-area data:

• Results from existing surveys should be explored for their potential use to model estimates in conjunction with data from administrative records for smaller areas and for smaller population groups.

• Administrative records require more attention in order to provide more frequent estimates for small geographic areas. We endorse the proposal by the Census Bureau to develop income and poverty estimates for families and households for small areas, using available annual income data from tax records. We urge that such work also consider the use of administrative records from the Aid to Families with Dependent Children, Food Stamps, and other special programs that provide information on the low-income population.

• We encourage additional work by federal agencies to provide small-area estimates on other topics such as education and employment—key items for funding and management decisions for small areas throughout the decade.

Administrative records for small areas could be used in three ways. First, program data from administrative records can be analyzed by geographic area, without requiring a geographic database or linkage to other program data. Such data as school enrollments and hospital admissions can be summarized and mapped for the geographic areas available in the record system itself. Federal program data are available centrally for many important types of small-area data (e.g., tax records for income and poverty estimates). The panel believes that high priority should be given to the expanded use of such records to prepare small-area estimates as an experiment with geocoding the data for existing areas. For this use of program data, the records may be used quickly for small-area estimates. The usefulness of the records is limited to the content of the records themselves, however, and no cross-tabulation can be done.

A second use of administrative record program data is to link the records to a geographic database for small areas down to individual blocks. For this use, the records require a street address or an address range. The advantage of this approach is that estimates for blocks could be aggregated to match various boundaries. For example, automobile ownership data could be linked to a geographic database and then aggregated for transportation planning zones. This use of administrative data would not require linking individual records. State and local government records, as well as federal records, would be potentially useful and it would be valuable to the Census Bureau in expanding its cooperation with state and local agencies.

Third, administrative record data can be linked at the household level to provide cross-tabulation information. Cross-tabulations require a geographic database with linked individual addresses and a record system that can be linked to a specific address.

These three types of uses of administrative records emphasize several points. First, it is possible to expand small-area estimates without record linkage. Second, an up-to-date geographic database is essential for some uses. Third, expanded use of administrative records requires cooperation with state and local governments.

Toward the goal of developing more frequent data for small areas, the panel recommends an expanded research program by the Census Bureau and greater cooperation between the Census Bureau and state and local governments.

Recommendation 8.1 The panel recommends that the Census Bureau work to improve the amount, quantity, and frequency of small-area intercensal data:

• **The Census Bureau should conduct experiments with federal administrative records for deriving more frequent small-area intercensal data estimates. At a minimum, the panel recommends that the Census Bureau geocode several large federal administrative record systems and use them to produce small-area estimates.**
• **The Census Bureau should work with state and local governments to enhance the quantity and frequency of small-area data.**

There is concern about the confidentiality of any research program that would use administrative records extensively. Confidentiality of the administrative records-based population program must be ensured, and safeguards for a program must be developed. Confidentiality concerns would vary, however, with the type of use of administrative records data. The three types of administrative records data uses differ in two important ways from the confidentiality concerns raised in Chapter 4 about an administrative records census. First, two of the three uses mentioned above do not involve matching or linkage of individual records. Major improvements could be made in intercensal small-area estimates without program data linkage, and those uses should be exploited. Second, an administrative records census would require a more expanded linkage of federal, state, and local records than that entertained for cross-tabulated intercensal estimates. For intercensal small-area estimates, important work on such topics as poverty and program participation can be conducted by state and local areas with limited use of administrative records data. Finally, small-area estimates using federal program data do not require creation of a central data bank, as would be necessary for an administrative records census.

ASSESSMENT OF CURRENT METHODS

This section provides a brief assessment of the feasibility of the currently known methodologies to meet needs for small-area intercensal data: mid-decade censuses, new surveys, augmenting existing surveys, and model-based estimates. (The use of administrative records is covered separately below.)

Mid-Decade Censuses

One approach to obtaining intercensal data would be to conduct a mid-decade census. In late 1976, Congress mandated but did not fund such an activity. A wide variety of possible approaches was explored in the early 1980s for possible implementation in 1985, ranging from a full census to a large, mid-decade survey activity, but funding was never provided. To our knowledge, a mid-decade activity was not considered at all for 1995.

If carried out at a minimum level of effort, a mid-decade census could provide many of the desired data, certainly at the state level and, most likely, at the level of large counties and incorporated places with a single estimate for a combined group of smaller counties within the state. With regard to cost, estimates in the early 1980s began at around $100 million and went as high as $1.1 billion, the total cost of the 1980 decennial census.

Although it is quite clear that the nation now recognizes the need for more current data than provided by the last decennial census and, as noted earlier, that a legislative mandate already exists for a mid-decade activity, it seems equally clear that neither Congress nor the Census Bureau is looking to this approach as a means of providing intercensal data.

New and Special Surveys

A very large survey would be required to produce subnational estimates. Depending on the design and desired reliability, a survey several times larger than the CPS would be required to make annual estimates for all states and major metropolitan areas. A survey to produce annual estimates for all U.S. counties, for example, would probably require a sample size of several million interviews, and estimates for smaller geographic units would need even larger sample sizes.

Although the point at which a special survey becomes a mid-decade exercise is open to argument, the key issue is the level of subnational geography for which estimates will be provided. Any requirement for county-level information that will be obtained through visiting households bears with it a significant funding burden, even with such compromises as collapsing all counties within a state below a given population or characteristic size into a single balance-of-state area. The costs for such a survey would undoubtedly exceed $200 million. The costs for a national survey to provide reliable data at the level of census tracts or aggregations of census blocks would be far greater, surely approaching those of a mid-decade census. If data were limited to regions, divisions, or even the state level, then a special survey would be a viable option for obtaining the necessary detailed characteristic desired.

In connection with new surveys, we note the relevance of a continuous measurement survey (discussed in Chapter 6) as a resource in producing intercensal estimates for small areas. If such a program is developed and demonstrates its ability to produce reliable, accurate, and timely data at varying levels of subnational geography, it would immediately become an important element in any program to produce estimates for small levels of geography (i.e., census blocks). Again, at the national, state, and large metropolitan area level, it would provide annual or even quarterly direct estimates for the variety of subject matter included in the survey. When combined with other survey data or administrative records data, it could serve as a key element in a model-based series of estimates. Data derived from such a program also could serve as a benchmark estimate in model building or be used as an evaluation tool. Overall, if proven feasible, continuous measurement would be a significant addition to the arsenal of re- sources for preparing intercensal small-area estimates. However, there are major unanswered questions about how continuous measurement would relate to ongo- ing federal programs of intercensal surveys.

Augmenting Existing Surveys

Augmentation of existing surveys to provide data on a particular group is a feasible procedure under limited and controlled circumstances such as, for ex- ample, adding known Hispanic households to improve the reliability of esti- mates of data for Hispanics. This approach has been used in the CPS from time to time as a practical, efficient, and economical way to improve reliability for a particular group for which information is required. However, this approach cannot be used when the amount of necessary augmentation significantly ex- ceeds the presence of a specific characteristic within the existing sample, for example, for the Asian and Pacific Islander population.

More important, augmentation does *not* appear to be a feasible alternative to provide substate-level data, whatever the population characteristic of interest. Such an approach raises serious questions about whether augmentation is the best approach, the amount of sample augmentation required, and whether the approach would be consistent with the basic objectives of the survey being aug- mented, and neither overweigh nor compromise the basic survey.

We note that the CPS, as well as other national surveys, can be used to produce some subnational data, depending on the design and the degree of de- sired reliability, that is, on how the data will be used. Even before the CPS redesign in 1985, the files were being tabulated to provide information at such substate levels as region, division, states, and even for selected large metropoli- tan areas.[3] However, most of these estimates carried large sampling variances and were not published, although they were available in the public-use files.

In general, discussions about data collected in the census or the proposed continuous measurement survey rely primarily on mailout forms. Data from mail questionnaires differ from data collected in the CPS and most other federal household surveys that are collected by trained interviewers. Also, a great deal of research and testing over the years, and especially cognitive research underly- ing the recent CPS redesign, gives us much more information about the reliabil- ity of household survey estimates.

For the collection of small-area data, the sample for such surveys as the CPS would have to be spread out to many areas not represented in the CPS, since the CPS sample is selected to provide estimates for individual states and the nation as a whole. Expanding the CPS to provide county-level data, however, would not seem feasible or efficient under any set of criteria, since the contribution of the original CPS sample to the final estimates would be insignificant in many cases. Given the lack of any real benefit to the CPS, such "augmentation" should be viewed as totally independent and, thus, a special survey.

Model-Based Estimates

In recent years, most efforts to produce subnational data for intercensal periods, for areas smaller than the state level, have focused on the use of regression-based statistical models, generally involving the use of administrative data. The Census Bureau has used administrative record data extensively in preparing small-area estimates and, with the availability of both 1990 census results and some important new data from the IRS internal master file extract of federal tax returns, it has proposed a research project "to develop improved methodology for updating 1990 census estimates of household income distributions for small areas during the postcensal period" (Bureau of the Census, 1991a). If successful, estimates of the poverty population would be one of a number of summary measures derived from this work. The Census Bureau's research program, however, is well behind its original schedule; in fact, work has not yet begun on the first phase. When initiated, the plan calls for estimates to be produced on a biannual basis with a 2-year lag on the income reference year (e.g., 1993 income data would be published in the summer of 1995).

Outside the federal government, a number of attempts were made during the 1980s to produce selected postcensal estimates for states and counties. In an article reviewing these efforts, O'Hare (1993) concluded that the efforts have been haphazard and have produced mixed results. In the case of estimates for geographic units within states, the efforts were restricted to single states; in no instance was there any attempt to develop a model that could produce estimates for all counties in the United States or for counties in more than one state. The variables used in developing the estimates were quite varied from state to state, and their availability and timing also differed. More important, the variables that seemed most reliable in one case did not appear to be transferable to other cases. Given the experience to date, in fact, it may be necessary to examine an approach in which different models are developed for use in producing county-level or similar estimates in different states or groups of states, either because of the lack of comparable data elements, problems in timing, or research results that suggest different relationships across the states. If such an approach is feasible, it would suggest the possibility of an arrangement similar to the existing, cooperative venture between the federal government and the individual states, which was developed and nurtured by the Census Bureau in connection with its preparation of current population estimates.

ADMINISTRATIVE RECORDS

A major resource, both potential and realized, in the development and production of small-area estimates is the availability of the vast diversity of administrative records in the United States, both at all levels of government and for all categories of economic and social activity. From lists of those who have obtained driver's licenses to the vast repositories of records on those filing income tax returns, entering the country as immigrants or temporary workers, applying for Medicare coverage, receiving Social Security benefits, registering for unemployment benefits, receiving Food Stamps, applying for credit, subscribing to magazines, joining organizations, registering for school, receiving medical care or hospitalization, and applying for employment, the amount of information potentially available is huge. What appears to be, however, is not always so: the groups covered by the record systems may vary substantially, they may be out of date, and a given record system may not even fully cover what it purports to represent (it may be limited, incomplete, and even inaccurate). Furthermore, use of the files may be limited, or even precluded, by legal restrictions and questions of confidentiality and privacy.

In spite of various limitations, many administrative files already serve key roles in the production of diverse, current estimates covering a wide diversity of subjects—ranging from the Census Bureau's use of IRS files, to statistics derived from birth and death records, immigration statistics, and selected local files on housing starts and school enrollment—at national and subnational levels. The Bureau of Labor Statistics uses state unemployment insurance files as part of the data used to produce local-area estimates of labor market activity; the National Center for Education Statistics publishes estimates of school enrollment and a vast panoply of education data based on the system of records maintained by individual school systems; and the Bureau of Economic Analysis uses a vast diversity of administrative record data to produce its current estimates of gross domestic product and its compilation of national accounts. In many cases, the administrative files are used to produce summary statistics that in turn may be used directly or may become one input to a model-based product; in other cases, the focus is on the individual microrecord.

The use of administrative records has also been proposed to replace the decennial census (see Chapter 4) and to improve the coverage, accuracy, and efficiency of the census (see Chapter 5). In the latter case, administrative records have been used since the 1950s to assist in evaluating census results: the accuracy of census reporting of income has been validated through the matching of individual census returns against filed tax returns, addresses have been checked against local housing lists, and individuals found on selected lists have been checked against household rosters as an evaluation of census coverage. The 1980 census went a step further and used a very limited set of administrative record data directly to improve the quality of the count; thus, lists of welfare recipients and other hard-to-enumerate groups in selected large cities were used as a direct check on the enumeration, and follow-up activities were initiated if the names on the lists were not found to be recorded in the household. The 1990 census did not build on the experience of the earlier census: relatively little use was made of administrative records in conducting the census, and no tests concerning any expanded use of administrative records were incorporated in the 1990 research program. By contrast, planning for the 1995 census test includes an administrative record component, in which a number of microrecord files will be combined in an effort to reduce the differential undercount.[4]

Clearly, the efforts undertaken and the experience to date indicate that the use of administrative records can contribute substantially to the decennial census. The Census Bureau currently has a program to examine and document data in the major administrative record databases of federal and state governments. The panel relied on information from the Census Bureau's Administrative Record Information System (ARIS) for analysis of content and data quality analysis, presented in Appendix J.

Of interest in this chapter, however, is the use of administrative records as a unique component of intercensal estimates. Four factors render administrative record files a unique resource in developing intercensal small-area estimates of many of the socioeconomic characteristics covered in a decennial census, including both short- and long-form information. The first is the wide range of information available in the many different administrative record files; the second is the diversity of populations covered by administrative record files; the third is the extensive coverage of the various populations in the files; and the fourth is the broad geographic coverage of many of the record systems.

The first and most immediate requirement is for resources and effort to overcome the problems that inhibit the effective use of administrative record files. These include developing and maintaining an up-to-date annotated directory of the available administrative files; assessing the utility and quality of each file; arranging for prompt and continued access to the files deemed essential; establishing a system to integrate and unduplicate the various files; and deciding how the information on the different files can best be combined. At the same time, research efforts are needed for developing, testing, and refining the methodologies for the use of these files, alone or in concert with other data sources, to produce small-area estimates. It is important to note and recognize that the use of administrative records to produce subnational estimates that are consistent over both time and area and have credibility with users requires expertise in model development, access to the best data sources, adequate computing resources, and the time and funding necessary to plan, test, and evaluate alternative approaches.

The extensive nature of the effort needed can best be illustrated by considering the Census Bureau's proposal (1994b) to produce small-area intercensal estimates of income and poverty for counties, cities, and other incorporated places. The Census Bureau will be building on expertise developed over the past two decades through its efforts to produce models for small-area income estimation to meet the requirements of the general revenue sharing program and its subsequent work to produce median family 4-person income estimates based on the March CPS. For this project on income and poverty, the best data sources are located, for the most part, at the Census Bureau. One source is the basic 1990 census microdata files containing full detail on geographic identifiers and uncensored income data for all sample cases. (This file is not available for public use.) Another source is an extract of the information contained on the IRS individual master file containing more than 100 million federal individual income tax returns that the Census Bureau receives annually for research and population estimation purposes. The Census Bureau adds geographic codes that are consistent with the IRS's system of addressing. These codes are used to measure migration from place to place. In addition to these data, the Census Bureau proposes to use miscellaneous tax information documents (e.g., information on wages and salaries and miscellaneous income) to provide a more complete picture of assorted income and to improve the construction of income for households and families. The panel believes the Census Bureau should also consider initiating work with files from the Aid to Families with Dependent Children, Food Stamps, and other programs that are appropriate to the universe of low-income people. These other files, in addition to tax and income records, would greatly improve estimates of the number and location of low-income and poverty groups.

The third key source is the files created by linking the tax file extracts from the IRS individual master file with both the March CPS and the Survey of Income and Program Participation (SIPP).[5]

In the proposed estimates work, files will be linked, on a household-by-household basis, with the tax return of the survey respondent, using Social Security numbers. This link is a bridge for the socioeconomic information collected in the surveys, and the tax return data are expected to prove extremely valuable in the small-area estimation modeling process. Each of the files will have to undergo extensive cleansing and review to ensure that the geography as well as the data are complete and consistent. Since each of the files is national in coverage and produced by a single source, the Census Bureau will be spared the difficult, expensive, and very time-consuming activities of merging, standardizing, unduplicating, editing, and otherwise correcting files and data drawn from disparate and unrelated sources to produce usable data.

To develop and maintain a system for providing income and poverty estimates for about 40,000 geographic areas will require major computing resources: the 1990 census microdata file contains information for 17 million different households, and the IRS individual master file extract covers more than 100 million tax returns. Similarly, the staff and support required for the estimates project are significant. The Census Bureau estimates that funding and staff to support planning, testing, and evaluating alternative estimation approaches will cost around $4 million for the first 5 years, followed by annual funding of some $800,000 to operate the program. Some 15 months are planned for research, development, and evaluation, followed by a 6-month testing period, after which data will be released with a 2-year lag between the release and reference years. A major evaluation effort is planned following the availability of results from the 2000 census (assuming such data are collected), at which time improvements will be introduced into the estimation system; intercensal data will first be available in 2003.

This example highlights key factors needed for the production of small-area intercensal estimates. First, it includes comprehensive application of a variety of different methodologies—including census-based data, survey-based data, and administrative record data—to develop the estimates. Second, it has a benchmark source—in this case, the decennial census—both as a base from which to construct the intercensal estimate and as an independent measure in a future period to be used to evaluate the estimate. Third, it has the advantages of being able to match records through the use of a common identifier, as in this case, the Social Security number. Response rates to surveys, however, are negatively affected by the use of Social Security numbers. Moreover, as argued earlier in this chapter, the matching of individuals is not always needed for the use of administrative data for small-area estimates when the data are geographically coded. Fourth, it has the benefit of using administrative files in a single, standardized way for the entire nation. Finally, it draws together, under one sponsorship, data from disparate sources and so allows a focusing of resources to produce both an improved methodology and an improved set of estimates.

In sum, this example demonstrates that an organized program is needed to exploit the potential use of administrative records for small-area estimates. Administrative records have the potential for improving the nation's estimates for small areas, but it will take many years. It will require improvements in both the content and accuracy of administrative records and the ability to accurately and completely geographically reference the records to small areas.

Among the most valuable work that the Census Bureau could undertake would be to conduct experiments with administrative records for deriving more timely small-area estimates. At a minimum, geocoding several large administrative record systems in order to make intercensal small-area estimates would provide useful data and helpful experience. In addition, the Census Bureau might consider several other ways of enhancing the intercensal estimation program:

• When special census tests are conducted, select several geographic areas and then link administrative records to the household questionnaires. The experiments would examine the accuracy of residential addresses on administrative records, study the quality of the reporting data on records, and evaluate the usefulness of administrative records for broader use with the census and for deriving intercensal estimates. Such an experiment would provide information for estimating the costs of developing and improving administrative records for census and more timely intercensal uses.

•   Develop pilot projects with a few states and localities to experiment with ways to develop or improve small-area estimates using administrative records. These experiments need not produce data that are fully consistent across geographic areas.

•   Expand current programs to include age, sex, and race (including Hispanic status) estimates. The current methodology of preparing total population estimates using IRS files can be used to develop estimates by age, race, and sex. The Census Bureau has already experimented successfully in preparing such estimates for states and large metropolitan areas, using a 20 percent sample of Social Security numbers linked to the master IRS individual file. This could be expanded to linking *all* Social Security numbers to the file, for which the Census Bureau would need to obtain extracts from the Social Security Administration's files, which contain Social Security numbers, and information on age, sex, and race for all Social Security numbers ever issued, that is, the 100 percent file rather than a 20 percent sample. Estimates could be prepared for states, counties, and places.

•   Increase current research efforts on how best to unduplicate, link, and merge IRS information documents to the individual 1040 form files now used by the Census Bureau. Research suggests that this enhancement of the basic IRS file could increase population coverage to 97 to 98 percent and reduce geographic differentials in coverage. This is a most important step to significantly improve the accuracy of the small-area population estimates, as well as to increase face validity. A very useful by-product of such programs would be the improved estimates of gross migration flows by income characteristics for states and other geographic areas.

•   Immediately begin research on developing household and family estimates and size distributions from the IRS files. The research would involve exploring ways of converting tax-filing units to households and families. Current plans for TIGER (the Census Bureau's geographic-referencing database) and for maintaining a continuously updated master address file would assist this effort by making it possible to bring together all persons (or records) filing from the same housing unit (or address). Other linking and matching would need to be done to form families.

•   In addition to current plans to produce income and poverty estimates for small areas, primarily with the use of IRS, CPS, and SIPP data to model the estimates, undertake more research into using more direct estimation procedures by supplementing the data with such other files as Aid to Families with Dependent Children, Food Stamps, and aged beneficiaries—files directly related to the low-income population. In combination, such files may cover 90 percent or more of the population of interest. Research should include testing and developing 1990 estimates that are carried forward from 1980. Future work is needed on current estimates carried forward from 1990 and tested against a special census (or the 1995 test census) with additional focus on income. Pilot studies and case studies on developing income and poverty estimates could be expanded by carrying forward 1990 census figures to current dates using all the available administrative records for a select number of areas (and especially the planned 1995 test census areas) and evaluating results against special censuses.

Because of the size and complexity of the long-term development of improved small-area data, it is important to have a unit within the Census Bureau assigned the exclusive task of working on the use of administrative records for small-area estimates.

Recommendation 8.2 The panel recommends that the Census Bureau give a single unit sole responsibility to exploit administrative records and produce small-area intercensal estimates on a frequent basis. Its work on administrative records should examine geographic consistency and quality. The unit should develop methods for increasing geographic content; establishing consistency of federal, state, and local administrative data; augmenting content on national records; augmenting usefulness of the resulting information through modeling; and computerizing approaches to database management to facilitate the use of administrative data in a census. If the content of administrative records can be improved for use in preparing small-area estimates, that is desirable, but the major purpose of the unit would be to produce small-area intercensal estimates.

A GEOGRAPHIC REFERENCE SYSTEM
AND UPDATED ADDRESS FILE

The 1990 census relied heavily on a geographic database, called TIGER (Topologically Integrated Geographic Encoding and Referencing). The Census Bureau similarly plans to rely on a TIGER-type system for the 2000 census. There are two separate files in the geographic address system: a cartographic and an address database. TIGER itself is a cartographic database with physical features (such as roads, railroads, and rivers) and address ranges. The specific address lists are in a separate database so that TIGER does not itself reveal individual housing addresses (nor any information about the occupants of housing). TIGER can be linked to the address list for use in census planning and operations.

In the context of this chapter, a key question is whether a geographic database, such as TIGER, is critical for developing postcensal estimates, particularly small-area estimates. If so, then the geographic database needs to be maintained at some level throughout the decade. Some records have a geographic reference and can be geocoded without reference to other data, but for small-area estimates (and for linkage to other records), a geographic referencing system such as TIGER is needed. The availability of the TIGER database and its enhancement and support by private companies and federal and state agencies have opened the door for widespread small-area data analysis. Moreover, recent technological breakthroughs, including more powerful microcomputers and large-scale data storage on CD-ROM, have distributed the power of small-area data to many new users, who are now unlikely to accept more limited types of census data. The panel supports efforts to improve small-area data and to have the data and its geographic referencing available to a wide variety of users. We note, however, that the panel did not examine the cost of a continuously updated TIGER system or its alternatives.

It is the panel's understanding that the Census Bureau and the U.S. Postal Service are entering into an arrangement for sharing address lists and for updating geographic information on residential addresses on a continuous basis. The costs of maintaining such a system on a continuous basis have been estimated by census staff as roughly the same over a 10-year period as the costs for the one-time updating of an address and the associated geographic referencing system needed for the decennial census. If these cost data are confirmed, the panel endorses this activity.

In its proposed geographic activities for fiscal 1995 and the subsequent 3 fiscal years (1996 to 1998), the Bureau of the Census (1994a) would develop a continuously updated master address file linked to the TIGER geographic referencing database. As noted above, such an address file and associated geographic database were constructed for use in the 1990 census—as has been the case in prior censuses—but have not been updated during the past four years. Continuous updating of these files would provide a current database on housing units and their location for small geographic areas, a basic database for use in preparing intercensal estimates, and an address file for use in supporting household surveys conducted by the federal government. See the report of the Panel to Evaluate Alternative Census Methods (Steffey and Bradburn, 1994) for details on implementing such an activity.

The panel endorses the creation of a joint Census Bureau-U.S. Postal Service effort to create a continuously updated national address file, assuming that the 10-year cost is about the same as creating a file for the decennial census.

Recommendation 8.3 If the cost estimates for continually updating

the master address file and associated geographic-referencing database (including costs by the Census Bureau and others) are comparable to the cost of one-time updating just prior to the census, the panel recommends that development proceed. If the cost estimates are higher, then the clear advantages of the continuously updated address system should be weighed against the additional costs. If a decision is then made to continue, the Census Bureau should proceed with the necessary steps, including the necessary accompanying safeguards, to make the master address file available for statistical purposes to the federal statistical system and to cooperating state and local governments.

The full implementation of these recommendations would require some changes in the legislation governing Census Bureau operations, as discussed in the next section.

INTERAGENCY DATA SHARING

Title 13 of the U.S. Code, which governs the Census Bureau's mandate for data collection and how it distributes statistical information, limits its ability to share information.

In particular, Title 13 produces a one-way street for data exchange with the Census Bureau: agencies may give data to the Census Bureau, but the Census Bureau may not share any of its information with other agencies. For example, Title 13 requires the Census Bureau to safeguard the addresses of housing units, presumably because the list may contain illegal addresses from the perspective of local government housing law. There has been fear that local governments might use access to the Census Bureau's list to enforce housing regulations. Thus, although the Census Bureau develops its mailing list from public lists and in association with the U.S. Postal Service and through intensive canvassing by census personnel, it maintains the confidentiality of the address list itself. The inability of local governments to inspect and review the census mailing list has become a serious problem for census operations. City and local authorities often provide the Census Bureau with their list of housing units. The Census Bureau then comments on overall discrepancies but does not allow local authorities to scrutinize the census list. A closed mailing list fosters suspicions on the part of local authorities. It also does not allow the Census Bureau to work in full partnership with local officials for the improvement of the address list and its reconciliation with local records.

The one-way street for census address lists also affects the federal statistical system. The Census Bureau's interpretation of Title 13 prevents exchange of data with other statistical agencies that need geographic address files. Lack of access to census address lists creates unnecessary expense for the federal government because those agencies (the National Center for Health Statistics, for example) are forced to go out themselves to list addresses.

As an alternative, one might imagine a national housing register—a listing of housing addresses only, with no individual or family information—that was maintained collaboratively by the Census Bureau, the U.S. Postal Service, and local governments. Such a list would provide correct geographic locations and would be available for intercensal use and would, by its very nature, provide a continuous inventory of housing by small geographic areas. It would also be public (or available to local officials with restrictions for its use) and would avert one of the major disagreements of local officials with the decennial census: debates about the correct number of housing units in small areas. Such a reconciled, geographically referenced housing list would also improve the quality of the census count. Availability of a geographically referenced housing list, with addresses only, may require changes to Title 13, although with restrictions on the use of the address list for statistical uses only.

We note, however, that much can be done under the current provisions of Title 13. Expanded work with administrative records will require changes in access to some data for use by Census Bureau personnel to be linked to other records. Some records may require redesign. Some records may need improvements for accuracy, including information on residential address for proper allocation to the dwelling unit. All of these kinds of issues pertain to the participation of the Census Bureau and other agencies in teamwork to expand and improve the use of administrative records for intercensal use; none requires changes in Title 13.

CONCLUSION

Most efforts to date to meet the needs for intercensal small-area estimates have proven unsatisfactory. On one hand, the issue has been cost: to produce reliable survey-based information for such areas and for population subgroups within them (such as children ages 5 to 17, by race and ethnic origin) would require undertaking a major data-gathering activity approaching a census, with costs upward of $500 million. On the other hand, no major methodological improvements have been developed to produce current estimates for small areas, nor have there been new statistical applications to the problem of producing such data. Yet the need for such estimates continues to expand, especially as the emphasis in the formulation and implementation of public policy shifts in many areas from one of federal responsibility to state and local initiative in the allocation and distribution of public funds. Programs to locate public housing, examine the spread of AIDS, establish programs to assist the elderly poor or the unwed mother, for example, would all benefit from the availability of accurate, current, and consistent estimates of small geographic areas, such as counties or neighborhoods, and for selected population subgroups defined by race, ethnicity, education, and poverty status.

In light of the recognized need, the past decade has seen a number of conferences and seminars devoted to this topic, abroad as well as in this country, and researchers have explored a variety of approaches in attempting to produce intercensal estimates of selected characteristics for states and counties. Unfortunately, for the most part, the efforts have been haphazard and have produced mixed results. Nonetheless, researchers are continuing their efforts. One bright spot, noted above, is in providing population detail such as age, sex, race, and Hispanic origin, as well as children in poverty. It is quite clear, however, that much work remains to be done—and much time, effort, and resources will be required—to ensure that current research plans are translated into an operating program that can meet its objectives.

The panel concludes that the logical course is to provide strong support to the development of model-based estimates, especially those derived from the use of administrative record sources. Such efforts would include both work on analyzing and choosing the appropriate methodology and support for the establishment of the administrative records programs that are necessary to the success of the model. At the federal level, in particular, such an effort should include active support for an ongoing administrative records program that will provide, on a timely basis, the necessary detail at the substate level for model-based estimates. In the same vein, the relevant, current, federal surveys, such as CPS, SIPP, the Consumer Expenditures Survey, and the Health Interview Survey, should be reviewed to determine the applicability and potential of their subject matter to the model-based estimation process.

The likelihood that a comprehensive set of intercensal small-area estimates will be accomplished successfully in the very near future remains quite small. The encouraging aspects are the heightened recognition of the need for and importance of such data, the range of efforts now being devoted to accomplishing the goal of producing valid and reliable small-area estimates, and the likelihood of adding some important new small-area estimates in the next few years.

NOTES

[1]For a discussion of many of these topics in the context of the 2000 census, see Steffey and Bradburn (1994).

[2]If there is an error in census coverage and the census is used as a benchmark for adjusting intercensal estimates, the census estimates will be affected by this error. Such propagation of error differs from the panel's concern that changes over time may swamp whatever was the original error in the one-time estimate.

[3]Some substate-level data have also been released by the Bureau of Labor Statistics, together with sampling errors (which are quite large).

[4]Administrative records are currently used for postcensal estimates: for example, the Census Bureau relies on vital statistics information, including records on marriages and divorce, to estimate the household structure in the years after a census.

[5]The March CPS collects information about household composition, demographics, and sources and amounts of income received for a nationally representative sample of about 60,000 households. The SIPP does the same for a sample of about 20,000 households and has much more extensive information about federal taxes.

References

Alexander, C.H.
   1993   A Continuous Measurement Alternative for the U.S. Census. Report CM-10, October 28.
            Bureau of the Census, U.S. Department of Commerce, Washington, D.C.
   1994a   Further Exploration of Issues Raised at the CNSTAT Requirements Panel Meeting. Mem-
            orandum to R.D. Tortora dated January 31. Continuous Measurement Research Series
            No. CM-13. Bureau of the Census, U.S. Department of Commerce, Washington, D.C.
   1994b   A Prototype Continuous Measurement System for the U.S. Census of Population and
            Housing. Paper prepared for the Annual Meeting of the Population Association of Amer-
            ica, Miami, Fla. continuous Measurement Research Series No. CM-17. Bureau of the
            Census, U.S. Department of Commerce, Washington, D.C.
Anderson, M.
   1988   *The American Census: A Social History.* New Haven, Conn.: Yale University Press.
Bean, F., B. Edmonston, and J. Passel, eds.
   1990   *Undocumented Migration to the United States: IRCA and the Experience of the 1980s.*
            Washington, D.C.: The Urban Institute Press.
Beresford, J.C.
   1993   Letter to R.D. Tortora dated September 13. The Right Data Company, Alexandria, Va.
   1994   Letter to B. Edmonston dated July 8, 1994. The Right Data Company, Alexandria, Va.
Bradburn, N.
   1992   Letter dated December 14 to B.E. Bryant, director, Bureau of the Census. Committee on
            National Statistics, National Research Council, Washington, D.C.
Bryant, B.E.
   1992   Results of the March Simplified Questionnaire Tests and Other Census 2000 Issues.
            Testimony delivered to the Subcommittee on Census and Population, House Committee
            on Post Office and Civil Service, July 1. Bureau of the Census, U.S. Department of
            Commerce, Washington, D.C.
   1993   Cenus-taking in a litigious, data-driven society. *Chance* 6(3):44-49.

Bureau of the Census
  1983   *1980 Census of Population, Chapter B-General Population Characteristics.* Washington, D.C.: U.S. Department of Commerce.
  1986   *1980 Census of Population and Housing—History, Part B, Chapter 5, Field Enumeration.* Washington, D.C.: U.S. Department of Commerce.
  1988a   Report of the Demographic Area Committee to Critique ISAS. September 2. Bureau of the Census, U.S. Department of Commerce, Washington, D.C.
  1988b   Report of the Demographic Area Committee to Critique the Proposed DCP. September 30. Bureau of the Census, U.S. Department of Commerce, Washington, D.C.
  1991a   Research Proposal to Improve Methods for Small Area Income Estimates. Bureau of the Census, U.S. Department of Commerce, Washington, D.C.
  1991b   *Technical Assessment of the Accuracy of Unadjusted Versus Adjusted 1990 Census Counts.* Report of the Undercount Steering Committee, June 21. Washington, D.C.: Bureau of the Census.
  1993a   Census Content and Questionnaire Design. Revision #2, December 9. Unpublished paper. Bureau of the Census, U.S. Department of Commerce, Washington, D.C.
  1993b   *Statistical Abstract of the United States, 1993.* Washington, D.C.: U.S. Department of Commerce.
  1994a   Funding for Geographic Support Activities: What Can and Cannot Be Done with Funding Requested in the FY 1995 Congressional Budget and Beyond. February 4. Geography Division, Bureau of the Census, U.S. Department of Commerce, Washington, D.C.
  1994b   The Small Area Income and Poverty Estimates Program for the 1990s. September. Housing and Household Economic Statistics Division, Bureau of the Census, U.S. Department of Commerce, Washington, D.C.
Census Data Quality Branch
  No date Implementation Test (IT) Mail Response Evaluation. Preliminary Report. Bureau of the Census, U.S. Department of Commerce, Washington, D.C.
Choldin, H.
  1994   *Looking for the Last Percent: The Controversy Over Census Adjustment.* New Brunswick: Rutgers University Press.
Citro, C.F., and M.L. Cohen, eds.
  1985   *The Bicentennial Census: New Directions for Methodology in 1990.* Panel on Decennial Census Methodology, Committee on National Statistics, National Research Council. Washington, D.C.: National Academy Press.
Citro, C.F., and G. Kalton, eds.
  1993   *The Future of the Survey of Income and Program Participation.* Panel to Evaluate the Survey of Income and Program Participation, Committee on National Statistics, National Research Council. Washington, D.C.: National Academy Press.
Cresce, A., S. Lapham, and S. Rolark
  1992   Preliminary evaluation of data from the race and ethnic origin questions in the 1990 census. 1992 Proceedings of the Social Statistics Section. Alexandria, Va.: American Statistical Association.
del Pinal, J. and S.J. Lapham
  1993   Impact of ethnic data needs in the United States. Pp. 447-475 in *Challenges of Measuring an Ethnic World: Science, Politics and Reality.* Statistics Canada and Bureau of the Census, U.S. Department of Commerce. Washington, D.C.: U.S. Government Printing Office.
Diffendal, G.
  1994   Block Level Analysis. May 10. Bureau of the Census, U.S. Department of Commerce, Washington, D.C.

Dillman, D.A., M.D. Sinclair, and J.R. Clark
  1993   The 1992 simplified questionnaire test: effects of questionnaire length, respondent-friendly design, and request for Social Security numbers on completion rates. Pp. 8-17 in *Proceedings of the 1993 Bureau of the Census Annual Research Conference.* Washington, D.C.: U.S. Department of Commerce.
Edmonston, B.
  1992   Nonresponse Rates for Census Questions, 1980 and 1990. Memorandum dated September 21 to the Federal Statistical System Working Group, Panel on Census Requirements for the Year 2000 and Beyond. Committee on National Statistics, National Research Council, Washington, D.C.
  1994   Census Cost Estimates. March 8. Panel on Census Requirements in the Year 2000 and Beyond, Committee on National Statistics, National Research Council, Washington, D.C.
Ericksen, E.P., and T.K. DeFonso
  1993   Beyond the net undercount: how to measure census error. *Chance* 6(4):38-43,14.
Fay, R.E.
  1988   *Evaluation of Census Coverage From the 1980 Post Enumeration Program (PEP): Census Population and Geocoding Errors as Measured by the E-Sample.* 1980 Census Preliminary Evaluation Results Memorandum No. 119. Washington, D.C.: Bureau of the Census.
Fellegi, I.P.
  1981   Comments. Pp. 51-68 in Congressional Research Service, *Using Cumulated Rolling Samples to Integrate Census and Survey Operations of the Census Bureau.* Prepared for the Subcommittee on Census and Population, Committee on Post Office and Civil Service, House of Representatives. Washington, D.C.: U.S. Government Printing Office.
Fienberg, S.E.
  1992   An adjusted census in 1990? The trial. *Chance* 5(3-4):28-38.
Gonzalez, M.E., D. Kasprzyk, and F. Scheuren
  1994   Nonresponse in federal surveys: an exploratory study. *Amstat News* 208 (April):1,6-7.
Green, S., and H.A. Scarr
  1993   Letter of Transmittal: U.S. Postal Service-Census Cooperation in Planning for the 2000 Decennial Census of Population and Housing. November 5. U.S. Postal Service and Bureau of the Census, U.S. Department of Commerce, Washington, D.C.
Grofman, B.
  1992   Expert witness testimony and the evolution of voting rights case law. Pp. 197-229 in B. Grofman and C. Davidson, eds., *Controversies in Minority Voting: The Voting Rights Perspective.* Washington D.C.: The Brookings Institution.
Hogan, H.
  1993   The 1990 post-enumeration survey: operations and results. *Journal of the American Statistical Association* 88(423):1047-1060.
Hogan, H., and G. Robinson
  1993   What the Census Bureau's coverage evaluation programs tell us about the differential undercount. Pp. 9-28 in *1993 Research Conference on Undercounted Ethnic Populations.* Bureau of the Census. Washington, D.C.: U.S. Department of Commerce.
Horvitz, D.G.
  1986   Statement to the Subcommittee on Census and Population, Committee on Post Office and Civil Service, House of Representatives, May 1. Research Triangle Institute, Research Triangle Park, N.C.
Irwin, R.
  1984   Feasibility of an Administrative Records Census in 1990. Special Report on the Use of Administrative Records. Administrative Records Subcommittee, Committee on the Use

of Administrative Records in the 1990 Census. Bureau of the Census, U.S. Department of Commerce, Washington, D.C.

Keeley, C.
1993   Could the Census Bureau Reduce the Undercount by Not Using a "Long Form?" Bureau of the Census, U.S. Department of Commerce, Washington, D.C.

Keller, J.
1993a   Census Cost Estimates: Response to Question 4 on Truncating and Sampling Nonre-sponse Follow-up. Facsimile message to B. Edmonston dated October 13. Bureau of the Census, U.S. Department of Commerce, Washington, D.C.
1993b   Cost Change Relative to 1990 Mail Response Rate (MRR). Table dated November 12. Bureau of the Census, U.S. Department of Commerce, Washington, D.C.
1994   Letter dated August 15 to M. Conrad, Panel on Census Requirements in the Year 2000 and Beyond. Bureau of the Census, U.S. Department of Commerce, Washington, D.C.

Kish, L.
1981   Population counts from cumulated samples. Pp. 5-50 in Congressional Research Service, *Using Cumulated Rolling Samples to Integrate Census and Survey Operations of the Census Bureau.* Prepared for the Subcommittee on Census and Population, Committee on Post Office and Civil Service, House of Representatives. Washington, D.C.: U.S. Government Printing Office.
1990   Rolling samples and censuses. *Survey Methodology* 16(1):63-79.

Kulka, R.A., N.A. Holt, W. Carter, and K.L. Dowd
1991   Self-reports of time pressures, concerns for privacy, and participation in the 1990 mail census. Pp. 33-54 in *Proceedings of the Bureau of the Census 1991 Annual Research Conference.* Washington, D.C.: U.S. Department of Commerce.

Mann, E.
1994   Race, Color and Related Concepts in the Decennial Censuses of the United States, 1790 to 1990. Paper commissioned by the Panel on Census Requirements in the Year 2000 and Beyond, Committee on National Statistics, National Research Council, Washington, D.C.

McKenney, N., and A. Cresce
1993   Measurement of ethnicity in the United States: Experiences of the U.S. Census Bureau. Pp. 173-223 in *Challenges of Measuring an Ethnic World: Science, Politics, and Reality.* Statistics Canada and Bureau of the Census, U.S. Department of Commerce. Washington, D.C.: U.S. Government Printing Office.

McKenney, N., C. Bennett, R. Harrison, and J. del Pinal
1993   Evaluating Racial and Ethnic Reporting in the 1990 Census. Paper presented at the 1993 Joint Statistical Meeting of the American Statistical Association, San Francisco, California

Miskura, S.M.
1992   Estimating the Full Cycle Costs for the Simplified Questionnaire Test (SQT). 2KS Memorandum Series, Design 2000, Book I, Chapter 30, #6, November 2. Bureau of the Census, U.S. Department of Commerce, Washington, D.C.
1993   Definition, Clarification and Issues: "One-Number Census." Memorandum for R.D. Tortora dated April 14, 1993. Bureau of the Census, U.S. Department of Commerce, Washington, D.C.

Murray, M.P.
1992   Census adjustment and the distribution of federal spending. *Demography* 29 (3):319-332.

Neece, L.
1993   Analysis of Potential Cost Reductions for the Truncated Nonresponse Follow-Up Census. Memorandum dated July 21 for J. Keller. Bureau of the Census, U.S. Department of Commerce, Washington, D.C.

Neece, L., and J. Pentercs
  1993   Analysis of Factors Associated with Census Cost Increases. Bureau of the Census, U.S. Department of Commerce, Washington, D.C.
  1994   1970, 1980, 1990 Decennial Census Cost Comparison. Year 2000 Research and Development Staff, Bureau of the Census, U.S. Department of Commerce, Washington, D.C.
New York State Department of Health
  1988   Experimental Estimates of Poverty, New York State Counties. N. Dunton and S. Leon. Paper presented at the National Conference in Applied Demography, Bowling Green, Ohio, September.
Office of Management and Budget
  1977   Statistical Directive 15: Race and Ethnic Standards for Federal Statistics and Administrative Reporting. Office of Management and Budget, Executive Office of the President, Washington, D.C.
O'Hare, W.P.
  1993   Assessing post-census state poverty estimates. *Population Research and Policy Review* 12:261-275.
Panel on Census Requirements in the Year 2000 and Beyond
  1993   *Planning the Decennial Census: Interim Report.* Committee on National Statistics, National Research Council. Washington, D.C.: National Academy Press.
Passel, J.S.
  1991   What census adjustment would mean. *Population Today* 19 (Summer):6-8.
Pentercs, J.
  1993a   Potential Cost Savings by Sampling for Nonresponse Follow-Up. Memorandum dated September 17 to J. Keller. Bureau of the Census, U.S. Department of Commerce, Washington, D.C.
  1993b   Response to Committee on National Statistic's Request for Cost Estimates. Memorandum dated December 15 to J. Keller. Bureau of the Census, U.S. Department of Commerce, Washington, D.C.
Redfern, P.
  1987   A Study on the Future of the Census of Population: Alternative Approaches. Eurostat Theme 3, Series C. Luxembourg: Office for Official Publications of the European Communities.
  1989   Population registers: some administrative and statistical pros and cons. *Journal of the Royal Statistical Society* Series A, 152(Part I):1-41.
Robinson, J.G., B. Ahmed, P. Das Gupta, and K. Woodrow
  1993   Estimation of population coverage in the 1990 U.S. census based on demographic analysis. *Journal of the American Statistical Association* 88(423):1061-1079.
Sailer, P., M. Weber, and E. Yau
  1993   How well can IRS count the population? Pp. 138-142 in *1993 Proceedings of the Government Statistics Section.* Alexandria, Va.: American Statistical Association.
Sailer, P., B. Windheim, and E. Yau
  1992   Toward a New Census Paradigm: Comparing Coverage of the Population in the Census and on Tax Documents. Paper presented at a meeting of the American Statistical Association, Boston, Mass.
  1993   How Well Can IRS Count the Population? Paper presented to a meeting of the Washington Statistical Society. Statistics of Income Division, Internal Revenue Service. June 8. U.S. Department of Treasury, Washington, D.C.
Scarr, H.A.
  1994   Review of the Census Bureau's Planning for the 2000 Census. Written testimony submitted to the House Subcommittee on Census, Statistics, and Postal Personnel, Committee on the Post Office and Civil Service, U.S. House of Representatives. Bureau of the Census, U.S. Department of Commerce, Washington, D.C.

Schultze, C.L.
  1993   Letter dated November 17 to H.A. Scarr, acting director, Bureau of the Census. Commit-
          tee on National Statistics, National Research Council, Washington, D.C.

Shapiro, G.M., G. Diffendal, and D. Cantor
  1993   Survey undercoverage: major causes and new estimates of magnitude. Pp. 638-663 in
          Proceedings of the 1993 Bureau of the Census Annual Research Conference. Washing-
          ton, D.C.: U.S. Department of Commerce.

Shapiro, G., and D. Kostanich
  1988   High response error and poor coverage are severely hurting the value of household survey
          data. Pp. 443-448 in *1988 Proceedings of the Section on Survey Research Methods.*
          Alexandria, Va.: American Statistical Association.

Siegel, J.S.
  1975   Coverage of Population in the 1970 Census and Some Implications for Public Programs.
          Current Population Reports. Series P-23, No. 56. Bureau of the Census. Washington,
          D.C.: U.S. Department of Commerce.

Siegel, P.M.
  1993   The Impact of Content on Census Coverage. Memorandum. Population Division, Bu-
          reau of the Census, U.S. Department of Commerce, Washington, D.C.

Statistics Canada and Bureau of the Census
  1993   *Challenges of Measuring an Ethnic World: Science, Politics and Reality.* Proceedings of
          the Joint Canada-United States Conference on the Measurement of Ethnicity, April 1-3,
          1992. Washington, D.C.: U.S. Government Printing Office.

Steffey, D.L., and N.M. Bradburn, eds.
  1994   *Counting People in the Information Age.* Panel to Evaluate Alternative Census Method-
          ologies, Committee on National Statistics, National Research Council. Washington, D.C.:
          National Academy Press.

Thompson, J.H.
  1992   Documentation of the 1990 Census Mail Return Rates. DSSD 1990 REX Memorandum
          Series #Q-13, October 15, to Charles D. Jones. Bureau of the Census, U.S. Department of
          Commerce, Washington, D.C.

Tortora, R.
  1993   Handouts on Results of Appeals and Long Form Experiment (ALFE) to Meeting of the
          Panel on Census Requirements in the Year 2000 and Beyond. October 14. Bureau of the
          Census, U.S. Department of Commerce, Washington, D.C.

Treat, J.B.
  1993   1993 National Census Test Appeals and Long-Form Experiment, Long-Form Compo-
          nent. Final Report. Census Data Quality Branch, Bureau of the Census, U.S. Department
          of Commerce, Washington, D.C.

U.S. General Accounting Office
  1990   *Federal Formula Programs: Outdated Population Data Used to Allocate Most Funds.*
          GAO/HRD-90-145. Washington, D.C.: U.S. General Accounting Office.
  1992   *Decennial Census: 1990 Results Show Need for Fundamental Reform.* GAO/GGD-92-
          94. Washington, D.C.: U.S. General Accounting Office.

Waters, M.C.
  1990   *Ethnic Options: Choosing Identities in America.* Berkeley: University of California
          Press.

Wolter, K.M.
  1991   Accounting for America's uncounted and miscounted. *Science* 253:12-15.

Zitter, M., and D. Levine
  1991   Needs for Small-Area Data for the Nation. Committee on National Statistics, National
          Research Council, Washington, D.C.

Appendices

A
Basic Information on
Census Questionnaires

This appendix summarizes information on the content of the decennial censuses, 1960-1990. In general, the number of items for which data are obtained in the census and the major content areas have remained about the same over this period. The 1990 long-form questionnaire (which includes the short-form questions) is shown in Figure A.1 (although the dimensions of the census form have been altered to fit into this book, the content is the same as on the original form). All households received the short form; a sample of households received the long form. The short form is the first 7 pages and page 32 of Figure A.1. The actual short form delivered to households in 1990 was 4 pages. The appendix also provides information on the number of households receiving and responding to the questionnaires in the 1970-1990 censuses.

SHORT-FORM AND LONG-FORM QUESTIONNAIRE CONTENT

Table A.1 is a summary of total population and housing items asked in the short- and long-form questionnaires. The summary shows great stability in the number of short-form population items, which are limited to basic demographic information. There has been a decline in the number of short-form housing items; hence, the burden of the short form on the population has declined somewhat over time. The number of long-form items (population and housing combined) grew from 49 items in 1960 to 64 items in 1970 and 65 items in 1980, declining to 58 items in 1990 (the Office of Management and Budget played a role in this reduction—see Chapter 6). In the 1970 census, the use of matrix sampling reduced the burden of the long form on individual households (the 1960 census also used matrix sampling but to a more limited extent).

The table indicates that the burden of the long form has progressively declined in terms of the sampling rate. Twenty-five percent of households were designated to receive the long form in 1960, 20 percent in 1970, 19 percent on average in 1980, and 16 percent on average in 1990. The 1970 census used a type of matrix sampling for both population and housing items: 15 percent of households received a markedly shorter long form, and 5 percent received a longer long form; some items were common to both forms, producing a 20 percent sample for those items.

The 1960 census also employed matrix sampling but to a more limited extent from the perspective of responding households. Different forms were used in large cities of 50,000 or more population and other areas; each contained a couple of questions unique to the form. In addition, in conventionally enumerated areas in 1960 (see below), 20 percent of households were asked one set of housing items by enumerators, and 5 percent were asked another set; some items were asked in common, producing a 25 percent sample for those items. In the remaining areas, however, which covered about 80 percent of households, every household in the 25 percent sample was asked to fill out and mail back a long form with all of the sample questions for the type of place (large city or other). Enumerators then transcribed the answers to computer-readable forms, transcribing the answers for 25, 20, or 5 percent of households, depending on the item (see Table A.2).

Table A.2 lists the various detailed items on the census. The housing portion of the long-form questionnaire no longer includes such items as possession of a washing machine or other appliances. The population portion of the long-form questionnaire, over time, has included more questions on disability and ancestry (although the question on birthplace of parents was deleted after 1970) and fewer on marriage and schooling. The greatest number of questions are related to employment, occupation, and income. For the income question, each added income source (e.g., pensions) is counted as a separate item because the respondent must consciously disaggregate the preceding year's income into component parts

QUESTIONNAIRE RECEIPT AND RESPONSE

Table A.3 lists the total number of both vacant and occupied housing units and the number of occupied housing units (households) in 1970, 1980, and 1990. Total housing units have increased over time from 69 million in 1970 to 102 million in 1990; total households have increased from 64 million to 92 million over the same period. Also shown are the number of households receiving the short and long forms and, for each form type, the number receiving and returning a form by mail. (Other households were visited by an enumerator to pick up their form.)

Assessing changes over time in the willingness of households to cooperate with the census, specifically, their willingness to mail back a form, is difficult because of changes in methodology.[1] The 1960 census was an exploratory attempt at mailback questionnaires and was limited to the long form (for this reason, Table A.3 does not include figures for 1960). The U.S. Postal Service (USPS) delivered unaddressed short forms for households to fill out and wait for enumerator pick-up. At the time of pick-up in areas of the country containing about 80 percent of the housing, enumerators left long forms at every fourth unit (25%) to be completed and returned by mail. (This was termed the two-stage procedure.) In the remaining areas, enumerators obtained answers to the long-form items from every fourth unit at the same time as they picked up the short form. (This was termed the single-stage or conventional procedure.)

In 1970, the USPS delivered questionnaires to addresses on a mailing list developed by the Census Bureau for areas containing about 60 percent of the housing. Four-fifths of housing units received a short form and the other one-fifth received one of two versions of the long form. In these mailout/mailback census areas, about 87 percent of households (occupied housing units) returned a questionnaire. The mail return rate (based on occupied housing units) was 87.8 percent for the short form and 85.5 percent for the long form, a difference of 2.3 percentage points. In the remaining conventionally enumerated areas containing about 40 percent of the housing, households received an unaddressed short form and were then visited by an enumerator who picked up the short form and, at every fifth household (20%), administered one of two versions of the long form.

In 1980, the mailout/mailback census areas covered about 96 percent of the housing. Overall, about 19 percent of housing units received the long form. In places with an estimated population of less than 2,500, the sampling rate was 1 in 2 (50%). In all other areas, it was 1 in 6 (17%). In the mailout/mailback areas, about 81 percent of households mailed back their questionnaire. The mail return rate (based on occupied housing units) was 81.6 percent for the short form and 80.1 percent for the long form, a difference of 1.5 percentage points.

In 1990, the mailout/mailback areas covered about 95 percent of the housing. (In most of these areas, the USPS delivered the questionnaires, but, in some areas, census enumerators made the delivery—see Appendix B.) Overall, about 17 percent of the housing units received a long form. In places (such as counties and incorporated places) with an estimated 1988 population of less than 2,500, the sampling rate was 1 in 2 (50%). Based also on precensus estimates, very populous census tracts (or equivalents) had a sampling rate of 1 in 8 (12.5%). All other areas had a sampling rate of 1 in 6 (17%). In the mailout/mailback areas, 74 percent of households returned their questionnaires. For both long and short forms, mail return rates (based on occupied housing units) were lower for

1990 than 1980. The long form return rate in 1990 was 4.5 percentage points below the short form mail return rate (70.4 percent versus 74.9 percent).

NOTE

[1]For descriptions of census methodology in the 1960, 1970, and 1980 censuses, see Citro and Cohen (1985:Chap. 3); for a description of the 1990 census methodology, see Appendix B. For official mail return rates (based on occupied housing units), see Chapter 6.

REFERENCE

Citro, C.F., and M.L. Cohen
    1985   *The Bicentennial Census: New Directions for Methodology in 1990.* Panel on Decennial
           Census Methodology, Committee on National Statistics, National Research Council.
           Washington, D.C.: National Academy Press.

TABLE A.1 Questions on the Decennial Census, 1960-1990, Totals[a]

Questionnaire Item	1960	1970	1980	1990
Short-form population items	5	5	6	6
Short-form housing items[b]	12	13	9	7
Combined short-form items	17	18	15	13
Long-form population items	23	37	37	35
15% long form		25		
5% long form		30		
Long-form housing items	26	27	28	23
15% long form		13		
5% long form		22		
Combined long-form items	49	64	65	58
15% long form		38		
5% long form		52		
Grand total short- and long-form items	66	82	80	71
On 15% long form		56		
On 5% long form		70		

SOURCE: Compiled by staff from reviewing census questionnaires.

NOTE: The 1980 and 1990 censuses used one long form with a variable sampling rate depending on the estimated population size of the area; the overall long-form sampling rate was about 19 percent of households in 1980 and 17 percent in 1990.

The 1970 census used matrix sampling, with two long forms, one containing items asked of 15 percent of the households and the other containing items asked of 5 percent; some items were common to both forms (producing a 20% sample).

The 1960 census also used matrix sampling, but to a lesser extent and with a complex design that is difficult to summarize. A few long-form housing items were asked only in large cities of 50,000 or more; a few other long-form housing items were asked only outside large cities. In addition, in areas using the conventional, single-stage procedure (see text), enumerators asked long-form questions of 25 percent of households overall, but asked some housing questions of only 20 percent of households and other housing questions of only 5 percent. In areas using the two-stage procedure, 25 percent of households were asked to fill out and mail back either the large city or other area questionnaire with all of the long-form items. However, enumerators subsequently transcribed some of the housing items for only 20 percent of households and other housing items for only 5 percent. Hence, the combined number of long-form population and housing items in the 1960 census, from the perspective of households asked to respond, ranged from 40-42 items in conventional areas to 48 items in two-stage areas outside large cities (compared with 49 items in the table).

[a]Totals should not be regarded as exact, as there is some interpretation as to what constitutes a separate item.

[b]Several items on vacant units are omitted because enumerators fill out these items, not household members.

TABLE A.2 Questions on the Decennial Census: 1960-1990 (S indicates short form; L indicates long form)

Questionnaire Item	1960	1970	1980	1990
Population items				
Age (and/or date of birth)	S	S	S	S
Sex	S	S	S	S
Race	S	S	S	S
Hispanic origin		L[b]	S	S
Relationship to household head	S	S	S	S
Marital status	S	S	S	S
Age at or date of first marriage	L	L[b]	L	
Married more than once	L	L[b]	L	
If remarried, was first marriage ended by death?		L[b]	L	
Number of children ever born to mother	L	L	L	L
School attendance/education attainment	L	L	L	L
Public or private school	L	L	L	L
Vocational training		L[b]		
Place of birth (short-form item in New York State in 1960)	L	L	L	L
Place of birth of mother and father	L	L[a]		
Citizenship (short-form item in New York State in 1960 and not asked elsewhere in that year)		L[b]	L	L
Year of immigration		L[b]	L	L
Language spoken at home (if born abroad in 1960)	L	L[a]	L	L
How well English spoken			L	L
Ancestry			L	L
Veteran status/period of service (for men only in 1960 and 1970)	L	L[a]	L	L
Years of military service				L
Place of residence 5 years ago	L	L[a,b]	L	L
Year moved to present residence (see housing item on year household head moved into unit)	L	L[a]		
Work disability		L[b]	L	L
Transportation disability			L	
Disabled for going outside the home alone				L
Disabled for taking care of personal needs				L
Duration of disability		L[b]		
Employment status	L	L	L	L
Hours worked in preceding week	L	L	L	L
Industry	L	L	L	L
Occupation	L	L	L	L
Class of worker	L	L	L	L
Place of work	L	L[a]	L	L

TABLE A.2 Continued

Means of transportation to work	L	L[a]	L	L
Commuting time			L	L
Carpooling			L	L
Year last worked	L	L	L	L
Weeks worked in preceding year	L	L	L	L
Hours worked per week in preceding year			L	L
Weeks unemployed in preceding year			L	
Activity 5 years ago		L	L	
Occupation 5 years ago		L[b]		
Industry 5 years ago		L[b]		
Class of worker 5 years ago		L[b]		
Income from earnings	L	L	L	L
Income from nonfarm self-employment (nonfarm plus farm self-employment in 1960)	L	L	L	L
Income from farm self-employment		L	L	L
Income from Social Security		L	L	L
Income from public assistance		L	L	L
Income from interest, dividends, rents			L	L
Income from pensions				L
All other income	L	L	L	L
Housing items				
Tenure—owned or rented	S	S	S	S
Number of rooms	S	S	S	S
Units at address	S[c]	S	S	S
Type of property	S[c]	S	S	S
Value (short-form item in large cities, long-form item otherwise in 1960)	S	S	S	S
Contract rent (short-form item in large cities, long-form item otherwise in 1960)	S	S	S	S
Does the rent include any meals				S
Access to unit	S[c]	S	S	
Condominium status			S	L
Condition	S[c]			
Water supply	S	S		
Toilet facilities	S	S		
Bathing facilities	S	S		
Complete plumbing facilities			S	L
Kitchen, cooking facilities	S	S	L	L
Telephone available	L	S	L	L
Basement	L[a]	S		
Utilities				
Electricity costs (for renters only in 1960 and 1970)	L	L	L	L
Gas costs (for renters only in 1960 and 1970)	L	L	L	L

continued on next page

TABLE A.2 Continued

Water costs	L	L	L	L
(for renters only in 1960 and 1970)				
Oil, coal, etc. costs	L	L	L	L
(for renters only in 1960 and 1970)				
Real estate taxes (for owners only)			L	L
Homeowners insurance			L	L
Whether have mortgage			L	L
Mortgage payment			L	L
(whether includes taxes and insurance)				
Whether have second mortgage			L	L
Payment for second mortgage(s)/loans				L
Condominium or mobile home fee				L
Farm residence/sales of farm products	L	L	L	L
(asked only outside large cities in 1960)				
Second home		L[b]		
Year structure built	L	L	L	L
Year household head moved into unit			L	L
(replaced pop. item on year moved in)				
Number of units in structure	L[a,c]	L	L	
Whether home mobile or fixed	L			
Number of stories		L[b]	L	
Elevator	L[a]	L[b]	L	
(asked only in large cities in 1960 combined with question on number of stories)				
Number of bathrooms	L[a]	L[a]	L	
Number of bedrooms	L[b]	L[b]	L	L
Source of water	L[a]	L[a]	L	L
(asked only outside large cities in 1960)				
Sewage disposal	L[a]	L[a]	L	L
(asked only outside large cities in 1960)				
Heating equipment	L	L	L	
Heating fuel	L[b]	L[b]	L	L
Cooking fuel		L[b]	L	
Water heating fuel		L[b]	L	
Radio sets	L[b]	L[b]		
(battery-operated only in 1970)				
Clothes washer	L[b]	L[b]		
Clothes dryer	L[b]	L[b]		
Home food freezer	L[b]	L[b]		
Air conditioning	L[b]	L[a]	L	
Television sets	L[b]	L[b]		
Whether television equipped for UHF		L[b]		
Dishwasher		L[b]		
Automobiles	L[a,b]	L[a]	L	L
(20% item in large cities, 5% item outside large cities in 1960)				
Vans or trucks			L	

TABLE A.2 Continued

SOURCE: Compiled by staff from reviewing census questionnaires.

[a]Indicates the 15 percent long form in the 1970 census and the items that were transcribed on a 20 percent basis in the 1960 census..

[b]Indicates the 5 percent long form in the 1970 census and the items that were transcribed on a 5 percent basis in the 1960 census.

[c]Item obtained by enumerator observation.

TABLE A.3 Number of Households Receiving the Census Questionnaires, 1970, 1980, and 1990, in millions

	1970	1980	1990
Total number of housing units[a]	68.7	88.4	102.3
Total number of households[b]	63.5	80.4	91.9
Number of households receiving short form	51.0	65.6	76.2
Households receiving short form for mailback[c]	31.2	62.8	70.9
Households returning short form by mail	27.4	51.3	53.1
Number of households receiving long form	12.4	14.8	15.7
Households receiving long form for mailback[c]	7.6	14.2	13.9
Households returning long form by mail	6.5	11.3	9.8

SOURCE: This table is based on information in Bureau of the Census memoranda, June 7, June 16, and September 3, 1994, from Florence Abramson to Meyer Zitter and Juanita Tamayo Lott.

NOTE: Because of rounding, mail return rates (based on occupied housing units) calculated from this table will not agree exactly with published rates.

[a]The total number of housing units includes both vacant and occupied units.

[b]Households are occupied housing units. The numbers of households receiving the short and long forms in the 1990 census include estimates for 3 million households for which definitive information regarding the type of form is not readily determined.

[c]For the 1970 and 1980 censuses, includes households in the mailout/mailback areas; for the 1990 census, includes households in the mailout/mailback and update/leave/mailback areas.

CENSUS '90

OFFICIAL 1990
U.S. CENSUS FORM

Thank you for taking time to complete and return this census questionnaire. It's important to you, your community, and the Nation.

The law requires answers but guarantees privacy.

By law (Title 13, U.S. Code), you're required to answer the census questions to the best of your knowledge. However, the same law guarantees that your census form remains confidential. For 72 years--or until the year 2062--only Census Bureau employees can see your form. No one else--no other government body, no police department, no court system or welfare agency--is permitted to see this confidential information under any circumstances.

How to get started--and get help.

Start by listing on the next page the names of all the people who live in your home. Please answer all questions with a black lead pencil. You'll find detailed instructions for answering the census in the enclosed guide. If you need additional help, call the toll-free telephone number to the left, near your address.

Please answer and return your form promptly.

Complete your form and return it by April 1, 1990 in the postage-paid envelope provided. Avoid the inconvenience of having a census taker visit your home.

Again, thank you for answering the 1990 Census.
Remember: Return the completed form by April 1, 1990.

Para personas de habla hispana --
(For Spanish-speaking persons)

Si usted desea un cuestionario del censo en español, llame sin cargo alguno al siguiente número: **1-800-CUENTAN**
                          (o sea 1-800-283-6826)

U.S. Department of Commerce
BUREAU OF THE CENSUS
FORM **D-2**

OMB No. 0607-0628
Approval Expires 07/31/91

FIGURE A.1 Long-form questionnaire, 1990 census.

Page 1

The 1990 census must count every person at his or her "usual residence." This means the place where the person lives and sleeps most of the time.

1a. List on the numbered lines below the name of each person living here on Sunday, April 1, including all persons staying here who have no other home. If EVERYONE at this address is staying here temporarily and usually lives somewhere else, follow the instructions given in question 1b below.

Include	Do NOT include
• Everyone who usually lives here such as family members, housemates and roommates, foster children, roomers, boarders, and live-in employees	• Persons who usually live somewhere else
• Persons who are temporarily away on a business trip, on vacation, or in a general hospital	• Persons who are away in an institution such as a prison, mental hospital, or a nursing home
• College students who stay here while attending college	• College students who live somewhere else while attending college
• Persons in the Armed Forces who live here	• Persons in the Armed Forces who live somewhere else
• Newborn babies still in the hospital	
• Children in boarding schools below the college level	
• Persons who stay here most of the week while working even if they have a home somewhere else	• Persons who stay somewhere else most of the week while working
• Persons with no other home who are staying here on April 1	

Print last name, first name, and middle initial for each person. Begin on line 1 with the household member (or one of the household members) in whose name this house or apartment is owned, being bought, or rented. If there is no such person, start on line 1 with any adult household member.

	LAST	FIRST	INITIAL		LAST	FIRST	INITIAL
1				7			
2				8			
3				9			
4				10			
5				11			
6				12			

1b. If EVERYONE is staying here only temporarily and usually lives somewhere else, list the name of each person on the numbered lines above, fill this circle ⟶ ○ and print their usual address below. DO NOT PRINT THE ADDRESS LISTED ON THE FRONT COVER.

House number	Street or road/Rural route and box number	Apartment number

City	State	ZIP Code

County or foreign country	Names of nearest intersecting streets or roads

NOW PLEASE OPEN THE FLAP TO PAGE 2 AND ANSWER ALL QUESTIONS FOR THE FIRST 7 PEOPLE LISTED. USE A BLACK LEAD PENCIL ONLY.

Page 2

	PERSON 1
Please fill one column ➡ for each person listed in Question 1a on page 1.	Last name First name Middle initial

2. How is this person related to PERSON 1?

Fill ONE circle for each person.

If **Other relative** of person in column 1, fill circle and print exact relationship, such as mother-in-law, grandparent, son-in-law, niece, cousin, and so on.

START in this column with the household member (or one of the members) in whose name the home is owned, being bought, or rented.

If there is no such person, start in this column with any adult household member.

■

3. Sex

Fill ONE circle for each person.

○ Male   ○ Female

4. Race

Fill ONE circle for the race that the person considers himself/herself to be.

     If **Indian (Amer.)**, print the name of the enrolled or principal tribe. ⟶

     If **Other Asian or Pacific Islander (API)**, print one group, for example: Hmong, Fijian, Laotian, Thai, Tongan, Pakistani, Cambodian, and so on. ⟶

     If **Other race**, print race. ⟶

○ White
○ Black or Negro
○ Indian (Amer.) (Print the name of the enrolled or principal tribe.) ⌐
    ⌐   ¬
○ Eskimo
○ Aleut   Asian or Pacific Islander (API)

○ Chinese   ○ Japanese
○ Filipino ■   ○ Asian Indian
○ Hawaiian   ○ Samoan
○ Korean   ○ Guamanian
○ Vietnamese   ○ Other API ⌐
    ⌐   ¬
○ Other race (Print race) ⌐

5. Age and year of birth

   a. Print each person's age at last birthday. Fill in the matching circle below each box.

   b. Print each person's year of birth and fill the matching circle below each box.

a. Age	b. Year of birth
	1
0 ○ 0 ○ 0 ○	1 ● 8 ○ 0 ○ 0 ○
1 ○ 1 ○ 1 ○	9 ○ 1 ○ 1 ○
2 ○ 2 ○	2 ○ 2 ○
3 ○ 3 ○	3 ○ 3 ○
4 ○ 4 ○	■ 4 ○ 4 ○
5 ○ 5 ○	5 ○ 5 ○
6 ○ 6 ○	6 ○ 6 ○
7 ○ 7 ○	7 ○ 7 ○
8 ○ 8 ○	8 ○ 8 ○
9 ○ 9 ○	9 ○ 9 ○

6. Marital status

Fill ONE circle for each person.

○ Now married   ○ Separated
○ Widowed   ○ Never married
○ Divorced

7. Is this person of Spanish/Hispanic origin?

Fill ONE circle for each person.

     If **Yes, other Spanish/Hispanic**, print one group. ⟶

○ No (not Spanish/Hispanic)
○ Yes, Mexican, Mexican-Am., Chicano
○ Yes, Puerto Rican ■
○ Yes, Cuban
○ Yes, other Spanish/Hispanic
    (Print one group, for example: Argentinean, Colombian, Dominican, Nicaraguan, Salvadoran, Spaniard, and so on.) ⌐
    ⌐   ¬

FOR CENSUS USE ⟶

○

○

PLEASE ALSO ANSWER HOUSING QUESTIONS ON PAGE 3 ⟶

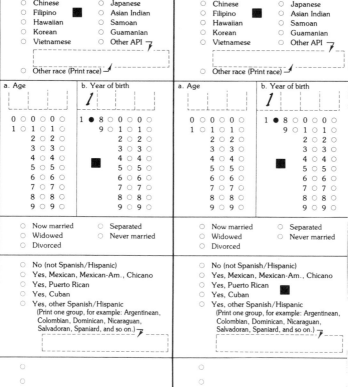

PERSON 2	PERSON 3
Last name	Last name
First name Middle initial	First name Middle initial

If a RELATIVE of Person 1:

PERSON 2:
- ○ Husband/wife
- ○ Natural-born or adopted son/daughter
- ○ Stepson/ stepdaughter
- ○ Brother/sister
- ○ Father/mother
- ○ Grandchild
- ○ Other relative ⌐

If NOT RELATED to Person 1:
- ○ Roomer, boarder, or foster child
- ■ Housemate, roommate
- ○ Unmarried partner
- ○ Other nonrelative

- ○ Male   ○ Female

- ○ White
- ○ Black or Negro
- ○ Indian (Amer.) (Print the name of the enrolled or principal tribe.)⌐
- ○ Eskimo
- ○ Aleut

Asian or Pacific Islander (API)
- ○ Chinese
- ■ Filipino
- ○ Hawaiian
- ○ Korean
- ○ Vietnamese
- ○ Japanese
- ○ Asian Indian
- ○ Samoan
- ○ Guamanian
- ○ Other API ⌐
- ○ Other race (Print race) ⌐

a. Age   b. Year of birth   1

0 ○	0 ○	0 ○		1 ●	8 ○	0 ○	0 ○	0 ○	
1 ○	1 ○	1 ○		9 ○		1 ○	1 ○	1 ○	
	2 ○	2 ○				2 ○	2 ○	2 ○	
	3 ○	3 ○				3 ○	3 ○	3 ○	
	4 ○	4 ○		■		4 ○	4 ○	4 ○	
	5 ○	5 ○				5 ○	5 ○	5 ○	
	6 ○	6 ○				6 ○	6 ○	6 ○	
	7 ○	7 ○				7 ○	7 ○	7 ○	
	8 ○	8 ○				8 ○	8 ○	8 ○	
	9 ○	9 ○				9 ○	9 ○	9 ○	

- ○ Now married
- ○ Widowed
- ○ Divorced
- ○ Separated
- ○ Never married

- ○ No (not Spanish/Hispanic)
- ○ Yes, Mexican, Mexican-Am., Chicano
- ○ Yes, Puerto Rican
- ○ Yes, Cuban
- ○ Yes, other Spanish/Hispanic (Print one group, for example: Argentinean, Colombian, Dominican, Nicaraguan, Salvadoran, Spaniard, and so on.) ⌐

- ○
- ○

PERSON 3:

If a RELATIVE of Person 1:
- ○ Husband/wife
- ○ Natural-born or adopted son/daughter
- ○ Stepson/ stepdaughter
- ○ Brother/sister
- ○ Father/mother
- ○ Grandchild
- ○ Other relative ⌐

If NOT RELATED to Person 1:
- ○ Roomer, boarder, or foster child
- ■ Housemate, roommate
- ○ Unmarried partner
- ○ Other nonrelative

- ○ Male   ○ Female

- ○ White
- ○ Black or Negro
- ○ Indian (Amer.) (Print the name of the enrolled or principal tribe.)⌐
- ○ Eskimo
- ○ Aleut

Asian or Pacific Islander (API)
- ○ Chinese
- ■ Filipino
- ○ Hawaiian
- ○ Korean
- ○ Vietnamese
- ○ Japanese
- ○ Asian Indian
- ○ Samoan
- ○ Guamanian
- ○ Other API ⌐
- ○ Other race (Print race) ⌐

- ○ Now married
- ○ Widowed
- ○ Divorced
- ○ Separated
- ○ Never married

- ○ No (not Spanish/Hispanic)
- ○ Yes, Mexican, Mexican-Am., Chicano
- ○ Yes, Puerto Rican ■
- ○ Yes, Cuban
- ○ Yes, other Spanish/Hispanic (Print one group, for example: Argentinean, Colombian, Dominican, Nicaraguan, Salvadoran, Spaniard, and so on.) ⌐

- ○
- ○

PLEASE ALSO ANSWER HOUSING QUESTIONS ON PAGE 3

PERSON 4	PERSON 5

Last name

First name — Middle initial

Last name

First name — Middle initial

If a RELATIVE of Person 1:

○ Husband/wife ○ Brother/sister
○ Natural-born ○ Father/mother
  or adopted ○ Grandchild
  son/daughter ○ Other relative ⟶
○ Stepson/
  stepdaughter

If NOT RELATED to Person 1:

○ Roomer, boarder, ○ Unmarried
  or foster child   partner
○ Housemate, ■ ○ Other
  roommate   nonrelative

○ Male ○ Female

○ White
○ Black or Negro
○ Indian (Amer.) (Print the name of the
  enrolled or principal tribe.)⟶

○ Eskimo
○ Aleut   Asian or Pacific Islander (API)

○ Chinese ○ Japanese
○ Filipino ■ ○ Asian Indian
○ Hawaiian ○ Samoan
○ Korean ○ Guamanian
○ Vietnamese ○ Other API ⟶

○ Other race (Print race)⟶

a. Age | b. Year of birth

1

0 0 0 0 0 | 1 ● 8 0 0 0 0
1 ○ 1 ○ 1 ○ | 9 ○ 1 ○ 1 ○
    2 ○ 2 ○ | 2 ○ 2 ○
    3 ○ 3 ○ | 3 ○ 3 ○
    4 ○ 4 ○ | ■   4 ○ 4 ○
    5 ○ 5 ○ | 5 ○ 5 ○
    6 ○ 6 ○ | 6 ○ 6 ○
    7 ○ 7 ○ | 7 ○ 7 ○
    8 ○ 8 ○ | 8 ○ 8 ○
    9 ○ 9 ○ | 9 ○ 9 ○

○ Now married ○ Separated
○ Widowed ○ Never married
○ Divorced

○ No (not Spanish/Hispanic)
○ Yes, Mexican, Mexican-Am., Chicano
○ Yes, Puerto Rican ■
○ Yes, Cuban
○ Yes, other Spanish/Hispanic
  (Print one group, for example: Argentinean,
  Colombian, Dominican, Nicaraguan,
  Salvadoran, Spaniard, and so on.) ⟶

○

○

PERSON 5

If a RELATIVE of Person 1:

○ Husband/wife ○ Brother/sister
○ Natural-born ○ Father/mother
  or adopted ○ Grandchild
  son/daughter ○ Other relative ⟶
○ Stepson/
  stepdaughter

If NOT RELATED to Person 1:

○ Roomer, boarder, ○ Unmarried
  or foster child   partner
○ Housemate, ■ ○ Other
  roommate   nonrelative

○ Male ○ Female

○ White
○ Black or Negro
○ Indian (Amer.) (Print the name of the
  enrolled or principal tribe.)⟶

○ Eskimo
○ Aleut   Asian or Pacific Islander (API)

○ Chinese ○ Japanese
○ Filipino ■ ○ Asian Indian
○ Hawaiian ○ Samoan
○ Korean ○ Guamanian
○ Vietnamese ○ Other API ⟶

○ Other race (Print race)⟶

a. Age | b. Year of birth

1

0 0 0 0 0 | 1 ● 8 0 0 0 0
1 ○ 1 ○ 1 ○ | 9 ○ 1 ○ 1 ○
    2 ○ 2 ○ | 2 ○ 2 ○
    3 ○ 3 ○ | 3 ○ 3 ○
    4 ○ 4 ○ | ■   4 ○ 4 ○
    5 ○ 5 ○ | 5 ○ 5 ○
    6 ○ 6 ○ | 6 ○ 6 ○
    7 ○ 7 ○ | 7 ○ 7 ○
    8 ○ 8 ○ | 8 ○ 8 ○
    9 ○ 9 ○ | 9 ○ 9 ○

○ Now married ○ Separated
○ Widowed ○ Never married
○ Divorced

○ No (not Spanish/Hispanic)
○ Yes, Mexican, Mexican-Am., Chicano
○ Yes, Puerto Rican ■
○ Yes, Cuban
○ Yes, other Spanish/Hispanic
  (Print one group, for example: Argentinean,
  Colombian, Dominican, Nicaraguan,
  Salvadoran, Spaniard, and so on.) ⟶

○

○

PERSON 6	PERSON 7
Last name	Last name
First name — Middle initial	First name — Middle initial

If a RELATIVE of Person 1:

PERSON 6:
- ○ Husband/wife
- ○ Natural-born or adopted son/daughter
- ○ Stepson/ stepdaughter
- ○ Brother/sister
- ○ Father/mother
- ○ Grandchild
- ○ Other relative

If NOT RELATED to Person 1:
- ○ Roomer, boarder, or foster child
- ○ Housemate, roommate ■
- ○ Unmarried partner
- ○ Other nonrelative

- ○ Male
- ○ Female

- ○ White
- ○ Black or Negro
- ○ Indian (Amer.) (Print the name of the enrolled or principal tribe.)
- ○ Eskimo
- ○ Aleut

Asian or Pacific Islander (API)
- ○ Chinese
- ○ Filipino ■
- ○ Hawaiian
- ○ Korean
- ○ Vietnamese
- ○ Japanese
- ○ Asian Indian
- ○ Samoan
- ○ Guamanian
- ○ Other API

- ○ Other race (Print race)

a. Age | **b. Year of birth**

```
0 ○ 0 ○ 0 ○     1 ● 8 ○ 0 ○ 0 ○
1 ○ 1 ○ 1 ○     9 ○ 1 ○ 1 ○
    2 ○ 2 ○         2 ○ 2 ○
    3 ○ 3 ○         3 ○ 3 ○
    4 ○ 4 ○  ■      4 ○ 4 ○
    5 ○ 5 ○         5 ○ 5 ○
    6 ○ 6 ○         6 ○ 6 ○
    7 ○ 7 ○         7 ○ 7 ○
    8 ○ 8 ○         8 ○ 8 ○
    9 ○ 9 ○         9 ○ 9 ○
```

- ○ Now married
- ○ Widowed
- ○ Divorced
- ○ Separated
- ○ Never married

- ○ No (not Spanish/Hispanic)
- ○ Yes, Mexican, Mexican-Am., Chicano
- ○ Yes, Puerto Rican
- ○ Yes, Cuban
- ○ Yes, other Spanish/Hispanic
  (Print one group, for example: Argentinean, Colombian, Dominican, Nicaraguan, Salvadoran, Spaniard, and so on.)

- ○
- ○

PERSON 7:

If a RELATIVE of Person 1:
- ○ Husband/wife
- ○ Natural-born or adopted son/daughter
- ○ Stepson/ stepdaughter
- ○ Brother/sister
- ○ Father/mother
- ○ Grandchild
- ○ Other relative

If NOT RELATED to Person 1:
- ○ Roomer, boarder, or foster child
- ○ Housemate, roommate ■
- ○ Unmarried partner
- ○ Other nonrelative

- ○ Male
- ○ Female

- ○ White
- ○ Black or Negro
- ○ Indian (Amer.) (Print the name of the enrolled or principal tribe.)
- ○ Eskimo
- ○ Aleut

Asian or Pacific Islander (API)
- ○ Chinese
- ○ Filipino ■
- ○ Hawaiian
- ○ Korean
- ○ Vietnamese
- ○ Japanese
- ○ Asian Indian
- ○ Samoan
- ○ Guamanian
- ○ Other API

- ○ Other race (Print race)

a. Age | **b. Year of birth**

```
0 ○ 0 ○ 0 ○     1 ● 8 ○ 0 ○ 0 ○
1 ○ 1 ○ 1 ○     9 ○ 1 ○ 1 ○
    2 ○ 2 ○         2 ○ 2 ○
    3 ○ 3 ○         3 ○ 3 ○
    4 ○ 4 ○  ■      4 ○ 4 ○
    5 ○ 5 ○         5 ○ 5 ○
    6 ○ 6 ○         6 ○ 6 ○
    7 ○ 7 ○         7 ○ 7 ○
    8 ○ 8 ○         8 ○ 8 ○
    9 ○ 9 ○         9 ○ 9 ○
```

- ○ Now married
- ○ Widowed
- ○ Divorced
- ○ Separated
- ○ Never married

- ○ No (not Spanish/Hispanic)
- ○ Yes, Mexican, Mexican-Am., Chicano
- ○ Yes, Puerto Rican ■
- ○ Yes, Cuban
- ○ Yes, other Spanish/Hispanic
  (Print one group, for example: Argentinean, Colombian, Dominican, Nicaraguan, Salvadoran, Spaniard, and so on.)

- ○
- ○

NOW PLEASE ANSWER QUESTIONS H1a—H26 FOR THIS HOUSEHOLD

H1a. Did you leave anyone out of your list of persons for Question 1a on page 1 because you were not sure if the person should be listed — for example, someone temporarily away on a business trip or vacation, a newborn baby still in the hospital, or a person who stays here once in a while and has no other home?

○ Yes, please print the name(s) ○ No
and reason(s). ↗

----

b. Did you include anyone in your list of persons for Question 1a on page 1 even though you were not sure that the person should be listed — for example, a visitor who is staying here temporarily or a person who usually lives somewhere else?

○ Yes, please print the name(s) ○ No
and reason(s). ↗

H2. **Which best describes this building?** Include all apartments, flats, etc., even if vacant.

○ A mobile home or trailer
○ A one-family house detached from any other house
○ A one-family house attached to one or more houses
○ A building with 2 apartments
○ A building with 3 or 4 apartments
○ A building with 5 to 9 apartments
○ A building with 10 to 19 apartments
○ A building with 20 to 49 apartments
○ A building with 50 or more apartments
○ Other

H3. **How many rooms do you have in this house or apartment?** Do NOT count bathrooms, porches, balconies, foyers, halls, or half-rooms.

○ 1 room   ○ 4 rooms   ○ 7 rooms
○ 2 rooms   ○ 5 rooms   ○ 8 rooms
○ 3 rooms   ○ 6 rooms   ○ 9 or more rooms

H4. Is this house or apartment —

○ Owned by you or someone in this household with a mortgage or loan?
○ Owned by you or someone in this household free and clear (without a mortgage)?
○ Rented for cash rent?
○ Occupied without payment of cash rent?

If this is a ONE-FAMILY HOUSE —
H5a. **Is this house on ten or more acres?**

○ Yes   ○ No

b. **Is there a business (such as a store or barber shop) or a medical office on this property?**

○ Yes   ○ No

Answer only if you or someone in this household OWNS OR IS BUYING this house or apartment —
H6. **What is the value of this property; that is, how much do you think this house and lot or condominium unit would sell for if it were for sale?**

○ Less than $10,000   ○ $70,000 to $74,999
○ $10,000 to $14,999   ○ $75,000 to $79,999
○ $15,000 to $19,999   ○ $80,000 to $89,999
○ $20,000 to $24,999   ○ $90,000 to $99,999
○ $25,000 to $29,999   ○ $100,000 to $124,999
○ $30,000 to $34,999   ○ $125,000 to $149,999
○ $35,000 to $39,999   ○ $150,000 to $174,999
○ $40,000 to $44,999   ○ $175,000 to $199,999
○ $45,000 to $49,999   ○ $200,000 to $249,999
○ $50,000 to $54,999   ○ $250,000 to $299,999
○ $55,000 to $59,999   ○ $300,000 to $399,999
○ $60,000 to $64,999   ○ $400,000 to $499,999
○ $65,000 to $69,999   ○ $500,000 or more

Answer only if you PAY RENT for this house or apartment —
H7a. **What is the monthly rent?**

○ Less than $80   ○ $375 to $399
○ $80 to $99   ○ $400 to $424
○ $100 to $124   ○ $425 to $449
○ $125 to $149   ○ $450 to $474
○ $150 to $174   ○ $475 to $499
○ $175 to $199   ○ $500 to $524
○ $200 to $224   ○ $525 to $549
○ $225 to $249   ○ $550 to $599
○ $250 to $274   ○ $600 to $649
○ $275 to $299   ○ $650 to $699
○ $300 to $324   ○ $700 to $749
○ $325 to $349   ○ $750 to $999
○ $350 to $374   ○ $1,000 or more

b. **Does the monthly rent include any meals?**

○ Yes   ○ No

FOR CENSUS USE

A. Total persons

B. Type of unit

Occupied	Vacant
○ First form	○ Regular
○ Cont'n	○ Usual home elsewhere

C1. Vacancy status

○ For rent   ○ For seas/
○ For sale only   rec/occ
○ Rented or   ○ For migrant
sold, not   workers
occupied   ○ Other vacant

C2. Is this unit boarded up?

○ Yes   ○ No

D. Months vacant

○ Less than 1   ○ 6 up to 12
○ 1 up to 2   ○ 12 up to 24
○ 2 up to 6   ○ 24 or more

E. Complete after

○ LR   ○ TC   ○ QA   JIC 1
○ P/F ○ RE   ○ I/T ○
○ MV   ○ ED   ○ EN

○ P0   ○ P3   ○ P6
○ P1   ○ P4   ○ IA   JIC 2
○ P2   ○ P5   ○ SM   ○

F. Cov.

○ 1b   ○ 1a   ○ 7   ○ H1

G. DO   **ID**

A. Total persons digits and census use number grids:

○ ○
I I
2 2
3
4
5
6
7
8
9

0	0	0	0	0	0	0	0	0	0	0
I	I	I	I	I	I	I	I	I	I	I
2	2	2	2	2	2	2	2	2	2	2
3	3	3	3	3	3	3	3	3	3	3
4	4	4	4	4	4	4	4	4	4	4
5	5	5	5	5	5	5	5	5	5	5
6	6	6	6	6	6	6	6	6	6	6
7	7	7	7	7	7	7	7	7	7	7
8	8	8	8	8	8	8	8	8	8	8
9	9	9	9	9	9	9	9	9	9	9

Page 4

H8. When did the person listed in column 1 on page 2 move into this house or apartment?

- ○ 1989 or 1990
- ○ 1985 to 1988
- ○ 1980 to 1984
- ○ 1970 to 1979
- ○ 1960 to 1969
- ○ 1959 or earlier

H9. How many bedrooms do you have; that is, how many bedrooms would you list if this house or apartment were on the market for sale or rent?

- ○ No bedroom
- ○ 1 bedroom
- ○ 2 bedrooms
- ○ 3 bedrooms
- ○ 4 bedrooms
- ○ 5 or more bedrooms

H10. Do you have COMPLETE plumbing facilities in this house or apartment; that is, 1) hot and cold piped water, 2) a flush toilet, and 3) a bathtub or shower?

- ○ Yes, have all three facilities
- ○ No

H11. Do you have COMPLETE kitchen facilities; that is, 1) a sink with piped water, 2) a range or cookstove, and 3) a refrigerator?

- ○ Yes
- ○ No

H12. Do you have a telephone in this house or apartment?

- ○ Yes
- ○ No

H13. How many automobiles, vans, and trucks of one-ton capacity or less are kept at home for use by members of your household?

- ○ None
- ○ 1
- ○ 2
- ○ 3
- ○ 4
- ○ 5
- ○ 6
- ○ 7 or more

H14. Which FUEL is used MOST for heating this house or apartment?

- ○ Gas: from underground pipes serving the neighborhood
- ○ Gas: bottled, tank, or LP
- ○ Electricity
- ○ Fuel oil, kerosene, etc.
- ○ Coal or coke
- ○ Wood
- ○ Solar energy
- ○ Other fuel
- ○ No fuel used

H15. Do you get water from —

- ○ A public system such as a city water department, or private company?
- ○ An individual drilled well?
- ○ An individual dug well?
- ○ Some other source such as a spring, creek, river, cistern, etc.?

H16. Is this building connected to a public sewer?

- ○ Yes, connected to public sewer
- ○ No, connected to septic tank or cesspool
- ○ No, use other means

H17. About when was this building first built?

- ○ 1989 or 1990
- ○ 1985 to 1988
- ○ 1980 to 1984
- ○ 1970 to 1979
- ○ 1960 to 1969
- ○ 1950 to 1959
- ○ 1940 to 1949
- ○ 1939 or earlier
- ○ Don't know

H18. Is this house or apartment part of a condominium?

- ○ Yes
- ○ No

If you live in an apartment building, skip to H20.

H19a. Is this house on less than 1 acre?

- ○ Yes — *Skip to H20*
- ○ No

b. In 1989, what were the actual sales of all agricultural products from this property?

- ○ None
- ○ $1 to $999
- ○ $1,000 to $2,499
- ○ $2,500 to $4,999
- ○ $5,000 to $9,999
- ○ $10,000 or more

PLEASE ALSO ANSWER THESE QUESTIONS FOR YOUR HOUSEHOLD

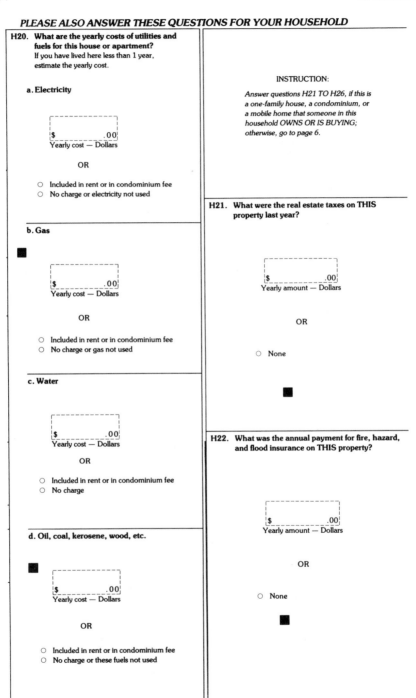

H20. What are the yearly costs of utilities and fuels for this house or apartment?
If you have lived here less than 1 year, estimate the yearly cost.

a. Electricity

```
$ _____ .00
```
Yearly cost — Dollars

OR

○ Included in rent or in condominium fee
○ No charge or electricity not used

b. Gas

```
$ _____ .00
```
Yearly cost — Dollars

OR

○ Included in rent or in condominium fee
○ No charge or gas not used

c. Water

```
$ _____ .00
```
Yearly cost — Dollars

OR

○ Included in rent or in condominium fee
○ No charge

d. Oil, coal, kerosene, wood, etc.

```
$ _____ .00
```
Yearly cost — Dollars

OR

○ Included in rent or in condominium fee
○ No charge or these fuels not used

INSTRUCTION:

Answer questions H21 TO H26, if this is a one-family house, a condominium, or a mobile home that someone in this household OWNS OR IS BUYING; otherwise, go to page 6.

H21. What were the real estate taxes on THIS property last year?

```
$ _____ .00
```
Yearly amount — Dollars

OR

○ None

H22. What was the annual payment for fire, hazard, and flood insurance on THIS property?

```
$ _____ .00
```
Yearly amount — Dollars

OR

○ None

H23a. Do you have a mortgage, deed of trust, contract to purchase, or similar debt on THIS property?

- ○ Yes, mortgage, deed of trust, or similar debt ⎫
- ○ Yes, contract to purchase ⎬ *Go to H23b*
- ○ No — *Skip to H24a* ⎭

■

b. How much is your regular monthly mortgage payment on THIS property? Include payment only on first mortgage or contract to purchase.

┌─────────────────┐
│ $_____.00 │
└─────────────────┘
Monthly amount — Dollars

OR

- ○ No regular payment required — *Skip to H24a*

c. Does your regular monthly mortgage payment include payments for real estate taxes on THIS property?

■

- ○ Yes, taxes included in payment
- ○ No, taxes paid separately or taxes not required

d. Does your regular monthly mortgage payment include payments for fire, hazard, or flood insurance on THIS property?

- ○ Yes, insurance included in payment
- ○ No, insurance paid separately or no insurance

■

H24a. Do you have a second or junior mortgage or a home equity loan on THIS property?

- ○ Yes
- ○ No — *Skip to H25*

■

b. How much is your regular monthly payment on all second or junior mortgages and all home equity loans?

┌─────────────────┐
│ $_____.00 │
└─────────────────┘
Monthly amount — Dollars

OR

- ○ No regular payment required

■

Answer ONLY if this is a CONDOMINIUM —

H25. What is the monthly condominium fee?

┌─────────────────┐
│ $_____.00 │
└─────────────────┘
Monthly amount — Dollars

■

Answer ONLY if this is a MOBILE HOME —

H26. What was the total cost for personal property taxes, site rent, registration fees, and license fees on this mobile home and its site last year? Exclude real estate taxes.

┌─────────────────┐
│ $_____.00 │
└─────────────────┘
Yearly amount — Dollars

Please turn to page 6. ➔

Page 6

PERSON 1

Last name   First name   Middle initial

8. In what U.S. State or foreign country was this person born?

(Name of State or foreign country; or Puerto Rico, Guam, etc.)

9. Is this person a CITIZEN of the United States?

- ○ Yes, born in the United States — *Skip to 11*
- ○ Yes, born in Puerto Rico, Guam, the U.S. Virgin Islands, or Northern Marianas
- ○ Yes, born abroad of American parent or parents
- ○ Yes, U.S. citizen by naturalization
- ○ No, not a citizen of the United States

10. When did this person come to the United States to stay?

- ○ 1987 to 1990
- ○ 1985 or 1986
- ○ 1982 to 1984
- ○ 1980 or 1981
- ○ 1975 to 1979
- ○ 1970 to 1974
- ○ 1965 to 1969
- ○ 1960 to 1964
- ○ 1950 to 1959
- ○ Before 1950

11. At any time since February 1, 1990, has this person attended regular school or college?
Include only nursery school, kindergarten, elementary school, and schooling which leads to a high school diploma or a college degree.

- ○ No, has not attended since February 1
- ○ Yes, public school, public college
- ○ Yes, private school, private college

12. How much school has this person COMPLETED?
Fill ONE circle for the highest level COMPLETED or degree RECEIVED. If currently enrolled, mark the level of previous grade attended or highest degree received.

- ○ No school completed
- ○ Nursery school
- ○ Kindergarten
- ○ 1st, 2nd, 3rd, or 4th grade
- ○ 5th, 6th, 7th, or 8th grade
- ○ 9th grade
- ○ 10th grade
- ○ 11th grade
- ○ 12th grade, **NO DIPLOMA**
- ○ **HIGH SCHOOL GRADUATE** - high school DIPLOMA or the equivalent (For example: GED)
- ○ Some college but no degree
- ○ Associate degree in college - Occupational program
- ○ Associate degree in college - Academic program
- ○ Bachelor's degree (For example: BA, AB, BS)
- ○ Master's degree (For example: MA, MS, MEng, MEd, MSW, MBA)
- ○ Professional school degree (For example: MD, DDS, DVM, LLB, JD)
- ○ Doctorate degree (For example: PhD, EdD)

13. What is this person's ancestry or ethnic origin?
(See instruction guide for further information.)

(For example: German, Italian, Afro-Amer., Croatian, Cape Verdean, Dominican, Ecuadoran, Haitian, Cajun, French Canadian, Jamaican, Korean, Lebanese, Mexican, Nigerian, Irish, Polish, Slovak, Taiwanese, Thai, Ukrainian, etc.)

14a. Did this person live in this house or apartment 5 years ago (on April 1, 1985)?

- ○ Born after April 1, 1985 — *Go to questions for the next person*
- ○ Yes — *Skip to 15a*
- ○ No

b. Where did this person live 5 years ago (on April 1, 1985)?

(1) Name of U.S. State or foreign country

(If outside U.S., print answer above and skip to 15a.)

(2) Name of county in the U.S.

(3) Name of city or town in the U.S.

(4) Did this person live inside the city or town limits?

- ○ Yes
- ○ No, lived outside the city/town limits

15a. Does this person speak a language other than English at home?

- ○ Yes
- ○ No — *Skip to 16*

b. What is this language?

(For example: Chinese, Italian, Spanish, Vietnamese)

c. How well does this person speak English?

- ○ Very well
- ○ Well
- ○ Not well
- ○ Not at all

16. When was this person born?

- ○ Born before April 1, 1975 — *Go to 17a*
- ○ Born April 1, 1975 or later — *Go to questions for the next person*

17a. Has this person ever been on active-duty military service in the Armed Forces of the United States or ever been in the United States military Reserves or the National Guard? If service was in Reserves or National Guard only, see instruction guide.

- ○ Yes, now on active duty
- ○ Yes, on active duty in past, but not now
- ○ Yes, service in Reserves or National Guard only — *Skip to 18*
- ○ No — *Skip to 18*

b. Was active-duty military service during —
Fill a circle for each period in which this person served.

- ○ September 1980 or later
- ○ May 1975 to August 1980
- ○ Vietnam era (August 1964—April 1975)
- ○ February 1955—July 1964
- ○ Korean conflict (June 1950—January 1955)
- ○ World War II (September 1940—July 1947)
- ○ World War I (April 1917—November 1918)
- ○ Any other time

c. In total, how many years of active-duty military service has this person had?

Years

PLEASE ANSWER THESE QUESTIONS FOR PERSON 1 ON PAGE 2

18. Does this person have a physical, mental, or other health condition that has lasted for 6 or more months and which —

a. Limits the kind or amount of work this person can do at a job?

○ Yes   ○ No

b. Prevents this person from working at a job?

■ ○ Yes   ○ No

19. Because of a health condition that has lasted for 6 or more months, does this person have any difficulty —

a. Going outside the home alone, for example, to shop or visit a doctor's office?

○ Yes   ○ No

b. Taking care of his or her own personal needs, such as bathing, dressing, or getting around inside the home? ■

○ Yes   ○ No

If this person is a female —

20. How many babies has she ever had, not counting stillbirths? Do not count her stepchildren or children she has adopted.

None 1 2 3 4 5 6 7 8 9 10 11 12 or more
○ ○ ○ ○ ○ ○ ○ ○ ○ ○ ○ ○   ○

21a. Did this person work at any time LAST WEEK?

○ Yes — Fill this circle if this person worked full time or part time. (Count part-time work such as delivering papers, or helping without pay in a family business or farm. Also count active duty in the Armed Forces.)

○ No — Fill this circle if this person did not work, or did only own housework, school work, or volunteer work. — *Skip to 25*

■

b. How many hours did this person work LAST WEEK (at all jobs)? Subtract any time off; add overtime or extra hours worked.

[_____] Hours

22. At what location did this person work LAST WEEK?
If this person worked at more than one location, print where he or she worked most last week.

■ **a. Address (Number and street)** ⌐

[_____]

(If the exact address is not known, give a description of the location such as the building name or the nearest street or intersection.)

b. Name of city, town, or post office ⌐

[_____]

c. Is the work location inside the limits of that city or town?

■ ○ Yes   ○ No, outside the city/town limits

d. County ⌐

[_____]

e. State ⌐   **f. ZIP Code** ⌐

[_____]   [_____]

23a. How did this person usually get to work LAST WEEK? If this person usually used more than one method of transportation during the trip, fill the circle of the one used for most of the distance.

○ Car, truck, or van   ○ Motorcycle
○ Bus or trolley bus   ○ Bicycle
○ Streetcar or trolley car ○ Walked
○ Subway or elevated   ○ Worked at home ⌐
○ Railroad   *Skip to 28* ◄
○ Ferryboat   ■ ○ Other method
○ Taxicab

If "car, truck, or van" is marked in 23a, go to 23b. Otherwise, skip to 24a.

b. How many people, including this person, usually rode to work in the car, truck, or van LAST WEEK? ■

○ Drove alone   ○ 5 people
○ 2 people   ○ 6 people
○ 3 people   ○ 7 to 9 people
○ 4 people   ○ 10 or more people

24a. What time did this person usually leave home to go to work LAST WEEK?

[_____] ○ a.m.
            ○ p.m.

b. How many minutes did it usually take this person to get from home to work LAST WEEK?

[_____] ■ Minutes — *Skip to 28*

25. Was this person TEMPORARILY absent or on layoff from a job or business LAST WEEK?

○ Yes, on layoff
○ Yes, on vacation, temporary illness, labor dispute, etc.
○ No

26a. Has this person been looking for work during the last 4 weeks?

○ Yes
○ No — *Skip to 27*

b. Could this person have taken a job LAST WEEK if one had been offered?

○ No, already has a job ■
○ No, temporarily ill
○ No, other reasons (in school, etc.)
○ Yes, could have taken a job

27. When did this person last work, even for a few days?

○ 1990 ⎫   ○ 1980 to 1984 ⎫ Skip
○ 1989 ⎬ Go   ○ 1979 or earlier ⎬ to 32
○ 1988 ⎪ to   ○ Never worked   ⎭
○ 1985 to 1987 ⎭ 28 ↓

28-30. CURRENT OR MOST RECENT JOB ACTIVITY. Describe clearly this person's chief job activity or business last week. If this person had more than one job, describe the one at which this person worked the most hours. If this person had no job or business last week, give information for his/her last job or business since 1985.

Please turn the page and answer questions for Person 2 listed on page 1.

28. Industry or Employer

a. For whom did this person work?
If now on active duty in the Armed
Forces, fill this circle ⟶ ○ and print the
branch of the Armed Forces.

> [   ]

(Name of company, business, or other employer)

b. What kind of business or industry was this?
Describe the activity at location where employed.

> [   ]

(For example: hospital, newspaper publishing,
mail order house, auto engine manufacturing,
retail bakery)

c. Is this mainly — Fill ONE circle

○ Manufacturing   ○ Other (agriculture,
○ Wholesale trade   construction, service,
○ Retail trade   government, etc.)

29. Occupation

a. What kind of work was this person doing?

> [   ]

(For example: registered nurse, personnel manager,
supervisor of order department, gasoline engine
assembler, cake icer)

**b. What were this person's most important activities
or duties?**

> [   ]

(For example: patient care, directing hiring policies,
supervising order clerks, assembling engines,
icing cakes)

30. Was this person — Fill ONE circle

○ Employee of a PRIVATE FOR PROFIT company or
  business or of an individual, for wages, salary, or
  commissions
○ Employee of a PRIVATE NOT-FOR-PROFIT,
  tax-exempt, or charitable organization
○ Local GOVERNMENT employee (city, county, etc.)
○ State GOVERNMENT employee
○ Federal GOVERNMENT employee
○ SELF-EMPLOYED in own NOT INCORPORATED
  business, professional practice, or farm
○ SELF-EMPLOYED in own INCORPORATED
  business, professional practice, or farm
○ Working WITHOUT PAY in family business or farm

**31a. Last year (1989), did this person work, even for a
few days, at a paid job or in a business or farm?**

○ Yes
○ No — *Skip to 32*

b. How many weeks did this person work in 1989?
Count paid vacation, paid sick
leave, and military service.

> [   ] Weeks

**c. During the weeks WORKED in 1989, how many
hours did this person usually work each week?**

> [   ] Hours

32. INCOME IN 1989 —
Fill the "Yes" circle below for each income source
received during 1989. Otherwise, fill the "No" circle.
If "Yes," enter the total amount received during 1989.

For income received jointly, see instruction guide.
If exact amount is not known, please give best estimate.

If net income was a loss, write "Loss" above
the dollar amount.

**a. Wages, salary, commissions, bonuses, or tips
from all jobs** — Report amount before deductions
for taxes, bonds, dues, or other items.

○ Yes ⟶ $ .00
○ No   Annual amount — Dollars

**b. Self-employment income from own nonfarm
business, including proprietorship and
partnership** — Report NET income after
business expenses.

○ Yes ⟶ $ .00
○ No   Annual amount — Dollars

c. Farm self-employment income — Report NET
income after operating expenses. Include earnings
as a tenant farmer or sharecropper.

○ Yes ⟶ $ .00
○ No   Annual amount — Dollars

**d. Interest, dividends, net rental income or royalty
income, or income from estates and trusts** —
Report even small amounts credited to an account.

○ Yes ⟶ $ .00
○ No   Annual amount — Dollars

e. Social Security or Railroad Retirement

○ Yes ⟶ $ .00
○ No   Annual amount — Dollars

**f. Supplemental Security Income (SSI), Aid to
Families with Dependent Children (AFDC), or
other public assistance or public
welfare payments.**

○ Yes ⟶ $ .00
○ No   Annual amount — Dollars

g. Retirement, survivor, or disability pensions —
Do NOT include Social Security.

○ Yes ⟶ $ .00
○ No   Annual amount — Dollars

**h. Any other sources of income received regularly
such as Veterans' (VA) payments,
unemployment compensation, child support,
or alimony** — Do NOT include lump-sum payments
such as money from an inheritance or the sale
of a home.

○ Yes ⟶ $ .00
○ No   Annual amount — Dollars

33. What was this person's total income in 1989?
Add entries in questions 32a through 32h; subtract
any losses. If total amount was a loss, write "Loss"
above amount.

○ None   OR $ .00
              Annual amount — Dollars

If this is the last person listed in question 1a on page 1, go to the back of the form.

Page 8

PERSON 2

Last name   First name   Middle Initial

8. In what U.S. State or foreign country was this person born?

(Name of State or foreign country; or Puerto Rico, Guam, etc.)

9. Is this person a CITIZEN of the United States?

- ○ Yes, born in the United States — *Skip to 11*
- ○ Yes, born in Puerto Rico, Guam, the U.S. Virgin Islands, or Northern Marianas
- ○ Yes, born abroad of American parent or parents
- ○ Yes, U.S. citizen by naturalization
- ○ No, not a citizen of the United States

10. When did this person come to the United States to stay?

- ○ 1987 to 1990
- ○ 1985 or 1986
- ○ 1982 to 1984
- ○ 1980 or 1981
- ○ 1975 to 1979
- ○ 1970 to 1974
- ○ 1965 to 1969
- ○ 1960 to 1964
- ○ 1950 to 1959
- ○ Before 1950

11. At any time since February 1, 1990, has this person attended regular school or college?
Include only nursery school, kindergarten, elementary school, and schooling which leads to a high school diploma or a college degree.

- ○ No, has not attended since February 1
- ○ Yes, public school, public college
- ○ Yes, private school, private college

12. How much school has this person COMPLETED?
Fill ONE circle for the highest level COMPLETED or degree RECEIVED. If currently enrolled, mark the level of previous grade attended or highest degree received.

- ○ No school completed
- ○ Nursery school
- ○ Kindergarten
- ○ 1st, 2nd, 3rd, or 4th grade
- ○ 5th, 6th, 7th, or 8th grade
- ○ 9th grade
- ○ 10th grade
- ○ 11th grade
- ○ 12th grade, **NO DIPLOMA**
- ○ **HIGH SCHOOL GRADUATE** - high school DIPLOMA or the equivalent (For example: GED)
- ○ Some college but no degree
- ○ Associate degree in college - Occupational program
- ○ Associate degree in college - Academic program
- ○ Bachelor's degree (For example: BA, AB, BS)
- ○ Master's degree (For example: MA, MS, MEng, MEd, MSW, MBA)
- ○ Professional school degree (For example: MD, DDS, DVM, LLB, JD)
- ○ Doctorate degree (For example: PhD, EdD)

13. What is this person's ancestry or ethnic origin?
(See instruction guide for further information.)

(For example: German, Italian, Afro-Amer., Croatian, Cape Verdean, Dominican, Ecuadoran, Haitian, Cajun, French Canadian, Jamaican, Korean, Lebanese, Mexican, Nigerian, Irish, Polish, Slovak, Taiwanese, Thai, Ukrainian, etc.)

14a. Did this person live in this house or apartment 5 years ago (on April 1, 1985)?

- ○ Born after April 1, 1985 — *Go to questions for the next person*
- ○ Yes — *Skip to 15a*
- ○ No

b. Where did this person live 5 years ago (on April 1, 1985)?

(1) Name of U.S. State or foreign country

(If outside U.S., print answer above and skip to 15a.)

(2) Name of county in the U.S.

(3) Name of city or town in the U.S.

(4) Did this person live inside the city or town limits?

- ○ Yes
- ○ No, lived outside the city/town limits

15a. Does this person speak a language other than English at home?

- ○ Yes
- ○ No — *Skip to 16*

b. What is this language?

(For example: Chinese, Italian, Spanish, Vietnamese)

c. How well does this person speak English?

- ○ Very well
- ○ Well
- ○ Not well
- ○ Not at all

16. When was this person born?

- ○ Born before April 1, 1975 — *Go to 17a*
- ○ Born April 1, 1975 or later — *Go to questions for the next person*

17a. Has this person ever been on active-duty military service in the Armed Forces of the United States or ever been in the United States military Reserves or the National Guard? If service was in Reserves or National Guard only, see instruction guide.

- ○ Yes, now on active duty
- ○ Yes, on active duty in past, but not now
- ○ Yes, service in Reserves or National Guard only — *Skip to 18*
- ○ No — *Skip to 18*

b. Was active-duty military service during —
Fill a circle for each period in which this person served.

- ○ September 1980 or later
- ○ May 1975 to August 1980
- ○ Vietnam era (August 1964—April 1975)
- ○ February 1955—July 1964
- ○ Korean conflict (June 1950—January 1955)
- ○ World War II (September 1940—July 1947)
- ○ World War I (April 1917—November 1918)
- ○ Any other time

c. In total, how many years of active-duty military service has this person had?

Years

PLEASE ANSWER THESE QUESTIONS FOR PERSON 2 ON PAGE 2

18. Does this person have a physical, mental, or other health condition that has lasted for 6 or more months and which —

a. Limits the kind or amount of work this person can do at a job?

   ○ Yes   ○ No

b. Prevents this person from working at a job?

■   ○ Yes   ○ No

19. Because of a health condition that has lasted for 6 or more months, does this person have any difficulty —

a. Going outside the home alone, for example, to shop or visit a doctor's office?

   ○ Yes   ○ No

b. Taking care of his or her own personal needs, such as bathing, dressing, or getting around inside the home? ■

   ○ Yes   ○ No

If this person is a female —

20. How many babies has she ever had, not counting stillbirths? Do not count her stepchildren or children she has adopted.

None 1 2 3 4 5 6 7 8 9   10   11   12 or more
 ○   ○ ○ ○ ○ ○ ○ ○ ○ ○ ○   ○   ○   ○

21a. Did this person work at any time LAST WEEK?

   ○ Yes — Fill this circle if this person worked full time or part time. (Count part-time work such as delivering papers, or helping without pay in a family business or farm. Also count active duty in the Armed Forces.)

   ○ No — Fill this circle if this person did not work, or did only own housework, school work, or volunteer work. — *Skip to 25*

■

b. How many hours did this person work LAST WEEK (at all jobs)? Subtract any time off; add overtime or extra hours worked. ⌐ ¬ Hours

22. At what location did this person work LAST WEEK?

If this person worked at more than one location, print where he or she worked most last week.

■ **a.** Address (Number and street) ⌐

(If the exact address is not known, give a description of the location such as the building name or the nearest street or intersection.)

b. Name of city, town, or post office ⌐

c. Is the work location inside the limits of that city or town?

■   ○ Yes   ○ No, outside
                           the city/town limits

d. County ⌐

e. State ⌐   **f.** ZIP Code ⌐

23a. How did this person usually get to work LAST WEEK? If this person usually used more than one method of transportation during the trip, fill the circle of the one used for most of the distance.

  ○ Car, truck, or van   ○ Motorcycle
  ○ Bus or trolley bus   ○ Bicycle
  ○ Streetcar or trolley car ○ Walked
  ○ Subway or elevated   ○ Worked at home ⌐
  ○ Railroad   *Skip to 28*
  ○ Ferryboat   ■   ○ Other method
  ○ Taxicab

If "car, truck, or van" is marked in 23a, go to 23b. Otherwise, skip to 24a.

b. How many people, including this person, usually rode to work in the car, truck, or van LAST WEEK?   ■

  ○ Drove alone   ○ 5 people
  ○ 2 people   ○ 6 people
  ○ 3 people   ○ 7 to 9 people
  ○ 4 people   ○ 10 or more people

24a. What time did this person usually leave home to go to work LAST WEEK?

⌐ ¬   ○ a.m.
          ○ p.m.

b. How many minutes did it usually take this person to get from home to work LAST WEEK?

⌐ ¬   ■
  Minutes — *Skip to 28*

25. Was this person TEMPORARILY absent or on layoff from a job or business LAST WEEK?

  ○ Yes, on layoff
  ○ Yes, on vacation, temporary illness, labor dispute, etc.
  ○ No

26a. Has this person been looking for work during the last 4 weeks?

  ○ Yes
  ○ No — *Skip to 27*

b. Could this person have taken a job LAST WEEK if one had been offered?

  ○ No, already has a job   ■
  ○ No, temporarily ill
  ○ No, other reasons (in school, etc.)
  ○ Yes, could have taken a job

27. When did this person last work, even for a few days?

  ○ 1990   ⎫ Go   ○ 1980 to 1984   ⎫ Skip
  ○ 1989   ⎬ to   ○ 1979 or earlier   ⎬ to 32
  ○ 1988   ⎭ 28   ○ Never worked   ⎭
  ○ 1985 to 1987

28-30. CURRENT OR MOST RECENT JOB ACTIVITY. Describe clearly this person's chief job activity or business last week. If this person had more than one job, describe the one at which this person worked the most hours. If this person had no job or business last week, give information for his/her last job or business since 1985.

Please turn to the next page and answer the questions for Person 3 on page 2.

28. **Industry or Employer**

a. **For whom did this person work?**
If now on active duty in the Armed Forces, fill this circle ⟶ ○ and print the branch of the Armed Forces.

_____

(Name of company, business, or other employer)

b. **What kind of business or industry was this?**
Describe the activity at location where employed.

_____

(For example: hospital, newspaper publishing, mail order house, auto engine manufacturing, retail bakery)

c. **Is this mainly — Fill ONE circle**

○ Manufacturing   ○ Other (agriculture,
○ Wholesale trade   construction, service,
○ Retail trade   government, etc.)

29. **Occupation**

a. **What kind of work was this person doing?**

_____

(For example: registered nurse, personnel manager, supervisor of order department, gasoline engine assembler, cake icer)

b. **What were this person's most important activities or duties?**

_____

(For example: patient care, directing hiring policies, supervising order clerks, assembling engines, icing cakes)

30. **Was this person — Fill ONE circle**

○ Employee of a PRIVATE FOR PROFIT company or business or of an individual, for wages, salary, or commissions

○ Employee of a PRIVATE NOT-FOR-PROFIT, tax-exempt, or charitable organization

○ Local GOVERNMENT employee (city, county, etc.)
○ State GOVERNMENT employee
○ Federal GOVERNMENT employee
○ SELF-EMPLOYED in own NOT INCORPORATED business, professional practice, or farm
○ SELF-EMPLOYED in own INCORPORATED business, professional practice, or farm
○ Working WITHOUT PAY in family business or farm

31a. **Last year (1989), did this person work, even for a few days, at a paid job or in a business or farm?**

○ Yes
○ No — *Skip to 32*

b. **How many weeks did this person work in 1989?**
Count paid vacation, paid sick leave, and military service.

[_____] Weeks

c. **During the weeks WORKED in 1989, how many hours did this person usually work each week?**

[_____] Hours

32. **INCOME IN 1989 —**
Fill the "Yes" circle below for each income source received during 1989. Otherwise, fill the "No" circle. If "Yes," enter the total amount received during 1989.
For income received jointly, see instruction guide.
If exact amount is not known, please give best estimate.
If net income was a loss, write "Loss" above the dollar amount.

a. **Wages, salary, commissions, bonuses, or tips from all jobs** — Report amount before deductions for taxes, bonds, dues, or other items.

○ Yes ⟶ $ [_____].00
○ No   Annual amount — Dollars

b. **Self-employment income from own nonfarm business, including proprietorship and partnership** — Report NET income after business expenses.

○ Yes ⟶ $ [_____].00
○ No   Annual amount — Dollars

c. **Farm self-employment income** — Report NET income after operating expenses. Include earnings as a tenant farmer or sharecropper.

○ Yes ⟶ $ [_____].00
○ No   Annual amount — Dollars

d. **Interest, dividends, net rental income or royalty income, or income from estates and trusts** — Report even small amounts credited to an account.

○ Yes ⟶ $ [_____].00
○ No   Annual amount — Dollars

e. **Social Security or Railroad Retirement**

○ Yes ⟶ $ [_____].00
○ No   Annual amount — Dollars

f. **Supplemental Security Income (SSI), Aid to Families with Dependent Children (AFDC), or other public assistance or public welfare payments.**

○ Yes ⟶ $ [_____].00
○ No   Annual amount — Dollars

g. **Retirement, survivor, or disability pensions —** Do NOT include Social Security.

○ Yes ⟶ $ [_____].00
○ No   Annual amount — Dollars

h. **Any other sources of income received regularly such as Veterans' (VA) payments, unemployment compensation, child support, or alimony** — Do NOT include lump-sum payments such as money from an inheritance or the sale of a home.

○ Yes ⟶ $ [_____].00
○ No   Annual amount — Dollars

33. **What was this person's total income in 1989?**
Add entries in questions 32a through 32h; subtract any losses. If total amount was a loss, write "Loss" above amount.

○ None   OR $ [_____].00
                   Annual amount — Dollars

If this is the last person listed in question 1a on page 1, go to the back of the form.

Page 10

PERSON 3

Last name — First name — Middle initial

8. In what U.S. State or foreign country was this person born?

(Name of State or foreign country; or Puerto Rico, Guam, etc.)

9. Is this person a CITIZEN of the United States?

○ Yes, born in the United States — *Skip to 11*
○ Yes, born in Puerto Rico, Guam, the
   U.S. Virgin Islands, or Northern Marianas
○ Yes, born abroad of American parent or parents
○ Yes, U.S. citizen by naturalization
○ No, not a citizen of the United States

10. When did this person come to the United States to stay?

○ 1987 to 1990   ○ 1970 to 1974
○ 1985 or 1986   ○ 1965 to 1969
○ 1982 to 1984   ○ 1960 to 1964
○ 1980 or 1981   ○ 1950 to 1959
○ 1975 to 1979   ○ Before 1950

11. At any time since February 1, 1990, has this person attended regular school or college?
Include only nursery school, kindergarten, elementary school, and schooling which leads to a high school diploma or a college degree.

○ No, has not attended since February 1
○ Yes, public school, public college
○ Yes, private school, private college

12. How much school has this person COMPLETED?
Fill ONE circle for the highest level COMPLETED or degree RECEIVED. If currently enrolled, mark the level of previous grade attended or highest degree received.

○ No school completed
○ Nursery school
○ Kindergarten
○ 1st, 2nd, 3rd, or 4th grade
○ 5th, 6th, 7th, or 8th grade
○ 9th grade
○ 10th grade
○ 11th grade
○ 12th grade, **NO DIPLOMA**
○ **HIGH SCHOOL GRADUATE** - high school
   DIPLOMA or the equivalent (For example: GED)
○ Some college but no degree
○ Associate degree in college - Occupational program
○ Associate degree in college - Academic program
○ Bachelor's degree (For example: BA, AB, BS)
○ Master's degree (For example: MA, MS, MEng,
   MEd, MSW, MBA)
○ Professional school degree (For example: MD,
   DDS, DVM, LLB, JD)
○ Doctorate degree
   (For example: PhD, EdD)

13. What is this person's ancestry or ethnic origin?
(See instruction guide for further information.)

(For example: German, Italian, Afro-Amer., Croatian, Cape Verdean, Dominican, Ecuadoran, Haitian, Cajun, French Canadian, Jamaican, Korean, Lebanese, Mexican, Nigerian, Irish, Polish, Slovak, Taiwanese, Thai, Ukrainian, etc.)

14a. Did this person live in this house or apartment 5 years ago (on April 1, 1985)?

○ Born after April 1, 1985 — *Go to questions for*
                                    the next person
○ Yes — *Skip to 15a*
○ No

b. Where did this person live 5 years ago (on April 1, 1985)?

(1) Name of U.S. State or foreign country

(If outside U.S., print answer above and skip to 15a.)

(2) Name of county in the U.S.

(3) Name of city or town in the U.S.

(4) Did this person live inside the city or town limits?

○ Yes
○ No, lived outside the city/town limits

15a. Does this person speak a language other than English at home?

○ Yes   ○ No — *Skip to 16*

b. What is this language?

(For example: Chinese, Italian, Spanish, Vietnamese)

c. How well does this person speak English?

○ Very well   ○ Not well
○ Well   ○ Not at all

16. When was this person born?

○ Born before April 1, 1975 — *Go to 17a*
○ Born April 1, 1975 or later — *Go to questions*
                                    for the next person

17a. Has this person ever been on active-duty military service in the Armed Forces of the United States or ever been in the United States military Reserves or the National Guard? If service was in Reserves or National Guard only, see instruction guide.

○ Yes, now on active duty
○ Yes, on active duty in past, but not now
○ Yes, service in Reserves or National
   Guard only — *Skip to 18*
○ No — *Skip to 18*

b. Was active-duty military service during —
Fill a circle for each period in which this person served.

○ September 1980 or later
○ May 1975 to August 1980
○ Vietnam era (August 1964—April 1975)
○ February 1955—July 1964
○ Korean conflict (June 1950—January 1955)
○ World War II (September 1940—July 1947)
○ World War I (April 1917—November 1918)
○ Any other time

c. In total, how many years of active-duty military service has this person had?

Years

PLEASE ANSWER THESE QUESTIONS FOR PERSON 3 ON PAGE 2

18. Does this person have a physical, mental, or other health condition that has lasted for 6 or more months and which —

a. Limits the kind or amount of work this person can do at a job?

○ Yes   ○ No

b. Prevents this person from working at a job?

■ ○ Yes   ○ No

19. Because of a health condition that has lasted for 6 or more months, does this person have any difficulty —

a. Going outside the home alone, for example, to shop or visit a doctor's office?

○ Yes   ○ No

b. Taking care of his or her own personal needs, such as bathing, dressing, or getting around inside the home? ■

○ Yes   ○ No

If this person is a female —

20. How many babies has she ever had, not counting stillbirths? Do not count her stepchildren or children she has adopted.

None 1 2 3 4 5 6 7 8 9 10 11 12 or more
○ ○○○○○○○○○ ○ ○ ○

21a. Did this person work at any time LAST WEEK?

○ Yes — Fill this circle if this person worked full time or part time. (Count part-time work such as delivering papers, or helping without pay in a family business or farm. Also count active duty in the Armed Forces.)

■ ○ No — Fill this circle if this person did not work, or did only own housework, school work, or volunteer work. — *Skip to 25*

b. How many hours did this person work LAST WEEK (at all jobs)? Subtract any time off; add overtime or extra hours worked.

```
                          Hours
```

22. At what location did this person work LAST WEEK?

If this person worked at more than one location, print where he or she worked most last week.

■ **a. Address (Number and street)** ⌐

```
```

(If the exact address is not known, give a description of the location such as the building name or the nearest street or intersection.)

b. Name of city, town, or post office ⌐

```
```

c. Is the work location inside the limits of that city or town?

■ ○ Yes   ○ No, outside the city/town limits

d. County ⌐

```
```

e. State ⌐   **f. ZIP Code** ⌐

```
```

23a. How did this person usually get to work LAST WEEK? If this person usually used more than one method of transportation during the trip, fill the circle of the one used for most of the distance.

○ Car, truck, or van   ○ Motorcycle
○ Bus or trolley bus   ○ Bicycle
○ Streetcar or trolley car ○ Walked
○ Subway or elevated   ○ Worked at home ⌐
○ Railroad   *Skip to 28*
○ Ferryboat   ■   ○ Other method
○ Taxicab

If "car, truck, or van" is marked in 23a, go to 23b. Otherwise, skip to 24a.

b. How many people, including this person, usually rode to work in the car, truck, or van LAST WEEK? ■

○ Drove alone   ○ 5 people
○ 2 people   ○ 6 people
○ 3 people   ○ 7 to 9 people
○ 4 people   ○ 10 or more people

24a. What time did this person usually leave home to go to work LAST WEEK?

```
                    ○ a.m.
                    ○ p.m.
```

b. How many minutes did it usually take this person to get from home to work LAST WEEK?

```
            ■ Minutes — Skip to 28
```

25. Was this person TEMPORARILY absent or on layoff from a job or business LAST WEEK?

○ Yes, on layoff
○ Yes, on vacation, temporary illness, labor dispute, etc.
○ No

26a. Has this person been looking for work during the last 4 weeks?

○ Yes
○ No — *Skip to 27*

b. Could this person have taken a job LAST WEEK if one had been offered?

○ No, already has a job ■
○ No, temporarily ill
○ No, other reasons (in school, etc.)
○ Yes, could have taken a job

27. When did this person last work, even for a few days?

○ 1990   ⎫ Go   ○ 1980 to 1984 ⎫ Skip
○ 1989   ⎬ to   ○ 1979 or earlier ⎬ to 32
○ 1988   ⎭ 28   ○ Never worked   ⎭
○ 1985 to 1987 ⎭

28-30. CURRENT OR MOST RECENT JOB ACTIVITY. Describe clearly this person's chief job activity or business last week. If this person had more than one job, describe the one at which this person worked the most hours. If this person had no job or business last week, give information for his/her last job or business since 1985.

Please turn to the next page and answer the questions for Person 4 on page 2.

28. Industry or Employer

a. For whom did this person work?

If now on active duty in the Armed
Forces, fill this circle ⟶ ○ and print the
branch of the Armed Forces.

_____

(Name of company, business, or other employer)

b. What kind of business or industry was this?

Describe the activity at location where employed.

_____

(For example: hospital, newspaper publishing,
mail order house, auto engine manufacturing,
retail bakery)

c. Is this mainly — Fill ONE circle

○ Manufacturing   ○ Other (agriculture,
○ Wholesale trade   construction, service,
○ Retail trade   government, etc.)

29. Occupation

a. What kind of work was this person doing?

_____

(For example: registered nurse, personnel manager,
supervisor of order department, gasoline engine
assembler, cake icer)

**b. What were this person's most important activities
or duties?**

_____

(For example: patient care, directing hiring policies,
supervising order clerks, assembling engines,
icing cakes)

30. Was this person — Fill ONE circle

○ Employee of a PRIVATE FOR PROFIT company or
business or of an individual, for wages, salary, or
commissions
○ Employee of a PRIVATE NOT-FOR-PROFIT,
tax-exempt, or charitable organization
○ Local GOVERNMENT employee (city, county, etc.)
○ State GOVERNMENT employee
○ Federal GOVERNMENT employee
○ SELF-EMPLOYED in own NOT INCORPORATED
business, professional practice, or farm
○ SELF-EMPLOYED in own INCORPORATED
business, professional practice, or farm
○ Working WITHOUT PAY in family business or farm

**31a. Last year (1989), did this person work, even for a
few days, at a paid job or in a business or farm?**

○ Yes
○ No — Skip to 32

b. How many weeks did this person work in 1989?

Count paid vacation, paid sick
leave, and military service.

_____ Weeks

**c. During the weeks WORKED in 1989, how many
hours did this person usually work each week?**

_____ Hours

32. INCOME IN 1989 —

Fill the "Yes" circle below for each income source
received during 1989. Otherwise, fill the "No" circle.
If "Yes," enter the total amount received during 1989.

For income received jointly, see instruction guide.

If exact amount is not known, please give best estimate.

If net income was a loss, write "Loss" above
the dollar amount.

**a. Wages, salary, commissions, bonuses, or tips
from all jobs —** Report amount before deductions
for taxes, bonds, dues, or other items.

○ Yes ⟶ $ .00
○ No
         Annual amount — Dollars

**b. Self-employment income from own nonfarm
business, including proprietorship and
partnership —** Report NET income after
business expenses.

○ Yes ⟶ $ .00
○ No
         Annual amount — Dollars

c. Farm self-employment income — Report NET
income after operating expenses. Include earnings
as a tenant farmer or sharecropper.

○ Yes ⟶ $ .00
○ No
         Annual amount — Dollars

**d. Interest, dividends, net rental income or royalty
income, or income from estates and trusts —**
Report even small amounts credited to an account.

○ Yes ⟶ $ .00
○ No
         Annual amount — Dollars

e. Social Security or Railroad Retirement

○ Yes ⟶ $ .00
○ No
         Annual amount — Dollars

**f. Supplemental Security Income (SSI), Aid to
Families with Dependent Children (AFDC), or
other public assistance or public
welfare payments.**

○ Yes ⟶ $ .00
○ No
         Annual amount — Dollars

g. Retirement, survivor, or disability pensions —
Do NOT include Social Security.

○ Yes ⟶ $ .00
○ No
         Annual amount — Dollars

**h. Any other sources of income received regularly
such as Veterans' (VA) payments,
unemployment compensation, child support,
or alimony —** Do NOT include lump-sum payments
such as money from an inheritance or the sale
of a home.

○ Yes ⟶ $ .00
○ No
         Annual amount — Dollars

33. What was this person's total income in 1989?
Add entries in questions 32a through 32h; subtract
any losses. If total amount was a loss, write "Loss"
above amount.

○ None   OR $ .00
              Annual amount — Dollars

If this is the last person listed in question 1a on page 1, go to the back of the form.

Page 12

PERSON 4

Last name _____ First name _____ Middle initial

8. In what U.S. State or foreign country was this person born?

(Name of State or foreign country; or Puerto Rico, Guam, etc.)

9. Is this person a CITIZEN of the United States?

- ○ Yes, born in the United States — *Skip to 11*
- ○ Yes, born in Puerto Rico, Guam, the U.S. Virgin Islands, or Northern Marianas
- ○ Yes, born abroad of American parent or parents
- ○ Yes, U.S. citizen by naturalization
- ○ No, not a citizen of the United States

10. When did this person come to the United States to stay?

- ○ 1987 to 1990
- ○ 1985 or 1986
- ○ 1982 to 1984
- ○ 1980 or 1981
- ○ 1975 to 1979
- ○ 1970 to 1974
- ○ 1965 to 1969
- ○ 1960 to 1964
- ○ 1950 to 1959
- ○ Before 1950

11. At any time since February 1, 1990, has this person attended regular school or college?
Include only nursery school, kindergarten, elementary school, and schooling which leads to a high school diploma or a college degree.

- ○ No, has not attended since February 1
- ○ Yes, public school, public college
- ○ Yes, private school, private college

12. How much school has this person COMPLETED?
Fill ONE circle for the highest level COMPLETED or degree RECEIVED. If currently enrolled, mark the level of previous grade attended or highest degree received.

- ○ No school completed
- ○ Nursery school
- ○ Kindergarten
- ○ 1st, 2nd, 3rd, or 4th grade
- ○ 5th, 6th, 7th, or 8th grade
- ○ 9th grade
- ○ 10th grade
- ○ 11th grade
- ○ 12th grade, **NO DIPLOMA**
- ○ **HIGH SCHOOL GRADUATE** - high school DIPLOMA or the equivalent (For example: GED)
- ○ Some college but no degree
- ○ Associate degree in college - Occupational program
- ○ Associate degree in college - Academic program
- ○ Bachelor's degree (For example: BA, AB, BS)
- ○ Master's degree (For example: MA, MS, MEng, MEd, MSW, MBA)
- ○ Professional school degree (For example: MD, DDS, DVM, LLB, JD)
- ○ Doctorate degree (For example: PhD, EdD)

13. What is this person's ancestry or ethnic origin?
(See instruction guide for further information.)

(For example: German, Italian, Afro-Amer., Croatian, Cape Verdean, Dominican, Ecuadoran, Haitian, Cajun, French Canadian, Jamaican, Korean, Lebanese, Mexican, Nigerian, Irish, Polish, Slovak, Taiwanese, Thai, Ukrainian, etc.)

14a. Did this person live in this house or apartment 5 years ago (on April 1, 1985)?

- ○ Born after April 1, 1985 — *Go to questions for the next person*
- ○ Yes — *Skip to 15a*
- ○ No

b. Where did this person live 5 years ago (on April 1, 1985)?

(1) Name of U.S. State or foreign country

(If outside U.S., print answer above and skip to 15a.)

(2) Name of county in the U.S.

(3) Name of city or town in the U.S.

(4) Did this person live inside the city or town limits?

- ○ Yes
- ○ No, lived outside the city/town limits

15a. Does this person speak a language other than English at home?

- ○ Yes
- ○ No — *Skip to 16*

b. What is this language?

(For example: Chinese, Italian, Spanish, Vietnamese)

c. How well does this person speak English?

- ○ Very well
- ○ Well
- ○ Not well
- ○ Not at all

16. When was this person born?

- ○ Born before April 1, 1975 — *Go to 17a*
- ○ Born April 1, 1975 or later — *Go to questions for the next person*

17a. Has this person ever been on active-duty military service in the Armed Forces of the United States or ever been in the United States military Reserves or the National Guard? If service was in Reserves or National Guard only, see instruction guide.

- ○ Yes, now on active duty
- ○ Yes, on active duty in past, but not now
- ○ Yes, service in Reserves or National Guard only — *Skip to 18*
- ○ No — *Skip to 18*

b. Was active-duty military service during —
Fill a circle for each period in which this person served.

- ○ September 1980 or later
- ○ May 1975 to August 1980
- ○ Vietnam era (August 1964—April 1975)
- ○ February 1955—July 1964
- ○ Korean conflict (June 1950—January 1955)
- ○ World War II (September 1940—July 1947)
- ○ World War I (April 1917—November 1918)
- ○ Any other time

c. In total, how many years of active-duty military service has this person had?

_____ Years

PLEASE ANSWER THESE QUESTIONS FOR PERSON 4 ON PAGE 2

18. Does this person have a physical, mental, or other health condition that has lasted for 6 or more months and which —

a. Limits the kind or amount of work this person can do at a job?

○ Yes   ○ No

b. Prevents this person from working at a job?

■   ○ Yes   ○ No

19. Because of a health condition that has lasted for 6 or more months, does this person have any difficulty —

a. Going outside the home alone, for example, to shop or visit a doctor's office?

○ Yes   ○ No

b. Taking care of his or her own personal needs, such as bathing, dressing, or getting around inside the home? ■

○ Yes   ○ No

If this person is a female —

20. How many babies has she ever had, not counting stillbirths? Do not count her stepchildren or children she has adopted.

None 1 2 3 4 5 6 7 8 9 10 11 12 or more
○ ○ ○ ○ ○ ○ ○ ○ ○ ○ ○ ○ ○

21a. Did this person work at any time LAST WEEK?

○ Yes — Fill this circle if this person worked full time or part time. (Count part-time work such as delivering papers, or helping without pay in a family business or farm. Also count active duty in the Armed Forces.)

■ ○ No — Fill this circle if this person did not work, or did only own housework, school work, or volunteer work. — *Skip to 25*

b. How many hours did this person work LAST WEEK (at all jobs)? Subtract any time off; add overtime or extra hours worked.

[_____] Hours

22. At what location did this person work LAST WEEK?

If this person worked at more than one location, print where he or she worked most last week.

a. Address (Number and street) ⌐

[_____]

(If the exact address is not known, give a description of the location such as the building name or the nearest street or intersection.)

b. Name of city, town, or post office ⌐

[_____]

c. Is the work location inside the limits of that city or town?

■ ○ Yes   ○ No, outside the city/town limits

d. County ⌐

[_____]

e. State ⌐   **f. ZIP Code ⌐**

[_____]   [_____]

23a. How did this person usually get to work LAST WEEK? If this person usually used more than one method of transportation during the trip, fill the circle of the one used for most of the distance.

○ Car, truck, or van   ○ Motorcycle
○ Bus or trolley bus   ○ Bicycle
○ Streetcar or trolley car   ○ Walked
○ Subway or elevated   ○ Worked at home ⌐
○ Railroad   *Skip to 28*
○ Ferryboat   ■   ○ Other method
○ Taxicab

If "car, truck, or van" is marked in 23a, go to 23b. Otherwise, skip to 24a.

b. How many people, including this person, usually rode to work in the car, truck, or van LAST WEEK? ■

○ Drove alone   ○ 5 people
○ 2 people   ○ 6 people
○ 3 people   ○ 7 to 9 people
○ 4 people   ○ 10 or more people

24a. What time did this person usually leave home to go to work LAST WEEK?

[_____] ○ a.m.
                        ○ p.m.

b. How many minutes did it usually take this person to get from home to work LAST WEEK? ■

[_____] Minutes — *Skip to 28*

25. Was this person TEMPORARILY absent or on layoff from a job or business LAST WEEK?

○ Yes, on layoff
○ Yes, on vacation, temporary illness, labor dispute, etc.
○ No

26a. Has this person been looking for work during the last 4 weeks?

○ Yes
○ No — *Skip to 27*

b. Could this person have taken a job LAST WEEK if one had been offered?

○ No, already has a job ■
○ No, temporarily ill
○ No, other reasons (in school, etc.)
○ Yes, could have taken a job

27. When did this person last work, even for a few days?

○ 1990   ○ 1980 to 1984   Skip
○ 1989   Go   ○ 1979 or earlier to 32
○ 1988   to   ○ Never worked
○ 1985 to 1987 28

28-30. CURRENT OR MOST RECENT JOB ACTIVITY. Describe clearly this person's chief job activity or business last week. If this person had more than one job, describe the one at which this person worked the most hours. If this person had no job or business last week, give information for his/her last job or business since 1985.

Please turn to the next page and answer the questions for Person 5 on page 2.

28. Industry or Employer

a. For whom did this person work?
If now on active duty in the Armed Forces, fill this circle ────► ○ and print the branch of the Armed Forces.

(Name of company, business, or other employer)

b. What kind of business or industry was this?
Describe the activity at location where employed.

(For example: hospital, newspaper publishing, mail order house, auto engine manufacturing, retail bakery)

c. Is this mainly — Fill ONE circle

○ Manufacturing   ○ Other (agriculture,
○ Wholesale trade   construction, service,
○ Retail trade   government, etc.)

29. Occupation

a. What kind of work was this person doing?

(For example: registered nurse, personnel manager, supervisor of order department, gasoline engine assembler, cake icer)

b. What were this person's most important activities or duties?

(For example: patient care, directing hiring policies, supervising order clerks, assembling engines, icing cakes)

30. Was this person — Fill ONE circle

○ Employee of a PRIVATE FOR PROFIT company or business or of an individual, for wages, salary, or commissions
○ Employee of a PRIVATE NOT-FOR-PROFIT, tax-exempt, or charitable organization
○ Local GOVERNMENT employee (city, county, etc.)
○ State GOVERNMENT employee
○ Federal GOVERNMENT employee
○ SELF-EMPLOYED in own NOT INCORPORATED business, professional practice, or farm
○ SELF-EMPLOYED in own INCORPORATED business, professional practice, or farm
○ Working WITHOUT PAY in family business or farm

31a. Last year (1989), did this person work, even for a few days, at a paid job or in a business or farm?

○ Yes
○ No — *Skip to 32*

b. How many weeks did this person work in 1989?
Count paid vacation, paid sick leave, and military service.

[____] Weeks

c. During the weeks WORKED in 1989, how many hours did this person usually work each week?

[____] Hours

32. INCOME IN 1989 —
Fill the "Yes" circle below for each income source received during 1989. Otherwise, fill the "No" circle.
If "Yes," enter the total amount received during 1989.
For income received jointly, see instruction guide.
If exact amount is not known, please give best estimate.
If net income was a loss, write "Loss" above the dollar amount.

a. Wages, salary, commissions, bonuses, or tips from all jobs — Report amount before deductions for taxes, bonds, dues, or other items.

○ Yes ──► $ [_____] .00
○ No   Annual amount — Dollars

b. Self-employment income from own nonfarm business, including proprietorship and partnership — Report NET income after business expenses.

○ Yes ──► $ [_____] .00
○ No   Annual amount — Dollars

c. Farm self-employment income — Report NET income after operating expenses. Include earnings as a tenant farmer or sharecropper.

○ Yes ──► $ [_____] .00
○ No   Annual amount — Dollars

d. Interest, dividends, net rental income or royalty income, or income from estates and trusts — Report even small amounts credited to an account.

○ Yes ──► $ [_____] .00
○ No   Annual amount — Dollars

e. Social Security or Railroad Retirement

○ Yes ──► $ [_____] .00
○ No   Annual amount — Dollars

f. Supplemental Security Income (SSI), Aid to Families with Dependent Children (AFDC), or other public assistance or public welfare payments.

○ Yes ──► $ [_____] .00
○ No   Annual amount — Dollars

g. Retirement, survivor, or disability pensions — Do NOT include Social Security.

○ Yes ──► $ [_____] .00
○ No   Annual amount — Dollars

h. Any other sources of income received regularly such as Veterans' (VA) payments, unemployment compensation, child support, or alimony — Do NOT include lump-sum payments such as money from an inheritance or the sale of a home.

○ Yes ──► $ [_____] .00
○ No   Annual amount — Dollars

33. What was this person's total income in 1989?
Add entries in questions 32a through 32h; subtract any losses. If total amount was a loss, write "Loss" above amount.

○ None   OR $ [_____] .00
                  Annual amount — Dollars

If this is the last person listed in question 1a on page 1, go to the back of the form.

Page 14

PERSON 5

Last name   First name   Middle initial

8. In what U.S. State or foreign country was this person born?

(Name of State or foreign country; or Puerto Rico, Guam, etc.)

9. Is this person a CITIZEN of the United States?

- ○ Yes, born in the United States — *Skip to 11*
- ○ Yes, born in Puerto Rico, Guam, the U.S. Virgin Islands, or Northern Marianas
- ○ Yes, born abroad of American parent or parents
- ○ Yes, U.S. citizen by naturalization
- ○ No, not a citizen of the United States

10. When did this person come to the United States to stay?

- ○ 1987 to 1990
- ○ 1985 or 1986
- ○ 1982 to 1984
- ○ 1980 or 1981
- ○ 1975 to 1979
- ○ 1970 to 1974
- ○ 1965 to 1969
- ○ 1960 to 1964
- ○ 1950 to 1959
- ○ Before 1950

11. At any time since February 1, 1990, has this person attended regular school or college?
Include only nursery school, kindergarten, elementary school, and schooling which leads to a high school diploma or a college degree.

- ○ No, has not attended since February 1
- ○ Yes, public school, public college
- ○ Yes, private school, private college

12. How much school has this person COMPLETED?
Fill ONE circle for the highest level COMPLETED or degree RECEIVED. If currently enrolled, mark the level of previous grade attended or highest degree received.

- ○ No school completed
- ○ Nursery school
- ○ Kindergarten
- ○ 1st, 2nd, 3rd, or 4th grade
- ○ 5th, 6th, 7th, or 8th grade
- ○ 9th grade
- ○ 10th grade
- ○ 11th grade
- ○ 12th grade, **NO DIPLOMA**
- ○ **HIGH SCHOOL GRADUATE** - high school DIPLOMA or the equivalent (For example: GED)
- ○ Some college but no degree
- ○ Associate degree in college - Occupational program
- ○ Associate degree in college - Academic program
- ○ Bachelor's degree (For example: BA, AB, BS)
- ○ Master's degree (For example: MA, MS, MEng, MEd, MSW, MBA)
- ○ Professional school degree (For example: MD, DDS, DVM, LLB, JD)
- ○ Doctorate degree (For example: PhD, EdD)

13. What is this person's ancestry or ethnic origin?
(See instruction guide for further information.)

(For example: German, Italian, Afro-Amer., Croatian, Cape Verdean, Dominican, Ecuadoran, Haitian, Cajun, French Canadian, Jamaican, Korean, Lebanese, Mexican, Nigerian, Irish, Polish, Slovak, Taiwanese, Thai, Ukrainian, etc.)

14a. Did this person live in this house or apartment 5 years ago (on April 1, 1985)?

- ○ Born after April 1, 1985 — *Go to questions for the next person*
- ○ Yes — *Skip to 15a*
- ○ No

b. Where did this person live 5 years ago (on April 1, 1985)?

(1) Name of U.S. State or foreign country

(If outside U.S., print answer above and skip to 15a.)

(2) Name of county in the U.S.

(3) Name of city or town in the U.S.

(4) Did this person live inside the city or town limits?

- ○ Yes
- ○ No, lived outside the city/town limits

15a. Does this person speak a language other than English at home?

- ○ Yes
- ○ No — *Skip to 16*

b. What is this language?

(For example: Chinese, Italian, Spanish, Vietnamese)

c. How well does this person speak English?

- ○ Very well
- ○ Well
- ○ Not well
- ○ Not at all

16. When was this person born?

- ○ Born before April 1, 1975 — *Go to 17a*
- ○ Born April 1, 1975 or later — *Go to questions for the next person*

17a. Has this person ever been on active-duty military service in the Armed Forces of the United States or ever been in the United States military Reserves or the National Guard? If service was in Reserves or National Guard only, see instruction guide.

- ○ Yes, now on active duty
- ○ Yes, on active duty in past, but not now
- ○ Yes, service in Reserves or National Guard only — *Skip to 18*
- ○ No — *Skip to 18*

b. Was active-duty military service during —
Fill a circle for each period in which this person served.

- ○ September 1980 or later
- ○ May 1975 to August 1980
- ○ Vietnam era (August 1964—April 1975)
- ○ February 1955—July 1964
- ○ Korean conflict (June 1950—January 1955)
- ○ World War II (September 1940—July 1947)
- ○ World War I (April 1917—November 1918)
- ○ Any other time

c. In total, how many years of active-duty military service has this person had?

Years

PLEASE ANSWER THESE QUESTIONS FOR PERSON 5 ON PAGE 2

18. Does this person have a physical, mental, or other health condition that has lasted for 6 or more months and which —

a. Limits the kind or amount of work this person can do at a job?

○ Yes   ○ No

b. Prevents this person from working at a job?

■   ○ Yes   ○ No

19. Because of a health condition that has lasted for 6 or more months, does this person have any difficulty —

a. Going outside the home alone, for example, to shop or visit a doctor's office?

○ Yes   ○ No

b. Taking care of his or her own personal needs, such as bathing, dressing, or getting around inside the home? ■

○ Yes   ○ No

If this person is a female —

20. How many babies has she ever had, not counting stillbirths? Do not count her stepchildren or children she has adopted.

None 1 2 3 4 5 6 7 8 9 10 11 12 or more
○   ○ ○ ○ ○ ○ ○ ○ ○ ○ ○ ○ ○

21a. Did this person work at any time LAST WEEK?

○ Yes — Fill this circle if this person worked full time or part time. (Count part-time work such as delivering papers, or helping without pay in a family business or farm. Also count active duty in the Armed Forces.)

■   ○ No — Fill this circle if this person did not work, or did only own housework, school work, or volunteer work. — *Skip to 25*

b. How many hours did this person work LAST WEEK (at all jobs)? Subtract any time off; add overtime or extra hours worked.

[_____] Hours

22. At what location did this person work LAST WEEK?

If this person worked at more than one location, print where he or she worked most last week.

■   **a. Address (Number and street) ⌐**

[_____]

(If the exact address is not known, give a description of the location such as the building name or the nearest street or intersection.)

b. Name of city, town, or post office ⌐

[_____]

c. Is the work location inside the limits of that city or town?

■   ○ Yes   ○ No, outside
                     the city/town limits

d. County ⌐

[_____]

e. State ⌐   **f. ZIP Code ⌐**

[_____]   [_____]

23a. How did this person usually get to work LAST WEEK? If this person usually used more than one method of transportation during the trip, fill the circle of the one used for most of the distance.

○ Car, truck, or van   ○ Motorcycle
○ Bus or trolley bus   ○ Bicycle
○ Streetcar or trolley car ○ Walked
○ Subway or elevated   ○ Worked at home ⌐
○ Railroad   *Skip to 28* ◄
○ Ferryboat   ○ Other method
○ Taxicab   ■

If "car, truck, or van" is marked in 23a, go to 23b. Otherwise, skip to 24a.

b. How many people, including this person, usually rode to work in the car, truck, or van LAST WEEK? ■

○ Drove alone   ○ 5 people
○ 2 people   ○ 6 people
○ 3 people   ○ 7 to 9 people
○ 4 people   ○ 10 or more people

24a. What time did this person usually leave home to go to work LAST WEEK?

[_____]   ○ a.m.
                ○ p.m.

b. How many minutes did it usually take this person to get from home to work LAST WEEK?

[_____] ■ Minutes — *Skip to 28*

25. Was this person TEMPORARILY absent or on layoff from a job or business LAST WEEK?

○ Yes, on layoff
○ Yes, on vacation, temporary illness, labor dispute, etc.
○ No

26a. Has this person been looking for work during the last 4 weeks?

○ Yes
○ No — *Skip to 27*

b. Could this person have taken a job LAST WEEK if one had been offered?

○ No, already has a job ■
○ No, temporarily ill
○ No, other reasons (in school, etc.)
○ Yes, could have taken a job

27. When did this person last work, even for a few days?

○ 1990 ⌐   ○ 1980 to 1984 ⌐
○ 1989   *Go*   ○ 1979 or earlier   *Skip*
○ 1988   *to*   ○ Never worked ⌐   *to 32*
○ 1985 to 1987 ⌐ *28*

28-30. CURRENT OR MOST RECENT JOB ACTIVITY. Describe clearly this person's chief job activity or business last week. If this person had more than one job, describe the one at which this person worked the most hours. If this person had no job or business last week, give information for his/her last job or business since 1985.

Please turn to the next page and answer the questions for Person 6 on page 2.

28. Industry or Employer

a. For whom did this person work?
If now on active duty in the Armed Forces, fill this circle ———→ ○ and print the branch of the Armed Forces.

_____

(Name of company, business, or other employer)

b. What kind of business or industry was this?
Describe the activity at location where employed.

_____

(For example: hospital, newspaper publishing, mail order house, auto engine manufacturing, retail bakery)

c. Is this mainly — Fill ONE circle

○ Manufacturing ○ Other (agriculture,
○ Wholesale trade construction, service,
○ Retail trade government, etc.)

29. Occupation

a. What kind of work was this person doing?

_____

(For example: registered nurse, personnel manager, supervisor of order department, gasoline engine assembler, cake icer)

b. What were this person's most important activities or duties?

_____

(For example: patient care, directing hiring policies, supervising order clerks, assembling engines, icing cakes)

30. Was this person — Fill ONE circle

○ Employee of a PRIVATE FOR PROFIT company or business or of an individual, for wages, salary, or commissions
○ Employee of a PRIVATE NOT-FOR-PROFIT, tax-exempt, or charitable organization
○ Local GOVERNMENT employee (city, county, etc.)
○ State GOVERNMENT employee
○ Federal GOVERNMENT employee
○ SELF-EMPLOYED in own NOT INCORPORATED business, professional practice, or farm
○ SELF-EMPLOYED in own INCORPORATED business, professional practice, or farm
○ Working WITHOUT PAY in family business or farm

31a. Last year (1989), did this person work, even for a few days, at a paid job or in a business or farm?

○ Yes
○ No — *Skip to 32*

b. How many weeks did this person work in 1989?
Count paid vacation, paid sick leave, and military service.

_____ Weeks

c. During the weeks WORKED in 1989, how many hours did this person usually work each week?

_____ Hours

32. INCOME IN 1989 —
Fill the "Yes" circle below for each income source received during 1989. Otherwise, fill the "No" circle. If "Yes," enter the total amount received during 1989.

For income received jointly, see instruction guide.

If exact amount is not known, please give best estimate.

If net income was a loss, write "Loss" above the dollar amount.

a. Wages, salary, commissions, bonuses, or tips from all jobs — Report amount before deductions for taxes, bonds, dues, or other items.

○ Yes ——→
○ No |$ .00|
Annual amount — Dollars

b. Self-employment income from own nonfarm business, including proprietorship and partnership — Report NET income after business expenses.

○ Yes ——→
○ No |$ .00|
Annual amount — Dollars

c. Farm self-employment income — Report NET income after operating expenses. Include earnings as a tenant farmer or sharecropper.

○ Yes ——→
○ No |$ .00|
Annual amount — Dollars

d. Interest, dividends, net rental income or royalty income, or income from estates and trusts — Report even small amounts credited to an account.

○ Yes ——→
○ No |$ .00|
Annual amount — Dollars

e. Social Security or Railroad Retirement

○ Yes ——→
○ No |$ .00|
Annual amount — Dollars

f. Supplemental Security Income (SSI), Aid to Families with Dependent Children (AFDC), or other public assistance or public welfare payments.

○ Yes ——→
○ No |$ .00|
Annual amount — Dollars

g. Retirement, survivor, or disability pensions — Do NOT include Social Security.

○ Yes ——→
○ No |$ .00|
Annual amount — Dollars

h. Any other sources of income received regularly such as Veterans' (VA) payments, unemployment compensation, child support, or alimony — Do NOT include lump-sum payments such as money from an inheritance or the sale of a home.

○ Yes ——→
○ No |$ .00|
Annual amount — Dollars

33. What was this person's total income in 1989?
Add entries in questions 32a through 32h; subtract any losses. If total amount was a loss, write "Loss" above amount.

○ None OR |$ .00|
Annual amount — Dollars

If this is the last person listed in question 1a on page 1, go to the back of the form.

Page 16

PERSON 6

Last name   First name   Middle initial

8. In what U.S. State or foreign country was this person born?

(Name of State or foreign country; or Puerto Rico, Guam, etc.)

9. Is this person a CITIZEN of the United States?

- ○ Yes, born in the United States — *Skip to 11*
- ○ Yes, born in Puerto Rico, Guam, the U.S. Virgin Islands, or Northern Marianas
- ○ Yes, born abroad of American parent or parents
- ○ Yes, U.S. citizen by naturalization
- ○ No, not a citizen of the United States

10. When did this person come to the United States to stay?

- ○ 1987 to 1990
- ○ 1985 or 1986
- ○ 1982 to 1984
- ○ 1980 or 1981
- ○ 1975 to 1979
- ○ 1970 to 1974
- ○ 1965 to 1969
- ○ 1960 to 1964
- ○ 1950 to 1959
- ○ Before 1950

11. At any time since February 1, 1990, has this person attended regular school or college?
Include only nursery school, kindergarten, elementary school, and schooling which leads to a high school diploma or a college degree.

- ○ No, has not attended since February 1
- ○ Yes, public school, public college
- ○ Yes, private school, private college

12. How much school has this person COMPLETED?
Fill ONE circle for the highest level COMPLETED or degree RECEIVED. If currently enrolled, mark the level of previous grade attended or highest degree received.

- ○ No school completed
- ○ Nursery school
- ○ Kindergarten
- ○ 1st, 2nd, 3rd, or 4th grade
- ○ 5th, 6th, 7th, or 8th grade
- ○ 9th grade
- ○ 10th grade
- ○ 11th grade
- ○ 12th grade, **NO DIPLOMA**
- ○ **HIGH SCHOOL GRADUATE** - high school DIPLOMA or the equivalent (For example: GED)
- ○ Some college but no degree
- ○ Associate degree in college - Occupational program
- ○ Associate degree in college - Academic program
- ○ Bachelor's degree (For example: BA, AB, BS)
- ○ Master's degree (For example: MA, MS, MEng, MEd, MSW, MBA)
- ○ Professional school degree (For example: MD, DDS, DVM, LLB, JD)
- ○ Doctorate degree (For example: PhD, EdD)

13. What is this person's ancestry or ethnic origin?
(See instruction guide for further information.)

(For example: German, Italian, Afro-Amer., Croatian, Cape Verdean, Dominican, Ecuadoran, Haitian, Cajun, French Canadian, Jamaican, Korean, Lebanese, Mexican, Nigerian, Irish, Polish, Slovak, Taiwanese, Thai, Ukrainian, etc.)

14a. Did this person live in this house or apartment 5 years ago (on April 1, 1985)?

- ○ Born after April 1, 1985 — *Go to questions for the next person*
- ○ Yes — *Skip to 15a*
- ○ No

b. Where did this person live 5 years ago (on April 1, 1985)?

(1) Name of U.S. State or foreign country

(If outside U.S., print answer above and skip to 15a.)

(2) Name of county in the U.S.

(3) Name of city or town in the U.S.

(4) Did this person live inside the city or town limits?

- ○ Yes
- ○ No, lived outside the city/town limits

15a. Does this person speak a language other than English at home?

- ○ Yes
- ○ No — *Skip to 16*

b. What is this language?

(For example: Chinese, Italian, Spanish, Vietnamese)

c. How well does this person speak English?

- ○ Very well
- ○ Well
- ○ Not well
- ○ Not at all

16. When was this person born?

- ○ Born before April 1, 1975 — *Go to 17a*
- ○ Born April 1, 1975 or later — *Go to questions for the next person*

17a. Has this person ever been on active-duty military service in the Armed Forces of the United States or ever been in the United States military Reserves or the National Guard? If service was in Reserves or National Guard only, see instruction guide.

- ○ Yes, now on active duty
- ○ Yes, on active duty in past, but not now
- ○ Yes, service in Reserves or National Guard only — *Skip to 18*
- ○ No — *Skip to 18*

b. Was active-duty military service during —
Fill a circle for each period in which this person served.

- ○ September 1980 or later
- ○ May 1975 to August 1980
- ○ Vietnam era (August 1964—April 1975)
- ○ February 1955—July 1964
- ○ Korean conflict (June 1950—January 1955)
- ○ World War II (September 1940—July 1947)
- ○ World War I (April 1917—November 1918)
- ○ Any other time

c. In total, how many years of active-duty military service has this person had?

Years

PLEASE ANSWER THESE QUESTIONS FOR PERSON 6 ON PAGE 2

18. **Does this person have a physical, mental, or other health condition that has lasted for 6 or more months and which —**
    a. **Limits the kind or amount of work this person can do at a job?**
       ○ Yes   ○ No

    b. **Prevents this person from working at a job?**
       ■   ○ No

19. **Because of a health condition that has lasted for 6 or more months, does this person have any difficulty —**
    a. **Going outside the home alone, for example, to shop or visit a doctor's office?**
       ○ Yes   ○ No

    b. **Taking care of his or her own personal needs, such as bathing, dressing, or getting around inside the home?** ■
       ○ Yes   ○ No

If this person is a female —

20. **How many babies has she ever had, not counting stillbirths?** Do not count her stepchildren or children she has adopted.
    None 1 2 3 4 5 6 7 8 9 10 11 12 or more
    ○   ○ ○ ○ ○ ○ ○ ○ ○ ○ ○   ○   ○

21a. **Did this person work at any time LAST WEEK?**
    ○ Yes — Fill this circle if this person worked full time or part time. (Count part-time work such as delivering papers, or helping without pay in a family business or farm. Also count active duty in the Armed Forces.)

    ○ No — Fill this circle if this person did not work, or did only own housework, school work, or volunteer work. — *Skip to 25*
    ■

    b. **How many hours did this person work LAST WEEK (at all jobs)?** Subtract any time off; add overtime or extra hours worked.
    [_____] Hours

22. **At what location did this person work LAST WEEK?**
    If this person worked at more than one location, print where he or she worked most last week.
    ■
    a. **Address (Number and street)** ⌐
    [_____]

    (If the exact address is not known, give a description of the location such as the building name or the nearest street or intersection.)

    b. **Name of city, town, or post office** ⌐
    [_____]

    c. **Is the work location inside the limits of that city or town?**
    ■
       ○ Yes   ○ No, outside
                          the city/town limits

    d. **County** ⌐
    [_____]

    e. **State** ⌐   f. **ZIP Code** ⌐
    [_____]   [_____]

23a. **How did this person usually get to work LAST WEEK?** If this person usually used more than one method of transportation during the trip, fill the circle of the one used for most of the distance.

    ○ Car, truck, or van   ○ Motorcycle
    ○ Bus or trolley bus   ○ Bicycle
    ○ Streetcar or trolley car ○ Walked
    ○ Subway or elevated   ○ Worked at home ⌐
    ○ Railroad   *Skip to 28*
    ○ Ferryboat   ■   ○ Other method
    ○ Taxicab

    If "car, truck, or van" is marked in 23a, go to 23b. Otherwise, skip to 24a.

    b. **How many people, including this person, usually rode to work in the car, truck, or van LAST WEEK?** ■

    ○ Drove alone   ○ 5 people
    ○ 2 people   ○ 6 people
    ○ 3 people   ○ 7 to 9 people
    ○ 4 people   ○ 10 or more people

24a. **What time did this person usually leave home to go to work LAST WEEK?**
    [_____]   ○ a.m.
                   ○ p.m.

    b. **How many minutes did it usually take this person to get from home to work LAST WEEK?**
    [_____] ■ Minutes — *Skip to 28*

25. **Was this person TEMPORARILY absent or on layoff from a job or business LAST WEEK?**

    ○ Yes, on layoff
    ○ Yes, on vacation, temporary illness, labor dispute, etc.
    ○ No

26a. **Has this person been looking for work during the last 4 weeks?**
    ○ Yes
    ○ No — *Skip to 27*

    b. **Could this person have taken a job LAST WEEK if one had been offered?**
    ○ No, already has a job ■
    ○ No, temporarily ill
    ○ No, other reasons (in school, etc.)
    ○ Yes, could have taken a job

27. **When did this person last work, even for a few days?**
    ○ 1990   ⎫ Go   ○ 1980 to 1984 ⎫ Skip
    ○ 1989   ⎪ to   ○ 1979 or earlier ⎬ to 32
    ○ 1988   ⎬ 28   ○ Never worked ⎭
    ○ 1985 to 1987 ⎭

28-30. **CURRENT OR MOST RECENT JOB ACTIVITY.** Describe clearly this person's chief job activity or business last week. If this person had more than one job, describe the one at which this person worked the most hours. If this person had no job or business last week, give information for his/her last job or business since 1985.

Please turn to the next page and answer the questions for Person 7 on page 3.

28. Industry or Employer

a. For whom did this person work?
If now on active duty in the Armed Forces, fill this circle ──► ○ and print the branch of the Armed Forces.

(Name of company, business, or other employer)

b. What kind of business or industry was this?
Describe the activity at location where employed.

(For example: hospital, newspaper publishing, mail order house, auto engine manufacturing, retail bakery)

c. Is this mainly — Fill ONE circle

○ Manufacturing ○ Other (agriculture,
○ Wholesale trade   construction, service,
○ Retail trade   government, etc.)

29. Occupation

a. What kind of work was this person doing?

(For example: registered nurse, personnel manager, supervisor of order department, gasoline engine assembler, cake icer)

b. What were this person's most important activities or duties?

(For example: patient care, directing hiring policies, supervising order clerks, assembling engines, icing cakes)

30. Was this person — Fill ONE circle

○ Employee of a PRIVATE FOR PROFIT company or business or of an individual, for wages, salary, or commissions
○ Employee of a PRIVATE NOT-FOR-PROFIT, tax-exempt, or charitable organization
○ Local GOVERNMENT employee (city, county, etc.)
○ State GOVERNMENT employee
○ Federal GOVERNMENT employee
○ SELF-EMPLOYED in own NOT INCORPORATED business, professional practice, or farm
○ SELF-EMPLOYED in own INCORPORATED business, professional practice, or farm
○ Working WITHOUT PAY in family business or farm

31a. Last year (1989), did this person work, even for a few days, at a paid job or in a business or farm?

○ Yes
○ No — *Skip to 32*

b. How many weeks did this person work in 1989?
Count paid vacation, paid sick leave, and military service.

[_____] Weeks

c. During the weeks WORKED in 1989, how many hours did this person usually work each week?

[_____] Hours

32. INCOME IN 1989 —
Fill the "Yes" circle below for each income source received during 1989. Otherwise, fill the "No" circle. If "Yes," enter the total amount received during 1989.
For income received jointly, see instruction guide.
If exact amount is not known, please give best estimate.
If net income was a loss, write "Loss" above the dollar amount.

a. Wages, salary, commissions, bonuses, or tips from all jobs — Report amount before deductions for taxes, bonds, dues, or other items.

○ Yes ──► $[_____].00
○ No   Annual amount — Dollars

b. Self-employment income from own nonfarm business, including proprietorship and partnership — Report NET income after business expenses.

○ Yes ──► $[_____].00
○ No   Annual amount — Dollars

c. Farm self-employment income — Report NET income after operating expenses. Include earnings as a tenant farmer or sharecropper.

○ Yes ──► $[_____].00
○ No   Annual amount — Dollars

d. Interest, dividends, net rental income or royalty income, or income from estates and trusts — Report even small amounts credited to an account.

○ Yes ──► $[_____].00
○ No   Annual amount — Dollars

e. Social Security or Railroad Retirement

○ Yes ──► $[_____].00
○ No   Annual amount — Dollars

f. Supplemental Security Income (SSI), Aid to Families with Dependent Children (AFDC), or other public assistance or public welfare payments.

○ Yes ──► $[_____].00
○ No   Annual amount — Dollars

g. Retirement, survivor, or disability pensions — Do NOT include Social Security.

○ Yes ──► $[_____].00
○ No   Annual amount — Dollars

h. Any other sources of income received regularly such as Veterans' (VA) payments, unemployment compensation, child support, or alimony — Do NOT include lump-sum payments such as money from an inheritance or the sale of a home.

○ Yes ──► $[_____].00
○ No   Annual amount — Dollars

33. What was this person's total income in 1989?
Add entries in questions 32a through 32h; subtract any losses. If total amount was a loss, write "Loss" above amount.

○ None OR $[_____].00
Annual amount — Dollars

If this is the last person listed in question 1a on page 1, go to the back of the form.

Page 18

PERSON 7

Last name .... First name .... Middle initial

8. In what U.S. State or foreign country was this person born? ⌐

[_____]

(Name of State or foreign country; or Puerto Rico, Guam, etc.)

9. Is this person a CITIZEN of the United States?

○ Yes, born in the United States — *Skip to 11* ■
○ Yes, born in Puerto Rico, Guam, the
    U.S. Virgin Islands, or Northern Marianas
○ Yes, born abroad of American parent or parents
○ Yes, U.S. citizen by naturalization
○ No, not a citizen of the United States

10. When did this person come to the United States to stay?

○ 1987 to 1990 ■	○ 1970 to 1974
○ 1985 or 1986	○ 1965 to 1969
○ 1982 to 1984	○ 1960 to 1964
○ 1980 or 1981	○ 1950 to 1959
○ 1975 to 1979	○ Before 1950

11. At any time since February 1, 1990, has this person attended regular school or college?
Include only nursery school, kindergarten, elementary school, and schooling which leads to a high school diploma or a college degree.

○ No, has not attended since February 1
○ Yes, public school, public college
○ Yes, private school, private college ■

12. How much school has this person COMPLETED?
Fill ONE circle for the highest level COMPLETED or degree RECEIVED. If currently enrolled, mark the level of previous grade attended or highest degree received.

○ No school completed
○ Nursery school ■
○ Kindergarten
○ 1st, 2nd, 3rd, or 4th grade
○ 5th, 6th, 7th, or 8th grade
○ 9th grade
○ 10th grade
○ 11th grade
○ 12th grade, **NO DIPLOMA**
○ **HIGH SCHOOL GRADUATE** - high school
    DIPLOMA or the equivalent (For example: GED)
○ Some college but no degree
○ Associate degree in college - Occupational program
○ Associate degree in college - Academic program
○ Bachelor's degree (For example: BA, AB, BS)
○ Master's degree (For example: MA, MS, MEng,
    MEd, MSW, MBA)
○ Professional degree (For example: MD,
    DDS, DVM, LLB, JD) ■
○ Doctorate degree
    (For example: PhD, EdD)

13. What is this person's ancestry or ethnic origin? ⌐
(See instruction guide for further information.)

[_____]

(For example: German, Italian, Afro-Amer., Croatian,
Cape Verdean, Dominican, Ecuadoran, Haitian, Cajun,
French Canadian, Jamaican, Korean, Lebanese, Mexican,
Nigerian, Irish, Polish, Slovak, Taiwanese, Thai,
Ukrainian, etc.)

14a. Did this person live in this house or apartment 5 years ago (on April 1, 1985)?

○ Born after April 1, 1985 — *Go to the back page*
○ Yes — *Skip to 15a*
○ No

b. Where did this person live 5 years ago (on April 1, 1985)?

(1) Name of U.S. State or foreign country ⌐

[_____]

(If outside U.S., print answer above and skip to 15a.)

(2) Name of county in the U.S. ⌐

[_____]

(3) Name of city or town in the U.S. ⌐

[_____]

(4) Did this person live inside the city or town limits?

○ Yes
○ No, lived outside the city/town limits

15a. Does this person speak a language other than English at home?

○ Yes   ○ No — *Skip to 16*

b. What is this language? ⌐

[_____]

(For example: Chinese, Italian, Spanish, Vietnamese)

c. How well does this person speak English?

○ Very well   ○ Not well
○ Well   ○ Not at all

16. When was this person born?

○ Born before April 1, 1975 — *Go to 17a*
○ Born April 1, 1975 or later — *Go to the back page*

17a. Has this person ever been on active-duty military service in the Armed Forces of the United States or ever been in the United States military Reserves or the National Guard? If service was in Reserves or National Guard only, see instruction guide.

○ Yes, now on active duty
○ Yes, on active duty in past, but not now
○ Yes, service in Reserves or National
    Guard only — *Skip to 18*
○ No — *Skip to 18*

b. Was active-duty military service during —
Fill a circle for each period in which this person served.

○ September 1980 or later
○ May 1975 to August 1980
○ Vietnam era (August 1964—April 1975)
○ February 1955—July 1964
○ Korean conflict (June 1950—January 1955)
○ World War II (September 1940—July 1947)
○ World War I (April 1917—November 1918)
○ Any other time

c. In total, how many years of active-duty military service has this person had?

[_____] Years

PLEASE ANSWER THESE QUESTIONS FOR PERSON 7 ON PAGE 3

18. Does this person have a physical, mental, or other health condition that has lasted for 6 or more months and which —

a. Limits the kind or amount of work this person can do at a job?

○ Yes   ○ No

b. Prevents this person from working at a job?

■ ○ Yes   ○ No

19. Because of a health condition that has lasted for 6 or more months, does this person have any difficulty —

a. Going outside the home alone, for example, to shop or visit a doctor's office?

○ Yes   ○ No

b. Taking care of his or her own personal needs, such as bathing, dressing, or getting around inside the home? ■

○ Yes   ○ No

If this person is a female —

20. How many babies has she ever had, not counting stillbirths? Do not count her stepchildren or children she has adopted.

None 1 2 3 4 5 6 7 8 9 10 11 12 or more
○   ○ ○ ○ ○ ○ ○ ○ ○ ○   ○   ○   ○

21a. Did this person work at any time LAST WEEK?

○ Yes — Fill this circle if this person worked full time or part time. (Count part-time work such as delivering papers, or helping without pay in a family business or farm. Also count active duty in the Armed Forces.)

■ ○ No — Fill this circle if this person did not work, or did only own housework, school work, or volunteer work. — *Skip to 25*

b. How many hours did this person work LAST WEEK (at all jobs)? Subtract any time off; add overtime or extra hours worked.

[_____] Hours

22. At what location did this person work LAST WEEK?

If this person worked at more than one location, print where he or she worked most last week.

■ **a. Address (Number and street)** ⌐

[_____]

(If the exact address is not known, give a description of the location such as the building name or the nearest street or intersection.)

b. Name of city, town, or post office ⌐

[_____]

c. Is the work location inside the limits of that city or town?

■ ○ Yes   ○ No, outside the city/town limits

d. County ⌐

[_____]

e. State ⌐   **f. ZIP Code** ⌐

[_____]   [_____]

23a. How did this person usually get to work LAST WEEK? If this person usually used more than one method of transportation during the trip, fill the circle of the one used for most of the distance.

○ Car, truck, or van   ○ Motorcycle
○ Bus or trolley bus   ○ Bicycle
○ Streetcar or trolley car   ○ Walked
○ Subway or elevated   ○ Worked at home ⌐
○ Railroad   *Skip to 28*
○ Ferryboat   ■   ○ Other method
○ Taxicab

If "car, truck, or van" is marked in 23a, go to 23b. Otherwise, skip to 24a.

b. How many people, including this person, usually rode to work in the car, truck, or van LAST WEEK? ■

○ Drove alone   ○ 5 people
○ 2 people   ○ 6 people
○ 3 people   ○ 7 to 9 people
○ 4 people   ○ 10 or more people

24a. What time did this person usually leave home to go to work LAST WEEK?

[_____]   ○ a.m.
             ○ p.m.

b. How many minutes did it usually take this person to get from home to work LAST WEEK?

[_____] Minutes — *Skip to 28*   ■

25. Was this person TEMPORARILY absent or on layoff from a job or business LAST WEEK?

○ Yes, on layoff
○ Yes, on vacation, temporary illness, labor dispute, etc.
○ No

26a. Has this person been looking for work during the last 4 weeks?

○ Yes
○ No — *Skip to 27*

b. Could this person have taken a job LAST WEEK if one had been offered?

○ No, already has a job   ■
○ No, temporarily ill
○ No, other reasons (in school, etc.)
○ Yes, could have taken a job

27. When did this person last work, even for a few days?

○ 1990   ⎫ Go   ○ 1980 to 1984   ⎫ Skip
○ 1989   ⎬ to   ○ 1979 or earlier ⎬ to 32
○ 1988   ⎪ 28   ○ Never worked   ⎭
○ 1985 to 1987 ⎭

28-30. CURRENT OR MOST RECENT JOB ACTIVITY. Describe clearly this person's chief job activity or business last week. If this person had more than one job, describe the one at which this person worked the most hours. If this person had no job or business last week, give information for his/her last job or business since 1985.

28. Industry or Employer

a. For whom did this person work?
If now on active duty in the Armed
Forces, fill this circle ———————▶ ○ and print the
branch of the Armed Forces.

_____

(Name of company, business, or other employer)

b. What kind of business or industry was this?
Describe the activity at location where employed.

_____

(For example: hospital, newspaper publishing,
mail order house, auto engine manufacturing,
retail bakery)

c. Is this mainly — Fill ONE circle

○ Manufacturing   ○ Other (agriculture,
○ Wholesale trade   construction, service,
○ Retail trade   government, etc.)

29. Occupation

a. What kind of work was this person doing?

_____

(For example: registered nurse, personnel manager,
supervisor of order department, gasoline engine
assembler, cake icer)

**b. What were this person's most important activities
or duties?**

_____

(For example: patient care, directing hiring policies,
supervising order clerks, assembling engines,
icing cakes)

30. Was this person — Fill ONE circle

○ Employee of a PRIVATE FOR PROFIT company or
   business or of an individual, for wages, salary, or
   commissions
○ Employee of a PRIVATE NOT-FOR-PROFIT,
   tax-exempt, or charitable organization
○ Local GOVERNMENT employee (city, county, etc.)
○ State GOVERNMENT employee
○ Federal GOVERNMENT employee
○ SELF-EMPLOYED in own NOT INCORPORATED
   business, professional practice, or farm
○ SELF-EMPLOYED in own INCORPORATED
   business, professional practice, or farm
○ Working WITHOUT PAY in family business or farm

**31a. Last year (1989), did this person work, even for a
few days, at a paid job or in a business or farm?**

○ Yes
○ No — *Skip to 32*

b. How many weeks did this person work in 1989?
Count paid vacation, paid sick
leave, and military service.

_____ Weeks

**c. During the weeks WORKED in 1989, how many
hours did this person usually work each week?**

_____ Hours

32. INCOME IN 1989 —
Fill the "Yes" circle below for each income source
received during 1989. Otherwise, fill the "No" circle.
If "Yes," enter the total amount received during 1989.

For income received jointly, see instruction guide.
If exact amount is not known, please give best estimate.
If net income was a loss, write "Loss" above
the dollar amount.

**a. Wages, salary, commissions, bonuses, or tips
from all jobs —** Report amount before deductions
for taxes, bonds, dues, or other items.

○ Yes ——▶
○ No $ .00
             Annual amount — Dollars

**b. Self-employment income from own nonfarm
business, including proprietorship and
partnership —** Report NET income after
business expenses.

○ Yes ——▶
○ No $ .00
             Annual amount — Dollars

c. Farm self-employment income — Report NET
income after operating expenses. Include earnings
as a tenant farmer or sharecropper.

○ Yes ——▶
○ No $ .00
             Annual amount — Dollars

**d. Interest, dividends, net rental income or royalty
income, or income from estates and trusts —**
Report even small amounts credited to an account.

○ Yes ——▶
○ No $ .00
             Annual amount — Dollars

e. Social Security or Railroad Retirement

○ Yes ——▶
○ No $ .00
             Annual amount — Dollars

**f. Supplemental Security Income (SSI), Aid to
Families with Dependent Children (AFDC), or
other public assistance or public
welfare payments.**

○ Yes ——▶
○ No $ .00
             Annual amount — Dollars

g. Retirement, survivor, or disability pensions —
Do NOT include Social Security.

○ Yes ——▶
○ No $ .00
             Annual amount — Dollars

**h. Any other sources of income received regularly
such as Veterans' (VA) payments,
unemployment compensation, child support,
or alimony —** Do NOT include lump-sum payments
such as money from an inheritance or the sale
of a home.

○ Yes ——▶
○ No $ .00
             Annual amount — Dollars

33. What was this person's total income in 1989?
Add entries in questions 32a through 32h; subtract
any losses. If total amount was a loss, write "Loss"
above amount.

○ None   OR
          $ .00
          Annual amount — Dollars

Please continue onto the next page.

Please make sure you have . . .

1. FILLED this form completely.

2. ANSWERED Question 1a on page 1.

3. ANSWERED Questions 2 through 7 for each person you listed in Question 1a.

4. ANSWERED Questions H1a through H26 on pages 3, 4, and 5.

5. ANSWERED the questions on pages 6 through 19 for each person you listed in Question 1a.

Also . . .

6. PRINT here the name of a household member who filled the form, the date the form was completed, and the telephone number at which a person in this household can be called.

Name			Date	
Telephone number ⟶	Area code	Number	○ Day ○ Night	

Then . . .

7. FOLD the form the way it was sent to you.

8. MAIL it back by April 1, or as close to that date as possible, in the envelope provided; no stamp is needed. When you insert your completed questionnaire, please make sure that the address of the U.S. Census Office can be seen through the window on the front of the envelope.

NOTE — If you have listed more than 7 persons in Question 1a, please make sure that you have filled the form for the first 7 people. Then mail back this form. A census taker will call to obtain the information for the other people.

Thank you very much.

The Census Process

The process of conducting the 1990 decennial census involved a complex set of operations.[1] The major components of the 1990 census included the following:

- address register/control file;
- questionnaire mailout/mailback;
- self-enumeration;
- sampling (long form);
- nonresponse follow-up;
- coverage improvement (including promotion, publicity, outreach);
- coverage evaluation;
- data capture, editing, and processing;
- efficient staffing and field organization;
- geographic tools and materials;
- research and experimentation; and
- a multitude of products in a variety of formats to meet the needs of a broad range of users.

These activities were carried out over a period of time both concurrently and sequentially; however, the data collection process itself falls into four basic procedures essentially carried out sequentially, as follows:

(1) developing a mailing list, that is, a list of addresses of all housing units in the country—the list is in effect a master address control file;

(2) mailing census questionnaires to each address on the list, which the householders are to fill out and return by mail;

(3) following up those addresses that fail to report; and

(4) carrying out simultaneously a number of processes designed to assure as complete coverage as possible.

This appendix reviews the basic data collection procedures for the 1990 census, beginning with descriptions by year of the census process for developing the mailing list, collecting the data, and field operations (opening of offices). Subsequent sections describe the 1990 census process for follow-up operations, coverage improvement, local review, and the Post-Enumeration Survey.

DEVELOPMENT OF MAILING LIST
(MASTER ADDRESS CONTROL FILE)

1988

• Computerized address lists for nearly 60 million housing units (mostly for metropolitan areas) were purchased from commercial vendors. These addresses were assigned to census geography (down to the block level) by using a combination of the automated geocoding capabilities of the TIGER system and clerical geocoding using other sources. The resulting automated address control file then was used to conduct the advance post office check (APOC) by the U.S. Postal Service (USPS), which identified missing addresses and those that needed corrections or were not recognizable for mail delivery.

• An address list for another 30 million housing units (mostly in more rural areas) was created by having census enumerators canvass the areas and record the mailing address of each housing unit. This operation was called 1988 prelist. The enumerators also noted the location of each unit on a map (for use in finding the unit later if other visits were needed). These computer-generated maps were one of the first major products of the new TIGER system. The addresses were keyed to form the automated address control file for these areas. That file then was used in 1989 for an advance post office check by the USPS.

1989

• For the address control file that was based on the purchased vendor files, the list was updated for APOC changes, and then the addresses were printed out by block (grouped together to form roughly equal-sized workloads, called address register areas [ARAs]). The list for each ARA was assigned to a census enumerator who canvassed each street and building in the ARA looking for (and adding) housing units not on the address list. This operation was called precanvass. Updates to the address list from the precanvass were made, and the resulting file was the basis for labeling the questionnaires to be mailed out for these areas in 1990.

- For the address control file created by the 1988 prelist, the address list was provided to the USPS for an APOC as well. In some cases, the addresses in these areas used mail delivery systems, such as rural route/box number, for which the address could not be located on the ground without additional information. As a result, most information on missing addresses and undeliverable addresses received from the APOC had to be checked in the field by census enumerators, if only to determine the correct census geographic block code. This operation was called APOC reconciliation. After the updates from APOC and APOC reconciliation were made to the automated address control file for these areas, the resulting file was the basis for labeling the questionnaires to be mailed out in 1990.

- For other rural areas (covering about 11 million housing units) for which most mailing addresses were of the type that could not be located on the ground without other information, census enumerators conducted the 1989 prelist (similar to the 1988 prelist described above). These addresses were not sent for an APOC, however, because they would not be used for a mailout census. Instead, they were used to label questionnaires that were delivered by census enumerators in 1990 during the update/leave/mailback operation (see below). This approach was used because the Census Bureau had found it very difficult in the past to list mailing addresses that were accurate enough for USPS delivery in some rural areas.

1990

- For areas for which the USPS would deliver addressed questionnaires in late March (basically, the areas for which the address list originally was purchased from vendors or compiled from the 1988 prelist), the list of addresses was reviewed again by the USPS in early March. Any new addresses identified from this check were added to the address control file and, if there was time, a mailing piece was prepared and mailed in hopes of obtaining a completed questionnaire by mail. Otherwise, the address was visited during nonresponse follow-up (see below) to obtain an interview.

COLLECTING THE DATA

There were three major collection methods for the 1990 census.

- The first data collection method was mailout/mailback, used primarily in urban and suburban areas to enumerate about 84 percent of total housing units. The Census Bureau compiled an address list in advance, and the USPS delivered questionnaires to the housing units on that list. The questionnaires were to be returned by mail when completed.

• The second data collection method was update/leave/mailback used in more rural areas, mainly in the South and Midwest, to enumerate about 11 percent of total housing units. (This method was also used in some high-rise, low-income urban areas, and a variation was used in urban areas having large numbers of boarded-up buildings.) Again, the Census Bureau compiled an address list in advance, but census enumerators (rather than USPS) delivered questionnaires to the housing units in those areas. The questionnaires were to be returned by mail when completed.

• The third data collection method was list/enumerate, used in the most sparsely populated areas, mainly in the West and Northeast, to enumerate about 5 percent of total housing units. Here, no precensus address list was compiled, but the USPS delivered an unaddressed short-form questionnaire to each unit. Then census enumerators canvassed door to door, listing all housing units, collecting completed questionnaires or completing them as necessary, including for units that did not receive one. In addition, at a predesignated subset of units, the enumerators collected responses to the sample (long-form) questions.

In March 1990, the major data collection efforts for the census began. These included the following:

• For mailout/mailback areas, the USPS delivered the labeled questionnaires on March 23. Most units received the short form containing only the questions asked of all households, but a predesignated sample of the units received the long form with additional questions. The mailing package included the questionnaire, instructions on how to fill out the form and to mail it back by April 1, and a motivational flyer to encourage response. One week later, the USPS delivered a postcard to each unit that reminded households to fill out the questionnaire and return it as soon as possible. The USPS returned about 5 percent of these questionnaires to the Census Bureau as undeliverable. Census enumerators were able to deliver about half of them by hand; the remainder did not receive a mailing piece, so they were physically enumerated during nonresponse follow-up.

• For update/leave/mailback areas, census enumerators delivered the labeled questionnaires while they canvassed each block looking for new or missed units. As in mailout areas, most units received a short form, but a predesignated sample received the long form. Besides the questionnaire, each unit also received the instructions and the motivational flyer used in mailout areas. Again, the household was asked to complete the questionnaire and mail it back by April 1. The USPS also delivered the reminder card in these areas on March 30.

• For list/enumerate areas, beginning in March, the USPS provided an unaddressed questionnaire package to each household. These packages included instructions on how to complete the form and to hold the completed form for pick-up by a census enumerator. In addition to visiting each unit to pick up the questionnaires, the enumerators also canvassed their assigned areas to list each address. For units that did not receive a questionnaire, and for units in which the household had not yet completed the questionnaire (or needed assistance to do so), the enumerators completed it concurrently with the canvassing. In addition, using a predesignated sampling pattern, enumerators obtained answers to the additional questions using the long-form questionnaire.

• Special place enumeration also took place at this point. Examples of special places include group quarters, such as boarding houses, nursing homes, dormitories, rectories, convents, hospitals, YMCAs, YWCAs, and so forth. Enumerators visited these places to obtain the information from each resident. About 10 days before Census Day, the Census Bureau also conducted street and shelter enumeration to enumerate components of the homeless population. The first phase of the operation focused on physically enumerating persons staying in shelters for the homeless, while the second phase focused on physically enumerating homeless persons living outside of shelters, for example, on the street.

• In addition to the above, there were two other components to special place enumeration—transient enumeration and military enumeration. During transient enumeration, enumerators visited travel places at which guests were unlikely to have been reported at their usual place of residence or unlikely to have a permanent residence. These places included YMCAs, YWCAs, youth hostels, commercial campgrounds, and so forth. For military enumeration, special procedures were used to conduct the physical enumeration of domestic military and maritime personnel. The military bases and vessels were self-enumerating. The bases appointed a senior commissioned officer to serve as the enumeration project officer.

FIELD OPERATIONS (OPENING OF OFFICES)

1988

• To manage and process the 1988 prelist work, the first 110 field district offices were opened, as was the first of 7 processing offices. Minicomputers and other automated equipment and software were installed to handle both operations and administrative matters in these offices.

1989

• The remaining 339 field district offices (including nine in Puerto Rico) began opening in 1989 to prepare for their major activities in 1990. Also, 13 regional census centers opened to manage the 449 district offices for the data collection efforts in 1990. Finally, the remaining 6 processing offices were opened to prepare for their major activities in 1990. The opening of all these offices included hiring staff and installing various automated equipment and software, including minicomputers for all the district offices, regional census centers, and processing offices. In addition, the processing offices' electronic equipment was installed that would be used in 1990 to convert questionnaire data to computer-readable form.

- With the installation of the network of computers across all offices, the Census Bureau significantly increased the full-scale decentralized use of its new automated management information system (MIS). This system allowed detailed monitoring of costs, progress, staffing, and other information for all census activities in the district and processing offices. Depending on the size and critical nature of an operation, reports from each office were transmitted to headquarters as often as daily, but more typically they were weekly reports. Throughout the census, this system offered a major improvement in the ability of management officials to track the status of operations, costs, staffing, and possible problem areas in real time. Thus the Census Bureau could take corrective action "midstream" for many operations, a capability that did not exist for any previous census.

1990 FIELD OPERATION—FOLLOW-UP

Mail Return

Once the delivery of questionnaires had been completed, the forms began to arrive by mail in the district or processing office serving each area. Mail returns for Type 1 district offices (which covered hard-to-enumerate areas in central cities) went to the processing offices for check-in.[2] For all other district offices, the mail returns went to that office directly, as did questionnaires completed by enumerators during list/enumeration or special place enumeration. Both the processing offices and district offices used automated equipment to check in the forms by scanning a bar code on the return envelope. The associated listing in the address control file then could be coded to show a questionnaire had been received for that unit. At the conclusion of the check-in phase, each listing not so coded represented a case that would have to be visited by an enumerator during nonresponse follow-up.

Questionnaires checked in at the processing offices immediately were sent for data capture using electronic equipment to produce computer-readable data. This concurrent processing scheme was new for 1990—in previous censuses, this phase did not occur until all physical enumeration was completed. Using the resulting computer file of data, the processing offices conducted an automated edit, or review, of the data to identify which households had not provided complete data or otherwise would need telephone or personal visit follow-up. For questionnaires checked in at the district offices, a similar edit was done by clerks using the actual paper questionnaires. Clerks in both the processing and district offices then attempted to contact these households by telephone to obtain the additional information needed to complete the questionnaire. When this could not be done, and depending on the extent or type of missing data, some of these units later had to be visited by enumerators during field follow-up (see below).

Daily reports on the mail return check-in rates for each district office were transmitted to headquarters through the MIS. This information was used to project the likely workload for nonresponse follow-up that was expected to require over 200,000 temporary enumerators to visit a projected 30 million units over a 2-month period. By the end of April, the Census Bureau had to determine the actual number of persons to hire and to begin preparing lists of addresses that had not returned a questionnaire. The response rate (from all households— occupied and vacant) was 63 percent, significantly lower than the projected 70 percent, and as a result, the Census Bureau needed to hire more enumerators for nonresponse follow-up, which in turn led to a request to Congress (which was approved) for an emergency supplemental appropriation of about $110 million.

Nonresponse Follow-Up

For the nonresponse follow-up, enumerators were provided with a complete address list for their assignment area. The units for which no questionnaire had been received were coded as such. In multiunit buildings and for most rural areas, the listing also provided the surname (if available) of households that had returned a questionnaire. This information was used to help the enumerator locate the nonresponse case in situations for which addresses/unit designations were not clear-cut. During nonresponse follow-up, enumerators were required to make as many as six attempts to contact a household member and complete the questionnaire. If this was not possible after three personal visits and (if possible) three telephone calls at different times and on different days, the enumerator attempted to obtain at least basic information on the household members from a knowledgeable source, such as a neighbor or building manager.

Because the nonresponse follow-up had to be completed in a timely fashion so that other operations could be conducted, each district office was authorized to begin a close-out phase once 95 percent or so of the operation had been completed. During this phase, enumerators made one more visit to each remaining case to obtain as complete an interview as possible. Because of very high workloads and/or staffing problems, some offices took up to 6 weeks longer than planned to complete this operation. To reduce these problems and prevent even longer delays, the Census Bureau raised the pay rate in selected areas to attract additional staff and to motivate many part-time staff to work more hours.

Field Follow-Up

After the nonresponse follow-up was completed, the next major operation (field follow-up) was conducted for two reasons:

• For each unit that had been classified as vacant or deleted by a nonresponse follow-up enumerator, a different enumerator was sent to verify this status. Past experience had shown that a significant number of such cases (perhaps up to 10 percent) actually were occupied units. This vacant/delete check was the first of several post-Census Day coverage improvement operations.

• For mail-return questionnaires that had failed the automated or clerical edit, and for which follow-up by telephone was not possible, an enumerator visited the household to obtain information needed to complete the questionnaires.

OTHER COVERAGE IMPROVEMENTS

In addition to the vacant/delete check component of field follow-up, a number of other coverage improvement efforts took place after the conclusion of nonresponse follow-up.

• The "Were you counted?" campaign provided an opportunity for persons who believed they had been missed to report data for their household on a form printed in newspapers, distributed through other mechanisms, or by calling one of the toll-free telephone numbers. These questionnaires then were processed during the search/match operation (see below).

• The parolee/probationer check was conducted because research had shown this group may have been disproportionately undercounted in previous censuses. Each state and the District of Columbia were asked to participate by distributing questionnaires through parole and probation officers to those under their jurisdiction. The parolees and probationers were asked to provide their Census Day address, and completed forms from this operation then were processed during the search/match operation (see below).

• During the search/match operation, forms received from various activities were checked against completed questionnaires to see if the persons on the forms needed to be added to the census questionnaire for the reported Census Day address. This had to be done because these types of cases might otherwise result in duplication. For example, a "Were you counted?" questionnaire might be sent in by someone who did not know that another household member had mailed back the original questionnaire for the address. Similarly, parolees or probationers might have been reported as a household member by someone on a regular census questionnaire. This approach also was needed to process individual forms filled out by persons temporarily away from home in hotels; military personnel at U.S. bases or on shipboard; and whole households who were at a second home or temporary address, but reported their usual home was elsewhere.

• Between late July and early October, the Census Bureau recanvassed over 500,000 blocks containing about 15 million housing units, or about 15 percent of all housing units. This operation, called the housing coverage check, was done for these blocks based on a variety of data sources, most of them internal to the Census Bureau. The sources included:

— on-going internal count review analyses that were based on comparing 1980 data, new construction and demolition data, and the preliminary 1990 count;

— results of earlier postal checks and local knowledge in the district offices about where significant new construction had taken place such that the address list creation and updating might need further review;

— a review of correspondence or media reports that indicated areas or buildings that might have been missed; and

— a review of the "Were you counted?" calls and forms to look for clusters of unenumerated households.

These blocks were systematically canvassed to identify and list missing addresses. The recanvass identified 300,000 housing units as potential adds. Enumerators visited each of these and obtained an interview if the housing unit was in existence on April 1, 1990.

LOCAL REVIEW

Local review was an attempt to bring to bear local knowledge, records, data, and other types of evidence to improve the accuracy and completeness of the count at small levels of geography. The local review program was designed to provide local officials an opportunity to review aggregate counts and provide supporting evidence while the census field offices were still open and field rechecks were possible. The Census Bureau provided local offices with a booklet explaining the program, a technical guide containing specific guidelines, and detailed census maps showing boundaries for tracts and blocks, so that local officials could compile their own data, especially housing unit estimates, at the block level for comparisons with the counts to be provided by the Bureau. Local offices were asked to provide "hard evidence" of possible discrepancies and enumeration problems at the ED level. Significant discrepancies would then be examined and resolved in a variety of ways including recanvassing.

Over the period from August 1987 to September 1988, the Census Bureau offered the first round of training to local officials for the local review program that would take place in 1990. Officials from about 39,000 functioning governmental units in the United States were offered training on how to prepare for and conduct reviews of preliminary housing counts resulting from the 1990 census.

In summer 1989, the Census Bureau offered the second round of local review training (similar to the first round described above) to officials from the 39,000 local governments.

In fall 1989, the precensus local review program was conducted. This involved about 21,000 local governments within areas covered by the mailout/mailback methodology (the areas where the address list originally was purchased from vendors or compiled from the 1988 prelist). The remainder of the 39,000 local governments were located in areas where update/leave/mailback or list/enumerate would be used and were not eligible for precensus local review because the initial address list was not available. That is, the update/leave/mailback areas used addresses from the 1989 prelist, and this address file still was being processed at the time of precensus local review. For list/enumerate areas, the addresses would not be listed until March when enumerators canvassed those areas for that purpose and to pick up completed questionnaires.

For this program, the Census Bureau sent the involved local governments maps and preliminary housing counts developed from the address file so that these could be compared to local information. For those places where the local government identified blocks for which their count differed significantly from the preliminary census count, the Census Bureau sent enumerators to those blocks to conduct a recanvass. In some cases this added new units, but in other cases it only required that the geographic code be corrected (that is, the unit had been assigned to the wrong block in the address file). For units added from this program, questionnaires were labeled for the mailout in late March.

In late August 1990, the Census Bureau sent to 39,000 local governments preliminary housing unit and group quarters counts, by block, for the postcensus local review. As with the precensus review, the local governments were asked to report discrepancies between these counts and their local data. The Census Bureau then recanvassed all blocks with significant differences to make sure units had not been missed or geocoded to the wrong block. After unduplicating the list of blocks with the housing coverage check, about 5.5 million units in about 150,000 blocks were recanvassed during this operation. In December, each governmental unit that participated received a listing showing the net change in the housing count for each block identified as a potential problem.

POST-ENUMERATION SURVEY

At the conclusion of the nonresponse follow-up operation, the Census Bureau also began the Post-Enumeration Survey (PES). This survey was conducted to reenumerate a sample of households so that the results later could be compared to census results to measure undercount and overcount errors in the census. The results of the PES along with data from other research, such as demographic analysis, provided the information needed to measure and evaluate the completeness of coverage of the census and to adjust the census count for the incomplete coverage if so desired. Although officially the census counts were not adjusted, these coverage evaluation measures are used in a number of ways in the postcensal estimates program.

NOTES

[1]This appendix is largely a rearrangement and extraction of material from Bureau of the Census (1991). See Citro and Cohen (1985:Chap. 3) for a description of the census process for the 1960, 1970, and 1980 censuses.

[2]Type 2 district offices covered the balance of mail areas; Type 3 district offices covered the conventional list/enumerate areas.

REFERENCES

Bureau of the Census
  1991   Planning and Conducting the 1990 Decennial Census. June. Bureau of the Census, U.S.
           Department of Commerce, Washington, D.C.
Citro, C.F., and M.L. Cohen, eds.
  1985   *The Bicentennial Census: New Directions for Methodology in 1990.* Panel on Decennial
           Census Methodology, Committee on National Statistics, National Research Council.
           Washington, D.C.: National Academy Press.

C

Data Requirements for Reapportionment and Redistricting

One of the first tasks of the panel was to examine the requirements for the decennial census to satisfy data needs for reapportionment of the U.S. Congress and the redrawing of congressional, state, and local districts for purposes of political representation. The Constitution of the United States mandates in article I, section 2, that "Representatives and direct Taxes shall be apportioned among the several States which may be included within this Union, according to their respective numbers. . . . The actual Enumeration shall be made within three Years after the first Meeting of the Congress of the United States, and within every subsequent Term of ten Years, in such Manner as they shall by Law direct." Hence, the requirement to support congressional reapportionment, which, in turn, entails redrawing congressional district boundaries, represents the absolute bedrock on which the U.S. decennial census rests.[1]

The panel reviewed data requirements for reapportionment and redistricting (at the federal, state, and local levels) that stem from the Constitution (including amendments) and also from other statutes (e.g., the Voting Rights Act, Title 13 of the U.S. Code), judicial interpretation, and administrative practice. The panel sought to determine how open to interpretation the requirements might be, so that, in turn, it could consider the fullest possible range of census designs in the spirit of a "zero-based" assessment of the most cost-effective ways to conduct

---

With the exception of the information on the August 1994 ruling of the U.S. Court of Appeals for the Second Circuit on the 1990 census adjustment issue, this appendix appeared in the panel's 1993 interim report, *Planning the Decennial Census: Interim Report.*

future censuses. Specifically, the panel considered the possibility that designs that made use of sampling and administrative records, which might offer cost savings and other benefits for the census, could satisfy data requirements for reapportionment and redistricting.

REAPPORTIONMENT

As noted above, the U.S. Constitution mandates the conduct of an "enumeration" every 10 years for the purpose of reapportionment of the U.S. House of Representatives.[2] The interpretation of the word *enumeration* is obviously key to an assessment of whether census designs that involve sampling or administrative records could serve this fundamental purpose. A second important consideration is that reapportionment must be effected simultaneously for the entire country—one cannot reapportion in some areas in one year and in other areas in another.

The Role of Sampling

A legal review prepared by the Congressional Research Service (Lee, 1993) concludes that, for the purpose of reapportionment, there needs to be an attempt to account for every inhabitant in the country: a sample census, no matter how large, cannot satisfy the constitutional requirement.[3] Similarly, "rolling census" designs, in which different parts of the population are surveyed each year without even a minimal census of the entire population at any one time, would not satisfy the requirement. (The rolling census designs proposed by Horvitz, 1986, and Kish, 1981, 1990, are in this category.) Other rolling census designs, namely, those that do include a minimal census every tenth year, would satisfy the constitutional requirement. (The designs proposed by Herriot et al., 1989, and Alexander, 1993, are of this type; see Chapter 6 for further discussion of the potential and problems of rolling census or continuous measurement designs that include a minimal decennial census together with rolling surveys.)

Lee (1993) draws the conclusion that an attempt at a complete count is constitutionally required from a review of the meaning of the word *enumeration* at the time the Constitution was adopted and subsequent legislative and judicial history.[4] In particular, two sections of Title 13 of the U.S. Code (which pertains to the Census Bureau) address the topic of sampling in the decennial census. Section 195, adopted in 1957, states that "*except* [emphasis added] for the determination of population for purposes of apportionment of Representatives in Congress among the several States, the Secretary shall, if he considers it feasible, authorize the use of the statistical method known as 'sampling' in carrying out the provisions of this title." Section 141(a) appears to be more liberal, in that it authorizes the secretary of commerce to take a decennial census every 10 years "in such form and content as he may determine, including the use of sampling procedures and special surveys." Lee (1993) states that the courts have reconciled the two sections by holding that the Census Bureau may use sampling procedures in the census, but only in addition to more traditional methods of enumeration (see, e.g., *Carey v. Klutznick* [1980, Southern District, New York]; other relevant cases are referenced below).

Although a sample census and some rolling census designs appear precluded on constitutional grounds, the use of sampling as part of the census process appears compatible with the spirit of the constitutional, legislative, and judicial history regarding enumeration, so long as the process includes an effort to reach all inhabitants. Specifically, designs that use sampling for the follow-up stage of census operations (after an initial attempt has been made to deliver a questionnaire to every household or person) and for coverage improvement programs (including adjustments based on sample surveys) would appear to meet the data requirements for reapportionment.

Several court cases (in addition to *Carey v. Klutznick*) have explicitly upheld the constitutionality of an adjustment, citing the importance of having as accurate data as possible for reapportionment and redistricting (see Lee, 1993:18-20; NCSL Reapportionment Task Force, 1989:4-5).[5] In *City of New York v. U.S. Department of Commerce* (1990, Eastern District, New York), the court stated that it "is no longer novel or, in any sense, new law to declare that statistical adjustment of the decennial census is both legal and constitutional. This Court has already recognized that Article I, Section 2 require[s] that the census be as accurate as practicable." Subsequently, the Eastern District Court in New York reaffirmed the conclusion that "the Constitution is not a bar to statistical adjustment" (*City of New York v. U.S. Department of Commerce*, 1993). Although the court upheld the constitutionality of adjustment, it ruled that the decision of the secretary of commerce not to adjust the 1990 census results followed the guidelines developed by the Commerce Department for the adjustment decision and could not be deemed to be arbitrary or capricious.

The question of the legality of sampling for nonresponse follow-up has never been explicitly raised in the courts; however, language used in the court cases just cited clearly seems to support its use. For example, in *Carey v. Klutznick* (1980, Southern District, New York), the court held that the Census Bureau may use sampling procedures in addition to a traditional enumeration. In *Young v. Klutznick* (1980, Eastern District, Michigan), the court noted that, since 1970, the census has not been a "simple straight forward headcount" but instead "a relatively accurate estimate of the population developed through the use of self-enumeration by questionnaire, statistical techniques, and computer control devices." The court held that section 195 of Title 13 did not prohibit the use of statistical techniques in the census. (As Lee [1993:20] observed, the court appeared to treat "statistical techniques" as equivalent to "sampling.")[6]

There are precedents for designs that use sampling in the later stages of the census process. In the 1970 census, two coverage improvement programs were conducted on a sample basis, and the results were used to add people to the census by an imputation procedure.[7] In the 1990 census, a postenumeration survey was conducted of a sample of housing units for purposes of evaluating the completeness of the population count and developing adjusted counts on the basis of the sample survey results. These adjusted counts were not used for reapportionment, but the court-ordered process under which they were developed certainly contemplated that they might be so used (see *City of New York v. U.S. Department of Commerce*, 1989, 1990, Eastern District, New York).

Most recently, in an August 1994 ruling, the U.S. Court of Appeals for the Second Circuit vacated the decision in *City of New York v. U.S. Department of Commerce* (1993) that upheld the secretary's decision not to adjust the 1990 census and remanded the case back to the lower court for reconsideration. The appellate court agreed with the lower court's view that Title 13 does not bar the use of sampling for a statistical adjustment of the initial census enumeration, and also with its assessment that statistical adjustment is feasible and would have improved the 1990 census counts and reduced the disproportionate undercounting of minority groups. The appellate court, however, disagreed with the basis on which the lower court upheld the secretary's decision against adjustment, namely, the arbitrary and capricious standard of review in the Administrative Procedures Act. The appellate court argued that a higher standard of review should prevail, stating that the decision not to adjust the 1990 census must be shown to be necessary to a legitimate governmental interest, or it cannot be upheld, and remanding the case back to the lower court "for further proceedings not inconsistent with this opinion."

The court's reasoning was as follows: the states and the federal government are required by the equal protection clause of the Fourteenth Admendment and the due process clause of the Fifth Amendment to strive to ensure that the vote of every citizen counts equally; there was a demonstrated differential undercount in the 1990 census that disadvantaged identifiable minority groups in this regard; and the means by which to improve the count by statistical adjustment were available. The circuit court concluded that the "plaintiffs amply showed that the Secretary did not make the required effort to achieve numerical accuracy as nearly as practicable, and that the burden thus shifted to the Secretary to justify his decision not to adjust the census in a way that the court found would for most purposes be more accurate and lessen the disproportionate counting of minorities" (*City of New York v. U.S. Department of Commerce*, 1994, Second Circuit Court of Appeals).

Role of Administrative Records

The use of administrative records (e.g., income tax and Social Security records) to provide complete population data for reapportionment raises a different set of issues from the use of sampling. The use of records is probably not consistent with most people's idea of a census, in that there would be no attempt to contact all the people on or close to a designated Census Day. However, such use could be viewed as meeting the constitutional requirements for reapportionment, if there were an administrative records system (or a combination of systems) that, when used for purposes of a census, could be determined to contain data for all inhabitants (or as close to the total of all inhabitants as has been achieved for traditional U.S. censuses), with the records assigned to the correct state of residence. See Chapter 4 for discussion of both the potentials and the problems of exploiting administrative records for the U.S. census.

There is no body of legal opinion on which to base an assessment of the constitutionality of an administrative records census. However, both Lee (1993:30) and Barnett (1993) conclude that a census based on administrative records would be likely to be held by the courts to be constitutional if it could be demonstrated that the data were accurate.

With regard to the more limited use of administrative records as part of the U.S. census process, there are several precedents. The nonhousehold sources program was an administrative records-based operation to improve coverage in the 1980 census (Citro and Cohen, 1985:94,200). It involved matching several lists to census records for selected census tracts in urban district offices. The lists used were driver's license records, immigration records, and public assistance records in New York City. Enumerators visited addresses of people identified from the match who might have been omitted from the count. The parolee/probationer check was an administrative records-based coverage improvement program adopted in the 1990 census (Ericksen et al., 1991:43-47). As part of this operation, probation officers in large cities and smaller cities with large minority populations were asked by census enumerators to verify addresses of parolees and probationers obtained from records. These addresses were matched against the census, and all cases of nonmatches were added to the census, with no attempt at a personal follow-up. In other words, this program added individuals to the census based solely on administrative records, as might be done for a census entirely based on administrative records.

Both programs had serious problems of implementation that indicate needed areas for further research and development to improve the data quality and cost-effectiveness of coverage improvement efforts that make use of administrative records. The 1980 nonhousehold sources program had very low payoff in terms of additions to the census count. A total of about 6.8 million records were checked against the census, but only 130,000 people were added to the count as a result of the matching and field follow-up operations (Citro and Cohen, 1985:200). The parolee/probationer check had a high error rate. An estimated 53 percent of the additions to the census count as a result of this program (about 250,000 people) were erroneous enumerations, that is, people who were already counted or who should not have been included for some other reason (Ericksen et al., 1991:44).

REDISTRICTING ON THE BASIS OF TOTAL POPULATION

Legal Foundations

Reapportionment of the U.S. Congress or a state or local legislature carries the implication that district boundaries should be redrawn to accommodate changes in the number of seats allotted to the jurisdiction and, even if that number does not change, to accommodate changes in the distribution of population so that a vote in one district carries about the same weight as a vote in another. Indeed, in the nineteenth century, Congress typically passed a statute at the time of each census that required all states, whether or not they gained or lost seats, to redistrict and to establish single-member districts that were contiguous, compact, and as nearly equal in population as practicable (Durbin and Whitaker, 1991:4-5).[8] After the 1920 census, however, Congress declined to reapportion the House because of the concerns of rural interests about the tremendous population growth in the cities, particularly from immigration. In 1929, Congress passed an act that provided for automatic reapportionment upon delivery of the population counts after each census, but it set no standards for redistricting. The courts held that the omission of such standards was intentional, and, since then, it has been up to the courts themselves to provide for any standards (Durbin and Whitaker, 1991:4-5).[9]

From the 1920s through the 1950s, the courts generally declined to intervene in the political thicket of redistricting, and congressional and state legislative districts became increasingly more unequal in population size. Many states chose not to redistrict after a census, unless they gained or lost seats, and those that did often paid little attention to achieving population equality across districts. Very large deviations in population, generally favoring rural over urban and suburban districts, were quite common. After the 1960 round of reapportionment and redistricting, the largest congressional district in the United States had over five times the population of the smallest district; the 20 most populous districts had a combined population of 14 million compared with a combined population of 4.6 million for the 20 smallest districts. Disparities among state legislative districts were even greater (Baker, 1986:258).

A 1967 law required single-member congressional districts. Also, the Voting Rights Act, as interpreted by the courts and administrative practice, led to de facto standards with regard to the representation of minorities. (The Voting Rights Act was enacted in 1965 and has been extended and amended several times since then.)

The landmark "one-person, one-vote" Supreme Court decisions, beginning in the early 1960s, changed the requirements for redistricting drastically. In the first of these cases, *Baker v. Carr* (1962), which involved Tennessee state legislative districts, the court held that reapportionment and redistricting matters were subject to judicial review under the equal protection clause of the Fourteenth

Amendment. In *Wesberry v. Sanders* (1964), the court held, under article 1 of the Constitution, that congressional districts must be as nearly equal in population as practicable. In *White v. Weiser* (1973), the court rejected a Texas congressional redistricting plan in which the smallest district was about 4 percent smaller than the largest district, and in *Karcher v. Daggett* (1983), the court in a 5 to 4 decision rejected a New Jersey congressional redistricting plan in which the smallest district was only 0.7 percent smaller than the largest district. The court held that the state could have avoided such a deviation, as it had rejected a plan with a population deviation of only 0.45 percent. Furthermore, the court ruled, the state had failed to show that the deviation in its approved plan was needed to achieve a legitimate goal (Parker, 1989:61; see also Durbin and Whitaker, 1991:12; and Ehrenhalt, 1983:56-57).

Whether the Supreme Court will continue to view virtually absolute population equality among congressional districts as an overriding constitutional requirement is, of course, not certain. Although *Karcher v. Daggett* (1983) is certainly indicative of a strict interpretation, the decision was a close one (5 to 4), and language in both the concurring and dissenting opinions at least raises the possibility that the court could modify its pursuit of absolute population equality in the future.[10]

Over the same period, the Supreme Court issued decisions that greatly affected state and local as well as congressional redistricting. In *Reynolds v. Sims* (1964), the court held that, under the Fourteenth Amendment, both houses of a state legislature must be apportioned on a population basis.[11] Moreover, although mathematical exactness may be impossible, states should strive for population equality. Generally, however, the courts have allowed more deviation among state legislative seats than among congressional districts. The guidelines appear to be that deviations of up to 10 percent in the size of state districts are constitutionally acceptable, although they can be challenged on other grounds (e.g., racial discrimination). Deviations between 10 and 16 percent are presumed to be unconstitutional, but states can try to justify them; deviations above 16 percent are usually viewed as completely unacceptable (Parker, 1989:57-58; see also O'Rourke, 1980:22).

Census Data for Redistricting

After the 1970 census, the states could obtain population counts for geographic areas as small as city blocks, which were defined in urbanized areas and in other localities that contracted with the Census Bureau, and for enumeration districts in unblocked areas. However, no special data files or reports were provided specifically to meet redistricting needs. In 1975 Congress required the Census Bureau to provide decennial census population tabulations to state officials for purposes of legislative reapportionment or redistricting within 1 year after the census date (i.e., under the current schedule, by April 1 of census year plus one) (Public Law 94-171; section 141(c) of Title 13). States can specify the geographic areas for which they require tabulations, provided that their requirements satisfy Census Bureau criteria and are transmitted to the Bureau no later than 3 years prior to the census date; if no special areas are identified, the Census Bureau is to provide "basic tabulations of population." In practice, basic tabulations have come to mean tabulations for individual blocks, the smallest area of geography identified in census data products.

After the 1980 census, the P.L. 94-171 data file provided by the Census Bureau contained the following information: total population; white; black; American Indian, Eskimo, and Aleut; Asian and Pacific Islander; and other races; and a separate count of Hispanics. Data were provided for states, counties, minor civil divisions, places, voting districts (when specified by the state), census tracts or block numbering areas, enumeration districts or block groups, and blocks. The number of blocks identified in the 1980 census was 2.5 million, an increase from 1.7 million in 1970. Blocks were identified in all urbanized areas, all incorporated places of 10,000 or more population, and other areas for which a state or local government contracted with the Census Bureau to define block boundaries. The average population per block was estimated in the 1980 census at about 70 people, and the average population per enumeration district at about 600 people (Bureau of the Census, 1982:56,67,79). Voting precincts identified by the states were generally the size of an enumeration district or group of blocks.

In 1990, the P.L. 94-171 file was expanded to include, in addition to the 1980 content, cross-tabulations of all items by age (under 18 and 18 years and over), a cross-tabulation of race by Hispanic origin, and a count of occupied housing units (included in response to requests from other users).[12] The geographic areas identified in 1990 were the same as in 1980, except that enumeration districts as a concept no longer existed, and blocks—about 10 million in all—were defined for the entire country (Bureau of the Census, 1992:82-83).

Although P.L. 94-171 requires the Census Bureau to furnish decennial census tabulations to the states, the courts have clearly held that the states may use other data sources for redistricting purposes. Over time, however, the states, on their own initiative and prodded by the courts, have come to rely almost exclusively on census data to prepare redistricting plans.

In the 1960s and 1970s, several court cases held that a state could use other than decennial census data for congressional and other kinds of legislative districts (NCSL Reapportionment Task Force, 1989:12-13). In 1966, citing Hawaii's special military and tourist populations, the Supreme Court in *Burns v. Richardson* held that the state could redistrict on the basis of numbers of registered voters. However, this decision was reached after the court determined that the results would not have been substantially different from those based on total citizen population. In *Kirkpatrick v. Preisler* (1969), the court implied that the eligible voter population could be the basis for redistricting if identified properly and applied uniformly. In *Ely v. Klahr* (1971), the court cautioned that a new plan for Arizona legislative districts could use registered voter data only if the results would not differ substantially from what would have resulted "from the use of a permissible population base."

In the 1980s, the case law generally reflected the position that alternative sources of data could be used if they were applied uniformly and the results were comparable to those under a plan based on the total or total citizen population. For example, the District Court in Massachusetts upheld the use of a state census for legislative redistricting in *McGovern v. Connolly* (1986). However, a district court struck down a New Mexico plan that was based on number of votes cast, and, in 1982, the District Court in Hawaii struck down Hawaii's state legislative plan that used registered voters, finding that the results did not "substantially approximate" those based on total population. In the same case (*Travis v. King*, 1982), the District Court struck down Hawaii's congressional redistricting plan, also based on registered voters, as unconstitutional: "[P]ursuant to Article I, Sec. 2 of the Constitution states must depend on total federal census figures to apportion congressional districts within their boundaries."

Recent cases dealing with the issue of adjustment of the census for coverage errors have generally upheld the view that the states need not use census data, at least not exclusively (Lee, 1993:5-6). For example, in reviewing *Young v. Klutznick*, the appeals court (1981, 6th Circuit) held that states are not constitutionally required to use census data supplied by the Census Bureau for redistricting, but can use adjusted population figures, so long as the adjustment was thoroughly documented and systematically applied. In *City of Detroit v. Franklin* (1992, Eastern District, Michigan), the court noted that *Karcher v. Daggett* did not hold that states must use census figures in redistricting but rather must use "the best population data available." In *Senate of the State of California v. Mosbacher*, the appeals court (1992, 9th Circuit) held that the Census Bureau was under no obligation to release adjusted data, but, if the state knew the census data were underrepresentative of the population, it could and should use noncensus data, in addition to the official count, for redistricting. In a recent case, *City of New York v. U.S. Department of Commerce* (1993, Eastern District, New York), the court found that there was a public interest in having available data tapes containing adjusted 1990 census counts down to the block level for the entire United States. The court ruled that the plaintiffs, who had acquired these tapes from the Census Bureau as part of the court-ordered process for deciding whether to adjust the census, could make the tapes publicly available.[13]

Over time, virtually all states have come to rely on census population counts for legislative redistricting. When states have used other bases, such as registered voters, they have generally had to obtain census data to demonstrate to the courts that their data would not give a substantially different result from census data. Although the court cases on adjustment noted above appear to give considerable discretion to the states in their choice of population data, they deal largely with the question of whether to use the official census counts or adjusted figures that are also based on the census. It seems clear that population counts for redistricting are a practical, if not precisely a constitutional, required use of the U.S. census.

Required Level of Geographic Detail

Over time, the need for block data from the census for redistricting has also become a practical requirement: although not mandated, block data are treated by most parties as if they were mandatory. The driving force behind this focus on block data appears to come from the stipulations of the courts that there be virtually no deviation among congressional districts in population size and very little deviation among state legislative districts.

In fact, not all states actually use block data in the redistricting process; many use data for election precincts or voting districts for which they have specified the boundaries to the Census Bureau (under the provisions of P.L. 94-171). These districts are generally the size of a block group or *enumeration district* in the old terminology. Commenting on the 1980 census P.L. 94-171 data program, officials of 33 states said they preferred working with block totals, and 15 states indicated they preferred working with voting district summaries. A total of 28 states, however, wanted to see voting district summaries for the entire state, and 8 states wanted to see such summaries for portions of the state in order to relate voting data to the block or precinct population data (Romig, 1983:9-10; see also Bureau of the Census, 1983; for a preliminary assessment of reactions to the 1990 P.L. 94-171 program, see National Conference of State Legislatures, 1992). The Census Bureau requires that voting district boundaries follow streets or other geographic features so that they align with census geographic boundaries; however, the precincts need not and typically do not align with geographic levels larger than the block (e.g., they often cut census tract boundaries). Hence, the Census Bureau has used block data to provide voting district summaries for the states that request them.

As noted above, the courts have given primacy to the population equality of districts over such other criteria as compactness or contiguity. The result has often been the creation of very peculiar-looking districts, as state legislative majorities seek to redraw district boundaries in a manner that maximizes partisan advantage.[14] Indeed, another force to retain blocks as the basic unit for redistricting is the widespread use of voting data (e.g., percent Democratic and Republican) in conjunction with census data to determine district boundaries. Typically, the people who work on redistricting want to look at several years of voting data because precinct boundaries change frequently: a common practice is to allocate precinct voting data to blocks and reaggregate the blocks to try out various redistricting plans to determine their political advantage.

All of this manipulation of small-area data has been made possible by computers and the advent of the Census Bureau's TIGER geocoding system. Indeed, one firm that assisted about half the states with redistricting after the 1990 census expressed the wish that census data could be provided for block faces (i.e., sides of blocks). The widespread use of computers as a data processing and mapping tool has made it easy for legislators to examine a variety of plans in order to determine the best one from their point of view. In turn, this behavior has made it necessary to have a database that can be reaggregated in many ways.[15]

Role of Sampling and Administrative Records

It seems clear that the provision of population figures by block is, for all practical purposes, a burden that the U.S. census must satisfy. Even if the restrictions on allowable deviations in population size were to be relaxed somewhat in the future, small-area data would still be required to provide the basic units for definition of legislative districts. This requirement all but eliminates the sample census design, even if such a design were otherwise determined to be constitutional and feasible. The sample size would have to be so large it would practically preclude any cost savings compared with a complete count census.

There appears to be no constitutional barrier to the use of sampling as part of the census process and hence no reason to rule out its use a priori, but questions have been raised about the quality of block-level data that might result under designs that incorporate sampling. For example, a factor in the decision not to use adjusted census counts in 1990 or, more recently, for intercensal estimates, was the belief that the adjustment factors developed on the basis of the postenumeration survey were not sufficiently reliable for small geographic areas (Bryant, 1993). Certainly, the merits of sampling as part of the census process require thorough research to determine its effect on total error and the costs of implementing various types of sample operations. It is possible, however, that the net effects could be positive: for example, careful sampling for nonresponse follow-up, at an appropriate sampling rate, might reduce costs and also reduce total error by decreasing nonsampling error more than the added variability due to sampling. Moreover, it is critical to keep in mind that block data are the input to redistricting, not the output. So long as the block data are of sufficient quality that, when aggregated to the congressional or other district level, the quality of the estimated population of the larger area is high, then the data requirements for redistricting would be served.

Census designs that make use of administrative records might also meet the practical requirement for population totals at the block level for redistricting purposes, if a number of problems can be overcome. One problem for the purpose of redistricting—which is likely to be much more severe than the corresponding problem for congressional reapportionment—concerns the accuracy of the addresses in administrative records systems, which may be out of date or pertain to a business or another individual (e.g., a tax preparer).

REDISTRICTING ON THE BASIS OF
RACIAL OR ETHNIC COMPOSITION

All of the above discussion of data needs for reapportionment and redistricting has focused on total population figures. The civil rights movement of the 1950s and 1960s led to legislation, court decisions, and administrative practices that moved another requirement front and center, namely, the need for data on race and ethnic origin for purposes of legislative redistricting.[16]

Legal History

The Voting Rights Act, originally passed in 1965 (P.L. 89-110) and extended and amended in 1970, 1975, 1982, and 1992, has led to the practical necessity for race and ethnicity data from the census (see Laney, 1992, for a history of the act). The act nowhere actually stipulates the use of census data, although it does require the director of the Census Bureau to make a number of determinations. But interpretations of the act by the courts and the Justice Department have virtually mandated the need for census data in redistricting.

The original intention of the Voting Rights Act was to make it possible for blacks in the South to obtain the opportunity to participate in elections, an opportunity that was often denied them by unreasonable literacy tests and other barriers to registration and voting. The act, as enacted in 1965, prohibited (in section 2) under the authority of the Fifteenth Amendment the enactment of any election law to deny or abridge voting rights on account of race or color. It further specified (in section 4) that any state or county that had any test or device as a condition for voter registration on November 1, 1964, and in which the number of registered or actual voters fell below 50 percent of the total voting-age population in the 1964 presidential election could not use a literacy test or any other test or device to screen potential voters. Finally, it provided (in section 5) that any covered jurisdiction (i.e., any jurisdiction required to drop voting tests under section 4) had to submit "any voting qualification or prerequisite to voting, or standard, practice, or procedure with respect to voting" adopted after November 1, 1964, for "preclearance" to the U.S. Department of Justice or the U.S. District Court for the District of Columbia to determine that there was no abridgement of the right to vote on the basis of race or color.

The 1970 amendments to the Voting Rights Act outlawed literacy tests and other devices in all jurisdictions, not just those in covered jurisdictions, and extended coverage to jurisdictions that had such tests in November 1, 1968, and in which there was less than 50 percent registration or turnout in the 1968 presidential election. The effect of this provision was to cover subdivisions in northern and western as well as southern states.

The 1975 amendments to the act included a major new provision that, on the basis of the equal protection clause of the Fourteenth Amendment, extended coverage under the act to protect the voting rights of language minorities, defined to be people of Spanish heritage, American Indians, Asian Americans, and Alaskan Natives. The preclearance provisions of the act (i.e., the requirement to submit proposed changes in voting procedures to the Justice Department for approval) were applied to any jurisdiction (counties and independent cities in most states and townships in others) for which the Census Bureau determined that more than 5 percent of the voting-age citizens were of a single-language minority, election materials had been printed only in English for the November 1972 elections, and less than 50 percent of all voting-age citizens in the jurisdiction had registered or voted in the 1972 presidential election. This provision covered the states of Alaska, Arizona, and Texas and political subdivisions in eight other states.

The 1982 amendments to the act kept the basic provisions intact, but made some changes. The amendments extended the preclearance section of the act (likewise the provision for examiners and election observers in covered jurisdictions) to the year 2007, but also provided that Congress reexamine them in 1997. (Jurisdictions can petition for release from the provisions at an earlier date, but they must meet a stiff set of criteria for release.) Another provision stated that the standard of proof for judging an election law to be discriminatory under section 2 (as well as section 5) was no longer discriminatory intent, but, rather, discriminatory *result*. As somewhat of a counterbalance, still another provision stated that minorities had no *right* to proportional representation, but that the courts could consider the lack of representation as part of the totality of circumstances in cases brought under the Voting Rights Act.

Finally, although not related to redistricting data needs per se, the act, as amended, included a provision (section 203) that is currently satisfied by using data from the census long form. This provision, as first adopted in 1975, required jurisdictions (counties, cities, or townships) to provide election materials and oral assistance in another language as well as English in areas for which the Census Bureau determined that 5 percent of the voting-age citizens were of a single-language minority and the illiteracy rate in English of the minority (defined as failure to complete fifth grade) was greater than the illiteracy rate in English of the entire nation. The 1982 act amendments asked the Census Bureau to investigate the usefulness of 1980 census long-form questions on mother tongue and English-speaking ability for determining coverage under bilingual assistance provisions. On the basis of the Census Bureau's research, the definition of a covered area became one in which 5 percent of the citizens of voting age comprised a group of people who spoke a single minority language and who said they did not speak English very well and who had a higher illiteracy rate than the nation as a whole. The result of this change was to reduce the number of covered areas from about 500 following the 1970 census to about 200 following the 1980 census; about 300 covered areas were identified after the 1990 census. The 1992 amendments extended the bilingual voting assistance provisions to 2007 and made some additional minor changes to the definition (see Bureau of the Census, 1976; Kominski, 1985, 1992).

With regard to data needs for redistricting, it is section 5 of the Voting Rights Act, with its requirement for federal review and preclearance—not only of tests for voting registration but of any "standard, practice, or procedure with respect to voting"—that has led to the practical necessity for census figures on race and ethnicity by block for redistricting.[17] A key case that supported the use of section 5 to review many aspects of states' (and counties' and cities') electoral systems was *Allan v. Board of Elections* (1969), in which the Supreme Court held that such changes as moving from single-member to multimember districts were "practices or procedures" that were subject to review under section 5 because they had the potential of "diluting" the black vote. The Justice Department quickly moved to instruct legal officers in covered jurisdictions to clear every change in voting procedure. Whereas only 323 voting changes were received by the Department for preclearance between 1965 and 1969, almost 5,000 were submitted between 1969 and 1975 (Thernstrom, 1979:59).[18]

From 1965 to 1988, the Justice Department most often objected to three ways of setting up electoral systems on the grounds that they would have resulted in abridging or diluting the voting power of blacks, Hispanics, or other protected minority voters (Parker, 1989:Table 6.1): municipal annexations (1,088 of 2,167 total objections over the period); changing from single-member districts to at-large voting (472 objections); and redistricting plans that lessened the effectiveness of minority votes, for example, such schemes as dividing concentrations of minority voters into adjoining majority-white areas or minimizing the number of minority districts by placing minority voters in as few districts as possible (248 objections). Congress also specifically expressed an interest in having redistricting plans reviewed by providing in the 1975 amendments that jurisdictions covered as of 1965 could not seek release from coverage until 1982 and by extending that date in the 1982 amendments to 1984. These dates were enacted to ensure that there would be time for Justice Department or court review of redistricting plans based on the 1980 census in those jurisdictions (Laney, 1992:18, 24).

Role of the Census

As noted above, the data files provided to the states by the Census Bureau (under P.L. 94-171) include race and ethnicity counts by blocks—and voting districts if specified by the state—in addition to total population. The 1990 file added a cross-tabulation of race by Hispanic origin. In a survey of reactions to the 1990 redistricting data program, 32 states said they used the race and ethnicity data, and 3 said positively that they did not (National Conference of State Legislatures, 1992:8). As noted above, not all states are covered by the preclearance provisions of the Voting Rights Act, although, potentially, redistricting plans in any state can be challenged under section 2. Overall, it seems clear that, for many states, the data are an important input to the redistricting process.

Whether this situation will continue unchanged in the future is unclear. The preclearance procedures of the Voting Rights Act are scheduled to be reviewed by Congress in 1997 and, in any event, to expire in 2007. However, the language of the 1982 amendments, although not guaranteeing the right to proportional representation, states that minority representation is a factor to be considered by the courts. Also, historically, the preclearance provisions have been extended every time the act has come up for renewal. It would seem prudent to expect that the census in the year 2000 and most likely in the year 2010 will need to supply block-level data on race and ethnicity for purposes of legislative redistricting.[19]

Adding a characteristic such as race or ethnicity to census requirements raises the issue of measurement error and, for designs that make use of administrative records, the issue of data availability. See Chapter 7 for a discussion of several questions and concerns with regard to obtaining race and ethnicity data from the census.

NOTES

[1]The provision in article 1, section 2 (also in article 1, section 9) that required direct taxes to be based on the census was effectively repealed by the Sixteenth Amendment, ratified in 1913, which stated that "the Congress shall have power to lay and collect taxes on incomes, from whatever source derived, without apportionment among the several States, and without regard to any census or enumeration."

[2]The current reapportionment formula, which uses the method of "equal proportions," was written into law at the time of the 1940 census (Anderson, 1988:189).

[3]For the panel's review of legal issues, a report was requested from the Congressional Research Service (CRS). The CRS review was prepared by Margaret Lee (1993), an attorney with its American Law Division. Lee's report was reviewed internally by the Congressional Research Service. The panel then asked three constitutional scholars with expertise on census issues to review the CRS report and to offer their opinions on several census issues of interest to the panel (e.g,. the use of sampling in the census). The panel relied on the consensus of these scholars as well as its own judgment for its interpretation of the CRS report.

[4]Lee (1993:1) notes that the wording changed from "census" to "enumeration" during the course of the Constitutional Convention. She could find no reason for the change but speculates that the negative references to censuses in the Bible may have been a reason (see also Anderson, 1988:10). However, the phrase "census or enumeration" appears in article I, section 9, of the Constitution, which deals with the levying of direct taxes. Lee (1993:2) notes that, in the dictionaries of the time, "enumerate" had the meaning of "to reckon up singly," and "enumeration" had the meaning of "the act of counting over."

[5]These cases include *Young v. Klutznick* (1980, Eastern District, Michigan), *City of Philadelphia v. Klutznick* (1980), and *City of New York v. U.S. Department of Commerce* (1990, Eastern District, New York). *Cuomo v. Baldrige* (1987, Southern District, New York) also implicitly assumes that an adjustment would be constitutional.

[6]In work commissioned by the panel, Barnett (1993) and Issacharoff (1993) agree with Lee (1993) that court decisions to date allow for the use of statistical methods, including sampling, as part of the census process. They go even further to offer arguments whereby the Constitution, which allows Congress complete discretion to determine the method for taking the census, might be interpreted to permit the use of methods that do not involve any physical enumeration at all. In their view, the key legal requirement is that the population figures be obtained by the most reliable methods possible.

[7]The 1970 national vacancy check involved a resurvey of 13,500 housing units originally classified as vacant (about 0.2 percent of all such units). On the basis of the findings, imputation procedures were used to reclassify 8.5 percent of all vacant units as occupied and to impute persons to these units, amounting to 0.5 percent of the total population count. The postenumeration post office check was conducted in rural areas of 16 southern states. The Postal Service checked the address lists developed by enumerators for completeness, and Census Bureau staff followed up a sample of missed addresses in the field. On the basis of the results, census records were imputed for 1.3 percent of the population in these areas, representing 0.2 percent of total U.S. population (see Citro and Cohen, 1985:189-193).

[8]Until 1911, with one exception, Congress increased the size of the House of Representatives at each reapportionment, so that no state lost congressional seats. The exception occurred when the size of the House was decreased from 242 members following the 1830 census to 232 members following the 1840 census. In 1911, the size of the House was fixed at 435 seats.

[9]See Anderson (1988:Ch.6) for a review of reapportionment and redistricting history and the relationship to the census.

[10] One commentator (Baker, 1986:275-276) claims that a majority of the Supreme Court no longer truly supports the ideal of strict mathematical equality for congressional districts but has felt constrained by precedent. He argues that Congress should pass legislation that would permit a reasonable degree of popu-

lation variance among districts and require other desirable criteria, such as compactness and contiguity.

[11]This decision effectively abolished systems that assigned a minimum number of seats to each county or other jurisdiction no matter how small in size, although one exception occurred for a Wyoming state legislative redistricting plan. On the day the Supreme Court issued *Karcher v. Daggett* (1983), it also issued *Brown v. Thomson* (also a 5 to 4 decision), which upheld a plan that gave a seat to one county that was significantly smaller in size than the other districts. The court accepted the state's argument that this deviation from the ideal was justified to permit one isolated county to retain the seat it had been granted in 1913. Two members of the majority issued an opinion saying that they agreed with the decision only because the deviation from population equality involved just one county (Parker, 1989:61).

[12]The additional items provided in the 1990 P.L. 94-171 file were available from the 1980 census as well but only in data files that were released at a later date than the 1980 P.L. 94-171 file; hence, they were not available for redistricting on a timely basis.

[13]Previously, the Department of Commerce had released adjusted census data for the nation, states, counties, and cities; it had also released to Congress adjusted data for half of the census blocks.

[14]In *Davis v. Bandemer* (1986), the Supreme Court held that partisan political gerrymandering was subject to judicial review, but it set a high standard for successfully bringing such a case, stating that plaintiffs must do more than show that a redistricting plan makes winning elections more difficult (Durbin and Whitaker, 1991:13-14).

[15]This discussion of redistricting practices draws heavily on information provided to the panel staff by Kimball Brace, president of Election Data Services, Inc., Washington, D.C. See also Ehrenhalt (1983) for an overview of the redistricting experience following the 1980 census; and Henry (1989), who notes that half the states used computers for tabulation purposes in the 1980 redistricting cycle and that (as of 1989) several firms were ready with integrated computerized tabulating and mapping systems for the 1990 cycle.

[16]Ethnic origin in the context of redistricting generally refers to Spanish or Hispanic origin. In addition to total population and information on race and ethnicity, many states want data on the voting-age population. These data were added to the P.L. 94-171 data file in 1990, and 28 states reported using them (National Conference of State Legislatures, 1992:8). The requirements for the census as the source of such data are not considered further here. It can well be argued that age—and sex—are essential characteristics to obtain simply to establish the existence of an individual and to help ensure that people are not double-counted.

[17]Parker (1989:59-63) notes that challenges to redistricting plans on the grounds that they are racially discriminatory can be brought under section 2 of

the act as well as the more frequently invoked section 5. Hence, although the preclearance provisions of section 5 currently apply to fewer than half the states (in some cases, just to selected jurisdictions in the state; see Laney, 1992), all states must worry about the racial composition of legislative districts if they are to avoid challenges under the Voting Rights Act.

[18]See Davidson (1992), Grofman et al. (1992), Karlan and McCrary (1988), Kousser (1992), and Thernstrom (1979, 1987) for discussions of the history and implications of the Voting Rights Act from different perspectives.

[19]Some analysts involved with redistricting efforts to comply with the Voting Rights Act have argued that it is also important to provide small-area data on citizenship from the census as part of the P.L. 94-171 data files (e.g., see Gobalet and Lapkoff, 1993). They find that citizenship rates among the Hispanic population vary greatly across small areas. Because voters must be citizens, legislative districts may not adequately represent the potential voting strength of the Hispanic population unless citizenship status is known. To provide data on citizenship in the P.L. 94-171 files would likely require asking for this information on the census short form.

REFERENCES

Alexander, C.
    1993   Untitled [notes on continuous measurement designs]. Draft paper. Bureau of the Census, U.S. Department of Commerce, Washington, D.C.

Anderson, M.
    1988   *The American Census: A Social History.* New Haven, Conn.: Yale University Press.

Baker, G.E.
    1986   Whatever happened to the reapportionment revolution in the United States? Pp. 257-276 in Bernard Grofman and Arend Lijphart, eds., *Electoral Laws and Their Political Consequences.* New York: Agathon Press, Inc.

Barnett, L.D.
    1993   Comments on *Congressional Research Service Report for Congress: Legal Issues for Census 2000.* Paper prepared for the Panel on Census Requirements in the Year 2000 and Beyond, Committee on National Statistics, National Research Council. School of Law, Widener University.

Bryant, B.E.
    1993   Decision of the Director of the Bureau of the Census on whether to use information from the 1990 Post-Enumeration Survey (PES) to adjust the base for the intercensal population estimates produced by the Bureau of the Census. *Federal Register* 58(1):69-78.

Bureau of the Census
    1976   *Language Minority, Illiteracy, and Voting Data Used in Making Determinations for the Voting Rights Act Amendments of 1975 (Public Law 94-73).* Current Population Reports, Population Estimates and Projections, Series P-25, No. 627. Washington, D.C.: U.S. Department of Commerce.
    1982   *1980 Census of Population and Housing, Users' Guide, Part A. Text.* PHC80-R1-A. Washington, D.C.: U.S. Department of Commerce.
    1983   *Stakeholders' Conference on Public Law 94-171 Program.* 1990 Planning Conference Series No. 3. Washington, D.C.: U.S. Department of Commerce.

1992   *1990 Census of Population and Housing, Guide, Part A. Text.* 1990 CPH-R-1A. Washington, D.C.: U.S. Department of Commerce.

Citro, C.F., and M.L. Cohen, eds.
1985   *The Bicentennial Census: New Directions for Census Methodology in 1990.* Panel on Decennial Census Methodology, Committee on National Statistics, National Research Council. Washington, D.C.: National Academy Press.

Davidson, C.
1992   The Voting Rights Act: A brief history. Pp. 7-51 in Bernard Grofman and Chandler Davidson, eds., *Controversies in Minority Voting: The Voting Rights Act in Perspective.* Washington, D.C.: The Brookings Institution.

Durbin, T.M., and L.P. Whitaker
1991   *Congressional and State Reapportionment and Redistricting: A Legal Analysis.* Congressional Research Service Report for Congress, 91-292-A. Washington, D.C.: U.S. Government Printing Office.

Ehrenhalt, A.
1983   Reapportionment and redistricting. Pp. 44-71 in Thomas E. Mann and Norman J. Ornstein, eds., *The American Elections of 1982.* Washington, D.C.: American Enterprise Institute for Public Policy Research.

Ericksen, E.P., L.F. Estrada, J.W. Tukey, and K.M. Wolter
1991   Report on the 1990 Decennial Census and the Post-Enumeration Survey, Appendix A: The Census Process. Report submitted by members of the Special Advisory Panel to the Secretary, U.S. Department of Commerce, Washington, D.C.

Gobalet, J.G., and S. Lapkoff
1993   Voting Rights Act Issues in Political Redistricting. Paper prepared for the Population Association of America annual meeting, Cincinnati, Ohio. Lapkoff & Gobalet Demographic Research, Inc., Oakland, California.

Grofman, B., L. Handley, and R.G. Niemi
1992   *Minority Representation and the Quest for Voting Equality.* Cambridge, Eng.: Cambridge University Press.

Henry, C.
1989   The impact of new technology and new census data on redistricting in the 1990s. Pp. 67-74 in William P. O'Hare, ed., *Redistricting in the 1990s: A Guide for Minority Groups.* Washington, D.C.: Population Reference Bureau, Inc.

Herriot, R.A., D.V. Bateman, and W.F. MCCarthy
1989   The decade census program—a new approach for meeting the nation's needs for subnational data. In *Proceedings of the Social Statistics Section.* Alexandria, Va.: American Statistical Association.

Horvitz, D.G.
1986   Statement to the Subcommittee on Census and Population, Committee on Post Office and Civil Service, House of Representatives, May 1. Research Triangle Institute, Research Triangle Park, N.C.

Issacharoff, S.
1993   Comments on Congressional Research Service Report for Congress: Legal Issues for Census 2000. Paper prepared for the Panel on Census Requirements in the Year 2000 and Beyond, Committee on National Statistics, National Research Council. School of Law, University of Texas, Austin.

Karlan, P.S., and P. McCrary
1988   Book review: Without fear and without research: Abigail Thernstrom on the Voting Rights Act. *The Journal of Law & Politics* 4(4):751-777.

Kish, L.
1981   Population counts from cumulated samples. Pp. 5-50 in Congressional Research Service, *Using Cumulated Rolling Samples to Integrate Census and Survey Operations of the*

Census Bureau. Prepared for the Subcommittee on Census and Population, Committee on Post Office and Civil Service, House of Representatives. Washington, D.C.: U.S. Government Printing Office.

1990   Rolling samples and censuses. *Survey Methodology* 16(1):63-79.

Kominski, R.

1985   Final Report—Documentation of Voting Rights Act Determinations. Unpublished memorandum to Paul Siegel. Bureau of the Census, U.S. Department of Commerce, Washington, D.C.

1992   1992 Voting Rights Act Bilingual Ballots Determinations. Unpublished memorandum for the record. Bureau of the Census, U.S. Department of Commerce, Washington, D.C.

Kousser, J.M.

1992   The Voting Rights Act and the two Reconstructions. Pp. 135-176 in Bernard Grofman and Chandler Davidson, eds., *Controversies in Minority Voting—The Voting Rights Act in Perspective.* Washington, D.C.: The Brookings Institution.

Laney, G.P.

1992   *The Voting Rights Act of 1965, As Amended: Its History and Current Issues.* Congressional Research Service Report for Congress, 92-578-GOV. Washington, D.C.: U.S. Government Printing Office.

Lee, M.M.

1993   *Legal Issues for Census 2000.* Congressional Research Service Report 93-177-A. Washington, D.C.: U.S. Government Printing Office.

National Conference of State Legislatures

1992   Customer Feedback for the 1990 Census Redistricting Data Program—A Preliminary Summary. Prepared for Discussion at the National Conference of State Legislatures Annual Meeting, Cincinnati, Ohio.

NCSL Reapportionment Task Force

1989   *Reapportionment Law: The 1990s.* Denver, Colo.: National Conference of State Legislatures.

O'Rourke, T.G.

1980   *The Impact of Reapportionment.* New Brunswick, N.J.: Transaction Books.

Panel on Census Requirements in the Year 2000 and Beyond

1993   *Planning the Decennial Census: Interim Report.* Committee on National Statistics, National Research Council. Washington, D.C.: National Academy Press.

Parker, F.R.

1989   Changing standards in voting rights law. Pp. 55-66 in William P. O'Hare, ed., *Redistricting in the 1990s: A Guide for Minority Groups.* Washington, D.C.: Population Reference Bureau, Inc.

Romig, C.L.

1983   *Evaluation of the 1980 Census and the Legislative Reapportionment Process.* Denver, Colo.: National Conference of State Legislatures.

Thernstrom, A.M.

1979   The odd evolution of the Voting Rights Act. *The Public Interest* 55(Spring):49-76.

1987   *Whose Votes Count? Affirmative Action and Minority Voting Rights.* Cambridge, Mass.: Harvard University Press.

D

Research Uses of Census Data

The 1990 census constitutes the one of the most important sources of U.S. data for basic and applied social research across the decade of the 1990s and will retain its importance into the long-term future. While the primary use of census data may be more limited in some fields (e.g. economics), the census is often used indirectly for weighting sample surveys or for serving as the denominators for demographic rates. Decennial census data are of primary importance in three different respects. First, taken in themselves, they constitute the basic data for extensive research into U.S. society, the economy, the work force, housing stock, and population distribution, as well as the characteristics of the nation and its various regions. The census is the only source of comparable data for all geographic regions in the nation. Similarly, for many purposes it is the only large-scale source of data for minority groups and for other special populations, such as specific income, age, or occupation groups. Second, census data are often necessary for research on noncensus data, such as school, hospital, legal, and administrative records, and provide the necessary denominators for calculating rates and proportions in many arenas of research. Third, the data are vital to the design of research, including the most obvious example—the drawing of survey samples.

Census data are indispensable for a wide range of research questions, programs, and instructional programs. A large cadre of established researchers and newcomers (including graduate students) awaits the release of census data every 10 years. After the 1990 census, these social scientists were ready to mine the data to describe what happened during the 1980s, to confirm or refute the hypotheses of extant studies, to exploit new opportunities for study of small geographic areas, and to examine temporal changes.

RESEARCH VALUE

Much of our knowledge of social transformations over recent decades has been obtained from analyses of census data. The decennial census has developed into an indispensable tool of government and a servant of many other purposes. A small number of questions deemed suitable and necessary for the government to ask has sufficed to delineate many of the most important features of the nation's peoples and their principal activities. Age, sex, race, ethnicity, family relationship, parenthood, place of current and previous residence, birthplace, education, employment, income—these topics covered in the census provide raw data for specification and analysis of each of the social and economic transformations mentioned above, and for an endless array of reports and research by public and private agencies.

The census of 1940 was the first to go beyond the traditional complete enumeration and employ sampling for some questions. Sampling continued in subsequent censuses, with a roughly 1-in-8 sample used in the 1990 census for most census data. Development of sampling theory and methods and the need for much more frequent temporal detail on many topics gave rise to a wide variety of federal, state, and privately sponsored surveys from the 1940s to the present. These surveys have not replaced the need for the census to provide data for small geographic areas, for small and widely dispersed population groups (such as American Indians), and for a benchmark for intercensal surveys.

Forms of Census Data

The Census Bureau releases decennial census data in two forms. One form is aggregated data for geographic units and administrative jurisdictions. The aggregated data are for varying geographic sizes ranging from city blocks to metropolitan statistical areas (MSAs) to states. Aggregated data are made available in published form that are widely available in libraries and research centers and in summary tapes. The Census Bureau released a number of different summary tape files containing an immense quantity of census data arranged by geographic category. The data consist of detailed tabulations for each geographic area and tables by conventional categories, such as age and race. A typical table might show the population by age, sex, and race for census tracts for a city. Such a table would allow an educational planner to note the elementary school-age population for Asian children for small areas for purposes of planning the needs for bilingual language instruction. With the aid of the Census Bureau's TIGER software for geographical referencing, aggregated data may be further combined to any collection of geographic units, including local service areas, congressional districts, and areas generated by the researcher. Given further information, changes in areas can be projected. A typical research task is to project the size and characteristics of a particular ethnic or age group using birth, mortality, and migration rates.

A second form of census data are Public Use Microdata Sample (PUMS) files. PUMS files provide data for a sample of housing units, as well as for each individual residing in those housing units. Geographic identification in the 1990 PUMS files extends down to areas of 100,000 or more people. This level of identification allows analysis of specific cities, groups of cities, and counties or groups of counties that reach the threshold of at least 100,000 population. PUMS files do not include any individual-level identification and are analogous to the data of common sample surveys of persons or households, but on a much larger scale. PUMS files for 1990 have sample sizes of 1 and 5 percent of the nation's population, including about 2.5 million and 12.5 million persons in the samples, respectively. The large PUMS data files permit research of literally ten of millions of observations, including the creation of samples of minority populations that cannot be found in any other available national sample. Although the PUMS files sacrifice the geographic detail of aggregated census data, they compensate by freeing the researcher to produce tables that do not appear in the aggregated data. For example, race, ethnicity, gender, income, and employment can be related to fertility, age, or any other characteristic—a multivariate association that does not exist in the aggregated data.

Census data for 1990 are a snapshot of the structure and characteristics of the nation's population and of its geographic and jurisdictional components as of April 1. The value of the data are greatly enhanced, moreover, by the ready availability of computer-readable data from earlier censuses. Comparable PUMS files are available for earlier censuses of population and housing. Access to historical PUMS census data is described later. Aggregate data for essentially comparable geographic units and jurisdictions for 1980 and 1970 can be combined with 1990 census data for research on changes over time.

The research value of these comparable sources is apparent. Data from several censuses and related sources support research into change in size and age structure of population groups, comparison of cohorts over time, and examination of comparable population groups at different times. Thus, period, age, and cohort effects can be examined, and changes in living conditions, income, housing, and other aspects of the well-being of population groups can be traced through time.

Identification of patterns and rates of change allows projections into the future size, characteristics, and distribution of the population. These projections have fundamental importance to the formulation and evaluation of public policies. They allow estimation of the kinds and extent of services that will be required or demanded in the future and the magnitude of social resources necessary to meet those needs and demands. As an example, the nature and adequacy of the housing of particular groups can be assessed. Projections of the future size of the population, its household size, and its residential patterns together will present patterns of home ownership, and provide a basis for estimating the housing needs of the future for particular metropolitan and rural areas as well as for the nation.

As a further example, census materials provide data on the number of children ever born, marital status, family and household size, and family relationships within households for immigrant groups. Knowledge of time trends in these variables (*not* available from vital statistics nor in sufficient sample sizes from any national survey) provides a basis for estimating future fertility and family trends of particular population groups and, in this way, facilitate understanding of future national population growth and identification of the local social services and support needs that are likely to confront those population groups in the future. In similar fashion, census data support exploration of the relationship between health and functional abilities, on the one hand, and socioeconomic status on the other. Knowledge of that relationship provides further support for estimation of future service needs and costs.

Advantages of PUMS Files

Researchers are well aware of the general utility of the census Public Use Microdata Sample (PUMS) files. Research-manipulable data for large numbers of individual units—persons, families, or households—provide an enormously powerful tool in contemporary social science and have fueled and been fueled by new statistical and analytical methods. Where the large data files are of such scale and proven utility as the national censuses, the potential becomes great. By working with individual microdata files, researchers realize several gains over working with published tabulations.

(1) *Maximum feasible comparability.* Data in PUMS files can be recoded or regrouped from existing detailed codes. The existing detailed coding of occupational titles, for example, can be recoded into different groups of occupations, of the researcher's selection, for new research projects.

(2) *Multivariate analysis.* Research can undertake multivariate analysis to explore new hypotheses and models of such complexity as current techniques and sample size allow. Published tabulations usually include only a few variables in each table, with information sacrificed to effect groupings that highlight the data while still fitting on the page, and with combinations of variables that reflect a particular view of which associations among variables would be of general interest.[1]

(3) *Attain comparability in data organization.* The most effective time-series analysis, whether the intervals are 1 year or 10 years, requires that the researcher be able to attain comparability in the organization of data and main-

tain control over treatment of age. In general, there are three distinct forms of analysis that may be used in the study of trends with census data:

(a) Aggregate analysis of trends, for which the researcher seeks to attain maximum comparability on all variables. Age is primarily a defining attribute (as in specifying population of labor-force age or reproductive age). Comparisons may be made of single variables or patterns of relationships among variables at each census date.

(b) Between-cohort analysis comparing persons of the same age at successive times. If a cohort is defined as those persons born in a given time interval, this style of analysis permits comparison of successive cohorts on successive variables as educational attainment at age 25, or on patterns of relationship such as the number of children ever born at wife's age 45-49 years to a variety of social and economic attributes of wife and husband.

(c) Within-cohort analysis tracing life-cycle patterns. For persons born during 1940-1950, for example, measures of male and female labor-force participation may be examined for successive ages as the cohorts grow older—ages 20-30 years in the 1970 census, ages 30-40 years in the 1980 census, and ages 40-50 years in the 1990 census.

By combining types (b) and (c), additional interpretative potential is gained. Life-cycle patterns and trends for different cohorts may be compared. Matching these to the specific dates of observation used for aggregate comparisons brings all three styles of analysis together for joint assessment of what are frequently identified as period, cohort, and age effects.

Examples of Research

It would be impossible to describe or list, for even a small portion, the many research applications that aggregated and PUMS census data support. It is possible to give a few examples as provided by various scholars (taken from descriptions in Rockwell and Austin, 1991).

Aging of the Population

The aging of the population is an increasingly common experience among industrial nations with lower fertility levels. The "baby boom" generation in the United States will enter late middle age at the beginning of the twenty-first century, transforming the society from a primarily young one (in the 1970s) to a predominantly old one. Heightened research attention is being given to examining the nature of the elderly population, and decennial census data are one of the chief tools used in such examinations. Researchers are increasingly aware of the heterogeneity of the elderly population. A chief topic pursued is the varied retirement situations of older individuals. Retirement has come to be referenced, rather ambiguously, by both the sources of one's income and the extent of one's labor-force activity. Data from the 1990 census on labor-force activity and on income sources are used to distinguish alternative states of retirement among the elderly population, ranging from those who either never worked or previously worked and currently receive a retirement form of income, to those who work part or full time and receive a retirement form of income.

Additional research questions concerning the elderly also require the type of geographic specificity presented by decennial census data. The nature and extent of geographic concentration of the elderly have important policy consequences for planning and for cost-effective service delivery. Knowledge of the spatial distribution of older individuals permits the testing of generalizations about "unique" living conditions of the elderly that have already begun to break down our rather simplistic views about this segment of the population. Included in this nexus of factors are such 1990 census indicators as disability or severe health limitations, living arrangements and households composition, alternative sources of income, and the relative size of the older population groups in various locales. No single other source of research data contains the diversity of indicators or contextual richness necessary for examining the condition of the older population of the nation.

Race Relations

A major component of the study of race relations in the United States focuses on racial residential segregation. An extensive literature, based on research conducted over the past three decades, has demonstrated variation in the degree to which racial groups live in close proximity only to members of their own racial or ethnic group. The consequences of racial residential segregation, for both racial and ethnic minority groups as well as for society as a whole, are enormous, affecting the distribution of political power in cities, quality of education received, and the differential socialization of children and adults. Decennial census data contain the basic information used to measure racial residential segregation and to construct widely used indexes of racial concentrations and of contact with persons of different racial or ethnic groups. Researchers use the aggregated data from the 1990 census to measure this type of segregation and to compare results with similar data from the 1970 and 1980 censuses. Such measurements permit researchers to investigate the economic consequences of residential segregation, as well as to probe into racial attitudes and discriminatory practices that may promote different levels of racial segregation in various locales. While early results of investigations tend to show a decline in residential segregation since 1980, the pattern is uneven, with some ethnic groups exhibiting increases in segregated living areas over the past decade. A great deal more research will be conducted on this topic, covering both metropolises and less urbanized areas across the whole country.

Education

Census data are essential for research on the process of education and for examination of the consequences of education on individuals' life chances. Educational researchers use information from the decennial censuses to control their other analyses and research results for demographic variables. Such investigations, for example, use small-area census data to explore the socioeconomic context within which individuals' educational attainment occurs. Attributes such as a neighborhood's median years of school completed, average income, and employment patterns have been found to have a profound impact on educational outcomes of persons residing in them. Among the important research investigations that are conducted with census data are studies of the effect of school desegregation on employment chances of members of minority groups and the degree to which school cohorts are segregated on factors such as racial composition, graduation rates, migration, income, and housing quality. Such studies of the importance of context on individual behavior and actions are greatly enhanced by using maps to display the geographic distribution of various demographic and economic characteristics of the population.

Concentrated Poverty

In the mid-1980s, analyses of census data revealed a large increase during the 1970s in the number of urban neighborhoods in which more than 40 percent of the households had incomes below the official poverty line. The number of people living in such areas also increased dramatically. A large proportion of these people were blacks living in a handful of the nation's largest cities.

These rather straightforward tabulations attracted research attention to a set of issues that were emerging in social policy debates. Is there something about geographically concentrated poverty that is distinctive? Is there a "natural order of the inner-city ghetto" that changes the character of ghetto problems and requires different kinds of interventions? In the 1930s and the 1950s, national social policy included a major component directed toward slum clearance and urban renewal. In the 1960s and 1970s, these programs were less favored than efforts focused on general economic vitality. In the 1980s, an increasing number of social science articles and books raised new concerns about the urban poor, persistent poverty, the growth of an "underclass," and the neighborhood and community problems of the "disadvantaged."

Researchers began to use a much richer array of census data in the 1980s, along with noncensus data keyed to census geography, to document levels and changes in a medley of indicators of undesirable social conditions. With the availability of 1990 census data within the past 2 years, these earlier studies are now being replicated, updated, and expanded. One example of the kinds of questions now being researched is: Do poor single parents living in an urban poverty area have different behaviors and life prospects than poor single parents in other circumstances? Census data are essential to the analysis of such issues, although they are rarely sufficient in themselves.

During the last two decades, much of the best and most innovative research on issues of poverty, race, and class was fueled from new national sample surveys such the Panel Survey on Income Dynamics (PSID), General Social Survey, Current Population Survey, Survey on Income and Program Participation, and National Longitudinal Survey. The rediscovery in the late 1980s of neighborhoods and slums required social scientists to turn some of their attention to other kinds of data. Because of the limited sample sizes and sample designs, sample surveys are relatively weak for the study of geographically concentrated phenomena. They can be strengthened by the incorporation of contextual data from the census; for example, the PSID has successfully linked its individual and family data to contextual information for census tracts and counties in which its sample families live. Only the decennial census offers the abundant detail needed for research that makes use of small areas throughout the entire nation.

The 1990 census offers two dramatic innovations to facilitate this research and also to spur development of new modes of analysis and hence new ways of thinking about these issues. One innovation is delineation of small areas (census blocks) throughout the entire country, with enormous quantities of aggregate data available for each area. The second innovation is new technology for manipulating census spatial data and matching noncensus data to census geography: the TIGER system. Social scientists have rapidly increasing accessibility to powerful personal computer systems and work stations required for use of these new tools. Research that 30 years ago could only be done with one of the world's most powerful computers and with a team of skilled programmers and analysts can now be accomplished by a single researcher at a personal computer.

Global Change

One of the most pressing fundamental and applied research tasks of the present and coming decades concerns the interrelation between human and natural processes as they affect the natural environment and the quality—or the possibility for some areas in the long term—of human life. These are, of course, issues of global significance, but they must be addressed at the local, regional, and national levels as well. For research into social processes as they affect and are affected by the natural environment, the census provides data on population distribution and density, and limited data on land use, resource consumption, and certain kinds of effluent production. The census data thus allow research into the relation between human habitation, activities, and behavior on the one hand,

and environmental hazards and environmental deterioration on the other. The geographically comprehensive nature of the data and their geographic resolution allow research to be conducted at multiple levels and aids in assessing the environmental impact of specific localities on each other and on regional and larger areas. The availability of data from earlier censuses, as well as other sources, allows projections of environmental change and human activities and better identification of the patterns of human behavior that retard or accelerate adverse environmental change.

The low level of geographic aggregation characteristic of census data combined with the availability of TIGER files contributes in important ways to the achievement of these goals. At present, the census is probably the only source of national data on social and economic processes that can be effectively linked through geographical information systems to satellite-produced remote sensing data measuring natural processes. In these terms, the census materials afford what may be at this time a unique opportunity to explore directly the relations between natural and human processes.

DEVELOPMENT OF CENSUS MICRODATA FILES

The incredible volume of raw data produced by census enumeration has compelled the Census Bureau to be a persistent innovator in techniques of mass data processing. Successive developments in punched card technology, machine-readable coding, and computers enabled the Census Bureau to keep up with the processing demands and to issue an ever-expanding shelf of publications. During the 1940s and 1950s there were occasional instances in which published tabulations were deemed inadequate and particular users made arrangements for special tabulations. During the past 30 years, there has been the development and expanded access to large census microdata files containing individual anonymous records.

Development of PUMS Files

With increased demand for access to census data, the Census Bureau in 1962 released a 1-in-1,000 public-use sample from the 1960 census basic record files (coded so as to preclude breach of confidentiality rules) to the community of researchers (academic, governmental, and business). This first public sample of individual census data provided researchers with their own census database and freedom to tabulate or manipulate without the constraints imposed by a fixed set of printed tables in bound volumes.

Access by social scientists to large files of data at the individual and household level is a comparatively recent development of profound significance to social research. At the time of release of the 1960 0.1 percent sample, only a few research centers had access to both computers and programs to make use of the computer tapes, and most researchers either struggled with punched card tabulation machines or neglected the new data resource. By the time of the 1970 census, computer technology had improved, accessibility of researchers to appropriate hardware and software had become more common, and the increasing statistical sophistication of social scientists led to a variety of analytical techniques that depended on computer data processing and analysis. The distinctions between survey research (defined traditionally to exclude the decennial census) and demographic research (traditionally based on work with limited sets of published cross-tabulations) became blurred, to the benefit of both traditions.

The use of large census data files for social science research has increased steadily since 1962. Despite a series of initial difficulties with the 1960 0.1 percent public-use sample file, researchers soon became so accustomed to it that they ceased acknowledging the file's sponsors (the Census Bureau) and simply cited the 1960 1-in-1,000 census sample data. Several 1.0 percent public-use sample tapes from the 1970 census were released as routine census products, along with many other alternatives to the traditional bound sets of tables, and a 1.0 percent public-use sample from the 1960 census was subsequently produced by the Census Bureau in the 1970s, providing a large comparable sample for the 1960 and 1970 censuses.

Development of Summary Tape Files

Summary tape files are selected census items and cross-tabulation arranged by geography. The files contain information for states, places, and small areas down to the census block.

The 1970 census was the first census for which summary tape files were released as regular products, in addition to the printed reports (tapes from the 1960 census that had been made solely to generate printed reports were made available on request; relatively few copies were released outside of the Census Bureau). Summary tape files from the 1970 and later censuses covered more subjects and provided more geographic detail than the reports. In 1980 and 1990, the summary tape files were expanded in geography and content (e.g., the long-form data in 1980 were made available for block groups in addition to census tracts) and, in some cases, replaced the published reports entirely (e.g., no block data were printed in 1980 or 1990, but they were available in the summary tape files).

Historical Census Files

As soon as the social science research community became familiar with the feasibility, flexibility, and virtues of the 1960 and 1970 public-use samples, the idea took hold of producing public-use samples from earlier censuses. Social historians were particularly interested in the nineteenth century censuses, and were spurred by the public availability (without confidentiality restrictions) of microfilm copies of the original manuscript enumeration forms. Demographers and many other social scientists were particularly interested in the two censuses preceding 1960. The 1940 census was the first "modern" census—the first with a question on income and a wide range of other social and economic information, the first to use sampling (to collect long-form data), and the first to be designed and planned by a full-time professional staff that included social scientists. Starting in the 1960s, demographers began to express an interest at professional meetings in constructing public-use samples from the 1940 and 1950 censuses. By the late 1970s, the Census Bureau had prepared cost estimates and preliminary procedural plans for 1940 and 1950 public-use census samples. Eventually, with financial support from several federal agencies and strong encouragement from social science researchers, the first samples from historical censuses (1940 and 1950) were produced.

During the past 20 years, work has continued on taking samples from much earlier censuses, from 1850 onward. Just recently, public-use samples have been completed of the 1850 and 1880 censuses (Ruggles, 1993). Work on the 1850 census manuscripts began in September 1992 to take a 1 percent sample of the free population of the United States.[2] The 1850 enumeration was the first individual-level census in the United States and is therefore the first census for which a public-use microdata sample is possible. The 1850 census included questions on fertility, urban and rural residence, foreign-born status, occupation, and household relationship. The new public-use sample allows the construction of tabulations on a wide range of topics that are not covered in census publications or were incompletely tabulated. Availability of the 1850 PUMS files will provide an important baseline for historical studies. The availability of the 1850 census microdata will extend the current series of census PUMS data back to a period prior to the Civil War, filling in a critical gap in the study of long-term social change.

The 1880 PUMS files is a 1 percent sample of the 1880 census. The 1880 census was innovative in a number of ways: it had improved completeness of coverage, enhanced accuracy of enumeration, and included a greater range and detail of questions. For the 1880 census, the supervision of enumerators was shifted from a part-time responsibility of U.S. Marshals to 150 census supervisors who were specifically appointed for the purpose. It was the first census to inquire about marital status, a critical variable for analysis of fertility and household arrangement. A question on relationship to head of family was added, which makes it possible to distinguish immediate family relatives from secondary individuals and allows construction of a wide variety of variables on family structure. Other valuable new questions in the 1880 census included birthplace of father and mother, condition of health, married within the past year, and number of months unemployed during the census year.

The preliminary 1850 PUMS files are now available, including 177,000 individuals and representing 90 percent of the final sample. The penultimate version of the 1880 PUMS files are also now available, consisting of information on 503,000 individuals. Work for producing the 1850 and 1880 PUMS files was supported by grants from the National Science Foundation and the National Institute for Child Health and Human Development.

At the same time that work has proceeded on censuses from the nineteenth century, researchers have worked with the Census Bureau to take samples from the remaining censuses of the twentieth century. With the recent availability of the 1850 and 1880 censuses, 11 census PUMS files are now available from 1850 to 1990 (1850, 1880, 1900, 1910, 1920, 1940, 1950, 1960, 1970, 1980, and 1990) offering a usable and accessible data series of 140 years of major changes in U.S. society. These historical files are our most important quantitative resource for the study of social change. Altogether, they provide individual-level data on 65 million Americans from the middle of the nineteenth century to near the beginning of the twenty-first.

ACCESS TO CENSUS DATA

Researchers have access to census data in two ways. One approach is to purchase census data directly from the Census Bureau. The Census Bureau releases census data in a variety of formats, including printed tabulations, computer tapes, floppy diskettes, and CD-ROMs. A second approach is to obtain data from one of several organizations that preprocess census data and release them in a form that is easier to analyze. The Inter-university Consortium for Political and Social Research (ICPSR), a nonprofit organization supported by about 360 member institutions (primarily colleges and universities) that is located at the University of Michigan, provides a common source of census data for researchers. Other sources of census data include state data centers, individual universities, and groups organized to provide data on a consortium basis. (The Association of Public Data Users, for example, purchased and recopied the 1980 and 1990 data for its members.)

Role of the Inter-University Consortium for Political and Social Research

All census PUMS and summary tape files are maintained at the Inter-university Consortium for Political and Social Research (ICPSR) and are inexpensive and accessible to researchers. Researchers affiliated with the 360 institutional members of ICPSR have access to census data (especially the PUMS data from the census from 1850 to 1990) without charge. Individuals at nonmember institutions also have access to census data for a nominal charge—well below the rate charged by the Census Bureau. In the event that an institution is unable to pay the charge, limited amounts of data are provided by ICPSR to individuals at nonmember institutions without charge.

The advantages of census data are well recognized. But an awareness of general potential is not a sufficient specification of benefits to weigh in the balance against the rather high costs of producing PUMS files. During the past 30 years the specific benefits of the PUMS data have been demonstrated many times. Financial support has been given by the federal government, by state and local governments, and by research foundations for the preparation, distribution, and use of PUMS data to thousands of researchers and research agencies for several decades. To cite one example for 1990 PUMS data: the ICPSR acquired census data and provided training and assistance for access to the data. ICPSR contributed $270,000 of its membership fees to the project. Additional support was received from the Census Bureau, the National Science Foundation, and jointly from the National Institute of Child Health and Human Development and the National Institute on Aging, each of the three contributing about $250,000 individually.

Underutilization

In principle, the widespread research use of census data demonstrates that the continued collection and creation of public-use data files are in the public interest. A set of fundamental questions about the character of U.S. society and how it has been changing exists; those questions can receive better answers from social science researchers only if census data files are produced and reasonably accessible.

The inventory of topics and questions in the census is, of course, not complete. The census can never be complete or provide the sole data set for research. Because social science, like all science, responds to new techniques and new data sources as well as to the continually cumulating body of prior work, forecasting developments is difficult. As a case in point, when the 0.1 percent sample file from the 1960 census was first released, the sponsors at the Census Bureau were disappointed by the slow rate of purchases and utilization. The subsequent experience has been one of extraordinary frequent and diverse use of the 1960 sample files and of the subsequent census public-use files that have been released.

Still, there are difficulties in access to 1990 census public-use files. Census files are large and complicated. Researchers who try to use the large 5 percent PUMS files for the 1990 census find that they receive several dozen computer tapes, that the initial processing of the tapes requires trained computer programming staff, and that there is considerable cost and time required to ready the data for analysis.

Online Access

One of the most important recent developments in access to census data has been the online availability of 1980 and 1990 1 percent PUMS data. The Consortium for International Earth Science Information Network (CIESIN), located in Saginaw, Michigan maintains both the 1980 and 1990 PUMS data on workstations. Users can dial the telephone number, on one of several lines, for the Saginaw workstations, access either the 1980 or 1990 data, request specific tabulations or descriptive statistics, and receive the requested data back in typically 5-8 seconds.

CIESIN's computers are online continuously and allow users to obtain instantaneously tabulations for any population of interest. For example, a user might be interested in the labor-force status for Hispanic and black men and women, aged 18-24 years, who completed 4 years of high school and who live in a specific metropolitan area or a specific state. One might want to compare their unemployment rates to the national average or to compare the 1990 rates to 1980. CIESIN's workstation computer and online software allow researchers to obtain such tabulation almost instantly.

The widespread and continuous use of census data on the CIESIN's computer is evidence that there is strong demand for even greater accessibility to census data. There are now more researchers using the CIESIN census data in a single day than used the 1960 PUMS data in the 1960s over the entire decade. The future trends seem to be the development of increasingly easier access to public-use census samples, probably with improved online systems and greater user-friendly CD-ROMs, for the 2000 census.

NOTES

[1]PUMS data support a great deal of multivariate analysis that can be tailored to specific research questions. Although the summary tape files with aggregated data may limit the particular cross-tabulations available, aggregated data have often been used for studies of residential settlement, especially residential segregation, based on the spatial analysis of particular social groups.

[2]Individual microdata were not collected from the slave population in the 1850 census.

REFERENCES

Rockwell, R.C., and E.W. Austin
  1991   1990 U.S. Census Data Project. Proposal submitted to the National Science Foundation. Inter-university Consortium for Political and Social Research, Ann Arbor, Mich.
Ruggles, S.
  1993   Historical Census Projects: Integrated Public Use Microdata Series. Social History Research Laboratory, University of Minnesota, Minneapolis.

APPENDIX

E

State and Local Needs for Census Data

As part of its study of census data needs, the panel undertook a survey of state data centers to determine their requirements for data content, the priority of key features of census data, and comments on alternative census designs. Our survey consisted of requests for:

- documents or summaries of specific examples of how census data are used;
- descriptions of innovative uses of census materials, especially the use of small-area data (census tracts, blocks, or aggregates of blocks);
- information on programs that rely on census data and demonstrate the critical role of census data for major public programs and policies;
- a list and brief explanation of essential data;
- comments on five components of alternative census designs (geographic detail; timeliness of data; content; accuracy of data; and a geographic referencing system, e.g., TIGER); and
- comments on four classes of alternative census designs (current design, census with intercensal surveys, expanded use of administrative records, and a minimal census with cumulated surveys).

This appendix is based on a background paper prepared for the panel by Michele Conrad entitled "State and Local Needs for Census Data: A Survey of State Data Centers."

State data centers serve as clearinghouses for census data in their states and responded to our survey on the state's needs for data, as well as the needs of county and city governments, businesses, and other data center affiliates (non-profit associations, etc). We report on responses provided by 18 states: Alabama, Alaska, California, Hawaii, Illinois, Indiana, Iowa, Maine, Maryland, Michigan, Minnesota, Montana, New Hampshire, New York, North Carolina, Oklahoma, South Carolina, and Wisconsin.

In focusing on state and local needs for census data, first the general census data categories (general demographic, race and ethnicity, immigration, labor force and occupation, education, disability, transportation, income and poverty, and housing) and their uses are discussed. This is followed by a discussion of specific uses of census data; uses of data for meeting state and federal legislative requirements, preparing state and federal grants applications, public health and social service programs, community planning and development, environmental uses, and economic uses are discussed. Next, the appendix addresses the level of geographic detail needed by states and local jurisdictions for performing their work. Finally, general conclusions regarding the needs reported by state data centers are presented.

USES OF CENSUS DATA: AN OVERVIEW

Small-area census data are essential to state and local governmental agencies for descriptive analyses, assessments, and planning related to public-policy decision making, including the day-to-day decision-making process. Those purposes include, but are not limited to: meeting state and federal legislative requirements, allocating funds for social service programs and assessing the need and effects of public health and social service programs, community planning and development, environmental monitoring, and economic analyses. Census data are used to describe neighborhoods, which helps private and public agencies understand their community's needs and target program and policy efforts effectively. The actual data items used to meet the policy objectives of the states and local communities are varied, but data at the county, municipal, tract, census block group, and census block levels are frequently used to inform the decision-making process and achieve public-policy goals of the state and local governments and community groups. Based on the survey responses, it is apparent that census data are important for being able to accurately describe the demographic diversity within a county or city for understanding the society and the ability to make government more effective. More important, however, is that the census is the only reliable source of accurate small-area data available to them.

Census data are used for everything from selecting a site for a major power plant or community day-care center to planning the construction of a new road or bridge to distributing federal funds. State and local governments use census data to prepare analyses related to population trends; community and economic development plans; long-range plans and recommendations for land-use transportation, community facilities, public utilities, recreation, housing, and other community improvements and developments; grant applications for federal- and state-funded projects; designation of enterprise zones; reapportionment and redistricting, library service area designations, and population aggregations. With all of these uses of census data, it is easy to imagine a great demand for census data products. One data center reported that the demand for census data has grown dramatically—in 1983, that center received fewer than 1,000 inquiries for census data; in 1993, it received over 8,000 inquiries.

School districts, university students, housing authorities, the farm programs, consultants for sewer and water districts, grant applicants, state tax assessors, utility companies, soil conservation services, grocery store chains, hospitals and health clinics, various state and local government agencies, municipalities, housing developers, newspaper reporters, accountants, the United Way, media consultants, banks, transportation agencies, libraries, and other types of businesses and industries are among the users of census data. The data requested range from population estimates to economic data to types of employment. Specific examples of uses are:

(1) the use of statistics on the total number of households, including the number of households below the poverty level, by a housing development corporation to gain support for a housing rehabilitation project that would provide affordable rental housing;

(2) the use of educational attainment data and age cohort statistics used in planning an adult basic education program;

(3) the use of tract-level data to create maps showing concentrations of immigrant populations, as well as maps showing housing units using public and private sewerage and water systems;

(4) the use of zip code data to prepare profiles of age, race, sex, income, education, occupation, and type of employment by zip code area;

(5) the use of census block-level data from summary tapes, aggregated to user-defined areas, to prepare a demographic profile of city communities and neighborhoods;

(6) the use of census data to create maps showing an area's population change from 1970 to 1990; and

(7) the use of census data to create census tract maps showing the change in household income from 1970 to 1990.

The survey of state data centers asked for state and local requirements, based on the overall experiences with thousands of requests for census data, for general data categories. The survey grouped census data into nine categories: general demographic data, race and ethnicity, immigration, labor force and occupation, education, disability, transportation, income and poverty, and housing.

Summarizing, first of all, the general replies from all state data centers, Table E.1 shows the priority or importance the data centers place on the various categories of census data. (It should be noted that not all survey respondents provided a ranking for every data item.) The variation among items reported as being essential by some data centers and eligible for elimination by others suggests that states often have very different uses and needs for data. Several respondents noted, in fact, that every data item on the 1990 census has a constituency, and that eliminating any item would be a problem for at least some community of users.

CENSUS DATA CATEGORIES

As noted above, the first part of our survey asked for information on the uses made of various categories and specific items from the census questionnaire. The broad categories are: general demographic, race and ethnicity, immigration, labor force and occupation, education, disability, transportation, income and poverty, and housing.

General Demographic Data

General demographic data, as defined by our survey, includes: population items (including residence, age, race, and sex), household relationship, migration and place of birth, fertility and marital history. These data are used to describe the way U.S. citizens live and are frequently combined with noncensus data for rate calculations. Each category is discussed in turn.

Population by age, race, and sex is essential at the block level and is the backbone for demographic analyses and establishment of incidence rates. The data are used for many federal reports and grants, research, area profiles, land-use planning, labor-force estimates based on residence (in cooperation with the Bureau of Labor Statistics), determination of voting-age populations, school facility planning, and licensing.

Household relationship helps to identify high-risk areas, such as those areas with high concentrations of single, female-headed families, high unemployment, and high drop-out rates; federal reports and grants; research; area profiles; planning and evaluation purposes; household projections; and determining and targeting areas where social services are needed.

Migration is crucial for understanding migration from state to state and within states, as well as for understanding who is moving. Data on migration are also used for population estimates, federal reports and grants, and research. For states such as Alaska, where heavy annual migration in and out of the state fluctuates by season, the movement of people between states and counties between decennial censuses is tracked using the change of address information on IRS tax returns.

Although a number of respondents indicated that place of birth is not crucial, they did indicate that it is a useful item. According to one of the data centers, place of birth is the only migration measure available for subcounty geographic levels.

Responses to the use of fertility data were inconsistent. Several data centers noted that the data were essential; others noted that they were important or useful, but not necessary. Those in the former category noted that fertility data are important because the census is the only source of that data for subcounty geographic levels. They are also used and necessary for various federal reports and grants, research, area profiles, and population projections. A few data centers, however, indicated that state vital statistics units sometimes provide better and more current information than the census.

Several states noted that marital history data are essential or important and used for federal reports and grants, research, and area profiles, with some reporting that the census is the only source of marital history information at subcounty geographic levels. A few data centers noted that they are not frequently used or not essential. One data center reported that state vital statistics provide better and more current information than the census.

Race, Hispanic Origin, and Ancestry

The data centers reported almost unanimously that race is an essential data item. Most of the centers cited the need for the data for reapportionment and redistricting purposes, as well as for compliance with and enforcement of the Voting Rights Act. Race data are also essential for grants applications; housing, social service, and community planning; affirmative action compliance assessments, as well as for education, health care, and employment services. A way of addressing multiple racial background in the census was advocated.

Most of the data centers reported that Hispanic origin item is essential. Hispanic status is used for reapportionment and redistricting and for meeting Voting Rights Act requirements. The data are also used for state and local planning and evaluation. Because of the steady growth of the Hispanic population, a number of states have a greater need than in previous years for information so that the Hispanic population can be better served.

The responses on the ancestry item covered a wide range: essential, not crucial, used very little, eliminate. Data centers that found it essential or important noted the item's cultural significance and use for urban analyses at the tract and block-group levels. Ancestry data are used in some states to obtain information on people of multiple racial backgrounds.

Immigration: Citizenship, Year of Entry, and Language

Citizenship data are used to develop plans for immigrant and refugee services and for distributing state funds. Year of entry data were reported by a majority of data centers as being used by government demographers and others, but otherwise not essential or frequently used or requested. One data center, however, reported that year of entry data are essential because foreign immigration is becoming the largest component of growth in its area, as well as in many other areas.

Language data are used to determine areas where information should be distributed in a language other than English or where language assistance might be needed. It was reported that there are few or no sources other than the census that will yield language data at low levels of geography.

Labor Force and Occupation

Data categories included under labor force and occupation in our survey are employment status, work and employment in prior year, and veteran status.

Data on employment status are used widely as an economic tool for labor-force and employment projections and affirmative action plans. Employment data may also be linked to income and poverty data for various types of analyses.

These data are used to assess the effects of structural changes in economies (e.g., the closing of a sugar plantation in Hawaii), as well as to assess the economic potential of an area for potential new industries.

According to our respondents, the most frequent use of veteran status data is for health and program analysis for the veteran population.

Education: School Enrollment and Highest Grade Completed

School enrollment data are a widely used indicator and in some states are used as a measure of accountability for the education system. For example, Hawaii creates social and economic profiles for school areas that are used in planning processes. Enrollment data are used for labor-force and other economic analyses and may be used to compare age data with local school censuses and projections. The Alaska State Data Center noted that enrollment data are available from the state Department of Education.

Data on education levels are used by the departments of education and educational leaders to measure programmatic impact, and many communities use the data to attract industry. It is critical to many states is assessing the type of work force in an area, for economic analyses of areas, and for economic development profiles. Some states routinely tie educational attainment to occupation and income characteristics and find the data very important when broken out by race. Finally, the data are used by some jurisdictions in gauging improvement.

Disability

Although many of the data centers indicated that disability is an essential census item, and some said that increased data collection is needed, not all state data centers reported that it is essential. Those that found it to be a high priority item cited the data's use by social service and public works agencies for grants and social service grants applications and planning (including transportation planning), as well as its use for compliance with the Americans with Disabilities Act. Respondents who did not find the item essential indicated that the data are not widely used because the disabled population is well-documented with noncensus sources.

Transportation

Transportation data are used for assessing commuting patterns, locating new roads, and transportation planning. Commuting pattern information is used as an economic tool. For instance, commuting data from the 1990 census helped to show a growing economic link between the Baltimore and Washington, D.C. areas. Transportation data needs and uses are discussed in Appendix G.

Income and Poverty

Based on survey responses, the income and poverty data are, for many areas, the most important data gleaned from the census. Income and poverty data are used extensively for every planning and analysis that can be imagined. The data are used by the private sector for, among other things, targeting customers, and by the public sector for, among other things, determining areas with low to moderate income households for providing services. The data are used, obviously, for area economic profiles, but also for grants, housing applications, housing analyses, establishing job training service areas and programs. The data are also vital indicators of an area's current economic status.

Housing

Respondents reported that housing data are useful in looking at housing demand, for housing applications, analyses of housing conditions and development plans, area profiles, etc. Data on septic and sewered systems are essential for some areas in developing sewer service area plans. The data area also essential for land-use plans and community development block-grant programs. Uses and needs for housing data are discussed in Appendix H.

USES OF CENSUS DATA

Uses of Census Data for State and Federal Legislative Requirements

In an effort to meet state and federal legislative requirements, small-area census data are often used to assess compliance with laws. The Minnesota state data center also noted that many state statutes rely on small-area income, poverty, and housing census data for the distribution of funds.

One of the most frequently mentioned uses of census data was the use of block-level data to meet federal reapportionment and redistricting deadlines. (Appendix C discusses reapportionment and redistricting in detail.) For example, in California, census data are used for reapportionment of state senate and assembly districts, county supervisorial districts, school districts, and city council districts. Montana uses sample items at the block and block-group level for redistricting.

Many other federal laws, however, require the use of census data. For instance, the Community Development Block Grant Program (CDBG), as mandated by the Housing and Community Development Act of 1974; the comprehensive housing affordability strategies (CHAS); the CHAS Anti-Poverty Plan; the National Affordable Housing Act of 1990; and the Housing and Community Development Act (HCDA) of 1992 all require census data at the census tract and block levels. The census data are necessary for local jurisdictions to prove eligibility for funding and for implementation of the programs, e.g., identification of areas where a project or service can be developed and provided. The census data are used to identify areas of poverty concentration, minority concentration, overcrowding, and substandard housing. Without the data described above, it would be impossible to comply with the application submission requirements of the programs, and the programs could not be implemented as mandated by Congress. Finally, without the data, many needy areas would not be able to prove eligibility for funds. Some examples of uses that are legislatively mandated follow.

• Small-area transportation data items, such as mode of transportation to work and vehicle occupancy are used by transportation and environmental agencies to assess environmental impacts related to federal guidelines or mandates, including requirements of the Intermodal Surface Transportation Efficiency Act of 1991.

• The Illinois Department of Public Health cited the use of block- and tract-level data for health assessment studies related to toxic waste clean-up of Super Fund sites on the national priority list—a federally mandated program. The demographic and housing characteristics near Super Fund sites are analyzed using census data.

• Title I of the National Affordable Housing Act of 1990 requires that local, county, and state governments submit a housing assistance strategy program in order to receive federal funding. Census data are required to identify areas of poverty and minority concentration, overcrowding, and substandard housing.

In addition to the federal requirements listed above, many state laws require the use of census data for program purposes.

• California Government Code 65302(b) requires local traffic circulation documentation to make an assessment of the needs of those who depend on public transportation (low income, elderly, and disabled).
• In Minnesota, the Mobile Health Clinic, which travels in and around poverty stricken areas of the state providing services, is required by legislation.
• Also in Minnesota, the home visiting program, which works to prevent child abuse and neglect, is required by Minnesota statutes.

Uses of Census Data for State and Federal Grants Applications

Census data are a necessary input for many federal and state grants applications. The Community Development Block Grant program is an example of census data used for completing and certifying grants applications. In California, census data are required for most grant applications for county, city, and small community programs. In addition to the Community Development Block Grant, the Urban County Grant Fund, also administered by the U.S. Department of Housing and Urban Development (HUD), requires census data for the grant application (Title I of the Housing and Community Development Act of 1974). CDBG housing and other grant applications are prepared using census data on population, number of households, income, vacant housing units (number of), occupied housing units (number of), seasonal housing units (number of), owners (number of), renters (number of), median value of owner-occupied housing, median contract rent, renter vacancy rate, homeowner vacancy rate, female head of households, minorities, median age, population over age 65, and housing units constructed before 1940. The information for the applications is needed by county, city, village, township, census tract, and in some cases block groups. Census data are also needed to complete Comprehensive Housing Assistance Plans and to prepare annual reports.

Uses of Census Data for Public Health and Social Service Programs

Federally funded social service and human resource agencies that provide services to low-income and minority populations often require census data at tract or other levels to determine eligibility for program participation. Census data are used to identify areas needing programs and funding for programs that offer counseling, child care information, referral services, and drug and alcohol education. In some cases, state laws require the distribution of state resources on a per capita basis based on census data (in particular, population and poverty data). The Illinois Department of Public Health reported using census data daily for vital statistics and planning purposes.

The ability to measure aspects of a community's health is very important. A clear picture of community health status is needed to focus resources where they are needed most. Data are required for prevention program policy, planning, and evaluation processes, and for certain reporting requirements for state and federal agencies (such as disease counts and rates). The data most needed are age, sex, race/ethnicity by census tract and over time (preferably yearly). Data that are very helpful, but not critical are poverty status, households, persons/household, housing units, housing units/acre, persons/acre, educational attainment, place of birth, and household income. Without census data, many public health and social service agencies would not be able to meet their responsibilities and, in the long run, the public's health could suffer.

Census data are used to help state departments and agencies for child welfare predict trends in child abuse, foster care, socioeconomic needs, number of children in foster care and/or receiving social services, cost of services in the future, and household composition. At least one state's laws mandate the use of census data to formulate rationale for child care funding priorities. Census data are frequently used by child care service programs to identify, by race/ethnicity and income, areas where there are children with parents in the work force; child care subsidies are made based on those data. Census data also help county mental health agencies provide specific, mandated levels of service to children and help them plan for the services and apply for funding for those services.

In one example of data used for public health and social service programs provided to the panel, census data were used by a state public health official to order flu vaccine. The official was planning to order far too much vaccine, and the census data enabled him to see that ordering less would be adequate.

Identifying the need and eligibility for Head Start programs, which are mandated to serve families with the greatest need, is an important use of census data. The data are used to certify eligibility for federal and state funding of the Head Start program and to target areas where the program is needed.

An innovative use of census data is being made by the Asian American Health Forum. The forum is attempting to link census tract data with health data from Hawaii's Health Surveillance Program. Census tract is used as the common variable. The ability to link the data in this way will enable socioeconomic data to be related to health issues for areas in the state, enabling the populations most at risk and in need of services to be served more effectively.

Geographic coding of welfare recipients to help create a better understanding of welfare dependency can be attained through the use of census data. Coding welfare recipients geographically allows welfare data to be correlated with census data at the census tract level. In turn, cross-sectional statistical analysis can be performed and profiles of welfare recipients can be developed. Those analyses and profiles can help target populations for programs designed to move them to self-sufficiency. According to one of the respondents, census data are the only statistically reliable means of determining dependency rates for populations most at risk of welfare dependency.

Uses of Census Data for Community Planning and Development

Many community planning efforts require small-area census data to help determine, implement, and follow up on courses of action. Data required by most planning projects include population, age, race, income, employment, and housing. Federal Environmental Protection Agency mandates require many local governments to upgrade or replace water systems, sewage systems, and solid waste facilities. The funds for those projects are obtained through grants from the Farmers Home Administration, Community Development Block Grants, and, in some cases, state endowment programs. Census data are required for all of the grants applications and for administration of the programs mentioned above. In addition, HUD's new HOME program requires census data for grant applications and program administration. In order to qualify recipients, many federal programs require either census information or independent surveys that will provide the necessary qualifying data. As discussed above, recipients of Community Development Block Grants must have a certain percent of low-to-moderate income households. Municipalities or special purpose districts (fire or sewer districts) may apply for CDBG grants; however, because special purpose districts sometimes cross municipal lines, tract- or block-group data must be used for their grant applications. Since the grants may be used to develop infrastructure, data at smaller levels of geography are crucial for economic development. In one state, tract-level data are used to study characteristics of community areas, which are aggregates of census tracts. Those community areas can divide, for instance, a large city, into a number of geographic units. Census data aggregated to the community-area level are used extensively to create local community fact books, for health studies, for vital statistics analyses, and for all types of planning. Also, census data are the only source of comprehensive and consistent historical data, which are important in tracking changes in an area and in documenting urban decay. Historical and comparative research on areas that once thrived and are now in economic and physical decay helps pinpoint factors that contribute to the phenomenon of urban decay.

The following are some examples of data used for community planning and development purposes.

• Census data at the city-wide level are used for preparing and updating general plans, e.g., land use and housing elements and for infrastructure planning. If census data were not available, the state would incur significant costs in developing, standardizing, and enforcing data collection and reporting criteria. In addition, cities would incur tremendous costs to collect their own data.

• The census provides data on social, structural, labor-force, and economic change to planning agencies. Those data are used for planning roads, water and sewage systems (including wastewater treatment systems), and landfill and waste systems; evaluating public services and facilities; economic development and redevelopment projects; traffic analysis and hazardous material transportation; budget forecasting and fiscal planning; and developing social programs for the elderly, disabled, low-income, and foreign born.

A brief description of data uses for school districts, law enforcement, library services, and emergency planning follows.

School Districts

Some state codes require that school districts calculate the average the number of students in poverty and the number of school-age children in families receiving AFDC based on census data. School districts also use census data to develop demographic profiles of the students and community to better understand their educational needs, which in turn helps them plan facilities for K-12 schools. In Minnesota, for example, school districts rely on the census for many needs: child poverty assessments and analyses, enrollment-based facilities planning, and distributing school funding. Because school districts do not correlate to any other established geographic boundary, it is necessary to aggregate data from the smallest available census area to create an accurate picture of the school district's demographic characteristics. Those demographic profiles of the school districts help the educational planners and administrators determine the need for bilingual instruction programs and other special services that may be warranted in the schools.

Law Enforcement

Law enforcement training programs in some states are developed using census data. Trends and events that may impact the future of law enforcement and local communities are assessed using census data. Census data are used by city police departments for program design, workload distribution forecasting, patrol design, and analysis of crime and demographic data. In one instance, a state court system was able to discern that the crime-prone age group (16-26 years old) would be expanding. Census data also help to predict and analyze crime trends and statistics to help in investigations.

The San Diego County Automated Regional Justice Information System is one system that uses census data for those purposes. The San Diego City Police

Department has a computerized dispatch system that relies on census tract- and block-level data that are linked to police officers' patrols. A geographic file assigns a tract and block number to calls coming into the system. Patrol officers on the beat are assigned to investigate the call.

Library Services

Libraries use data for their grant applications (required by the Library Services and Construction Act). They also assist users who cannot afford to purchase census data. In addition, census data are used to analyze library service areas (census tract aggregations) to determine the type of services, materials, and programs that should be offered.

Emergency Planning

General demographic, housing, social, and economic information is especially important for areas where natural disasters (hurricanes, earthquakes, or volcanic eruptions) occur. In those instances, data are needed quickly so that emergency services can be implemented and the impact of the disaster can be assessed. For example, California uses census data to develop earthquake hazard assessments. Those assessments evaluate the potential damage and population affected by a given level of an earthquake centered in a given area, as well as the cost of actual damage and displacement. In addition, data on employment by work zone are used to estimate the daytime population in the event of a major catastrophe. Necessary treatment, services, and evacuation plans are based on daytime population in many larger cities. This was true for Hawaii during and after Hurricane Iniki, Florida after Hurricane Andrew, and California after the 1994 earthquake.

Uses of Census Data for Environmental Planning

Census data, particularly block-group and block-level data, are used to create land-use and land-cover maps, land-use projections, and socioeconomic profiles and projections (including sustainable growth analyses for areas) that affect the environment. This was done, for example, in Maryland for the governor's Chesapeake Bay Work Group Tributary Watershed Strategy. In California, the Air Quality Management Plan requires preparation of an air-quality element that identifies and analyzes population trends, commuting patterns, and land-use characteristics and their effect on the environment. In Minnesota, the Environmental Quality Board released an in-depth study of sustainable growth based on evaluation and mapping of census items at the block-group level.

In addition to the uses described above, census data are used also to identify and describe population segments exposed to environmental hazards, such as studies of populations living in close proximity to hazardous waste sites (i.e., Three Mile Island in Pennsylvania).

Economic Uses of Census Data:
Employment, Labor Force, and Economic Development Analyses

Designation of enterprise zones, affirmative action compliance, employment and labor-force analyses, and analyses of local economies are among the economic uses made of census data. Census data on occupation and labor force are used to analyze regional economic growth, as well as plans for future development. Census data are used to target state and federally funded job training programs to areas where those services are needed. For those purposes, according to survey respondents, census labor-force and employment/unemployment data are the only reliable indicators of joblessness at the small-area level. In Oklahoma, for example, income data at the block-group level are used to certify state enterprise zones for tax incentives—a legislatively mandated use. Income, poverty, and other socioeconomic characteristics are crucial at least at the census tract level for those areas. The California enterprise zones program identifies economically depressed areas and offers state incentives designed to encourage business investment and the creation of jobs. Another legislated California program, the Target Area Contract Preference Act, is designed to encourage and facilitate job maintenance and job development in areas that are identified and qualify as economically distressed and declining areas. Also, in New York, poverty and employment data are used to test the eligibility for the smallest places at the tract level for the Economic Development Zone Program.

In some states, small-area labor-force, employment, and occupation data are used to analyze local economies, including creating employment projections. One state prepared a report, based on 1990 census state- and county-level data, that analyzed occupational categories of the civilian labor force by sex and race.

In Alaska, monthly labor-force estimates are allocated to county-equivalent level; those estimates are prepared using census data. The data, which are used to adjust more current employment estimates from monthly samples to a residence basis, provide the correlations necessary to estimate the category of self-employed, unpaid family, and private household work employment. Census employment data are also used in Alaska to project patterns of occupational separations due to death and retirement. For those projections, worker occupations are cross-tabulated by age.

Detailed data on occupation by race and sex (which are available only from the census and only at the county and state levels) are used heavily by existing and potential employers to meet federal equal employment requirements or to identify the composition of the labor force of an area. Data on education, income, labor force, occupation, race and ethnicity, and sex are used for affirmative action purposes. For example, California's Office of Federal Contract Compliance Programs mandates the use of census data to establish labor market availability; and an affirmative action plan, including the use of census data, is required by the Eight Factor Analysis (Chapter 60-2.11,b). In addition, Executive Order 11246 of the U.S. Civil Rights Act mandates the use of census data to develop affirmative action plans. In Hawaii, Chinese, Korean, Filipino, Hawaiian, and Japanese race categories are used for affirmative action compliance analyses.

In preparing economic analyses and grant applications for counties and communities in Wisconsin, data on the farm and nonfarm populations, median age, educational attainment, minority population, employment categories, occupational data, income and poverty data, race, population by age and by sex, and place of work are utilized. An important use of census data is to aid in assessing the potential impact of an economic disruption, such as the closing of a large automobile manufacturer or a military base, on an area.

The Economic Development Division of the Office of Hawaiian Affairs seeks to identify economic needs, investigate and develop business programs, and advocate legislation that supports economic development and financial assistance for Native Hawaiian businesses. It also attempts to develop strategies for identifying barriers that prevent equal access to employment and works to develop ways of improving job skills and increasing the employability of Native Hawaiians. Census data provide the basic statistical data on income, poverty, education, employment, industry, and occupation data that are required for the division's work.

SMALL-AREA DATA NEEDS FOR GEOGRAPHICALLY DETAILED DATA

Small-area data are used to allocate funds and provide assistance in needy areas. Without the data, it would be difficult to understand differences between various racial/ethnic groups, to describe the demographic diversity in a city or county, and consequently to understand society. A detailed census, according to state data centers, is the only way to measure the basic characteristics of the population. It can help document society's problems, a necessary step to being able to solve them. Although a large state survey may be able to provide the necessary data, those surveys would take time and money to develop and implement. Evidence of the need for small-area data is that villages with as few as 1,000 residents must respond to the same environmental, development, and other concerns as large cities and counties. Those reporting requirements of smaller areas demand the same level of economic and demographic data as large cities and counties. The North-Central Alabama Regional Council of Governments cited a need for more geographic detail for small rural areas with less than 200 population. One sentiment echoed by most of the data centers is that the decennial census provides the only comprehensive socioeconomic database with reliable data down to the block level.

Data at the tract, block group, block, and place levels allow state and local governments to describe neighborhoods and are crucial to the governments' ability to conduct analyses and to make decisions about planning, program funding, and community development. State, county, place, tract, and zip code data are most frequently requested by users (including businesses, governmental units, and nonprofit organizations). Data for tracts and small minor civil divisions (less than 2,500 population) are frequently requested from the Wisconsin state data center, but there are few requests for block and block-group data. One of the data centers stated that the requested census data are primarily at the tract, block group, and block levels. In some cases, however, particularly in rural areas, detailed zip codes and minor civil divisions were reported as being sufficient. According to the data centers, geography must be as small as possible to do proper and accurate microanalyses; in most cases, geography larger than a census tract is useless. One data center suggested that there may be a need for a new geographic division between the tract and block levels and the elimination of the block level because it is used less. It was also noted by a data center that the need for small-area data will only remain important if the data are accurate.

According to the data centers, all 1990 content is essential at the tract/block numbering area level and above. Income, poverty, and socioeconomic characteristics were reported separately as being crucial at least at the tract level. Areas with highly diverse populations have an especially great need for census data at the tract level so that areas with special needs can be identified and served.

Although it was reported that income, poverty, and other socioeconomic characteristics are essential at the tract level, some data centers indicated that those data are also important to have at the block-group level. It was also reported that all or almost all 1990 sample data are essential at the block-group level. Some sample items are not as crucial to have at the block-group level; among those items are place of birth, ancestry, veteran status, citizenship, year of entry, condominium status, and number of bedrooms.

As reported by the Maryland Office of Planning and the North Carolina Office of State Planning, complete count (short form or 100 percent) data items are valuable and necessary at the block level, if only for the purpose of aggregating the data to user-defined, nonstandard areas (neighborhoods, legislative districts, market areas, school districts, fire and other emergency districts, etc.) and areas smaller than census tracts. It was noted that expanded use of user-defined areas might address small area needs for sample data. The Minnesota state planning agency reported that housing information, used to create state population and household estimates, is needed at the block level. Because data at geographic areas larger than the block level can cross jurisdictional boundaries, those levels of geography are unusable for developing population and household estimates. Block data were also reported as being important for urban areas with population above a few thousand residents.

According to our respondents, place-level data are also important. One data center affiliate cited a critical need for employment, labor-force participation, total income and income by category, household composition, housing stock, education, race, migration, and disability characteristics at the place level. That affiliate, however, noted that place-level data for some areas frequently involve the same trade-offs in reporting detail, accuracy, timeliness, and content as do block and tract-level data. That affiliate also said that if the long form were eliminated or the 1-in-2 sampling ratio were discontinued, there would be no substitute source for their data.

CONCLUSIONS

In reviewing the responses to the survey, several general themes emerged. First, it is difficult to say that any data item or level of geography can be discarded. As several centers noted, all of the data items are used by some group or agency for some purpose, whether for federally mandated reporting or for long-range local transportation planning or for economic analyses of an area. Second, all of the centers expressed a desire and need for current small-area data that are accurate at various levels of geography (e.g., tracts, block groups, and blocks). Third, the census is the only source of much of the data, and the centers reported that for them the census is the only source for obtaining reliable data.

TABLE E.1 Importance of Data Items as Reported by State Data Centers

	Number of States Reporting						
Item	Essential	Very Important	Important	Less Important, but Useful	Not Used, Used Infrequently, Infrequently Requested	Unimportant, Not Essential	Eliminate
Residence	14			1			
Household relationship	14			2			
Migration	10			3			
Place of birth	7			3		3	
Fertility	7		3	1		2	
Marital history	4	1	1		2	3	
Race	16		1				
Spanish/Hispanic origin	11		2	1			
Ancestry	4		3	2	3	1	1
Citizenship	1		3	1	2	5	1
Year of entry	2		1	1	2	5	1
Language	4		5	1	1	3	1
School enrollment	8		2	3		2	
Highest grade completed	9		3	2		2	
Employment status	9		3	3[a]		1[b]	
Work and employment experience in prior year	7		2	1	1		
Veteran status	3		1	2	1	4	1
Disability	7[c]		3	2	1	1	1
Transportation	6		2	4		2	

Income	17[d]		2		
Poverty	17		2		
Housing	10[e]	1	4[f]	3	1

Note: 18 states provided information on the importance of data items; however, not all states offered replies for every census item.

[a]Data on industry are not frequently requested from the California State Data Center.

[b]New Hampshire reported that employment status may not be useful below the county level in New Hampshire because labor can easily cross county lines, and suggested that the ability to obtain employment status through noncensus sources should be investigated.

[c]One state data center reported that more detailed information on disability and handicapped status is needed; another center suggested eliminating some detail.

[d]The California State Data Center reported that the source of income is not in high demand.

[e]Several respondents suggested that some characteristics may be eliminated.

[f]Some respondents reported that some items are vital; other items are not frequently used or requested from the state data centers.

APPENDIX

F

Business Uses of Census Data

Census data are used by many in the private sector, by for- and not-for-profit organizations. Retail establishments and restaurants, banks and other financial institutions, media and advertising, insurance companies, utility companies, health care providers, and many other segments of the business world use census data. In the past, household-level data on consumers at the zip-code and census-tract levels have been classified by characteristics such as age, sex, and income. Increasingly, however, individual households are contacted by direct mail or some other type of direct media (e.g., newspaper inserts). This appendix contains some examples of uses of census data by various segments of the business community—evidence of the great use of census data by businesses is provided by the Division of Research and Statistical Services of the South Carolina Budget and Control Board (the state data center for census information in South Carolina), which estimated that 35 percent of the annual requests received for census data are from businesses.

Small-area data are important for many business applications. Some businesses use small-area data as a substitute for household-level data. More important, however, is the ability to aggregate the small-area census data to nonstandard geographic areas—for example for business trade areas. As long as these data are available, businesses can create aggregations of data into areas for which data have never been published. The smaller the level of geography for which data are available, the more creatively businesses can create aggregations and the more precisely they can define the geographic area.

Several key types of small-area census data (at tract and other geographic levels) are used for business purposes: age; education; employment; housing unit age, tenure, heating fuel, type, value, and rent; income; occupation; persons in household; phone availability; race and ethnicity; commute to work; and vehicles per household. Products—such as maps showing the concentration of a specific racial or ethnic group by specific areas (e.g., county, census tract, or zip code) or maps showing moderate-, high-, or low-income areas—can be produced using census data. Data also can be used to create consumer profiles, which can help in targeting advertising to current and potential customers; finding new customers; and analyzing locations, selecting sites, and competing against other businesses in a market area. Both the maps and consumer profiles (which may also be linked to a map) are used by businesses to target their markets more effectively. As the use of geographic information systems has grown, the demand for small-area geographic data has also grown. And, in turn, the newfound congruence of accessible geographically referenced small-area data is promoting the use of small-area census data for business purposes even further.

For example, a retail corporation with plans to expand could analyze potential markets before selecting sites. A specific case study (Kintner et al., 1994) involved examining and assessing various markets for a corporation's planned expansion. Several potential markets were selected by the corporation for the expansion, and the corporation wanted to determine which of the potential markets would be the most successful. Although the company's staff would make the final decision about the exact location of the sites, consultants were hired to analyze the potential revenue for each market. First, the consultants developed a model for analyzing the potential markets. The model took into account a number of variables—such as population, number of firms employing 100 or more workers, number of vehicles entering the county, and size of the transient population—that could help predict the viability of a site in areas selected for analysis. Some data were from business sources, but census data provided an essential component for analysis. Information on existing markets was used in the model to help determine its accuracy. Then, the predicted revenues for each of the existing locations generated by the model were compared with the actual revenues of those markets, enabling the corporation to assess and identify the strengths and weaknesses of the model. Next, data were collected for the potential new markets. By adding the new data to the model, revenue estimates were created for the potential markets, and the markets were ranked based on their predicted revenue. Markets that were the most promising were selected for additional analyses and reviewed by the corporation's staff, who then were able to select the best markets for the corporation's expansion.

It is clear to the panel that businesses use small-area data creatively and effectively for a number of applications, and that small-area census data are important to those applications. However, it is difficult to foresee the effects of a loss of small-area census data. There could be a negative impact on efficiency and competitiveness—impacts that would be difficult to measure.

This appendix describes the business uses of census data for a variety of industries, including retail and restaurant, banks and other financial institutions, media and advertising, insurance, utilities, health care, nonprofit, and others. The review is not exhaustive of all industries, nor comprehensive in the many ways that census data are used. Rather, the purpose is to highlight several common uses, for a variety of industries, to illustrate the specific ways census data are used to reach business decisions and to improve business marketing. The examples cited below are taken from Thomas and Kirchner (1991), a recent publication on desktop marketing that describes ways that demographic data are used by businesses.

RETAIL AND RESTAURANT

Retail and service businesses, such as restaurants, use data to decide where to locate their stores and how to effectively market their goods and services. A retail chain might use population, poverty, income, and labor-force data for a state and for a city or county to study the possibility of a retail outlet. For example, county-level population figures for women aged 16-34 years could be used to help determine the location for a maternity shop. Or a children's clothing retailer could use age data, income data, and retail statistics to select a location.

A fast-food restaurant chain was able to better target employee recruiting efforts and improve service by analyzing concentrations of the population with desirable employee traits/lifestyle characteristics (including longevity of employment). To accomplish this task, the restaurant chain identified the characteristics of its current base of employees and located areas with high concentrations of potential employees—a population whose characteristics were the same as the most successful current employees. In creating the profile of current employees, past and present employees with at least 6 months of service with the restaurant were categorized into 1 of 50 categories based on census block-group characteristics of their neighborhoods. The categories were charted according to the percentage of total current employees falling into the category. Using the data, the restaurant was able to identify categories of workers that were likely to become restaurant employees and determine areas where they lived. Recruiting efforts were targeted to those areas using mail and newspaper advertisements, among other techniques. The restaurant has found this ability to be useful in existing markets and new markets, and it has helped reduce turnover in the restaurants, resulting in improved customer service (Thomas and Kirchner, 1991:55-60).

For selecting restaurant sites, a general area, as well as specific sites for the restaurant can be evaluated. By looking at selected demographic data by specific levels of geography (e.g., counties and zip codes) the characteristics of the potential customers can be determined. Employment data at those same levels may also be evaluated. These analyses taken together can help the restaurateur select the best site for a successful restaurant (Thomas and Kirchner, 1991:61-63).

BANKS AND OTHER FINANCIAL INSTITUTIONS

Like retailers and restaurateurs, banks and other financial institutions can select the best locations for branch offices by analyzing population, demographic, and economic data from the census. More importantly, however, banks and financial institutions require median household income and income distributions by census tracts to ensure compliance with federal mortgage lending guidelines regarding race, and for meeting other regulatory requirements, particularly the Community Reinvestment Act, Home Mortgage Disclosure Act, and the Federal Insurance Improvement Act of 1992.

For example, the Community Reinvestment Act mandates that financial institutions meet deposit and credit needs in the communities they serve. The federal agencies that supervise financial institutions are required to assess whether the financial institutions in an area are meeting the needs of the community. To assess its compliance with the mandates of the Community Reinvestment Act, a bank wanted to determine the ratio of its loans to its deposits. Using customer data and a software system that is able to link demographic and client information, the bank was able to determine the loan-to-deposit ratio for its service areas. Thus, the bank was able to assess itself whether it was complying with the Community Reinvestment Act before the regulatory agencies conducted their audits. If there were areas with a discrepancy between deposits and loans, the bank would be able to make corrections in those areas (Thomas and Kirchner, 1991:114-116).

Census data can be used by banks to develop locally focused marketing programs. For example, a bank can determine the potential success of a particular new service by looking at how and where to market the service. A demographic profile of service areas based on age, deposits, household income, and credit use can be created. By grouping and mapping the frequency of the four variables mentioned above, along with a consumer profile, areas where the service is likely to be used can be identified. Those areas then can be targeted for promotion and implementation of the new service (Thomas and Kirchner, 1991:93-97).

In trying to determine if acquiring a competing banking institution (Bank B) would be a feasible and profitable way to expand and diversify its services, Bank A wanted to assess the proximity of Bank B's branches to its existing branches, the comparability of existing customers of Bank A with Bank B, and the comparability of services offered by both banks. The population (current and future projected) of the areas surrounding branches was compared, and income estimates for Bank B's locations were analyzed by census tract level (Thomas and

Kirchner, 1991:102-108). Using these analyses, Bank A is able to make the best decision about acquiring the competing bank.

A bank can analyze the potential performance of new and existing markets by developing a profile for evaluating those markets. By combining demographic characteristics of data on national financial behavior with demographic data for a particular market, a profile of the bank's service area can be developed. Using the average state performance of branches as a benchmark, the bank can determine the amount of increased business for areas performing below the state average if those areas grow to the state average level. This can help the bank determine areas for increased market analysis and marketing efforts, while also pinpointing markets that are performing at or above the state average that need to be maintained and protected from competitors (Thomas and Kirchner, 1991:111-113).

MEDIA AND ADVERTISING

Newspapers use census data in stories to profile the demographics of blocks, neighborhoods, towns, cities, counties, states, and other geographic areas. Census data also provide demographic background for other stories of general and specific interest to the public, e.g., what are the socioeconomic characteristics of areas with the most lawlessness in the Los Angeles riots? What is the most "middle class" tract in L.A. County? And what are commuter travel patterns in Orange County? Examples included in responses to the panel's survey of state data centers (see Appendix E) noted that all variables to the block-group level in various census geographic files can be used to describe the demographic and economic characteristics of places and areas. Also reported in a survey response was that the *Los Angeles Times* recently used 1990 census data in more than 300 news stories within one year.

The collection of consumer zip codes may be used to create a consumer profile for an area. For instance, a radio station might collect a caller's zip code and link it to demographic data to develop profiles of listener preferences (Thomas and Kirchner, 1991:34). In turn, the station can determine the potential success of a particular radio format for a given area and target marketing campaigns accordingly. Those profiles can also be linked with ratings information and used to optimize advertising revenue.

A cable television company analyzed purchase of pay-per-view events by census tract maps (Thomas and Kirchner, 1991:37) and created customer profiles by block-group level. Those customer profiles assisted the company in focussing its marketing efforts to specific customers. For example, pay-per-view sporting events can be marketed to the subscribers that are most likely to purchase the event, rather than to the entire customer base, thus increasing the advertising value.

INSURANCE COMPANIES

In a case study, an insurance company wanted to determine if some of its offices had allowed policies to lapse more than others. The company first wanted to determine if sites with high lapse rates were located in areas with high-risk customers. To determine the different characteristics between lapsed customers and continuing customers, the company created a profile of current customers, as well as a profile of lapsed customers. Based on the profile, the company determined that the continuing customers were generally more affluent and more family-oriented. When the profile for continuing customers was compared to the profile for lapsed customers, the company found that lapsed customers "tended to be more downscale than average" (Thomas and Kirchner, 1991:119). Using the data, the company was able to estimate what the performance of various offices should be, based on their geographic locations. For example, some of the offices were located in areas where the population could be characterized as high-lapse customers. Those offices, it was determined, could expect lower overall performance (Thomas and Kirchner, 1991:117-121).

UTILITY COMPANIES

Utility companies use census data to target low-income areas or areas with special needs, as well as for market research. Most utility companies have special lower rates for poorer, elderly, or disabled customers. Census data help companies note special areas for individual contact and special services and rates. An electric or gas company can use customer records to determine their share of the market. Using customer address information, a utility company can determine areas where it might be desirable to increase customer volume through greater name recognition. Other companies are using census maps to plot the location of their utility lines so they can quickly reference the proximity of lines to population areas.

HEALTH CARE PROVIDERS

Health care providers use census data to determine the need for additional hospital services, physicians, urgent care facilities, or other type of medical services in an area. For example, a hospital used data to study population trends when looking into building an off-site facility in a rural area, so that better health care could be provided to residents in that area. Using characteristics such as race, age, sex, and income for the health service area, a provider can determine if there is a need for additional doctors or other health services in an area. By estimating the need for services in an area, the best site for a doctor's office can be determined (Thomas and Kirchner, 1991:130-136). A hospital's selection of urgent care center sites is aided by analyzing patient records (including address and other information about use of the hospital's health care services). Information that may be used in the analysis includes physician's name, reason for hospital admission, distance from the hospital, and insurance coverage. Those variables can be geocoded and aggregated by physician or group practice and mapped to show concentration of use, need for services, type of services provided, etc. (Thomas and Kirchner, 1991:137-140). The same type of analyses can help determine a need for certain health services, e.g., mammography, obstetrical, or family practice services, in a particular area.

NONPROFIT ORGANIZATIONS

Nonprofit organizations, such as community advocacy groups and rural health clinics, need small-area census data to define and describe the needs of the population. Community-wide data does not always adequately describe a neighborhood or service area. For example, a rural health clinic would use census data for a special federal designation based on location and population served. Such clinics provide access to important medical services and establish reimbursement rates for services to ensure that clinics can remain in service. Community service organizations help small communities prepare grant applications for funding based on census data. Those same organizations also help evaluate and target community needs for fundraising campaigns. Local chambers of commerce rely on census data to keep businesses, attract new businesses, and assist established businesses market their products locally. A neighborhood housing service organization working to improve the quality of life of low- and moderate-income residents of communities would likely use census data to draft proposals and prepare applications for federally funded programs.

OTHER USERS

The examples above touch on only a few of the innumerable business uses of census data. Other uses and users include:

• real estate appraisal companies that use census data to establish an inventory of existing real estate, the current and future demand for real estate, and the value of that real estate.
• attorneys, who use census data, for example, to ensure equitable racial/ethnic representation on juries and to show the disparate impact of housing practices on particular classes of the population.
• telecommunications firms, which might determine the percent of the population in a particular area that graduated from high school for marketing purposes.

In addition, there are firms that use small-area census data in developing software systems that assist businesses in choosing sites, targeting populations, creating marketing strategies, etc. Those products are sold for marketing and demographic uses like those described above. Many of the private suppliers who develop business software systems for marketing and other purposes use block-group level data in creating the user-defined areas for their programs. Although it could be argued that block-level data are inaccurate, when the data are aggregated (even for small aggregations), the accuracy improves considerably. For these companies and business users, the need for small-area census data is focused on the ability to conveniently aggregate small-area data to user-defined areas, for which accuracy is likely to be acceptable, rather than on the use and accuracy of individual block-group data. The development, existence, and use of the products create a large market for census data and ultimately increases the overall value of the census.

As of 1991, other businesses that use census data in their products include:

• CACI has several marketing information systems that are used by businesses in assessing sites and developing consumer profiles. One of CACI's database systems contains census geography, and telephone exchange and zip-code areas. Another of its database systems facilitates the creation of area profiles for targeting marketing efforts; this system classifies over 200,000 census block groups into 44 lifestyle categories. CACI also annually publishes a series of data on cities, counties, and zip-code areas (Thomas and Kirchner, 1991:208-209).

• Claritas Corporation works mostly in the financial and media arenas. One of its marketing software systems allows for data manipulation and market analysis, mapping, and the preparation of reports. The system can be customized by users to fit their individual needs. A second Claritas system groups areas into 40 types for targeting consumers in those areas. The groups, which are based on census data and records of consumer purchases, can then be linked to other data available. Other products available from Claritas include Census Bureau demographic data, TIGER mapping files, and data on businesses (Thomas and Kirchner, 1991:210-211).

• Donnelley Marketing Inc. has a database of over 85 million households and supplies population estimates based on census tract data. One of its database systems includes data on demographics, retail sales, and lifestyles. The system was initially used by retail business and real estate developers in site selection applications, but it is also currently used by financial service organizations, media, government agencies, and health care providers. Another database system classifies neighborhoods into 47 different lifestyles, and is available at the block-group, census-tract, and zip-code levels, and can be linked with other data, including a company's own customer files (Thomas and Kirchner, 1991:215-216).

• National Decision Systems provides marketing services to a variety of business in the United States, including retail, restaurant, insurance, and advertising. It provides services such as target marketing, market analysis, site evaluation, and direct marketing. One of its database systems merges business data with census data. The system classifies every U.S. household into one of 50 market categories. Those categories can then be used for a variety of marketing purposes. In addition, a business's information on its own customers can be incorporated into a specialized program designed by the client and National Decision Systems (Thomas and Kirchner, 1991:218-219).

In addition, there are several marketing and demographic information firms that produce marketing and demographic analysis programs specifically for use by the health care industry.

REFERENCES

Kintner, H.J., T.W. Merrick, P.A. Morrison, and P.R. Voss
  1994   *Demographics: A Casebook for Business and Government.* Boulder, Colo.: Westview Press.
Thomas, R.K., and R.J. Kirchner
  1991   *Desktop Marketing: Lessons from America's Best.* Ithaca, N.Y.: American Demographics Books.

Use of Decennial Census Data in Transportation Planning

This appendix reviews the history of the use of census data in transportation planning, the types of data available, and experience with the use of data in actual practice.[1] Responses to a survey questionnaire mailed to states and metropolitan planning organizations to determine the past and planned use of census data are summarized. The relationship of census data to current legislative requirements for transportation planning is discussed, as well as the options and costs involved in replacing the data if they are not collected in the 2000 census.

The U.S. Department of Transportation (DOT), as well as state and local transportation planning organizations, have relied on the consistent data collection provided by the decennial census for travel-to-work characteristics and vehicle availability information since 1960 when transportation items were first added to the census. Information from the decennial census is used by the DOT as a comprehensive database supporting development of new policies and programs as benchmark data with which to evaluate the impacts and overall effectiveness of previously implemented programs.

Decennial census data for small areas such as census tracts and traffic analysis zones are used by state and metropolitan transportation planning agencies to meet the provisions of the Intermodal Surface Transportation Efficiency Act of 1991 (ISTEA), which require a comprehensive transportation planning process at both the state and metropolitan levels. The census provides the baseline origin-destination data on local work trips, household characteristics, and worker characteristics for use in travel forecasting models and for monitoring carpooling, public transit use, and other travel behavior. These data are now provided to all the states and metropolitan planning agencies as a special tabulation in the Census Transportation Planning Package (CTPP) at a cost of only $10 per 1,000 population or 1 cent per capita. Funding for the CTPP comes from funds available through ISTEA.

The census data on commuter travel flows and characteristics also are used to evaluate and select projects, develop traffic congestion management systems, and identify transportation corridors needing capacity expansion. Further, travel-to-work and vehicle availability data from the census for small areas are used by state and metropolitan planning organizations to prepare vehicular travel and pollutant emissions profiles, compute regional average rates of vehicle occupancy in the commute to work and evaluate the impact of long range transportation plans on air quality in compliance with the Clean Air Act Amendments of 1990. Finally, census data on the geographic distribution of persons with work disabilities and mobility limitations are used by local transit operators to provide service levels that are fully accessible to all segments of the population under the Americans with Disabilities Act.

The federal legislative initiatives cited above—the Intermodal Surface Transportation Efficiency Act of 1991, the Clean Air Act Amendments of 1990, and the Americans with Disabilities Act—delineate the national interest in rebuilding the transportation infrastructure, improving environmental quality, and providing a fully accessible system for accommodating the mobility needs of a diverse population. To respond to these statutes, policy and program development at the federal, state, and local levels needs to be based on decennial census data that provide a context for evaluating past trends and preparing forecasts of the future. The high levels of current use by both state transportation agencies and metropolitan planning organizations, along with the low cost of obtaining and disseminating the data lead to the conclusion that *abandoning the tradition of nationwide survey uniformity and geographic consistency of data provided by the decennial census would result in high costs and disruption to program development and evaluation at all levels of government.*

The continued collection of transportation data in the decennial census is under review. In response to congressional criticism, the Census Bureau is taking a zero-based approach to 2000 census planning. A major thrust of this approach is to question the justification for collecting data on topics such as place of work, mode of transportation to work, travel time, carpooling, time of departure for work, disabled persons with mobility limitations, and number of vehicles available to each household as part of the decennial census. This appendix reviews the history of the use of census data in transportation planning, the types of data available, and experience with the use of data in actual practice. Since the 1990 census results have only recently become available for transportation planning applications, much of this appendix deals with experiences with the 1980 census data. Discussion of the 1990 census is included wherever possible. The historical review of transportation data takes the perspective of building on the experience of previous censuses as has been its tradition in the past.

HISTORY OF TRANSPORTATION QUESTIONS IN THE CENSUS

The inclusion of transportation items is a fairly recent occurrence in the history of the decennial census. Although the first census was conducted in 1790, questions pertaining to transportation did not appear until 1960 when three such questions were asked on a 25-percent sample basis. The population items in 1960 included questions on each worker's place of work (city, county, and state) and means of transportation to work; the housing items included a question on the number of automobiles available for use by the members of each household. The principal impetus for adding the question on place of work to the 1960 census was the need for data on commuting interchanges for use as an indicator of economic integration between large cities and their suburbs as part of the criteria for delineating metropolitan statistical areas. The commuting data from the census were certainly of interest to transportation planners, but urban transportation planning in the early 1960s was still being done on the basis of locally conducted origin-destination surveys.

By 1970, with the development by the Census Bureau of Address Coding Guides (ACGs) and Dual Independent Map Encoding (DIME) files, interest in the census as a source of transportation planning data increased considerably. The ACGs and DIME files provided the capability of geographically coding place-of-work addresses within the urbanized portion of metropolitan areas down to the level of the census block. The 1970 census again asked questions on place of work, means of transportation to work, and automobile availability. However, the place-of-work question asked for the actual street address of the respondent's workplace, and these addresses were coded to census blocks within the areas covered by ACGs and DIME files. The DOT contracted with the Bureau of the Census to create a series of special tabulations in a transportation planning package. Metropolitan Planning Organizations (MPOs) obtained the data tabulated for their traffic zones on a cost-reimbursable basis.

Between 1970 and 1980, several developments resulted in significant expansion in the number of transportation items included in the decennial census. The energy crisis of the early 1970s and the subsequent ongoing concern for the nation's supply of nonrenewable energy sources brought about a sharp increase in the need for statistics for transportation planning and policy formulation. From 1975 to 1977, under the sponsorship of the DOT, the Census Bureau conducted for the first time journey-to-work surveys in 60 metropolitan areas and a national survey in 1975, all as part of the Annual Housing Survey. In recognition of the growing need for analysis of these data, a Journey-to-Work Statistics Branch was created within the bureau's Population Division to carry out the technical planning and developmental work pertaining to the collection, processing, tabulation, and analysis of journey-to-work data from the decennial census and periodic surveys. Also during the decade, the cost of conducting metropolitan origin-destination surveys increased rapidly, and the DOT began to encourage local agencies to look to the decennial census as an alternative source for cost-effective transportation planning data.

Thus, due to the significant increase in the need for transportation data at all levels of government, the 1980 census included eight transportation items: six population questions and two housing questions. On the population side, in addition to questions on place of work and means of transportation to work, the 1980 census asked about carpooling arrangements, the number of riders in the carpool, travel time from home to work, and whether persons had a disability that limited or prevented their use of public transportation. On the housing side, the automobile availability question was supplemented with an additional question on the number of light trucks and vans available for use by members of each household.

Once again for the 1980 census, the DOT contracted with the Census Bureau to create a series of special tabulations in a Transportation Planning Package. MPOs obtained the data tabulated for their traffic analysis zones on a cost-reimbursable basis. To increase the utility of the census data for local transportation planning, the Census Bureau developed an innovative procedure to assign incomplete place-of-work responses to census blocks so that they too could be tabulated at the traffic analysis zone level.

THE 1990 CENSUS

The 1990 census transportation statistics program marked the continued refinement of transportation data available from the census, technical improvement in the geographic coding of place-of-work responses to small areas within metropolitan regions, and the creation and dissemination of innovative transportation data products. The 1990 census again included questions on place of work, means of transportation to work, carpooling, carpool occupancy, and travel time to work. An important new question on time of departure from home to work was added to the census questionnaire to allow tabulation of commuting patterns and characteristics by peak hours of travel. The questions on the number of automobiles available to each household and the number of trucks or vans available to each household were combined into one question on the total number of vehicles (cars, trucks, and vans) available. The question on public transportation disability was replaced with a more general questions that identified persons whose disabilities limited their ability to get around outside the home.

Two innovative technical advancements in place-of-work coding were made for 1990. The first innovation was the joint development by the Census Bureau and the DOT of the Census/Metropolitan Planning Organization Cooperative Assistance Program. This program gave local MPOs the opportunity to assist the Census Bureau in improving the accuracy of place-of-work data for their region. Planning organizations took part in three activities: providing files of employers and their locations to the Census Bureau, working with major employers to ensure that their employees reported accurate workplace addresses, and assisting the Census Bureau in identifying the locations of workplaces that census clerks could not code. Over 300 MPOs took part in these cooperative activities. The Federal Highway Administration (FHWA) made the costs incurred by the MPOs for this work an eligible activity for use of federal aid highway planning funds.

The second advancement in place-of-work coding was the implementation by the Census Bureau of an automated place-of-work coding system. Place-of-work addresses were keyed to create machine-readable files that were then matched to address coding and major employer files to assign geographic codes to the place-of-work responses. Cases that could not be coded on the computer were sorted and clustered and referred to clerks for research and computer-assisted clerical coding. The automation of place-of-work coding allowed the Census Bureau to accomplish the coding operation efficiently and cost effectively.

THE URBAN TRANSPORTATION PLANNING PACKAGE (UTTP)

The availability of block-level data on commuting origins and destinations from the 1970 census made possible the development for the first time of the Urban Transportation Planning Package (UTPP). The 1970 UTPP was a special tabulation of census data for individual metropolitan areas tailored to the geographic areas that are used in transportation planning. Local transportation planning organizations prepared specifications for the blocks that made up their traffic analysis zones, and the Census Bureau then produced a standard set of tabulations for those zones on a cost-reimbursable basis. Specifications for the content of the UTPP were submitted to the bureau by FHWA. About 120 UTPPs were prepared after the 1970 census.

The Census Bureau again produced the UTPP after the 1980 census. This time specifications were developed and submitted to the Bureau by an ad hoc committee of transportation planners under the auspices of the Transportation Research Board, an organizational component of the National Research Council. Funding for development of the necessary computer programs and administration of the 1980 project was provided by the DOT. The number of packages produced increased to over 150.

Significant innovations in the dissemination of the journey-to-work data were achieved for the 1990 census. Two transportation planning packages were produced: statewide packages for each state and the District of Columbia and urban packages for the transportation study area defined by each MPO. Production of the transportation planning packages by the Census Bureau was sponsored by the state departments of transportation under a pooled funding arrangement with the American Association of State Highway and Transportation Officials (AASHTO). This pooled funding arrangement supported the production of data for the entire country instead of only those areas that decided to purchase the data as in previous censuses. Funding to develop the 1990 CTPP program was provided by the FHWA and the Federal Transit Administration (FTA). The total cost was $2.6 million or about $10 per 1,000 persons compared to $12 per 1,000 persons in 1980 (1980 dollars). The number of packages produced (both state and metropolitan) increased to 415 for the 1990 census.

The 1990 CTPP continued the program established in 1970 and conducted in 1980 in the same general format. A working group was established to develop the specifications for the 1990 CTPP for both the metropolitan data set and the statewide data set. This ad hoc group consisted of members from AASHTO, the National Association of Regional Councils, FHWA, FTA, the Census Bureau, plus experts in the field from states and MPOs. A similar group developed the 1980 UTPP.

The statewide tabulations were the first product produced from the 1990 CTPP. A file was produced for each state, containing data for the households, persons, and workers who live in each city and county in the state, data on all workers working in each city and county in the state, and data on commuter flows between counties and cities. The urban tabulations were similar to the data provided in the statewide package, except that the data were tabulated on the basis of census tracts or traffic analysis zones. The urban data were delivered after the delivery of the statewide packages. An urban package was produced for each metropolitan area for which the Census Bureau had an address coding capability. To make the CTPP data easily accessible and widely available, the DOT's Bureau of Transportation Statistics released the CTPPs on CD-ROM with software to display and retrieve the data from a personal computer.

Use of the 1980 UTPP Data—A Case Study

Since the early 1970s, the Delaware Valley Regional Planning Commission (DVRPC), the metropolitan planning organization for the Philadelphia region, has relied on census data for transportation planning and travel forecasting because of rising costs of large-scale data collection such as regional home interviews, employment, and land-use surveys. DVRPC used the 1970 census data to check and validate traffic simulation models for producing traffic analyses based on up-to-date information. Census work trips, housing statistics, car ownership, employed persons, and employment data were used to estimate trip generation and distribution patterns between transportation simulation zones. In addition, information about the journey to work and other characteristics of workers has been used by DVRPC, local and state governments, transit operating agencies, and private corporations to make a variety of decisions on transportation and locational matters.

Uses of the 1980 UTPP in the Delaware Valley region were similar to those applications outlined in the Transportation Planners' Guide to Using the 1980

Census (Sosslau, 1983). These include the study of bus circulation patterns, location of park-and-ride lots and express bus service, study of accessibility and special population segments, analysis of highway and transit trips, planning of highway and public transportation systems, planning and analysis of projects, update of traffic simulation models, analysis of work-trip trends, location of shopping centers and service industries, analysis of parking requirements, and studies of employment.

DVRPC used census data in various studies and continues to use such data in transportation planning and nontransportation planning activities because it is the only comprehensive information at the regional and local levels. The six major uses of the 1980 UTPP in the Delaware Valley region are:

- *Establishing a Database for Transportation Planning* DVRPC prepared a data bank for transportation planning at the block-group and tract levels. This information includes population, employment, work trips, car ownership, and other socioeconomic variables required for traffic simulation and transportation analysis and planning. Such data were extracted from the 1980 UTPP. All data items were edited for reasonableness based on other census data and DVRPC surveys, traffic counts, and employment files. These data were used in most transportation system and project planning studies.

- *Preparation of Data Summaries and Evaluation of Trends* DVRPC completed a report on the journey-to-work trends in the Delaware Valley region (Delaware Valley Regional Planning Commission, 1994). This report compared the 1970 and 1980 journey-to-work information, means of transportation for commuting to work, employed persons, and employment at the county and regional levels. It also analyzed the commuting flow between the counties of the Delaware Valley region and surrounding counties and cities. The report was well received by planners and decision makers because it provided factual information about trends in development and travel patterns in the region. Other tables showed the trends in employment and mode of travel for all DVRPC counties.

- *Update of DVRPC Traffic Simulation Models* The DVRPC travel forecasting models were updated using the 1980 UTPP. The 1970 UTPP was used to check and update the DVRPC traffic simulation models. These models were updated again using 1980 census data. The DVRPC travel simulation models follow the traditional steps of trip generation, trip distribution, modal split, and travel assignment and utilize the computer programs included in the federally sponsored Urban Transportation Planning System (UTPS).

- *Use in Highway and Transit Corridor Studies* The 1980 UTPP data, especially the journey-to-work information, were used in three transit corridor studies by DVRPC to check the travel demand or ridership for each transit submode, including high-speed rail line, express bus and park-and-ride service, and local bus service. The use of these data minimized any large-scale data collection and decreased the rising costs of surveys required for transportation planning.

• *Application in Strategic Planning and Economic Development* DVRPC used the 1980 UTPP information on employment to evaluate the significant changes in the type and location of industries and commercial establishments. This evaluation resulted in recommendations and strategies aimed at attracting new industries and high-technology firms to the Delaware Valley. Also, employment information was useful in the redevelopment of declining areas of old urban centers and provision of the required physical improvements for their rehabilitation.

• *Provision of 1980 UTPP Data to Public Agencies and Private Corporations* Finally, DVRPC provided the 1980 UTPP data to any public or private agency involved in planning or urban studies. This included studies for housing, finance, real estate, health facilities, social services, economic base, and economic development. Planning agencies and private companies in the Delaware Valley region were interested in obtaining the UTPP information for their various studies.

Summary

Generally, the 1980 UTPP for the Delaware Valley region contained data of good quality for transportation planning, economic base and employment location studies, urban development analysis, and planning and evaluation of public services. However, the evaluation of UTPP data indicates a few programming, statistical, and bias problems. Most of these problems were resolved before DVRPC used the UTPP for trend analyses, information purposes, traffic simulation, highway and transit project studies, and strategic planning. The errors in the 1980 data were generally smaller than those found in the 1970 UTPP. Trip and employment information should be adjusted before it is used in transportation planning studies because it does not include all workers or jobs.

DIFFERENCES BETWEEN CENSUS AND TRAVEL SURVEY DATA

Most of the tabulations of the CTPP and its predecessor, the UTPP, focus on workers and their travel. The balance is about households, vehicles, and persons. Vehicles include automobiles, trucks, and vans available to a household. Mode of transportation is synonymous with the census term "means of transportation."

Journey-to-work questions asked in the census differ in some respects from those usually asked by planners in travel surveys (McDonnell, 1984). Several points should be kept in mind when census data about work trips are used:

1. The address where the individual works most often is recorded in the

census questionnaire. When a worker holds two jobs, the second job location is not entered.

2. Some workers go to different work locations on a given day. If such workers report to a central location, this location is to be entered as the workplace. If there is no central location and the worker went to various work locations, the smallest geographic area common to the starting places (for example, Westchester County, New York) is to be entered.

3. The data imply direct trips from residence to workplace and do not request information about indirect work trips (stops on the way to work).

4. The census asks about work "at any time last week." Thus, typical (usual) workday information is received rather than average workday information. The difference between an average day and a typical day is significant in transportation planning because on an average day some 10-20 percent of all workers may not commute from home to work for one reason or another.

5. The census asks how the person "usually" got to work the previous week. This approach does not measure periodic use of transit among commuters who drive or carpool, but also use transit on some days of the week.

6. Similarly, questioning about "usual" carpool size in the census probably results in overestimation of carpool size. Carpools are usually formed on a given day, a carpool member might not go to work, might be out of town, and so on, resulting in a number of passengers lower than that reported for the usual case.

7. The census asks where the respondent was employed "last week." It does not ask, as travel surveys do, whether a trip to work was made "yesterday."

8. Journey-to-work questions are asked of both full-time and part-time workers, and only the combined responses were reported by the Census Bureau.

For the reasons listed above, transportation planners need to adjust census data for use in planning models, as described below.

Journey-to-Work Adjustments

The Washington Metropolitan Council of Governments compared census journey-to-work data with those collected by the MPO (Wickstrom, 1984). The census source in this case was a supplementary journey-to-work survey conducted by the Census Bureau for the U.S. Department of Housing and Urban Development as part of the 1977 Annual Housing Survey. The journey-to-work supplement was similar in form to the 1980 census questionnaire.

The census questionnaire asked where the respondent was employed "last week." It did not ask, as travel surveys usually do, whether a trip to work was made "yesterday." In Washington, D.C., it was found that a factor of 0.85 was required to adjust the census "usual-day" data to travel demands on a specific day as sought by transportation planners.

Public transit trips tended to be underreported in the census data because only the usual mode was requested. A Washington, D.C. survey of transit riders showed that only 89 percent of bus riders and 76 percent of rail riders used public transit 4 or more days per week. For both forms of transit combined, 85 percent were regular users.

Comparisons also were made of person work trips and transit work trips. For the Washington, D.C. region, census data were a little more than 6 percent low for total trips and a little more than 5 percent low for transit trips.

Overall employment data were also compared. The census data did not count second jobs and, except in areas where commutershed information was available, the failure to count work trips into the region from counties outside the SMSA resulted in underreporting the volume of travel demands.

Problems Inherent in Census Data

The 1980 census UTPP journey-to-work data were reviewed extensively and utilized in the transportation planning process in the Washington, DC area. There were more than 75,000 individual records representing 1,650,000 workers in 1980. It should be recognized that the census data brought some inherent problems as well as provided a new data source for transportation analysts and planners.

The following problems were inherent in the data:

1. There were certain basic definitional differences between the way the census viewed the journey to work and an actual trip. Transportation planners would prefer information on the most recent journey-to-work trip, including data on places that were travelled on the way to work. Actual trips often involve some other intermediate trip purpose and, hence, differ from census information on the "usual" journey to work.

2. Comparisons of census employment location coding with an independent data source indicated that more effort was needed to code accurately to the traffic zone or district level. Although trips to downtown and to urban areas were compatible, trips to outlying suburban centers were underrepresented in most cases.

3. Not all trips were coded to the zone level of geography.

4. Certain key data items useful for transportation planning were not collected in the census. This included information on the cost of parking, departure and arrival times for the work trip (peak hour, peak period, and nonpeak), and a listing of all modes of travel used. The peak hour data were subsequently collected in the 1990 census.

5. Considerable additional staff effort was needed to produce a file considered suitable for use in recalibrating models or for use at the individual planning project level.

Positive Aspects of Census Data

The following positive conclusions may be made based on experience with using the 1980 UTPP for the Washington, D.C. area:

1. The census data were used extensively. It is unlikely that any other comprehensive data source could have been developed and used within the time and cost associated with the census data.

2. The parts of the UTPP that provided zone of residence, zone of work, and zone-to-zone commuter-flow data were used the most. The county-to-county totals were also extremely useful.

3. Because the Baltimore and Washington, D.C. areas were tabulated as one region in the UTPP, there was an opportunity to obtain data that were not handled adequately by two separate data collection and study processes in the two regions.

4. Although not a file of individual workers, the data were capable of being used for model verification and development. The data verified the need for revisions to travel forecasting procedures.

5. Acceptance of the census data by participants in the planning process, including elected officials, was high.

USE OF DECENNIAL CENSUS DATA BY TRANSPORTATION PLANNING AGENCIES

To gain insight into the extent to which 1980 decennial census data were used by transportation planning agencies, we mailed a questionnaire to 28 such agencies throughout the United States. Both state departments of transportation and MPOs were contacted. Similar questions also were asked of those agencies about their planned use of the 1990 census data. Questions asked included: (1) type of census data used, (2) use of the data, (3) usefulness of the data in addressing federal requirements, (4) degree of difficulty expected in order to replace the data, (5) method of replacing the data, and (6) whether or not funds and staff would be available to replace the data.

Twenty-two agencies (almost 80 percent) responded to the questionnaire. Of these, 10 were state departments of transportation and 12 were MPOs. The ten states included California, Texas, Wisconsin, Washington, Florida, Minnesota, Maryland, Ohio, North Carolina, and New York. The 12 MPOs included Pittsburgh, Philadelphia, Denver, Chicago, San Francisco, Washington, D.C., Boston, Los Angeles, New York, San Diego, Baltimore, and Charlotte.

Tables G.1 and G.2 show the overall response from all 22 agencies. Separate summaries are made for the past use of 1980 data and the planned use of the 1990 data.

Work-trip data by mode of travel and origin-destination data by zone along with socioeconomic data were used in 1980 by 18 of the 22 respondents. The lowest use reported (15 agencies) was associated with the employment by place-of-work information. All categories, including household and population data, as well as use of the special cross-tabulations provided by the CTPP showed an increase in planned use by agencies for the 1990 data when compared to 1980.

Heavy use was made of the data for providing inputs to travel forecasting models (and as a check of model results) and for corridor studies. Long-range planning, transit planning, and alternatives analysis also ranked high on the list.

All categories of planned use for 1990 data showed marked increases, with 20 of the 22 agencies planning use of the data in transit planning and corridor studies. Fifteen of the agencies also responded positively to the three categories that reflect new federal requirements through the Clean Air Act Amendments and the Intermodal Surface Transportation Efficiency Act—congestion management, transportation control measures, and conformity determination.

In regard to agency responses as to the usefulness of the census data in addressing federal requirements, 20 of the 22 responding agencies reported that the data were either essential or very useful in meeting the requirements for the development of statewide or metropolitan area plans. Seventeen reported the same degree of usefulness in meeting alternatives analysis requirements. Transit planning and the new requirement of developing congestion management plans were similarly noted by 15 agencies. Results were similar for both states and MPOs (not shown separately here), with three-quarters of the MPOs adding air-quality conformity requirements to the list.

Eighteen of the 22 agencies said that they would experience great difficulty in replacing the work-trip data by mode (by traffic analysis zone) or the origin-destination data (zone-zone). Fifteen reported that replacing the special tabulations from the CTPP would prove very difficult. Only the employment data provided were not cited as being very difficult to replace by a majority of the respondents. MPOs reported a greater degree of difficulty in all categories listed and by a considerable margin. Since the 1980 census did not contain a statewide element, and since the states had not received the 1990 data at the time of the survey, the lower response rate by states is understandable.

When asked how the census data would be replaced (if not available), 19 of the 22 agencies cited a home interview as the most likely method. Some cited workplace surveys, roadside or transit surveys, or secondary sources as alternatives. MPOs were more inclined toward home interviews, with states citing secondary sources more frequently.

When asked if funds and staff could be made available to replace the census data with some alternative collection activity, only 1 of the 22 agencies responding gave a "yes" answer to this question. This agency, a state department of transportation, reported that it does not rely on census data because its planning needs require data in a more timely manner than census can provide (2 to 3 year lag). Eleven agencies reported that staff and funds could probably be made available, while 10 said that replacing the data was unlikely. Of these, 5 were states and 5 MPOs.

RELATIONSHIP OF CENSUS DATA TO
LEGISLATIVE REQUIREMENTS

Data from the decennial census are the backbone of the statistical system that supports the transportation planning process of our nation. The DOT, as well as state and local transportation planning agencies, have relied on the consistent data collection provided by the decennial census since 1960 when transportation questions were first added to the census questionnaire. Today, these organizations are increasingly reliant on census data to implement the requirements of the Intermodal Surface Transportation Efficiency Act of 1991 and the Clean Air Act Amendments of 1990.

In its October 1993 report, *Transportation Infrastructure: Better Tools Needed for Making Decisions on Using ISTEA Funds Flexibly*, the U.S. General Accounting Office (GAO) concluded that current-travel demand models must be improved to provide better information for analyzing the impact of transportation projects on air quality. The GAO urged the Secretary of Transportation to ensure that the next generation of travel-demand models and analytical procedures being developed by the DOT's Travel Model Improvement Program (TMIP) help states and localities address their transportation priorities and comply with both the air-quality standards set forth in the Clean Air Act and the intent of the ISTEA that a total systems approach be used in decision making. In its official response to the GAO report, the DOT stated that it is imperative that the decennial census continue the transportation data used in these models that are the key to the ultimate success of the TMIP.

Significant innovations in the dissemination of the journey-to-work data also were achieved for the 1990 census. Two transportation planning packages were produced: statewide packages for each state and the District of Columbia and urban packages for the transportation study area defined by each metropolitan planning organization. Production of the transportation planning packages by the Census Bureau was sponsored by the state departments of transportation under a pooled funding arrangement with the American Association of State Highway and Transportation Officials. This pooled funding arrangement supported the preparation of data for the entire country instead of only those areas that decided to purchase the data as in previous censuses. Funding to develop the 1990 Census Transportation Planning Package Program (CTPP) was provided by the FHWA and the FTA. CTPP funding totaled $2.6 million for both programming and production of the statewide and urban packages.

Transportation data from the decennial census are used by the DOT as a comprehensive database supporting development of new policies and programs, and as benchmark data with which to evaluate the impacts and overall effectiveness of previously implemented programs.

The DOT works in partnership with states and local governments to assess project and corridor-level impacts of implemented plans, programs, and specific projects. In supporting the ISTEA and the Clean Air Act, as well as other federal legislation such as the National Environmental Protection Act, Title 6 of the Civil Rights Act of 1964, the Uniform Relocation Assistance Act, and the Highway Safety Act, decennial census data facilitate a consistent level of responsible federal oversight and review of state and local plans and programs. For example, census data are an important tool in the environment review process required under the National Environmental Protection Act to assess the potential impacts of yet-to-be implemented projects. In consideration of the Clean Air Act, journey-to-work data from the 2000 census will provide important feedback on the overall effectiveness of today's national air-quality agenda. To respond to the requirements of the Americans with Disabilities Act for fully accessible transportation to all segments of the population, census data on persons with mobility limitations that are traditionally provided by the census provide an opportunity for the DOT to conduct a nationwide assessment of service needs.

Intermodal Surface Transportation Efficiency Act Legislative Requirements

The 1991 legislative requirements of the Intermodal Surface Transportation Efficiency Act (ISTEA) for census data include four specific categories, described below.

Comprehensive Planning Provisions

The ISTEA contains specific provisions requiring comprehensive transportation planning processes on a statewide basis, as well as at the metropolitan area level. States, local governments, and regional agencies must analyze the impacts of transportation plans, policies, and programs. The procedures involved are very data-intensive, and small-area data from the decennial census provide much of the required information. Principal among these procedures is travel forecasting.

The function of transportation models is to replicate how people travel, to model their travel to and from different locations, by time of day, purpose, and mode. Models are used to forecast how people will travel in the future, with assumptions made about transportation infrastructure development and changes, land-use changes, parking cost and availability, and changes in individual travel behavior. By building these models, planners can evaluate different alternatives. For example, will adding carpool lanes along a particular highway reduce or increase congestion in the future and increase transit service? For most travel models, the forecasting horizon is 20-30 years. Thus, data from the 1990 census are used to test the reliability of current models to predict 1990 travel behavior and to then forecast travel in 2000, 2010, and 2020.

The decennial census provides the baseline of household and person characteristics, origins and destinations of work trips, and travel characteristics for small areas such as traffic analysis zones used in regional and local travel demand modeling efforts. These forecasts are used by state, regional, and local agencies to develop, test, and refine methods for projecting future travel needs at the regional, subarea, and corridor levels. Using these models for travel forecasting allows analysis of alternative highway, transit, and multimodal developments with various policy scenarios.

In addition to supplying data for travel forecasting, the decennial census provides important information for transportation planners to monitor trends in travel behavior. Census data permit the tracking of travel times and peak hours of travel by mode of travel and by residence and work location. The census also provides estimates and data for trend analyses of rates of carpooling and public transit use in the journey to work.

Transportation Improvement Program: Project Selection

The ISTEA specifically requires that statewide and metropolitan transportation plans address broad issues such as land development and demographic growth, impacts of transportation facilities on population segments, and regional mobility and congestion levels. These plans must give consideration to the social, economic, and environmental effects, including air-quality effects, of transportation plans and programs. Projects contained in transportation improvement programs must be found to conform to the emissions reduction schedules in a state implementation plan. Census data on commuter travel flows and travel behavior patterns provide important baseline values against which transportation improvement program projects can be evaluated and selected.

Traffic Congestion Management

The ISTEA requires states, in cooperation with metropolitan planning organizations, to develop traffic congestion management systems. Transportation control measures and travel demand management programs often use census data on the journey to work as baseline values from which to establish goals for increasing average vehicle occupancy and for decreasing single occupant vehicles. Census data can also be used for preparing a comprehensive profile of peak period commuter flows by area and time of day.

Corridor Preservation

The ISTEA provides a planning framework for early identification of transportation corridors needing some form of capacity expansion. Small-area data from the census provide a basis for defining these corridors and the number and characteristics of residents and jobs affected.

Clean Air Act Amendments of 1990 Legislative Requirements

Regions cited for being in nonattainment of federal air-quality standards must comply with Environmental Protection Agency and DOT requirements under the Clean Air Act Amendments of 1990 (CAAA). The transportation/air-quality planning requirements of the CAAA require state and local public agencies to prepare comprehensive vehicular travel and pollutant emissions profiles. To prepare these profiles requires analysis of detailed household and worker characteristics, means of travel, commuting patterns, and journey-to-work trip lengths obtained from the decennial census.

The CAAA also requires severely polluted areas to compute regional average rates of vehicle occupancy in the commute to work. The census provides these data in a consistent manner nationwide.

Under the CAAA, preparation of the state implementation plan and the comprehensive urban transportation planning process must be coordinated. Transportation facilities and projects proposed as part of the long-range transportation plan must be evaluated for their impact on air quality. Thus, forecasted travel volumes along specific routes are translated into forecasted traffic volumes, speeds, and subsequent emissions. The results are used in conformity analyses of state implementation plan. Data from the decennial census are used to calibrate and verify the travel simulation and forecasting models used to develop these parameters.

Other Legislative Requirements

Understanding regional travel patterns assists transit agencies in developing new services and revising existing services. These services may include vanpools and carpools, in addition to fixed-rail and fixed-route bus services. Small-area census data for traffic analysis zones on journey-to-work characteristics are used for route planning, market analysis, publicity, and advertising.

The Americans with Disabilities Act requires states and local transit operators, with oversight and policy review by the DOT, to provide service levels that are fully accessible to all segments of the population. Data from the census that describe the geographic distribution of persons with disabilities that limit their ability to get around outside the home are used to develop and improve transportation services for this specific population.

STATE AND LOCAL USES

Decennial census data for small areas such as census tracts and traffic analysis zones are used by states and metropolitan planning organizations to meet the provisions of the ISTEA, the Clean Air Act, and the Americans with Disabilities Act.

In the survey described earlier, 11 of the 12 MPOs responding stated that they used all of the categories of the census data listed in the questionnaire with the exception of the employment data (75 percent utilization). Uses included application to all planning items required by the federal government, including the new requirements imposed by ISTEA and the Clean Air Act. The data were deemed either essential or very useful by a large majority of respondents for these purposes.

Work-trip data by mode and origin-destination data, along with the special tabulations from the CTPP, were cited as the most difficult to replace. Home interview surveys, along with workplace and roadside or transit surveys would be required to replace the data. Five of the 12 MPOs reported that adequate staff and funding would be made available to replace the census data.

State transportation agencies reported significantly higher planned use of the 1990 census data than the actual use of the 1980 data. (Special statewide tabulations were made available as part of the CTPP in 1990 for the first time). All items were reported used by a majority of the states responding for 1980 and by 8 of the 10 in 1990. At the time of the survey (in late 1993), state agencies were receiving 1990 data, but had not yet begun actual use.

As was the case with the MPOs, state uses for the data included a heavy emphasis on inputs to travel forecasting models, including use as a base year, for the development of model parameters, and especially as a check of model results (9 of 10). These models are used extensively to provide data and forecasts in meeting Clean Air Act Amendment requirements. Heaviest use of the census data was for corridor studies, alternatives analysis, and transit planning application (all 8 of 10). Nine of the 10 states responding reported that the data were most useful for statewide and regional transportation planning. Other items cited were congestion management (a new federal requirement along with statewide planning), transit planning, and alternatives analysis.

Work-trip data by mode were cited as the most difficult to replace by 8 of 10 states. Besides home interview surveys, the use of secondary source data would be the most likely way that states would replace the census data. Five of the 10 states stated that it would be unlikely that adequate funding would be made available to replace the census data.

COST AND FEASIBILITY OF REPLACING
CENSUS TRANSPORTATION DATA

At a sampling rate of 1 in 6 households and a cost of $2.6 million to prepare, program, tabulate, and distribute the CTPP, the unit cost to provide the journey-to-work and associated data to states and MPOs totals less than 25 cents per household interviewed.

The majority of state and metropolitan agencies surveyed indicated that they would substitute home interview surveys if census data were not available. Costs of urban home interview surveys generally range between $70 and $100 per household. Because of the high cost, sampling rates for home interview surveys are also much lower than that of the census, typically on the order of 1 in 20 (0.5 percent). The 1990 CTPP also includes statewide summaries as well as urban. Home interview surveys collect data on all trips made by the household, however, so a direct cost comparison is difficult. Most urban areas collect home interviews in addition to census data. Because of the detailed geography (tract and traffic zone) and mode of travel information, other work-related surveys that do not provide such information are not comparable.

Even if home interviews are conducted or an alternative survey methodology is found, they would not be national in scope, but only state or local in nature. Many agencies have indicated that they lack money or staff to replace the census. Transportation planning agencies require such detail since the mathematical models using the data are in widespread use to simulate a base year and then to forecast future travel by mode.

Approximately 80 percent of the states and MPOs surveyed plan to use the 1990 census journey-to-work data to provide inputs to such models and to establish a base year. Approximately 90 percent of the agencies plan to use the data as a check of such models and to use the data in transit and corridor studies.

Perhaps the only real alternative to the provision of census journey-to-work information would be to greatly expand the Nationwide Personal Transportation Survey, now conducted every 5 years by the DOT. Its present sample size of about 25,000 households would have to be expanded by at least a factor of 20 to provide even a minimal sample to obtain adequate geographical data suitable for use by state and metropolitan agencies. That cost is estimated at $50 million, or 20 times the current cost of the Census Transportation Planning Package.

The high levels of current use by both state transportation and metropolitan planning agencies, along with the low cost of obtaining and disseminating the data, lead to the conclusion that abandoning the tradition of nationwide survey uniformity and geographic consistency of data provided by the decennial census would result in high costs and disruption to program development and evaluation at all levels of government.

NOTE

[1]The panel acknowledges the assistance of Philip Fulton, associate director of the Department of Transportation's Bureau of Transportation Statistics, and George V. Wickstrom, a transportation planning consultant in Kensington, Maryland, for their assistance in preparing this appendix. Dr. Fulton prepared materials on the history of transportation data in the census and the use of census data to meet federal legislative requirements. Mr. Wickstrom coordinated the survey of state transportation and metropolitan planning agencies of their use of census data for their programs. Both Dr. Fulton and Mr. Wickstrom provided drafts of their work that were used in the panel's deliberations and in preparation of this appendix.

REFERENCES

Delaware Valley Regional Planning Commission
   1994   *The Journey-to-Work Trends in the Delaware Valley Region 1970-1980.*   Philadelphia, Pa.: Delaware Valley Regional Planning Commission.
McDonnell, J.J.
   1984   The urban transportation planning package. Pp. 11-15 in *Census Data and Urban Transportation Planning in the 1980s.*   Transportation Research Record 981.   Transportation Research Board, National Research Council.   Washington, D.C.: Transportation Research Board.
Sosslau, A.B.
   1983   *Transportation Planner's Guide to Using the 1980 Census.* Washington, D.C.: Federal Highway Administration, U.S. Department of Transportation.
U.S. General Accounting Office
   1993   *Transportation Infrastructure: Better Tools Needed for Making Decisions on Using ISTEA Funds Flexibly.* GAO/RCED-94-25. Washington, D.C.: U.S. General Accounting Office.
Wickstrom, G.V.
   1984   Experience with the 1980 census urban transportation planning package in the Washington metropolitan area. Pp. 91-95 in *Census Data and Urban Transportation Planning in the 1980s.* Transportation Research Record 981.   Transportation Research Board, National Research Council.   Washington, D.C.: Transportation Research Board.
   1994   The Use of Decennial Census Data in Transportation Planning.   May.   Paper prepared for the Bureau of Transportation Statistics, U.S. Department of Transportation, Washington, D.C.

TABLE G.1 Type of Transportation Data Used by State Transportation Agencies and Metropolitan Planning Agencies (22 agencies reporting)

Items	Number		Percentage	
	1980	1990	1980	1990
Type of Data Used				
Household, population	17	19	77	86
Other socioeconomic	18	21	82	95
Employment	15	17	68	77
Trip characteristics	18	20	82	91
Origin-destination	18	19	82	86
Cross-tabs (CTPP)	16	18	73	82
Uses for the Data				
As inputs to models	16	18	73	82
As a base year	12	18	55	82
To develop model parameters	13	18	59	82
As a check of model results	14	19	64	86
Purpose of Use				
Long-range planning/TIP	15	16	68	73
Corridor studies	16	0	73	91
Alternatives analysis	15	18	68	82
Transit planning	15	0	68	91
Congestion management[a]	—	16	—	73
TCM analysis[a]	—	15	—	68
Air quality evaluation	13	16	59	73
Conformity determination[a]	—	15	—	68
Monitoring	12	15	55	68
Other	1	2	5	7

[a]These purposes are new federal requirements that were added to census data requirements by legislation enacted since the 1980 census.

Source: Wickstrom (1994:Table 4).

TABLE G.2 Usefulness and Alternative Sources of Transportation Data
for State Transportation Agencies and Metropolitan Planning Agencies (22
agencies reporting), 1990 Census

Items	Number	Percentage
Usefulness of the Data for (essential or very useful):		
Statewide and regional transportation plan	20	91
Program development	14	64
Conformity requirements	14	64
Congestion management	15	68
Transit planning	15	68
Traffic control measures	11	50
Alternatives analysis	17	77
Monitoring and evaluation	11	50
Other	4	18
Difficulty to Replace Data (very difficult):		
Socioeconomic data (by zone)	13	59
Employment data (by zone)	8	36
Work-trip data by mode (by zone)	18	82
Origin-destination data (by zone)	17	77
Special tabulations in CTPP	15	68
Most Likely Way to Replace Data:		
Conduct or expand home interviews	19	86
Conduct workplace surveys	13	59
Conduct roadside or transit surveys	13	59
Use secondary source data	13	59
Other new data collection	7	32
Could Funds and Staff Be Made Available	Yes Probably Unlikely	
	1 11 10	

Source: Wickstrom (1994:Table 5).

H

Census Data Needs for Housing and Urban Development

In 1992, the Office of Management and Budget (OMB) requested department and agency heads to identify topics to be included in the 2000 census. The Department of Housing and Urban Development's (HUD) response stated that "HUD cannot fulfill its mission of making communities work for people without the use of census data in developing, administering, and monitoring HUD programs" (Cisneros, 1993:1). HUD uses census data to allocate funds to cities and local jurisdictions most in need of assistance, such as in the assisted housing Community Development Block Grants (CDBG) or Emergency Shelter Grants (ESG). HUD relies heavily on detailed, small-area information only available through a census-like source in monitoring HUD-funded, locally administered programs. Developing a national urban policy and assessing the condition of

The panel was assisted in the preparation of this chapter by Mary Nenno, visiting fellow at the Urban Institute. Ms. Nenno worked with the panel in contacting state and metropolitan housing and urban development officials about their perceptions of census data requirements. She also provided technical advice on the exposition of housing and urban development. The panel also acknowledges the assistance of four housing experts who provided background papers. Roberta F. Garber, a consultant in Westerville, Ohio, prepared a paper on the use of census data in housing policy development. F. Edward Geiger, III, an official with Pennsylvania's Department of Community Affairs, provided a paper on the quality of housing quality statistics. Mr. Geiger received advice and suggestions from Natalie S. Geiger and Dr. Marshall A. Geiger. Franklin F. James, professor of public policy at the University of Colorado at Denver, prepared a paper on the priorities for housing data from future censuses. Thomas B. Cook, deputy director of the California Department of Housing and Community Development, prepared a paper on state and local housing policy development. This appendix also draws on information reported in Cisneros (1993).

urban areas depend largely on measurements made for cities, towns, and counties by the Census Bureau in the decennial enumeration.

Communities are at the heart of HUD's mission, and it needs to continue having information about these integral components of America's cities. Census tracts are the essential building blocks for such community information. HUD uses tract-level data in implementing its own and other federal programs. For example, HUD staff uses tract data to identify qualified census tracts for mortgage revenue bonds and low-income housing tax credits. CDBG program staff monitor the distribution of program assistance using data at the tract- and block-group level. HUD's office of Fair Housing and Equal Opportunity requires census tract-level data to conduct fair housing compliance reviews mandated by Title 6 of the Civil Rights Act of 1964. HUD's field office economists use tract data in performing market analyses required under the Federal Housing Administration (FHA) insurance programs. Location decisions for HUD-assisted housing require tract-level information to avoid undue concentrations of persons living in poverty.

After looking at the array of census 2000 options and reviewing its data needs, HUD (Cisneros, 1993) concluded that the content and design used in 1990 and other recent censuses come closest to meeting the department's needs.

FEDERAL LEGISLATIVE AND CENSUS DATA REQUIREMENTS

Federal legislation specifies census data be used by HUD in several areas. Only a few housing items are strictly "mandated" in the census. Mandated items are census questions that federal legislation specifically requires to be collected in the census. In the narrow legal sense of "mandated" there are several housing items, including number of rooms, tenure, year built, that are required to be collected in the census. Most of the mandated items are listed in federal block-grant formulas.

Because of their reliability and accuracy and for geographic consistency across the nation, census data are especially important for housing and urban development programs. The precision and reliability of population and housing items available from a 1990 census "level of content" seem to be adequate for purposes of HUD (Cisneros, 1993). According to HUD (Cisneros, 1993) reliability and accuracy of the "expanded content" and "continuous measurement" approaches would not be adequate for distributing or allocating funds since sampling errors at low levels of aggregation can result in serious misallocations of resources. And, coverage would not be sufficient for adequate evaluation of urban conditions or community development. Also, the realiability and accuracy of current surveys for income and poverty data would not be adequate for establishing program eligibility and distributing or allocating funds, again because sampling errors at low levels of aggregation can cause serious misallocations of resources. As a result, current surveys would not be adequate for assessing urban conditions, housing needs of disabled Americans, and CDBG effectiveness.

This section first describes small-area geographic detail needed and then the content of census items that are required by federal legislation.

Small-Area Geographic Detail

The level of aggregation required for allocating funds in the CDBG and HOME programs is generally the unit of government. Allocation of funds using income and poverty counts for the CDBG, ESG, and HOME programs ususally also requires aggregation to the unit of government. For many participating jurisdictions, however, data must be available at the census place level to construct "CDBG urban counties." These urban counties represent the balance of counties that contain one or more entitlement cities. In addition, the CDBG program requires that local governments develop community programs to target benefits to low- and moderate-income individuals. This must be done at the block-group level. Fair housing compliance reviews under Title 6 of the Civil Rights Act of 1964, affirmative fair housing marketing reviews under Title 8 of the Civil Rights Act of 1968, and Home Mortgage Disclosure Act compliance reviews require data at the census tract level and block group level. Identification of qualifying census tracts and difficult development areas for low-income housing tax credits and mortgage revenue bonds also requires the use of tract-level data.

Reporting on the conditions of urban areas requires assessment of concentrations and distributions of activities and needs across neighborhoods, i.e., census tracts. The finest levels of aggregation for these uses of data are at the jurisdiction or census place level for comprehensive housing affordability strategies development, CDBG, Fair Housing, and Section 202 elderly and handicapped. And, for calculating income limits and fair market rents, data at the county level are required. Income limits for various assisted housing programs must be defined for separate housing markets—cities, counties, or groups of counties

Census Content

There are several key items in the census that are needed for the administration of HUD programs: population counts; housing; income and poverty; labor-market information; mobility, health, ethnicity, and language; and homeless population. This section reviews each of these important data items and the federal legislation that requires the information.

Population Counts

Among the most essential census information for HUD are data on persons, households, and family counts by family type, age, disabilities, race, and marital status. These data are used to allocate funds; set income limits; report on housing program accomplishments, needs, and urban conditions; assist local governments in planning; enforce civil rights laws; and identify needy areas and families. For example, this information, along with other data elements, is used to allocate CDBG, ESG, HOME Investment Funds, Section 8 Housing certificates and vouchers, and Section 202 (elderly and handicapped) funds. More effective targeting and more equitable distribution of resources are the goals of such data-driven allocation formulas.

Enforcement and monitoring of the Civil Rights Act of 1964 and the FHA are also carried out through use of these data. Court cases concerning housing discrimination against families with children require such data as evidence. This information is used by local government units to develop timely and well-designed comprehensive housing affordability strategies, which are required to establish eligibility for receiving funds from CDBG, HOME, and other HUD programs. More effective targeting of the low-income housing tax credits and mortgage revenue bonds programs can be achieved by using these data in designating qualified census tracts and difficult to develop areas. These data are under consideration for determining eligibility for new programs such as enterprise zones and community development banks. Congressionally required reports, such as the President's National Urban Policy Report, the State of Fair Housing and Civil Rights Data on HUD Program Applicants and Beneficiaries, and Worst Case Housing Needs, require the use of these data. These data are also used in combination with other data items to set income limits that reflect regional variation in housing costs for several programs, including HUD-assisted housing, Farmers Home Administration, Resolution Trust Corporation, and Treasury Department programs.

One problem, however, is that the 1990 census categories used for race and ethnicity allow an "other race" option. This makes it difficult for HUD and other federal civil rights enforcement agencies to use census data with program data collected and categorized according to OMB guidelines on racial and ethnic information, which do not include an "other race" category.

Housing

A central requirement for census data for HUD is information on housing, including data on tenure, cost, rent, value, utilities, quality, size, structure types, amenities, and physical conditions. The 1990 data on housing are used to allocate funds; make grants; establish fair market rents; set income limits; report on housing programs, needs, and urban conditions; assist local governments in planning; enforce civil rights laws; and identify needy areas and families. For example, this information, along with other data elements, is used to allocate CDBG, ESG, HOME Investment Funds, Section 8 Housing certificates and vouchers, and Section 202 (elderly and handicapped) funds. The goals of the allocations formulas are more effective targeting and more equitable distribution of resources.

Information on rent paid, tenure, number of bedrooms, plumbing and kitchen facilities, utility costs, year moved in, and quality is used to calculate fair market rents used in the Section 8 Housing certificate and voucher program. Enforcement and monitoring of the Civil Rights Acts of 1964 and 1968, the Home Mortgage Disclosure Act, and the Fair Housing Act are also carried out through use of these data. This information is used by local government units to develop timely and well-designed comprehensive housing affordability strategies, which are required to establish eligibility for receiving funds under CDBG, HOME, and other HUD programs. FHA underwriting for single- and multifamily insurance also makes use of these data to undertake market and feasibility analyses. More effective targeting of the low-income housing tax credits and mortgage revenue bonds programs can be achieved by using these data for designating qualified census tracts and difficult development areas.

Congressionally required reports, such as the President's National Urban Policy Report and Worst Case Housing Needs, require use of these data. Like population data, these data are used in combination with other data items in setting income limits that reflect regional variation in housing costs for several programs and agencies, including HUD-assisted housing, Farmers Home Administration, Resolution Trust Corporation, and Treasury Department programs.

Two problems arise, however, with the use of 1990 data. First, collection of rent information using the same set of precoded rent intervals for all areas of the country and all bedroom sizes presents serious accuracy problems in calculating fair market rents when rents exceed $750 per month. Second, the 1990 census categorizations used for race and ethnicity allow an "other race" option, making it difficult for HUD and other federal civil rights enforcement agencies to use census data with program data collected and categorized according to OMB guidelines on racial and ethnic information.

Income and Poverty

Income information and numbers of persons in poverty are used in several HUD programs. For example, income information for local areas collected in the census is used to define low, very low, and moderate incomes for eligibility determinations in conventional public housing, Section 8 Housing voucher and certificate programs (existing, new construction, and moderate and substantial rehabilitation); rent supplements, CDBG targeting (low- and moderate-income benefit requirement); allocation of funds in the CDBG, Fair Share, Emergency

Shelter Grants, Section 202 elderly housing and HOME programs; developing comprehensive housing affordability strategies by local governments; reporting on worst case housing needs; and identifying qualified census tracts and difficult development areas for low-income housing tax credit and mortgage revenue bond programs. HUD income limits and estimates are used by numerous other agencies and organizations: the Federal Reserve Board, Treasury, Farmers Home Administration, Resolution Trust Corporation, Federal Deposit Insurance Corporation, Federal Housing Finance Board, Federal National Mortgage Corporation, and Federal Home Loan Mortgage Corporation. The 1990 census data on income and poverty are used to define income eligibility limits for rent supplements and conventional public housing. The income limits are also being used by the Federal Reserve Board, U.S. Treasury Department, Farmers Home Administration, Resolution Trust Corporation, Federal Deposit Insurance Corporation, Federal Housing Finance Board, Federal National Mortgage Corporation, and Federal Home Loan Mortgage Corporation. In addition, census data are being used to report on conditions and needs for housing and urban development, assist local governments in planning, and enforce civil rights laws.

Labor Market Information

These data—education, school attendance, employment and unemployment, work location, transportation, industry, occupation, type of firm, and number of weeks worked—are used in assessing the condition of urban areas in the President's Urban Policy Report and in assessing and evaluating the effectiveness of the CDBG program. Secretary Cisneros has initiated a new process of monitoring the condition of cities that uses information from the 1990 census.

Mobility, Health, Ethnicity, and Language

The 1990 census data on mobility, health, ethnicity, and language have been used in the National Urban Policy Report, CHAS development, Section 202 grants, the CDBG evaluation, and in fair housing compliance and enforcement. Information on health conditions and health limitations is used in the Section 202 Elderly Housing Grant Program (now Supportive Housing for Persons with Disabilities Program). The President's National Urban Policy Report has used of information on ethnicity, 5-year mobility, language, and health conditions as indicators of urban conditions. Comprehensive housing affordability strategies developed by local governments are required to use information on health difficulties in assessing local needs. Evaluation of the CDBG program has made use of the information on mobility and language.

Homeless Population

The Emergency Shelter Grants, Supportive Housing Demonstration, Supplemental Assistance for Facilities to Assist the Homeless, and Section 8 Moderate Rehabilitation Single Room Occupancy—programs created by the McKinney Act—require allocation of funds, determination of eligibility, and identification of areas with severe homelessness problems. At present these funds are awarded using competitive procedures or proxy measures.

Current procedures for census data on the homeless lack adequate coverage, reasonable reliability, and accuracy. While the shelter and street night enumeration (S-night) count is reasonable in the areas where it was done, there was no universal cooperation at the local jurisdiction level.[1] The street count suffers because of numerous methodological and enumeration problems.

The shelter count on the homeless from the S-night operation was used by HUD to assess alternative approaches for allocating homeless assistance by formula. At present, funds for homeless populations are generally allocated and programs are administered at the jurisdiction level. The street count, however, was not considered to be sufficiently accurate for allocating funds.

PROGRAM USES OF CENSUS DATA

Comprehensive Housing Affordability Strategies

As mentioned above, there are only a few housing items specifically mandated by legislation. There are other housing items in the census, however, that are required for effective program and policy purposes. Data on telephones, kitchen, rents, number of bedrooms, plumbing, and number of rooms are routinely used in HUD program work. At the moment, these data are updated annually using the American Housing Survey (AHS) and the consumer price index.

One of the most important current uses of census data by HUD is for the CHAS legislation. CHAS data are assembled to help give states and areas submitting their CHAS applications equal access to data. CHAS requirements include calculating the annual median family income for the area and adjusting it for family size. HUD looked at other possible tabulations for local area housing strategies, but after examining a number of options and after comprehensive discussion with state and local housing officials, it was decided that the CHAS data tabulations would offer the most accurate, equitable information for making housing decisions.

For the CHAS data, HUD obtained decennial census data tapes from the Census Bureau, processed them, and then published a databook. At the same time, the Census Bureau produced equivalent tabulations for many areas of the nation and released them on CD-ROMs. HUD has offered many workshops on the use of the CHAS data, usually conducted with private consultants. Consultants to HUD work with state and local governments so that local agencies can prepare census data for HUD applications and program monitoring.

With the available CD-ROMs, published databook, and software, local and state agencies are able to define specific geographic areas. They examine different household types and define the low-income and poverty universe for the population in the geographic areas. Next, they analyze housing costs for various income groups. Finally, they calculate the composition of the population for affordability groups. Such a procedure helps to ensure that all parts of the nation—in different regions, as well as urban, suburban, and rural areas—are treated equally by HUD in assisting groups who lack affordable housing.

The strengths of 1990 census data for a local agency are access to the data (with a microcomputer and a CD-ROM reader) and software that enables them to make local decisions about housing areas. The current system for handling CHAS data has one major attraction: there is remarkable trust at the local level in the quality of the data. All the data were collected nationwide at the same time, with comparable questions asked of respondents in different states. No other local housing data provide such comparability. Local administrative data on housing, for example, vary markedly in the definition of a household or family. For instance, different metropolitan housing agencies use different definitions of "dependents." Administrative data have variations in the coverage of the lower income groups, which make the data worrisome for decisions about housing affordability. Finally, few local or state agencies have made quality checks on their housing data. With the CHAS data, housing officials are able to examine neighborhoods, which are re-emerging as a central focus for urban policy. A key use of the small-area data in the census is the ability to define neighborhoods locally.

Housing Policy Development

One example of the use of census data at the local level is that of the Mid-Ohio Regional Planning Commission, which in 1990 contracted with Roberta F. Garber Consulting and Ohio Capital Corporation for Housing to prepare a five-year CHAS for the city of Columbus and Franklin County (see Garber, 1994). This joint city-county planning process was intended not only to meet HUD's requirements for the CHAS, but, more importantly, to reach consensus among a broad array of public, private, and nonprofit actors regarding affordable housing goals and strategies.

One of the most challenging parts of this process was the collection, analysis, and presentation of data on affordable housing needs and the affordable housing market to the 35-member CHAS planning committee. Data were gathered from surveys, locally generated reports, focus groups, the 1990 census, and the 1991 AHS. Data analysis and presentation were key for successfully reaching consensus on policy directions. There were, however, a number of obstacles to overcome.

Census data have inherent limitations in their use for housing policy development. First, they provide little direct data on physical housing conditions. Data on the year a structure was built and the number of vacant, boarded-up units, overlaid with data on household income or poverty, can help target areas in an urban community where there is a high likelihood of deteriorated housing. Data on units lacking complete plumbing and kitchen facilities—though useful in rural areas—have little relationship to housing conditions in urban areas. The other indicator of housing problems—extent of overcrowding—may or may not relate to housing condition and is a fairly minor housing problem in Columbus and Franklin County.

Second, until HUD requested special tabulations from the 1990 census in a CHAS databook, there was no way to use census data to understand the characteristics of households with housing problems. The special HUD tabulations available in 1993 were valuable in developing the most recent 5-year CHAS for Columbus and Franklin County. For the first time, data that described the number and characteristics of persons with housing cost burden, severe housing cost burden, overcrowding, and units lacking complete plumbing and kitchens were available. In addition, data on the affordability of the local housing stock and of vacant housing units were provided. For Columbus and Franklin County, it was possible to use the CHAS data book to determine, for example, that nearly 80 percent of renter households with severe cost burden (paying more than 50 percent of their income for rent and utilities) also had incomes below 30 percent of area median income. This indicated that most of the programs subsidizing the production of affordable rental housing, such as the low-income housing tax credits program, are still not serving the housing needs of the community. Typically those programs are designed to serve households at 50 to 60 percent of area median income. These data resulted in strategies to make significant changes in the city of Columbus and Franklin County housing programs in order to target the use of CDBG and HOME program funds to projects that serve households with the greatest need.

Although the CHAS data book was a great improvement in the availability of census data for affordable housing policy development, a major area of data was still missing, specifically, data that cross-tabulated housing condition with housing cost burden. The availability of these data is important because of the common perceptions local community leaders have about housing problems— that most housing problems involve poor housing conditions or lack of available affordable units. As a result of this misperception, strategies generally involve housing rehabilitation or new construction.

Fortunately, larger cities like Columbus have another data resource, the AHS, that provides a great deal of data on housing conditions and numerous cross-tabulations of data on housing condition with data on other household characteristics. The AHS indicated that 80 percent of households with "worst case housing needs" in Columbus and Franklin County had *only severe cost burden as a housing problem*; only 17 percent lived in substandard housing. The availability of these data has significant implications for housing policy: for many households, what is commonly thought of as a "housing problem" is in reality as much or more so an "income problem." This is particularly true for Columbus and Franklin County, where there are also comfortable vacancy rates. This suggests a need to focus on economic self-sufficiency and rental assistance as integral parts of an affordable housing strategy. However, it should be noted that responding to the income support needs for families with high rent burdens involves more than assistance from HUD, which has a priority mission to improve the condition/supply of housing and condition of neighborhoods; it also involves other federal departments whose missions are focused on income and family support. In addition, 17 percent of households living in substandard housing is not insignificant, especially if condition of structure is related to neighborhood condition. Decennial census data are a critical resource for identifying local housing needs that go beyond one federal department of the local housing agency.

Unfortunately, the AHS also has a major limitation. It only aggregates data on a jurisdictional basis. There are no census tract-level or neighborhood-level data. Neighborhood-level planning and policy development are required for the CHAS, for the new HUD consolidated plan, and for the strategic planning process for the empowerment zone and enterprise community program. Lack of subarea data on housing conditions creates a significant void in planning at this scale. It is increasingly evident that housing, economic, and social data on a neighborhood basis—blocks and census tracts—are essential in designing and carrying out effective local programs. Recent studies have emphasized that it is important to measure neighborhood quality, as well as the quality of housing structures (Newman and Schnare, 1994). For smaller communities it may be possible to conduct windshield surveys to determine neighborhood housing conditions. For larger urban areas, this process can take years. In addition, lack of AHS subarea data makes it difficult to clearly describe to suburban officials the housing problems in their communities that need to be addressed.

Another example of the use of decennial census data for housing policy development is that of the California Department of Housing and Community Development. The deputy director of the department, Thomas B. Cook (1994), cites the use of these data in state housing planning, including the state review of required local housing planning documents, evaluation of financial assistance applications for both state and federal funds, and technical assistance both in the preparation of local planning documents and local loan and grant applications. This includes the use of small-area data from the census. The state has acquired and uses 1980 and 1990 cross-tabulations of population and housing items at state and substate levels. It also utilizes decennial data as a benchmark for surveys that update information between census periods.

In conclusion, the need for the housing data provided in the decennial census certainly has not decreased in recent years, and in fact will continue to grow as the federal government adds increasing planning requirements to its programs. The focus on comprehensive and strategic planning means that housing data are important not only for housing planning, but also for planning related to economic development, welfare reform, crime reduction, and transportation. A minimal level of data is included in the census. Without special HUD data runs and the AHS, it would be very difficult to accurately link investments of resources with real needs. Unfortunately for rural areas, these other data resources are not available at low levels of geography, leaving the decennial census as the primary database. Fewer census questions pertaining to housing will only make it more difficult to effectively target scarce public and private resources.

Analysis, Development, and Evaluation of Urban Policy Initiatives

A loss of small-area data from the census would forestall a variety of important urban research and would impede the effective implementation of a number of urban programs that currently rely on such data. Many urban processes can be meaningfully examined and documented only using small-area census data.

Urban Poverty, Need, and Economic Trends

Poverty has become concentrated in massive and growing neighborhoods within cities. Data describing socioeconomic and demographic characteristics of census tracts or blocks are used to track the dimensions and causes of this type of poverty. Census small-area data can also permit at least crude analysis of mobility patterns in and out of poverty-stricken areas. The data are also used to analyze the effects that living in such areas has on the opportunities and achievements of residents. There is no substitute for census data as a basis for such analyses.

Over the past 20 years, urban experts have documented the importance of small-area geographic specialization of urban economies. Researchers have shown that office and retail trade trends in the downtowns of American cities have differed significantly from those elsewhere in big cities. Thus, place-of-work data describing trends in central business districts are helpful for documenting this trend. Such data have been provided from the decennial census.

Indeed, there is a general shortage of up-to-date employment information for even the municipalities. The Census Bureau's *County Business Patterns* provides annual data for counties, however, most cities are not coterminous with counties. The Census Bureau has the ability to compile a "city business patterns" data series, though such an effort would require financial support. Such a report would he invaluable for local, state, and federal economic development planning.

Research has shown that geographic access to jobs is a major determinant of unemployment and employment in urban areas. Thus, information on the spatial locations of workers and jobs is important for understanding unemployment. Those data also help in the analysis of urban workers' transportation needs. Federal laws such as the Intermodal Surface Transportation Efficiency Act and the Clean Air Act impose complex planning requirements on states and local governments that can only be accomplished using small-area data on housing, population, employment, and other characteristics of small areas that determine transportation demands. Local governments have a panoply of planning needs that also require such data.

The geographic level of detail required for such research and planning is difficult or impossible to specify without detailed knowledge of the particular area. Therefore, small-area data that enable the researcher or policy analyst to combine small areas flexibly into meaningful areas for analysis are needed.

Housing and Neighborhoods

Small-area data help document the characteristics and trends—physical and social—in urban neighborhoods. They also help identify and document the effects of abandonment, revitalization, social transition, and so forth.

Neighborhood patterns of income, race, and ethnicity have been shown again and again to affect the development of a neighborhood or community. Overall patterns of segregation are important indicators and determinants of housing, neighborhood, school, and job opportunities facing racial and ethnic minorities in urban areas. Studies of neighborhood segregation obviously require small-area data. Indeed, it is clear that the smaller the area the better the data. Census blocks play a central role in research on segregation.

Urban Programs

The loss of small-area data would hinder the implementation of many of the most important urban programs in the nation. The loss would be particularly great for recently implemented urban programs.

If federal resources are to be used most efficiently, they must be accurately targeted to the places and people who need them most. Many federal programs use measures of local need in allocation formulas or eligibility standards. Some programs, such as the Community Development Block Grants, attempt to measure community need or distress using formulas that reflect conditions in entire municipalities or counties.

The most exciting new urban programs are being implemented at the neighborhood scale (e.g., community development programs). Community development efforts can sometimes effect fundamental change in a community by instituting a comprehensive effort that has the support of residents, property owners, local governments, and others affected by the programs. The first new federal economic development initiatives in almost 20 years—enterprise and empowerment zones—also are targeted to either areas smaller than a municipality or overlapping areas of more than one locality. Small-area data are needed to evaluate the effects of these programs on the socioeconomic, demographic, and housing conditions in the community. Such data are also needed to target assistance and support to community development organizations.

Census data are also being used to target federal, state, and local efforts to ameliorate large concentrations of poverty.

ALTERNATIVE SOURCES OF CENSUS DATA

Many areas of the country (counties, cities, and towns) are not included or identified in the sample-based surveys. Sample sizes in small areas are too small to provide any confidence in the data.

Alternative sources of data on population; housing; income and poverty; labor markets; and mobility, health, ethnicity, and language include the Current Population Survey (for income and poverty data, the March supplement), AHS (conducted nationally every other year), and the AHS large metropolitan area data (collected for selected areas every four years). These surveys are sample-based and have fairly small sample sizes and very low levels of precision and accuracy. This is especially true for population data, income and poverty data, and labor market information, which have statutory requirements that specify the level of aggregation needed for meeting program and funding requirements.

A second alternative source is HUD administrative records, which capture information from the part of the population already receiving benefits from HUD programs. These records are limited, however, because they only cover a part of the population. Areas or families needing assistance cannot be identified with these records. Also, because the records contain little information on labor market characteristics, they not be very useful for obtaining labor market information. Model-based estimates cannot be used because they artificially reduce the amount of variance, which leads to incorrect allocations. Such estimates also rely on strong assumptions that are difficult to defend. These estimates could not be used to obtain labor market information because they are not independent assessments of program outcomes and conditions.

A final source for housing data is the use of random digit dialing telephone surveys. Such surveys have been used to determine fair market rents; however, they would be extremely costly to use in the 2,700 market areas for which data are needed.

As could be expected, there are no other consistent estimates on the homeless that cover all areas and places on a national basis. Prior survey estimates of the homeless are dated (a national survey was conducted in 1984), did not measure the number of homeless (i.e., measured shelter bed capacity), or did not provide reliable estimates at the local level.

PRIORITIES FOR HOUSING DATA

Data From Future Censuses

There is the possibility that future censuses may not continue to provide data for small geographic areas such as census tracts, census blocks, and small cities or towns. The loss of such data would have profound, adverse impacts on federal urban policy and research and would impede the effective targeting and administration of a number of important urban programs. It would also harm state and local policy and programs. Vitally important urban research and urban programs would be crippled if high-quality data for small areas are not provided by the Census Bureau in the future.

Franklin J. James, professor of public policy at the University of Colorado at Denver, previous director of the U.S. Department of Housing and Urban Development's legislative and urban policy staff and still active in urban policy organizations, notes that high-quality data for small areas are necessary for accuracy in defining urban conditions (James, 1994):

> I have a variety of experience which enables me to judge the value of such small area data. As the director of HUD's Legislative and Urban Policy Staff, I was involved in the urban policy development during President Carter's administration. I remain active in urban policy research. Recently, HUD asked me to assist in preparing a background paper on urban economic development issues for President Clinton's urban policy. Moreover, I am on research advisory committees which keep me up to date on research and policy issues. Examples are the advisory committee of the Community Development Research Center of the New School for Social Research, and the research advisory panel of the Federal National Mortgage Association.

Improving Data on the Condition of Housing Structures

Research and analysis of housing quality has been hampered by the lack of useful data. While independent researchers could undertake housing surveys to fill this gap, such surveys would be too costly or lack the credibility and reliability of data produced by the Census Bureau. Unfortunately, the decennial census is not an adequate source for housing quality statistics, and other Census Bureau data have significant limitations too. With only minimal additions to the decennial census, data on housing quality could be expanded tremendously, thus making existing Census Bureau data considerably more useful.

Outdated and Too Little Data

The only real indicators of housing quality in the decennial census are the questions regarding lack of a full bath and lack of a complete kitchen. Through the middle of this century, indoor plumbing was a reasonable gauge of the quality of a home. However, these two housing features have outlived their usefulness since only about 1 percent of all housing units in the United States lack complete plumbing facilities (Bureau of the Census, 1993).

F. Edward Geiger, III, senior policy analyst of the Pennsylvania Department of Community Development, emphasizes the need for improved data in the decennial census on condition of housing structures for individual communities and by census tracts and makes recommendations for additional condition items (see Table H.1; see also Geiger, 1994). This need is critical in Pennsylvania because 72 percent of Pennsylvania's housing stock is over 30 years old and only 42 percent of the state's municipalities have enacted building codes (Bureau of the Census, 1992). Yet, a scant 1-2 percent of the state's housing would be considered substandard using lack of kitchen or bath as the measure of decent quality housing (Bureau of the Census, 1992). Common sense tells us that this decennial census information does not measure up to the task.

The AHS is the most comprehensive source of housing quality data in the nation. The survey covers roughly 150,000 housing units and contains a wealth of housing quality data. The AHS examines condition, structural features and equipment, financial characteristics, and even neighborhood quality (Bureau of the Census, 1991). However, even the AHS has its limitations. It does not provide data for individual communities (much less census tracts) and does not provide detailed reports for areas other than the 44 metropolitan areas covered by the survey.

Additional Decennial Census Questions

Assuming it is not feasible to expand the AHS to cover larger portions of the nation, a few minor additions to the decennial census's long form should be considered. Adding additional questions to the decennial census would improve the data available for all areas (including metropolitan and nonmetropolitan areas) and all levels of geography (state, county, county subdivisions, and tracts/block numbering areas). The additions would also provide the opportunity to generate even more detailed estimates of housing quality by extrapolating with data from the AHS.

The additional questions should cover the operation and breakdowns of major housing systems: plumbing, heating, electrical, and roofing. One or two questions about each of these housing features (about 8 questions in total) would vastly expand the housing quality information gathered at a relatively minimal cost compared to expanding the AHS to more homes in other areas of the country. (The existing questions about plumbing and kitchens might be eliminated to help limit the length of the census form.) Although example questions are suggested in Table H.1., the questions should be selected based on their relationship to other housing quality features covered in the AHS. With additional research, questions could be developed that would facilitate the extrapolation of housing quality data. For example, additional research might determine that x percent of homes having broken toilets also have serious leaks inside the structure from pipes or plumbing fixtures. If the decennial census gathered statistics on broken toilets, a good estimate of homes with leaking pipes would be available. Using this methodology, many housing quality features found in the AHS could be extrapolated from the slightly expanded decennial census. Both the actual census data and the extrapolated data could provide detailed information about the quality of housing in specific communities and other small geographic areas.

In addition to the research needed for extrapolation purposes, the added questions should be tested to determine how accurately this information can be self-reported in the long-form questionnaire. In order to truly improve housing quality data, the responses from the housing quality questions must be reliable.

One major issue neglected to this point is why the additional data on housing quality are needed. These additional data could be used to determine the level of funding for housing programs and how those funds should be used. Government agencies that fund housing programs could use this information to determine where additional monies are needed for housing rehabilitation rather than new construction. The expanded housing quality data also could be used to determine whether housing programs are effective. Over the long-term, it is unclear whether the quality of the housing stock is improving or declining. These additional data may help answer the question.

The private sector could also use the expanded housing quality data. Home repair and maintenance firms could use this information to target markets and determine the need for their products and services. The manufactured housing industry (commonly referred to as mobile home builders) could verify whether its housing is sound and durable. The industry could use the improved census data to compare the quality of manufactured homes to traditional, site-built housing.

Data for Small Areas

High-quality data for small areas are necessary for the accurate analysis and diagnosis of urban problems, and for the development, implementation, and evaluation of urban programs. Survey data such as the Current Population Survey or the AHS can frequently substitute for census data when the focus is on large geographic areas such as the nation, populous states, or major metropolitan areas. Indeed, survey data are sometimes superior to census data for such purposes because survey questionnaires can be focused and fine tuned for particular tasks. However, it is prohibitively expensive to use surveys to describe situations and trends in small areas. For technical reasons, much the same sample size is required for accurate survey data for a small area as is required for a survey of a large area. Sample size is among the most important determinants of the costs of a data collection effort.

Small-area data from the Census Bureau have wide-ranging usefulness because they provide data of fundamental importance to a wide range of research and policy analysis, such as demographic information, labor-force and employment information, and income and housing descriptions. From the vantage point of the federal government, it is much more efficient to provide such basic data from the census than to finance or require others to finance the large numbers of special surveys that would be needed to replace census data for small areas. The marginal cost of adding additional data items to an ongoing survey or census is small. Similarly, the potential savings from dropping individual questions is also small if other survey parameters are unchanged. Moreover, the loss of quality census data describing small areas would impede special surveys that might be done to replace the lost data. Currently, census data increase the efficiency of special surveys. Generic data from the census can help target special survey efforts to the places where the survey is most appropriate and facilitate the design of efficient lists for more detailed sample surveys. The data provided by the census are used to delineate areas for special studies. This targeting function increases the efficiency of a large number of special surveys in small areas.

CONSEQUENCES OF NOT COLLECTING CENSUS DATA

There would be severe consequences for HUD programs if census data were not available for population and housing characteristics. First, HUD would be unable to meet legislatively mandated requirements for several programs—community development block grants, emergency shelter grants, low-income housing tax credits, and mortgage revenue bonds. Second, lower levels of accuracy and precision associated with other data sources would lead to poorly targeted programs, inefficient use of limited federal resources, and seriously inequitable distributions of program benefits. Third, HUD would not be able to effectively carry out its civil rights and fair housing responsibilities.

There would be other consequences if census data were lacking for special characteristics. Without census data on income and poverty, HUD would be unable to meet legislatively mandated requirements for several programs—community development block grants, emergency shelter grants, low-income housing tax credits, and mortgage revenue bonds. Second, lower levels of accuracy and precision associated with other data sources would lead to poorly targeted programs, inefficient use of limited federal resources, and seriously inequitable distributions of program benefits. Without census data on labor markets, the

President's Urban Policy Report would not be able to report on the required conditions or would have to rely on other unsatisfactory sources. CDBG evaluation would be difficult or impossible. Lack of information on disabilities would lessen the ability of HUD to effectively target Section 202 grants, for local governments to include this special needs group in their CHAS, and for the Office of Fair Housing and Equal Opportunity to determine need for accessible housing. Without census data on the homeless, decisions concerning funding allocations, program design, and national priorities will continue to be made in an information vacuum.

NOTE

[1]S-night was a national operation as part of the 1990 census to count the homeless population and others not covered by the ususal census-taking procedures. The operation was conducted in two phases: the shelter phase and the street phase. During the shelter phase, census enumerators collected data on persons found in shelters (emergency shelters, and shelters for abused women and runaways). During the street phase, census enumerators collected data on persons found at selected street locations and other areas where the homeless might spend the night (e.g., abandoned buildings, parks, and vacant lots). For more information on S-night operations, see Barrett, et al., 1992.

REFERENCES

Barrett, D.F., I. Anolik, and F.H. Abramson
    1992   The 1990 Census Shelter and Street Night Enumeration. Paper presented at the annual meeting of the American Statistical Association, Boston, Mass. Bureau of the Census, Washington, D.C.

Bureau of the Census
    1991   *What is the American Housing Survey?* Washington, D.C.: U.S. Department of Commerce.
    1992   Age of Pennsylvania's Housing Stock: 1990 Census of Population and Housing, Summary Tape File 3A, prepared by Pennsylvania State Data Center, May.
    1993   *Statistical Abstract of the United States, 1993.* Washington, D.C.: U.S. Department of Commerce.

Cisneros, H.G.
    1993   Response of the Department of Housing and Urban Development to Office of Management and Budget Request to Identify Topics to Be Included in the 2000 Census. Letter and Attachment to Philip Lader, Office of Management and Budget, June 18.

Cook, T.B.
    1994   Letter dated March 3 to B. Edmonston. Division of Housing Policy Development, Department of Housing and Community Development, Sacramento, Calif.

Garber, R.F.
    1994   Use of Decennial Census Data in Housing Policy Development. Paper prepared for the Panel on Census Requirements in the Year 2000 and Beyond, Committee on National Statistics, National Research Council, Washington, D.C.

Geiger, F.E. III
   1994   Improving the Quality of Housing Quality Statistics. April. Paper prepared for the Panel
            on Census Requirements in the Year 2000 and Beyond, Committee on National Statistics,
            National Research Council, Washington, D.C.
James, F.J.
   1994   Priorities for Data from Future Censuses. Memorandum dated April 20 to B. Edmonston.
            Panel on Census Requirements in the Year 2000 and Beyond. Graduate School of Public
            Affairs, University of Colorado, Denver, Colo.
Newman, S.J., and A.B. Schnare
   1994   *Back to the Future: Housing Policy for the Next Century.* Baltimore, Md.: Johns
            Hopkins University.
Pennsylvania Department of Community Affairs
   1994   *Municipalities without Building Codes: Local Land Use Controls in Pennsylvania,* 2nd
            ed. Harrisburg, Pa.: Pennsylvania Department of Community Affairs.

TABLE H.1 Suggested Additional Decennial Census Questions on Housing Condition

Census Question	Data Need Addressed
During the past year, have all the toilets in this housing unit been broken for 6 hours or more?	Availability of adequate toilet and wastewater disposal
During the past year have plumbing problems prevented you from using a sink, bath, or shower for longer than 6 hours?	Presence of adequate plumbing system
Were you uncomfortably cold last winter for more than 24 hours because of problems affording or operating heating equipment in your home?	Affordability and operation of heating system
Did your heating equipment last winter break down at least 3 times for 6 hours or more?	Adequate maintenance and repair of heating equipment
Does your home have any exposed wiring?	Presence of serious electrical hazards
Does your home have any room where all the electrical outlets do not work?	Adequate maintenance and operation of electrical system
Did you have water leaks in your home because the roof remained unrepaired for longer than 3 months?	Adequate roof construction and maintenance
Did you have water leaks in your home because the windows, walls, or doors remained unrepaired for longer than 3 months?	Soundness of structure and maintenance (other than roof)

Source: Geiger (1994).

I

Alternative Ways to Produce
Intercensal Small-Area Data

There are alternative ways to improve small-area data for the nation. The panel began its deliberation by considering ways to reduce census costs by possibly reducing the content of the decennial census. We also considered the problem of the timeliness of the estimates. Our review of alternative ways to meet the needs for intercensal small-area estimates suggests that there are some sensible low-cost efforts that could begin now. Available administrative records could be exploited immediately to provide more frequent estimates for small geographic areas. The decennial census, however, is needed to provide a benchmark for these estimates. Initial work should strive to provide annual estimates for smaller geographic areas for a few key variables: population and housing counts and estimates of the population by sex, age, race, income, and poverty status. Later work might strive to provide estimates by education and school enrollment.

It would be difficult for state and local governments to replace the current data collected by the census long form if it were dropped. Available administrative records can provide only limited univariate data (see Appendix J). With geographic references for several different administrative records, limited correlated information (e.g., high-crime areas with high poverty rates) could be gleaned. But for several examples of state and local planning, it is apparent that there is no reasonable substitute—at present—for census long-form data.

Small-area data users rely greatly on data provided by the decennial census. Appendix E provides background information on some important census data uses documented by state data centers. Appendix F illustrates the variety of census data uses by businesses. There seems to be little support for dropping data from the census and replacing it with other alternatives until data from these alternatives are available, used and tested, and preferred as a replacement to the census. A variety of census data users have informed the panel that they primarily rely and wish to rely on the census for small-area data. Small-area data users have, however, indicated the value of more timely small-area estimates from the Census Bureau, the value of a mid-decade census or a large mid-decade sample survey, and the value of being able to provide geographically referenced estimates from administrative records. These alternatives deserve further study. None of the alternatives, however, are feasible replacements for the census at this time.

We turn to an examination of several case studies on improving intercensal small-area data. The first case study discusses methods used by the Department of Defense for estimating the number of persons qualified for military service. The second study discusses the procedures used by the Bureau of Labor Statistics to provide monthly employment and unemployment estimates for states, the District of Columbia, and 2,600 labor-market areas. The third case study describes Census Bureau work to prepare annual estimates of income and poverty. The last case study examines possible ways to improve subnational estimates for the migrant and seasonal farmworker population.

QUALIFIED MILITARY POPULATION

A recent workshop convened by the Committee on National Statistics, at the request of the Department of Defense, assessed alternative techniques to develop small-area estimates of those qualified for military service (Committee on National Statistics, 1989). The ultimate aim of the workshop was to decide what method would provide the "best" estimates of the qualified military persons available in small areas (usually counties) on an annual basis for the country. Such estimates would offer a common basis for comparative recruiting goals, at small areas, within the armed services.

For military recruitment into the enlisted ranks, the key concept for data estimates is the qualified military available (QMA), defined as the number of male high school graduates, ages 17-21 years, who mentally and physically qualify and are of suitable moral character. The QMA is the current target population by the armed services for new military recruits. Women are excluded from the current QMA because the services are oversubscribed in their recruitment of women.

Preparing small-area estimates for the QMA may be thought of as a successive narrowing of the target population. The step-down approach at estimating the QMA, at any geographic level, starts with the base population and successively restricts the nonqualifying groups. The remaining group is the QMA. The approach for county estimates for the QMA is as follows:[1]

• *Base population.* The first step is to make a local-area estimate of the male population ages 17-21 years residing in the country. The estimates exclude the institutionalized population (those living in a college dormitory or military base or residing in some other institution) and are subdivided by race and ethnic group. To prepare these estimates, the decennial census data (released in the 5 percent Public Use Microdata Sample [PUMS]) are used. Census data are then aged for future years and corrected for internal migration and net international migration.

• *Educationally qualified.* From the base population, an estimate is generated of those educationally qualified, defined as someone who has completed high school or its equivalent. Data on high school completion rates by age, sex, and race and ethnicity for counties are taken from the decennial census PUMS files.

• *Mentally qualified.* Aptitude qualification for the armed services is based on a minimum score on the Armed Forces Qualification Test (AFQT). The various services set different minimum grades for qualification so that the small-area estimates need to provide a distribution of AFQT scores for each county. Several steps are followed to prepare county estimates for AFQT scores. Data on 11,878 youths in the National Longitudinal Survey, sponsored by the Department of Labor, are used to prepare county estimates for various AFQT categories. A large set of variables is then used, within race and ethnic groups, to predict AFQT scores. In general, the level of education and socioeconomic status of areas are the best predictors of a county's AFQT scores. The prediction equations, however, vary for race and ethnic groups.

• *Physically qualified.* There are no adequate data on methods for estimating local differentials in expected disqualification rates for failure to meet physical standards. In practice, the physical disqualification rate for armed forces applicants is about 14 percent. Based on the National Health and Nutrition Examination Survey, conducted by the National Center for Health Statistics, the medical fitness of military service determined that 22 percent of males and 25 percent of females were disqualified (Committee on National Statistics, 1989:13). Obesity was the leading cause of disqualification. Given the present data, there appears to be no feasible approach to preparing small-area estimates for the physically qualified.

• *Morally qualified.* The workshop did not address the topic of estimating moral qualification rates for small areas. No estimates of the morally qualified are used for current Department of Defense estimates.

The example of preparing small-area estimates for the population qualified for military service illustrates issues for data needs and methods. Regarding data needs, the estimates rely on a combination of decennial census data (with detailed, multivariate information for small areas, by race and ethnicity) and survey data. Survey data, even with limited coverage of small areas (e.g., counties), are used in statistical modeling to provide data useful for small-area estimates. Other existing survey data sets on public enrollment and the number of high school graduates might provide sources of additional data. Data sets are inadequate, however, for modeling moral and/or physical standards for local areas.

Regarding methods, estimates of the QMA illustrate that much can be done with careful attention to available data. Although estimates can be made for small counties and areas, there is concern about the quality of the estimates. The accuracy of small-area estimates varies with the size of the area, as well as the amount of money spent on the methodology. To the extent feasible, regression sample-data methods from survey data offer a way to improve more frequent local estimates.

EMPLOYMENT ESTIMATES

Monthly employment and unemployment estimates are prepared by the Bureau of Labor Statistics (BLS) for the 50 states, the District of Columbia, and over 2,600 labor-market areas (see Bureau of Labor Statistics, 1994). The process of making these monthly small-area estimates involves the use of sample surveys, administrative records, and statistical modeling. The local unemployment estimates are used to determine local-area eligibility for such federal programs as the Job Training and Partnership Act, the Economic Dislocation and Worker Adjustment Assistance Act, and the Urban Development Action Grant program.

State Estimates

The Current Population Survey (CPS) produces reliable monthly estimates of employment and unemployment for the country as a whole and for the 11 largest states. The CPS also provides reliable annual estimates for all states, the District of Columbia, and selected large metropolitan areas. Its sample size is not large enough to produce reliable monthly estimates for most states (the 39 smaller states), the District of Columbia, and smaller geographic areas.

For the 39 states and the District of Columbia that do not have monthly CPS estimates, statistical techniques (regression analysis) are used. Regression models are based on historical and current relationships within each state's economy, as reflected by data from the CPS, the BLS survey of employers, and states' unemployment insurance system. The regression models for states use the same explanatory variables, but the coefficients are unique for each state. The employment models also include trend and seasonal components to account for movements in the CPS not captured by the BLS's survey of employers. Similarly, the unemployment models use trend and seasonal components to capture the state's historical relationship between the unemployment insurance claims and unemployment measured by the CPS.

Once each year, the monthly estimates from the regression models are calibrated, or adjusted, to the annual average CPS state estimates. This calibration sets the annual average of the regression models to the CPS annual average, while preserving the distinctive monthly seasonal pattern of the regression model estimates.

Substate Estimates

CPS monthly estimates are reliable for the largest two metropolitan areas— New York City and the Los Angeles-Long Beach metropolitan area. Estimates for other metropolitan areas and for the 2,600 labor-market areas are made with an indirect statistical procedure. First, preliminary estimates are made for employment and unemployment in the local market areas. The estimates are then adjusted to the state totals. And, finally, the estimates are corrected to benchmark data.

Preliminary civilian employment estimates are based on the Current Employment Statistics (CES) survey that provides place-of-work data. Census data are used to derive factors for adjusting place-of-work to place-of-residence data for several categories of employment. These factors are applied to CES data to provide adjusted employment estimates by place of residence. Estimates for employment not included in the CES—agricultural workers, nonagricultural self-employed and unpaid family workers, and private household workers—are added to the CES estimates.

Preliminary unemployment estimates are based on the aggregate of estimates for three groups: (1) persons who were previously employed in industries covered by state unemployment insurance laws, (2) those not previously employed in industries not covered by those laws, and (3) those who were entering the labor force for the first time or reentering after having been out of the labor force for a period of time.

After preliminary estimates of employment and unemployment are made for metropolitan areas and for the 2,600 local-market areas, the sums of the estimates are totaled for each state. The estimates are proportionately adjusted so that the state sums add to the independently estimated state totals for employment and unemployment.

At the end of each year, substate estimates are revised for CES-based employment figures, corrections to unemployment claims, and updated historical relationships. The revised estimates are readjusted to sum to the state benchmark data for estimates of employment and unemployment.

INCOME AND POVERTY[2]

Income

The Bureau of the Census prepares annual estimates by states of median family income of four-person families to meet the needs as an eligibility criterion of the Low Income Home Energy Assistance Program—a block grant program administered within the Department of Health and Human Services. The annual four-person family income estimates are also important to data users as the only source of intercensal state-specific family income estimates produced by the Census Bureau.

Methodology

The income estimates program utilizes census, sample surveys, and administrative records data to update small-area decennial information. Estimates of four-person median family incomes by state utilize the most recent data available from the following three data sources: (1) March Current Population Survey (CPS) from the Bureau of the Census, (2) decennial census of population from the Bureau of the Census, and (3) per capita personal income estimates from the Bureau of Economic Analysis (BEA).

The CPS is a monthly labor force survey of about 60,000 households across the country. Each March, the monthly survey is supplemented with questions that ask household respondents about their money income received during the previous year. Survey results are published annually by the Census Bureau.[3] The CPS provides estimates of median incomes for four-person families annually at the national level. Though CPS data may also be tabulated at the state level, the sampling variability of state estimates from the CPS is large enough to make their direct use inadvisable for program purposes.

The decennial census provides income values for calendars years 1979 and 1989 that utilize the same money income concept as the annual CPS estimates, with negligible sampling error at the state level.

The Bureau of Economic Analysis (BEA) produces annual estimates of personal per capita income based on this income concept for states and other geographic areas. The estimates provide an overall indication of relative incomes among states and of change over time for particular states, even though personal per capita income is only indirectly related to median incomes of four-person families. The BEA estimates, though conceptually different from census income data, are essentially free from sampling error.

The main difference between the BEA and CPS income concepts is that the BEA personal income relates to income from all sources, while CPS income relates only to money income and adjustments are made accordingly. The BEA series is developed from a variety of government statistics, the most important being the federal tax records of the Department of Treasury, the insurance files of the Social Security Administration, and state unemployment records collected by the U.S. Department of Labor.

Estimation Models

Prior to 1984, the estimation procedure consisted of five main steps:

1. State median family income estimates for four-person families and respective standard errors were directly calculated form CPS data.
2. Another set of state estimates of four-person family income was developed by carrying forward census median estimates using the percent change in state BEA per capita personal income.
3. A regression estimate was then developed to predict the CPS estimates from the adjusted census medians from the preceding step.
4. A composite estimate was formed as a weighted average of the regression and CPS sample estimates.
5. Finally, the composite estimate for each state was constrained to a range that was equal to the CPS estimate, plus or minus one standard error.

After the 1980 census, a comparison of estimates from the census with comparable estimates from the estimation model afforded an opportunity to assess the merits of the model and to modify it. The major impetus for the revisions was the year-to-year variability of some of the state estimates. As before, the revised methodology employed sample estimates of four-person median family income from the CPS. Unlike the previous methodology, however, a second sample estimate was considered for each state. This second variable is a weighted average of estimated state median incomes for three- and five-person families. By introducing this second variable into the estimation model, the amount of sample information reflected in the estimate of four-person medians for each state was roughly doubled.

Changes in the 1984-1989 methodology are summarized below:

1. As in the earlier methodology, a regression equation was fitted to the CPS four-person estimated medians. In the new equation however, two variables were used: (a) a proportional adjustment of the census median for changes in BEA per capita income and (b) a reduction in the adjustment in case of a "regression toward the mean" which might arise if BEA per capita income did not perfectly measure the proportional changes in the income distribution.

It was found that the inclusion of the unadjusted median improved the predictive power of the regression.

2. In the revised model, a second regression equation was simultaneously fitted to the weighted average of three- and five-person medians.

3. The composite estimate in the revised model utilized both regression equations along with the CPS sample estimates.

4. Since the revised methodology essentially doubled the use of sample data in forming the composite estimates, the standard error constraint of the original equation model was eliminated. The comparison to the census results suggested that the estimates were more accurate, on the average, without the constraint.

Time Frame

In updating the state median income estimates annually, the Bureau of the Census uses the most recent data available from its March CPS and BEA's per capita income estimates.[4] However, the availability of such data results in a 3 year difference between the time frame of the March CPS and BEA income data and the fiscal year in which the estimates are in effect. For example, the state median income estimates for fiscal year 1992 were published in March 1991. The estimates are based, in part, on 1989 family income from the March 1990 CPS, which became available in August 1990 and BEA's 1989 state per capita income estimates which became available in September 1990.

Therefore, the state median income estimates do not represent projected data for a fiscal year. Instead, the estimates represent the most recent estimates available for use in a fiscal year.

Poverty

Subnational estimates of poverty are not now prepared by the Census Bureau (or any other agency of the U.S. government). At the moment, the development of such estimates is still in the research and experimentation stages. More recently, the Census Bureau has been exploring ways to develop such estimates in connection with potential congressional legislation mandating the preparation of current estimates of income and poverty for small areas, including most government jurisdictions and school districts (Poverty Data Improvement Act of 1993).

Although precise methodology is still in the developmental stages, lacking direct estimates from appropriate administrative records, the broad outline of the methodology would require integration and statistical estimation processes of the following data:

• the basic 1990 decennial census micro-data files containing "full" detail on geographic identifiers and complete income data for all sample cases. This file is not available for public use.

• an extract of the information contained on the IRS Individual Master File

(IMF) containing more than 100 million federal individual income tax returns that the Census Bureau receives annually for research and population estimation purposes. The Bureau of the Census adds geographic codes based on taxfilers' addresses that are internally consistent within the Internal Revenue Service's system of addressing. These codes are used to measure migration from place to place.

• files created by linking the IMF tax file extracts with both the March CPS and the Survey of Income and Program Participation (SIPP). The March CPS collects information about sources and amounts of income. The SIPP has much more extensive information about federal taxes. In the proposed estimates work, both of these files will be linked, on a case-by-case basis, with the tax return of the survey respondent. This linkage, made possible by collection of social security numbers in the survey, brings together the information from tax returns with the socioeconomic information collected in the surveys. This link provides a "bridge" between the Census Bureau data and the tax return data that is required in the small area estimation modeling process. Modeling and statistical estimation techniques are the processes by which changes in income and poverty at the national level are used to update the small-area data for the last decennial census. In addition, considering the population universe being estimated, additional administrative records such as AFDC or food stamp files would be extremely important and valuable for use in the estimation process.

Thus, the prospective methodology for such small-area estimates illustrates a number of important factors to be borne in mind in contemplating the production of small-area intercensal estimates: (1) a most comprehensive application, in which a variety of different data sets, including census based data, survey based data, and administrative record data, and different methodologies are brought together and utilized in developing the estimates; (2) the importance of having a "benchmark" source—in this case, the decennial census—both as a base from which to construct the intercensal estimate, and as an independent measure in a future period to be used to evaluate the methodology; (3) the advantages of and benefits to be derived from the ability to match records through the use of a common identifier, whether, as in this case, the Social Security number, an address, or some other common reference identifier; and (4) the clear advantage of using administrative files from a single, standardized source that covers the entire nation. And, finally, it demonstrates the advantages and strengths of drawing together, under one sponsorship, the diversity of disparate sources and, in so doing, allows a focusing of resources and a combining of data sources to produce both an improved methodology and a more reliable, more accurate set of estimates.

Work to date by the Bureau of the Census on income and poverty estimates has relied on tax files from the Internal Revenue Service. Proposed work will include using miscellaneous tax documents to provide a more complete picture of assorted income and to improve the construction of income for households and families. The panel urges the Bureau of the Census to also initiate work with the Aid to Families with Dependent Children (AFDC), Food Stamps, and other files that are appropriate to the universe of low-income persons. These other files, in addition to tax and income records, would greatly improve estimates of the number and location of low-income and poverty groups.

MIGRANT AND SEASONAL FARMWORKERS

The federal government currently spends over $550 million annually on farmworker programs. Among the major federal programs for farmworkers are migrant education, food stamps, Head Start, the Job Training and Partnership Act, migrant health, and housing assistance. There are few reliable data available for program planning or for purposes of allocating resources to state or local jurisdictions. At the moment, each of the federal programs either relies on decennial census data or carries out its own limited data gathering. Although these separate data collection activities add up to significant expenditures, unconnected research does not contribute to a general national database on the farmworker population.

Data collection on farmworkers begins with four facts:

(1) Farmworkers are hard to find. They often do not have mail addresses and are widely scattered in selected agricultural areas. They often reside in camps, temporary housing, or buildings converted to residential space. Special procedures are needed to canvass an area and to locate the residences of farmworkers.

(2) Farmworkers are seasonal. They do not work as farmworkers throughout the year. To address the seasonality issue, data collection must take place throughout the year, with data collected in different times in different areas, depending on the farming season.

(3) Farmworkers are migratory. The higher geographic mobility of farmworkers is a special challenge for data collection. An area with a high number of farmworkers during farm season may have no workers at other times of the year. The issue of geographic mobility can be addressed by collecting work and residence histories, and then calculating the distribution of farmworkers in the country at given times of the year. This approach also provides estimates of where farmworkers reside when they are not working in agriculture.

(4) Farmworkers are often foreign-born. A substantial proportion of farmworkers are not English-speaking or, if competent in English, do not read or write English. The largest proportion of foreign-born farmworkers are Mexican-origin and Spanish-speaking. Other foreign-born farmworkers are from Central America (and may speak native Indian languages) and Haiti.

Limitations of Census Data

Farmworkers have been an extremely difficult group to enumerate in past decennial censuses for all the reasons discussed above. Estimates prepared by groups working with farmworkers suggest that the 1990 census counted and identified only about 25-35 percent of the persons who are farmworkers at some time during the year (Kissam, 1991; Gabbard, et al., 1993).

Underidentification of farmworkers in the census stems from two different causes: undercount and nonidentification. Undercount problems stem from the difficulties of locating and enumerating farmworkers at the time of the census. Because of the nontraditional housing of farmworkers, geographic mobility, and limited English-language ability, farmworkers experience a high rate of total household omissions from the census. Also, some farmworkers and their families reside outside of the United States (primarily in Mexico) at the time of census enumeration.

Nonidentification of farmworkers occurs when there is a failure to identify correctly that someone is a farmworker. The census long-form questionnaire asks questions about occupation, but the questions pertain to the occupation at the time of the census or, for unemployed persons, for the last job. Many "farmworkers" are unemployed or are employed temporarily in nonagricultural work when the census is taken (on April 1 for the 1990 census). Analysis of the National Agricultural Worker Survey data suggests that more than 25 percent of farmworkers were working temporarily in some other occupation at the time of the 1990 census (Gabbard, et al., 1993).

To give one example, estimates from three alternative data sources place the number of farmworkers in California in the range of 560,000 to 720,000 for the period around 1990; the mid-range estimate by experts of the number of farmworkers—in terms of an occupational definition of "farmworker"—was about 640,000 (Gabbard, et al., 1993). The 1982 Census of Agriculture reported 980,000 farmworkers in California. As reported in the 1990 census, however, there was a count of 182,000 farmworkers, or about 25-32 percent of the alternative estimates. Using the mid-range estimate of 640,000, the census count underidentified the number of farmworkers by about 72 percent.

Persons reported as farmworkers in the decennial census also suffer from sample bias. The census collects data on persons who reported that they were farmworkers at the time of the census. These farmworkers tend to be those who are employed on a regular basis throughout the year, who work permanently in agriculture. Such permanent workers tend to be English-speaking and socially and economically better off. The portrait of farmworkers, as pictured in the census, does not give an accurate portrait of people or their families who work as farmworkers.

Although more research on the problems of differential undercount and nonidentification of farmworkers in the census would be helpful, it is difficult to see how the decennial census could be improved to provide an accurate count or description of farmworkers. To make an improved count, three changes would be needed: (1) to canvass farmworkers through the crop seasons, (2) to ask retrospective questions on job and residence history, and (3) to expand dramatically the intensity of effort to locate farmworkers and interview them in their native languages. It would not be cost effective to design the census, with its national focus and attempted coverage of the entire population, for this purpose, as compared to other alternatives such as special sample surveys. Moreover, a census would provide a count at one point in time and would lack the up-to-date estimates that might be obtained from improved intercensal estimates.

If alternative estimates of the farmworker population could be made, for small areas and for intercensal periods, federal and state farmworker programs could rely on alternative data for funding allocations and for assigning program resources. Farmworker groups and federal and state agencies working with farmworkers might explore the possibility of using sample surveys and administrative records to improve small-area data on farmworkers and their dependents. One possible way to obtain intercensal information on farmworkers is outlined below.

A National Sample Survey

The prior discussion leads to two propositions. First, the decennial census cannot provide reliable counts of the farmworker population. The census takes place at one point in time (when many farmworkers are not working in agriculture). The census count could not be redesigned to include a job and residence history (questions that would be needed in order to estimate the distribution and size of the farmworker population). High-quality data on farmworkers require more expensive canvassing and personal interviewing (in several languages) than can ordinarily be achieved in the census. Second, the number and characteristics of the farmworker population change substantially over time. More frequent intercensal estimates of the farmworker population are needed in order to provide well-targeted program resources. The census cannot provide these estimates.

To remedy this situation and to decrease the inappropriate reliance of federal allocations for farmworkers on the census, one proposal would be to initiate a national sample survey of farmworkers, in conjunction with statistical modeling for small-area estimates. An integrated program of surveys and statistical modeling would:

- estimate the program-eligible seasonal and migrant farmworker population for each state on an annual basis to improve resource allocation;
- describe the characteristics of the farmworker population and their dependents for each state to improve program planning and evaluation; and

• estimate the farmworker population for small areas by statistical modeling on a periodic basis to improve the targeting of programs and resource allocation.

Mines (1993) has outlined an integrated approach to annual intercensal estimates for the farmworker population. The approach would involve adjusting a
sample survey on farmworkers to two benchmarks: (1) crops and livestock
workers and (2) fishing, food processing, and forest products workers. Farm and
livestock workers are already covered in the Quarterly Agricultural Labor Survey, sponsored by the Department of Agriculture. The Quarterly Agricultural
Labor Survey provides quarterly employment estimates for 17 states with the
vast majority of the nation's food production and processing.[5] Only a small
proportion of workers in the fishing, food processing, and forest products industry are farmworkers; these industries provide data through the quarterly unemployment insurance reports for estimating employment levels. As a first observation, required benchmark data exist for adjusting survey results to national
estimates of farmworkers.

A national sample survey of farmworkers and their characteristics, including their industry of employment, could be combined with employment benchmark data to produce accurate estimates of the total population of farmworkers
in each region and state and an estimate of dependents in each state on an annual
basis.

The design of a national sample survey of farmworkers would build on the
experience of the surveys of migrant and seasonal farmworkers over the past
decade. There are an estimated 3.25 million farmworkers in the nation, including about 2.25 million workers in crop agriculture, another 500,000 livestock
workers, and about 500,000 in nonfarm sectors. Workers would be sampled
through employers on a periodic basis throughout the year to avoid seasonality
issues. The interviews would be conducted away from the workplace in the
native languages of the farmworkers.

A regionally stratified areal probability sample would involve samples in
about 300 counties, with approximately 725 respondents per state per year for
the 17 states with the bulk of farmworkers. This design would need approximately 20,000 interviews per year. Estimates for the remaining 33 states could
be made by grouping states with similar weather and crops, using smaller sample
sizes in the aggregated areas.

Some federal programs, such as the migrant education program, require
information on ex-farmworkers. To meet these program requirements in an cost-
effective manner, follow-up interviews could be conducted on a subsample of
initial interviews: 8,000 follow-up interviews would provide annual estimates
on ex-farmworkers for 11 agricultural regions of the country.

Mines (1993) estimated that there would be an annual cost of $6 million for
a survey program such as the one outlined above. The cost estimates include the

costs of sampling lists, conducting the annual sample survey, improving the Quarterly Agricultural Labor Survey and extending it to Puerto Rico, and adjusting the survey estimates for industry employment benchmarks.

Not included in the cost estimates is the cost of a third stage of the program to provide small-area estimates. Annual state estimates of the number and characteristics of farmworkers and their dependents could rely on statistical modeling to estimate small-area data. Although no specific proposals are available on ways to make these estimates, data from the Census of Agriculture (including information on crops and employment levels) may offer a suitable context for estimating, at least once every 5 years, the number and characteristics of farmworkers and their dependents for counties and rural program areas. Annual estimates for similar small areas could be made by assuming annual changes for states and then prorating the changes by assuming the geographic distribution estimated with Census of Agriculture data. Such small-area estimates would have two great attractions compared to decennial census data: they would be more accurate about numbers and characteristics and they could be revised more frequently.

NOTES

[1]Different branches of the armed services vary in their approach to local-level estimates of the QMA population. The description in this appendix is the approach taken by the Marine Corps and Navy (Navy Personnel Research and Development Center, 1987).

[2]Source: Extracted from U.S. Bureau of the Census, "Estimates of Median Four-Person Family Income by State, 1974-1989." *Current Population Reports Technical Paper 61*, January 1992.

[3]March 1990 CPS income estimates were published in a report entitled, "Money Income and Poverty Status in the United States: 1989," Series P-60, No. 168.

[4]Income data from the 1990 decennial census for 1989 became available in 1992 for updating the evaluation of the state median income estimates.

[5]The 17 states with the bulk of farmworkers are Alaska, Arizona, California, Florida, Hawaii, Michigan, Minnesota, New Mexico, New York, North Carolina, Oklahoma, Oregon, Pennsylvania, Texas, Virginia, Washington, and Wisconsin.

REFERENCES

Bureau of Labor Statistics
  1994   *Local Area Unemployment Statistics.* Washington, D.C.: U.S. Department of Labor.
Committee on National Statistics
  1989   *Small-Area Estimates for Military Personnel Planning: Report of a Workshop.* Washington, D.C.: National Academy Press.

Gabbard, S., E. Kissam, and P.L. Martin
    1993   The impact of migrant travel patterns on the undercount of Hispanic farm workers. Pp.
            207-245 in *Proceedings of the 1993 Research Conference on Undercounted Ethnic Popu-
            lations*. Bureau of the Census. Washington, D.C.: U.S. Department of Commerce.
Kissam, E.
    1991   Out in the Cold: Causes and Consequences of Missing Farmworkers in the 1990 Census.
            July. La Cooperative Campesina de California, Sacramento, Calif.
Mines, R.
    1993   Estimation and Description of Farmworkers by State: An Integrated Approach. U.S.
            Department of Labor, Washington, D.C.
Navy Personnel Research and Development Center
    1987   Estimating the Youth Population Qualified for Military Service. E.W. Curtis et al. Au-
            gust. Personnel Research and Development Center, San Diego, Calif.

J

Content and Quality of Federal and State Administrative Records

The Bureau of the Census has established an Administrative Record Information System (ARIS) (for more information on ARIS, see Gates and Palacios, 1993) that provides current information about the content, nature, and availability of over 60 federal administrative record systems and more than 400 state systems.

Table J.1 summarizes the subject content (population) available from a selected set of federal administrative records. These files are comprehensive in their coverage for specific universes and, in total, are estimated to or are likely to include most if not all of the population usually enumerated in the census (excluding the homeless and the institutional populations that can be obtained from other administrative records). These files would play important roles in any census activities involving administrative records.

Not included in this summary are a number of special files with restricted universes, e.g., Veterans Administration files (disability and education files), Office of Personnel Management, and the Indian Health Service, which may have some utility but lack the broad scope and appeal for present purposes.

FEDERAL FILES

The federal files summarized in Table J.1 include:

(1) *Internal Revenue Service (IRS) Individual Master File.* This is essentially the information available on each individual income tax return (1040). Furthermore, matching to other information returns—1099s, W-2s, and other

IRS documents—would provide links to employers and place of work and considerably increase population coverage.

(2) *Master Beneficiary Record and the Supplemental Security Record of the Social Security Administration (SSA).* Provides some income items not always reported in IRS returns as well as information for many nonfilers. Monthly benefit amounts for Social Security recipients and Supplemental Security Income (for very low income recipients only) are included.

(3) *Numident File (SSA).* This is the basic file of Social Security numbers (SSNs) assigned. Information obtained from application for SSN (the SS-5) form. This is the key file for finding an individual's SSN and for other matching and linking purposes.

(4) *Summary Earnings File (SSA).* This is where individual earnings received under covered employment are posted and maintained as a permanent record for computing Social Security benefit entitlements.

(5) *Health Insurance Master Entitlement File (HCFA).* This is the "medicare" file and provides comprehensive coverage for those 65 years and older.

Some content issues (even for the limited amount available):

Address: Mailing address with major overlap with home address. It's been estimated that 10-20 percent of IRS addresses on individual tax returns may not be the address of residence. Work with information documents may reduce this percentage considerably. Similarly, addresses of beneficiaries include many financial institutions, but it may be possible to obtain home addresses from the Health Care Financing Administration (HCFA) files. There is the further issue of reference date of address relative to census day.

For census purposes the ability to geocode addresses to the smallest lands of geography is paramount, and this ability will be affected by the nature of addresses. Research carried out by the staff of the population division of the Census Bureau using a 1-in-1,000 sample of the 1988 individual income tax file (Form 1040) informs us on this aspect of the problem. Specifically, the results showing the types of addresses in the IRS files were as follows: city style, 81.3%; rural routes, 9.0%; and P.O. boxes, 7.7%.

The percentages varied significantly by state, with 9 states having 90 percent or greater city-style addresses, and at the other extreme, 6 states with less than 50 percent of city-style type. Furthermore, less than half the counties had such addresses in excess of 50 percent. Continuing research at the Census Bureau suggested that TIGER/Address Control File (i.e., TIGER update with the 1990 Census Address Control File) should be able to code 64.4 percent of all IRS addresses (Form 1040) in the United States. About 9 percent are not codable because of rural routes, 8 percent P.O. boxes, 2 percent for other reasons; and 17 percent were potentially codable but not coded mainly because of street misspellings, bad abbreviations, or miskeying. Improved address standardization should reduce these problems to a minimum. Present work on enhancing TIGER and proposals for developing and maintaining a continuous updated master address file (MAF) should overcome present shortcomings due to the nature of addresses and in the coding systems (see Schneider, 1992; Sater, 1992, 1993).

Race: Uncertain quality and poor coverage especially for new birth cohorts. Before 1980, SSA obtained only three categories: white, black, and other. After 1980, the SS-5 calls for 5 categories: white (non-Hispanic), black (non-Hispanic), Hispanic, Asian and Pacific Islanders, American Indian, or Alaskan Native. Furthermore, in recent years, race is not provided for those applying for SSN for their children at birth using the birth record. Overall, race is not reported in the SSA files as follows:

Current beneficiaries (approximately 42 million)	1.5%
Supplemental Security Income (SSI) recipients (6 million)	3.3%
Wage earners (130 million)	3.0%
Social Security numbers issued 1980-1991 (90 million)	15.2%

Self-reporting, third-party reporting (birth and death records for example), and consistency of reporting over time also affect comparability of data between and within various records systems.

Relationship and household composition: Ability to reconstruct households and family composition from the records requires considerable research.

Occupation: Not clear on comparability with census classifications.

Industry and class of work: Presumably available from employer's name and employer identification number (EIN), but reference time not clear.

Note again that the summary is based on information extracted from the Census Bureau ARIS file. Discussions with program administrators may refine or modify some of the entries.

In general, not too much is known about the quality, consistency, and comparability of the various subject items in administrative records. A priori expectations vary between systems and particular characteristics. For example, income data from IRS records, age (date of birth) from birth records, or earning information from the Summary Earnings Record would be expected to be most accurate—in fact they represent standards against which we evaluate accuracy of reporting of these items in other systems. Addresses of persons receiving benefits also falls into this category, except, as noted earlier, mailing addresses do not necessarily reflect addresses of residence. Much research and evaluation would be required to fully understand the quality, including consistency and comparability, of other information in this federal record system.

STATE FILES

A summary of the content status of various state administrative record systems is provided in Table J.2. Twelve systems are summarized ranging from the broad (perhaps comprehensive) coverage of state income tax files and driver's license records to the more limited universe of birth records and probation and parolee files. Not all states have record systems covering the types of programs indicated, and a large number of program agencies failed to respond to this survey. In general, state programs and their files are much more limited than the federal system in the percentage of the population covered.

In terms of content, census-type information (long form) is available on only a very limited basis and in many cases only partially reported. Name, age, sex, and address (mail or residence) are almost universally available. Most of the other items are infrequently included, although income is reported most of the time on five record systems (income tax, AFDC, food stamps, unemployment insurance, and worker's compensation), but little is known on available detail or comparability with census data.

As stated, although little is known specifically about the quality (loosely defined) of the individual record items, the Census Bureau survey did attempt to elicit information from file managers on what is known about the quality of its data. Table J.3 provides an accuracy assessment of the state record systems and summarizes survey responses to a series of questions designed to inform on quality aspects of the files. The table shows how many program managers answered "yes" to such questions as to whether studies were carried out relative to record and file accuracy, comparability, and other type studies. The survey did not ask for the results of the studies, but a "yes" response presumes that such information should be forthcoming from the originating agencies (see Figure J.1).

REFERENCES

Gates, G.W., and H.L. Palacios
   1993   ARIS: an administrative records information resource for statisticians. Pp. 189-193 in *1993 Proceedings of the Government Statistics Section.* Alexandria, Va.: American Statistical Association.

Sater, D.
   1992   Geographic Coding Research—Types of Addresses on Income Tax Returns. Memorandum to J. Knott dated February 6. Population Division, Bureau of the Census, U.S. Department of Commerce, Washington, D.C.

   1993   *Geographic Coding of Administrative Records—Past Experience and Current Research.* Technical Working Paper No. 2. Population Division, Bureau of the Census. Washington, D.C.: U.S. Department of Commerce.

Schneider, P.J.
   1992   Year 2000 Census Research Administrative Records Geographic Coding Research. Memoranda to S. Miskura dated June 8, June 15, and June 29. Population Division, Bureau of the Census, U.S. Department of Commerce, Washington, D.C.

TABLE J.1 Content of Selected Federal Administrative Records (all files except the decennial census contain Social Security numbers)

Census Subjects (population only)	IRS (including information documents)	Social Security Files			HCFA Health Insurance Master Record
		Master Beneficiary Record	Numident File	Summary Earning Record	
Name	x	x	x	x	x
Address	x	x	—	—	x
Relationship and/or household composition	(partial)	—	—	—	—
Sex	—	x	x	x	x
Race (15 categories)	—	w, b, other	(2)	(2)	w, b, other
Age	(1) (primary taxpayer)	x	x	—	x
Marital status	x	x	—	—	—
Spanish (4 categories)	—	Surname in 5 states	(2)	Spanish	—
State or country of birth	—	—	x	—	—
Citizenship	—	—	—	—	—
Year of immigration	—	—	—	—	—
School enrollment	—	—	—	—	—
Level of education	—	—	—	—	—
Ancestry/ethnic origin	—	—	—	—	—
Place of residence (5 years ago)	—	—	—	—	—
Language spoken at home	—	—	—	—	—
Ability to speak English	—	—	—	—	—
Military service/veteran status	—	—	—	—	—
Disability	(1)	x (if receiving disability benefits)	x (if receiving disability benefits)	x (if disabled)	x (if disabled before age 65)

	Individual returns: 9-12 months Information returns: 12-15 months	Updated daily	Updated daily	Updated weekly	Updated daily
Children ever born	—	—	—	—	—
Labor force/employment/ work experience	—	—	—	—	—
Place of work	(3)	—	—	—	—
Commuting items	—	—	—	—	—
Occupation	x	—	—	—	—
Industry	(3)	—	—	—	—
Class of worker	(3)	—	—	—	—
Income (gross)	x	—	—	—	—
Income—wage/salary self-employment, farm	x	—	—	covered earnings	—
Income—Social Security, pensions, other retirement	x	monthly benefits	—	—	—
Income—public assistance, etc.	—	SSI	—	—	—
Income—dividend/interest, etc.	x	—	—	—	—
Income—all other	x	—	—	—	—
Timing/availability	Individual returns: 9-12 months Information returns: 12-15 months	Updated daily	Updated daily	Updated weekly	Updated daily

Notes: x indicates content item available in the record system; — indicates content item is not available in the record system.

(1) Indication of +65; Indication of blindness.

(2) Numbers issued before 1980 - white, black, other; after 1980 - white (non-Hispanic), black (non-Hispanic), Asian, American Indian or Alaskan Native, and Hispanic; race and Spanish not available for those obtaining SSN at birth, an option available starting in 1990.

(3) Employer's name and EIN; last or current employer.

Source: Administrative Records Information System, Program and Policy Development Office, Bureau of the Census.

TABLE J.2 Content of Twelve Major Administrative Record Systems
Maintained by 52 Jurisdictions (50 states, the District of Columbia, and
Puerto Rico)

Information	Birth Records	Death Records	Income Tax Records	Auto Registration	Driver's License Records
Reporting cases	45	45	31	34	40
Eligible cases	52	52	43	52	52
Name	45	44	30	33	40
SSN	14	41	26	9	32
Date of birth	43	44	4	9	40
Sex	44	44	1	4	39
Marital status	25	43	21	0	0
Race	43	44	0	0	13
Hispanic origin	38	39	0	0	5
Mail address	32	12	28	25	32
Residence address	32	28	12	23	37
Other geograph.	45	44	29	31	39
Place of birth	38	41	0	1	2
Phone	1	0	8	0	2
Income	0	0	29	0	0
Occupation	10	32	2	0	0
Education	25	37	0	0	0
Health	33	7	1	1	10

Note: Each column indicates the number of jurisdictions, out of 52, that maintain content
items in the particular record system. The total column displays the total number of major
state systems containing the content item (the maximum number in the column is 624, if all
jurisdictions maintain all the content items in every major record system).

Source: Administrative Records Information System, Program and Policy Development
Office, Bureau of the Census.

AFDC Records	Food Stamp Records	Unemp. Insurance Records	Worker's Comp. Records	Parollee Records	Probation Records	Prisoner Records	Total
29	31	41	32	32	30	42	432
51	51	52	52	51	45	52	605
29	30	41	32	32	30	42	428
29	29	34	28	25	23	36	326
29	30	33	30	32	29	42	365
29	29	34	31	31	30	40	356
19	16	9	18	24	19	38	232
26	25	32	3	30	29	41	286
22	21	26	0	23	24	34	232
22	23	34	26	14	15	16	279
20	18	18	22	18	15	29	272
22	24	34	25	25	26	37	381
6	3	2	0	19	17	35	164
20	20	31	15	9	7	12	125
28	29	30	25	8	6	4	159
5	3	16	23	13	10	20	134
17	13	17	2	23	19	33	186
13	12	8	21	14	15	22	157

TABLE J.3 Accuracy Assessment of 12 Major State Record Systems, 1992

System Type	Record Accuracy	File Accuracy	Data Comparability Multiple Sources	Data Comparability Similar Collection	Statistical Studies	Samples	Eligible States	Control Number of States Responding
Birth	35	20	12	31	41	31	52	45
Death	26	14	9	27	44	27	52	45
Income tax	6	11	2	1	20	19	43	31
Auto registration	4	0	2	2	11	10	52	34
Driver's licenses	6	2	4	4	15	11	52	40
AFDC	16	7	9	9	15	24	51	29
Food stamps	16	7	12	8	15	25	51	31
Unemployment	22	10	10	13	20	20	52	41
Workers' compensation	9	4	1	6	16	8	52	32
Parole	12	6	4	6	18	12	51	32
Probation	9	7	7	3	18	12	45	30
Prisoner	12	10	5	12	29	17	52	42

Note: Each column indicates the number of jurisdictions with particular accuracy assessments out of 52 jurisdictions.

Source: Administrative Records Information System, Program and Policy Development Office, Bureau of the Census.

b. Record Accuracy

(1) Have any research studies or audits been completed assessing the extent of missing data within a record or on the accuracy of the data on the file?

1 ☐ Yes – *Specify and provide a copy, if available* ↘

2 ☐ No
3 ☐ Don't know

(2) Are any research studies or audits currently being planned or in progress assessing the extent of missing data within a record or accuracy of the data on the file?

1 ☐ Yes – *Specify what is being done and by whom (name, address, telephone number)* ↘

2 ☐ No
3 ☐ Don't know

FORM ARIS-1 (6-9-92)

FIGURE J.1 Administrative File Information Request, Extract of Survey Questions from Section D, Quality of Data. Source: Administrative File Information Request, Form ARIS-1, Program and Policy Development Office, Bureau of the Census.

Section D. CURRENT DESCRIPTION OF FILE – Continued

5c. File Accuracy

(1) Have any research studies or audits been done to assess the completeness of the file? That is, have any studies been done to measure the file's population coverage?

1 ☐ Yes – *Specify what studies have been done and provide a copy of the available documentation* ↗

2 ☐ No
3 ☐ Don't know

(2) Are any research studies currently being planned or in progress to assess the completeness of the file?

1 ☐ Yes – *Specify what is being done and by whom (name, address, phone number)* ↗

2 ☐ No
3 ☐ Don't know

d. Data Comparability

(1) If the file is derived from multiple sources (e.g., branch offices reporting to a state office), have any quality control studies been done to determine if source agencies are supplying comparable data (i.e., are the data from all sources referencing the same time frame, providing the same level of accuracy, etc.)?

1 ☐ Yes, such studies have been done – *Specify by whom and when such studies were done, and provide a copy, if available* ↗

_____

_____

_____

2 ☐ No
3 ☐ Don't know

(2) Have any studies been done to determine how data from your state compare with similar data collected in other states?

1 ☐ Yes – *Please specify when such studies were done and who did them. Please provide a copy of any pertinent documentation, if available* ↗

_____

_____

_____

_____

2 ☐ No
3 ☐ Don't know

FORM ARIS-1 (6-9-92)

Section D. CURRENT DESCRIPTION OF FILE – Continued

5e. (1) Describe any statistical studies which have been done using this file: ↗

a ☐☐ Don't know of any statistical studies
b ☐☐ No statistical studies have been done

(2) Have samples been drawn from this file?

a ☐ Yes – *Please describe the sample file (e.g., size of sample, whether sample file is an extract or entire data set, intended use, etc.)* ↗

b ☐☐ No – *Skip to question D6*
c ☐☐ Don't know – *Skip to question D6*

(3) What kinds of statistical analyses have been done using these samples?

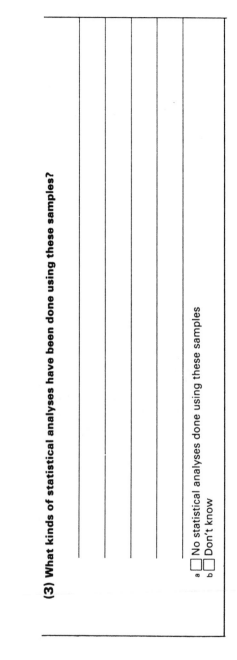

a ☐ No statistical analyses done using these samples

b ☐ Don't know

K
Quality of Current Data on Race and Ethnicity

REQUIREMENTS FOR RACE AND ETHNICITY DATA SINCE 1970

In recent times, requirements for race and ethnicity data have changed to meet new demands for federal laws and to adjust to a changing population. For racial minorities and persons of Hispanic origin, such data have been required for a range of federal and state laws pertaining to political representation and equal opportunity. For the 1970, 1980, and 1990 censuses, the Census Bureau devised specific research, testing, and evaluation of items related to race and ethnicity. This was consistent not only with new policy needs, but also because the 1970 census was the start of the use of self-identification on the questionnaire. During this period, the Census Bureau engaged in extensive outreach programs to improve the participation of racial and ethnic minorities in the decennial census. One other factor also increased attention to race and ethnicity data: the removal of national origin restrictions on immigration with the passage of amendments to the 1965 Immigration and Nationality Act resulted in the growth of previously smaller ethnic groups, especially among Asians and Hispanics.

These factors taken together resulted in greater visibility of racial and ethnic groups in several ways. First, there has been a growing number of racial minorities and people of Hispanic origin. Minorities accounted for 1 of 4 U.S. resi-

---

Much of the discussion in this appendix is taken from papers by McKenney et al. (1993) and Cresce et al. (1992).

dents in 1990 and are projected to be 1 in 3 for the 2000 census. Second, there is a growing diversity within minority groups by nativity, national origin, and socioeconomic status. Finally, there is a greater recognition that people have multiple racial and ethnic identities.

COLLECTION OF RACE AND ETHNICITY DATA IN THE CENSUS

Beginning with the 1970 census, the Census Bureau provided data on race and Hispanic origin to meet several statutory requirements, enacted in recent decades. For all practical purposes, the Voting Rights Act of 1965 and as amended requires the director of the Census Bureau to provide decennial census data, including race and Hispanic origin, for bilingual election determinations. Public Law 94-311 (15 U.S.C. 1516a) requires the collection of Hispanic origin data in censuses and surveys since 1976. Race and Hispanic origin data are provided to the states for legislative redistricting (Public Law 94-171) and to the Department of Justice for the review of redistricting plans. The Census Bureau collects and tabulates race and Hispanic-origin data in compliance with the federal Statistical Directive 15.[1] In addition, the Census Bureau provides race and ethnicity data to other government agencies for their use in meeting statutory requirements and program needs.

In the past 30 years, the Census Bureau has placed increasing efforts on providing detailed and comprehensive classification of race and ethnicity. For the 1970, 1980, and 1990 censuses, additional categories for race and ethnicity were included in the questionnaires. The Census Bureau implemented research and testing programs and extensive consultations on race, Hispanic origin, and ancestry items in response to requests from different groups and laws in response to growing federal data needs primarily related to civil rights compliance.

The Census Bureau has utilized an evolutionary process for developing these categories. In terms of understanding Hispanic status, it introduced a Spanish-origin item on the long form in the 1970 census that was later refined in 1980 and 1990 for the short form. With respect to racial status, the 1980 and 1990 censuses became more inclusive of the Asian and Pacific Islander groups, and the American Indian and Alaskan Native populations. The coding of write-ins for the "other race" category was introduced in 1980 and 1990 to obtain data on smaller groups and to improve the quality of data. In addition, the 1980 census introduced an ancestry item to replace the "place of birth of parents" question that had been on the census since 1870. The question was designed to reflect a more general ethnic identity into the third and later generations. Use of these items for field tests and actual census enumeration has been accompanied by outreach and promotion programs to minority communities.

The Census Bureau has invested considerable resources in editing and coding responses into the current categories. Entries in "other race" responses numbered 9.8 million in 1990. Write-ins from the race item numbered over 300 separate race responses and approximately 600 different American Indian tribes. The Hispanic-origin item elicited 70 different origin write-in responses, and the ancestry item, an open-ended item, elicited over 600 ancestry groups. Use of a computer-automated coding operation in the 1990 census greatly improved the quality of operation in terms of decreased clerical errors and reduced costs. Even with this automated system, however, the Census Bureau encountered difficulties in aggregating some 250,000 race write-ins that indicated mixed racial or ethnic identities or nationalities and write-ins without a clear racial connotation.

The 1990 census produced unprecedented amounts of data on racial groups and people of Hispanic origin, documenting the transformation of the United States to a multiethnic and multiracial society with 1 of 4 being black, Hispanic, Asian and Pacific Islander, or American Indian and Alaskan Native. It also documented the growth of new immigrants with significant impact on the Asian and Hispanic populations. Of the total foreign-born population, nearly 44 percent arrived between 1980 and 1990. One-third of population growth for this period was due to immigrants. If current levels of immigration continue—with the latest projections of 880,000 net immigrants a year—another 10 million or so immigrants will be added to the U.S. population by the year 2000.

The Census Bureau's evaluation of data on race and ethnicity from the 1990 census revealed that broad generalizations about the accuracy of the race and ethnicity data are not appropriate. Various statistical measures suggested that the overall quality of the data was good; however, the evaluations also showed persistent problems related to question wording and respondent's understanding of the questions. These problems are of major concern because: (1) they have a substantial impact on the quality of the data for small geographical areas and for such relatively smaller racial and ethnic groups as American Indians; (2) these data are used for drawing political boundaries for very small geographical areas and funding allocations; (3) there is some evidence that a higher proportion of the population had difficulties with answering the race and ethnicity questions in 1990 than in 1980 (Cresce et al., 1992:6); and (4) some studies suggest that the current concepts may not be the most appropriate for a changing population (Hirschman, 1993; Lieberson, 1993).

ALLOCATION RATES

If a respondent did not provide answers to each question to the census, special procedures were made by the Census Bureau to impute (or allocate) the response. Not all items were allocated, including ancestry. The Hispanic-origin item continued to have the highest allocation rate (10 percent) of any item collected on the short form (see Table K.1). By contrast, the rate was much lower for the race item at 2.0 percent. The allocation rates for the 100 percent items for 1990, particularly for Hispanic origin, were significantly higher than those for the 1980 census. The higher rates were due partially to the decision, based on budget limitations, to cut back on field follow-up for the short-form questionnaires that failed field content edit. The Census Bureau studies, however, show that the national figures hide great variability in the allocation rate for race and Hispanic origin, and that the variability for the national average is likely to be clustered in certain localities. For example, 1990 census allocation rates were substantially higher, above 20 percent, for both race and Hispanic origin in some census tracts of Los Angeles County. Furthermore, the variability has a great effect on some population groups. For instance, over 62 percent of black Mexicans were allocated in the census (del Pinal, 1994). These relatively high allocation rates can have potentially adverse effects on small-area analysis such as those on residential segregation.

All major race groups, except American Indians, Eskimos, and Aleuts, experienced increases in short-form allocations. The "other race" category experienced the highest rate of computer allocations in 1990 and the largest increase from the 1980 rate (see Table K.2).

The high nonresponse to the ancestry and Hispanic-origin items is also of concern. It may in part reflect respondents' perception that the race, Hispanic origin, and ancestry questions are asking for the same information and may lead some respondents to not answer all three items. Some researchers have suggested that the Census Bureau explore ways of combining these questions to reduce nonresponse rates and perhaps to reduce inconsistent reporting in these items as well (Farley, 1993). Efforts to shorten the census long form might also force consideration of a combined question if the census is still to gather ancestry data.

MEASURES OF INCONSISTENCY

Measures of inconsistency also provided evidence, however, of some misreporting in certain race and Hispanic-origin categories and of moderate inconsistency in ancestry reporting. Persons identifying in the American Indian, other Asian and Pacific Islander and other race categories of the race item and in the other Hispanic category of the Hispanic-origin item showed high inconsistency rates in their responses to these items. This is of concern because these are the write-in categories for the race and Hispanic-origin items. It may indicate a need for the Census Bureau to further examine the presentation and instructions for the write-in entries on the race and Hispanic items and to better understand how respondents perceive and interpret these questions.

The levels of inconsistency are especially important and of concern for the American Indian population because of its relatively small size and the importance of the data to develop and fund programs for American Indian tribal and Alaska native village governments. In addition to this inconsistent reporting, instances of Asian Indians reporting themselves or their children as American

Indians and possible overreporting of Cherokees indicate that further research is needed on reporting on response to the American Indian category of the race item. The growth of the American Indian population at a rate greater than can be explained by natural increase and improved methods makes it one of the more important populations for studying how and why persons change their racial identities over time.

The level of inconsistent reporting in the other Asian Pacific Islander, other race, and other Hispanic categories is of importance, because it seems to reflect reporting problems among immigrant populations that have grown rapidly during the past two decades. Immigrants are projected to represent ever increasing percentages of the U.S. population. A thorough understanding of how these respondents interpret and respond to other race and Hispanic-origin questions is therefore essential to the Census Bureau's ability to devise and implement questions that provide high-quality data on these groups.

With some exceptions, it seems to be foreign-born people and both foreign- and native-born Hispanics that had the highest levels of inconsistent reporting on the race questions. Foreign-born people showed considerably more inconsistency on the race item than native-born ones. White foreign-born people had only moderate consistency in race reporting, perhaps due to the greater ancestral diversity in the white racial group. By contrast, native-born people had the greatest inconsistency reporting in the Hispanic-origin items.

Both foreign-born and native-born Hispanics overreported in the other race and other Asian Pacific Islanders categories of the race item, but underreported in the white, black, and Asian and Pacific Islander categories. Shifting, largely by Hispanics, between the other race and white categories led to an underreporting of the white population and overreporting of the other race population in the census. Over 97 percent of people reporting in the other category were of Hispanic origin.

Inconsistent reporting by the foreign-born and Hispanic populations may in part reflect unfamiliarity with or different interpretations and meanings of the concepts of race and Hispanic origin. Both race and Hispanic origin are subjective or culturally specific items that lack a universal definition, and foreign-born people may have a different understanding of these concepts. For Hispanics, inconsistent reporting might also reflect ambiguities arising from the listing of several sociocultural or national origin groups in the race item. Some respondents may try to indicate identification with a Hispanic national origin group comparable to other groups specified in the race item. Preliminary findings from cognitive research by the Census Bureau indicates that foreign-born Hispanics, foreign-born Asian and Pacific Islanders, and foreign-born blacks view the concept of race differently from the native U.S. population. For example, foreign-born Hispanics and foreign-born Asians and Pacific Islanders view race in terms of national origin or language.

LIMITATIONS OF THE RACE AND
HISPANIC ORIGIN QUESTIONS

The race and Hispanic-origin questions continue to be confusing to some census respondents. Information provided to census staff in the data collection stages (telephone inquires to the field and processing offices) indicated that a substantial number of people did not understand how to answer the race question. Inquiries about the race question came from persons who: (1) were confused by the listing of sociocultural groups and wanted to provide an ethnic group (e.g., Polish or Jamaican); (2) were Hispanic and did not understand the response categories; and (3) were of mixed parentage or were the parents of interracial children and wanted to report a multiple race.

LIMITATIONS OF THE ANCESTRY QUESTION

The ancestry question provided data of only moderate quality, in part because of its open-ended format. Unlike the race and Hispanic-origin items, people could identify more than one ancestry. Consistency between 1980 and 1990 in reporting in the general types of ancestry is evidence that the question worked reasonably well in 1990. However, consistency in reporting levels for specific ancestry groups deserves attention. Several ancestries used as examples in the instructions showed implausibly large increases over 1980, whereas ancestries dropped from the instructions decreased substantially. The most noted example was "English," which was used in 1980 but deleted in 1990. In terms of ranking, English was first in 1980 with 49,598,000 responses.[2] In 1990, it ranked third with 38,736,000 responses.[3] Similarly, "French" responses numbered 12,892,000 in 1980 when it was used as an example but fell to 10,320,000 in 1990 when it was not an example. "Cape Verdean" was a 1990 example that yielded 50,772 responses. This is in contrast to a count of 23,215 in 1980 when it was not an example. "Cajun" was an example for 1990 but not in 1980; the combined Acadian/Cajun response number in 1990 was 668,271. Unfortunately, there was no comparable figure for 1980 as these responses, deemed too few to warrant their own code, were coded as "French" in the Census Bureau's 1980 code list. Although there may be other reasons for these changes, such as increase or decrease in immigration and changes in coding procedures, such "example effects" must be of considerable concern if write-ins are to be used to capture groups not now listed (for example, Arabs) or to capture an identity that combines racial status and ancestry in one item.

This pattern of ancestry inconsistency reporting also reflected high rates of intermarriage and of geographic and social mobility among people of European descent. Waters (1990) notes that European-origin groups have a great range of choices and options in how they choose to identify when there are a wide range of options and the specific ethnic identification may be situational and flexible.

The examples presented on the census questionnaire can influence the reporting, as can general social conditions about favorable or unfavorable attitudes toward specific ethnic groups. With the high intermarriage rates for several Asian and Pacific Islander and Hispanic populations, these groups will also grow more important as the pool of people with identity options increases.

STRENGTHS OF THE RACE AND ANCESTRY QUESTIONS

Racial and ethnicity categories for 2000 and beyond may usher yet new ways of defining group identity as well as disadvantaged populations. The high rates of immigration, from both traditional and nontraditional sources of immigrants, and the increase of interracial unions and births in the last 20 years are the most visible alternate responses to the current race, Hispanic-origin, and ancestry items. The Census Bureau and other researchers initially assumed that these responses may suggest a lack of understanding of current race and ethnicity categories. Subsequent assumptions are that new immigrants and persons of multiple race or ancestry may have a different concept or lack of identification with these categories. Their socioeconomic characteristics also reflect these differences.

Research across different groups is instructive in this regard. Snipp's work (1989) on the 1980 American Indian population underscores the multiple and differential meanings of race. Although American Indians are not an immigrant group, they have a high rate of intermarriage. This group has witnessed a tremendous increase (beyond natural growth and an explanation of better coverage due to outreach programs) that is due to shifts in self-identification. Snipp differentiated three groups: (1) persons who identified as American Indian by race and ancestry (numbered 947,500), (2) persons identified as American Indian by race of multiple ancestry (numbered 269,700), and (3) persons who were not American Indian by race but claimed Indian ancestry (numbered 5,537,600). These groups differed in socioeconomic status and patterns of language. Snipp concluded that Americans of Indian descent were more similar to middle-class Americans and did not conform to a common perception of Americans Indians as a culturally distinct population of economically disadvantaged individuals. This common perception was more pertinent to people who consistently identified their race and ethnicity as American Indian. American Indians of multiple ancestry were a diverse group.

Utilizing race, Hispanic origin, and ancestry based on the 1990 public-use microdata samples, Farley (1994) concluded that there was a need to define populations by more than race. He classified 63 mutually exclusive categories by Hispanic origin, race, ancestry, and nativity. In a ranking of these groups by percent living in households with incomes below the poverty line, the top 10 groups included 4 that identified themselves as black by race, 4 as Hispanic origin, 1 American Indian, and 1 Vietnamese. In an examination of households of foreign-born people with incomes five times or more the poverty line, 6 identified as white by race and 4 as Asian. Native-born whites and native-born blacks fared less well than their foreign-born counterparts.

In the case of Hispanics, preliminary research by del Pinal (1992) based on the Current Population Survey explored the effects of various combinations of race and Hispanic-origin categories on the level of selected socioeconomic indicators. He found that Hispanics are nearly 10 percent of the white category and about 1.5 percent of all blacks. He argues that, on one hand, due to the relatively disadvantaged position of Hispanics, their inclusion in the white category tends to attenuate the difference between whites and other race categories on several important socioeconomic characteristics (e.g., labor force status, educational attainment, poverty level, family income) and that, at a minimum, Hispanics should be removed from the white category. On the other hand, the overlap between black and other numerically smaller race categories with Hispanic origin is small and, for now, does not adversely affect the analytical results of basic socioeconomic indicators.

The Census Bureau's analysis indicates that race and ethnicity are complex matters and not likely to be suitably enumerated with one or two questions. The analysis provides some evidence that the question might be more consistent with *some* respondents' concepts and self-perception, for example, by allowing respondents to identify with more than one race group; to report as multiracial; to treat "Hispanic" as equivalent to a race group; and to combine the race and Hispanic-origin items. At the same time, other respondents might find such changes less consistent with their concepts and self-perceptions. The implications of any such changes for providing data needed for legislative and programmatic purposes clearly require thorough research. In addition, because of the complexity of race and ethnicity, any proposed changes to these items requires consultation with affected groups and data users. Such consultation must occur concurrently with testing.

Testing of the race questions before the 1990 census showed that questions with write-in responses for subgroups within a category may produce data as reliable as that from questions with prespecified categories. Questions for write-in responses hold advantages in capturing groups not represented by the detailed categories of the race question. At the same time, benefits of write-in questions must be weighted against their higher processing costs. The Census Bureau's ability to process write-in data in a timely fashion should be considered.

Census Bureau evaluations have been confirmed by other data users. In recent years with the growth of new populations, Statistical Directive 15 has been questioned as being outdated and not reflecting the current and foreseeable population. New immigrants often identify themselves by national origin rather than major categories. Other populations of more than one race or ethnicity find it difficult to choose only one category. There is acknowledgment by federal agencies and other data users that some populations do not easily fit into existing categories or want to be reclassified from one category to another.

The House Subcommittee on Census, Statistics, and Postal Personnel held a set of hearings in 1993 on the federal standard noting the need for a review of the standards. In preparation for a review of the standard, the Office of Management and Budget requested the Committee on National Statistics to conduct a workshop of key stakeholders to articulate the issues. The workshop, held in February 1994, found that the current categories have broad usage beyond the federal statistical system and have become reified as absolute standards. And yet, many individuals do not readily identify with a single, broad, homogeneous, and mutually exclusive category used in standard classifications. Some prefer multicultural classifications and others prefer subcategories of the broader categories. Such findings are consistent with the Census Bureau's experience with stakeholders. Any revisions to the federal standard will require examination of the Census Bureau's collection, use, and presentation of race and ethnicity data, which are broader than that of most federal agencies. This is of particular importance as the census provides the benchmark for other federal data.

It seems clear that to ensure data of high quality and to identify race and ethnicity concepts that are appropriate for the changing racial and ethnic populations of the United States, the Census Bureau must conduct a comprehensive research and testing program for the 2000 census and establish an even more extensive long-range program of research and testing.

NOTES

[1]OMB Statistical Directive 15 has set forth the race and ethnicity standards for federal administrative and statistical reporting since 1977. Directive 15 acknowledges four racial groups (American Indian or Alaskan Native, Asian or Pacific Islander, Black, and White) and two ethnic categories (Hispanic Origin and Not of Hispanic Origin). OMB is currently in the process of reviewing the race and ethnicity classifications.

[2]This number includes people who indicate more than one ancestry.

[3]1980 figures are from U.S. Bureau of the Census, *1990 Census of the Population* Supplementary Report, "Ancestry of the Population by State." PC80-S1-10. Figures for 1990 are from U.S. Bureau of the Census, Ethnic and Hispanic Branch, Population Division, "1990 Detailed Ancestry Groups for States," CPH-L-97, a supplement to the 1990 CP-S-1-2, "Detailed Ancestry Groups for States."

REFERENCES

Cresce, A., S. Lapham, and S. Rolark
   1992   Preliminary Evaluation of Data from the Race and Ethnic Origin Questions in the 1990 Census. Paper presented at the annual meeting of the American Statistical Association, Boston.

del Pinal, J.
   1992   *Exploring Alternative Race-Ethnic Comparison Groups in Current Population Surveys.* Current Populations Reports, Special Studies, Series P23-182. Washington, D.C.: Bureau of the Census.
   1994   Social Science Principles: Forming Race-Ethnic Categories for Policy Analysis. Paper presented at the Workshop on Race and Ethnicity Classification: An Assessment of the Federal Standard for Race and Ethnicity Classification, February 17-18. Committee on National Statistics, National Research Council, Washington, D.C.

Farley, R.
   1993   Questions about Race, Spanish Origin and Ancestry: Findings from the Census of 1990 and Proposals for the Census of 2000. Testimony before the Subcommittee on Census, Statistics and Postal Personnel, Committee on Post Office and Civil Service, U.S. House of Representatives.
   1994   The Experience of Federal Agencies Measuring Race in Accord with Directive #15. Comments at the Workshop on Race and Ethnicity Classification: An Assessment of the Federal Standard for Race and Ethnicity Classification, February 17-18. Committee on National Statistics, National Research Council, Washington, D.C.

Hirschman, C.
   1993   How to measure ethnicity: an immodest proposal. Pp. 547-560 in *Challenges of Measuring an Ethnic World: Science, Politics and Reality.* Statistics Canada and Bureau of the Census, U.S. Department of Commerce. Washington, D.C.: U.S. Government Printing Office.

Lieberson, S.
   1993   The enumeration of ethnic and racial groups in the census: some devilish principles. Pp. 23-35 in *Challenges of Measuring an Ethnic World: Science, Politics and Reality.* Statistics Canada and Bureau of the Census, U.S. Department of Commerce. Washington, D.C.: U.S. Government Printing Office.

McKenney, N.C., Bennett, R. Harrison, and J. del Pinal
   1993   Evaluating Racial and Ethnic Reporting in the 1990 Census. Paper presented at the 1993 annual meeting of the American Statistical Association, San Francisco.

Snipp, C.M.
   1989   *American Indians: The First of This Land.* New York: Russell Sage Foundation.

U.S. General Accounting Office
   1993   *Census Reform: Early Outreach and Decisions Needed on Race and Ethnic Questions.* GAO/GGD-93-36. Washington, D.C.: U.S. Government Printing Office.

Waters, M.C.
   1990   *Ethnic Options: Choosing Identities in America.* Berkeley: University of California Press.

TABLE K.1 Comparative Allocation Rates of Population Questions Asked of Total Population (in percent)

Item	1980	1990
Sex	0.8	1.2
Marital status	1.3	2.0
Race	1.5	2.0
Age	2.9	2.4
Relationship	2.1	2.6
Hispanic origin	4.2	10.0

Source: U.S. General Accounting Office (1993).

TABLE K.2 Total Allocation Rates by Race for the United States: 1990 and 1980

Race	100 Percent (short form)		Sample (long form)	
	1990	1980	1990	1980
Total	2.0	1.5	1.2	1.5
White	1.7	1.3	1.0	1.5
Black	2.9	1.6	1.6	1.7
American Indian, Eskimo, Aleut	2.5	3.1	1.7	1.5
Asian and Pacific Islander	2.7	2.1	1.6	1.6
Other race	6.4	3.9	3.2	1.8

Source: Cresce et al. (1992).

Allocation Rates

This appendix describes the impact of nonresponse on the quality of the various questions in the 1990 census. Specifically, the following tables show allocation rates—the number of people or households (in terms of percentages) for which a specific question was not answered and a response for the missing value was created. The overall process of creating responses for missing values for census questions is referred to as "imputation," which consists of two major components: (1) *allocation*, in which missing values for individual items are filled in on the basis of other reported information for the person or household (or from other persons or households nearby with similar characteristics); and (2) *substitution*, in which *all* of the information for a person or a household is created (usually referred to as whole person or whole household substitution). Altogether about 1.6 million persons and 750,000 households were substituted in the 1990 census, adding about 0.8 percent to the overall imputation rate. Whole person or whole household substitution applies only to the processing of short-form items; in creating data files of responses to the long form, people or households in the long-form sample for whom no information is available are accounted for by reweighting the remaining sample cases.

Item nonresponse rates and allocation rates serve at least two important purposes: (1) to inform users about the quality of individual items as reflected in the rates and suggest caution in their use; and (2) to alert the Census Bureau to possible problems associated with specific items. The problems may reflect aspects of question wording or design, or respondent reluctance or inability to answer questions in particular areas, among other concerns.

ALLOCATION RATES FOR SHORT-FORM POPULATION ITEMS BY FORM TYPE

Table L.1 shows allocation rates for short-form population items for all household members, blacks, and Hispanics, separately for people receiving the short form ("100%") and people receiving the long form ("sample").[1] Rates are also shown for the "worst" 10 percent of census tracts in the country—worst in terms of those having the highest overall rates of allocation.

Tabulating allocation rates for items common to the short and long forms by type of form permits one to understand the impact of census processing and follow-up rules on nonresponse and allocation rates. Census procedures in 1990 called for questionnaires mailed back to processing offices to be reviewed and edited for consistency in reporting of related items and for missing or incomplete responses. Rules were established for determining whether a questionnaire "passed edit" and was moved along for processing, or "failed edit" and was set aside and scheduled for follow-up. For "failed edit" cases, census personnel in the various offices attempted to contact households by telephone, and when this failed or could not be done, they scheduled a field visit by enumerators to obtain the missing or otherwise incomplete information. For cost and other reasons, however, the rules specified that only a sample of "failed edit" short-form cases for which telephone contact was unsuccessful would be scheduled for follow-up. Thus, only 1 in 10 of the short-form questionnaires that failed edit were sent for follow-up, whereas essentially all long forms that failed edit were followed up. As a result, the items on the short form had substantially higher allocation rates than the same items appearing on the long form (see Table L.1).

The impact of this differential treatment of short and long forms (in terms of follow-up) is especially reflected in the allocation rates for Spanish origin overall and for all short-form population items for the worst 10 percent tracts. Thus, the allocation rate for Spanish origin was 10.5 percent of short forms but only 3.4 percent of long forms. The rate for Spanish origin in the worst 10 percent tracts was 19.0 percent of short forms but only 5.4 percent of long forms. Overall, allocation rates for the basic population items—namely age, sex, and race—averaged between 2 and 3 percent of short forms and 1 percent of long forms.

ALLOCATION RATES ON LONG FORMS BY RESPONSE TYPE

Table L.2 shows 1990 allocation rates for selected short-form and long-form population items for people in households that received the long form, by whether the household mailed back the form ("household respondent") or the form was obtained by an enumerator in the follow-up stage of census operations ("enumerator-filled"). (Enumerated-filled forms also include all forms obtained in the list/enumerate areas—see Appendix B.)

With few exceptions, allocation rates are substantially higher for forms obtained by enumerators than for forms filled out by the household. Household respondent allocation rates, however, are not "pure" rates, in that many partially completed questionnaires were given to enumerators for completion. Thus, the rates are lower than if they had been computed before item nonresponse follow-up. Unfortunately, information is not available on allocation rates before such follow-up. On the other hand, higher allocation rates for enumerator-filled questionnaires should not be unexpected because enumerators deal with reluctant populations, who failed to answer the census initially, perhaps after several attempts by census field personnel to collect the information. These results suggest that follow-up enumerators frequently have limited success in obtaining missing information.

ALLOCATION RATES ON LONG FORMS BY RACE AND GEOGRAPHIC RESIDENCE

Tables L.3 and L.4 show 1990 census allocation rates for selected short- and long-form population and housing items for people or households that received the long form, by race of the household head and type of geographic area of residence, respectively. Tables L.5 and L.6 show the same information for the worst 10 percent census tracts. Also, there are four tables for each of five selected states (Tables L.6-L.26), which show for each state equivalent information to that in Tables L.3-L.6. The five states are California, Illinois, Iowa, New York, and Tennessee. (Allocation rates in comparable race/ethnicity, geographic, and subject detail are available for all 50 states from the Census Bureau.) Overall, the rates shown in the accompanying tables are illustrative of the whole range of rates implicit in all census tabulations and data products.

The results indicate that allocation rates for long-form (sample) items, such as income, education, and employment, are generally higher than rates for the basic short-form (100%) items appearing on the long form. Whereas allocation rates for 100 percent items for the total population (see Table L.3) are between 1 and 3 percent, the rates for many sample items are between 5 and 10 percent, with an occasional item, such as property taxes, having a rate of over 10 percent. And in the worst cases—for example, in the worst 10 percent tracts—allocation rates in excess of 20 percent are not unusual.

The income item is of interest because of its pervasive use in many cross-tabulations and as an overall measure of economic well-being. Unlike the usual allocation rates that indicate the number of people or households (as a percent) for which a missing entry was allocated, the figures for income represent the number of people (as a percent) for whom a specified percentage of their total income was allocated. Thus, referring to Table L.3, one-half of one percent of the total population had less than 10 percent of their income allocated; 11.7 percent had 100 percent of their income allocated; and, adding across the 5 categories, 13.4 percent had some of their income allocated.[2]

REFERENCE

Citro, C.F., and G. Kalton, eds.
   1993   *The Future of the Survey of Income and Program Participation.*   Panel to Evaluate the
          Survey of Income and Program Participation, Committee on National Statistics, National
          Research Council. Washington, D.C.:   National Academy Press.

NOTES

[1]The rates for people receiving the short form include substitutions as well as allocations, which accounts for a fraction of the difference—0.8 percentage points on average—between the short-form and long-form allocation rates for short-form items.

[2]In terms of aggregate household income, Census Bureau staff estimate that 19 percent was allocated in the census. By comparison, 20 percent of aggregate household income is allocated in the March Current Population Survey, and 11 percent of total income is allocated in the Survey of Income and Program Participation (Citro and Kalton, 1993:Table 3-6).

TABLE L.1 Allocation Rates for Short-Form Population Items, 1990 Census, Total Population and Population in Worst 10 Percent Census Tracts, by Type of Form Received: Short-Form (100%) or Long Form (Sample)[a]

Item	Total		Black Non-Hispanic		Hispanic	
	100%	Sample	100%	Sample	100%	Sample
U.S. total						
Relationship	3.3	1.9	6.1	3.3	5.9	3.5
Sex	1.9	0.9	3.4	1.4	2.6	1.1
Race	2.6	1.1	3.4	1.3	9.4	4.3
Age	3.1	0.9	5.6	1.6	3.9	1.5
Marital status	3.1	1.4	5.9	2.2	5.7	2.7
Spanish origin	10.5	3.4	18.4	5.3	7.8	1.8
Worst 10 percent census tracts						
Relationship	8.5	3.8	8.7	4.1	9.8	5.0
Sex	5.1	1.3	5.2	1.4	4.6	1.4
Race	7.8	2.8	5.2	1.6	17.3	8.0
Age	7.9	1.9	8.2	2.1	6.5	2.1
Marital status	8.2	2.8	8.4	2.5	9.5	3.3
Spanish origin	19.0	5.4	23.1	6.8	12.6	2.5

Note: These allocation rates are based on a special tabulation of the 1990 census files and reflect the "final" disposition of each census item or category. They cover the household population only, excluding people in group quarters. The rates shown here may differ from rates shown in other tables of this report or in census publications because of differences in universe or category definitions (e.g., whether the universe is all people or just household members) and because of differences between final and preliminary rates.

[a]Allocation rates for short forms include substitutions (see text). The worst 10 percent census tracts are the 10 percent with the highest overall allocation rates among all tracts.

TABLE L.2 Allocation Rates for Selected Population Items, 1990 Census, for People Receiving the Long Form, by Type of Response: Household Respondent vs. Enumerator-Filled

Item	Household Respondent[a]	Enumerator-Filled[b]
Relationship	1.7	2.3
Sex	0.9	0.8
Race	1.0	1.5
Age	0.8	1.2
Marital status	1.5	1.1
Spanish origin	4.2	1.8
Place of birth	4.3	7.1
Education level	3.8	6.1
English ability	3.8	7.4
Veteran status	4.0	7.0
Work disability	8.3	8.0
Mobility disability	4.7	6.4
Self-care	3.5	6.7
Employment status	3.0	6.2
Place of work	9.0	12.7
Occupation	7.9	12.5
Income (100% allocated)[c]	9.1	19.1

Note: These allocation rates are based on a special tabulation of the 1990 census files and reflect the "final" disposition of each census item or category They cover the household population only. Rates by type of response have not previously been tabulated or published.

[a]Also includes partially completed questionnaires given to enumerators for follow-up for incomplete entries.

[b]Includes long forms obtained by enumerators in the follow-up stage of census operations from households that failed to mail back their form; also includes all long forms obtained in the list/enumerate areas in which households in the sample were asked to respond at the time of the enumerator's visit (see Appendix B).

[c]Rate is percent of people with 100 percent of their total income allocated (all other rates are percent of people with the item allocated).

TABLE L.3 Allocation Rates for Selected Items, U.S., by Race/Ethnicity, 1990 Census (number of persons in thousands)

Item	Total (242,050)	White Non-Hispanic (183,680)	Black Non-Hispanic (28,065)	Hispanic (21,415)	Asian Pacific Islander Non-Hispanic (6,848)	American Indian Non-Hispanic (1,811)
100 percent population items						
Relationship	1.90	1.47	3.28	3.50	2.65	2.55
Sex	0.85	0.72	1.40	1.09	1.05	1.71
Race	1.14	0.74	1.26	4.33	1.14	1.22
Age	0.91	0.73	1.59	1.45	1.12	1.49
Marital status	1.40	1.11	2.22	2.68	1.66	1.78
Spanish origin	3.36	3.26	5.31	1.75	2.85	4.50
100 percent housing items						
Rooms	0.44	0.41	0.60	0.52	0.42	0.64
Tenure	1.43	1.37	1.74	1.67	1.19	1.67
Value	3.24	3.17	4.37	2.98	2.09	5.11
Rent	1.28	1.22	1.73	1.03	0.86	1.47
Sample housing items						
Complete plumbing	1.70	1.67	2.00	1.69	1.48	2.03
Complete kitchen	1.74	1.72	2.02	1.72	1.48	2.09
Heating fuel	2.86	2.67	3.83	3.45	3.00	4.50
Condominium	3.35	3.09	4.43	4.41	4.36	4.04
Electric cost	5.49	4.95	8.98	6.39	5.24	6.90
Property taxes	12.11	11.06	22.03	15.89	13.57	15.93

Sample population items						
Place of birth	5.06	4.03	9.95	7.43	4.97	5.94
Education level	4.47	3.64	7.63	7.34	5.14	5.44
English ability	4.76	3.68	8.32	9.01	6.41	6.19
Veteran status	4.78	3.97	8.56	7.43	5.11	5.78
Work disability	8.35	7.77	11.54	9.90	7.71	9.02
Mobility disability	5.15	4.50	8.15	7.10	5.73	5.63
Self-care disability	5.80	5.15	8.87	7.74	6.34	6.08
Employment status	3.82	2.93	7.96	6.68	4.51	4.78
Place of work	9.96	8.40	16.49	16.23	13.39	12.28
Occupation	9.14	7.92	15.25	12.93	9.63	10.43
Income: >0-9% allocated	0.63	0.63	0.70	0.61	0.54	0.55
Income: 10-19%	0.08	0.09	0.08	0.05	0.05	0.09
Income: 20-49%	0.26	0.27	0.28	0.16	0.13	0.28
Income: 50-99%	0.73	0.74	0.87	0.55	0.50	0.99
Income: 100%	11.72	10.10	20.34	15.87	11.19	13.51

Note: These allocation rates are based on a special run of the 1990 census files and reflect the "final" disposition of each census item or category. They cover the household population only. In the case of housing items, they refer to occupied units. Rates were tabulated separately for Hispanic and non-Hispanic groups. Thus, all racial/ethnic groups are mutually exclusive in that the racial categories shown cover "non-Spanish" only (e.g., white non-Hispanic, black non-Hispanic, etc.). For income, the allocation rates refer to the percent of people for whom a specified percentage of their income was allocated (e.g., greater than zero to 9%, 10-19%, etc.). The rates shown here may differ from rates shown in other tables of this report or in census publications because of differences in universe or category definitions (e.g., whether the universe is all people or just household members) and because of differences between final and preliminary rates.

TABLE L.4 Allocation Rates for Selected Items, U.S. by Selected Geography, 1990 Census (number of persons in thousands)

Item	Central Cities of Large MSAs (75,065)	Balance of Large MSAs (71,180)	Central Cities of Small MSAs (20,975)	Balance of Small MSAs (20,621)	Non-MSAs, Urban (19,742)	Non-MSAs, Rural (34,466)
100 percent population items						
Relationship	2.35	1.68	1.84	1.71	1.62	1.71
Sex	0.92	0.78	0.81	0.83	0.82	0.87
Race	1.46	0.96	1.05	0.96	0.97	1.08
Age	1.13	0.76	0.83	0.76	0.84	0.92
Marital status	1.59	1.29	1.44	1.33	1.27	1.31
Spanish origin	3.61	2.96	3.60	3.32	3.61	3.39
100 percent housing items						
Rooms	0.48	0.38	0.42	0.41	0.44	0.50
Tenure	1.39	1.38	1.30	1.57	1.28	1.72
Value	2.99	2.64	2.88	3.63	3.36	4.63
Rent	1.35	1.12	1.13	1.23	1.23	1.64
Sample housing items						
Complete plumbing	1.60	1.53	1.42	1.72	1.59	2.54
Complete kitchen	1.64	1.56	1.47	1.76	1.64	2.60
Heating fuel	2.91	2.39	2.37	2.83	2.63	4.22
Condominium	3.48	3.02	3.06	3.19	3.32	4.02
Electric cost	6.17	4.81	5.07	5.00	5.30	6.04
Property taxes	13.47	10.82	12.21	11.33	11.07	13.41

Sample population items					
Place of birth	6.66	4.18	4.36	4.14	4.17	4.88
Education level	5.58	3.87	3.82	3.82	3.71	4.52
English ability	6.10	4.00	4.04	4.02	3.95	4.78
Veteran status	5.92	4.04	4.25	4.13	4.13	4.87
Work disability	9.25	7.55	7.61	7.91	7.68	9.13
Mobility disability	6.22	4.71	4.52	4.56	4.22	4.94
Self-care disability	6.93	5.42	5.14	5.19	4.77	5.45
Employment status	5.34	3.15	3.26	2.99	3.08	3.12
Place of work	11.53	8.98	8.30	9.15	9.55	10.35
Occupation	10.79	7.80	8.02	8.13	8.14	10.28
Income: >0-9% allocated	0.61	0.59	0.60	0.67	0.64	0.76
Income: 10-19%	0.08	0.07	0.09	0.09	0.10	0.11
Income: 20-49%	0.23	0.21	0.28	0.26	0.33	0.34
Income: 50-99%	0.67	0.62	0.80	0.74	0.88	0.97
Income: 100%	13.54	10.30	10.64	10.69	10.78	12.43

Note: These allocation rates are based on a special tabulation of the 1990 census files and reflect the "final" disposition of each census item or category. They cover the household population only. In the case of housing items, they refer to occupied units. For income, the allocation rates refer to the percent of people for whom a specified percentage of their income was allocated (e.g., greater than zero to 9%, 10-19%, etc.). The rates shown here may differ from rates shown in other tables of this report or in census publications because of differences in universe or category definitions (e.g., whether the universe is all people or just household members) and because of differences between final and preliminary rates.

MSA: Metropolitan Statistical Area. Large MSAs are those with 500,000 or more population.

TABLE L.5 Allocation Rates for Selected Items, Worst 10 Percent Census Tracts, by Race/Ethnicity, 1990 Census (number of persons in thousands)[a]

Item	Total (20,037)	White Non-Hispanic (5,505)	Black Non-Hispanic (9,810)	Hispanic (3,894)	Asian Pacific Islander Non-Hispanic (627)	American Indian Non-Hispanic (152)
100 percent population items						
Relationship	3.75	2.14	4.12	4.97	3.82	5.70
Sex	1.31	0.96	1.44	1.36	1.45	4.22
Race	2.75	1.10	1.62	7.98	1.47	3.56
Age	1.90	1.39	2.06	2.10	1.77	4.48
Marital status	2.38	1.45	2.52	3.27	2.04	4.37
Spanish origin	5.40	4.86	6.84	2.46	4.46	12.04
100 percent housing items						
Rooms	0.72	0.64	0.76	0.74	0.68	2.13
Tenure	1.86	1.59	1.99	2.07	1.52	3.60
Value	5.04	4.56	5.40	5.18	4.24	9.32
Rent	1.85	1.61	2.18	1.46	1.14	3.84
Sample housing items						
Complete plumbing	2.17	1.87	2.32	2.38	1.95	3.56
Complete kitchen	2.18	1.91	2.32	2.39	1.92	3.33
Heating fuel	4.29	3.63	4.45	5.23	4.30	7.69
Condominium	4.72	3.87	4.98	5.72	5.61	6.35
Electric cost	9.02	6.42	10.98	9.27	7.22	10.17
Property taxes	20.22	14.36	25.55	20.88	18.18	21.28

Sample population items

Place of birth	11.35	7.19	13.54	12.09	8.05	13.20
Education level	8.95	5.58	10.06	11.10	8.20	10.53
English ability	10.21	5.83	11.03	14.42	10.77	12.03
Veteran status	9.66	6.16	11.18	11.86	8.55	10.75
Work disability	12.84	10.05	14.27	14.13	11.13	13.59
Mobility disability	9.30	6.35	10.65	10.90	8.34	10.37
Self-care disability	10.05	7.09	11.43	11.60	8.97	10.72
Employment status	9.51	5.66	11.28	11.65	8.42	10.31
Place of work	18.82	11.33	21.54	25.74	20.92	20.90
Occupation	17.38	11.14	20.48	20.70	15.65	18.89
Income: >0-9% allocated	0.74	0.69	0.77	0.79	0.64	0.55
Income: 10-19%	0.08	0.09	0.09	0.95	0.04	0.07
Income: 20-49%	0.27	0.29	0.29	0.18	0.16	0.25
Income: 50-99%	0.80	0.78	0.91	0.57	0.50	0.84
Income: 100%	20.47	13.28	24.60	22.58	16.32	19.27

Note: These allocation rates are based on a special tabulation of the 1990 census files and reflect the "final" disposition of each census item or category. They cover the household population only. In the case of housing items, they refer to occupied units. Rates were tabulated separately for Hispanic and non-Hispanic groups. Thus, all racial/ethnic groups are mutually exclusive in that the racial categories shown cover "non-Spanish" only (e.g., white non-Hispanic, black non-Hispanic, etc.). For income, the allocation rates refer to the percent of people for whom a specified percentage of their income was allocated (e.g., greater than zero to 9%, 10-19%, etc.). The rates shown here may differ from rates shown in other tables of this report or in census publications because of differences in universe or category definitions (e.g., whether the universe is all people or just household members) and because of differences between final and preliminary rates.

[a]The worst 10 percent census tracts are the 10 percent with the highest overall rates of allocation among all tracts.

TABLE L.6 Allocation Rates for Selected Items, Worst 10 Percent Census Tracts, by Selected Geography, 1990 Census (number of persons in thousands)[a]

Item	Central Cities of Large MSAs (15,307)	Balance of Large MSAs (2,125)	Central Cities of Small MSAs (1,141)	Balance of Small MSAs (384)	Non-MSAs, Urban (414)	Non-MSAs, Rural (666)
100 percent population items						
Relationship	3.89	3.27	3.29	3.31	2.99	3.50
Sex	1.27	1.27	1.34	1.71	1.62	2.07
Race	2.89	2.62	1.73	2.35	1.99	2.40
Age	1.92	1.75	1.57	1.73	1.99	2.38
Marital status	2.36	2.31	2.54	2.27	2.29	2.78
Spanish origin	5.40	4.25	5.64	4.86	7.53	7.75
100 percent housing items						
Rooms	0.71	0.75	0.58	0.73	0.73	1.26
Tenure	1.82	1.85	1.69	2.23	1.78	3.08
Value	5.08	4.36	4.55	4.94	5.15	6.39
Rent	1.86	1.79	1.58	1.90	1.88	3.16
Sample housing items						
Complete plumbing	2.18	2.07	1.74	2.28	1.96	3.19
Complete kitchen	2.18	2.12	1.80	2.31	1.85	3.26
Heating fuel	4.39	3.70	3.41	3.91	3.62	6.05
Condominium	4.76	4.45	4.30	4.46	4.72	5.76
Electric cost	9.50	7.33	7.60	6.62	7.39	8.05
Property taxes	22.05	17.58	18.02	15.24	14.77	15.79

Sample population items

Sample population items					
Place of birth	12.26	8.06	7.24	8.35	8.83
Education level	9.55	6.50	6.60	6.32	7.28
English ability	10.95	7.35	7.31	7.22	7.89
Veteran status	10.36	7.04	6.49	6.99	7.74
Work disability	13.46	10.72	10.24	10.04	11.64
Mobility disability	9.94	6.92	6.75	6.45	7.48
Self-care disability	10.70	7.59	7.51	7.14	8.17
Employment status	10.40	6.36	5.77	6.38	6.53
Place of work	20.24	13.04	13.06	14.57	14.33
Occupation	18.65	13.06	12.53	12.56	14.26
Income: >0-9% allocated	0.75	0.74	0.71	0.81	0.82
Income: 10-19%	0.08	0.11	0.09	0.08	0.08
Income: 20-49%	0.26	0.33	0.29	0.35	0.31
Income: 50-99%	0.79	0.97	0.88	0.97	0.87
Income: 100%	21.64	16.76	15.03	16.06	16.82

Note: These allocation rates are based on a special tabulation of the 1990 census files and reflect the "final" disposition of each census item or category. They cover the household population only. In the case of housing items, they refer to occupied units. For income, the allocation rates refer to the percent of people for whom a specified percentage of their income was allocated (e.g., greater than zero to 9%, 10-19%, etc.). The rates shown here may differ from rates shown in other tables of this report or in census publications because of differences in universe or category definitions (e.g., whether the universe is all people or just household members) and because of differences between final and preliminary rates.

MSA: Metropolitan Statistical Area. Large MSAs are those with 500,000 or more population.

[a]The worst 10 percent census tracts are the 10 percent with the highest overall rates of allocation among all tracts.

TABLE L.7 Allocation Rates for Selected Items, California by Race/Ethnicity, 1990 Census (number of persons in thousands)

Items	Total (29,025)	White Non-Hispanic (16,670)	Black Non-Hispanic (1,994)	Hispanic (7,408)	Asian Pacific Islander Non-Hispanic (2,710)	American Indian Non-Hispanic (190)
100 Percent Population Items						
Relationship	2.61	1.78	3.67	4.08	2.87	2.38
Sex	0.99	0.80	1.25	1.31	1.08	1.36
Race	1.85	0.78	1.04	4.74	1.06	1.05
Age	1.08	0.79	1.52	1.62	1.07	0.91
Marital status	1.81	1.21	2.48	2.97	1.79	1.31
Spanish origin	2.81	3.06	4.83	1.67	2.84	4.09
100 Percent Housing Items						
Rooms	0.48	0.46	0.59	0.51	0.40	0.43
Tenure	1.29	1.23	1.38	1.53	1.10	1.41
Value	2.59	2.59	3.56	2.62	1.79	4.17
Rent	1.00	1.07	1.31	0.78	0.75	1.07
Sample Housing Items						
Complete plumbing	1.34	1.30	1.61	1.39	1.31	1.38
Complete kitchen	1.38	1.35	1.64	1.42	1.28	1.47
Heating fuel	2.51	2.28	3.10	3.04	2.75	2.91
Condominium	3.50	3.10	4.11	4.45	4.38	3.29
Electric cost	5.73	5.41	9.09	5.83	5.06	7.03
Property taxes	11.52	10.39	19.77	14.53	12.39	14.78

Sample Population Items

Item						
Place of birth	5.67	4.32	9.92	7.74	5.12	5.28
Education level	5.50	4.01	8.58	8.25	5.17	5.07
English ability	5.98	3.97	8.97	9.71	6.50	5.21
Veteran status	5.51	4.29	9.95	7.76	4.93	5.49
Work disability	8.71	7.93	12.49	10.13	7.66	9.03
Mobility disability	5.79	4.84	9.34	7.43	5.45	5.38
Self-care disability	6.46	5.53	10.00	8.08	6.03	5.99
Employment status	4.83	3.59	9.33	7.01	4.40	4.43
Place of work	11.75	9.06	16.52	17.23	13.44	11.07
Occupation	10.20	8.55	16.65	13.19	9.39	9.49
Income: >0-9% allocated	0.55	0.57	0.52	0.53	0.53	0.45
Income: (10-19%)	0.07	0.08	0.06	0.03	0.04	0.08
Income: (20-49%)	0.20	0.24	0.23	0.14	0.13	0.25
Income: (50-99%)	0.60	0.65	0.70	0.47	0.48	0.79
Income: 100%	12.23	10.30	20.05	15.80	10.50	12.78

Note: These allocation rates are based on a special run of the 1990 census files and reflect the "final" disposition of each census item or category. They cover the household population only. In the case of housing items, they refer to occupied units. Rates were tabulated separately for Hispanic and non-Hispanic groups. Thus, all racial/ethnic groups are mutually exclusive in that the racial categories shown cover "non-Spanish" only (e.g., white non-Hispanic, black non-Hispanic, etc.). For income, the allocation rates refer to the percent of people for whom a specified percentage of their income was allocated (e.g., greater than zero to 9%, 10-19%, etc.). The rates shown here may differ from rates shown in other tables of this report or in census publications because of differences in universe or category definitions (e.g., whether the universe is all people or just household members) and because of differences between final and preliminary rates.

TABLE L.8 Allocation Rates for Selected Items, California by Selected Geography, 1990 Census (number of persons in thousands)

Items	Central Cities of Large MSAs (12,271)	Balance of Large MSAs (13,105)	Central Cities of Small MSAs (1,226)	Balance of Small MSAs (1,216)	Non-MSAs, Urban (625)	Non-MSAs, Rural (582)
100 Percent Population Items						
Relationship	2.87	2.36	2.93	2.78	2.03	2.01
Sex	1.04	0.96	0.98	1.06	0.80	0.97
Race	2.04	1.66	2.32	1.93	1.49	1.40
Age	1.21	0.99	1.02	1.05	0.83	0.93
Marital status	1.90	1.64	2.49	2.25	1.73	1.39
Spanish origin	2.98	2.55	3.70	3.09	3.24	2.34
100 Percent Housing Items						
Rooms	0.49	0.43	0.53	0.50	0.61	0.71
Tenure	1.24	1.23	1.40	1.73	1.52	2.24
Value	2.55	2.26	3.31	4.33	3.58	4.33
Rent	0.97	0.97	1.23	1.13	1.19	1.65
Sample Housing Items						
Complete plumbing	1.30	1.34	1.20	1.48	1.31	2.25
Complete kitchen	1.32	1.38	1.20	1.61	1.30	2.35
Heating fuel	2.51	2.34	2.71	3.18	2.80	4.29
Condominium	3.58	3.40	3.49	3.60	3.23	4.44
Electric cost	5.97	5.37	6.05	6.33	5.55	6.73
Property taxes	11.69	11.10	12.51	12.63	11.84	13.26

Sample Population Items						
Place of birth	6.40	5.10	5.52	5.37	4.27	5.28
Education level	6.23	4.94	5.35	5.25	4.12	5.24
English ability	6.81	5.29	5.93	5.78	4.59	5.95
Veteran status	6.18	4.92	5.71	5.50	4.34	5.63
Work disability	9.29	8.12	9.09	8.91	8.09	9.22
Mobility disability	6.35	5.31	6.06	5.64	4.75	5.50
Self-care disability	7.02	6.01	6.69	6.17	5.38	5.98
Employment status	5.52	4.24	5.08	4.64	3.82	4.30
Place of work	12.40	11.21	11.51	12.54	10.18	10.84
Occupation	11.01	9.41	10.31	10.82	8.80	11.34
Income: >0-9% allocated	0.54	0.54	0.64	0.66	0.58	0.66
Income: (10-19%)	0.06	0.06	0.08	0.10	0.08	0.11
Income: (20-49%)	0.20	0.19	0.23	0.30	0.28	0.36
Income: (50-99%)	0.58	0.57	0.68	0.75	0.83	0.96
Income: 100%	12.95	11.47	12.68	13.00	10.57	13.41

Note: These allocation rates are based on a special tabulation of the 1990 census files and reflect the "final" disposition of each census item or category. They cover the household population only. In the case of housing items, they refer to occupied units. For income, the allocation rates refer to the percent of people for whom a specified percentage of their income was allocated (e.g., greater than zero to 9%, 10-19%, etc.). The rates shown here may differ from rates shown in other tables of this report or in census publications because of differences in universe or category definitions (e.g., whether the universe is all people or just household members) and because of differences between final and preliminary rates.

MSA: Metropolitan Statistical Area. Large MSAs are those with 500,000 or more population.

TABLE L.9 Allocation Rates for Selected Items, Worst 10 Percent Census Tracts Nationally, California Portion, by Race/Ethnicity, 1990 Census (number of persons in thousands)[a]

Items	Total (2,397)	White Non-Hispanic (412)	Black Non-Hispanic (625)	Hispanic (1,150)	Asian Pacific Islander Non-Hispanic (193)	American Indian Non-Hispanic (9)
100 Percent Population Items						
Relationship	4.69	2.53	4.67	5.64	3.73	1.98
Sex	1.44	1.06	1.26	1.70	1.31	1.51
Race	4.56	1.22	1.48	7.97	1.36	1.43
Age	1.99	1.40	1.93	2.32	1.49	0.78
Marital status	2.85	1.74	2.87	3.36	2.11	1.62
Spanish origin	3.88	4.67	6.32	2.26	3.90	4.60
100 Percent Housing Items						
Rooms	0.68	0.67	0.74	0.66	0.56	0.36
Tenure	1.70	1.60	1.61	1.92	1.43	1.75
Value	4.51	4.39	4.74	4.34	4.46	4.11
Rent	1.21	1.34	1.75	0.85	0.67	0.93
Sample Housing Items						
Complete plumbing	1.71	1.88	1.80	1.57	1.46	0.97
Complete kitchen	1.72	1.89	1.84	1.57	1.36	1.03
Heating fuel	3.36	3.40	3.15	3.54	3.33	2.64
Condominium	4.95	4.25	4.72	5.68	5.06	5.06
Electric cost	7.75	6.64	10.61	6.59	5.54	6.48
Property taxes	17.20	12.76	21.76	17.75	14.31	16.20

Sample Population Items

Item						
Place of birth	10.33	6.60	12.83	10.83	7.03	8.48
Education level	10.20	5.88	10.72	12.06	7.12	7.21
English ability	11.71	5.74	11.34	14.50	10.05	9.58
Veteran status	9.96	6.17	11.82	11.11	7.21	7.48
Work disability	12.74	10.16	15.00	13.00	10.36	12.87
Mobility disability	9.43	6.34	11.25	10.21	6.91	7.09
Self-care disability	10.04	7.00	11.81	10.85	7.40	7.41
Employment status	9.50	5.57	12.14	10.21	6.93	7.81
Place of work	20.22	11.55	20.60	24.29	18.43	15.56
Occupation	17.25	11.56	21.68	18.09	13.68	14.66
Income: >0-9% allocated	0.52	0.58	0.58	0.49	0.43	0.34
Income: (10-19%)	0.05	0.08	0.06	0.03	0.04	0.03
Income: (20-49%)	0.21	0.26	0.25	0.15	0.23	0.49
Income: (50-99%)	0.63	0.80	0.75	0.49	0.55	0.82
Income: 100%	19.05	12.47	23.49	20.56	12.94	15.37

Note: These allocation rates are based on a special tabulation of the 1990 census files and reflect the "final" disposition of each census item or category. They cover the household population only. In the case of housing items, they refer to occupied units. Rates were tabulated separately for Hispanic and non-Hispanic groups. Thus, all racial/ethnic groups are mutually exclusive in that the racial categories shown cover "non-Spanish" only (e.g., white non-Hispanic, black non-Hispanic, etc.). For income, the allocation rates refer to the percent of people for whom a specified percentage of their income was allocated (e.g., greater than zero to 9%, 10-19%, etc.). The rates shown here may differ from rates shown in other tables of this report or in census publications because of differences in universe or category definitions (e.g., whether the universe is all people or just household members) and because of differences between final and preliminary rates.

[a]The worst 10 percent census tracts are the 10 percent with the highest overall rates of allocation among all tracts for the country as a whole. The universe here is those tracts that fall in California.

TABLE L.10 Allocation Rates for Selected Items, Worst 10 Percent Census Tracts Nationally, California Portion, by Selected Geography, 1990 Census (number of persons in thousands)[a]

Items	Central Cities of Large MSAs (1,684)	Balance of Large MSAs (505)	Central Cities of Small MSAs (117)	Balance of Small MSAs (77)	Non-MSAs, Urban (7)	Non-MSAs, Rural (8)
100 Percent Population Items						
Relationship	4.76	4.36	5.34	4.59	4.01	3.37
Sex	1.40	1.58	1.39	1.53	1.28	1.92
Race	4.51	4.89	3.73	4.87	5.40	2.98
Age	1.99	1.96	1.80	2.32	1.45	2.53
Marital status	2.73	2.86	4.30	3.10	4.91	3.00
Spanish origin	4.01	3.28	4.54	3.71	3.77	4.91
100 Percent Housing Items						
Rooms	0.65	0.73	0.61	0.86	0.95	2.49
Tenure	1.61	1.94	1.56	2.20	1.57	5.69
Value	4.54	4.30	4.04	5.29	3.86	6.29
Rent	1.17	1.28	1.28	1.98	2.61	0.99
Sample Housing Items						
Complete plumbing	1.68	1.93	1.01	1.74	2.52	3.68
Complete kitchen	1.67	1.94	1.26	1.89	3.64	3.59
Heating fuel	3.30	3.31	3.36	4.25	4.88	8.50
Condominium	5.00	5.07	4.02	4.19	4.76	6.37
Electric cost	8.06	6.79	6.57	8.11	7.95	9.79
Property taxes	17.69	17.07	16.17	13.79	16.42	16.20

Sample Population Items						
Place of birth	10.90	9.40	8.11	8.08	5.90	7.66
Education level	10.73	9.14	8.24	8.82	7.39	9.48
English ability	12.43	9.99	10.35	9.72	8.75	9.04
Veteran status	10.64	8.31	8.50	7.59	7.78	8.71
Work disability	13.29	11.02	12.50	12.01	10.60	14.06
Mobility disability	9.96	7.96	8.51	8.40	8.16	10.15
Self-care disability	10.56	8.60	9.31	8.80	7.97	11.57
Employment status	10.27	7.57	7.85	7.29	6.50	8.96
Place of work	21.32	18.25	15.88	16.66	10.73	13.89
Occupation	18.40	14.59	14.09	15.22	13.44	14.75
Income: >0-9% allocated	0.50	0.53	0.71	0.75	1.08	0.48
Income: (10-19%)	0.05	0.05	0.05	0.07	0.08	0.00
Income: (20-49%)	0.20	0.22	0.16	0.34	0.49	0.03
Income: (50-99%)	0.60	0.65	0.60	0.98	0.98	0.63
Income: 100%	20.04	16.90	15.50	16.52	16.64	16.00

Note: These allocation rates are based on a special tabulation of the 1990 census files and reflect the "final" disposition of each census item or category. They cover the household population only. In the case of housing items, they refer to occupied units. For income, the allocation rates refer to the percent of people for whom a specified percentage of their income was allocated (e.g., greater than zero to 9%, 10-19%, etc.). The rates shown here may differ from rates shown in other tables of this report or in census publications because of differences in universe or category definitions (e.g., whether the universe is all people or just household members) and because of differences between final and preliminary rates

MSA: Metropolitan Statistical Area. Large MSAs are those with 500,000 or more population.

[a]The worst 10 percent census tracts are the 10 percent with the highest overall rates of allocation among all tracts for the country as a whole. The universe here is those tracts that fall in California.

TABLE L.11 Allocation Rates for Selected Items, New York by Race/Ethnicity, 1990 Census (number of persons in thousands)

Items	Total (17,447)	White Non-Hispanic (12,143)	Black Non-Hispanic (2,480)	Hispanic (2,090)	Asian Pacific Islander Non-Hispanic (659)	American Indian Non-Hispanic (48)
100 Percent Population Items						
Relationship	2.38	1.63	4.03	4.32	3.49	3.44
Sex	0.91	0.73	1.53	1.16	1.08	1.71
Race	1.76	0.78	1.73	7.50	1.12	2.08
Age	1.23	0.92	2.22	1.84	1.40	1.74
Marital status	1.58	1.19	2.41	2.83	1.55	2.23
Spanish origin	3.89	3.43	7.42	2.32	3.73	6.88
100 Percent Housing Items						
Rooms	0.56	0.48	0.84	0.71	0.64	1.07
Tenure	1.50	1.38	1.84	1.93	1.35	1.79
Value	4.34	4.11	6.99	5.96	2.83	5.66
Rent	1.94	1.88	2.47	1.66	1.33	1.96
Sample Housing Items						
Complete plumbing	2.27	2.08	3.00	2.66	2.25	2.49
Complete kitchen	2.30	2.13	3.02	2.66	2.19	2.62
Heating fuel	4.37	3.70	6.53	6.30	4.86	4.94
Condominium	3.95	3.42	5.64	5.25	5.27	4.03
Electric cost	7.77	6.54	12.45	10.65	7.88	10.76
Property taxes	14.19	12.95	29.92	21.37	17.97	19.33

Sample Population Items						
Place of birth	8.05	5.54	16.03	12.94	8.14	11.62
Education level	6.11	4.26	11.31	10.17	7.91	7.73
English ability	6.98	4.56	12.49	13.69	10.55	7.94
Veteran status	6.70	4.72	12.58	11.59	9.00	8.55
Work disability	10.54	8.98	15.64	14.25	11.17	12.34
Mobility disability	7.27	5.67	12.34	10.82	9.04	8.14
Self-care disability	8.15	6.55	13.30	11.63	9.82	8.95
Employment status	6.44	4.24	13.00	11.90	8.78	7.19
Place of work	14.88	10.78	26.35	27.06	23.73	18.12
Occupation	12.36	9.11	22.20	20.91	15.73	16.40
Income: >0-9% allocated	0.77	0.70	0.97	1.01	0.64	0.59
Income: (10-19%)	0.08	0.09	0.07	0.05	0.05	0.05
Income: (20-49%)	0.26	0.27	0.24	0.21	0.14	0.20
Income: (50-99%)	0.69	0.72	0.77	0.53	0.50	0.84
Income: 100%	15.43	12.18	26.18	22.62	17.13	20.05

Note: These allocation rates are based on a special run of the 1990 census files and reflect the "final" disposition of each census item or category. They cover the household population only. In the case of housing items, they refer to occupied units. Rates were tabulated separately for Hispanic and non-Hispanic groups. Thus, all racial/ethnic groups are mutually exclusive in that the racial categories shown cover "non-Spanish" only (e.g., white non-Hispanic, black non-Hispanic, etc.). For income, the allocation rates refer to the percent of people for whom a specified percentage of their income was allocated (e.g., greater than zero to 9%, 10-19%, etc.). The rates shown here may differ from rates shown in other tables of this report or in census publications because of differences in universe or category definitions (e.g., whether the universe is all people or just household members) and because of differences between final and preliminary rates.

TABLE L.12 Allocation Rates for Selected Items, New York by Selected Geography, 1990 Census (number of persons in thousands)

Items	Central Cities of Large MSAs (10,736)	Balance of Large MSAs (4,064)	Central Cities of Small MSAs (359)	Balance of Small MSAs (780)	Non-MSAs, Urban (438)	Non-MSAs, Rural (1,069)
100 Percent Population Items						
Relationship	2.82	1.81	1.48	1.29	1.46	1.56
Sex	1.03	0.81	0.62	0.53	0.68	0.67
Race	2.31	0.93	0.72	0.70	0.74	0.91
Age	1.51	0.88	0.56	0.55	0.69	0.80
Marital status	1.74	1.41	1.24	1.15	1.18	1.22
Spanish origin	4.30	3.29	3.56	2.92	3.36	3.14
100 Percent Housing Items						
Rooms	0.64	0.43	0.36	0.35	0.43	0.47
Tenure	1.53	1.44	1.28	1.41	1.21	1.68
Value	4.78	3.70	3.83	3.84	3.69	4.75
Rent	2.03	1.83	1.35	1.39	1.32	1.82
Sample Housing Items						
Complete plumbing	2.42	2.04	1.28	1.88	1.49	2.59
Complete kitchen	2.47	2.02	1.29	1.94	1.52	2.69
Heating fuel	5.00	3.35	2.60	2.99	2.74	4.06
Condominium	4.36	3.35	2.45	2.83	2.91	3.78
Electric cost	8.62	6.66	6.22	5.40	5.94	6.33
Property taxes	15.58	12.49	13.71	12.20	15.06	15.03

Sample Population Items						
Place of birth	10.26	4.77	4.22	3.58	3.97	4.57
Education level	7.49	4.06	3.51	3.34	3.17	4.09
English ability	8.78	4.29	3.48	3.45	3.38	4.32
Veteran status	8.27	4.27	3.67	3.52	3.65	4.41
Work disability	11.88	8.47	7.67	7.68	7.40	9.14
Mobility disability	8.65	5.27	4.39	4.42	4.22	5.08
Self-care disability	9.55	6.22	5.05	5.11	4.87	5.77
Employment status	8.46	3.47	2.80	2.32	2.74	2.71
Place of work	18.82	9.16	6.35	7.39	9.34	9.58
Occupation	15.12	8.34	7.19	6.98	7.27	8.51
Income: >0-9% allocated	0.78	0.74	0.62	0.70	0.65	0.83
Income: (10-19%)	0.08	0.09	0.11	0.08	0.11	0.10
Income: (20-49%)	0.24	0.25	0.29	0.31	0.34	0.37
Income: (50-99%)	0.65	0.69	0.92	0.74	0.94	0.95
Income: 100%	17.97	11.72	10.43	10.00	9.94	11.30

Note: These allocation rates are based on a special tabulation of the 1990 census files and reflect the "final" disposition of each census item or category. They cover the household population only. In the case of housing items, they refer to occupied units. For income, the allocation rates refer to the percent of people for whom a specified percentage of their income was allocated (e.g., greater than zero to 9%, 10-19%, etc.). The rates shown here may differ from rates shown in other tables of this report or in census publications because of differences in universe or category definitions (e.g., whether the universe is all people or just household members) and because of differences between final and preliminary rates.

MSA: Metropolitan Statistical Area. Large MSAs are those with 500,000 or more population.

TABLE L.13 Allocation Rates for Selected Items, Worst 10 Percent Census Tracts Nationally, New York Portion, by Race/Ethnicity, 1990 Census (number of persons in thousands)[a]

Items	Total (3,974)	White Non-Hispanic (760)	Black Non-Hispanic (1,779)	Hispanic (1,253)	Asian Pacific Islander Non-Hispanic (1,556)	American Indian Non-Hispanic (13)
100 Percent Population Items						
Relationship	4.27	2.78	4.43	4.89	4.44	6.10
Sex	1.41	1.21	1.59	1.25	1.36	2.57
Race	4.32	1.46	1.95	9.59	1.53	4.54
Age	2.23	2.08	2.42	2.09	1.82	2.33
Marital status	2.55	1.67	2.58	3.08	2.10	3.38
Spanish origin	5.91	5.67	8.32	2.57	5.74	13.16
100 Percent Housing Items						
Rooms	0.89	0.85	0.94	0.81	1.03	1.82
Tenure	1.94	1.63	1.95	2.21	1.87	2.70
Value	7.49	6.52	8.08	9.02	4.78	8.28
Rent	2.28	2.47	2.57	1.83	1.40	2.28
Sample Housing Items						
Complete plumbing	3.01	2.53	3.22	3.04	3.18	3.06
Complete kitchen	3.03	2.64	3.25	3.03	2.92	3.15
Heating fuel	6.58	5.46	6.94	7.01	6.61	5.52
Condominium	5.59	4.51	6.01	5.75	6.64	4.76
Electric cost	11.46	8.81	12.97	11.69	9.72	10.03
Property taxes	27.85	19.87	33.29	30.34	26.17	25.08

Sample Population Items

Place of birth	15.60	11.31	17.97	15.34	11.02	15.48
Education level	11.27	7.77	12.50	11.71	10.64	13.61
English ability	13.59	8.69	13.81	16.31	13.78	14.00
Veteran status	12.61	8.47	13.96	13.59	12.43	14.89
Work disability	15.77	12.81	17.04	16.21	14.17	17.43
Mobility disability	12.15	8.90	13.59	12.44	11.31	12.46
Self-care disability	13.06	9.74	14.58	13.26	12.14	13.01
Employment status	13.29	9.10	14.67	14.38	12.25	13.20
Place of work	27.93	17.94	29.72	32.80	29.36	29.05
Occupation	22.76	15.15	24.79	25.44	20.75	23.55
Income: >0-9% allocated	0.98	0.81	1.02	1.06	0.92	0.44
Income: (10-19%)	0.07	0.09	0.07	0.06	0.06	0.10
Income: (20-49%)	0.24	0.34	0.23	0.22	0.13	0.26
Income: (50-99%)	0.72	0.84	0.80	0.56	0.48	1.04
Income: 100%	24.43	16.96	27.69	25.24	21.96	27.23

Note: These allocation rates are based on a special tabulation of the 1990 census files and reflect the "final" disposition of each census item or category. They cover the household population only. In the case of housing items, they refer to occupied units. Rates were tabulated separately for Hispanic and non-Hispanic groups. Thus, all racial/ethnic groups are mutually exclusive in that the racial categories shown cover "non-Spanish" only (e.g., white non-Hispanic, black non-Hispanic, etc.). For income, the allocation rates refer to the percent of people for whom a specified percentage of their income was allocated (e.g., greater than zero to 9%, 10-19%, etc.). The rates shown here may differ from rates shown in other tables of this report or in census publications because of differences in universe or category definitions (e.g., whether the universe is all people or just household members) and because of differences between final and preliminary rates.

[a]The worst 10 percent census tracts are the 10 percent with the highest overall rates of allocation among all tracts for the country as a whole. The universe here is those tracts that fall in New York.

TABLE L.14 Allocation Rates for Selected Items, Worst 10 Percent Census Tracts Nationally, New York Portion, by Selected Geography, 1990 Census (number of persons in thousands)[a]

Items	Central Cities of Large MSAs (3,795)	Balance of Large MSAs (150)	Central Cities of Small MSAs (10)	Balance of Small MSAs ( )	Non-MSAs, Urban (15)	Non-MSAs, Rural (5)
100 Percent Population Items						
Relationship	4.28	4.64	2.48		2.07	2.58
Sex	1.38	2.08	1.13		1.07	0.61
Race	4.40	3.13	0.90		0.97	1.39
Age	2.20	3.01	1.52		1.28	1.98
Marital status	2.52	3.64	1.77		1.30	1.19
Spanish origin	5.91	5.81	5.10		7.41	3.10
100 Percent Housing Items						
Rooms	0.86	1.73	0.35		0.99	0.30
Tenure	1.94	1.93	1.50		1.95	1.90
Value	7.55	6.72	6.98		7.09	5.17
Rent	2.24	3.62	1.20		1.87	0.78
Sample Housing Items						
Complete plumbing	3.00	3.72	1.06		0.96	2.49
Complete kitchen	3.03	3.50	1.47		1.59	2.84
Heating fuel	6.60	6.69	4.09		2.34	4.15
Condominium	5.59	5.96	3.11		2.60	4.74
Electric cost	11.47	11.94	10.81		7.77	6.22
Property taxes	28.58	23.25	23.27		11.79	15.07

Sample Population Items

Place of birth	15.79	12.14	12.29	6.90	7.53
Education level	11.33	10.68	9.10	5.28	5.91
English ability	13.73	11.36	8.56	5.94	4.84
Veteran status	12.75	10.30	8.24	5.63	7.39
Work disability	15.86	14.25	12.45	11.82	11.46
Mobility disability	12.23	11.10	9.64	6.31	9.23
Self-care disability	13.14	11.94	10.96	6.95	8.77
Employment status	13.48	9.92	7.59	4.94	3.25
Place of work	28.46	18.60	17.95	12.05	9.19
Occupation	23.03	18.00	19.31	11.75	10.39
Income: >0-9% allocated	0.98	0.99	0.80	0.83	1.23
Income: (10-19%)	0.07	0.09	0.22	0.08	0.00
Income: (20-49%)	0.24	0.28	0.44	0.44	0.57
Income: (50-99%)	0.72	0.74	0.87	1.23	0.87
Income: 100%	24.60	21.46	22.96	14.00	14.92

Note: These allocation rates are based on a special tabulation of the 1990 census files and reflect the "final" disposition of each census item or category. They cover the household population only. In the case of housing items, they refer to occupied units. For income, the allocation rates refer to the percent of people for whom a specified percentage of their income was allocated (e.g., greater than zero to 9%, 10-19%, etc.). The rates shown here may differ from rates shown in other tables of this report or in census publications because of differences in universe or category definitions (e.g., whether the universe is all people or just household members) and because of differences between final and preliminary rates.

MSA: Metropolitan Statistical Area. Large MSAs are those with 500,000 or more population.

[a]The worst 10 percent census tracts are the 10 percent with the highest overall rates of allocation among all tracts for the country as a whole. The universe here is those tracts that fall in New York.

TABLE L.15 Allocation Rates for Selected Items, Iowa by Race/Ethnicity, 1990 Census (number of persons in thousands)

Items	Total (2,677)	White Non-Hispanic (2,574)	Black Non-Hispanic (43)	Hispanic (30)	Asian Pacific Islander Non-Hispanic (22)	American Indian Non-Hispanic (7)
100 Percent Population Items						
Relationship	1.13	1.10	1.85	1.66	2.41	0.87
Sex	0.62	0.61	0.92	0.54	1.11	1.38
Race	0.67	0.62	0.70	4.16	1.27	1.38
Age	0.66	0.63	1.29	1.38	1.30	1.19
Marital status	1.09	1.04	3.04	1.96	2.23	1.05
Spanish origin	3.35	3.37	3.91	1.54	2.89	2.30
100 Percent Housing Items						
Rooms	0.29	0.29	0.71	0.43	0.14	0.32
Tenure	1.05	1.05	1.07	1.63	1.04	0.99
Value	3.36	3.38	3.81	1.16	2.08	3.25
Rent	1.24	1.25	1.47	0.82	0.66	1.79
Sample Housing Items						
Complete plumbing	2.17	2.19	1.49	2.08	1.24	1.04
Complete kitchen	2.19	2.20	1.82	1.83	1.83	1.40
Heating fuel	2.87	2.88	2.53	3.12	3.11	1.80
Condominium	3.26	3.23	4.21	3.96	5.50	2.12
Electric cost	4.92	4.87	7.67	6.08	4.65	4.46
Property taxes	10.97	10.90	18.77	13.23	9.88	12.61

Sample Population Items						
Place of birth	3.60	3.54	5.79	5.01	4.28	3.92
Education level	3.22	3.15	4.71	5.16	4.37	5.23
English ability	3.35	3.28	5.01	5.46	5.08	5.03
Veteran status	3.40	3.35	5.74	5.18	3.67	4.26
Work disability	7.74	7.74	8.42	7.59	6.81	8.96
Mobility disability	4.05	4.01	5.23	6.15	4.77	3.68
Self-care disability	4.58	4.55	5.38	6.60	5.50	3.54
Employment status	1.92	1.85	4.51	4.40	3.03	2.76
Place of work	8.24	8.15	10.38	12.45	10.76	10.92
Occupation	8.08	8.05	9.96	8.58	7.92	7.23
Income: >0-9% allocated	0.79	0.79	0.97	0.62	0.60	1.52
Income: (10-19%)	0.12	0.12	0.18	0.01	0.22	0.21
Income: (20-49%)	0.37	0.37	0.40	0.28	0.09	0.00
Income: (50-99%)	0.99	0.99	1.28	0.47	0.41	0.61
Income: 100%	8.87	8.69	16.93	14.41	9.52	11.33

Note: These allocation rates are based on a special run of the 1990 census files and reflect the "final" disposition of each census item or category. They cover the household population only. In the case of housing items, they refer to occupied units. Rates were tabulated separately for Hispanic and non-Hispanic groups. Thus, all racial/ethnic groups are mutually exclusive in that the racial categories shown cover "non-Spanish" only (e.g., white non-Hispanic, black non-Hispanic, etc.). For income, the allocation rates refer to the percent of people for whom a specified percentage of their income was allocated (e.g., greater than zero to 9%, 10-19%, etc.). The rates shown here may differ from rates shown in other tables of this report or in census publications because of differences in universe or category definitions (e.g., whether the universe is all people or just household members) and because of differences between final and preliminary rates.

TABLE L.16 Allocation Rates for Selected Items, Iowa by Selected Geography, 1990 Census (number of persons in thousands)

Items	Central Cities of Large MSAs (53)	Balance of Large MSAs (28)	Central Cities of Small MSAs (666)	Balance of Small MSAs (433)	Non-MSAs, Urban (627)	Non-MSAs, Rural (869)
100 Percent Population Items						
Relationship	1.25	0.94	1.28	1.16	1.11	1.01
Sex	0.63	0.57	0.63	0.62	0.61	0.62
Race	0.57	0.58	0.74	0.60	0.62	0.69
Age	0.45	0.57	0.73	0.57	0.69	0.63
Marital status	0.94	0.88	1.19	0.97	1.04	1.12
Spanish origin	3.11	3.38	3.44	3.30	3.33	3.32
100 Percent Housing Items						
Rooms	0.29	0.27	0.26	0.28	0.30	0.32
Tenure	0.66	1.70	1.07	0.96	0.91	1.19
Value	2.22	3.44	2.42	2.89	2.78	4.71
Rent	0.83	0.90	0.99	1.10	1.10	1.84
Sample Housing Items						
Complete plumbing	1.89	2.71	1.78	1.79	1.51	3.21
Complete kitchen	1.82	2.66	1.77	1.77	1.58	3.23
Heating fuel	2.19	3.75	2.53	2.45	2.10	4.00
Condominium	3.34	3.44	3.10	2.69	2.87	3.97
Electric cost	3.91	5.20	4.74	3.78	4.87	5.72
Property taxes	9.38	12.16	8.86	8.52	7.29	16.15

Sample Population Items						
Place of birth	3.48	2.80	3.38	2.99	3.26	4.34
Education level	2.96	3.48	2.81	2.78	2.61	4.19
English ability	3.24	4.28	3.09	2.77	2.70	4.28
Veteran status	3.22	4.20	3.11	2.82	2.80	4.36
Work disability	6.79	8.24	6.64	6.57	6.96	9.83
Mobility disability	3.55	4.78	3.81	3.68	3.51	4.84
Self-care disability	4.42	4.97	4.38	4.22	4.04	5.33
Employment status	2.34	2.27	2.21	1.62	1.78	1.92
Place of work	5.64	8.16	5.87	6.66	8.39	11.12
Occupation	5.89	8.85	6.23	6.28	6.78	11.57
Income: >0-9% allocated	0.86	1.16	0.60	0.67	0.72	1.04
Income: (10-19%)	0.15	0.13	0.10	0.09	0.12	0.15
Income: (20-49%)	0.29	0.39	0.29	0.25	0.40	0.46
Income: (50-99%)	0.63	0.69	0.83	0.76	0.96	1.28
Income: 100%	8.15	8.84	8.91	7.91	8.39	9.71

Note: These allocation rates are based on a special tabulation of the 1990 census files and reflect the "final" disposition of each census item or category. They cover the household population only. In the case of housing items, they refer to occupied units. For income, the allocation rates refer to the percent of people for whom a specified percentage of their income was allocated (e.g., greater than zero to 9%, 10-19%, etc.). The rates shown here may differ from rates shown in other tables of this report or in census publications because of differences in universe or category definitions (e.g., whether the universe is all people or just household members) and because of differences between final and preliminary rates.

MSA: Metropolitan Statistical Area. Large MSAs are those with 500,000 or more population.

TABLE L.17 Allocation Rates for Selected Items, Worst 10 Percent Census Tracts Nationally, Iowa Portion, by Race/Ethnicity, 1990 Census (number of persons in thousands)[a]

Items	Total (26)	White Non-Hispanic (14)	Black Non-Hispanic (9)	Hispanic (1)	Asian Pacific Islander Non-Hispanic (2)	American Indian Non-Hispanic (less than 1)
100 Percent Population Items						
Relationship	2.40	2.21	1.86	1.09	7.70	0.00
Sex	0.93	0.40	1.47	0.00	2.08	14.15
Race	1.61	1.00	1.03	13.79	6.17	0.00
Age	1.15	0.77	1.03	0.54	5.50	0.00
Marital status	3.15	1.96	5.07	4.90	2.51	0.00
Spanish origin	4.43	4.09	4.88	0.00	6.78	0.00
100 Percent Housing Items						
Rooms	0.45	0.37	0.67	0.00	0.00	0.00
Tenure	1.46	0.90	1.86	9.70	4.30	0.00
Value	4.10	1.86	5.83	0.00	16.67	100.00
Rent	1.47	1.26	2.26	0.00	0.00	0.00
Sample Housing Items						
Complete plumbing	2.31	2.74	1.66	0.00	2.03	0.00
Complete kitchen	2.72	3.17	1.81	0.00	4.30	0.00
Heating fuel	3.45	3.53	2.88	0.00	8.61	0.00
Condominium	4.86	4.29	5.42	6.72	8.86	0.00
Electric cost	7.66	6.47	9.26	0.00	13.42	44.00
Property taxes	16.67	14.59	19.44	0.00	14.39	100.00

Sample Population Items

Place of birth	6.28	4.84	7.56	5.08	11.98	10.38
Education level	4.54	3.02	5.94	2.94	10.21	11.34
English ability	5.13	4.14	5.53	4.65	12.23	0.00
Veteran status	5.81	4.49	7.18	5.44	11.01	15.71
Work disability	9.34	8.06	10.40	2.87	18.45	15.71
Mobility disability	6.00	4.96	6.74	0.00	15.03	0.00
Self-care disability	5.46	4.38	6.26	0.00	14.37	0.00
Employment status	4.48	3.10	6.03	2.58	10.63	0.00
Place of work	8.30	5.52	11.58	8.51	20.84	7.69
Occupation	9.39	7.15	13.22	0.00	15.28	0.00
Income: >0-9% allocated	1.35	1.71	0.96	0.00	0.38	0.00
Income: (10-19%)	0.12	0.05	0.26	0.00	0.00	0.00
Income: (20-49%)	0.25	0.26	0.31	0.00	0.00	0.00
Income: (50-99%)	1.55	1.56	1.78	2.23	0.00	0.00
Income: 100%	13.46	9.40	20.22	2.79	16.07	37.50

Note: These allocation rates are based on a special tabulation of the 1990 census files and reflect the "final" disposition of each census item or category. They cover the household population only. In the case of housing items, they refer to occupied units. Rates were tabulated separately for Hispanic and non-Hispanic groups. Thus, all racial/ethnic groups are mutually exclusive in that the racial categories shown cover "non-Spanish" only (e.g., white non-Hispanic, black non-Hispanic, etc.). For income, the allocation rates refer to the percent of people for whom a specified percentage of their income was allocated (e.g., greater than zero to 9%, 10-19%, etc.). The rates shown here may differ from rates shown in other tables of this report or in census publications because of differences in universe or category definitions (e.g., whether the universe is all people or just household members) and because of differences between final and preliminary rates.

[a]The worst 10 percent census tracts are the 10 percent with the highest overall rates of allocation among all tracts for the country as a whole. The universe here is those tracts that fall in Iowa.

TABLE L.18 Allocation Rates for Selected Items, Worst 10 Percent Census Tracts Nationally, Iowa Portion, by Selected Geography, 1990 Census (number of persons in thousands)[a]

Items	Central Cities of Large MSAs ()	Balance of Large MSAs ()	Central Cities of Small MSAs (26)	Balance of Small MSAs ()	Non-MSAs, Urban ()	Non-MSAs, Rural ()
100 Percent Population Items						
Relationship			2.40			
Sex			0.93			
Race			1.61			
Age			1.15			
Marital status			3.15			
Spanish origin			4.43			
100 Percent Housing Items						
Rooms			0.45			
Tenure			1.46			
Value			4.10			
Rent			1.47			
Sample Housing Items						
Complete plumbing			2.31			
Complete kitchen			2.72			
Heating fuel			3.45			
Condominium			4.86			
Electric cost			7.66			
Property taxes			16.67			

Sample Population Items

Place of birth	6.28
Education level	4.54
English ability	5.13
Veteran status	5.81
Work disability	9.34
Mobility disability	6.00
Self-care disability	5.46
Employment status	4.48
Place of work	8.30
Occupation	9.39
Income: >0-9% allocated	1.35
Income: (10-19%)	0.12
Income: (20-49%)	0.25
Income: (50-99%)	1.55
Income: 100%	13.46

Note: These allocation rates are based on a special tabulation of the 1990 census files and reflect the "final" disposition of each census item or category. They cover the household population only. In the case of housing items, they refer to occupied units. For income, the allocation rates refer to the percent of people for whom a specified percentage of their income was allocated (e.g., greater than zero to 9%, 10-19%, etc.). The rates shown here may differ from rates shown in other tables of this report or in census publications because of differences in universe or category definitions (e.g., whether the universe is all people or just household members) and because of differences between final and preliminary rates.

MSA: Metropolitan Statistical Area. Large MSAs are those with 500,000 or more population.

[a]The worst 10 percent census tracts are the 10 percent with the highest overall rates of allocation among all tracts for the country as a whole. The universe here is those tracts that fall in Iowa.

422

TABLE L.19 Allocation Rates for Selected Items, Tennessee by Race/Ethnicity, 1990 Census (number of persons in thousands)

Items	Total (4,748)	White Non-Hispanic (3,932)	Black Non-Hispanic (746)	Hispanic (29)	Asian Pacific Islander Non-Hispanic (29)	American Indian Non-Hispanic (12)
100 Percent Population Items						
Relationship	1.46	1.26	2.53	1.34	2.26	1.30
Sex	0.76	0.65	1.35	0.94	0.95	0.97
Race	0.76	0.68	1.06	2.62	1.03	0.75
Age	0.72	0.61	1.27	0.66	1.17	0.60
Marital status	1.33	1.15	2.22	2.28	1.81	0.63
Spanish origin	3.21	3.07	3.96	3.15	2.51	2.65
100 Percent Housing Items						
Rooms	0.33	0.32	0.38	0.40	0.38	0.06
Tenure	1.19	1.15	1.48	0.76	0.58	0.40
Value	3.76	3.74	4.06	2.77	1.69	2.03
Rent	1.01	0.98	1.15	0.78	0.23	0.21
Sample Housing Items						
Complete plumbing	2.11	2.14	1.99	1.40	1.62	1.82
Complete kitchen	2.17	2.21	1.94	1.65	2.12	1.19
Heating fuel	3.21	3.17	3.48	2.56	3.52	3.73
Condominium	3.60	3.45	4.45	3.60	5.42	4.21
Electric cost	5.46	4.87	8.95	6.03	7.13	5.70
Property taxes	13.13	11.87	24.27	12.61	17.62	16.77

Sample Population Items						
Place of birth	4.11	3.61	6.78	4.29	3.43	3.15
Education level	3.92	3.56	5.85	4.49	4.57	2.94
English ability	4.10	3.67	6.37	5.01	5.33	3.78
Veteran status	4.26	3.93	6.20	5.07	3.82	3.97
Work disability	7.74	7.57	8.92	6.99	5.43	7.58
Mobility disability	4.27	3.99	5.89	5.19	4.68	3.42
Self-care disability	4.86	4.57	6.52	5.84	4.84	3.66
Employment status	2.79	2.36	5.33	3.09	2.90	2.73
Place of work	8.48	7.81	12.66	9.94	10.79	7.32
Occupation	7.95	7.35	11.68	7.62	8.30	7.30
Income: >0-9% allocated	0.70	0.69	0.73	0.40	0.37	0.72
Income: (10-19%)	0.09	0.09	0.08	0.07	0.06	0.06
Income: (20-49%)	0.27	0.27	0.29	0.31	0.16	0.11
Income: (50-99%)	0.73	0.70	0.92	0.57	0.40	0.88
Income: 100%	11.58	10.44	18.26	11.37	12.36	10.74

Note: These allocation rates are based on a special run of the 1990 census files and reflect the "final" disposition of each census item or category. They cover the household population only. In the case of housing items, they refer to occupied units. Rates were tabulated separately for Hispanic and non-Hispanic groups. Thus, all racial/ethnic groups are mutually exclusive in that the racial categories shown cover "non-Spanish" only (e.g., white non-Hispanic, black non-Hispanic, etc.). For income, the allocation rates refer to the percent of people for whom a specified percentage of their income was allocated (e.g., greater than zero to 9%, 10-19%, etc.). The rates shown here may differ from rates shown in other tables of this report or in census publications because of differences in universe or category definitions (e.g., whether the universe is all people or just household members) and because of differences between final and preliminary rates.

TABLE L.20 Allocation Rates for Selected Items, Tennessee by Selected Geography, 1990 Census (number of persons in thousands)

Items	Central Cities of Large MSAs (1,307)	Balance of Large MSAs (1,076)	Central Cities of Small MSAs (438)	Balance of Small MSAs (384)	Non-MSAs, Urban (448)	Non-MSAs, Rural (1,095)
100 Percent Population Items						
Relationship	1.91	1.23	1.56	1.39	1.19	1.26
Sex	0.97	0.56	0.86	0.75	0.76	0.68
Race	0.83	0.63	0.75	0.81	0.67	0.81
Age	1.07	0.53	0.64	0.58	0.61	0.61
Marital status	1.46	1.19	1.25	1.24	1.14	1.45
Spanish origin	3.66	2.70	3.30	2.87	3.30	3.22
100 Percent Housing Items						
Rooms	0.37	0.23	0.34	0.39	0.30	0.35
Tenure	1.15	1.14	1.08	1.37	1.01	1.35
Value	3.03	3.13	2.87	4.52	3.64	5.02
Rent	1.05	0.98	0.80	1.08	1.04	1.06
Sample Housing Items						
Complete plumbing	1.71	2.04	1.87	2.35	2.03	2.76
Complete kitchen	1.77	2.01	1.98	2.32	2.18	2.86
Heating fuel	2.70	3.05	2.67	3.63	2.95	4.23
Condominium	3.56	3.25	3.37	4.07	3.78	3.83
Electric cost	6.54	4.60	4.68	4.98	5.32	5.48
Property taxes	16.85	11.93	13.21	12.17	12.16	11.62

Sample Population Items						
Place of birth	5.06	3.31	3.53	4.02	3.61	4.21
Education level	4.48	3.43	3.55	3.55	3.48	4.21
English ability	4.77	3.63	3.84	3.59	3.45	4.32
Veteran status	4.73	3.74	4.10	4.20	3.82	4.46
Work disability	7.77	6.84	6.75	7.85	7.32	9.12
Mobility disability	4.84	3.87	3.95	4.11	3.61	4.46
Self-care disability	5.47	4.42	4.50	4.77	4.21	5.00
Employment status	3.80	2.22	2.72	2.52	2.34	2.46
Place of work	9.09	6.71	9.11	10.48	7.73	8.93
Occupation	8.93	6.80	7.04	7.61	7.36	8.67
Income: >0-9% allocated	0.62	0.67	0.62	0.75	0.69	0.82
Income: (10-19%)	0.07	0.07	0.07	0.11	0.11	0.11
Income: (20-49%)	0.28	0.22	0.27	0.29	0.33	0.27
Income: (50-99%)	0.68	0.65	0.72	0.70	0.87	0.82
Income: 100%	13.28	10.37	10.43	11.05	11.15	11.55

Note: These allocation rates are based on a special tabulation of the 1990 census files and reflect the "final" disposition of each census item or category. They cover the household population only. In the case of housing items, they refer to occupied units. For income, the allocation rates refer to the percent of people for whom a specified percentage of their income was allocated (e.g., greater than zero to 9%, 10-19%, etc.). The rates shown here may differ from rates shown in other tables of this report or in census publications because of differences in universe or category definitions (e.g., whether the universe is all people or just household members) and because of differences between final and preliminary rates.

MSA: Metropolitan Statistical Area. Large MSAs are those with 500,000 or more population.

TABLE L.21 Allocation Rates for Selected Items, Worst 10 Percent Census Tracts Nationally, Tennessee Portion, by Race/Ethnicity, 1990 Census (number of persons in thousands)[a]

Items	Total (116)	White Non-Hispanic (42)	Black Non-Hispanic (72)	Hispanic (1)	Asian Pacific Islander Non-Hispanic (1)	American Indian Non-Hispanic (less than 1)
100 Percent Population Items						
Relationship	2.25	0.95	3.05	0.00	0.87	0.00
Sex	1.08	0.57	1.36	0.95	0.77	0.00
Race	1.07	0.73	1.23	7.28	0.00	0.00
Age	1.67	1.51	1.70	0.95	7.05	0.00
Marital status	2.09	1.44	2.40	6.65	4.54	0.00
Spanish origin	4.71	5.07	4.47	1.42	8.70	7.11
100 Percent Housing Items						
Rooms	0.42	0.52	0.36	0.00	0.00	0.00
Tenure	1.07	0.70	1.38	0.00	0.00	0.00
Value	4.59	3.86	5.34	0.00	8.93	0.00
Rent	1.29	1.23	1.35	0.00	0.91	0.00
Sample Housing Items						
Complete plumbing	2.01	2.05	2.00	0.00	2.83	0.00
Complete kitchen	1.95	2.30	1.70	0.00	2.83	0.00
Heating fuel	4.07	4.01	3.85	0.00	18.59	7.38
Condominium	4.54	4.37	4.55	2.77	12.53	0.00
Electric cost	8.63	6.49	10.14	5.53	15.35	9.02
Property taxes	21.05	15.21	26.53	7.04	78.43	36.96

Sample Population Items

Place of birth	7.19	4.36	8.82	1.90	10.72	13.71
Education level	5.85	3.87	7.00	2.50	8.45	16.67
English ability	6.73	4.51	8.10	0.00	9.85	10.11
Veteran status	6.25	4.73	7.36	0.00	10.66	0.00
Work disability	8.99	7.74	9.88	7.53	11.04	7.45
Mobility disability	5.83	4.70	6.58	2.28	11.79	0.00
Self-care disability	6.47	5.43	7.18	2.28	11.79	0.00
Employment status	5.50	3.57	6.78	1.88	14.18	5.59
Place of work	12.97	8.14	17.10	16.26	26.28	11.39
Occupation	11.92	8.72	14.36	13.35	19.49	5.22
Income: >0-9% allocated	0.65	0.47	0.80	0.00	0.00	0.00
Income: (10-19%)	0.08	0.04	0.11	0.00	0.00	0.00
Income: (20-49%)	0.28	0.25	0.31	0.00	0.00	0.00
Income: (50-99%)	0.86	0.61	1.05	0.00	0.98	0.00
Income: 100%	16.79	12.79	19.62	12.66	19.90	4.97

Note: These allocation rates are based on a special tabulation of the 1990 census files and reflect the "final" disposition of each census item or category. They cover the household population only. In the case of housing items, they refer to occupied units. Rates were tabulated separately for Hispanic and non-Hispanic groups. Thus, all racial/ethnic groups are mutually exclusive in that the racial categories shown cover "non-Spanish" only (e.g., white non-Hispanic, black non-Hispanic, etc.). For income, the allocation rates refer to the percent of people for whom a specified percentage of their income was allocated (e.g., greater than zero to 9%, 10-19%, etc.). The rates shown here may differ from rates shown in other tables of this report or in census publications because of differences in universe or category definitions (e.g., whether the universe is all people or just household members) and because of differences between final and preliminary rates.

[a]The worst 10 percent census tracts are the 10 percent with the highest overall rates of allocation among all tracts for the country as a whole. The universe here is those tracts that fall in Tennessee.

TABLE L.22 Allocation Rates for Selected Items, Worst 10 Percent Census Tracts Nationally, Tennessee Portion, by Selected Geography, 1990 Census (number of persons in thousands)[a]

Items	Central Cities of Large MSAs (99)	Balance of Large MSAs (4)	Central Cities of Small MSAs (12)	Balance of Small MSAs (O)	Non-MSAs, Urban (O)	Non-MSAs, Rural (1)
100 Percent Population Items						
Relationship	2.26	1.88	2.32			1.13
Sex	1.08	0.86	1.13			1.13
Race	1.03	1.13	1.41			1.13
Age	1.61	3.55	1.59			2.12
Marital status	2.06	1.40	2.15			9.05
Spanish origin	4.49	3.87	6.97			1.13
100 Percent Housing Items						
Rooms	0.43	0.53	0.39			0.00
Tenure	1.11	0.26	0.94			0.00
Value	4.98	1.69	3.04			19.05
Rent	1.34	4.35	0.21			7.14
Sample Housing Items						
Complete plumbing	1.93	1.40	2.70			5.16
Complete kitchen	1.79	1.40	3.14			6.35
Heating fuel	4.08	3.15	4.01			7.54
Condominium	4.32	2.71	6.51			7.54
Electric cost	8.56	10.25	8.85			9.13
Property taxes	21.45	19.90	20.21			11.32

Sample Population Items				
Place of birth	7.02	11.26	7.49	4.95
Education level	5.77	8.03	5.77	6.75
English ability	6.54	9.68	7.43	5.32
Veteran status	6.23	8.37	5.81	7.31
Work disability	8.88	10.92	9.14	13.24
Mobility disability	5.92	8.36	4.38	6.53
Self-care disability	6.48	10.29	5.30	7.49
Employment status	5.48	10.60	4.56	1.19
Place of work	12.61	20.47	12.83	13.36
Occupation	11.74	16.50	11.89	10.29
Income: >0-9% allocated	0.48	0.31	1.91	3.45
Income: (10-19%)	0.08	0.00	0.05	0.00
Income: (20-49%)	0.30	0.00	0.17	0.00
Income: (50-99%)	0.77	0.39	1.74	0.00
Income: 100%	16.62	21.95	16.57	20.35

Note: These allocation rates are based on a special tabulation of the 1990 census files and reflect the "final" disposition of each census item or category. They cover the household population only. In the case of housing items, they refer to occupied units. For income, the allocation rates refer to the percent of people for whom a specified percentage of their income was allocated (e.g., greater than zero to 9%, 10-19%, etc.). The rates shown here may differ from rates shown in other tables of this report or in census publications because of differences in universe or category definitions (e.g., whether the universe is all people or just household members) and because of differences between final and preliminary rates.

MSA: Metropolitan Statistical Area. Large MSAs are those with 500,000 or more population.

^aThe worst 10 percent census tracts are the 10 percent with the highest overall rates of allocation among all tracts for the country as a whole. The universe here is those tracts that fall in Tennessee.

TABLE L.23 Allocation Rates for Selected Items, Illinois by Race/Ethnicity, 1990 Census (number of persons in thousands)

Items	Total (11,145)	White Non-Hispanic (8,360)	Black Non-Hispanic (1,622)	Hispanic (866)	Asian Pacific Islander Non-Hispanic (270)	American Indian Non-Hispanic (20)
100 Percent Population Items						
Relationship	1.80	1.34	3.27	3.39	2.27	2.03
Sex	0.80	0.72	1.11	0.93	1.00	1.37
Race	1.01	0.62	1.27	4.34	0.72	1.32
Age	0.88	0.67	1.63	1.44	1.01	0.69
Marital status	1.22	0.97	1.83	2.41	1.29	1.04
Spanish origin	3.37	3.26	5.19	1.40	2.28	4.43
100 Percent Housing Items						
Rooms	0.41	0.36	0.70	0.50	0.45	0.08
Tenure	1.23	1.14	1.72	1.46	1.09	0.65
Value	3.22	3.12	4.48	3.35	2.17	3.99
Rent	1.38	1.19	2.15	1.08	0.66	1.40
Sample Housing Items						
Complete plumbing	1.36	1.33	1.65	1.34	0.82	1.61
Complete kitchen	1.42	1.40	1.70	1.38	0.92	1.18
Heating fuel	2.30	2.10	3.47	2.60	1.83	3.26
Condominium	2.86	2.58	4.06	3.97	3.53	3.60
Electric cost	5.66	4.89	10.03	6.87	4.72	6.21
Property taxes	9.00	8.07	19.71	12.83	9.25	10.83

Sample Population Items

Place of birth	5.01	3.65	10.93	7.44	3.76	5.55
Education level	4.36	3.30	8.44	7.34	3.66	5.49
English ability	4.57	3.25	9.13	9.09	5.14	5.53
Veteran status	4.48	3.43	9.22	7.29	3.88	5.62
Work disability	8.03	7.36	11.72	9.08	6.09	9.47
Mobility disability	5.13	4.32	8.88	7.03	4.35	5.38
Self-care disability	5.80	4.99	9.58	7.57	5.13	5.96
Employment status	3.72	2.49	9.29	6.82	3.06	4.22
Place of work	9.55	7.89	16.78	16.59	10.63	11.86
Occupation	9.12	7.55	17.09	13.15	7.28	8.73
Income: >0-9% allocated	0.64	0.65	0.59	0.63	0.60	0.97
Income: (10-19%)	0.09	0.09	0.09	0.04	0.04	0.05
Income: (20-49%)	0.26	0.27	0.28	0.11	0.12	0.28
Income: (50-99%)	0.71	0.71	0.85	0.47	0.50	0.97
Income: 100%	12.02	9.70	22.84	17.48	9.80	13.91

Note: These allocation rates are based on a special run of the 1990 census files and reflect the "final" disposition of each census item or category. They cover the household population only. In the case of housing items, they refer to occupied units. Rates were tabulated separately for Hispanic and non-Hispanic groups. Thus, all racial/ethnic groups are mutually exclusive in that the racial categories shown cover "non-Spanish" only (e.g., white non-Hispanic, black non-Hispanic, etc.). For income, the allocation rates refer to the percent of people for whom a specified percentage of their income was allocated (e.g., greater than zero to 9%, 10-19%, etc.). The rates shown here may differ from rates shown in other tables of this report or in census publications because of differences in universe or category definitions (e.g., whether the universe is all people or just household members) and because of differences between final and preliminary rates.

TABLE L.24 Allocation Rates for Selected Items, Illinois by Selected Geography, 1990 Census (number of persons in thousands)

Items	Central Cities of Large MSAs (3,370)	Balance of Large MSAs (4,410)	Central Cities of Small MSAs (753)	Balance of Small MSAs (718)	Non-MSAs, Urban (846)	Non-MSAs, Rural (1,048)
100 Percent Population Items						
Relationship	2.54	1.54	1.51	1.35	1.37	1.43
Sex	0.88	0.75	0.79	0.76	0.79	0.81
Race	1.63	0.75	0.75	0.68	0.72	0.79
Age	1.28	0.69	0.88	0.66	0.74	0.67
Marital status	1.44	1.17	1.16	1.00	0.98	1.08
Spanish origin	3.80	2.84	3.64	3.47	3.91	3.55
100 Percent Housing Items						
Rooms	0.52	0.32	0.41	0.40	0.40	0.44
Tenure	1.32	1.17	1.14	1.20	1.12	1.31
Value	4.01	2.45	2.65	3.54	3.45	4.64
Rent	1.48	1.20	1.38	1.40	1.31	1.54
Sample Housing Items						
Complete plumbing	1.23	1.11	0.97	1.60	1.01	3.28
Complete kitchen	1.25	1.18	0.97	1.62	1.13	3.45
Heating fuel	2.77	1.66	1.74	2.25	1.75	4.35
Condominium	3.12	2.55	2.56	2.70	2.30	4.16
Electric cost	6.81	4.40	5.74	6.12	5.67	6.70
Property taxes	11.43	7.33	8.35	9.56	7.61	12.82

Sample Population Items

Place of birth	8.07	3.33	3.96	3.72	3.36	5.23
Education level	6.51	3.13	3.39	3.38	3.11	5.00
English ability	7.08	3.20	3.54	3.37	3.17	5.03
Veteran status	6.58	3.26	3.57	3.56	3.29	5.23
Work disability	9.30	6.67	6.95	7.77	7.42	11.23
Mobility disability	6.76	4.28	4.18	4.45	3.75	5.72
Self-care disability	7.39	5.00	4.80	5.10	4.37	6.38
Employment status	6.38	2.57	2.96	2.45	2.47	2.42
Place of work	12.30	8.00	7.86	9.02	8.44	10.98
Occupation	12.56	6.92	7.68	8.21	7.47	11.30
Income: >0-9% allocated	0.55	0.62	0.65	0.66	0.72	0.96
Income: (10-19%)	0.07	0.08	0.10	0.10	0.12	0.13
Income: (20-49%)	0.23	0.21	0.30	0.24	0.36	0.40
Income: (50-99%)	0.68	0.58	0.78	0.78	0.83	1.18
Income: 100%	16.20	9.72	10.78	10.75	10.03	11.65

Note: These allocation rates are based on a special tabulation of the 1990 census files and reflect the "final" disposition of each census item or category. They cover the household population only. In the case of housing items, they refer to occupied units. For income, the allocation rates refer to the percent of people for whom a specified percentage of their income was allocated (e.g., greater than zero to 9%, 10-19%, etc.). The rates shown here may differ from rates shown in other tables of this report or in census publications because of differences in universe or category definitions (e.g., whether the universe is all people or just household members) and because of differences between final and preliminary rates.

MSA: Metropolitan Statistical Area. Large MSAs are those with 500,000 or more population.

TABLE L.25 Allocation Rates for Selected Items, Worst 10 Percent Census Tracts Nationally, Illinois Portion, by Race/Ethnicity, 1990 Census (number of persons in thousands)[a]

Items	Total (1,752)	White Non-Hispanic (382)	Black Non-Hispanic (1,042)	Hispanic (286)	Asian Pacific Islander Non-Hispanic (37)	American Indian Non-Hispanic (3)
100 Percent Population Items						
Relationship	3.24	1.79	3.51	4.21	2.76	2.68
Sex	1.03	0.87	1.11	0.93	1.07	1.73
Race	2.02	0.72	1.44	6.06	0.69	2.27
Age	1.65	1.14	1.81	1.75	1.93	0.66
Marital status	1.82	1.03	1.91	2.61	1.00	0.85
Spanish origin	4.89	4.27	6.01	1.64	4.31	7.62
100 Percent Housing Items						
Rooms	0.70	0.53	0.84	0.52	0.49	0.00
Tenure	1.66	1.24	1.93	1.56	1.15	0.93
Value	4.90	4.42	5.38	4.35	2.86	5.52
Rent	1.85	1.18	2.39	1.14	0.68	1.43
Sample Housing Items						
Complete plumbing	1.52	0.97	1.80	1.75	0.86	0.00
Complete kitchen	1.53	1.01	1.84	1.62	0.34	0.00
Heating fuel	3.34	2.82	3.68	3.29	2.39	3.80
Condominium	3.77	2.60	4.28	4.32	4.43	1.69
Electric cost	8.77	5.19	10.87	8.73	5.45	7.09
Property taxes	16.39	9.51	20.98	18.08	12.13	4.26

Sample Population Items						
Place of birth	10.50	5.93	12.47	10.06	5.67	9.83
Education level	8.26	4.33	9.55	9.30	5.67	10.19
English ability	9.14	4.44	10.33	11.63	7.59	9.85
Veteran status	8.54	4.63	10.17	9.35	5.63	8.58
Work disability	11.28	8.10	12.80	11.34	7.98	12.95
Mobility disability	8.42	5.08	9.82	9.05	5.50	9.72
Self-care disability	9.10	5.73	10.57	9.48	6.22	9.68
Employment status	8.64	4.18	10.58	9.26	5.53	7.89
Place of work	15.73	8.44	18.51	20.47	13.30	19.23
Occupation	16.18	9.49	19.36	17.63	9.65	17.43
Income: >0-9% allocated	0.59	0.59	0.60	0.59	0.35	2.22
Income: (10-19%)	0.08	0.09	0.09	0.04	0.04	0.00
Income: (20-49%)	0.27	0.32	0.29	0.14	0.20	0.00
Income: (50-99%)	0.81	0.75	0.90	0.60	0.40	1.90
Income: 100%	20.54	11.39	24.67	21.17	12.61	20.12

Note: These allocation rates are based on a special tabulation of the 1990 census files and reflect the "final" disposition of each census item or category. They cover the household population only. In the case of housing items, they refer to occupied units. Rates were tabulated separately for Hispanic and non-Hispanic groups. Thus, all racial/ethnic groups are mutually exclusive in that the racial categories shown cover "non-Spanish" only (e.g., white non-Hispanic, black non-Hispanic, etc.). For income, the allocation rates refer to the percent of people for whom a specified percentage of their income was allocated (e.g., greater than zero to 9%, 10-19%, etc.). The rates shown here may differ from rates shown in other tables of this report or in census publications because of differences in universe or category definitions (e.g., whether the universe is all people or just household members) and because of differences between final and preliminary rates.

[a]The worst 10 percent census tracts are the 10 percent with the highest overall rates of allocation among all tracts for the country as a whole. The universe here is those tracts that fall in Illinois.

TABLE L.26 Allocation Rates for Selected Items, Worst 10 Percent Census Tracts Nationally, Illinois Portion, by Selected Geography, 1990 Census (number of persons in thousands)[a]

Items	Central Cities of Large MSAs (1,503)	Balance of Large MSAs (139)	Central Cities of Small MSAs (87)	Balance of Small MSAs (10)	Non-MSAs, Urban (10)	Non-MSAs, Rural (2)
100 Percent Population Items						
Relationship	3.31	3.10	2.39	2.29	1.97	1.75
Sex	1.02	1.15	1.14	1.33	1.04	0.77
Race	2.16	1.41	1.05	1.15	0.55	0.26
Age	1.70	1.35	1.32	1.51	1.25	0.00
Marital status	1.80	2.09	1.81	2.18	1.22	0.21
Spanish origin	5.00	4.17	4.52	3.84	2.15	1.88
100 Percent Housing Items						
Rooms	0.70	0.80	0.62	0.30	0.78	0.51
Tenure	1.65	1.79	1.82	0.22	1.53	1.18
Value	5.13	3.87	3.66	5.26	6.47	0.00
Rent	1.81	2.64	1.86	2.17	1.32	0.52
Sample Housing Items						
Complete plumbing	1.52	1.44	1.64	1.24	1.21	1.35
Complete kitchen	1.54	1.48	1.40	2.61	0.73	0.84
Heating fuel	3.45	2.65	3.02	2.77	1.50	1.94
Condominium	3.79	3.54	3.80	3.10	3.60	5.14
Electric cost	8.93	8.37	7.86	7.61	3.88	1.10
Property taxes	17.19	14.98	11.95	11.90	9.28	9.01

Sample Population Items					
Place of birth	11.12	6.83	6.80	5.75	6.56	7.68
Education level	8.62	6.67	5.51	5.79	4.40	4.99
English ability	9.56	7.23	6.04	5.55	4.97	4.37
Veteran status	8.91	6.65	5.80	6.50	5.50	5.57
Work disability	11.55	10.12	9.05	12.44	6.82	6.15
Mobility disability	8.76	6.89	5.45	7.29	6.25	5.11
Self-care disability	9.41	7.87	6.15	7.72	6.64	5.64
Employment status	9.07	6.59	5.46	5.71	5.10	3.34
Place of work	16.19	14.14	10.69	14.05	20.10	7.49
Occupation	16.90	12.58	11.45	13.90	11.36	7.78
Income: >0-9% allocated	0.58	0.63	0.73	0.82	0.52	0.63
Income: (10-19%)	0.08	0.09	0.21	0.08	0.00	0.00
Income: (20-49%)	0.26	0.34	0.33	0.16	0.25	0.00
Income: (50-99%)	0.80	0.75	1.08	1.51	0.56	0.48
Income: 100%	21.18	17.34	16.16	16.09	15.10	9.16

Note: These allocation rates are based on a special tabulation of the 1990 census files and reflect the "final" disposition of each census item or category. They cover the household population only. In the case of housing items, they refer to occupied units. For income, the allocation rates refer to the percent of people for whom a specified percentage of their income was allocated (e.g., greater than zero to 9%, 10-19%, etc.). The rates shown here may differ from rates shown in other tables of this report or in census publications because of differences in universe or category definitions (e.g., whether the universe is all people or just household members) and because of differences between final and preliminary rates.

MSA: Metropolitan Statistical Area. Large MSAs are those with 500,000 or more population.

[a]The worst 10 percent census tracts are the 10 percent with the highest overall rates of allocation among all tracts for the country as a whole. The universe here is those tracts that fall in Illinois.

M
Census Data Requirements by Federal Agencies

In 1992, the Office of Management and Budget (OMB) requested federal agencies to document their statutory justification for decennial census data. Federal agencies provided a list of specific census items that they used, the statutory source supporting their use, the purpose of the data, and possible alternative sources of data.

OMB subsequently had Bureau of the Census staff code the federal agency responses by (1) census topic, (2) lowest level of geography required, and (3) requirement classification. Three levels of requirement classification were distinguished:

- Mandated—decennial census data *mandated* by legislation;
- Required—data specifically *required* by legislation, but decennial census not named as source, the census is the only or historical source of data;
- Programmatic—data used for agency *program*, planning, implementation, evaluation or to provide legal evidence.

From this review, it appears that *all* 1990 census items are needed for mandated, required, or programmatic purposes, as shown below (see Office of Management and Budget, 1994):

- **Mandated items.** For each person: age, sex, race, Hispanic origin, household relationship; for each housing unit: tenure; for a sample of persons: marital status, education, place of birth, citizenship, year of entry, language, veteran status, place of work, journey to work, and income; for a sample of housing units: number of rooms, vehicles, year structure built, and farm residence.

- **Required items**. For a sample of persons: disability, labor force status, occupation, industry, class of worker; for a sample of housing units: units in structure, rent, year moved in, number of bedrooms, plumbing, kitchen, fuels, utilities, and selected monthly ownership costs.
- **Program items**. For a sample of persons: ancestry, residence 5 years ago, children ever born, work status last year, and year last worked; for a sample of housing units: condominium, value of home, telephone, and water/sewer.

Table M.1 shows the geographic area requirements for mandated, required, and programmatic census items. With few exceptions, census data are needed for small areas. Most census data are needed for aggregations of blocks, census tracts, or minor civil divisions and places. The table is based on material provided by the Office of Management and Budget (1994). OMB is still receiving responses to its June 9, 1994, request for documentation from federal agencies.

REFERENCE

Office of Management and Budget
   1994   Memorandum on topics for inclusion in the year 2000 census for Heads of Departments and Agencies dated June 9, 1994 from Leon Panetta. With attachments. Office of Management and Budget, Executive Office of the President, Washington, D.C.

TABLE M.1 Overview of Mandated, Required, and Programmatic Decennial Census Topics by Lowest Level of Geography for Which Data Are Needed

Item	Lowest Level of Geography					
	Block	Aggregation of Blocks	Census Tract[a]	Place (with or without MCD)	County	State or Nation
Relationship	This item will be collected at the block level for coverage and other reasons.	Mandated— school district				
Sex	This item will be collected at the block level for coverage and other reasons. (Programmatic)	Mandated— school district				
Race	This topic will be collected at the block level for coverage and other reasons. (Programmatic)			Mandated		
Age	This topic will be collected at the block level for coverage and other reasons. (Programmatic)	Mandated— school district				

Hispanic origin			Mandated			This topic will be collected at the block level for coverage and other reasons. (Programmatic)
Marital status			Mandated			
Education			Mandated	Mandated—school district		
Place of birth, citizenship, year of entry			Mandated	Required—school district		
Ancestry					Programmatic	
Language			Mandated—school district		Programmatic	
Residence 5 years ago					Programmatic	
Disability			Required—school district			
Children ever born					Programmatic	
Veteran status		Programmatic	Programmatic—Zip code	Required		
Labor force status	Mandated	Required	Programmatic—Zip code	Required		

TABLE M.1 Continued

	Lowest Level of Geography					
Item	Block	Aggregation of Blocks	Census Tract[a]	Place (with or without MCD)	County	State or Nation
Occupation, industry, class of worker		Programmatic—Zip code		Required		
Place of work, journey to work		Required—traffic analysis zone			Mandated	
Work status last year			Programmatic			
Income	Programmatic	Mandated—school district				
Year last worked			Programmatic			
Units in structure		Programmatic	Required			
Rooms		Programmatic	Mandated			
Tenure	This topic will be collected at the block level for coverage and other reasons. (Programmatic)		Mandated			

Value	Programmatic		Programmatic
Rent	Programmatic	Required	
Year moved in			Required
Bedrooms	Programmatic	Required	
Plumbing	Programmatic	Required	
Kitchen	Programmatic	Required	
Telephone	Programmatic	Programmatic	
Vehicles	Required—traffic analysis zone		Mandated
Fuels	Programmatic		Required
Water/sewer	Programmatic		Programmatic
Year built	Programmatic	Mandated	Programmatic
Condominium		Programmatic	Programmatic

TABLE M.1 Continued

Item	Lowest Level of Geography					
	Block	Aggregation of Blocks	Census Tract[a]	Place (with or without MCD)	County	State or Nation
Acreage/farm		Mandated				
Utilities		Programmatic		Required		
Selected monthly ownership costs		Programmatic		Required		

NOTES: Mandated—decennial census data are specifically mandated by legislation. Required—data are specifically required by legislation; the census is the only or historical source. For each topic, the lowest level of geography for which data are needed is shown. Agencies providing input to the classification include Departments of Agriculture, Commerce, Defense, Education, Energy, Health and Human Services, Housing and Urban Development, Justice, Labor, Transportation, Veterans Affairs, Environmental Protection Agency, Equal Employment Opportunity Commission, the Federal Reserve, and National Science Foundation.

[a]Includes block numbering area (BNA).

Source: Office of Management and Budget (1994).

Groups and Individuals Consulted

This report would not have been possible without the contributions of many individuals and organizations. They include a wide variety of data users representing different subject areas, populations, and geographical areas. Staff from the legislative and executive branches also provided analyses and advice.

LEGISLATIVE BRANCH

Congressional Research Service

Margaret Mikyung Lee
Jennifer Williams

Congressional Committees

Kevin Fromer
TerriAnn Lowenthal
Shelley Wilkie Martinez
David McMillen
George Omas

General Accounting Office

Bruce Johnson
Jack Kaufman
Chris Mihm

Members of Congress

Representative Harold Rogers
Representative Thomas Sawyer

EXECUTIVE BRANCH

Department of Commerce, Bureau of the Census

Charles Alexander
Mike Batutis
Peter Bounpane
Leslie Brownrigg
William Butz
Don Dalzell
Jorge del Pinal
Greg Diffendal
Don Dillman
James Dinwiddie
Jerry Gates
Jay Keller
Joe Knott
Ed Kobilarcik
Elizabeth Martin
Robert Marx
Lawrence McGinn
Nampeo McKenney
Pat Melvin
Susan Miskura
Mary Mulry
Lorraine Neece
David Pemberton
Janice Pentercs
Gregg Robinson
Harry Scarr
Raj Singh
John Thompson
Robert Tortora
Signe Wetrogan
David Whitford
Henry Woltman

Department of Health and Human Services, National Center for Health Statistics

Monroe Sirken

Department of Housing and Urban Development

Duane McGough, Division of Housing and Demographic Analysis
John Nagoski, Data Systems Statistics Division
Kathy Nelson, Office of Policy Development

Department of Labor

William Barron, Bureau of Labor Statistics
Patrick Carey, Bureau of Labor Statistics
Mary Dzialo, Bureau of Labor Statistics
Rich Mines, Office of the Assistant Secretary for Policy
Wesley Schaible, Bureau of Labor Statistics

Department of Transportation

Philip Fulton, Bureau of Transportation Statistics

Department of Treasury, Internal Revenue Service

Peter Sailer
Fritz Scheuren
Ellen Yau

Office of Management and Budget

Maria Gonzalez
Katherine Wallman

2000 Census Advisory Committee

Honorable Ann Azari, Mayor, City of Ft. Collins

INDIVIDUALS

Larry Barnett, Widener University
Kimball Brace, Election Data Services, Inc.
Donald F. Cooke, Geographic Data Technology, Inc.
Jonathan Entin, Case Western Reserve University

Kenneth Hodges, Claritas/NPDC Inc.
Richard Irwin
Samuel Issacharoff, University of Texas, Austin, Texas
Daniel Levine, Westat, Inc.
Evelyn Mann, Consultant-Demographics, Jackson Heights, New York
Michael Murray, Bates College
Mary Nenno, Urban Institute, Washington, D.C.
William O'Hare, University of Louisville, Louisville, Kentucky
Martha F. Riche, Population Reference Bureau
Ed Spar, Council of Professional Associations on Federal Statistics
George Wickstrom
Arthur Young

ASSOCIATIONS

Lorraine Amico, National Governors' Association
William Barnes, National League of Cities
William Beeman, Committee for Economic Development
Richard Belous, National Planning Association
Rae Bond, National Governors' Association
Hamilton Brown, National Association of Towns and Townships
David Clawson, American Association of State Highway and Transportation
    Officers
Susan Collins, National Association of Realtors
Susan Doolittle, National Association of Business Economists
Dee Doyle, International Downtown Association
Jon Felde, National Conference of State Legislatures
Martin Fleming, Cahners Publishing Company, Inc.
Debbie Gona, Council of State Governments
Sharon Lawrence, National Association of Counties
Martin Lefkowitz, United States Chamber of Commerce, National Chamber
    Foundation
Fabian Linden, Consumer Research Center, The Conference Board, Inc.
Martha Marks, National Association of Industrial and Office Parks
Stacey Mazer, National Association of State Budget Officers
Kathryn Shane McCarty, National League of Cities
National Development Council
Thomas Palmerlee, Urban and Regional Information Systems Association
Ken Poole, National Council for Urban Economic Development
William Pound, National Conference of State Legislatures
Greg Schiffelbein, National Association of Development Organizations
Mary Schwartz, Urban Land Institute
Lance Simmons, U.S. Conference of Mayors

Ken Smalls, National Urban League
Victoria Sweeney, Advisory Commission on Intergovernmental Relations
Robert Woodson, National Center for Neighborhood Enterprise

MINORITY ORGANIZATIONS

Norman de Weaver, Indian and Native American Employment and Training
    Coalition
Charles Kamasaki, National Council of La Raza
Monica Kuumba, National Urban League
Billy Tidwell, National Urban League

FARMWORKER ORGANIZATIONS

Louis Flores, Gonzales and Flores
Ilena J. Jacobs, California Rural Legal Assistance
Ed Kissam, E. Kissam and Associates
Chris Paige, California Human Developmetn Corporation

HOUSING ORGANIZATIONS

James Allen, Department of Housing and Urban Development, City of
    Louisville, Kentucky
Charles Ballantine, Metropolitan Council, St. Paul, Minnesota
Thomas Cook, California Department of Housing and Community Development
David Crowe, National Association of Home Builders
Roberta F. Garber, Roberta F. Garber Consulting
Ed Geiger, Pennsylvania Department of Community Affairs
John Hoskins, Department of Planning, City of Seattle, Washington
Franklin James, Graduate School of Public Affairs, University of Colorado
Michael Piper, Washington Department of Community Development
Stephen Rudman, Bureau of Housing and Community Development, Portland,
    Oregon

CITY REPRESENTATIVES

Mark Brinson, Elkhart, Indiana
Carolyn Brown, Charleston, South Carolina
David Casciotti, Buffalo, New York
Sanford M. Cohen, New York, New York
Cindy Connick, New Orleans, Louisiana
Fernando Costa, Atlanta, Georgia
Buck Delventhal, San Francisco, California

Linda Dombrow, Syracuse, New York
Donald T. Dust, Newark, New Jersey
Dennis Evans, Highland Park, Michigan
Don Farrar, Meridian, Mississippi
Eric Friedli, Seattle, Washington
Heather Gilbert, New Haven, Connecticut
Urban Giordano, Paterson, New Jersey
David B. Goldin, New York, New York
Javier Guajardo, Austin, Texas
Neil De Haan, Elizabeth, New Jersey
Jessica Heinz, Los Angeles, California
Keith Henrichs, Charlotte, North Carolina
Harry Hines, Newark, New Jersey
Barbara Kaplan, Philadelphia, Pennsylvania
Jay Michaud, Chicago, Illinois
Norris Nordvold, Phoenix, Arizona
Juliette Okotie-Eboh, Detroit, Michigan
Jai P. Ryu, Baltimore, Maryland
Lynn Seth, Wilmington, Delaware
April Showers, York, Pennsylvania
May Lou Skerritt, New Haven, Connecticut
Allan Stern, Boston, Massachusetts
Robert Sweet, Binghamton, New York
Susan Taylor, Houston, Texas
Eleanor G. Tevnan, Elizabeth, New Jersey
James Walker, Wilmington, Delaware
Susan Weed, Chicago, Illinois
Cara White, Charleston, South Carolina
Jerry Wood, Houston, Texas
Karen Wilson, Miami, Florida

STATE DATA CENTERS

Annette Watters
Center for Business and Economic Research
University of Alabama
Tuscaloosa, Alabama

Kathryn Lizik
Alaska State Data Center
Juneau, Alaska

Betty Jeffries
Arizona Department of Security
Phoenix, Arizona

Sarah Breshears
State Data Center
University of Arkansas-Little Rock
Little Rock, Arkansas

Linda Gage
State Census Data Center
Department of Finance
Sacramento, California

Rebecca Picaso
Division of Local Government
Colorado Department of Local Affairs
Denver, Colorado

Bill Kraynak
Connecticut Office of Policy and Management
Hartford, Connecticut

Judy McKinney-Cherry
Delaware Development Office
Dover, Delaware

Gan Ahuja
Data Services Division
Washington, D.C.

Valerie Jugger
Florida State Data Center
Tallahassee, Florida

Marty Sik
Georgia Office of Planning and Budget
Atlanta, Georgia

Jan Nakamoto
Hawaii State Data Center
Honolulu, Hawaii

Alan Porter
Idaho Department of Commerce
Boise, Idaho

Suzanne Ebetsch
Illinois Bureau of the Budget
Springfield, Illinois

Laurence Hathaway
Indiana State Library
Indiana State Data Center
Indianapolis, Indiana

Beth Henning
State Library of Iowa
Des Moines, Iowa

Marc Galbraith
State Library of Kansas
Topeka, Kansas

Ron Crouch
College of Business and Public Administration
University of Louisville
Louisville, Kentucky

Karen Paterson
Office of Planning and Budget
Division of Administration
Baton Rouge, Louisiana

Jean Martin
Division of Economic Analysis and Research
Maine Department of Labor
Augusta, Maine

Robert Dadd
Maryland Department of State Planning
Baltimore, Maryland

Stephen Coelen
Massachusetts Institute for Social and Economic Research
University of Massachusetts
Amherst, Massachusetts

Eric Swanson
Michigan Information Center
Department of Management and Budget
Lansing, Michigan

David Birkholz
State Demographer's Office
Minnesota Planning
St. Paul, Minnesota

Rachel McNeely
Center for Population Studies
The University of Mississippi
University, Mississippi

Kate Graf
Missouri State Library
Jefferson City, Missouri

Patricia Roberts
Census and Economic Information Center
Montana Department of Commerce
Helena, Montana

Jerome Deichert
Nebraska State Data Center
University of Nebraska at Omaha
Omaha, Nebraska

Betty McNeal
Nevada State Library
Carson City, Nevada

Tom Duffy
Office of State Planning
Concord, New Hampshire

Connie O. Hughes
New Jersey Department of Labor
Trenton, New Jersey

Kevin Kargacin
Bureau of Business and Economic Research
University of New Mexico
Albuquerque, New Mexico

Robert Scardamalia
Department of Economic Development
Albany, New York

Francine Stephenson
North Carolina Office of State Planning
Raleigh, North Carolina

Richard Rathge
Department of Agricultural Economics
North Dakota State University
Fargo, North Dakota

Barry Bennett
Ohio Data Users Center
Ohio Department of Development
Columbus, Ohio

Jeff Wallace
Oklahoma State Data Center
Oklahoma Department of Commerce
Oklahoma City, Oklahoma

Maria Wilson-Figueroa
School of Urban and Public Affairs
Portland State University
Portland, Oregon

Michael Behney
Pennsylvania State Data Center
Pennsylvania State University at Harrisburg
Middletown, Pennsylvania

Paul Egan
Rhode Island Department of Administration
Providence, Rhode Island

Mike MacFarlane
South Carolina Budget and Control Board
Columbia, South Carolina

DeVee Dykstra
School of Business
University of South Dakota
Vermillion, South Dakota

Charles Brown
Tennessee State Planning Office
Nashville, Tennessee

Steve Murdock
Department of Rural Sociology
Texas A&M University System
College Station, Texas

Julie Johnsson
Office of Planning and Budget
State Capitol
Salt Lake City, Utah

Sybil McShane
Vermont Department of Libraries
Montpelier, Vermont

Dan Jones
Virginia Employment Commission
Richmond, Virginia

George Hough
Forecasting Division
Office of Financial Management
Olympia, Washington

Mary C. Harless
West Virginia Development Office
Charleston, West Virginia

Robert Naylor
Department of Administration
Demographic Services Center
Madison, Wisconsin

Wenlin Liu
Department of Administration and Information
Economic Analysis Division
Cheyenne, Wyoming

Biographical Sketches

CHARLES L. SCHULTZE is currently a senior fellow in economics at The Brookings Institution. Formerly, he was director of the U.S. Office of Management and Budget. His work has been primarily in macroeconomics and budgetary policy. He has often testified before Congress and in other forums on the statistical organization of the U.S. government. He served as chair of the Council of Economic Advisers during the Carter administration. He has a Ph.D. degree in economics from the University of Maryland.

MARGO ANDERSON is a professor of history at the University of Wisconsin, Milwaukee. She has done extensive research in the area of census history and on the history of statistics. She has published widely on the policy and historical development of the census, including *The American Census: A Social History* (1988). She has a Ph.D. degree in history from Rutgers University.

CONSTANCE F. CITRO is a member of the staff of the Committee on National Statistics. She is a former vice president and deputy director of Mathematica Policy Research, Inc., and was an American Statistical Association/National Science Foundation research fellow at the Bureau of the Census. For the Committee on National Statistics, she has served or is currently serving as study director for numerous studies, including the Panel on Poverty and Family Assistance, the Panel to Evaluate the Survey of Income and Program Participation, and the Panel on Decennial Census Methodology. She is a fellow of the American Statistical Association. She has a Ph.D. degree in political science from Yale University.

MICHELE L. CONRAD is a senior project assistant with the Committee on National Statistics. Previously she was the senior project assistant for the

Panel to Review Evaluation Studies of Bilingual Education, the Panel on Confidentiality and Data Access, and a number of workshops and conferences. She has a B.A. degree from the University of Pittsburgh.

DOUGLAS M. DUNN is a vice president with AT&T with responsibility for visual/multimedia communications strategy. After training in statistics, he worked at Bell Laboratories for several years before moving to AT&T, where he has served in many departments over the past 15 years. His main interests are data analysis, particularly time series, and uses of data in business. He serves on many community boards, including United Way, Boy Scouts, Woodruff Arts Center, Fisk University, and the United Negro College Fund. He has a Ph.D. degree in business administration (statistics) from the University of Michigan.

BARRY EDMONSTON is a study director with the Committee on National Statistics. He has been involved in demographic research and teaching at Stanford University and Cornell University, and he was senior research associate with the Program for Research on Immigration Policy at the Urban Institute. For the Committee on National Statistics, he has been study director for workshops on immigration statistics and on federal standards for race and ethnicity classification. He has done research on demographic methods, especially on the methodology of population projections, and on questions of immigration and immigration policy. He has a Ph.D. degree in demography from the University of Michigan.

IVAN P. FELLEGI is chief statistician of Canada and deputy minister in charge of Statistics Canada. He has served as the president of the Statistical Society of Canada and the International Statistical Institute. Previously, he served on the Panel on Decennial Census Methodology of the Committee on National Statistics. He is a fellow of the American Association for the Advancement of Science and an honorary fellow of the Royal Statistical Society. He has a Ph.D. degree in survey methodology from Carleton University.

STEPHEN E. FIENBERG is Maurice Falk professor of statistics and social science at Carnegie Mellon University. As former chair of the Committee on National Statistics, he was instrumental in the creation of its Panel on Decennial Census Methodology in the 1980s. He has testified a number of times before the Subcommittee on Census and Population of the U.S. House of Representatives, most recently in March 1991, and he has written extensively on the 1990 census process. He has a Ph.D. degree in statistics from Harvard University.

CHARLES P. KINDLEBERGER is director of research for the St. Louis Community Development Agency. He is a user of census information and has a long-standing affiliation with professional associations, such as the Urban and Regional Information Systems Association and the American Planning Association. He is now serving as chair of the Information Technology Division of the American Planning Association. He has an M.S. degree in urban and regional planning from the University of Pittsburgh.

MICHEL A. LETTRE is assistant director for planning data services with the Maryland Office of Planning. He has served as the governor's chief staff person on the redistricting advisory committee and also coordinated the governor's 1990 census promotion campaign. His office serves as the principal agency for the distribution of census data within the state of Maryland under the Census Bureau's state data center program. He has an M.S. degree in urban and public affairs from Carnegie Mellon University.

JUANITA TAMAYO LOTT is research associate/consultant to the Committee on National Statistics. She is president of Tamayo Lott Associates and contributing editor for the *Asian American Almanac*. She chaired the Census Bureau Advisory Committee on Asian and Pacific Islander Populations for the 1990 Census and has testified on race and ethnicity data for the House Subcommitee on Census, Statistics, and Postal Personnel. Previously she directed the program analysis division of the U.S. Commission on Civil Rights. She has an A.M. degree in sociology from the University of Chicago.

JAMES N. MORGAN is professor emeritus and emeritus senior research scientist at the University of Michigan, Institute for Social Research. He has been a professor of economics at the University of Michigan and is a pioneer in the use of survey research for understanding economic behavior. He is a member of the National Academy of Sciences. He has a Ph.D. degree in economics from Harvard University.

WILLIAM A. MORRILL is president of Mathtech, Inc., a small, applied research organization in Princeton, New Jersey. Formerly, he was an official in the U.S. Department of Health, Education, and Welfare and the U.S. Office of Management and Budget. He serves on the Commission on Behavioral and Social Sciences and Education of the National Research Council and previously was a member of the Committee on National Statistics. He has an M.P.A. degree from Syracuse University.

RICHARD F. MUTH is Fuller E. Calloway professor of economics at Emory University. His interests include spatial economics, the economics of housing and mortgage markets, and the economics of poverty and homelessness. He was formerly on the faculties of the University of Chicago, Washington University, and Stanford University. He has published extensively on spatial aspects of urban population distribution and housing markets. He has a Ph.D. degree in economics from the University of Chicago.

JANET L. NORWOOD is a senior fellow at the Urban Institute. She served as U.S. commissioner of labor statistics for 13 years, is a past president of the American Statistical Association, is a former vice president of the International Statistical Institute, and is a member of the Committee on National Statistics. She has testified often before congressional committees and has written extensively on measurement and statistical policy issues. She has a Ph.D. degree from the Fletcher School of Law and Diplomacy, Tufts University.

EROL R. RICKETTS is a senior research scholar at the City University of New York Graduate School's Center for Social Research. Formerly, he was a visiting scholar to the Russell Sage Foundation, and at the Rockefeller Foundation he administered policy analysis, research, and fellowship programs on urban poverty and the underclass. He has testified before Congress on race, ethnicity, and ancestry questions in the 1990 census and before the New York State Advisory Committee to the U.S. Commission on Civil Rights regarding the undercount in the 1990 census. He has a Ph.D. degree from the University of Chicago.

TERESA A. SULLIVAN is a professor of sociology and law, vice provost, and associate dean of graduate studies at the University of Texas at Austin. She serves on the Bureau of the Census's advisory committee on population statistics, which she chaired in 1991-1992. She has previously served on National Research Council panels on immigration statistics and on technology and women's employment. She has a Ph.D. degree in sociology from the University of Chicago.

KARL TAEUBER is professor of sociology at the University of Wisconsin, Madison. He specializes in race and ethnicity studies and has written extensively on trends in school and residential segregation. His experiences as an enumerator for the 1960 census spurred a continuing interest in census procedures. He has a Ph.D. degree in sociology from Harvard University.

JAMES TRUSSELL is professor of economics and public affairs at Princeton University, director of the University's Office of Population Research, and associate dean of the Woodrow Wilson School of Public and International Affairs. His publications are primarily in the areas of demographic methodology and reproductive health. He served for 6 years on the Bureau of the Census's advisory committee on population statistics, and he has served on many National Research Council panels. He has a Ph.D. in economics from Princeton University.

MEYER ZITTER is an independent demographic consultant and was formerly with the Bureau of the Census. He was chief of the Census Bureau's population division in the year leading to the 1980 census and later served as assistant director for international programs. He is a fellow of the American Statistical Association and a member of the International Statistical Institute and the International Union for the Scientific Study of Population. He has a B.B.A. degree from City College of New York.